THE ULTIMATE ENCYCLOPEDIA OF

SOCCER

THE ULTIMATE ENCYCLOPEDIA OF

SOCCER

The definitive illustrated guide to world soccer

General Editor: Keir Radnedge
Editor of World Soccer magazine

Foreword by Gary Lineker

PRIMA
Prima Publishing
P.O. Box 1260
Rocklin, CA 95677
(916) 632-4400

Prima Publishing, Rocklin, CA 95765

Printed and bound in Spain

95 96 97 98 10 9 8 7 6 5 4 3 2 1

ISBN 1-55958-702-4

Project editor: Martin Corteel
Project art direction: Russell Porter
Design: Stephen Cary
Production: Sarah Schuman

To Aidan, Lyndon, Noel and Christy

GENERAL EDITOR

KEIR RADNEDGE is the editor of the magazine *World Soccer*, the acknowledged authority on the international game. He has also worked on the *Daily Mail* sports desk since 1975, and now broadcasts regularly on international soccer for BBC Radio. He has scripted World Cup and many other soccer videos, includes the acclaimed *World Club Directory* among previous publications and was the 1990 British Sports Magazine Writer of the Year.

OTHER CONTRIBUTORS

COLIN BENSON is well known around the British game for his work in myriad media activities, including club programs, soccer videos, local radio commentaries and freelance contributions to many magazines.

IAN CRUISE, a self-confessed Luton Town fan, began his career in journalism with Hayters Sports Agency in London in 1986. Four years later he moved on to *Shoot!* magazine, where he now works as feature writer and sub-editor.

KEN GOLDMAN has been editor of *Soccer Coach Magazine* for 27 years and editor of *Normidian*, the North Middlesex referee's magazine, for 13 years. He has held coaching licenses for 27 years and has been a qualified referee since 1971.

JAMES HOOLEY joined the *Daily Mail* sports staff in London in 1976 and is now Chief Sub-Editor. He also reports on Premier League matches and basketball and has contributed to other soccer books, including *The Official History of Arsenal FC.*

MARK IRWIN is a past editor of *Shoot!* magazine, who became, in 1993, a partner in the Teamwork Sports Agency of London. A soccer journalist since leaving school in 1978, he reports on League soccer for the *Sunday Mirror* as well as contributing news and features for most of the English national newspapers and soccer magazines.

JOHN KELLY is a London-based freelance soccer writer, statistician and researcher. He is a regular contributor to *World Soccer* magazine and helps compile its comprehensive results and standings service. He worked as a consultant for one of the biggest play-by-mail soccer games. He also contributes to other soccer magazines around the world and claims Portman Road as his spiritual home.

DAVID PROLE was a veteran of what used to be known as Fleet Street before retiring from his position as a betting specialist on *The People*. Born in Liverpool and later a graduate of the *Hampstead and Highgate Express*, he is the author of six books on soccer, including *Football in London* and *Come On The Reds.*

DAN WOOG has been a soccer writer for 20 years. He is currently the executive youth editor of *Soccer America* magazine. He also contributes to 5 or 6 soccer magazines.

GENERAL EDITOR'S ACKNOWLEDGMENTS

Thanks are due to all those, seen and unseen, who worked so hard and with such enthusiasm to bring an ambitious project to fruition. Particular thanks to all my fellow writers for their contributions on the many and varied aspects of soccer considered in these pages. Thanks also to Steve Dobell, Peter Arnold and David Ballheimer for their work on the text; Sharon Hutton and Gina Wardrop for picture research; to special photographer Christine Donnier-Valetin; and to Nick Cooper and John Lucas for their help with the illustrations. To Ian Cook and Mark Wylie, curators of the Arsenal and the Manchester United Museums, respectively, for their assistance with special photography. Also to the production staff without whose efforts the late changes necessitated by events at the 1994 World Cup could not have been implemented. Last, but not least, to Martin Corteel, Executive Editor of Carlton Books, for keeping the show on the road from initial planning meeting to final print run.

Previous pages (left): **ROBERTO BAGGIO** *European Footballer of the Year in 1993;* (right) **SOCCER CRAZY** *A Brazilian fan bellows his appreciation*

CONTENTS

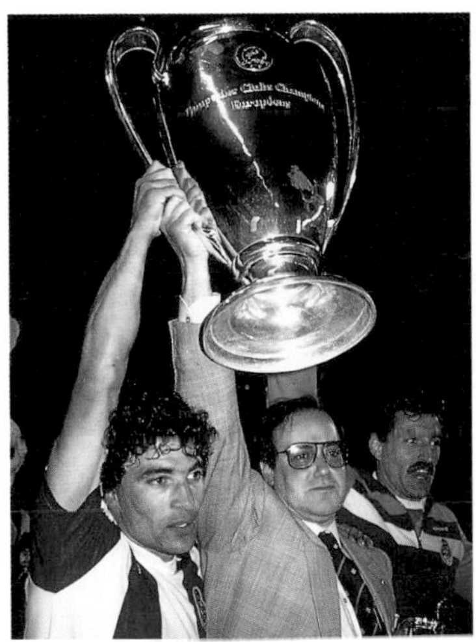
CLUBS *FC Porto – European Cup '87*

STADIUMS *Stadio Guiseppe Meazza*

PLAYERS *Carlos Valderrama*

Sondico
18

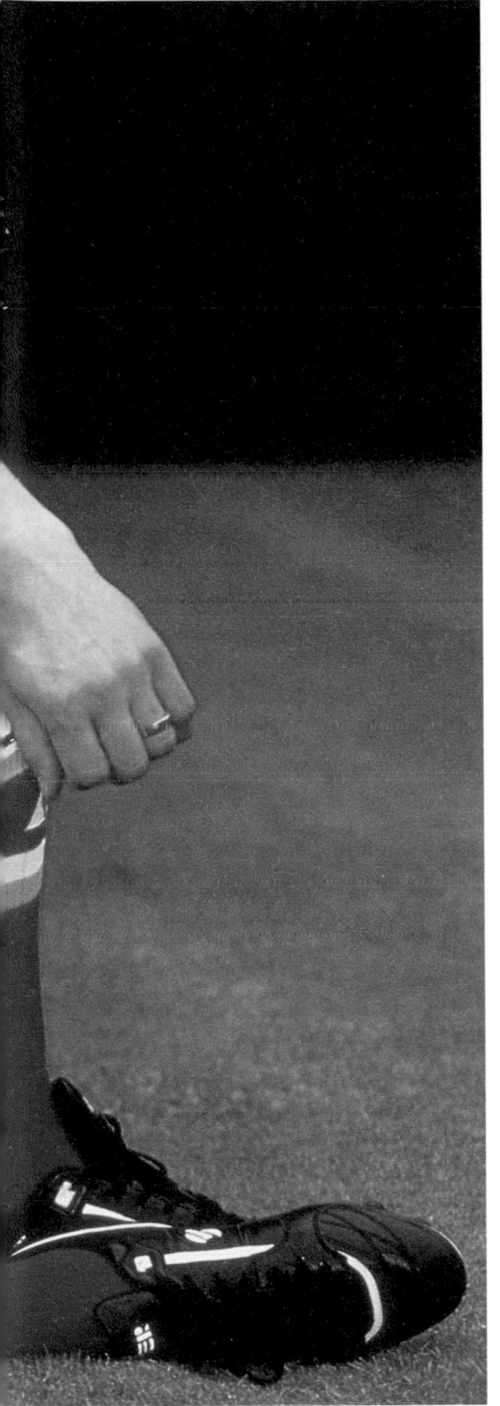

FOREWORD BY GARY LINEKER

So far as I'm concerned, the best thing about soccer is playing it. But there are other pleasures to be had from soccer and watching it, reading about it, talking about it and arguing about it are some of them. I suggest anybody who reads this encyclopedia will not only enjoy it for its own sake, but will be much better informed afterwards for those discussions and friendly arguments. What I like particularly about it is its international perspective – not least its extensive coverage of U.S. soccer.

My soccer career has been centered mainly in three English cities, Leicester, Liverpool and London, in a great Spanish city, Barcelona, and in Nagoya, a major port and key area for Japan's car industry.

At Leicester, my family was so keen on soccer they even moved homes to insure that I attended a soccer school rather than a rugby football one. Nobody thought this odd, and nobody thought my first soccer move – from Filbert Street to Goodison Park – was odd either. Everton rivaled Liverpool as the strongest team in the country, and it certainly was a good opportunity for me. Moving to Barcelona was different. Some shook their heads and said it was a mistake to leave "the strongest league in the world."

I don't agree with this assessment. It is the hardest league in the world, perhaps. But I think there are leagues where sharper, more skillful soccer is played. This is no reflection on British players. The game is more demanding than ever now, and with a 22-club Premier League and two Cup competitions, playing in England at the top level is very tiring. By comparison, the players in Serie A, the top Italian division, can more consistently produce their best form, and play better soccer, because they are fresher. There are fewer pressure games – this is true in Spain, too – and players can rise to the big occasion more readily. I hope the situation will improve in Britain as we move towards the European Championships in 1996.

I undoubtedly enjoyed one of my best club soccer memories with Barcelona – winning the European Cup-winners' Cup in 1989, an experience that compares with the two unforgettable games at Wembley in 1991 where Tottenham Hotspur beat Arsenal and then Nottingham Forest to win the FA Cup.

I knew there was no danger that this book would take the blind view that many English soccer followers have in undervaluing overseas football compared to our domestic game. The general editor, Keir Radnedge, is not editor of the magazine *World Soccer* for nothing, and I recall talking to him when he was invited by the J-League to study the boom in Japan, where I now play. He is as enthusiastic about the prospects there as I am.

In fact, this book covers the world game in such depth, that I don't mind admitting that a number of the two hundred or so international soccer players in the Great Players section were relatively new to me. There's a great deal of new and fascinating information about equipment, stadiums, culture, and all aspects of soccer. For me, it certainly is the "Ultimate" Encyclopedia of Soccer. I hope you get as much pleasure from it as I do.

Gary Lineker
March 1994

THE EARLY HISTORY OF SOCCER

The precise origin of Association football is unknown. Its modern format of 11 players against 11 in a confined area can be attributed to the British in the nineteenth century, but there is evidence of a form of soccer being played in China long before Julius Caesar brought the Roman game of harpastum to Britain.

AN ANCIENT BALL GAME

The game is mentioned in the Chinese writings of the Han Dynasty, dating back some two thousand years, while the Japanese too can point to a game called kenari which is some 14 centuries old. Ball games were also popular pursuits of the ancient Greeks as well as the Romans though it is difficult to pinpoint any of these as the origin of soccer.

Pollux describes harpastum in the following terms: "The players divided themselves into two bands. The ball was thrown upon the line in the middle. At the two ends behind the places where the players were stationed there were two other lines (which would seem to be equivalent to modern goal-lines), beyond which they tried to carry it, a feat that could not be done without pushing one another backward and forward." This description suggests that harpastum was indeed the origin of Rugby football and thus is as much the progenitor of Association football.

The early ball games in Britain seem to have started as annual events staged over Shrovetide. As a rule these contests began in the market-place and involved two teams of seemingly unlimited numbers trying to propel a ball into the opposite side's goal, which was usually some convenient spot not too remote from the center of town.

It was all very hostile, violent, and extremely dangerous. Householders had to barricade their lower windows as the mobs did battle along the streets. The hero was the fortunate player who eventually grounded the ball in goal. Not that it was always a ball. The followers of the rebel leader Jack Cade kicked a pig's bladder in the streets of London. In Chester the object of the boot was a little more distasteful. There the game originated as a celebration of victory over the marauding Danes, and the head of one of the vanquished

AN ANCIENT SPORT *This early drawing confirms that a game similar to soccer was played in a confined area as early as the sixteenth century*

BLOWING UP THE BALL FOR PALLO *It is assumed that Pallo was a forerunner to soccer*

army was used as a soccer. Later generations were content to boot a leather ball at their Shrove Tuesday festivals.

There is a record of London schoolboys playing organized football before Lent in 1175, and so popular had the game become in the streets of London in the reign of Edward II that the merchants, fearing this most robust and violent activity was affecting their trade, petitioned the king to prohibit the game. On April 13, 1314, Edward II issued the following proclamation forbidding the practice as leading to a breach of the peace: "Forasmuch as there is great noise in the city caused by hustling over large balls, from which many evils may arise, which God forbid; we command and forbid on behalf of the King, on pain of imprisonment, such game to be used in the city in future."

This was just one of many attempts to stamp out this popular activity. In 1349 Edward III tried to put an end to soccer because he felt the young men of the day were spending more time playing football than practicing archery or javelin throwing. He commanded his sheriffs to suppress "such idle practices." Similar orders were issued by Richard II, Henry IV and James III, without any lasting effect. One such Royal proclamation in 1491 forbade the people to participate in football and golf: it was to be an offense if "in a place of the realme ther be used futeball, golfe, or other sik unprofitable sports."

Despite these spoilsport measures the game flourished in the Tudor and Stuart epoch. It took Cromwell to effectively suppress the activity, after which the game did not come back into vogue until the Restoration. Samuel Pepys, writing a hundred years after the event, describes how, in the great freeze of January 1565, "the streets were full of footballs." There were still no rules, the game basically being an excuse for an uninhibited ruck. Sir Thomas Elyot, in a well-known book entitled *The Governour*, published in 1564, waxes indignantly against soccer, which he dismisses as "beastlike furie and extreme violence deserving only to be put in perpetual silence." But the lusty men of England were not to be denied their vigorous activity. During the reign of Elizabeth I football was played widely, and, in the absence of rules and referees, there were frequent and sometimes fatal accidents.

A SPLASH FROM THE PAST *The men of Ashbourne continue their tradition of the annual Shrove Tuesday game. The game dates back to the sixteenth century, but this encounter took place in 1952 with the rules almost entirely unchanged*

In the seventeenth century, football appears to have had various titles. In Cornwall it was termed "hurling," a name subsequently applied to hockey; while in Norfolk and parts of Suffolk it was known as "campynge" or "camping." Halliwell, in his *Dictionary of Archaic Words*, defines "camp" as "an athletic game of ball formerly in vogue in the Eastern Counties."

Carew, in his *Survey of Cornwall*, suggests that the Cornish were the first to adopt regular rules. He records that no one was permitted to "but or handfast under the girdle," which presumably meant that tripping, charging, or grabbing below the waist was prohibited. He goes on to state that it was also not allowed "to deal a foreball," which suggests that it was forbidden to pass forward, another similarity with Rugby football.

Such rules were obviously not in general use. Strutt, in his *Sports and Pastimes*, describes football thus: "When a match at Football is made, two parties, each containing an equal number of competitors, take the field and stand between two goals, placed at the distance of eighty or one hundred yards the one from the other. The goal is usually made with two sticks driven into the ground about two or three feet apart. The ball, which is commonly made of blown bladder and cased with leather, is delivered in the midst of the ground, and the object of each party is to drive it through the goal of their antagonists, which being achieved, the game is won.

"The abilities of the performers are best displayed in attacking and defending the goals, and hence the pastime was more frequently called a goal at Football than a game at Football. When the exercise becomes exceeding violent, the players kick each other's shins without the least ceremony, and some of them are overthrown at the hazard of their limbs."

It seems that "hacking" was as keenly relished in those days as it was when the game's modern renaissance began in the 1860s.

ROYAL DISPLEASURE *Football in the streets of London at the time of Edward II*

CODIFICATION OF ASSOCIATION FOOTBALL

Had soccer remained a regional pastime it could well have become altogether forgotten. It was the public schools and, in particular Oxford and Cambridge Universities, that dragged it from the almost aimless fury of multitudinous violence to bring shape and order to the game.

Even so, nearly all the older schools and the numerous clubs that mushroomed up in the wake of the Industrial Revolution had their own rules. Some allowed for the ball to be handled, some did not; some limited the number of participants on each side, some did not. Some favored hacking and tripping and grounding opponents by hand, while others barred these things.

The whole thing was chaotic to say the least and in 1846 the first serious attempts to unify a code of rules was instigated at Cambridge University by Messrs. H. de Winton and J.C. Thring, who met representatives from the major public schools with a view to formulating a standardized set of rules.

Their deliberations took seven hours 55 minutes and were published as the Cambridge Rules. These were well accepted and years afterwards, with very few alterations made, became the Association Rules. Unfortunately there is no copy of the original regulations, and the earliest set of rules to which those of the Football Association may be traced are those issued by Mr Thring in 1862 when he was the Assistant Master at Uppingham. These were the rules for what he termed "The Simplest Game," and as they are so important to the development of Association football as we know it today they are reproduced above. (The term "Soccer" is a popular derivative of Association football.)

The Football Association came into being in October 1863 following a meeting at the Freemasons' Tavern, Great Queen Street, London, "for the purpose of forming an Association with the object of establishing a definite code of rules for the regulation of the game." Representatives of all the major clubs were present and they appointed Mr A. Pember as president and Mr E.C. Morley as honorary secretary. Mr Morley was asked to write to the captains of the leading schools inviting them to cooperate in the movement but at a second meeting, held a few days later, it was revealed that replies from Harrow, Charterhouse and Westminster indicated they preferred to cling to their own rules.

At a third meeting a letter of acceptance was read from Mr Thring of Uppingham School and considerable progress was made with the laws, which were published on December 1, 1863. At the sixth meeting held that month the first committee of the Association was appointed.

It consisted of: Mr J.F. Alcock (Forest Club) – an elder brother of C.W. Alcock who came upon the scene later; Mr Warren (War Office); Mr Turner (Crystal Palace); Mr Steward (Crusaders) and the treasurer Mr Campbell (Blackheath); together with Pember and Morley.

It was at this meeting, however, that the "split" between the Rugby

Rules

THE SIMPLEST GAME

1. A goal is scored whenever the ball is forced through the goal and under the bar, except it be thrown by hand.

2. Hands may be used only to stop a ball and place it on the ground before the feet.

3. Kicks must be aimed only at the ball.

4. A player may not kick the ball whilst in the air.

5. No tripping up or heel kicking allowed.

6. Whenever a ball is kicked beyond the side flags, it must be returned by the player who kicked it, from the spot it passed the flag line, in a straight line towards the middle of the ground.

7. When a ball is kicked behind the line of goal, it shall be kicked off from that line by one of the side whose goal it is.

8. No player may stand within six paces of the kicker when he is kicking off.

9. A player is "out of play" immediately he is in front of the ball, and must return behind the ball as soon as possible. If the ball is kicked by his own side past a player, he may not touch or kick it, or advance, until one of the other side has first kicked it, or one of his own side has been able to kick it on a level with, or in front of him.

10. No charging allowed when a player is out of play; that is, immediately the ball is behind him.

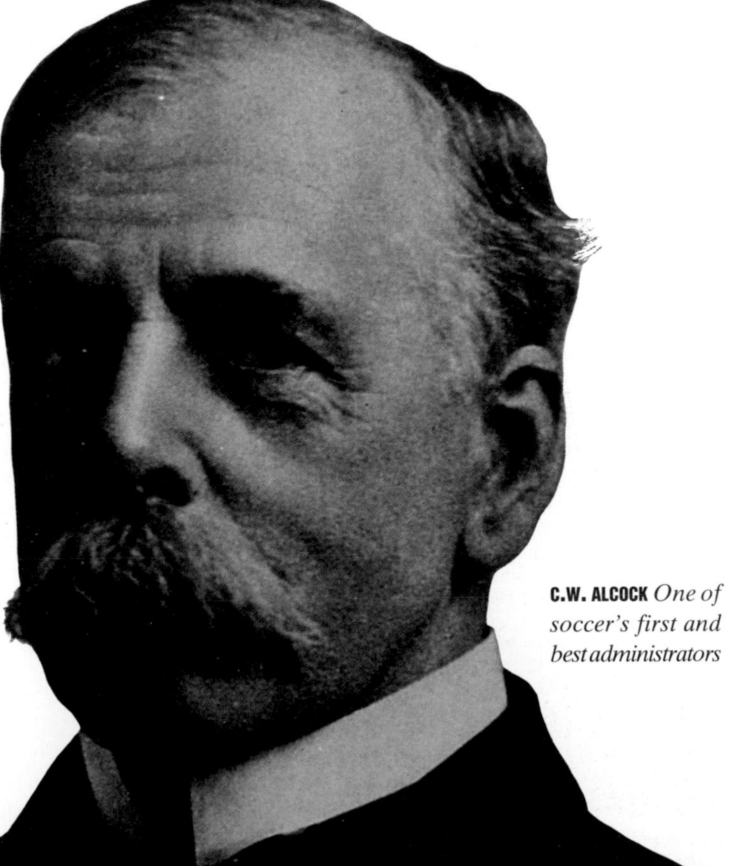

C.W. ALCOCK *One of soccer's first and best administrators*

Unionists (as they were now termed) and the Associationists occurred. Blackheath withdrew their membership, though Campbell agreed to stay in office as treasurer.

Although there were no further major upsets it seems there was still some uneasiness about the way the game should be played.

At the Association's annual meeting in February, 1866, a representative of the No Names (from Kilburn, north London) complained that only Barnes and Crystal Palace were playing strictly to Association rules. All present, apart from the Lincoln club who withdrew, agreed that no member clubs should ever play under any other rules.

The Association and the game grew steadily in public favor following the introduction of the FA Cup and international fixtures but the comparatively peaceful progress enjoyed until 1880 was followed by a decade of drastic reforms.

The number of the rules of the Association had by now increased from 10 to 15. Scotland still refused to adopt the English throw-in, or the English understanding of the offside rule; apart from that the two Associations were on friendly terms with each other.

But there loomed another crisis which was to become as significant as that which separated the Associationists from the Rugby followers. It was the advent of the paid player – the first professionals.

By now the membership of the FA, including clubs and affiliated associations, amounted to 128, of which 80 belonged to the South of England, 41 to the North, six to Scotland and one to Australia.

Amid persistent rumors that many of the northern contingent were paying men to play for them the following new rule (No 16) was added in 1882: "That any member of a club receiving remuneration or consideration of any sort above his actual expenses and any wages actually lost by any such player taking part in any match, shall be debarred from taking part in either cup, inter Association, or International contests, and any club employing such player shall be excluded from this Association."

OPIUM OF THE PEOPLE *Hampton scores for Aston Villa in the 1905 FA Cup Final against Newcastle at Crystal Palace*

The liberty to pay "wages lost" was extensively abused and this falling away from amateurism was seen by those in the south as a reflection of an unsportsmanlike spirit spreading through Northern and Midlands clubs.

Football had flourished with far greater rapidity in Scotland than in the rest of the UK and English clubs looked north of the border to strengthen their teams.

Blackburn Rovers, it was reported, "sooner than let Darwen reclaim Suter, had arranged to pay him £100 for his services" – and this at a time when footballers were supposed to be amateurs.

The FA at first turned a blind eye, but its hand was forced by the Sheffield, Lancashire, and Birmingham Associations, each of which held inquiries into charges of professionalism. In January 1883 an FA commission was appointed to look into the allegations. It consisted of: C.W. Alcock, N.L. Jackson, J.H. Cofield, T. Hindle and J.R. Harvey. They proved nothing. Yet the disquiet among the best amateur clubs continued and there was a veiled threat by some to boycott the FA Cup at the commencement of the 1883–84 season.

The row came to a head early in 1884 when the Upton Park Club lodged a complaint against Preston North End on the grounds of professionalism. The case attracted wide publicity and when William Sudell, the president of the Preston club and in effect the coach, admitted that they did pay their players and that he could prove that nearly every other important club in Lancashire and the Midlands did likewise, the cat was out of the bag.

Preston was disqualified from that season's FA Cup but the frankness of Sudell's confession brought home to the FA councilors the need to face reality. At their next committee meeting C.W. Alcock proposed "that the time has come for the legalization of professionalism." This was seconded by Dr Morley but was by no means a unanimous decision and a concerted battle to repress the move raged until July 1885 when the football professional was at last legalized.

The amateur/professional dispute rumbled on for years and affected other countries as well. In Argentina in the late 1920s amateur and professional leagues existed briefly in competition and it was the growth of professionalism which helped lead to the foundation of the World Cup, while the amateur-based Olympic Games lost credibility as a representation of the true strengths of each nation.

Simultaneously, British opposition to broken-time payments – the practice of making up players' wages for pay lost while playing football – provoked the departure of the four Home Countries from FIFA . . . costing them the right to participate in the first World Cups and, as the Hungarians proved with a decisive victory at Wembley in 1953, seriously hindering the technical development of the British game.

SOCCER DIASPORA

It could be argued that because in the early days of its development soccer in the United Kingdom was the pastime of the privileged few, it eventually became the game of the people. As communications and travel developed, British influence spread and sailors, soldiers, merchants, engineers, teachers and other professional classes took with them their sport, essentially cricket and football. Of the two games the latter gained greater popularity.

The pattern was repeated everywhere. A few Britons, possibly working, maybe just traveling, would bring out a ball and play the game and they would recruit and encourage the locals to join in.

Towards the end of the nineteenth century the game invaded Austria. There was a sizeable British colony in Vienna and their influence is manifest in the names of the two oldest clubs, the 1st Vienna FC and the Vienna Cricket and Football Club, from which FK Austria descended.

One of Vienna Cricket's most avid members was a little inside-forward named Hugo Meisl, who was to become an influential secretary of the Austrian Football Association. He recalled that the first ever game staged in Austria proper was between the Cricketers and Vienna on November 15, 1894. Cricketers won 4–0. In 1897 M.D. Nicholson was posted to the Vienna office of Thomas Cook and Sons and he became the most prominent English player in Austria's soccer history and the first president of the Austrian Football Union.

It was Meisl, though, who did most to spread the game on the continent. It was he who provided the driving force behind the launch of the Mitropa Cup – forerunner of today's European club events – and the Nations Cup competitions which popularized the game in central Europe.

Soccer has flourished in Hungary for longer than in almost any other European country. A young student returning from England imported the first soccer ball in the 1890s and two Englishmen, Arthur Yolland and Ashton, were included in the first Hungarian team. Before the First World War English teams had visited and impressed.

In Italy too the English played a great part in developing the game, as the names of some of the clubs reflect: Genoa Football and Cricket Club (founded by resident Englishmen) and Milan (not Milano). The game was introduced to Italy by a Turin businessman, Edoardo Bosio, in 1887, but Genoa, founded in 1892, were the first great club.

English boys at boarding school are claimed to have brought a rough type of soccer to Germany as early as 1865, though German football owes much to the enthusiasm of the two Schricker brothers. They actually borrowed money from their mother to help finance the first foreign tour ever made by a Football Association team, in 1899, which was a mixture of amateur and professional players. Steve Bloomer, the England and Derby County inside-right, went to Germany to coach and was interned during the First World War as was the highly influential coach, Jimmy Hogan.

Hogan was also to play a big part in the development of Dutch soccer. By 1908 Holland had 96 clubs and a competent national side under the direction of former England international Edgar Chadwick.

Football was introduced to Russia in 1887 by two Englishmen, the Charnock brothers, who ran a mill at Chrekhoro near Moscow. They acquired equipment from England but had insufficient money for shoes. Clement Charnock overcame the problem by getting a strap piercer at the mill to attach studs to the players' ordinary footwear. The Russians took to the game enthusiastically and by the late 1890s a Moscow League was in operation – the Charnocks' team, now called Morozovisti, winning the championship for the first five years in succession.

The first continental country to master soccer was perhaps Denmark. Coached by English professionals the Danes were the outstanding continental side in Europe in the early part of the twentieth century and reached the Final of the Olympic Games in 1908, where they lost, unluckily, 2–0 to Great Britain.

It had all started when an English boy studying at Soro Akademi, a famous Danish public school, received a soccer from home. There were other links too. The English "Football Club" was formed in Copenhagen in 1879 and two Englishmen, Smart and Gibson, were instrumental in popularizing the game.

Soccer was exported to all four corners of the world. In Brazil, British sailors were the first to play on their shores in 1874, and in 1878 men from the ship *Crimea* allegedly put on an exhibition match for Princess Isabel. But Charles Miller, born in São Paulo, the son of English immigrants, who came to England to study and returned ten years later with uniforms and two new soccer balls after playing for Southampton, is acknowledged as the true inspiration of the game in Brazil. Miller encouraged the British workers in establishments such as the Gas Company, the London Bank and the São Paulo Railway and the founders of the São Paulo Athletic Club — which was then soccer teams. The first real match was staged in April 1894 with the Rail team beating the Gas team 4–2.

The first club comprising mainly Brazilians was established in 1898: the Associaciao Athletica Mackenzie College in São Paulo. Thus the game in South America is as old as it is on the European continent. The British influence is seen clearly in the names of some of the club sides: Corinthians in Brazil; Liverpool and Wanderers in Uruguay; and Everton and Rangers in Chile, while Argentina boasts Newell's Old Boys and River Plate.

In Argentina although soccer was begun in the last century by British residents of Buenos Aires, it was slow to catch on with the locals. The national team of 1911 was full of Englishmen, though one, Arnold Hutton, a star forward, declined to play in one match because he had agreed to play rugby for his club. But it was Italian immigrants who really triggered the game's popularity there, as indeed they did through much of Latin America.

In Africa, as elsewhere, the British Colonial movement played a predominant part in introducing Association Football to the indigenous inhabitants. It is surprising, then, that in two of the major former British colonies, Australia and Canada, it is only now that soccer is emerging as a major sport.

GOLD RUSH *Great Britain beat Denmark in the 1908 Olympic Games Final*

THE MAJOR COMPETITIONS

The international soccer program has grown in piecemeal fashion since the first match between Scotland and England in 1872. Some competitions, like the Mitropa Cup, have faded and disappeared, but the strongest, like the World Cup for nations and the Copa Libertadores and the European Cup for clubs, flourish as a worldwide structure begins to take shape.

First there was the British Home Championship, the South American Championship and the Mitropa Cup for continental Europe's top clubs, then the World Cup itself . . . by the start of the 1930s the foundations of today's international competitive structure had been laid. The 1950s brought a further expansion, with the success of the European club cups and the launch of the European Championship. Each developing geographical region copied the competitive structures of Europe.

Now the sheer weight of the international list of teams has led soccer's world governing body, FIFA, into designing a worldwide schedule around which the game can organize into the next century.

To qualify for the World Cup, many nations played around a dozen matches. When the various international club competitions are added, the number of games played by the world's best becomes considerable.

THE WORLD CUP

The World Cup was conceived by FIFA's founders, but the driving force behind its launch was Frenchman Jules Rimet, the president of both FIFA and the French federation in the 1920s. The British had shunned FIFA's first meeting in Paris in 1904, and by the time the inaugural World Cup tournament was introduced in 1930 they had both joined and then withdrawn from the world governing body over the question of broken time payments for amateurs.

Italy, Holland, Spain, Sweden and Uruguay all applied to stage the tournament, but the European countries withdrew after an impassioned plea from the Latin Americans, who in 1930 would be celebrating a hundred years of independence. Uruguay would build a new stadium in Montevideo and would pay all travelling and hotel expenses for the competing nations. However, faced by a three-week boat trip each way, the Europeans were reluctant to participate, and two months before the competition not one European entry had been received. Meanwhile, Argentina, Brazil, Paraguay, Peru, Chile, Mexico and Bolivia had all accepted, as well as the United States.

The Latin American federations were bitter and threatened to withdraw from FIFA. Eventually France, Belgium, Yugoslavia and, under the influence of King Carol, Romania, all relented and travelled to Uruguay.

URUGUAY 1930
Triumph for ambitious party-throwers

Because of the limited response the 13 teams were split into four groups, with Uruguay, Argentina, Brazil and the USA the seeded nations.

On the afternoon of Sunday, July 13, France opened the tournament against Mexico, and in the 10th minute lost goalkeeper Alex Thepot, who was kicked in the jaw. Left-half Chantrel took over between the posts (there would be no substitutes

VICTORY AT LAST *Daniel Passarella holds the World Cup aloft in 1978*

14

for another forty years), but even with 10 men the French proved too good. Goals by Laurent, Langiller and Maschinot gave them a 3–0 advantage before Carreno replied for Mexico. Maschinot then grabbed a second to complete a 4–1 victory for France.

Two days later France lost to Argentina through a goal scored by Monti, nine minutes from time. The game had ended in chaos when Brazilian referee Almeida Rego blew for time six minutes early as Langiller raced through for a possible equalizer. In their next match, against Mexico, Argentina brought in young Guillermo Stabile, known as "El Infiltrador." He scored three goals in Argentina's 6–3 victory – in a game of five penalties – and finished as the top scorer of the tournament.

Argentina topped Group 1, while from Group 2 Yugoslavia qualified with victories over Brazil and Bolivia. The USA was most impressive in Group 4, reaching the semifinal without conceding a goal. However, their hit-on-the-break tactics were no match for Argentina, who cruised into the final 6–1. In the other semifinal Uruguay dispatched Yugoslavia by the same margin to set up a repeat of the 1928 Olympic final.

On this occasion Pablo Dorado shot Uruguay into a 12th-minute lead but Peucelle equalized and Argentina forged ahead in the 35th minute with a disputed goal by Stabile – who the Urugayans claimed was offside! Excitement grew when Pedro Cea made it 2–2 just after the break. In the 65th minute outside-left Santos Iriarte made it 3–2 for Uruguay, who underlined their victory with a fourth goal, smashed into the net by Castro in the closing seconds.

ITALY 1934
Tetchy Europeans battle it out

RESPITE *Italy prepare for extra time*

Uruguay is the only World Cup winner in history who did not defend their title. Upset by the Europeans' reluctance to participate in 1930, and plagued by players' strikes, they stayed at home.

No fewer than 32 countries – 22 from Europe, eight from the Americas and one each from Asia and Africa – contested a qualifying series in which even hosts Italy had to take part, and before the competition proper got under way the USA beat Mexico in Rome, but then fell 7–1 to Italy in Turin.

Of the 16 finalists, Italy and Hugo Meisl's "Wunderteam" were the clear favorites, though the Austrians, who were just past their peak, were taken to extra time by a spirited French side in the first knockout round. Belgium led Germany 2–1 at half-time, then crumbled as Conen, Germany's center-forward, completed a hat trick in a 5–2 win.

Brazil, beaten 3–1 by Spain, and Argentina, defeated 3–2 by Sweden, had traveled 8,000 miles to play one solitary game.

Spain forced Italy to a replay in the second round after a physical 1–1 draw was not resolved by extra time. In the replay, the following day, Meazza's 12th-minute header put Italy into the semifinals. Austria, who led Hungary 2–0 after 51 minutes through Horwarth and Zischek, then found themselves in what Meisl described as "a brawl, not an exhibition of football." Sarosi replied for Hungary from the penalty spot, but the Magyars' comeback was spoiled when Markos foolishly got himself sent off.

Italy and Austria now faced each other in the semifinals. A muddy field was not conducive to good soccer and Italy won when right-winger Guaita capitalized on a brilliant set-play routine, following a corner, to score in the 18th minute. Czechoslovakia, the conquerers of Romania and Switzerland joined Italy in the final after a 3–1 victory over Germany, with two goals by Nejedly.

In the final, Puc shot the Czechs into a deserved 70th-minute lead, Italian keeper Combi reacting late to the shot from 20 yards. Sobotka then squandered a fine opportunity and Svoboda rattled a post as the Czechs impressed with their short-passing precision. With eight minutes left the Slavs were still 1–0 ahead. Then left-winger Raimondo Orsi left Czech defenders in his wake as he dribbled through on goal. He attempted to shoot with his left but hit the ball with his right shoe. The ball spun crazily goalwards, and though Planicka got his fingers on it, he could not prevent a goal. Schiavio grabbed the Italian winner seven minutes into extra time. Italy was world champion.

FRANCE 1938
Italians make it two in a row

Europe was in turmoil, Argentina and Uruguay were absent but the tournament welcomed for the first time Cuba, Poland and the Dutch East Indies.

1930

Pool 1

France	4	Mexico	1
Argentina	1	France	0
Chile	3	Mexico	0
Chile	1	France	0
Argentina	6	Mexico	3
Argentina	3	Chile	1

	P	*W*	*D*	*L*	*F*	*A*	*Pts*
Argentina	3	3	0	0	10	4	6
Chile	3	2	0	1	5	3	4
France	3	1	0	2	4	3	2
Mexico	3	0	0	3	4	13	0

Pool 2

Yugoslavia	2	Brazil	1
Yugoslavia	4	Bolivia	0
Brazil	4	Bolivia	0

	P	*W*	*D*	*L*	*F*	*A*	*Pts*
Yugoslavia	2	2	0	0	6	1	4
Brazil	2	1	0	1	5	2	2
Bolivia	2	0	0	2	0	8	0

Pool 3

Romania	3	Peru	1
Uruguay	1	Peru	0
Uruguay	4	Romania	0

	P	*W*	*D*	*L*	*F*	*A*	*Pts*
Uruguay	2	2	0	0	5	0	4
Romania	2	1	0	1	3	5	2
Peru	2	0	0	2	1	4	0

Pool 4

USA	3	Belgium	0
USA	3	Paraguay	0
Paraguay	1	Belgium	0

	P	*W*	*D*	*L*	*F*	*A*	*Pts*
USA	2	2	0	0	6	0	4
Paraguay	2	1	0	1	1	3	2
Belgium	2	0	0	2	0	4	0

Semi-finals

Argentina	6	USA	1
Uruguay	6	Yugoslavia	1

Final

Uruguay	(1) 4	Argentina	(2) 2
Dorado, Cea, Iriarte, Castro		*Peucelle, Stabile*	

URUGUAY Ballesteros, Nasazzi (capt.), Mascheroni, Andrade, Fernandez, Gestido, Dorado, Scarone, Castro, Cea, Iriarte.

ARGENTINA Botasso, Della Torre, Paternoster, Evaristo J., Monti, Suarez, Peucelle, Varallo, Stabile, Ferreira (capt.), Evaristo M.

Leading scorers:
8 Stabile (Argentina); 5 Cea (Uruguay).

1934

First round

Italy	7	USA	1
Czech.	2	Romania	1
Germany	5	Belgium	2
Austria	3	France	2*
Spain	3	Brazil	1
Switzerland	3	Holland	2
Sweden	3	Argentina	2
Hungary	4	Egypt	2

Second round

Germany	2	Sweden	1
Austria	2	Hungary	1
Italy	1	Spain	1*
Italy	1	Spain	0®
Czech.	3	Switzerland	2

Semi-finals

Czech.	3	Germany	1
Italy	1	Austria	0

Third place match

Germany	3	Austria	2

Final

Italy	(0) 2	Czech.	(0) 1*
Orsi, Schiavio		*Puc*	

ITALY Combi (capt.), Monzeglio, Allemandi, Ferraris IV, Monti, Bertolini, Guaita, Meazza, Schiavio, Ferrari, Orsi.

CZECHOSLOVAKIA Planicka (capt.), Zenisek, Ctyroky, Kostalek, Cambal, Kreil, Junek, Svoboda, Sobotka, Nejedly, Puc.

Leading scorers:
4 Nejedly (Czechoslovakia), Schiavio (Italy), Conen (Germany).

*Notes: * After extra time ® Replay*

BACK TO BACK *Vittorio Pozzo brandishes the World Cup in Paris*

In the first round only Hungary, who beat the Dutch East Indies 6–0, and France 3–1 winners over Belgium—came through in 90 minutes, all the other ties going to extra time or replays. Defending champions Italy was saved by their goalkeeper Olivieri, who made a blinding save from Norwegian center-forward Brunyldsen in the last minute of the game to earn extra time, and Piola struck to see them through.

Brazil emerged from the mud of Strasbourg after an 11-goal thriller. A Leonidas hat trick gave the South Americans a 3–1 half-time lead, but the Poles ran riot after the break to force extra time. Willimowski scored four times but by then Leonidas had grabbed his fourth to help Brazil to a 6–5 win! The second round provided no shocks, though Brazil needed two games to eliminate Czechoslovakia and earn a semifinal joust with Italy, whose captain, Meazza, converted the winning penalty. In the other semifinal, Hungary beat Sweden, 5–1.

When Italy met Hungary in the final, Colaussi drilled Italy ahead in the sixth minute after a scintillating run almost the length of the field from Biavati, but Titkos equalized from close range within a minute. Then, with inside-forwards Meazza and Ferrari in dazzling form, Italy asserted themselves. Piola scored in the 15th minute, and Colaussi made it 3–1 in the 35th. In the 65th minute Sarosi forced the ball over the Italian line, but a magnificent back-heeled pass from Biavati set up Piola to smash in the decisive goal.

BRAZIL 1950
Hosts upstaged in final act

The first tournament after the war – for what was now known as the Jules Rimet Trophy – was to prove a thriller. Argentina refused to play in Brazil, and the Czechs and Scots declined to take their places, but England was there for the first time.

The competition was arranged, as in 1930, on a pool basis. Brazil won Pool 1 despite a 2–2 draw with Switzerland, and Uruguay topped two-team Pool 4, where they thrashed Bolivia 8–0. The shocks came in Pools 2 and 3. Italy started well enough, Riccardo Carapellese shooting them into a seventh-minute lead against Sweden. But by the break they were 2–1 down to goals from Jeppson and Sune Andersson. Jeppson grabbed another midway through the second half and, though Muccinelli replied and Carapellese hit the bar, this was Sweden's day. It was a setback the Italians were unable to overcome.

The greatest shock of all time, however, was to beset England. After a 2–0 victory over Chile, the game against the USA in Belo Horizonte seemed a formality. Instead it became a fiasco. England hit the bar and found goalkeeper Borghi unbeatable. Then in the 37th minute the impossible happened. Bahr shot from the left and Gaetjens got a touch with his head to divert the ball into the net. 1–0 to the USA!

There was no final in this competition, Brazil, Uruguay, Sweden and Spain qualifying for the Final Pool. The hosts were favorites as they faced Uruguay in the last game (a virtual final), a point ahead. A draw would make Brazil champions.

It proved a real thriller. Brazil's much-acclaimed inside-forward trio of Zizinho, Ademir and Jair, weaving gloriously through the Uruguayan defense, found goalkeeper Maspoli playing the game of his life. The giant Varela proved another stumbling block, as did Andrade. They cracked in the 47th minute, Friaca shooting past Maspoli. Uruguay's response was positive, and in the 65th minute Ghiggia's cross found Schiaffino unmarked – his thunderous shot gave Barbosa no hope. Brazil were shaken, the fizz went out of their game, and when Ghiggia ran in to shoot home in the 79th minute they were beaten. After 20 years the World Cup returned to Uruguay.

1938

First round

Switzerland	1	Germany	1*
Switzerland	4	Germany	2®
Cuba	3	Rumania	3*
Cuba	2	Rumania	1®
Hungary	6	Dutch E.Ind.	0
France	3	Belgium	1
Czech.	3	Holland	0*
Brazil	6	Poland	5*
Italy	2	Norway	1*

Second round

Sweden	8	Cuba	0
Hungary	2	Switzerland	0
Italy	3	France	1
Brazil	1	Czech.	1*
Brazil	2	Czech.	1®

Semi-finals

Italy	2	Brazil	1
Hungary	5	Sweden	1

Third place match

Brazil	4	Sweden	2

Final

Italy	(3) 4	Hungary	(1) 2
Colaussi (2), Piola (2)		*Titkos, Sarosi*	

ITALY Olivieri, Foni, Rava, Serantoni, Andreolo, Locatelli, Biavati, Meazza (capt.), Piola, Ferrari, Colaussi.

HUNGARY Szabo, Polgar, Biro, Szalay, Szucs, Lazar, Sas, Vincze, Sarosi (capt.), Szengeller, Titkos.

Leading scorers

8 Leonidas (Brazil); 7 Szengeller (Hungary); 5 Piola (Italy).

1950

First round Pool 1

Brazil	4	Mexico	0
Yugoslavia	3	Switzerland	0
Yugoslavia	4	Mexico	1
Brazil	2	Switzerland	2
Brazil	2	Yugoslavia	0
Switzerland	2	Mexico	1

	P	W	D	L	F	A	Pts
Brazil	3	2	1	0	8	2	5
Yugoslavia	3	2	0	1	7	3	4
Switzerland	3	1	1	1	4	6	3
Mexico	3	0	0	3	2	10	0

Pool 2

Spain	3	USA	1
England	2	Chile	0
USA	1	England	0
Spain	2	Chile	0
Spain	1	England	0
Chile	5	USA	2

	P	W	D	L	F	A	Pts
Spain	3	3	0	0	6	1	6
England	3	1	0	2	2	2	2
Chile	3	1	0	2	5	6	2
USA	3	1	0	2	4	8	2

Pool 3

Sweden	3	Italy	2
Sweden	2	Paraguay	2
Italy	2	Paraguay	0

	P	W	D	L	F	A	Pts
Sweden	2	1	1	0	5	4	3
Italy	2	1	0	1	4	3	2
Paraguay	2	0	1	1	2	4	1

Pool 4

Uruguay	8	Bolivia	0

	P	W	D	L	F	A	Pts
Uruguay	1	1	0	0	8	0	2
Bolivia	1	0	0	1	0	8	0

Final pool

Uruguay	2	Spain	2
Brazil	7	Sweden	1
Uruguay	3	Sweden	2
Brazil	6	Spain	1
Sweden	3	Spain	1
Uruguay	2	Brazil	1

	P	W	D	L	F	A	Pts
Uruguay	3	2	1	0	7	5	5
Brazil	3	2	0	1	14	4	4
Sweden	3	1	0	2	6	11	2
Spain	3	0	1	2	4	11	1

Deciding match

Uruguay	(0) 2	Brazil	(0) 1
Schiaffino, Ghiggia		*Friaca*	

URUGUAY Maspoli, Gonzales, M., Tejera, Gambetta, Varela, Andrade, Ghiggia, Perez, Miguez, Schiaffino, Moran.

BRAZIL Barbosa, Augusto, Juvenal, Bauer, Danilo, Bigode, Friaca, Ziziho, Ademir, Jair, Chico.

Leading scorers:

9 Ademir (Brazil); 6 Schiaffino (Uruguay); 5 Zarra (Spain).

*Notes: * After extra time ® Replay*

SWITZERLAND 1954

'Magic Magyars' found out by astute Germans

Hungary arrived in Zurich as the hottest ever World Cup favorites. The magic of Puskas, Hidegkuti and Kocsis had added a new dimension to the beautiful game and, what is more, had proved an unbeatable combination in the 1952 Olympic tournament.

No one was really surprised when the Magyars rattled in 17 goals in their opening pool matches against Korea and Germany. Kocsis scored four against the Germans but Hungary was left a significant legacy by their opponents, center-half Werner Liebrich delivering a fateful kick on Puskas that caused him to retire from the match in the 30th minute. It was an injury from which he never fully recovered during the remainder of the tournament. Hungary of course cruised into the quarterfinals, where they dispatched Brazil 4–2, but Germany had to win a play-off with Turkey to earn the right to face Yugoslavia.

NOT SO FAST *Morlock gets one back*

England began with a 4–4 draw with Belgium, yet secured a quarterfinal place with a 2–0 win over Switzerland. The Scots were not so successful. They failed to score and were beaten by Austria and Uruguay, neither of whom conceded a goal in their pool. Stanley Matthews and Schiaffino took the individual honors as Uruguay beat England 4–2, but the competition was sullied by a notorious clash between Brazil and Hungary, which was dubbed "The Battle of Berne." Three players were sent off, and a shameful fight ensued in the locker rooms afterwards. If that was infamous, then the match between Austria and Switzerland was incredible. The Swiss scored three in 20 minutes, and Austria replied with three in three minutes. In one seven-minute period, there were five goals! Finally, Austria came out 7–5 winners.

Puskas returned for the final, but it was a mistake. Although he scored the opening goal in a devastating start which saw Hungary score twice in eight minutes, his ankle was not fully recovered. Morlock replied for Germany in the 11th minute and Rahn blasted in two fine goals—the last only seven minutes from time—to win it for Germany.

SWEDEN 1958

Brazil teach the world a soccer lesson

Brazil enthralled the world in this competition, which was notable for the emergence of 4–2–4 and the outstanding individual talents of stars such as Didi, Garrincha, Vava and the teenager Pele. France too was to perform with style, Just Fontaine and Raymond Kopa providing the magic, while hosts Sweden provided their share of surprises.

West Germany headed Pool 1, where Northern Ireland, who had eliminated Italy in the qualifying rounds, caused an upset by beating Czechoslovakia in a play-off to earn a quarterfinal tie with France, who headed Pool 2 with Yugoslavia. Likewise Wales also made the quarterfinals, following a play-off with Hungary, and did themselves proud

1954

Pool 1

Yugoslavia	1	France	0
Brazil	5	Mexico	0
France	3	Mexico	2
Brazil	1	Yugoslavia	1

	P	*W*	*D*	*L*	*F*	*A*	*Pts*
Brazil	2	1	1	0	6	1	3
Yugoslavia	2	1	1	0	2	1	3
France	2	1	0	1	3	3	2
Mexico	2	0	0	2	2	8	0

Pool 2

Hungary	9	Korea	0
W. Germany	4	Turkey	1
Hungary	8	W. Germany	3
Turkey	7	Korea	0

	P	*W*	*D*	*L*	*F*	*A*	*Pts*
Hungary	2	2	0	0	17	3	4
W. Germany	2	1	0	1	7	9	2
Turkey	2	1	0	1	8	4	2
Korea	2	0	0	2	0	16	0

Play-off

W. Germany	7	Turkey	2

Pool 3

Austria	1	Scotland	0
Uruguay	2	Czech.	0
Austria	5	Czech.	0
Uruguay	7	Scotland	0

	P	*W*	*D*	*L*	*F*	*A*	*Pts*
Uruguay	2	2	0	0	9	0	4
Austria	2	2	0	0	6	0	4
Czech.	2	0	0	2	0	7	0
Scotland	2	0	0	2	0	8	0

Pool 4

England	4	Belgium	4
England	2	Switzerland	0
Switzerland	2	Italy	1
Italy	4	Belgium	1

	P	*W*	*D*	*L*	*F*	*A*	*Pts*
England	2	1	1	0	6	4	3
Italy	2	1	0	1	5	3	2
Switzerland	2	1	0	1	2	3	*2
Belgium	2	0	1	1	5	8	1

Play-off

Switzerland	4	Italy	1

Quarter-finals

W. Germany	2	Yugoslavia	0
Hungary	4	Brazil	2
Austria	7	Switzerland	5
Uruguay	4	England	2

Semi-finals

W. Germany	6	Austria	1
Hungary	4	Uruguay	2

Third-place match

Austria	3	Uruguay	1

Final

W. Germany (2) 3 Hungary (2) 2
Morlock, Rahn (2) — *Puskas, Czibor*

WEST GERMANY: Turek, Posipal, Kohlmeyer, Eckel, Liebrich, Mai, Rahn, Morlock, Walter O., Walter F (capt.), Schäfer.

HUNGARY: Grosics, Buzansky, Lantos, Bozsik, Lorant, Zakarias, Czibor, Kocsis, Hidegkuti, Puskas (capt.), Toth J.

Leading scorers

11 Kocsis (Hungary); 8 Morlock (W. Germany); 6 Probst (Austria), Hügi (Switzerland).

1958

Pool 1

W. Germany	3	Argentina	1
N. Ireland	1	Czech.	0
W.Germany	2	Czech.	2
Argentina	3	N. Ireland	1
W. Germany	2	N. Ireland	2
Czech.	6	Argentina	1

	P	*W*	*D*	*L*	*F*	*A*	*Pts*
W. Germany	3	1	2	0	7	5	4
Czech.	3	1	1	1	8	4	3
N. Ireland	3	1	1	1	4	5	3
Argentina	3	1	0	2	5	10	2

Play-off

N. Ireland	2	Czech.	1

Pool 2

France	7	Paraguay	3
Yugoslavia	1	Scotland	1
Yugoslavia	3	France	2
Paraguay	3	Scotland	2
France	2	Scotland	1
Yugoslavia	3	Paraguay	3

	P	*W*	*D*	*L*	*F*	*A*	*Pts*
France	3	2	0	1	11	7	4
Yugoslavia	3	1	2	0	7	6	4
Paraguay	3	1	1	1	9	12	3
Scotland	3	0	1	2	4	6	1

Pool 3

Sweden	3	Mexico	0
Hungary	1	Wales	1
Wales	1	Mexico	1
Sweden	2	Hungary	1
Sweden	0	Wales	0
Hungary	4	Mexico	0

	P	*W*	*D*	*L*	*F*	*A*	*Pts*
Sweden	3	2	1	0	5	1	5
Hungary	3	1	1	1	6	3	3
Wales	3	0	3	0	2	2	3
Mexico	3	0	1	2	1	8	1

Play-off

Wales	2	Hungary	1

Pool 4

England	2	Soviet Union	2
Brazil	3	Austria	0
England	0	Brazil	0
Soviet Union	2	Austria	0
Brazil	2	Soviet Union	0
England	?	Austria	2

	P	*W*	*D*	*L*	*F*	*A*	*Pts*
Brazil	3	2	1	0	5	0	5
England	3	0	3	0	4	4	3
Soviet Union	3	1	1	1	4	4	3
Austria	3	0	1	2	2	7	1

Play-off

Soviet Union	1	England	0

Quarter-finals

France	4	N. Ireland	0
W. Germany	1	Yugoslavia	0
Sweden	2	Soviet Union	0
Brazil	1	Wales	0

Semi-finals

Brazil	5	France	2
Sweden	3	W. Germany	1

Third place match

France	6	W. Germany	3

Final

Brazil (2) 5 Sweden (1) 2
Vava (2), Pele (2), Zagalo — *Liedholm Simonsson*

BRAZIL: Gilmar, Santos D., Santos N., Zito, Bellini (capt.), Orlando, Garrincha, Didi, Vava, Pele, Zagalo.

SWEDEN: Svensson, Bergmark, Axbom, Boerjesson, Gustavsson, Parling, Hamrin, Gren, Simonsson, Liedholm (capt.), Skoglund.

Leading scorers

13 Fontaine (France); 6 Pele (Brazil), Rahn (W. Germany); 5 Vava (Brazil), McParland (N..Ireland).

by limiting Brazil to one goal, inevitably scored by Pele. Brazil had comfortably emerged from Pool 4 without conceding a goal, but England was knocked out, when they lost 1–0 to Russia in another play-off.

The semifinals pitted Sweden against West Germany and Brazil against France. Hans Schaefer blasted West Germany into the lead with a spectacular volley from 25 yards. Sweden's equalizer from Skoglund should not have been given – Liedholm blatantly controlling the ball with a hand before setting up the chance. Juskowiak was sent off in the 57th minute, and Sweden took full advantage to clinch their final place with goals from Gren and Hamrin. Brazil took a second-minute lead against France thanks to a spectacular finish from Vava. Fontaine equalized within nine minutes, but Didi restored the lead for the South Americans, and in the second half young Pele ran riot with three more goals.

There was a sensational start to the final, when Liedholm kept his poise and balance to shoot Sweden into a fourth-minute lead. It was the first time in the tournament that Brazil had been behind. Six minutes later it was 1–1. Garrincha exploded down the right, and cut the ball back for Vava to run on to and fire firmly past Svensson. This was proving a fascinating spectacle. Pele slammed a shot against a post, Zagalo headed out from beneath the bar. In the 32nd minute the Garrincha-Vava combination struck again, and when Pele made it 3–1 in the 55th minute with a touch of sheer magic, the game was won. Bringing a dropping ball down on a thigh in a crowded penalty area, the youngster hooked it over his head, spun and volleyed thunderously into the net. Zagalo and Pele added further goals, either side of a dubious second Swedish goal from Agne Simonsson, who looked offside. There was no doubt that Brazil was the best in the world.

LAP OF HONOR *Brazil celebrates its first ever World Cup triumph in 1958*

CHILE 1962

Brazil without Pele still can't be matched

Brazil retained their world crown as Garrincha took center stage and 4–3–3 became the subtle change. But this was a World Cup marred by violence.

The Soviet Union and Yugoslavia comfortably overcame the Uruguayan and Colombian challenge in Group 1, while in Group 3 Brazil's only hiccup was a goalless draw with Czechoslovakia, who was to prove the surprise package of this tournament.

England got off to a bad start. Unable to break down the massed Hungarian defense after Springett was beaten by a thunderous long-range effort from Tichy, they equalized from a Ron Flowers penalty, but the impressive Albert clinched it for Hungary 18 minutes from time with a glorious individual goal. England did find some form to beat Argentina 3–1. Another Flowers penalty, a Bobby Charlton special and Jimmy Greaves clinched their first World Cup finals victory since 1954.

The Chile-Italy tie turned into a violent confrontation, with spitting, fighting, and two-footed tackles intended to maim. That referee Ken Aston sent only two players off was amazing in a game that sullied the name of soccer. Brazil, however, continued to thrill, even without the injured Pele, who was to take no further part after the group match against Mexico. Garrincha mesmerized England to defeat, then took Chile apart in the semifinal, only to be sent off for retaliation.

In Vina del Mar a mere 5,000 watched Czechoslovakia earn their final place at the expense of Yugoslavia, and the Czechs threatened to upset all the odds when Masopust cleverly gave them the lead over Brazil in the 16th minute. The equalizer, from Amarildo – Pele's replacement – was quickly registered but it was not until the 69th minute that Zito headed them into the lead. Vava made it 3–1 when goalkeeper Schroiff fumbled a lob.

SIMPLY THE BEST *Pele bides his time*

1962

Group 1

Uruguay	2	Colombia	1
Soviet Union	2	Yugoslavia	0
Yugoslavia	3	Uruguay	1
Soviet Union	4	Colombia	4
Soviet Union	2	Uruguay	1
Yugoslavia	5	Colombia	0

	P	*W*	*D*	*L*	*F*	*A*	*Pts*
Soviet Union	3	2	1	0	8	5	5
Yugoslavia	3	2	0	1	8	3	4
Uruguay	3	1	0	2	4	6	2
Colombia	3	0	1	2	5	11	1

Group 2

Chile	3	Switzerland	1
W. Germany	0	Italy	0
Chile	2	Italy	0
W. Germany	2	Switzerland	1
W. Germany	2	Chile	0
Italy	3	Switzerland	0

	P	*W*	*D*	*L*	*F*	*A*	*Pts*
W. Germany	3	2	1	0	4	1	5
Chile	3	2	0	1	5	3	4
Italy	3	1	1	1	3	2	3
Switzerland	3	0	0	3	2	8	0

Group 3

Brazil	2	Mexico	0
Czech.	1	Spain	0
Brazil	0	Czech.	0
Spain	1	Mexico	0
Brazil	2	Spain	1
Mexico	3	Czech.	1

	P	*W*	*D*	*L*	*F*	*A*	*Pts*
Brazil	3	2	1	0	4	1	5
Czech.	3	1	1	1	2	3	3
Mexico	3	1	0	2	2	3	2
Spain	3	1	0	2	2	3	2

Group 4

Argentina	1	Bulgaria	0
Hungary	2	England	1
England	3	Argentina	1
Hungary	6	Bulgaria	1
Argentina	0	Hungary	0
England	0	Bulgaria	0

	P	*W*	*D*	*L*	*F*	*A*	*Pts*
Hungary	3	2	1	0	8	2	5
England	3	1	1	1	4	3	3
Argentina	3	1	1	1	2	3	3
Bulgaria	3	0	1	2	1	7	1

Quarter-finals

Yugoslavia	1	W. Germany	0
Brazil	3	England	1
Chile	2	Soviet Union	1
Czech.	1	Hungary	0

Semi-finals

Brazil	4	Chile	2
Czech.	3	Yugoslavia	1

Third place match

Chile	1	Yugoslavia	0

Final

Brazil	(1) 3	Czech.	(1) 1
Amarildo, Zito, Vava		*Masopust*	

BRAZIL: Gilmar, Santos D., Mauro (capt.), Zozimo, Santos N., Zito, Didi, Garrincha, Vava, Amarildo, Zagalo.

CZECHOSLOVAKIA: Schroiff, Tichy, Novak (capt.), Pluskal, Popluhar, Masopust, Pospichal, Scherer, Kvasniak, Kadraba, Jelinek.

Leading scorers

4 Garrincha (Brazil), Vava (Brazil), Sanchez L. (Chile), Jerkovic (Yugoslavia), Albert (Hungary), Ivanov V. (USSR); 3 Amarildo (Brazil), Scherer (Czechoslovakia), Galic (Yugoslavia), Tichy (Hungary).

ENGLAND 1966

Victory for Ramsey's wingless wonders

IT'S ALL OVER NOW *Bobby Moore celebrates with England their extra-time victory over West Germany at Wembley*

For the first time in 32 years the host nation was to win the title. This was a series that had everything – passion, controversy, some fine soccer, and one of the greatest upsets of all time when North Korea knocked Italy out at Ayresome Park!

The tournament got off to a slow start, with England held 0–0 by Uruguay, but in Group 2 West Germany quickly displayed their potential with a 5–0 win over Switzerland. Brazil, alas, disappointed. Having beaten Bulgaria 2–0, they lost a classic encounter with Hungary, for whom Albert was the dominating factor, then succumbed to Portugal, whose striker Eusebio was to be one of the stars of the competition. The Soviet Union, efficient and technically sound, cruised through to the quarter-finals without alarm. For Italy, however, there was a rude awakening. Having lost 1–0 to the Soviets, they had to beat North Korea to stay in the competition, but what seemed a formality turned into a nightmare. In the 42nd minute Pak Doo Ik dispossessed Rivera, advanced and crashed a searing shot past Albertosi. It was the only goal. Italy was eliminated.

At Goodison Park there was a sensational opening to Korea's quarterfinal with Portugal. There was a goal in the opening minute, followed by a second and a third – and all for Korea. It was then that Eusebio proved his genius and, thanks to him and the towering Torres, the Portuguese clawed back from the deficit to win a sensational game 5–3.

The England–Portugal semifinal produced an emotional classic, Bobby Charlton upstaging the mercurial Eusebio with what many felt was his greatest game for England. This, unlike the bad-tempered quarterfinal shambles with Argentina, when Rattin was sent off and Geoff Hurst arrived as a new shooting star, was a wonderful advertisement for the game.

West Germany had edged out the Soviet Union, in a disappointing tie, to secure their place in the final, and there they struck the first blow through Haller. Hurst equalized and his West Ham colleague Martin Peters gave England the lead. But a scrambled goal from Weber just before time forced the game into extra time. In the 100th minute controversy raged. Alan Ball crossed, and Hurst coming in on the near post, hammered his shot goalwards. It thumped against the underside of the bar and dropped – but which side of the line? Swiss referee Dienst was not sure, but the Soviet linesman Bakhramov was. 3–2 England! Any feeling of injustice felt by the Germans was quickly irrelevant. Bobby Moore swept a long ball upfield for Hurst to chase, and the big striker slammed his shot into the roof of Tilkowski's net to become the first player ever to score a hat trick in a World Cup final.

1966

Group 1

England	0	Uruguay	0
France	1	Mexico	1
Uruguay	2	France	1
England	2	Mexico	0
Uruguay	0	Mexico	0
England	2	France	0

	P	*W*	*D*	*L*	*F*	*A*	*Pts*
England	3	2	1	0	4	0	5
Uruguay	3	1	2	0	2	1	4
Mexico	3	0	2	1	1	3	2
France	3	0	1	2	2	5	1

Group 2

W. Germany	5	Switzerland	0
Argentina	2	Spain	1
Spain	2	Switzerland	1
Argentina	0	W. Germany	0
Argentina	2	Switzerland	0
W. Germany	2	Spain	1

	P	*W*	*D*	*L*	*F*	*A*	*Pts*
W. Germany	3	2	1	0	7	1	5
Argentina	3	2	1	0	4	1	5
Spain	3	1	0	2	4	5	2
Switzerland	3	0	0	3	1	9	0

Group 3

Brazil	2	Bulgaria	0
Portugal	3	Hungary	1
Hungary	3	Brazil	1
Portugal	3	Bulgaria	0
Portugal	3	Brazil	1
Hungary	3	Bulgaria	1

	P	*W*	*D*	*L*	*F*	*A*	*Pts*
Portugal	3	3	0	0	9	2	6
Hungary	3	2	0	1	7	5	4
Brazil	3	1	0	2	4	6	2
Bulgaria	3	0	0	3	1	8	0

Group 4

Soviet Union	3	North Korea	0
Italy	2	Chile	0
Chile	1	North Korea	1
Soviet Union	1	Italy	0
North Korea	1	Italy	0
Soviet Union	2	Chile	1

	P	*W*	*D*	*L*	*F*	*A*	*Pts*
Soviet Union	3	3	0	0	6	1	6
North Korea	3	1	1	1	2	4	3
Italy	3	1	0	2	2	2	2
Chile	3	0	1	2	2	5	1

Quarter-finals

England	1	Argentina	0
W. Germany	4	Uruguay	0
Portugal	5	North Korea	3
Soviet Union	2	Hungary	1

Semi-finals

W. Germany	2	Soviet Union	1
England	2	Portugal	1

Third place match

Portugal	2	Soviet Union	1

Final

England (1) 4	W. Germany (1) 2*
Hurst (3), Peters	*Haller, Weber*

ENGLAND: Banks, Cohen, Wilson, Stiles, Charlton J., Moore (capt.), Ball, Hurst, Hunt, Charlton R., Peters.

WEST GERMANY: Tilkowski, Hottges, Schulz, Weber, Schnellinger, Haller, Beckenbauer, Overath, Seeler (capt.), Held, Emmerich.

Leading scorers

9 Eusebio (Portugal); 5 Haller (West Germany); 4 Beckenbauer (West Germany), Hurst (England), Bene (Hungary), Porkujan (USSR).

*Note: * After extra time*

MEXICO 1970
Beautiful soccer secures the Jules Rimet trophy

Soccer triumphed again in Mexico, where the colorful free-flowing Brazilians delighted, overcoming the heat, the altitude and, in a dramatic final, Italy – the masters of defensive caution.

There were no surprises in Groups 1 and 2 where the Soviet Union and Mexico and Italy and Uruguay qualified comfortably. The match between Brazil and England in Group 3 provided the outstanding tie of the series. In the 10th minute Jairzinho, a wonderful player of power and pace, delivered the perfect cross from the line. Pele timed his run and jump to perfection, and his header was hard and true, angled to bounce before passing just inside the left post. The shout of "Goal!" was already in the air when Gordon Banks, who had anticipated the ball going the other way, twisted athletically to pounce and incredibly push the wickedly bouncing ball over the bar. It was one of the greatest saves ever seen.

The only goal was scored in the second half by Jairzinho, who was to score in all of Brazil's six matches. England faltered in the quarterfinal. Without Banks, because of an upset stomach, they squandered a two-goal lead to lose to West Germany in extra time.

The semifinal between Italy and West Germany was dramatic. Having taken the lead through Boninsegna, Italy withdrew in the second half to protect their advantage. Given control of midfield, Germany took the initiative but did not equalize until the third minute of injury time through Schnellinger. In extra time, the goals came thick and fast: Müller for Germany, 1–2, Burgnich, then Riva for Italy, 3–2. Müller again, 3–3, before Rivera clinched it for Italy.

The final proved a marvelous affirmation of attacking soccer. Pele opened the scoring and made two more after Boninsegna had made it 1–1, capitalizing on a dreadful error by Clodoaldo. Gerson drove in a powerful cross-shot in the 66th minute, and the match was sewn up with goals from Jairzinho and Carlos Alberto.

TOTAL SOCCER *But Johan Cruyff could not overcome West Germany in '74*

WEST GERMANY 1974
Pyrrhic victory for 'Total Soccer'

European teams dominated this series in which West Germany regained the World Cup after 20 years. It was another triumph for positive tactics, as Holland and Poland – who had surprisingly eliminated England – demonstrated to the full the attributes of skill and technique. The term "Total Soccer" crept into the soccer vocabulary, with Cruyff, Neeskens and Rep leading the Dutch masters who abandoned the rigidity of 4–2–4 and 4–3–3 to introduce the concept of "rotation" play.

Half of the 16 competing nations had been eliminated after the first series of group matches. The two Germanys qualified for the second phase comfortably, as did Holland and Sweden, and Poland from Group 4, where Argentina just edged Italy on goal difference thanks to a 4–1 victory over Haiti, whom Italy had beaten 3–1.

Group 2 proved to be the most competitive. Brazil, now sadly without the retired Pele, could only draw 0–0 with Yugoslavia and Scotland. Zaïre was to be the key factor. Scotland defeated them 2–0, but Yugoslavia overwhelmed them 9–0 to clinch pole position on goal difference. As they went into the final round Scotland needed victory over Yugoslavia to win the group. They could only draw 1–1, and Brazil squeezed through, by virtue of one goal, thanks to a 3–0 win over Zaïre.

Holland looked impressive. They topped Group A to qualify for the Final without conceding a goal. Brazil, a shadow of their former selves, bowed out leaving us with one magic memory, their winning goal against East Germany. Jairzinho, standing on the end of the German wall facing a free kick, ducked as Rivelino crashed his shot towards him, the ball swerving past the bewildered goalkeeper Croy.

West Germany's passage was a little more uncertain. It hinged on their clash with the impressive Poles in the final game of Group B. On a waterlogged field they made their physical strength pay. Tomaszewski saved a Hoeness penalty, but the German atoned for his miss when his shot was deflected to "The Bomber,"

1970

Group 1

Mexico	0	Soviet Union	0
Belgium	3	El Salvador	0
Soviet Union	4	Belgium	1
Mexico	4	El Salvador	0
Soviet Union	2	El Salvador	0
Mexico	1	Belgium	0

	P	*W*	*D*	*L*	*F*	*A*	*Pts*
Soviet Union	3	2	1	0	6	1	5
Mexico	3	2	1	0	5	0	5
Belgium	3	1	0	2	4	5	2
El Salvador	3	0	0	3	0	9	0

Group 2

Uruguay	2	Israel	0
Italy	1	Sweden	0
Uruguay	0	Italy	0
Sweden	1	Israel	1
Sweden	1	Uruguay	0
Italy	0	Israel	0

	P	*W*	*D*	*L*	*F*	*A*	*Pts*
Italy	3	1	2	0	1	0	4
Uruguay	3	1	1	1	2	1	3
Sweden	3	1	1	1	2	2	3
Israel	3	0	2	1	1	3	2

Group 3

England	1	Romania	0
Brazil	4	Czech.	1
Romania	2	Czech.	1
Brazil	1	England	0
Brazil	3	Romania	2
England	1	Czech.	0

	P	*W*	*D*	*L*	*F*	*A*	*Pts*
Brazil	3	3	0	0	8	3	6
England	3	2	0	1	2	1	4
Romania	3	1	0	2	4	5	2
Czech.	3	0	0	3	2	7	0

Group 4

Peru	3	Bulgaria	2
W. Germany	2	Morocco	1
Peru	3	Morocco	0
W. Germany	5	Bulgaria	2
W. Germany	3	Peru	1
Morocco	1	Bulgaria	1

	P	*W*	*D*	*L*	*F*	*A*	*Pts*
W. Germany	3	3	0	0	10	4	6
Peru	3	2	0	1	7	5	4
Bulgaria	3	0	1	2	5	9	1
Morocco	3	0	1	2	2	6	1

Quarter-finals

W. Germany	3	England	2*
Brazil	4	Peru	2
Italy	4	Mexico	1
Uruguay	1	Soviet Union	0

Semi-finals

Italy	4	W. Germany	3*
Brazil	3	Uruguay	1

Third place match

W. Germany	1	Uruguay	0

Final

Brazil	4	Italy	1
Pele, Gerson, Jairzinho, Carlos Alberto		*Boninsegna*	

BRAZIL: Felix, Carlos Alberto (capt.), Brito, Piazza, Everaldo, Clodoaldo, Gerson, Jairzinho, Tostao, Pele, Rivelino.

ITALY: Albertosi, Cera, Burgnich, Bertini (Juliano), Rosato, Facchetti (capt.), Domenghini, Mazzola, De Sisti, Boninsegna (Rivera), Riva.

Leading scorers

9 Müller (West Germany); 7 Jairzinho (Brazil); 4 Pele (Brazil), Cubillas (Peru), Byscevietz (USSR), Seeler (West Germany).

*Note: * After extra time*

1974

Group 1

W. Germany	1	Chile	0
E. Germany	2	Australia	0
W. Germany	3	Australia	0
E. Germany	1	Chile	1
E. Germany	1	W. Germany	0
Chile	0	Australia	0

	P	W	D	L	F	A	Pts
E. Germany	3	2	1	0	4	1	5
W. Germany	3	2	0	1	4	1	4
Chile	3	0	2	1	1	2	1
Australia	3	0	1	2	0	5	1

Group 2

Brazil	0	Yugoslavia	0
Scotland	2	Zaïre	0
Brazil	0	Scotland	0
Yugoslavia	9	Zaïre	0
Scotland	1	Yugoslavia	1
Brazil	3	Zaïre	0

	P	W	D	L	F	A	Pts
Yugoslavia	3	1	2	0	10	1	4
Brazil	3	1	2	0	3	0	4
Scotland	3	1	2	0	3	1	4
Zaïre	3	0	0	3	0	14	0

Group 3

Holland	2	Uruguay	0
Sweden	0	Bulgaria	0
Holland	0	Sweden	0
Bulgaria	1	Uruguay	1
Holland	4	Bulgaria	1
Sweden	3	Uruguay	0

	P	W	D	L	F	A	Pts
Holland	3	2	1	0	6	1	5
Sweden	3	1	2	0	3	0	4
Bulgaria	3	0	2	1	2	5	2
Uruguay	3	0	1	2	1	6	1

Group 4

Italy	3	Haiti	1
Poland	3	Argentina	2
Italy	1	Argentina	1
Poland	7	Haiti	0
Argentina	4	Haiti	1
Poland	2	Italy	1

	P	W	D	L	F	A	Pts
Poland	3	3	0	0	12	3	6
Argentina	3	1	1	1	7	5	3
Italy	3	1	1	1	5	4	3
Haiti	3	0	0	3	2	14	0

Group A

Brazil	1	E. Germany	0
Holland	4	Argentina	0
Holland	2	E. Germany	0
Brazil	2	Argentina	1
Holland	2	Brazil	0
Argentina	1	E. Germany	1

	P	W	D	L	F	A	Pts
Holland	3	3	0	0	8	0	6
Brazil	3	2	0	1	3	3	4
E. Germany	3	0	1	2	1	4	1
Argentina	3	0	1	2	2	7	1

Group B

Poland	1	Sweden	0
W. Germany	2	Yugoslavia	0
Poland	2	Yugoslavia	1
W. Germany	4	Sweden	2
Sweden	2	Yugoslavia	1
W. Germany	1	Poland	0

	P	W	D	L	F	A	Pts
W. Germany	3	3	0	0	7	2	6
Poland	3	2	0	1	3	2	4
Sweden	3	1	0	2	4	6	2
Yugoslavia	3	0	0	3	2	6	0

Third place match

Poland 1 Brazil 0

Final

W. Germany (2) 2 Holland (1) 1
Breitner (pen), Müller — *Neeskens (pen)*

WEST GERMANY: Maier, Beckenbauer (capt.), Vogts, Schwarzenbeck, Breitner, Bonhof, Hoeness, Overath, Grabowski, Müller, Holzenbein.

HOLLAND: Jongbloed, Suurbier, Rijsbergen (De Jong), Haan, Krol, Jansen, Neeskens, Van Hanegem, Rep, Cruyff (capt.), Rensenbrink (Van de Kerkhof, R.).

Leading scorers 7 Lato (Poland); 5 Neeskens (Holland), Szarmach (Poland); 4 Müller (West Germany), Rep (Holland), Edstroem (Sweden).

Gerd Müller, who booked the date with Holland.

The Dutch produced the most dramatic opening to a final in the history of the competition. Right from the kick-off the ball was fluently played into the German area, where Cruyff was brought down by Hoeness. Neeskens calmly converted the first penalty awarded in a World Cup final to record the fastest final goal ever. And the Germans had yet to play the ball.

After being outplayed, West Germany got off the hook. Holzenbein was homing in on goal when he was tripped by Jansen, and Breitner duly rammed in the resultant penalty himself to make it 1–1. A 43rd-minute goal from Gerd Müller – his 68th, last and most important for his country – won the World Cup.

CLINCHER *Bertoni scores for Argentina*

ARGENTINA 1978

Tickertape triumph for hyper hosts

Ecstasy and euphoria greeted Argentina's eventual triumph on home soil, yet for neutrals the failure of Holland, as in 1974, to claim their rightful crown as the best team in the world left a void.

The home nation, backed by fanatical support and animated tickertape adoration in the River Plate Stadium, staged a colorful and dramatic tournament. Yet their passage to the final was not without controversy. Their opening game proved a torrid affair. Hungary took the lead in 12 minutes through Zombori only for Leopoldo Luque to equalize three minutes later. The Hungarians were to have two players sent off before Bertoni fired the winning goal. Italy and Argentina had already qualified for the second stage when they met to decide the final Group 1 places. The Italians played it tight and snatched the win through Bettega in the 67th minute.

In Group 2 Poland carried on where they left off in Germany, with slick precise play. The shock result featured Tunisia, who held West Germany to a goalless draw and could have won. Brazil once again failed to inspire, and only a fortunate 1–0 victory over Austria, who topped their group, squeezed them into the second phase. Scotland, the United Kingdom's only representatives, suffered humiliation. Rocked by a 3–1 defeat by Peru, they received a further blow to morale when Willie Johnston failed a drug test and was ordered home. A 1–1 draw with Iran added to the troubles, but they went out in style against Holland.

While Italy and West Germany played not to lose, Holland thrilled with their adventurous attitude. The "reprise" of the 1974 final between them and Germany provided one of the best games of this series. The final score was 2–2 and Holland were back in the final. Meanwhile Brazil's

1978

Group 1

Argentina	2	Hungary	1
Italy	2	France	1
Argentina	2	France	1
Italy	3	Hungary	1
Italy	1	Argentina	0
France	3	Hungary	1

	P	W	D	L	F	A	Pts
Italy	3	3	0	0	6	2	6
Argentina	3	2	0	1	4	3	4
France	3	1	0	2	5	5	2
Hungary	3	0	0	3	3	8	0

Group 2

W.Germany	0	Poland	0
Tunisia	3	Mexico	1
Poland	1	Tunisia	0
W. Germany	6	Mexico	0
Poland	3	Mexico	1
W. Germany	0	Tunisia	0

	P	W	D	L	F	A	Pts
Poland	3	2	1	0	4	1	5
W.Germany	3	1	2	0	6	0	4
Tunisia	3	1	1	1	3	2	3
Mexico	3	0	0	3	2	12	0

Group 3

Austria	2	Spain	1
Sweden	1	Brazil	1
Austria	1	Sweden	0
Brazil	0	Spain	0
Spain	1	Sweden	0
Brazil	1	Austria	0

	P	W	D	L	F	A	Pts
Austria	3	2	0	1	3	2	4
Brazil	3	1	2	0	2	1	4
Spain	3	1	1	1	2	2	3
Sweden	3	0	1	2	1	3	1

Group 4

Peru	3	Scotland	1
Holland	3	Iran	1
Scotland	1	Iran	1
Holland	0	Peru	0
Peru	4	Iran	1
Scotland	3	Holland	2

	P	W	D	L	F	A	Pts
Peru	3	2	1	0	7	2	5
Holland	3	1	1	1	5	3	3
Scotland	3	1	1	1	5	6	3
Iran	3	0	1	2	2	8	1

Group A

Italy	0	W. Germany	0
Holland	5	Austria	1
Italy	1	Austria	0
Austria	3	W.Germany	2
Holland	2	Italy	1
Holland	2	W. Germany	2

	P	W	D	L	F	A	Pts
Holland	3	2	1	0	9	4	5
Italy	3	1	1	1	2	2	3
W. Germany	3	0	2	1	4	5	2
Austria	3	1	0	2	4	8	2

Group B

Argentina	2	Poland	0
Brazil	3	Peru	0
Argentina	0	Brazil	0
Poland	1	Peru	0
Brazil	3	Poland	1
Argentina	6	Peru	0

	P	W	D	L	F	A	Pts
Argentina	3	2	1	0	8	0	5
Brazil	3	2	1	0	6	1	5
Poland	3	1	0	2	2	5	2
Peru	3	0	0	3	0	10	0

Third place match

Brazil 2 Italy 1

Final

Argentina (1)3 Holland (0)1*
Kempes (2), Bertoni — *Nanninga*

ARGENTINA: Fillol, Olguin, Galvan, Passarella (capt.), Tarantini, Ardiles (Larrosa), Gallego, Kempes, Bertoni, Luque, Ortiz (Houseman).
HOLLAND: Jongbloed, Krol (capt.), Poortvliet, Brandts, Jansen (Suurbier), Van de Kerkhof W., Neeskens, Haan, Rep (Nanninga), Rensenbrink, Van de Kerkhof R.

Leading scorers
6 Kempes (Argentina); 5 Rensenbrink (Holland), Cubillas (Peru).

*Note: * After extra time*

3–1 defeat of Poland left Argentina needing to beat Peru by at least four goals to make the final. They beat them by six in an exercise of shambles that tarnished the image of the whole competition.

The final, more dramatic than distinguished, saw Mario Kempes score twice as once more Holland fell at the final hurdle.

SPAIN 1982
Italy have the last laugh

Italy deservedly won the 1982 World Cup, after a slow start in which they drew all three games in Group 1 and qualified on the slenderest goal difference. West Germany, who was to finish runner-up, was on the wrong end of a shock 2–1 defeat in their opening tie against Algeria but, like Italy, got better as the tournament progressed.

England, in contrast, started with a bang then gradually eased up. Skipper Bryan Robson got them off to a dream start against France with a goal in 27 seconds, but although Ron Greenwood's team proved hard to beat, without the injured Keegan and Brooking they had little guile. The outstanding game was that between Italy and the favorites, Brazil. Three times Italy took the lead, twice Brazil came back to level the score in a classic that would not be matched for quality. Paulo Rossi, back after a two-year suspension, was the hero with a brilliant hat trick.

In the semifinals Rossi scored twice more to beat the impressive Poles, while West Germany and France, who had grown in stature and confidence following that initial setback against England, were involved in a pulsating thriller. With Platini, Tigana and Giresse at their teasing best, many fancied France as winners. In a tense 90 minutes they carved out the better chances but failed to make them count, then in extra-time fell victim on penalties after German keeper Harald Schumacher got away with an appalling foul on Battiston.

The less glamorous sides also had their moments. Algeria, Honduras and Kuwait caught the eye, and Northern Ireland – whose Norman Whiteside was, at 17, the youngest ever

CIAO BELLA *Marco Tardelli kisses the cup alongside Dino Zoff after Italy's triumph over West Germany in 1982*

1982

Group 1

Italy	0	Poland	0
Peru	0	Cameroon	0
Italy	1	Peru	1
Poland	0	Cameroon	0
Poland	5	Peru	1
Italy	1	Cameroon	1

	P	W	D	L	F	A	Pts
Poland	3	1	2	0	5	1	4
Italy	3	0	3	0	2	2	3
Cameroon	3	0	3	0	1	1	3
Peru	3	0	2	1	2	6	2

Group 2

Algeria	2	W. Germany	1
Austria	1	Chile	0
W. Germany	4	Chile	1
Austria	2	Algeria	1
Algeria	3	Chile	2
W. Germany	1	Austria	0

	P	W	D	L	F	A	Pts
W. Germany	3	2	0	1	6	3	4
Austria	3	2	0	1	3	1	4
Algeria	3	2	0	1	5	5	4
Chile	3	0	0	3	3	8	0

Group 3

Belgium	1	Argentina	0
Hungary	10	El Salvador	1
Argentina	4	Hungary	1
Belgium	1	El Salvador	0
Belgium	1	Hungary	1
Argentina	2	El Salvador	0

	P	W	D	L	F	A	Pts
Belgium	3	2	1	0	3	1	5
Argentina	3	2	0	1	6	2	4
Hungary	3	1	1	1	12	6	3
El Salvador	3	0	0	3	1	13	3

Group 4

England	3	France	1
Czech.	1	Kuwait	1
England	2	Czech.	0
France	4	Kuwait	1
France	1	Czech.	1
England	1	Kuwait	0

	P	W	D	L	F	A	Pts
England	3	3	0	0	6	1	6
France	3	1	1	1	6	5	3
Czech.	3	0	2	1	2	4	2
Kuwait	3	0	1	2	2	6	1

Group 5

Spain	1	Honduras	1
N. Ireland	0	Yugoslavia	0
Spain	2	Yugoslavia	1
N. Ireland	1	Honduras	1
Yugoslavia	1	Honduras	0
N. Ireland	1	Spain	0

	P	W	D	L	F	A	Pts
N. Ireland	3	1	2	0	2	1	4
Spain	3	1	1	1	3	3	3
Yugoslavia	3	1	1	1	2	2	3
Honduras	3	0	2	1	2	3	2

Group 6

Brazil	2	Soviet Union	1
Scotland	5	New Zealand	2
Brazil	4	Scotland	1
Soviet Union	3	New Zealand	0
Scotland	2	Soviet Union	2
Brazil	4	New Zealand	0

	P	W	D	L	F	A	Pts
Brazil	3	3	0	0	10	2	6
Soviet Union	3	1	1	1	6	4	3
Scotland	3	1	1	1	8	8	3
New Zealand	3	0	0	3	2	12	0

Group A

Poland	3	Belgium	0
Soviet Union	1	Belgium	0
Soviet Union	0	Poland	0

	P	W	D	L	F	A	Pts
Poland	2	1	1	0	3	0	3
Soviet Union	2	1	1	0	1	0	3
Belgium	2	0	0	2	0	4	0

Group B

W. Germany	0	England	0
W. Germany	2	Spain	1
England	0	Spain	0

	P	W	D	L	F	A	Pts
W. Germany	2	1	1	0	2	1	3
England	2	0	2	0	0	0	2
Spain	2	0	1	1	1	2	1

Group C

Italy	2	Argentina	1
Brazil	3	Argentina	1
Italy	3	Brazil	2

	P	W	D	L	F	A	Pts
Italy	2	2	0	0	5	3	4
Brazil	2	1	0	1	5	4	2
Argentina	2	0	0	2	2	5	0

Group D

France	1	Austria	0
N. Ireland	2	Austria	2
France	4	N. Ireland	1

	P	W	D	L	F	A	Pts
France	2	2	0	0	5	1	4
Austria	2	0	1	1	2	3	1
N. Ireland	2	0	1	1	3	6	1

Semi-finals

Italy	2	Poland	0
W. Germany	3	France	3*

(West Germany won 5–4 on pens)

Third place match

Poland	3	France	2

Final

Italy (0) 3 W. Germany (0) 1
Rossi, Tardelli Breitner
Altobelli

ITALY: Zoff (capt.), Bergomi, Cabrini, Collovati, Scirea, Gentile, Oriale, Tardelli, Conti, Graziani (Altobelli)(Causio), Rossi.

WEST GERMANY: Schumacher, Kaltz, Forster K., Stielike, Forster B., Breitner, Dremmler (Hrubesch), Littbarski, Briegel, Fischer (Müller, H.), Rummenigge (capt.).

Leading scorers

6 Rossi (Italy); 5 Rummenigge (West Germany); 4 Zico (Brazil), Boniek (Poland).

*Notes: * After extra time ® Replay*

to play in the finals – distinguished themselves in a win over Spain.

The final did not live up to its billing. There was not a shot on target in the opening 45 minutes including Cabrini's effort from a penalty. But in the second half the Germans paid, in fatigue, the price of their extra-time victory over France. Italy, inspired by the effort of Marco Tardelli and counter-attacking pace of Bruno Conti, were deserving winners – thus sealing a World Cup hat trick.

THEY SHALL NOT PASS *Karl-Heinz Rummenigge is stopped by Argentina's Oscar Ruggeri during the final in 1986*

MEXICO 1986

Divine intervention determines destiny of Cup

Mexico staged its second World Cup finals in the wake of a tragic earthquake, and set records all round with 52 matches played before 2,406,511 spectators.

West Germany continued their impressive World Cup record by reaching their fifth final, once again eliminating France at the semifinal stage, while Argentina overcame the impressive Belgiums to make a third final appearance. However, their 2-1 quarterfinal victory over England had been soured by the infamous "hand of God" incident, when Maradona knocked the ball past goalkeeper Peter Shilton with a hand to score the opening goal. There was no argument about Argentina's second goal, a brilliant solo run by the Argentinian ace taking him past three England defenders before he dispatched the ball into the back of the net.

Of the earlier games, the Soviet Union's 6–0 demolition of Hungary and Belgium's thrilling 4–3 victory over the Soviets in the second round were the most memorable. England muddled through after a desperate start, Carlos Manuel's lone strike giving Portugal a 1–0 win. Bobby Robson's team were then held 0–0 by Morocco. A Gary Lineker hat trick against Poland revived England's flagging fortunes and earned them a place in the second round.

In a dramatic final Argentina led 2–0 through Brown and Valdano before West Germany launched a remarkable recovery to equalize through Karl-Heinz Rummenigge and Völler. Burruchaga snatched the winner for Argentina's second World Cup title.

1986

Group A

Bulgaria	1	Italy	1
Argentina	3	South Korea	1
Italy	1	Argentina	1
Bulgaria	1	South Korea	1
Argentina	2	Bulgaria	0
Italy	3	South Korea	2

	P	W	D	L	F	A	Pts
Argentina	3	2	1	0	6	2	5
Italy	3	1	2	0	5	4	4
Bulgaria	3	0	2	1	2	4	2
South Korea	3	0	1	2	4	7	1

Group B

Mexico	2	Belgium	1
Paraguay	1	Iraq	0
Mexico	1	Paraguay	1
Belgium	2	Iraq	1
Paraguay	2	Belgium	2
Mexico	1	Iraq	0

	P	W	D	L	F	A	Pts
Mexico	3	2	1	0	4	2	5
Paraguay	3	1	2	0	4	3	4
Belgium	3	1	1	1	5	5	4
Iraq	3	0	0	3	1	4	0

Group C

Soviet Union	6	Hungary	0
France	1	Canada	0
Soviet Union	1	France	1
Hungary	2	Canada	0
France	3	Hungary	0
Soviet Union	2	Canada	0

	P	W	D	L	F	A	Pts
Soviet Union	3	2	1	0	9	1	5
France	3	2	1	0	5	1	5
Hungary	3	1	0	2	2	9	2
Canada	3	0	0	3	0	5	0

Group D

Brazil	1	Spain	0
N. Ireland	1	Algeria	1
Spain	2	N. Ireland	1
Brazil	1	Algeria	0
Spain	3	Algeria	0
Brazil	3	N. Ireland	0

	P	W	D	L	F	A	Pts
Brazil	3	3	0	0	5	0	6
Spain	3	2	0	1	5	2	4
N. Ireland	3	0	1	2	2	6	1
Algeria	3	0	1	2	1	5	1

Group E

W. Germany	1	Uruguay	1
Denmark	1	Scotland	0
Denmark	6	Uruguay	1
W. Germany	2	Scotland	1
Scotland	0	Uruguay	0
Denmark	2	W.Germany	0

	P	W	D	L	F	A	Pts
Denmark	3	3	0	0	9	1	6
W. Germany	3	1	1	1	3	4	3
Uruguay	3	0	2	1	2	7	2
Scotland	3	0	1	2	1	3	1

Group F

Morocco	0	Poland	0
Portugal	1	England	0
England	0	Morocco	0
Poland	1	Portugal	0
England	3	Poland	0
Morocco	3	Portugal	1

	P	W	D	L	F	A	Pts
Morocco	3	1	2	0	3	1	4
England	3	1	1	1	3	1	3
Poland	3	1	1	1	1	3	3
Portugal	3	1	0	2	2	4	2

Second round

Knock-out phase comprising the top two teams from each group plus the four best third-placed teams.

Mexico	2	Bulgaria	0
Belgium	4	Soviet Union	3*
Brazil	4	Poland	0
Argentina	1	Uruguay	0
France	2	Italy	0
W.Germany	1	Morocco	0
England	3	Paraguay	0
Spain	5	Denmark	1

Quarter-finals

France	1	Brazil	1*
(France won 4–3 on pens)			
W.Germany	0	Mexico	0*
(W Germany won 4–1 on pens)			
Argentina	2	England	1
Spain	1	Belgium	1*
(Belgium won 5–4 on pens)			

Semi-finals

Argentina	2	Belgium	0
W.Germany	2	France	0

Third place match

France	4	Belgium	2

Final

Argentina (1) 3	W.Germany (0) 2
Brown, Valdano, Burruchaga	*Rummenigge, Völler*

ARGENTINA: Pumpido, Cuciuffo, Olarticoechea, Ruggeri, Brown, Giusti, Burruchaga (Trobbiani), Batista, Valdano, Maradona (capt.), Enrique.

WEST GERMANY: Schumacher, Berthold, Briegel, Jakobs, Forster, Eder, Brehme, Matthäus, Allofs (Völler), Magath (Hoeness, D.), Rummenigge (capt.).

Leading scorers

6 Lineker (England); 5 Butragueño (Spain), Careca (Brazil), Maradona (Argentina); 4 Altobelll (Italy), Belanov (USSR), Elkjaer (Denmark), Valdano (Argentina).

*Note: * After extra time*

TOP OF THE WORLD *West German captain Lothar Mathäus celebrates victory over Argentina after the final in Rome*

ITALY 1990

Penalties decide in a tear-jerking anti-climax

The 14th World Cup finals did not live up to the setting. There was a distinct lack of goals, and a miserly shortage of great goals, but perhaps the saddest failure of all was on the part of the established stars who failed to enhance their reputations. The occasion was saved by the Italians themselves, for this was the People's World Cup.

It started dramatically with Cameroon beating the champions Argentina – Omam Biyik scoring the only goal. The Africans topped their group, with Argentina trailing in third place, and were later to frighten the life out of England when they took a 2–1 lead over them in the quarterfinals. Schillaci's tense expressions were to reflect the Italian mood. He scored the winner against Austria and the first against the Czechs as Italy comfortably headed Group A. Scotland was humiliated by Costa Rica, bounced back against Sweden, then crashed out to Brazil after taking them all the way. Scotland's gloom was contrasted by the Republic of Ireland's popular success, their shoot-out win over Romania earning them a tilt at the hosts in the quarterfinals. Belgium emerged as an impressive combination, but their journey ended when David Platt thumped home a brilliant volley to see England to the last eight.

The highlights included the drama in Milan, when Littbarski's goal seemed to have ended Colombia's dream before one of the great characters of the tournament, Carlos Valderrama, who had been carried off, returned to lay on an equalizer for Freddy Rincon. There was the reckless stupidity of Colombian goalkeeper René Higuita, the grace of Tomas Skuhravy, the Czech, striker and the magic of Yugoslavia's Stojkovic. The sheer theatre of West Germany blasting England in a penalty shoot-out, with Gascoigne sobbing.

But the lasting impression of Italia '90 was of the villain of the piece, Argentina, who robbed us of the grace of Brazil, and spoiled the script by beating Italy on penalties to reach a final they were to sully with their dour tactics and flagrant abuse of the rules, with two men sent off, until, ironically, they were beaten by a penalty.

1990

Group A

Italy	1	Austria	0
Czech.	5	USA	1
Italy	1	USA	0
Czech.	1	Austria	0
Italy	2	Czech.	0
Austria	2	USA	1

	P	W	D	L	F	A	Pts
Italy	3	3	0	0	4	0	6
Czech.	3	2	0	1	6	3	4
Austria	3	1	0	2	2	3	2
USA	3	0	0	3	2	8	0

Group B

Cameroon	1	Argentina	0
Romania	2	Soviet Union	0
Argentina	2	Soviet Union	0
Cameroon	2	Romania	1
Argentina	1	Romania	1
Soviet Union	4	Cameroon	0

	P	W	D	L	F	A	Pts
Cameroon	3	2	0	1	3	5	4
Romania	3	1	1	1	4	3	3
Argentina	3	1	1	1	3	2	3
Soviet Union	3	1	0	2	4	4	2

Group C

Brazil	2	Sweden	1
Costa Rica	1	Scotland	0
Brazil	1	Costa Rica	0
Scotland	2	Sweden	1
Brazil	1	Scotland	0
Costa Rica	2	Sweden	1

	P	W	D	L	F	A	Pts
Brazil	3	3	0	0	4	1	6
Costa Rica	3	2	0	1	3	2	4
Scotland	3	1	0	2	2	3	2
Sweden	3	0	0	3	3	6	0

Group D

Colombia	2	UAE	0
W. Germany	4	Yugoslavia	1
Yugoslavia	1	Colombia	0
W. Germany	5	UAE	1
W. Germany	1	Colombia	1
Yugoslavia	4	UAE	1

	P	W	D	L	F	A	Pts
W. Germany	3	2	1	0	10	3	5
Yugoslavia	3	2	0	1	6	5	4
Colombia	3	1	1	1	3	2	3
UAE	3	0	0	3	2	11	0

Group E

Belgium	2	South Korea	0
Uruguay	0	Spain	0
Belgium	3	Uruguay	1
Spain	3	South Korea	1
Spain	2	Belgium	1
Uruguay	1	South Korea	0

	P	W	D	L	F	A	Pts
Spain	3	2	1	0	5	2	5
Belgium	3	2	0	1	6	3	4
Uruguay	3	1	1	1	2	3	3
South Korea	3	0	0	3	1	6	0

Group F

England	1	Rep of Ireland	1
Holland	1	Egypt	1
England	0	Holland	0
Egypt	0	Rep of Ireland	0
England	1	Egypt	0
Holland	1	Rep of Ireland	1

	P	W	D	L	F	A	Pts
England	3	1	2	0	2	1	4
Rep of Ireland	3	0	3	0	2	2	3
Holland	3	0	3	0	2	2	3
Egypt	3	0	2	1	1	2	2

Second phase

Knock-out phase comprising the top two teams from each group plus the four best third-placed teams

Cameroon	2	Colombia	1*
Czech.	4	Costa Rica	1
Argentina	1	Brazil	0
W. Germany	2	Holland	1
Rep of Ireland	0	Rumania	0*
(Rep. of Ireland won 5–4 on pens)			
Italy	2	Uruguay	0
Yugoslavia	2	Spain	1*
England	1	Belgium	0*

Quarter-finals

Argentina	0	Yugoslavia	0*
(Argentina won 3–2 on pens)			
Italy	1	Rep of Ireland	0
W. Germany	1	Czech.	0
England	3	Cameroon	2*

Semi-finals

Argentina	1	Italy	1*
(Argentina won 4–3 on pens)			
W. Germany	1	England	1*
(West Germany won 4–3 on pens)			

Third place match

Italy	2	England	1

Final

W.Germany (0) 1 Argentina (0) 0
Brehme (pen)

West Germany: Illgner, Berthold (Reuter), Kohler, Augenthaler, Buchwald, Brehme, Littbarski, Hässler, Matthäus (capt.), Völler, Klinsmann.

Argentina: Goycochea, Lorenzo, Serrizuela, Sensini, Ruggeri (Monzon), Simon, Basualdo, Burruchaga (Calderon), Maradona (capt.), Troglio, Dezotti.

Leading scorers

6 Schillaci (Italy); 5 Skuhravy (Czechoslovakia); 4 Michel (Spain), Milla (Cameroon), Matthäus (West Germany), Lineker (England).

*Note: * After extra time*

USA 1994
Brazil's glory in Final shoot-out

History was made twice over at the 1994 World Cup finals. Brazil secured a fourth title to add to their triumphs in 1958, 1962 and 1970. But to do so they needed to win the first-ever penalty shoot-out at the end of extra time after a goalless final against Italy in the Rose Bowl in Pasadena.

FIFA introduced four radical measures in an attempt to improve the quality of the action: three points for a win instead of two in the first round group matches; a relaxation over the offside law by which play was to be stopped only if an attacking player was interfering with play; a crackdown on the tackle from behind in particular – for which a red card would be automatic – and violent conduct in general; and finally, injured players would be taken off the field immediately for treatment.

In simple statistical terms these changes added up to 15 sendings off and a record 235 bookings. But, on the positive side, they also computed to 141 goals in 52 matches, a match average of 2.71 and an improvement on Italia '90.

More Than a Game

The biggest shadow over the finals was cast by the death of Andres Escobar, the Colombian defender, who was killed a few days after returning back home to Medellin. The exact reason for his murder is not known – gambling losses, probably involving drug barons, is thought to be the cause – but what was certain was that the center-back had, inadvertantly, scored an own goal against the United States in Colombia's 2–1 defeat.

That victory for the US was probably the most significant single result in the finals because it virtually ensured the hosts a place in the second round. This success struck a chord with the domestic audience which helped carry the World Cup along on a wave of excitement and enthusiasm which surprised even the most optimistic of American soccer people.

However, the team of Group A was undoubtedly Romania, inspired by their attacking general Gheorghe Hagi. The well-organized Swiss team qualified in second place, but Colombia – among the pre-tournament favorites – played without conviction or pattern and were eliminated.

Group B offered clear favourites in Brazil and they did not disappoint their colorful, noisy and musical supporters. Brazil's strength was the striking partnership of Romario and Bebeto. Romario either scored or had a creative hand in 10 of Brazil's 11 goals. Brazil topped the group with Sweden second.

FIVE GOALS IN ONE MATCH *Russia's Oleg Salenko set an individual goal scoring record for the World Cup finals*

Group C included the formal Opening Match in which title holders Germany beat Bolivia 1–0. The Germans appeared labored, and Stefan Effenberg was expelled from the squad at the end of the first round for making a rude gesture towards jeering German fans in the narrow 3–2 win over South Korea. This was the other group which provided only two, rather than three, second round qualifiers. Germany finished top followed by Spain.

Maradona's Misery

In Group D Argentina's Diego Maradona was his team's attacking inspiration in the opening 4–0 win over Greece and in the 2–1 follow-up defeat of Nigeria, but it was after this game that he failed a dope test which showed traces of the banned stimulant ephedrine. The tournament was over for Maradona and Argentina lost their next game, without him, 2–0 to Bulgaria. The Bulgarians thus qualified for the second round despite having crashed 3–0 to the entertaining World Cup newcomers Nigeria in the group's opening match.

The tightest division was Group E, featuring Italy, the Republic of Ireland, Mexico and Norway, and the six matches produced only eight goals.

Ten Men Fight Back

Ireland shocked Italy with a 1–0 victory in their opening match, and Norway appeared on the verge of inflicting a second defeat on the group favorites when goalkeeper Gianluca Pagliuca was sent off. Remarkably, however, Italy fought back to win, 1–0, when defeat would have resulted in almost certain elimination. Wasting that numerical superiority cost Norway dearly. All four teams ended up with four points and zero goal difference, but Norway finished at the bottom of the group on goals scored and was thus eliminated.

Another favored team who struggled in the first round were Holland. They beat Saudi Arabia only 2–1 in their first match then lost an exciting duel 1–0 to Belgium next time out and escaped early elimination by defeating Morocco 2–1 in their final match, to qualify along with Belgium and World Cup newcomers Saudi Arabia – who beat Belgium 1–0 along the way.

> **"It's a death sentence. You can't have fun in this job. It will only be a pleasure if we win the World Cup."**
>
> *Carlos Alberto Parreira, Brazil coach*

The opening match of the second round saw Germany, as on the opening day, playing in Chicago. This time they defeated Belgium 3–2 in an exciting game which marked the successful two-goal return of veteran World Cup-winner Rudi Völler.

The Republic of Ireland committed defensive suicide against Holland, losing 2–0 on mistakes by fullback Terry Phelan and goalkeeper Packie Bonner. Spain had an easy time in beating Switzerland 3–0 and Sweden saw off Saudi Arabia 3–1. Brazil also spoiled the Americans' Independence Day holiday by defeating the hosts more easily than the 1–0 scoreline suggests. The other three second-round games were even more dramatic. Bulgaria defeated Mexico 3–1 on penalties – the first shoot-out of the finals – after an entertaining 1–1 draw, marred by two contentious sendings-off.

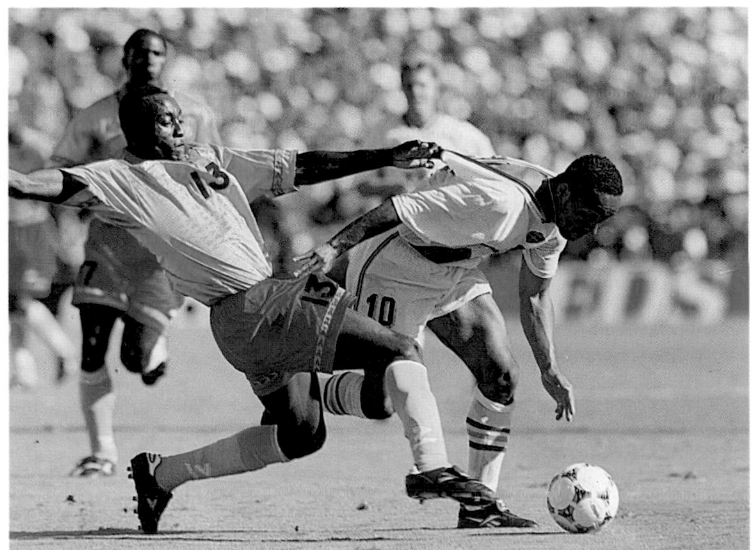

AFRICAN CHALLENGE *Nkongo of Cameroon tussles with Dahlin of Sweden*

A TANGO NOT A SAMBA *Romario and Baresi battle for supremacy in the Final at the Rose Bowl*

Hagi's Army March On

In Pasadena, Romania's Ilie Dumitrescu played the game of his life scoring twice and creating a third for Hagi in a 3–2 defeat of Argentina. Italy dramatically defeated Nigeria; with two minutes remaining the Italians were 1–0 down and had again been reduced to ten men by the dismissal, this time, of midfield substitute Gianfranco Zola. Roberto Baggio snatched an equalizer and as the Nigerians sagged in extra time, he scored again, from the penalty spot.

In the quarter-finals, Sweden, themselves down to 10 men after Stefan Schwarz was sent off, defeated Romania on penalties after a 2–2 draw.

Roberto Baggio confirmed his star rating with Italy's late second goal in their 2–1 victory over Spain. Another tight game saw Brazil defeat Holland 3–2, the first time an opposing team had put Brazil's defense under serious sustained pressure.

Completing the semifinal line-up was rank outsider Bulgaria. Germany went ahead through a Lothar Matthäus penalty. But the title holders conceded two last-gasp goals, from Hristo Stoichkov and Iordan Letchkov. It was Germany's earliest elimination since their quarter-final failure in 1962 and Bulgaria, who had played 16 matches at the finals without winning one before this tournament, moved into the semifinals.

That was to prove the end of the road. The two-goal brilliance of Roberto Baggio lifted Italy into their fifth final while, in the other semi-final, Brazil encountered few difficulties in defeating a lackluster and leg-weary Sweden 1-0.

Penalties in Pasadena

Italy gambled twice over, in playing superstar striker Roberto Baggio despite a hamstring strain and in recalling veteran sweeper Franco Baresi for his first appearance after a cartilage operation following his injury against Norway in the first round.

In fact, Baresi was Italy's man of the match. The game saw Brazil employing their technical brilliance to try to outflank Italy's defensive discipline while the Italians sat back and waited for the right moment to unleash their rapid counter-attacks.

It was a game of few chances, most of which fell to Brazil. Romario misplaced a first-half header and Mazinho couldn't quite capitalize on a half-chance when Pagliuca spilled a Branco free kick. In the 75th minute Pagliuca also allowed a long-range Mauro Silva effort to slip through his hands, but the ball bounced off the post and back into his arms. Pagliuca kissed the post in gratitude. Italy's best chance ended with Taffarel saving from Massaro.

Roberto Baggio went close with one effort in each half of extra time while Brazil should again have taken the lead in the 109th minute when the industrious Cafu crossed to the far post and Romario put the ball fractionally the wrong side of the post from four

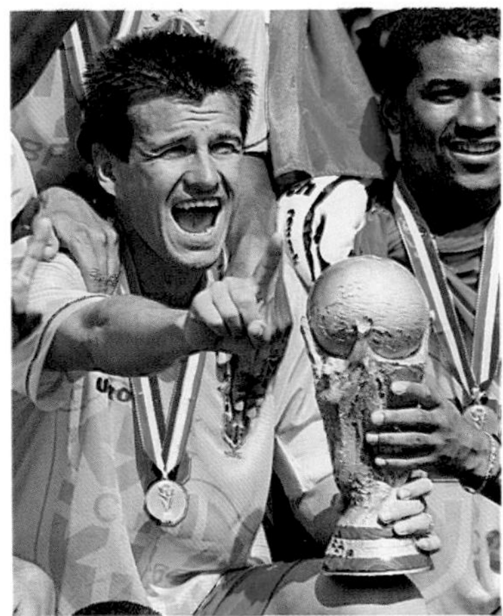

WE ARE THE CHAMPIONS *Dunga with the World Cup trophy*

yards out just beyond the far post.

In the penalty shoot-out, Taffarel benefited immediately when Baresi shot over. Baresi sank to his knees in despair. Pagliuca then saved from Marcio Santos and Italy went briefly ahead as Albertini scored from kick No 2. Romario squared for Brazil, Evani netted for Italy and Branco for Brazil. This was the point at which it fell apart for Italy as Taffarel saved from Massaro and Dunga shot what proved the vital Brazilian kick. Baggio needed to score with Italy's last kick of the five to keep his country alive. Instead, he scooped the ball over the bar. Brazil was back on top of the world.

1994

Group A

USA	1	Switzerland	1
Colombia	1	Romania	3
USA	2	Colombia	1
Romania	1	Switzerland	4
USA	0	Romania	1
Switzerland	0	Colombia	2

	P	W	D	L	F	A	Pts
Romania	3	2	0	1	5	5	6
Switzerland	3	1	1	1	5	4	4
USA	3	1	1	1	3	3	4
Colombia	3	1	0	2	4	5	3

Group B

Cameroon	2	Sweden	2
Brazil	2	Russia	0
Brazil	3	Cameroon	0
Sweden	3	Russia	1
Russia	6	Cameroon	1
Brazil	1	Sweden	1

	P	W	D	L	F	A	Pts
Brazil	3	2	1	0	6	1	7
Sweden	3	1	2	0	6	4	5
Russia	3	1	0	2	7	6	3
Cameroon	3	0	1	2	3	11	1

Group C

Germany	1	Bolivia	0
Spain	2	South Korea	2
Germany	1	Spain	1
South Korea	0	Bolivia	0
Bolivia	1	Spain	3
Germany	3	South Korea	2

	P	W	D	L	F	A	Pts
Germany	3	2	1	0	5	3	7
Spain	3	1	2	0	6	4	5
South Korea	3	0	2	1	4	5	2
Bolivia	3	0	1	2	1	4	1

Group D

Argentina	4	Greece	0
Nigeria	3	Bulgaria	0
Argentina	2	Nigeria	1
Bulgaria	4	Greece	0
Greece	0	Nigeria	2
Argentina	0	Bulgaria	2

	P	W	D	L	F	A	Pts
Nigeria	3	2	0	1	6	2	6
Bulgaria	3	2	0	1	6	3	6
Argentina	3	2	0	1	6	3	6
Greece	3	0	0	3	0	10	1

Group E

Italy	0	Rep of Ireland	1
Norway	1	Mexico	0
Italy	1	Norway	0
Mexico	2	Rep of Ireland	1
Rep of Ireland	0	Norway	0
Italy	1	Mexico	1

	P	W	D	L	F	A	Pts
Mexico	3	1	1	1	3	3	4
Rep of Ireland	3	1	1	1	2	2	4
Italy	3	1	1	1	2	2	4
Norway	3	1	1	1	1	1	4

Group F

Belgium	1	Morocco	0
Holland	2	Saudi Arabia	1
Belgium	1	Holland	0
Saudi Arabia	2	Morocco	1
Morocco	1	Holland	2
Belgium	0	Saudi Arabia	1

	P	W	D	L	F	A	Pts
Holland	3	2	0	1	4	3	6
Saudi Arabia	3	2	0	1	4	3	6
Belgium	3	2	0	1	2	1	6
Morocco	3	0	0	3	2	5	0

Second phase

Germany	3	Belgium	2
Spain	3	Switzerland	0
Saudi Arabia	1	Sweden	3
Romania	3	Argentina	2
Holland	2	Rep of Ireland	0
Brazil	1	USA	0
Nigeria	1	Italy	2*
Mexico	1	Bulgaria	1*

(*Bulgaria won 3–1 on pens*)

Quarter-finals

Italy	2	Spain	1
Holland	2	Brazil	3
Germany	1	Bulgaria	2
Sweden	2	Romania	2*

(*Sweden won 5–4 on pens*)

Semi-finals

Brazil	1	Sweden	0
Italy	2	Bulgaria	1

Third place match

Sweden	4	Bulgaria	0

Final

Brazil	0	Italy	0*

(*Brazil won 3–2 on pens*)

BRAZIL: Taffarel, Jorginho (Cafu 20), Aldair, Marcio Santos, Branco, Mazinho (Viola 106), Dunga (capt.), Mauro Silva, Zinho, Romario, Bebeto.

ITALY: Pagliuca, Mussi (Apolloni 34), Maldini, Baresi (capt.), Benarrivo, Berti, Albertini, D. Baggio (Evani 94), Donadoni, R. Baggio, Massaro.

Leading scorers

6 Salenko (Russia), Stoichkov (Bulgaria);
5 K. Andersson (Sweden), R. Baggio (Italy), Klinsmann (Germany), Romario (Brazil)
4 Batistuta (Argentina), Dahlin (Sweden), Raducioiu (Romania)

*Note: * After extra time*

INTERNATIONAL COMPETITIONS

FIFA UNDER-17 WORLD CHAMPIONSHIP

FIFA has made no secret of its desire to encourage soccer at the grass roots level, and the Under-17 (Junior) and Under-20 (Youth) World Championships are crucial elements of that process. The Under-17 World Championship in particular has shown that skillful soccer is not confined to Europe and South America. Of the five tournaments held so far, African countries have won three times and an Asian country once.

FIFA Under-17 World Championship Finals

1985 Nigeria 2, West Germany 0.
1987 Soviet Union 1, Nigeria 1.
Soviet Union won 4–2 on penalties.
1989 Saudi Arabia 2, Scotland 2.
Saudi Arabia won 5–4 on penalties.
1991 Ghana 1, Spain 0.
1993 Nigeria 2, Ghana 1.

FIFA UNDER-20 WORLD CHAMPIONSHIP

The World Youth Championship, as the Under-20 event is often known, reflects the gap between Europe and South America and the rest of the world which exists from this level up. The reasons for this are too numerous to list, but socio-economic problems and the strong club base in Europe and South America are certainly important factors. After nine tournaments, Africa and Asia have yet to win, although Qatar and Nigeria have been runners-up.

FIFA Under-20 World Championship Finals

1977 Soviet Union 2, Mexico 2.
Soviet Union won 9–8 on penalties.
1979 Argentina 3, Soviet Union 1.
1981 West Germany 4, Qatar 0.
1983 Brazil 1, Argentina 0.
1985 Brazil 1, Spain 0.
1987 Yugoslavia 1, West Germany 1.
Yugoslavia won 5–4 on penalties.
1989 Portugal 2, Nigeria 0.
1991 Portugal 0, Brazil 0.
Portugal won 4–2 on penalties.
1993 Brazil 2, Ghana 1.

HEAD GIRLS *The United States*

WOMEN'S WORLD CUP

Introduced in 1991, the Women's World Cup has massive potential, with over half the world's population eligible. FIFA is giving great encouragement to women's soccer and the first finals took place in China in the winter of 1991. Norway, the European runners-up, faced the USA in the final in Guangzhou, where the Americans won 2–1 with both goals coming from the undisputed star of women's soccer of the 1990s – Michelle Akers-Stahl.

Women's World Cup Finals

1991 USA 2, Norway 1.

OLYMPIC GAMES

Soccer has been part of the Olympic Games since 1908, but the validity of having a professional sport as part of an amateur festival has often been questioned. Indeed, it is reasonable to suggest that the main reason soccer is kept in the Olympic movement is because it is a great source of revenue. For example, at the Los Angeles games in 1984 and in Seoul in 1988, more people turned up to watch the soccer matches than any other sport, including track and field.

The whole amateur ideal of the Olympic Games seems at odds with soccer, which is predominantly a professional sport, and this crucial factor has caused many problems and controversies in the past. The most notable example was in 1928, when the four British Associations withdrew from FIFA in an argument over broken time payments.These were fees paid to players to compensate for loss of income from their regular jobs while they were away playing football. FIFA insisted that the International Olympic Committee accept the principle of these payments, and when the IOC agreed, the British walked out, boycotting the 1924 tournament along with Denmark.

Soccer was first played at the Olympics in 1896, when a scratch tournament involving select teams from Denmark, Athens and Izmir was organized. (The only recorded result was a 15–0 victory for the Danish XI against the Izmir XI.) In Paris in 1900, soccer was again included as a demonstration sport, with Upton Park FC, representing England, beating France 4–0 in the only game played. In 1904 in St Louis, three North American teams entered another demonstrationcompetition. Galt FC from Ontario represented Canada, with the St Louis Christian Brothers College and the St Rose Kickers of St Louis representing the United States. The Canadians won both their games, 7–0 and 4–0 respectively, to take the title.

However, soccer arrived as an accepted Olympic sport with the 1908 Games in London. The England amateur team (not a United Kingdom team), containing many of the best players in the country, won the title, beating Denmark 2–0 in the final at the White City Stadium. Vivian Woodward, one of the outstanding players of the day, scored the second goal at the White City, and led the England team four years later in Stockholm. Denmark, the best amateur team on the continent, was again England's final opponents, and again they ended up with only the silver medal. Berry, Walden and Hoare (twice) scored for England in a 4–2 win against a Danish side which contained Nils Middelboe, later to play

GOLD GETTERS *France's 1984 Olympic-winning side*

OPENING SALVO *Dobrovolski scores the Soviet Union's first goal in the 1988 final*

for Chelsea – one of Woodward's clubs.

The 1912 Stockholm Games were also notable for the introduction of the consolation tournament. This was for teams who were knocked out in the first round and who would otherwise have had to return home after playing only one match. Hungary won the first of these consolation tournaments, beating old rivals Austria 3–0 in the final.

The 1920 Games in Antwerp are remembered for the bad-tempered final between Belgium and Czechoslovakia. Trailing by two goals, the Czechs felt the referee was favoring the home side and walked off the field before the game had ended. They were duly disqualified by FIFA, and a tournament had to be quickly arranged to decide the silver and bronze medal winners. Spain, having won the consolation tournament, beat Holland 3–1 to claim the silver medal.

In 1924 the Games returned to Paris and a South American nation, Uruguay, appeared for the first time. The Uruguayans brought with them dazzling ball skills which most Europeans had never seen before.

They beat Yugoslavia 7–0 in the preliminary round, the United States 3–0 in the first, France 5–1 in the quarterfinals and Holland 2–1 in the semifinals. In the final, before 41,000 fans at Colombes, Uruguay fielded a team containing some of the greats of Uruguayan football: Nasazzi, Andrade, Vidal, Scarone, Petrone, Cea and Romano. Switzerland had no answer and was comprehensively beaten 3–0.

Four years later the Uruguayans returned, along with their great rivals Argentina, to take part in the 1928 Amsterdam Games. In the first round Uruguay defeated the hosts 2–0, while Argentina thrashed the United States 11–2, and both sides continued in similar fashion until they met in the final. The first match produced a 1–1 draw, and Uruguay won the replay 2–1 to retain the title.

Uruguay's success in 1924 and 1928 confirmed the emergence of South America as a soccer-playing continent to be reckoned with, and undoubtedly led to the idea of the World Cup. Indeed, 1928 can be regarded as a watershed year for the Olympic soccer tournament. Up until that date, the winners could justifiably claim to be the world champions. But with the 1930 World Cup, all that changed and the Olympic title assumed a less important role for the major players from Western Europe and South America. The 1932 Games in Los Angeles did not feature a soccer tournament, so Italy was the next Olympic champion, when they beat Austria 2–1 in the 1936 final in Berlin.

In London in 1948 Denmark gained some revenge for the 1908 and 1912 defeats by beating Great Britain 5–3 in the third place playoff. The title, though, went to Denmark's Scandinavian neighbors Sweden. The Swedes, featuring the famous "Grenoli" trio forward line of Gunnar Gren, Gunnar Nordahl and Nils Liedholm (all of whom later joined Milan), beat Yugoslavia 3–1 at Wembley, with Gren scoring twice.

Yugoslavia reached the Final again in Helsinki in 1952, but were unfortunate enough to come up against Hungary's "Magic Magyars." Ferenc Puskas and Zoltan Czibor scored in a 2–0 win — Hungary's only major title — and were part of a side almost identical to the one which lost the 1954 World Cup final.

The 1952 Games also marked the start of a new phase in the history of Olympic football, a period dominated by the Eastern Europeans. The spread of professionalism in the 1930s and 1940s meant that many countries could no longer send their full-strength side to the Olympics. The Eastern Bloc countries circumvented this problem by insisting that their players were amateurs, even though most were paid by the state to play football. Thus the period 1952 to 1976 was dominated by the "shamateurs" from the East.

A qualifying series was intro-

Winners

Olympic Games Finals

1908 *London:* England 2 (Chapman, Woodward), Denmark 0

1912 Stockholm: England 4 (Berry, Walden, Hoare 2), Denmark 2 (Olsen 2)

1920 *Antwerp:* Belgium 2 (Coppee, Larnoe 78), Czechoslovakia 0

1924 *Paris:* Uruguay 3 (Petrone, Cea, Romano), Switzerland 0. Att: 41,000

1928 *Amsterdam:* Uruguay 1 (Ferreira), Argentina 1 (Petrone) – *Amsterdam* (replay): Uruguay 2 (Figueroa, Scarone H.), Argentina 1 (Monti)

1936 *Berlin:* Italy 2 (Frossi 2), Austria 1 (Kainberger, K.). Att: 90,000

1948 *London:* Sweden 3 (Gren 2, Nordahl G.), Yugoslavia 1 (Bobek). Att: 60,000

1952 *Helsinki:* Hungary 2 (Puskas, Czibor), Yugoslavia 0. Att: 60,000

1956 *Melbourne:* Soviet Union 1 (Ilyin), Yugoslavia 0. Att: 120,000

1960 *Rome:* Yugoslavia 3 (Galic, Matus, Kostic), Denmark 1 (Nielsen, F.). Att: 40,000

1964 *Tokyo:* Hungary 2 (o.g., Bene), Czechoslovakia 1 (Brumovsky)

1968 *Mexico City:* Hungary 4 (Menczel, Dunai A.), Bulgaria 1 (Dimitrov)

1972 *Munich:* Poland 2 (Deyna 2), Hungary 1 (Varadi). Att: 50,000

1976 *Montreal:* East Germany 3 (Schade, Hoffmann, Hafner), Poland 1 (Lato). Att: 71,000

1980 *Moscow:* Czechoslovakia 1 (Svoboda), East Germany 0. Att: 70,000

1984 *Los Angeles:* France 2 (Brisson, Xuereb), Brazil 0. Att: 101,000

1988 *Seoul:* Soviet Union 2 (Dobrovolski, Savichev), Brazil 1 (Romario) aet. Att: 73,000

1992 *Barcelona:* Spain 3 (Abelardo, Quico 2), Poland 2 (Kowalczyk, Staniek). Att: 95,000

duced for the 1956 Melbourne Games, which was almost wrecked by the withdrawals of Egypt, Vietnam, China, Hungary, Poland, Turkey, Iran and Afghanistan, presumably because of the enormous distances and costs involved to get to Australia. The Soviet Union won the gold medal, beating poor old Yugoslavia 1–0 in the final in front of an amazing 120,000 crowd at the Melbourne Cricket Ground.

In 1960 the qualifying program was expanded from just 10 matches in 1956 to just under 100, divided along continental lines. Africa and Asia were awarded two berths at the finals, a crucial factor given that both continents only had one place each at the World Cup finals at the time. In this respect, the Olympics have been just as important to the African and Asian nations as the World Cup, especially since 1964 when both were given three berths. Yugoslavia made it fourth time lucky in Rome, beating Denmark 3–1 in the Final.

The Eastern European stranglehold on the competition continued throughout the 1960s and 1970s. Hungary clinched a hat trick of titles when they beat Czechoslovakia in 1964 in Tokyo and Bulgaria in 1968 in Mexico City; Poland ended the Hungarians' run by beating them 2–1 in the final in Munich in 1972; and East Germany made it seven in a row for Eastern Europe when they defeated the Poles 3–1 in Montreal in 1976.

It was clear that the system whereby Eastern European countries could enter full-strength teams, while everybody else could not, gave them an unfair advantage. So FIFA changed the rules for the 1980 tournament, preventing any European or South American who had played in a World Cup qualifier from taking part. The Eastern European countries had one last hurrah in Moscow, though, where Czechoslovakia beat East Germany 1–0. But the new eligibility ruling, even if only an unsatisfactory compromise, did break the monopoly in 1984, when France won gold in Los Angeles.

The 1988 tournament in Seoul featured a host of top-grade professional players and many emerging youngsters yet to play in the World Cup. Ironically, the Soviet Union again struck gold, beating Brazil 2–1 in the final. The tournament also conjured up one of the biggest shocks in Olympic football history when Zambia beat Italy 4–0.

For the 1992 Games in Barcelona the eligibility rule was again changed, with only players under the age of 23 allowed to take part (the UEFA Under-21 Championship now doubles as the Olympic qualifying tournament for Europe). The hosts Spain won the title by beating Poland 3–2 in a splendid final.

There is continued friction, however, between the IOC, which wants a tournament open to the full national sides of every country, and FIFA, which feels such a move would undermine their top competition, the World Cup. For now, the Olympic tournament remains the unofficial Under-23 world championship. For how long depends on whether or not FIFA and the IOC come closer together or grow further apart.

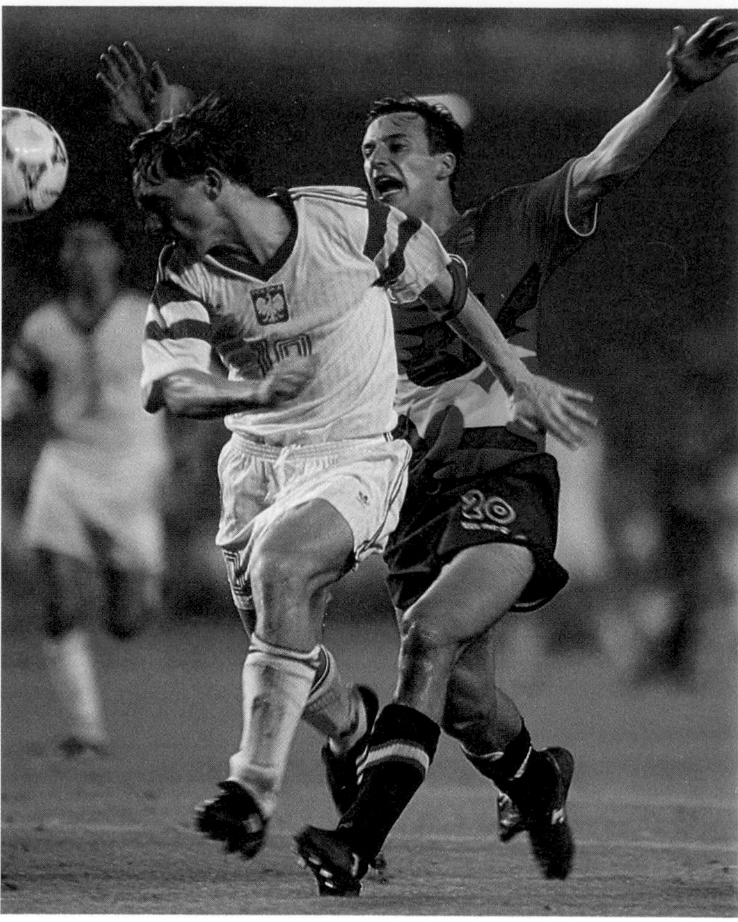

SPANISH GOLD *The hosts beat Poland 3–2 in Barcelona in 1992*

COPA AMERICA (SOUTH AMERICAN CHAMPIONSHIP)

The South American Championship is now the oldest running international competition in the world, following the demise of the British Home International Championship in 1984. The Copa America, as the competition has been known since 1975, is contested by the 10 members of CONMEBOL, the South American Confederation, and is 50 years older than its European equivalent.

The first tournament, in 1910, was not an official championship but is often considered to have been. Matches between River Plate rivals Argentina and Uruguay had been taking place regularly since 1901 in the Lipton and Newton Cups. The development of railways made broader competition a practical idea, and the Argentinians decided to arrange a tournament involving themselves, Uruguay, Brazil and Chile. The Brazilians withdrew before the tournament began, but on May 29, 1910, Uruguay and Chile contested the very first South American Championship match at the Gimnasia club in Buenos Aires.

Penarol star José Piendibene thus scored the first goal in the Copa America as Uruguay ran out 3–0 winners against a hugely inexperienced Chilean side. Seven days later Argentina had an even easier 5–1 victory over Chile, with the goal scorers' names, E. R. Brown, E. Brown and Susan, clearly demonstrating the strong British link.

The tournament has, on all except five occasions, been played on a group basis with no final match. (However, in 1919, 1922, 1937, 1949 and 1953, a championship play-off match decided the winners.)

Almost 40,000 crowded into the Gimnasia ground to see the great rivals, Argentina and Uruguay, battle it out for the inaugural title, but they were to be disappointed. The fans burned one stand and the match was abandoned before it started, amid reports of shootings inside the field. A day later a rearranged match was staged at Racing Club's field, where only 8,000 saw Argentina win 4–1, with goals by Vialle, Hayes, Hutton and Susan.

The Argentina vs. Uruguay "decider" has become a familiar feature of the tournament, as the two have dominated the championship over the years. This is somewhat surprising, because one would expect Brazil to be regularly among the honors. But, despite their proud record in the World Cup, Brazil's record in the Copa America is lamentable. The Brazilians have only ever won the tournament four times, in 1919, 1922, 1949 and 1989 – only once since 1950. This gives credence to the belief that, until recently, the tournament was held in some disdain by several countries. Certainly, it is not uncommon for countries to enter weak teams (without their European-based players), B teams and even youth sides. Indeed, 1975 was the first occasion on which all 10 CONMEBOL countries played.

The second tournament, in 1916, is also listed as unofficial ("extra-

COPA CAPTAIN *Ruggeri of Argentina with the trophy*

ordinario") and was organized as a celebration of Argentina's centenary as an independent country. Argentina and Uruguay again clashed in the "decider," with the Uruguayans avenging their defeat of six years previously.

Between 1916 and 1959 the tournament was held, on average, every two years in one country. Uruguay won six of the first 11 tournaments and have won regularly ever since. Argentina then gained the upper hand from the 1920s to the 1950s, winning 11 of the 18 tournaments staged during that period. Brazil's four victories have all been on home soil.

Successes for the rest of the South American nations have been few and far between. Peru won the first of their two titles in 1939, Paraguay triumphed in 1953 and 1979, and, most remarkably of all, Bolivia won in 1963 when they hosted the tournament. Although it was played at altitude, and although Brazil and Argentina fielded weakened teams, the victory remained Bolivia's finest moment until they qualified for the 1994 World Cup finals.

Argentina has played host nine times, Chile seven, Uruguay six, Peru five and the indifferent Brazilians only four. However, it was the Brazilians' misfortune that, when they were at their peak, in the 1960s, only two tournaments were staged. Indeed, the 1960s marked a decline in the championship as the continent's club championship, the Libertadores Cup, gained in importance. It is also true that the tournament suffered in this period because Argentina, Uruguay and especially Brazil increasingly sought lucrative friendly tours to Europe.

As the tournament expanded, it could not always be guaranteed that the "decider" would be the final match in the tournament, which forced the organizers to experiment with the format. After 1967 a seven-year gap ensued – the longest in the tournament's history – until the revamped 1975 competition, which featured a new format. The old system of playing all the games in one country was replaced with three groups playing home and away to decide the semifinal line-up, with the holders receiving a bye into the semi-finals. The winners were decided by points, not aggregate scores.

This system prevailed until the 1987 series, when the whole tournament was played in Argentina. This too was unsatisfactory, however, and in 1989 two groups of five were used to produce four teams to take part in a final round played on a league basis.

Brazil hosted the 1989 event and won their first title in 40 years, while Argentina won the 1991 tournament, their 14th title.

In 1993, in Ecuador, the tournament underwent another face-lift. Mexico and the United States were invited to take part as guests, and three first round groups were played to produce eight quarter-finalists. However, with only 12 entrants, that meant playing 18 matches in only 10 days to eliminate four teams! Having disposed of the four – Venezuela, Chile, Bolivia and the US – the tournament operated on a straightforward knock-out basis, with quarterfinals, semifinals, a third place play-off and a final.

Defending champions Argentina needed a penalty shoot-out to get past the emerging Colombians in the semi-final. One of the invited guests, Mexico, almost spoiled the party by reaching the final, where they lost 2–1 to Argentina. A Mexican victory would have been a huge embarrassment to CONMEBOL.

Winners

South American Championship

1910 *Buenos Aires*: 1st Argentina, 2nd Uruguay
1916 *Buenos Aires*: 1st Uruguay, 2nd Argentina
1917 *Montevideo*: 1st Uruguay, 2nd Argentina
1919 *Rio de Janeiro* (play-off): Brazil 1 (Friedenreich), Uruguay 0. Att: 28,000
1920 *Vina del Mar*: 1st Uruguay, 2nd Argentina
1921 *Buenos Aires*: 1st Argentina, 2nd Brazil
1922 *Rio de Janeiro* (play-off): Brazil 3 (Formiga 2, Neco), Paraguay 1 (Rivas G.). Att: 20,000
1923 *Montevideo*: 1st Uruguay, 2nd Argentina
1924 *Montevideo*: 1st Uruguay, 2nd Argentina
1925 *Buenos Aires*: 1st Argentina, 2nd Brazil
1926 *Santiago*: 1st Uruguay, 2nd Argentina
1927 *Lima*: 1st Argentina, 2nd Uruguay
1929 *Buenos Aires*: 1st Argentina, 2nd Paraguay
1935 *Lima*: 1st Uruguay, 2nd Argentina
1937 *Buenos Aires* (play-off): Argentina 2 (De la Mata 2), Brazil 0. Att: 80,000
1939 *Lima*: 1st Peru, 2nd Uruguay.
1941 *Santiago*: 1st Argentina, 2nd Uruguay
1942 *Montevideo*: 1st Uruguay, 2nd Argentina
1945 *Santiago*: 1st Argentina, 2nd Brazil
1946 *Buenos Aires*: 1st Argentina, 2nd Brazil
1947 *Guayaquil*: 1st Argentina, 2nd Paraguay
1949 *Rio de Janeiro* (play-off): Brazil 7 (Ademir Menezes 3, Tesourinha 2, Jair R. Pinto 2), Paraguay 0. Att: 55,000
1953 *Lima* (play-off): Paraguay 3 (Lopez A., Gavilan, Fernandez R.), Brazil 2 (Baltazar 2). Att: 35,000
1955 *Santiago*: 1st Argentina, 2nd Chile
1956 *Montevideo*: 1st Uruguay, 2nd Chile
1957 *Lima*: 1st Argentina, 2nd Brazil
1959 *Buenos Aires*: 1st Argentina, 2nd Brazil
1959 *Guayaquil*: 1st Uruguay, 2nd Argentina
1963 *Bolivia*: 1st Bolivia, 2nd Paraguay
1967 *Montevideo*: 1st Uruguay, 2nd Argentina
1975 *Bogota* (1st leg): Colombia 1 (Castro P.), Peru 0. Att: 50,000. *Lima* (2nd leg): Peru 2 (Oblitas, Ramirez O.), Colombia 0. Att: 50,000. *Caracas* (play-off): Peru 1 (Sotil), Colombia 0. Att: 30,000
1979 Asuncion (1st leg): Paraguay 3 (Romero C. 2, Morel M.), Chile 0. *Santiago* (2nd leg): Chile 1 (Rivas), Paraguay 0. Att: 55,000. *Buenos Aires* (play-off): Paraguay 0, Chile 0. Att: 6,000. (*Paraguay won on goal difference*)
1983 *Montevideo* (1st leg): Uruguay 2 (Francescoli, Diogo), Brazil 0. Att: 65,000 *Salvador* (2nd leg): Brazil 1 (Jorginho), Uruguay 1 (Aguilera). Att: 95,000
1987 *Buenos Aires*: Uruguay 1 (Bengochea), Chile 0. Att: 35,000
1989 *Brazil*: 1st Brazil, 2nd Uruguay
1991 *Chile*: 1st Argentina, 2nd Brazil
1993 *Guayaquil*: Argentina 2 (Batistuta 2), Mexico 1 (Galindo pen.). Att: 40,000

Notes: Details of finals or championship play-offs have been given where applicable. For all other tournaments, played on a league basis, only the first and second have been listed. The unofficial "extraordinarios" tournaments were: 1910, 1916, 1935, 1941, 1945, 1946, 1956 and 1959.

Ecuador also reached the semifinal, their best placing in the tournament.

The future for the Copa America is uncertain. Intead of Mexico and the United States, CONMEBOL is considering inviting Spain to participate in 1995, no doubt hoping that Spanish TV would pay handsomely for the broadcasting rights.

SOUTH AMERICAN YOUTH CUP

Started as early as 1954, the South American Youth Cup is the continent's leading event for younger players. Since 1977 it has also doubled as the qualifying tournament for the World Youth Cup, and has only ever been won by five countries.

South American Youth Cup

1954 Uruguay
1958 Uruguay
1964 Uruguay
1967 Argentina
1971 Paraguay
1974 Brazil
1975 Uruguay
1977 Uruguay
1979 Uruguay
1981 Uruguay
1983 Brazil
1985 Brazil
1987 Colombia
1988 Brazil
1991 Brazil
1993 Colombia

DUTCH COURAGE *Ruud Gullit takes on the Soviet defense in the 1988 European Championship final*

EUROPEAN CHAMPIONSHIP

The European Championship, surprisingly, was the last of the continental tournaments to get under way, and was yet another French innovation. Proposed in the mid-1950s by Henri Delaunay, secretary of the French football federation, the European Nations Cup, as the event was previously known, was designed to bring together the various regional tournaments such as the British Home International Championship, the Nordic Cup and the Central European Championship for the Dr Gero Cup.

Delaunay, sadly, died before the tournament got under way, but the trophy still bears his name, and his idea has grown into the second most important international competition after the World Cup. Held every four years, dovetailing neatly with the World Cup finals, the European Championship is a tough competition for which to qualify as there are only eight finals places, one of which is automatically claimed by the hosts.

The first tournament was held in 1959–60, and was played on a straightforward home and away knock-out basis. A four-team final series followed, though the hosts for the final matches were not decided until the semi-finalists were known. The very first European Championship match took place in Dublin on April 5, 1959, when the Republic of Ireland beat Czechoslovakia 2–0 in a preliminary round qualifier. Oddly, West Germany, Italy, Belgium, The Netherlands, Luxembourg, Sweden, Switzerland, Finland and the four British sides chose not to enter the first tournament.

The Eastern Bloc occupied three of the four semifinal slots in the 1960 finals, which France hosted. The Soviet Union received a bye in the quarterfinals after Spain, their opponents, withdrew because the Soviets were not deemed suitable opponents by the right-wing Franco government. In the semifinals, the Soviets beat Czechoslovakia 3–0 while the hosts lost 5–4 to Yugoslavia in a thrilling match. In the final, the Yugoslavs' all-out attack threatened to overrun the Soviets, but Lev Yashin responded with a string of fine saves. The Yugoslavs did take the lead, but the Soviets equalized almost immediately and made their superior physical strength count in extra time to win 2–1.

The 1964 finals tournament took place in Spain, where the hosts made good use of home advantage to win their only major trophy. The Spanish needed extra time to beat Hungary 2–1 in the semifinals, and thus set up a final showdown with the Soviet Union, who easily beat Denmark 3–0. Ironically, General Fran-

Finals

European Championship Finals

1960 *Paris:* Soviet Union 2 (Metreveli, Ponedelnik), Yugoslavia 1 (Galic). Att: 18,000
1964 *Madrid:* Spain 2 (Pereda, Marcelino), Soviet Union 1 (Khusainov). Att: 105,000
1968 *Rome:* Italy 1 (Domenghini), Yugoslavia 1 (Dzajic). Att: 85,000. Replay – *Home:* Italy 2 (Riva, Anastasi), Yugoslavia 0. Att: 85,000
1972 *Brussels:* West Germany 3 (Müller G. 2, Wimmer), Soviet Union 0. Att: 65,000
1976 *Belgrade:* Czechoslovakia 2 (Svehlik, Dobias), West Germany 2 (Müller D., Holzenbein) (aet). Czechoslovakia won 5–4 on penalties. Att: 45,000
1980 *Rome:* West Germany 2 (Hrubesch 2), Belgium 1 (Vandereycken). Att: 48,000
1984 *Paris:* France 2 (Platini, Bollone), Spain 0. Att: 47,000
1988 *Munich:* Holland 2 (Gullit, Van Basten), Soviet Union 0. Att: 72,000
1992 *Stockholm:* Denmark 2 (Jensen, Vilfort), Germany 0. Att: 37,000

co attended the final in Madrid and was doubtless pleased as Spain triumphed 2–1.

The qualifying tournament was expanded to eight groups for the 1968 event, as West Germany and Scotland took part for the first time, though neither reached the last four. Hosts Italy beat the Soviet Union in the first semifinal, but only by the rather dubious method of tossing a coin. World champions England also reached the semifinals, but was beaten 1–0 by Yugoslavia in a bad-tempered game in which Alan Mullery became the first English player to be sent off. England had to settle for victory in the third place play-off – their best ever performance in the event. The final went to a replay, where goals by Riva and Anastasi were too much for the exhausted Yugoslav players, who again had to be content with runners-up medals.

The Soviets reached their third final out of four in 1972, but were no match for the emerging West Germans, who beat England in the quarterfinals and hosts Belgium in the semis. The incomparable Gerd Müller was at his peak, and two goals by him in the final set up a 3–0 victory, and confirmed the Germans as favorites for the World Cup to be held two years later on their home soil.

The 1976 tournament threw up surprises from start to finish. England, Italy and France were eliminated in the qualifying round, and the semifinal line-up included two emerging nations, Czechoslovakia and Holland, World Cup holders West Germany and hosts Yugoslavia.

Both semifinals went to extra time, the Czechs beating the Dutch 3–1, thanks to two very late goals, and the West Germans defeating the Yugoslavs 4–2, with a hat trick by substitute Dieter Müller.

The Germans were clear favorites in the final, but the Czechs had other ideas. Goals by Svehlik and Dobias gave them a 2–0 lead inside half an hour, but the dogged Germans fought back, Holzenbein snatching an equalizer in the 89th minute. Extra time failed to separate the teams, and in the penalty shoot-out which followed, Antonin Panenka kept his nerve to chip his penalty past Sepp Maier and insure that justice was done.

ON ONE KNEE *Belgium's Millecamps tries to stop a German raider in 1980*

In 1980 the format for the final stages of the competition changed. The quarter-finals were abolished and the seven qualifying group winners proceeded straight to the finals along with the hosts, Italy, who received a bye direct to the final stage. The eight teams were divided into two groups of four, with the winners meeting in the final.

The Soviets failed to qualify for their "favorite" tournament, and the Yugoslavs also missed out, but there was a first ever finals appearance for Greece. Belgium proved the surprise package of the tournament, reaching the final after conquering England, Spain and hosts Italy in the group matches. West Germany won the other group with a little to spare and became the only nation to win the trophy twice when they beat the Belgians 2–1 with two goals from Horst Hrubesch – one early in the game, the other two minutes from time. The final was one of the few games to live up to expectations in a disappointing tournament marred by English hooligans.

The 1984 tournament was the best to date, with the flamboyant French in unstoppable form and playing at home, where new stadia were built and old ones refurbished. Semi-finals were re-introduced for the group winners and runners-up, and although the finals line-up did not include England, Holland, the Soviet Union or Italy, the quality of the football on show was not diminished.

Above all, France had Michel Platini to thank for their success. His nine goals in five games was a superb achievement as the French swept aside Denmark, Belgium and Yugoslavia in the group matches. Little respected Spain clinched the other group and then squeezed past the impressive Danes on penalties after a 1–1 draw in the semifinals. Portugal, in the finals for the first time, took France to extra time in the other semi in Marseille, then took the lead after 97 minutes, but eventually succumbed to goals by Domergue and Platini as the French won 3–2. The final was more conclusive. Platini and Bellone scored the goals as the host country won for the third time in seven events.

ON THE RUN *Denmark's Brian Laudrup outpaces Germany's Reuter in 1992*

The 1988 finals in West Germany included all Europe's big names, except the French, plus one new one: the Republic of Ireland. Jack Charlton's motley collection qualified for their first finals and were within nine minutes of reaching the semifinals, when a miscued header by Holland's Wim Kieft spun past Packie Bonner and into the net for the only goal.

England flopped disastrously, losing all three group matches, as the Soviet Union and Holland went through to meet Italy and West Germany respectively. With Rinus Michels in charge, the Dutch played irresistible soccer, beating the hosts 2–1 in the semifinal with a splendid goal by Marco Van Basten two minutes from time. Van Basten did even better in the final against the Soviets, crashing home a volley from an impossible angle to seal a 2–0 victory following Ruud Gullit's first-half opener.

Sweden hosted the 1992 finals, thus ensuring their first qualification, and they were joined in making their maiden voyage by Scotland. But the biggest surprise came from Denmark, last-minute replacements for the suspended Yugoslavia. To everybody's amazement, the Danes arrived with little time to prepare and walked off with the trophy!

Defending champions Holland impressed in the group matches, but were then victims of an old complaint: over-confidence. In the semifinal the Danes led twice in a 2–2 draw and then won 5–4 on penalties. In the other semi the Germans beat the hosts 3–2, having been two up, and looked set to claim their third European crown. But the hard-working, though injury-hit, Danish side confounded the experts by deservedly winning 2–0 with an outstanding display of counter-attacking soccer.

The 1996 tournament, to be held in England, will be expanded. With the fragmentation of the Soviet Union and Yugoslavia, many "new" countries have come on the scene, and UEFA faced great problems in coping with the increase in numbers. Clearly, the established system of an eight-team final tournament was no longer practical, and so the 1996 finals will feature 16 countries, with the hosts, as usual, receiving a bye, but the holders still having to qualify. The qualifying groups also have been expanded to cope with the increase. These changes will make it a little easier to qualify for the finals, but will put further strain on an already overcrowded international games list.

FRANCHI TROPHY

The Franchi Trophy is a challenge match between the champions of Europe and South America, and is named in memory of the late Artemio Franchi, a former president of UEFA. The trophy is not a regular event, and has only been held twice. France won the inaugural event in 1985 for Europe, Argentina levelling the series for the South Americans in 1992.

Franchi Trophy

1985 France	**1992** Argentina

EUROPEAN UNDER-21 CHAMPIONSHIP

Started in 1978, the European Under-21 Championship is Europe's top competition for up-and-coming players. Of the nine tournaments played, England, Italy and the Soviet Union have won twice, and the event now doubles up as the European qualifying tournament for the Olympic Games.

European Under-21 Championship Winners

1978 Yugoslavia	**1988** France
1980 Soviet Union	**1990** Soviet Union
1982 England	**1992** Italy
1984 England	**1994** Italy
1986 Spain	

EUROPEAN YOUTH CHAMPIONSHIP

This tournament began life, in 1948, as the European Junior Championship for Under-18s. The tournament was held every year until the mid-1980s, when a biennial format was tried, and subsequently abandoned. The competition changed its name to the European Youth Championship in 1981. England has the best overall record with nine victories, including a hat trick of titles between 1971 and 1973, and in 1993. Italy, surprisingly, has only won the title outright once, but in 1966 they shared it with the Soviet Union.

European Youth Championship Winners

1948 England	**1969** Bulgaria
1949 France	**1970** E. Germany
1950 Austria	**1971** England
1951 Yugoslavia	**1972** England
1952 Spain	**1973** England
1953 Hungary	**1974** Bulgaria
1954 Spain	**1975** England
1955 no final	**1976** Soviet Union
1956 no final	**1977** Belgium
1957 Austria	**1978** Soviet Union
1958 Italy	**1979** Yugoslavia
1959 Bulgaria	**1980** England
1960 Hungary	**1981** W. Germany
1961 Portugal	**1982** Scotland
1962 Romania	**1983** France
1963 England	**1984** Hungary
1964 England	**1986** E. Germany
1965 E. Germany	**1988** Soviet Union
1966 Soviet Union & Italy	**1990** Soviet Union
1967 Soviet Union	**1992** Turkey
1968 Czechoslovakia	**1993** England

STARS IN SYDNEY *Brazil in 1993*

AFRICAN NATIONS CUP

The African Nations Cup is the blue ribbon event of African soccer, and the tournament is as old as the Confederation of African Football itself. Held every two years in a nominated country, the tournament has grown from humble beginnings to embrace the whole continent.

The first finals took place in Khartoum in 1957 and involved only Sudan, Egypt and Ethiopia. South Africa were initially due to take part, and were scheduled to play Ethiopia in the semi-final, but would only send either an all-black team or an all-white team. The CAF insisted on a multi-racial team, South Africa refused and withdrew, and, until readmitted to the CAF in 1992, they took no further part in African or international soccer.

Egypt won the first tournament, with El Diba scoring all four goals in the 4–0 win over Ethiopia in the final. The same three nations took part in the second, which Egypt hosted in 1959. The tournament was played on a league basis, and Egypt retained the trophy by beating Ethiopia 4–0, with Gohri scoring a hat-trick, and Sudan 2–1. Ethiopia hosted the third tournament in 1962, where Tunisia and Uganda took part for the first time. This time around the Ethiopians prevented the Egyptians completing a hat trick of consecutive titles by beating them 4–2 in a final which went to extra time.

Ghana and Nigeria joined the fray for the 1963 tournament, held in Ghana, with two groups of three producing the two finalists – Ghana and Sudan. The hosts won 3–0 and went on to become the dominant force in African soccer during the decade, twice winning and twice finishing as runners-up.

Two years later, in Tunisia, the Ghanaians won again, this time beating the hosts 3–2 after extra time. A new rule allowing each country to field only two overseas-based players was also introduced in 1965, to encourage development of the game in Africa.

The tournament had by now grown from its original three to 18 entrants, and a qualifying tournament was introduced to produce eight finalists, with the hosts and holders qualifying for the final round automatically. Congo Kinshasa, as Zaïre was known, duly faced reigning champions Ghana in the 1968 final in Addis Ababa, and pulled off something of a shock by winning 1–0 with a goal by Kalala. Ghana returned for the 1970 final in Khartoum, but lost 1–0 to the hosts Sudan.

In 1972, in Yaounde, Zaïre's neighbors Congo won the title, beating Mali 3–2 in the Final. But Zaïre returned in 1974 to face Zambia in the final. A 2–2 draw in the first game was followed by a 2–0 win for Zaïre, who travelled to the World Cup finals a few months later as reigning African champions and the first African team to reach the finals of the world's premier event. Here Zaïre striker Ndaye scored twice in the first match and repeated the trick in the second – the first time that the African Nations Cup had required a replay.

Guinea won numerous club honours during the 1970s, but these triumphs were never reflected at national level. They came closest to winning the African title in 1976 in Ethiopia. A final round group replaced the semifinals and final, and Guinea needed a win in their final match against Morocco to take the title. Cherif gave them the lead after 33 minutes, but an equalizer by Baba four minutes from time gave Morocco a 1–1 draw and the title by a point.

Morocco, like their North African neighbors, have not done particularly well in the African Nations Cup. Despite qualifying for the World Cup finals on three occasions, 1976 remains Morocco's only African title. Given the success of North African clubs in continental competitions, it is curious that the national teams have not matched them.

Nigeria won their only African Nations Cup title on home soil in 1980. The semifinals featured the hosts, Algeria, Egypt and Morocco, but again the North Africans revealed a dislike for traveling. Paired with Algeria in the final, and spurred on by a crowd of 80,000 in Lagos, the

AFRICAN ART *Scene from the 1992 Nations Cup in Dakar, Senegal*

Nigerians won 3–0 with goals by Odegbami (two) and Lawal.

The 1982 tournament in Libya saw the return of Ghana to the African throne. The two-overseas-players rule, which had become impractical with so many of them earning a living in Europe, was abolished, and nations could choose their best line-ups once again. In the opening game of the tournament Libya beat Ghana 2–0, but both countries progressed to the final. This time around the Ghanaians made their greater experience count as they fought out a 1–1 draw before taking the trophy for a record fourth time with a 7–6 penalty shoot-out victory.

Cameroon emerged for their only victory in the 1984 finals in the Ivory Coast. Having squeezed past Algeria in the semifinals, on penalties, they beat Nigeria 3–1 in the final. Their team contained many who had performed so well at the 1982 World Cup finals in Spain, including the incomparable Roger Milla.

In 1986 Egypt hosted the tournament, which was marked by incidents on and off the field. A week before the tournament began, security police draftees in Egypt rioted. A curfew was imposed and there was the very real threat that the finals would have to be cancelled. Thankfully the curfew was lifted so that the tournament could take place, but tanks and armored cars still surrounded the stadiums to prevent further trouble.

On the field many teams complained about the standard of refereeing, and there were several angry outbursts from players and managers. Morocco manager José Faria was even prompted to describe one match as being rougher than the England vs. France Rugby Union international being staged at roughly the same time! Defending champions Cameroon again reached the final, where they met the hosts Egypt. The tournament as a whole had been laden with defensive play, and the final was no exception. After a dull 0–0 draw the hosts won 5–4 on penalties to the delight of the 100,000 crowd at Cairo's International Stadium.

Cameroon recovered from this disappointment by winning the 1988 title in Morocco. In the semifinals, they beat the hosts by a single goal while Nigeria needed penalties to get past Algeria. A crowd of 50,000 in Casablanca saw Cameroon win 1–0 with a goal by Emmanuel Kunde after 55 minutes.

Two years later, in Algiers, the Nigerians again reached the final. Unfortunately for them, they met the hosts and were again beaten by a single goal, from Oudjani after 38 minutes, in front of 80,000 fans. For the poor Nigerians, it was their third final defeat in four tournaments.

In 1992 a new name was added to the list of winners: the Ivory Coast. The tournament, held in Senegal for the first time, was expanded to 12 teams in the final round because of the ever-increasing number of countries taking part – even tiny nations such as Burkina Faso, Swaziland and the Seychelles now consider the African Nations Cup a worthwhile exercise. The Ivory Coast and their western neighbors Ghana reached the final, although the Ivorians needed penalties to overcome Cameroon in the semifinals. The final finished goalless and, in one of the most amazing penalty shoot-outs ever seen, the Ivory Coast won 11–10.

Zambia suffered a catastrophe in April 1993, when the plane carrying their squad to a World Cup match in Senegal crashed into the sea off Gabon, en route from a nations cup quailifier in Mauritius. All 30 people on board, including 18 players, died. But several European-based players were not on the flight, and the Zambians rebuilt their team around them, completed their qualifying matches and duly qualified for the 1994 finals in Tunisia. Neutrals must have been hoping that Zambia would win, but they fell to Nigeria who, in their fourth final in 10 years, finally triumphed

To overcome the problem of getting European-based players released, the biannual tournament is now held in the early part of the year, when most European countries are taking their winter break.

The tournament has come a long way since 1957, and worldwide TV companies are now showing greater interest in it. The presence of so many European-based players is partly responsible for this, and the future of Africa's top soccer event looks encouragingly bright.

ASIAN CUP

The Asian Cup, for national teams started in 1956 and, until the 1980 tournament, was dominated by South Korea and Iran. Since then Kuwait and Saudi Arabia have enjoyed success, reflecting the shift of power in Asian football towards the Arab states.

Asian Cup Finals

1956 South Korea 2, Israel 1
1960 South Korea 3, Israel 0
1964 Israel 2, India 0
1968 Iran 3, Burma 1
1972 Iran 2, South Korea 1
1976 Iran 1, Kuwait 0
1980 Kuwait 3, South Korea 0
1984 Saudi Arabia 2, China 0
1988 Saudi Arabia 0, South Korea 0 (*Saudia Arabia won 4–3 on penalties*)
1992 Japan 1, Saudi Arabia 0

Winners

African Nations Cup Finals

1957 *Khartoum:* Egypt 4 (El Diba 4), Ethiopia 0.
1959 *Cairo*: 1st Egypt, 2nd Sudan.
1962 *Addis Ababa*: Ethiopia 4 (Girma, Menguitsou 2, Italo), Egypt 2 (Badawi 2) (aet).
1963 *Accra*: Ghana 3 (Aggrey-Fynn, Mfum 2), Sudan 0.
1965 *Tunis*: Ghana 3 (Odoi 2, Kofi), Tunisia 2 (Chetali, Chaibi) (aet).
1968 *Addis Ababa:* Congo Kinshasa (Zaïre) 1 (Kalala), Ghana 0.
1970 *Khartoum*: Sudan 1 (El Issed), Ghana 0. Att: 12,000.
1972 *Yaounde*: Congo 3 (M'Bono 2, M'Pele), Mali 2 (Diakhite, Traore M.).
1974 *Cairo*: Zaire 2 (Ndaye 2), Zambia 2 (Kaushi, Sinyangwe) (aet).
Cairo (replay): Zaïre 2 (Ndaye 2), Zambia 0. Att: 1,000.
1976 *Addis Ababa*: 1st Morocco, 2nd Guinea.
1978 *Accra*: Ghana 2 (Afriye 2), Uganda 0. Att: 40,000.
1980 *Lagos*: Nigeria 3 (Odegbami 2, Lawal), Algeria 0. Att: 80,000.
1982 *Tripoli*: Ghana 1 (Al Hassan), Libya 1 (Beshari) (aet). (*Ghana won 7–6 on penalties.*) Att: 50,000
1984 *Abidjan*: Cameroon 3 (Ndjeya, Abega, Ebongue), Nigeria 0. Att: 50,000.
1986 *Cairo:* Egypt 0, Cameroon 0 (aet). (*Egypt won 5–4 on penalties.*) Att: 100,000.
1988 *Casablanca*: Cameroon 1 (Kunde), Nigeria 0. Att: 50,000.
1990 *Algiers*: Algeria 1 (Oudjani), Nigeria 0. Att: 80,000.
1992 *Dakar*: Ivory Coast 0, Ghana 0 (aet). (*Ghana won 11–10 on penalties.*) Att: 60,000.
1994 *Tunis*: Nigeria 2 (Amunike 2), Zambia 1 (Litana). Att: 25,000

ASIAN GAMES

The first Asian games were organized by India in 1951, and six countries brought teams for the soccer tournament. Since then the Asian Games football tournament has expanded to include most of the continent, and is effectively the region's second continental championship.

Asian Games Finals

1951 India 1, Iran 0
1954 Taiwan 5, South Korea 2
1958 Taiwan 3, South Korea 2
1962 India 2, South Korea 1
1966 Burma 1, Iran 0
1970 Burma 0, South Korea 0
1974 Iran 1, Israel 0
1978 North Korea 0, South Korea 0
1982 Iraq 1, Kuwait 0
1986 South Korea 2, Saudi Arabia 0
1990 Iran 0, North Korea 0
(Iran won 4–1 on penalties)

Note: in 1970 and 1978 the trophy was shared by the finalists.

CONCACAF CHAMPIONSHIP

The Central American Championship has been contested, under various formats and with varying numbers of participants, since 1941. Costa Rica's record is outstanding, with 10 victories, including a hat-trick between 1960 and 1963. The event became a serious regional championship in 1991, when Mexico and the USA joined in.

Renamed the CONCACAF Gold Cup, the final that year was won by the Americans against Honduras on penalties. In 1993, it was Mexico historically the strongest of the CONCACAF nations and the one with the greatest soccer pedigree, which triumphed.

CONCACAF Championship Winners

1941	Costa Rica	**1965**	Mexico
1943	El Salvador	**1967**	Guatemala
1946	Costa Rica	**1969**	Costa Rica
1948	Costa Rica	**1971**	Mexico
1951	Panama	**1973**	Haiti
1953	Costa Rica	**1977**	Mexico
1955	Costa Rica	**1981**	Honduras
1957	Haiti	**1985**	Canada
1960	Costa Rica	**1989**	Costa Rica
1961	Costa Rica	**1991**	USA
1963	Costa Rica	**1993**	Mexico

CLUB COMPETITIONS

WORLD CLUB CUP

The World Club Cup is not, as its name suggests, open to every side in the world. In reality it is a challenge match between the champions of Europe and the champions of South America. Asia, Africa and the rest of the world do not get a look in . . . yet. FIFA is now considering plans to expand the tournament to include the best teams from each of the continental confederations in a sort of world league. The idea is still in its infancy and may never come to fruition. But, if it were to happen, it is still likely that a European or South American team would win.

Henri Delaunay, UEFA general secretary, first suggested the idea of a challenge match between the champions of Europe and South America in a letter to CONMEBOL, the South American Confederation, in 1958. His idea provided the impetus for them to get the Copa Libertadores (the South American Club Cup) up and running because, at that stage, South America had no continental championship for its clubs, even though an event for national sides had been taking place since 1910.

Before 1980, matches in the World Club Cup, or Intercontinental Cup as it is sometimes known, were played on a home and away basis, and up until 1968 the result was decided by points, not the aggregate score. This meant that if the clubs won one match each or both were drawn, a decider had to be played. Until 1964 this decider had, for reasons never fully explained, to take place on the ground of the team who played at home in the second leg, giving them a massive advantage. Then for another four years the decider at least had to be played on that club's continent.

Despite these tortuous rules, the competition got off to a flying start in 1960, when Real Madrid met Penarol of Uruguay. Madrid had just won their fifth European Cup in a row, with a 7–3 demolition of Eintracht Frankfurt, while Penarol had become the first winners of the Copa

WORLD'S BEST *Nacional's Blanco faces Nottingham Forest's Francis in the 1981 World Club Cup in Tokyo*

Libertadores. The first leg, in Montevideo, produced a 0–0 draw, but in the return two months later Real Madrid pounded the Uruguayans 5–1. The Real forward line was one of the best ever, and contained Del Sol, Di Stefano, Gento and Puskas, who scored twice. A combined attendance of 200,000 saw the matches.

In 1961 it was Penarol's turn to chalk up five goals, this time against the emerging Portuguese eagles, Benfica. However, a solitary Coluna goal in the first leg meant a decider was necessary, and Penarol only just managed to win 2–1 at home against a Benfica side bolstered by a young Eusebio, who was specially flown in.

Benfica represented Europe again in 1962, but this time they ran headlong into Brazil's Santos . . . and Pele. The "Black Pearl" scored twice in Rio as Santos narrowly won 3–2, and then scored a breathtaking hat trick in Lisbon as Benfica crashed to a 5–2 home defeat. Santos became one of only four sides to retain the trophy when they beat Milan in 1963. Both teams won 4–2 at home, but the decider provided a nasty taste of things to come, with a player from each side sent off and a penalty deciding the outcome, in favor of the Brazilians, who were without Pele for the second and third games.

The next two editions were contested by Internazionale of Italy and Independiente of Argentina, with Inter winning on both occasions. A goal by Corso in a decider in Madrid was enough in 1964, and the following year Inter drew 0–0 away and won the home leg 3–0 to retain the trophy. Among the famous names in the Inter line-up were Suarez, Mazzola and Fachetti.

In 1966 Penarol returned to win for the third time, beating Real Madrid 2–0 in both legs, with Spencer scoring three of the Uruguayans' goals. From this encouraging start, the World Club Cup ran into severe problems in the late 1960s and early 1970s, largely owing to different styles of play and behavior.

The 1967 series paired Argentina's Racing Club with Scotland's Celtic. Feelings in Argentina were still running high over their 1966 World Cup quarter final elimination by England, and the matches degenerated into a bad-tempered farce. After a 1–0 Celtic win in Glasgow, the return in Buenos Aires was chaotic. Celtic goalkeeper Ronnie Simpson was struck by a missile from the crowd before the kick-off, and could not play. Racing won 2–1 to set up a decider, in Montevideo, which was doomed before it began. Celtic lost their composure under extreme provocation and had four men sent off after Basile had spat at Lennox. Racing also had two men sent off but won 1–0.

It was extremely unfortunate, therefore, that the next team to represent South America – for three years running – were Estudiantes de la Plata of Argentina, a team that was solely interested in winning, and would stop at nothing to do it. At home in 1968 they battered Manchester United, who had Nobby Stiles sent off for a gesture to a linesman and Bobby Charlton taken off with a shin injury caused by a kick from Pachame. In the return at Old Trafford, Medina and Best were sent off for fighting as, under the competition's revised rules, the Argentinians completed a 2–1 aggregate win. The violence was so bad that FIFA president Sir Stanley Rous was prompted to write a letter of complaint to the Estudiantes hierarchy.

The following year, 1969, Milan came off even worse than United. After winning 3–0 at home, Milan was savaged in Buenos Aires, where Combin had his nose broken and Prati was kicked in the back while receiving treatment, but managed to hold on for a 4–2 aggregate victory. Three Estudiantes players were imprisoned after the game for their outrageous behavior and were given severe suspensions at the request of the Argentinian president.

Sadly, Estudiantes did not learn their lesson, and things were as bad in 1970 when they played Feyenoord, who came out on top after drawing the drawing the first leg in Buenos Aires. In the return in Rotterdam, Feyenoord's bespectacled Van Deale had his glasses smashed early in the game but still scored the winner. Feyenoord made it known that they would not have taken part in a decider if it had been needed, and the following year their countrymen, Ajax, went a step further by refusing to play against Nacional of Uruguay. Panathinaikos, beaten finalists in

Winners

World Club Cup Finals

1960 *Montevideo*: Penarol 0, Real Madrid 0. Att: 75,000
Madrid: Real Madrid 5 (Puskas 2, Di Stefano, Herrera, Gento), Penarol 1 (Borges). Att: 125,000
1961 *Lisbon*: Benfica 1 (Coluna), Penarol 0. Att: 50,000
Montevideo: Penarol 5 (Sasia, Joya 2, Spencer 2), Benfica 0. Att: 56,000
Montevideo (play-off): Penarol 2 (Sasia 2), Benfica 1 (Eusebio). Att: 62,000
1962 *Rio de Janeiro*: Santos 3 (Pele 2, Coutinho), Benfica 2 (Santana 2). Att: 90,000
Lisbon: Benfica 2 (Eusebio, Santana), Santos 5 (Pele 3, Coutinho, Pepe). Att: 75,000
1963 *Milan*: Milan 4 (Trapattoni, Amarildo 2, Mora), Santos 2 (Pele 2). Att: 80,000
Rio de Janeiro: Santos 4 (Pepe 2, Almir, Lima), Milan 2 (Altafini, Mora). Att: 150,000
Rio de Janeiro (play-off): Santos 1 (Dalmo), Milan 0. Att: 121,000
1964 *Avellanada*: Independiente 1 (Rodriguez), Internazionale 0. Att: 70,000
Milan: Internazionale 2 (Mazzola, Corso), Independiente 0. Att: 70,000
Milan (play-off): Internazionale 1 (Corso), Independiente 0 (aet). Att: 45,000
1965 *Milan*: Internazionale 3 (Poiro, Mazzola 2), Independiente 0. Att: 70,000
Avellanada: Independiente 0, Internazionale 0. Att: 70,000
1966 *Montevideo*: Penarol 2 (Spencer 2), Real Madrid 0. Att: 70,000
Madrid: Real Madrid 0, Penarol 2 (Rocha, Spencer). Att: 70,000
1967 *Glasgow*: Celtic 1 (McNeill), Racing Club 0. Att: 103,000.
Avellanada: Racing Club 2 (Raffo, Cardenas), Celtic 1 (Gemmell). Att: 80,000
Montevideo (play-off): Racing Club 1 (Cardenas), Celtic 0. Att: 65,000.
1968 *Buenos Aires*: Estudiantes 1 (Conigliaro), Manchester United 0. Att: 65,000
Manchester: Manchester United 1 (Morgan), Estudiantes 1 (Veron). Att: 60,000
1969 *Milan*: Milan 3 (Sormani 2, Combin), Estudiantes 0. Att: 80,000
Buenos Aires: Estudiantes 2 (Conigliaro, Aguirre-Suarez), Milan 1 (Rivera). Att: 65,000. Milan won 4–2 on aggregate
1970 *Buenos Aires*: Estudiantes 2 (Echecopar, Veron), Feyenoord 2 (Kindvall, Van Hanegem). Att: 65,000
Rotterdam: Feyenoord 1 (Van Deale), Estudiantes 0. Att: 70,000 Feyenoord won 3–2 on aggregate.
1971 *Athens*: Panathinaikos 1 (Filakouris), Nacional (Uru) 1 (Artime). Att: 60,000
Montevideo: Nacional 2 (Artime 2), Panathinaikos 1 (Filakouris). Att: 70,000. Nacional won 3–2 on aggregate
1972 *Avellanada*: Independiente 1 (Sa), Ajax 1 (Cruyff). Att: 65,000.
Amsterdam: Ajax 3 (Neeskens, Rep 2), Independiente 0. Att: 60,000. Ajax won 4–1 on aggregate
1973 *Rome* (single match): Independiente 1 (Bochini 40), Juventus 0. Att: 35,000
1974 *Buenos Aires*: Independiente 1 (Balbuena 33), Atletico Madrid 0. Att: 60,000
Madrid: Atletico Madrid 2 (Irureta 21, Ayala 86), Independiente 0. Att: 45,000. Atletico won 2–1 on aggregate
1975 not played.
1976 *Munich*: Bayern Munich 2 (Müller, Kapellmann), Cruzeiro 0. Att: 22,000
Belo Horizonte: Cruzeiro 0, Bayern Munich 0. Att: 114,000. Bayern won 2–0 on aggregate
1977 *Buenos Aires*: Boca Juniors 2 (Mastrangelo, Ribolzi), Borussia Monchengladbach 2 (Hannes, Bonhof). Att: 50,000
Karlsruhe: Borussia Mönchengladbach 0, Boca Juniors 3 (Zanabria, Mastrangelo, Salinas). Att: 21,000. Boca Juniors won 5–2 on aggregate
1978 not played.
1979 *Malmö*: Malmö 0, Olimpia 1 (Isasi). Att: 4,000
Asuncion: Olimpia 2 (Solalinde, Michelagnoli), Malmö 1 (Earlandsson). Att: 35,000. Olimpia won 3–1 on aggregate
1980 *Tokyo*: Nacional (Uru) 1 (Victorino), Nottingham Forest 0. Att: 62,000
1981 *Tokyo*: Flamengo 3 (Nunes 2, Adilio), Liverpool 0. Att: 62,000
1982 *Tokyo*: Penarol 2 (Jair, Charrua), Aston Villa 0. Att: 62,000
1983 *Tokyo*: Gremio 2 (Renato 2), Hamburg SV 1 (Schroder). Att: 62,000
1984 *Tokyo*: Independiente 1 (Percudiani), Liverpool 0. Att: 62,000
1985 *Tokyo*: Juventus 2 (Platini, Laudrup M.), Argentinos Juniors 2 (Ereros, Castro) (aet). Att: 62,000 (*Juventus won 4–2 on penalties*)
1986 *Tokyo*: River Plate 1 (Alzamendi), Steaua Bucharest 0. Att: 62,000
1987 *Tokyo*: FC Porto 2 (Gomes, Madjer), Penarol 1 (Viera) (aet). Att: 45,000
1988 *Tokyo*: Nacional (Uru) 2 (Ostolaza 2), PSV Eindhoven 2 (Romario, Koeman R.) (aet). Att: 62,000 (*Nacional won 7–6 on penalties*)
1989 *Tokyo*: Milan 1 (Evani), Nacional (Col) 0 (aet). Att: 62,000
1990 *Tokyo*: Milan 3 (Rijkaard 2, Stroppa), Olimpia 0. Att: 60,000
1991 *Tokyo*: Red Star Belgrade 3 (Jugovic 2, Pancev), Colo Colo 0. Att: 60,000
1992 *Tokyo*: São Paulo 2 (Rai 2), Barcelona 1 (Stoichkov). Att: 80,000
1993 *Tokyo*: São Paulo 3 (Palinha, Cerezo, Müller), Milan 2 (Massaro, Papin). Att: 52,000

Notes:
From 1960 to 1979 ties were decided on points and not goal difference.
Since 1980 the tie has been played as a one-off match in Tokyo.

WORLD'S SECOND BEST *Liverpool lost to Independiente in 1984*

the European Cup, was appointed by UEFA to replace Ajax, and put up a brave performance before losing 3–2 on aggregate.

After such violent clashes, the value of the competition came into question, and it looked as if the World Club Cup would fade into history. Ajax did restore some credibility with a fine 4–1 aggregate win over Independiente in 1972, despite some rough treatment for Johan Cruyff, but the trend they started the year before continued throughout the 1970s.

Rather than risk their valuable players being mangled by the South Americans, Ajax, Liverpool, Bayern Munich and Nottingham Forest refused to take part, reducing the competition to a sideshow. On all but two occasions, 1975 and 1978 (when the competition was not held), the beaten European Cup finalists substituted for the real champions – Atletico Madrid even managing a victory in 1974 against Independiente, who were making the fourth of their six appearances in the event. Clearly this situation could not continue and it is, ironically, Japan we have to thank for the event's survival.

In 1980 the format of the World Club Cup was changed. The two-legged tie was replaced by a single game at the National Stadium in Tokyo. The car manufacturers Toyota sponsor the competition.

The tournament has now regained much of its credibility, and since 1980 the European and South American champions have consistently taken part. The South Americans won the first five matches played in Tokyo, with the Europeans enjoying more success in the second half of the decade. In 1991 Red Star Belgrade became the first Eastern European side to win when they beat Chile's Colo Colo 3–0. Since then Brazil's São Paulo has won the trophy twice.

FIFA would like the World Club Cup to become a truly worldwide event by the end of the century.

COPA LIBERTADORES (SOUTH AMERICAN CLUB CUP)

The Copa Libertadores is undoubtedly South America's premier club event, but has had a long history of problems both on and off the pitch. The competition was started in 1960 after a proposition from UEFA that the champions of South America should play against the European champions for the world title. A South American Champion Clubs Cup had been organized by Chile's Colo Colo as early as 1948, but the competition, won by Brazil's Vasco da Gama, was a financial disaster and was not staged again. But UEFA's success with the European Cup prompted CONMEBOL to consider giving the competition another chance, and the lucrative carrot of the World Club Cup swayed the balance in favor of trying again.

The first series was held in 1960, with seven of the continent's champions playing home and away matches on a knock-out basis, including the final. This has always been played over two legs, with games won, not goal difference, deciding the winners. Goal difference only came into the equation if the play-off failed to produce a winner, and is no longer relevant, since recently penalties have replaced the play-off.

At first there was little interest in the new event, largely because league championships have always been more popular than cup competitions in South America. Also, the large distances encountered in getting to away games – plus the large number of matches played – almost bankrupted the winners in the first decade of the competition. Worse still, as the Copa Libertadores grew in popularity and stature, it almost killed off the Copa America, which was not contested at all between 1967 and 1975 because clubs refused to release players while still in the cup.

The first two competitions were won by Penarol, and almost passed unnoticed. Alberto Spencer scored in both those victories, against Olimpia and Palmeiras, and he remains top scorer in the Copa Libertadores with over 50 goals.

In the following year, 1962, the format of the competition changed as more teams entered. The home-and-away knock-out method was replaced by groups, played for points, up until the Final. Penarol again appeared in the Final, against Santos, and the first of many unsavory incidents which have scarred the Copa Libertadores occurred.

The first leg, in Montevideo, passed peacefully with a 2–1 win for Santos, but the second leg took three and a half hours to complete! The game was suspended shortly after half-time, with Penarol leading 3–2, because the Chilean referee, Carlos Robles, had been hit by a stone and knocked unconscious. After discussions lasting 80 minutes he agreed to continue the game, but there was more trouble to follow.

Santos equalized just as a linesman, raising his flag, was knocked out by another stone from the terraces, prompting Robles to suspend the game once more. At a disciplinary hearing later, Robles claimed that the match had officially been suspended when Penarol were 3–2 up, and that he had only concluded the match to insure his own safety! So, the game was duly logged as a 3–2 win for Penarol, forcing a play-off which Santos won easily, 3–0.

Santos retained their trophy a year later, beating Boca Juniors home and away, but had been helped by the rule which gave the holders a bye into the semi-finals. With Pele in the Santos side, the Copa Libertadores received the image boost it needed. Interest in the competition increased dramatically, and by 1964 every CONMEBOL country entered.

Boca's run to the final was another important factor, as it encouraged the other Argentinian clubs to take the competition more seriously. (Uruguay had always regarded it as a serious event because it needed an outlet for Penarol and Nacional, who always finished first and second in the Uruguayan league.) Argentinian clubs now came to the fore as Independiente became champions in 1964, and retained the trophy in 1965. That year, a Uruguayan proposal to include league runners-up almost killed the tournament. The Brazilians refused to enter in 1966, as more matches would make it even less financially rewarding.

The 1966 tournament involved no fewer than 95 games—without the Brazilians—Penarol, the winners, playing 17 games to win the title. Here again, controversy occurred. A play-off with River Plate was needed in the final, and, having led 2–0 at half-time, River Plate eventually lost 4–2 after extra time. River had two former Penarol players in their side, Matosas and Cubilla, who both played badly and were accused of "selling" the game.

The 1967 final, between Argentina's Racing Club and Uruguay's Nacional, witnessed the birth of the South American clubs' win-at-all-costs approach to the competition, especially the Argentinians. The three-game final series was peppered with gamesmanship and rough play, a familiar sight in Copa Libertadores and World Club Cup finals to come.

Racing's win marked the beginning of a period of Argentinian dominance, especially by the small-town club Estudiantes de la Plata, who won the Copa Libertadores three years running (1968–70) on the back of a single Argentine championship in 1967. Estudiantes were the worst offenders when it came to gamesmanship. Every conceivable method was employed to distract opponents, from verbal harassment and time-wasting to spitting and even pricking opponents with pins when out of the referee's view! Estudiantes made few friends and very little money. Indeed, their hat trick of titles earned them a net loss of $1,600,000. As a result, their president committed suicide, the board resigned and their replacements were forced to sell the players at knock-down prices.

The second leg of their third final, against Penarol, ended in a free-for-all between both sets of players and reserves in the middle of the field. The disciplinary committee was extremely lenient, and then came down heavily on Boca Juniors a year later, after a battle between the players in a first-round tie against Peru's Sporting Cristal in Buenos Aires, which resulted in all of them being locked up in prison!

Top-level diplomatic negotiations earned the players' release the following day, and they were all promptly suspended by the clubs. Then, inexplicably, CONMEBOL punished Boca by closing their stadium for cup games, a strange move given that the fans were generally well-behaved on the day. Boca refused to accept this and duly turned up at their stadium for their next match, against Universitario of Peru, who did not – on the express orders of CONMEBOL's Peruvian president Salinas Fuller. Universitario were awarded the points and Boca was expelled from the competition . . . just another strange tale in the history of the Copa Libertadores.

With the ever-increasing disruption caused to domestic championships, Argentina joined Brazil in a boycott in 1969, prompting CONMEBOL to streamline the competition slightly by reducing the number of group matches. Argentina's Independiente then embarked on an unprecedented sequence of victories, winning the trophy four times in succession from 1972 to 1975.

The Brazilians, who returned in 1970, also began to enjoy some success, with Cruzeiro, Flamengo and Gremio winning between 1976 and 1983. Overall, however, Brazil's record in the tournament is as lamentable as her record in the Copa America. Brazilian clubs have won only seven times, compared with 15 for Argentina and eight for Uruguay. Indeed, between 1963 and 1979, Argentinian clubs appeared in all 17 finals, winning 12 of them.

Boca Juniors won the trophy for Argentina in 1977 and again in 1978, but in 1979 Olimpia of Paraguay broke the Argentina-Uruguay-Brazil domination of the competition. Olimpia's breakthrough marked a new era for the competition, which became more even and more open. Argentinian clubs still enjoyed success – Independiente, Argentinos Juniors and River Plate all tasted victory – but the "smaller" nations were starting to make an impres-

Winners

Copa Libertadores Finals

1960 *Montevideo*: Penarol 1 (Spencer), Olimpia 0
Asuncion: Olimpia 1 (Recalde), Penarol 1 (Cubilla). Att: 35,000

1961 *Montevideo*: Penarol 1 (Spencer), Palmeiras 0. Att: 50,000.
São Paulo: Palmeiras 1 (Nardo), Penarol 1 (Sasia). Att: 40,000

1962 *Montevideo*: Penarol 1 (Spencer), Santos 2 (Coutinho 2). Att: 50,000
Santos Santos 2 (Dorval, Mengalvio), Penarol 3 (Spencer, Sasia 2)
Buenos Aires (play-off): Santos 3 (Coutinho, Pele 2), Penarol 0. Att: 36,000

1963 *Rio de Janeiro*: Santos 3 (Coutinho 2, Lima), Boca Juniors 2 (Sanfilippo 2). Att: 55,000.
Buenos Aires: Boca Juniors 1 (Sanfilippo), Santos 2 (Coutinho, Pele). Att: 50,000

1964 *Montevideo:* Nacional (Uru) 0, Independiente 0
Avellaneda: Independiente 1 (Rodriguez), Nacional (Uru) 0

1965 *Avellaneda:* Independiente 1 (Bernao), Penarol 0
Montevideo: Penarol 3 (Goncalvez, Reznik, Rocha), Independiente 1 (De la Mata)
Santiago (play-off): Independiente 4 (Acevedo, Bernao, Avallay, Mura), Penarol 1 (Joya)

1966 *Montevideo*: Penarol 2 (Abaddie, Joya), River Plate 0. Att: 49,000
Buenos Aires: River Plate 3 (Onega E., Onega D., Sarnari), Penarol 2 (Rocha, Spencer). Att: 60,000
Santiago (play-off): Penarol 4 (Spencer 2, Rocha, Abbadie), River Plate 2 (Onega D., Solari). Att: 39,000

1967 *Avellaneda*: Racing Club 0, Nacional (Uru) 0. Att: 54,000
Montevideo: Nacional (Uru) 0, Racing Club 0. Att: 54,000
Santiago (play-off): Racing Club 2 (Cardozo, Raffo), Nacional (Uru) 1 (Esparrago). Att: 25,000

1968 *La Plata*: Estudiantes 2 (Veron, Flores), Palmeiras 1 (Servillio)
São Paulo: Palmeiras 3 (Tupazinho 2, Reinaldo), Estudiantes 1 (Veron)
Montevideo (play-off): Estudiantes 2 (Ribaudo, Veron), Palmeiras 0

1969 *Montevideo*: Nacional (Uru) 0, Estudiantes 1 (Flores). Att: 50,000
La Plata: Estudiantes 2 (Flores, Conigliaro), Nacional (Uru) 0. Att: 30,000

1970 *La Plata*: Estudiantes 1 (Togneri), Penarol 0. Att: 36,000.
Montevideo: Penarol 0, Estudiantes 0. Att: 50,000

1971 *La Plata*: Estudiantes 1 (Romeo), Nacional (Uru) 0. Att: 32,000
Montevideo: Nacional (Uru) 1 (Masnik), Estudiantes 0. Att: 62,000
Lima (play-off): Nacional (Uru) 2 (Esparrago, Artime), Estudiantes 0. Att: 42,000

1972 *Lima*: Universitario 0, Independiente 0. Att: 45,000
Avellaneda: Independiente 2 (Maglioni 2), Universitario 1 (Rojas). Att: 65,000

1973 *Avellaneda*: Independiente 1 (Mendoza), Colo Colo 1 (o.g.). Att: 65,000
Santiago: Colo Colo 0, Independiente 0. Att: 77,000
Montevideo (play-off): Independiente 2 (Mendoza, Giachello), Colo Colo 1 (Caszely). Att: 45,000

1974 *São Paulo*: São Paulo 2 (Rocha, Mirandinha), Independiente 1 (Saggioratto). Att: 51,000
Avellaneda: Independiente 2 (Bochini, Balbuena), São Paulo 0. Att: 48,000
Santiago (play-off): Independiente 1 (Pavoni), São Paulo 0. Att: 27,000

1975 *Santiago:* Union Espanola 1 (Ahumada), Independiente 0. Att: 43,000
Avellaneda: Independiente 3 (Rojas, Pavoni, Bertoni), Union Espanola 1 (Las Heras). Att: 52,000
Asuncion (play-off): Independiente 2 (Ruiz Moreno, Bertoni), Union Espanola 0. Att: 45,000

1976 *Belo Horizonte*: Cruzeiro 4 (Nelinho, Palinha 2, Waldo), River Plate 1 (Mas). Att: 58,000
Buenos Aires: River Plate 2 (Lopez, J., Gonzalez), Cruzeiro 1 (Palinha). Att: 45,000
Santiago (play-off): Cruzeiro 3 (Nelinho, Ronaldo, Joazinho), River Plate 2 (Mas, Urquiza). Att: 35,000

1977 *Buenos Aires*: Boca Juniors 1 (Veglio), Cruzeiro 0. Att: 50,000
Belo Horizonte: Cruzeiro 1 (Nelinho), Boca Juniors 0. Att: 55,000
Montevideo (play-off): Boca Juniors 0, Cruzeiro 0. Att: 45,000

1978 *Cali*: Deportivo Cali 0, Boca Juniors 0
Buenos Aires: Boca Juniors 4 (Perotti 2, Mastrangelo, Salinas), Deportivo Cali 0

1979 *Asuncion:* Olimpia 2 (Aquino, Piazza), Boca Juniors 0. Att: 45,000
Buenos Aires: Boca Juniors 0, Olimpia 0. Att: 50,000

1980 *Porto Alegre*: Internacional PA 0, Nacional (Uru) 0. Att: 80,000
Montevideo: Nacional (Uru) 1 (Victorino), Internacional PA 0. Att: 75,000

1981 *Rio de Janeiro*: Flamengo 2 (Zico 2), Cobreloa 1 (Merello). Att: 114,000
Santiago: Cobreloa 1 (Merello), Flamengo 0. Att: 61,000
Montevideo (play-off): Flamengo 2 (Zico 2), Cobreloa 0. Att: 35,000

1982 *Montevideo*: Penarol 0, Cobreloa 0. Att: 70,000
Santiago: Cobreloa 0, Penarol 1 (Morena). Att: 70,000

1983 *Montevideo*: Penarol 1 (Morena), Gremio 1 (Tita). Att: 65,000
Porto Alegre: Gremio 2 (Caio, Cesar), Penarol 1 (Morena). Att: 75,000

1984 *Porto Alegre*: Gremio 0, Independiente 1 (Burruchaga). Att: 55,000
Avellaneda: Independiente 0, Gremio 0. Att: 75,000

1985 *Buenos Aires*: Argentinos Juniors 1 (Comisso), America Cali 0. Att: 50,000
Cali: America Cali 1 (Ortiz), Argentinos Juniors 0. Att: 50,000
Asuncion (play-off): Argentinos Juniors 1 (Comizzo), America Cali 1 (Gareca). (*Argentinos Juniors won 5–4 on penalties*). Att: 35,000

1986 *Cali*: America Cali 1 (Cabanas), River Plate 2 (Funes, Alonso). Att: 55,000
Buenos Aires: River Plate 1 (Funes), America Cali 0. Att: 85,000

1987 *Cali*: America Cali 2 (Bataglia, Cabanas), Penarol 0. Att: 45,000
Montevideo: Penarol 2 (Aguirre, Villar), America Cali 1 (Cabanas). Att: 70,000
Santiago (play-off): Penarol 1 (Aguirre), America Cali 0. Att: 30,000

1988 *Rosario*: Newell's Old Boys 1 (Gabrich), Nacional (Uru) 0. Att: 45,000
Montevideo: Nacional (Uru) 3 (Vargas, Ostolaza , De Leon), Newell's Old Boys 0. Att: 75,000

1989 *Asuncion:* Olimpia 2 (Bobadilla, Sanabria), Atletico Nacional 0. Att: 50,000
Bogota: Atletico Nacional 2 (o.g., Usurriaga), Olimpia 0. (*Atletico Nacional won 5–4 on penalties*). Att: 50,000

1990 *Asuncion*: Olimpia 2 (Amarilla, Samaniego), Barcelona 0. Att: 35,000
Guayaquil: Barcelona 1 (Trobbiani), Olimpia 1 (Amarilla). Att: 55,000.

1991 *Asuncion*: Olimpia 0, Colo Colo 0. Att: 48,000
Santiago: Colo Colo 3 (Perez 2, Herrera), Olimpia 0. Att: 64,000

1992 *Rosario*: Newell's Old Boys 1 (Berizzo), São Paulo 0. Att: 45,000
São Paulo: São Paulo 1 (Rai), Newell's Old Boys 0. (*São Paulo won 3–2 on penalties*). Att: 105,000

1993 *São Paulo*: São Paulo 5 (o.g., Dinho, Gilmar, Rai, Muller), Universidad Catolica 1 (Almada). Att: 99,000
Santiago: Universidad Catolica 2 (Lunari, Almada), São Paulo 0. São Paulo won 5–3 on aggregate. Att: 50,000

sion. Chilean champions Cobreloa reached two successive finals in 1981 and 1982, and were followed by Colombia's America Cali, who lost three successive finals from 1985.

Uruguay came back into contention with wins by Nacional (1980 and 1988) and by Penarol (1982 and 1987), but no Argentinian or Uruguayan club has won the Copa Libertadores since 1988. In 1989 Nacional of Medellin won the trophy for Colombia for the first time, beating Olimpia 5–4 on penalties after a 2–2 aggregate draw. Olimpia returned the following year to win for the second time, beating Barcelona of Ecuador in the final, and made it a hat trick of final appearances in 1991 when they lost to Chile's Colo Colo.

In 1992 São Paulo beat Newell's Old Boys, of Argentina, to win Brazil's first Copa Libertadores for almost a decade. The São Paulo side, containing many Brazil internationals such as Rai, Cafu, Palinha and Muller, won again in 1993, beating Chile's Universidad Catolica 5–3 on aggregate, to become the first club to retain the trophy since 1978.

The Copa Libertadores is now a respectable, clean competition which attracts all the continent's leading clubs. There are still moments of controversy and high drama, but that is all part and parcel of South American football. Such is the excitement generated that it is worth putting up with the constantly changing format which, at present, involves five first-round groups, playing 60 matches to eliminate just five teams! The holders still receive a bye into the second round, which is a huge help, because any team progressing from the first round to ultimate victory will have to play a grueling 14 games on the way.

SOUTH AMERICAN RECOPA

The Recopa is basically a playoff between the winners of the Libertadores Cup and the Super Cup, and is thus South America's answer to the European Super Cup. Curiously, in 1990 Paraguay's Olimpia won the Recopa without having to play a match, because they also won the Libertadores and Super Cups.

South American Recopa Winners

1988 Nacional
1989 Boca Juniors
1990 Olimpia
1991 Colo Colo
1992 São Paulo
1993 São Paulo

SOUTH AMERICAN SUPER CUP

Introduced in 1988, the South American Super Cup, or Trofeo Havelange as it is known, is a competition for previous winners of the Libertadores Cup. The event, dismissed to start with as just another unnecessary tournament, is gaining in popularity and has the advantage of involving only the continent's top sides. Played at present on a knock-out basis, the competition may eventually change to a league format, which would effectively create a South American Super League.

South American Super Cup Winners

1988 Racing Club
1989 Boca Juniors
1990 Olimpia
1991 Cruzeiro
1992 Cruzeiro
1993 Botafogo

EUROPEAN CUP

It is not the oldest, or the biggest, and some would argue it is not even the best, but the European Champion Clubs' Cup – to give it its full title – is undoubtedly the premier European club event. Since its inception in 1956 the European Cup, as it is more commonly known, has become the most prized trophy in world club football. Reputations have been made and broken in the competition, which has always had an aura of romance and glamour about it.

The idea for the competition came, typically, from the French. Gabriel Hanot, a former international and then editor of the French daily sports paper *L'Equipe*, was angered by English newspaper claims that Wolverhampton Wanderers were the champions of Europe because they had beaten Honved and Moscow Spartak in friendlies.

Hanot decided to launch a competition to find the real champions of Europe and, in 1955, invited representatives of 20 leading clubs to Paris to discuss the idea. The meeting was attended by 15 clubs and it was agreed that the competition should begin in the 1955–56 season. FIFA supported the idea and consequently UEFA approved the tournament and took over its administration.

The clubs, restricted to the champions of each country plus the holders after the first series, play home and away on a knock-out basis, and the result is decided by the aggregate score – except in the final, which has always been a one-off match played at a neutral venue. Drawn ties used a play-off to produce a winner until 1967, when a new method was introduced, whereby the team scoring most away goals progressed. In the event of a draw even on away goals, a toss of a coin decided the winner until 1971, when penalty kicks were introduced. This may sound complicated but, compared with South American cup competitions, it is a simple formula which has stood the test of time well.

Sixteen teams entered the first tournament, though several were not really champions, merely replacements for teams who could not, or would not, take part. Chelsea, the English champions, stayed away on the short-sighted advice of the notoriously aloof Football League, while Hibernian, who had finished fifth, represented Scotland.

By a fortunate coincidence, just as the competition was launched, Real Madrid was blossoming into one of the greatest club teams the world has ever seen. In the final, fittingly played in Paris, Real faced a Stade de Reims side containing the legendary Raymond Kopa, who joined Real the following season. Despite leading twice, Reims could not cope with Real's deadly forwards, Alfredo Di Stefano, Hector Rial and Paco Gento, and lost 4–3.

Real went on to win the Cup for the next four years running, a feat which is unlikely to be matched in the modern game. Fiorentina (1957), Milan (1958), Reims again (1959) and Eintracht Frankfurt (1960) were all beaten in successive finals, with the match against Frankfurt being arguably the best final ever. In front of 135,000 fans at Hampden Park in Glasgow, Real thrashed the West German champions 7–3, with Ferenc Puskas, the "galloping major" of the great Hungarian team of the 1950s, scoring four goals and Di Stefano getting a hat-trick.

Real's run came to an end the following season in the second round, beaten by deadly rivals Barcelona, who went on to contest the Final with Portugal's Benfica – the newly emerging kings of Europe. Benfica

PARIS MATCH *Bayern Munich players celebrate victory in 1975*

NOT THIS TIME *Real Madrid's Dominguez saves during his team's 7–3 win over Eintracht Frankfurt in 1960*

contained the bulk of the Portuguese national team and would go on to play in five finals during the 1960s, winning two of them. The first, against Barcelona, was won without Eusebio, the Mozambique-born striker.

Eusebio was in the line-up the following year, though, when Benfica faced Real Madrid, and he scored twice as Benfica won 5–3 despite Puskas scoring another hat-trick for Real. The following season, 1963, the Lisbon Eagles appeared in their third consecutive Final, but lost 2–1 to Italy's Milan.

Milan's victory was the first of three for the city of Milan in the mid-1960s, as their city rivals Internazionale emerged to win the trophy in 1964 and 1965. Coached by the legendary Helenio Herrera, Inter fielded a host of international stars including Sarti, Burgnich, Facchetti, Jair from Brazil, Mazzola and the Spaniard Suarez. Their final victims were Real Madrid and Benfica.

Real returned to claim "their" crown in 1966 with a 2–1 win over Partizan Belgrade in Brussels. Of the 1950s attack all but Gento had gone, but Amancio and Serena proved worthy successors as both scored in the final. Real's sixth triumph still stands as a record, but it also marked the end of an era in the European Cup.

For the first 11 years of its existence, the Cup had only been won by clubs from Latin countries – Spain, Portugal and Italy – and of the first 22 finalists, 18 were from these three countries. Now the power-base of European club soccer shifted from the Mediterranean to northern Europe – Britain, Holland and Germany to be precise. The 1967 final paired Inter with Scotland's Celtic. The Scots, under the guiding hand of the great Jock Stein, won every competition open to them that season, ending up with a fine 2–1 win over the Italians in Lisbon. The breakthrough had been made, and Manchester United consolidated the position by becoming England's first winners the following season. Benfica was again the unfortunate loser in the final, at Wembley, where Matt Busby's side won 4–1 after extra time with goals by Bobby Charlton, George Best and a young Brian Kidd.

AT LAST *Matt Busby in 1968*

Milan regained the trophy in 1969, with a 4–1 demolition of Ajax in Madrid, but it was the last Latin success in the Cup for 17 years as Holland, Germany and then England dominated the trophy during the 1970s and early 1980s.

Feyenoord of Rotterdam were the first Dutch winners, in 1970, when they narrowly defeated Celtic 2–1 after extra time in Milan. Feyenoord's great rivals, Ajax, maintained Holland's position the following season when they beat Panathinaikos of Greece 2–0 at Wembley. It was the first of three consecutive titles for the Amsterdam club, which contained the bulk of the thrilling Dutch "total soccer" side of the 1970s. Johan Cruyff was the star of the show, but his impressive supporting cast included Johan Neeskens, Barrie Hulshoff, Wim Suurbier, Arie Haan, Rudi Krol and Piet Keizer.

Ajax's second victory was an impressive 2–0 win over Inter in Rotterdam, where Cruyff scored twice. The following year, 1973, Ajax beat Juventus in Belgrade with a solitary goal by the mercurial Johnny Rep. In the quarterfinals, Ajax had beaten Bayern Munich, and it was the West German champions who would dominate the Cup for the next three years.

Udo Lattek moulded Bayern into a highly effective unit, and players such as Franz Beckenbauer, Sepp Maier, Gerd Müller, Paul Breitner, Georg Schwarzenbeck and Uli Hoeness went on to form the core of the West German side which won the European Championship in 1972 and the World Cup in 1974. Bayern needed a replay to dispose of Atletico Madrid in the first of their three wins, Hoeness and Müller scoring two each in a 4–0 win after a 1–1 draw in Brussels. In 1975 they beat Leeds United 2–0 in a hotly-disputed match in Paris, after which distraught Leeds supporters trashed the stadium. Bayern's hat trick came with a 1–0 win over France's Saint-Etienne in Glasgow.

Then, in 1977, Liverpool clinched the first of six consecutive English victories with a 3–1 win over Germany's Borussia Mönchengladbach, veteran defender Tommy Smith scoring the decisive second goal. Liverpool, under Bob Paisley, retained the trophy at Wembley the following year by beating Belgium's Club Brugge. Kenny Dalglish, signed from Celtic to replace the Hamburg-bound Kevin Keegan, scored the only goal.

In 1979 a cruel twist of fate drew Liverpool with Brian Clough's Nottingham Forest in the first round. Forest had come up from the Second Division to win the title in successive seasons, and they out-fought Liverpool to win 2–0 on aggregate. In the Final, against Swedish rank outsiders Malmö, Britain's first million-pound soccer player, Trevor Francis, scored the only goal in a very tight game. Forest retained the Cup in 1980, ironically against Hamburg, who included Keegan in their side. On the night, the player who had twice been European Footballer of the Year was completely shackled by Forest's uncompromising Scottish centre-back Kenny Burns, and a single goal by winger John Robertson was enough for victory.

Liverpool returned for their third triumph the following season with a 1–0 win over Real Madrid in Paris, and Aston Villa became the fourth English winners in 1982, when they beat Bayern Munich 1–0 in Rotterdam. Hamburg broke the English monopoly in 1983 by beating Juventus 1–0, but it was only a brief respite. Liverpool, the most successful team in the history of English soccer, returned for the 1984 final and, against all the odds, beat AS Roma in Rome. After a 1–1 draw, Liverpool won 4–2 on penalties.

The period of English dominance was about to end, however, and the 1985 final at the Heysel Stadium in Brussels will always be remembered, not for the soccer, but for the appalling loss of life. Before the game, against Juventus, a group of English hooligans charged at the Italian fans behind one of the goals. A safety wall collapsed and 39 people, mostly Italian, lost their lives in the crush. Two weeks previously, 53 supporters had died in a fire at Bradford City's Valley Parade ground, leaving the image of English football at its lowest point ever.

Juventus won a meaningless game 1–0 with a Michel Platini penalty. More significantly, Liverpool were banned from European competitions indefinitely, while all English clubs were banned for five years. The ban took some of the gloss off the Cup because, without the English clubs, who had such a fine record in the competition, winning it was less satisfactory. Meanwhile the hooligan problem still remained.

WEMBLEY WINNERS *Barcelona players after their 1992 defeat of Sampdoria*

In 1986 Romania's Steaua Bucharest became the first Eastern European team to win the Cup, beating Barcelona – coached by Terry Venables – in Seville. The final, however, has to go down as one of the worst in the history of the tournament. It was still goalless after extra time, and the penalty shoot-out produced only two successful conversions – both for the Romanian army club.

Portugal's FC Porto won in 1987 in Vienna with a fine 2–1 win over the favorites Bayern Munich, having been a goal down. PSV Eindhoven became Holland's third European champions when they beat poor old Benfica in 1988. A dull 0–0 draw in Stuttgart was followed by a 6–5 penalty win for the Dutch team.

Milan then returned to reclaim the trophy. Free from the restrictions on importing foreign players, and backed by media magnate Silvio Berlusconi's money, Milan bought the best and beat the rest. Their Dutch axis of Frank Rijkaard, Ruud Gullit and Marco Van Basten steered them to a crushing 4–0 victory over Steaua in 1989, Gullit and Van Basten both scoring twice, while a single goal from Rijkaard was enough to beat the perennial bridesmaids Benfica in 1990.

In 1991 English clubs, though not Liverpool, were back in the running, but it was Yugoslavia's Red Star Belgrade and Marseille who met in the Final in Bari.

France, originators of the European Cup, was still hoping for a first ever victory . . . but the wait had to go on. Red Star abandoned their free-flowing, attacking style of play in favor of a blanket defense approach designed to stifle president Bernard Tapie's expensively assembled French champions. The plan worked. Red Star took the game to penalties and won the shoot-out 5–3 to become the second side from the East to be crowned European champions.

The format of the competition was radically changed in 1992, after direct pressure from Europe's bigger clubs who have made no secret of their desire to see a European Super League formed. The quarterfinals and semifinals were replaced with two groups of four, playing home and away, to produce the two finalists. Johan Cruyff's Barcelona took the Cup for the first time—completing a hat trick of European trophies—by beating Italy's Sampdoria 1–0 at Wembley with a rocket free-kick by Ronald Koeman.

Then, in 1993, came the biggest scandal the competition has ever witnessed. After 37 long years, the French drought in the European Cup seemed to have ended. Mar-

Winners

European Cup Finals

1956 *Paris*: Real Madrid 4 (Di Stefano, Rial 2, Marquitos), Stade de Reims 3 (Leblond, Templin, Hidalgo). Att: 38,000
1957 *Madrid*: Real Madrid 2 (Di Stefano, Gento), Fiorentina 0. Att: 124,000
1958 *Brussels*: Real Madrid 3 (Di Stefano, Rial, Gento), Milan 2 (Schiaffino, Grillo) (aet). Att: 67,000
1959 *Stuttgart*: Real Madrid 2 (Mateos, Di Stefano), Stade de Reims 0. Att: 80,000
1960 *Glasgow*: Real Madrid 7 (Di Stefano 3, Puskas 4), Eintracht Frankfurt 3 (Kress, Stein 2). Att: 127,621
1961 *Berne*: Benfica 3 (Aguas, o.g., Coluna), Barcelona 2 (Kocsis, Czibor). Att: 33,000
1962 *Amsterdam*: Benfica 5 (Aguas, Cavem, Coluna, Eusebio 2), Real Madrid 3 (Puskas 3). Att: 68,000
1963 *Wembley*: Milan 2 (Altafini 2), Benfica 1 (Eusebio). Att: 45,000
1964 *Vienna*: Internazionale 3 (Mazzola 2, Milani), Real Madrid 1 (Felo). Att: 72,000
1965 *Milan*: Internazionale 1 (Jair), Benfica 0. Att: 80,000
1966 *Brussels*: Real Madrid 2 (Amancio, Serena), Partizan Belgrade 1 (Vasovic). Att: 55,000
1967 *Lisbon*: Celtic 2 (Gemmell, Chalmers), Internazionale 1 (Mazzola). Att: 55,000
1968 *Wembley*: Manchester United 4 (Charlton 2, Best, Kidd), Benfica 1 (Graca) (aet). Att: 100,000
1969 *Madrid*: Milan 4 (Prati 3, Sormani), Ajax 1 (Vasovic). Att: 50,000
1970 *Milan*: Feyenoord 2 (Israel, Kindvall), Celtic 1 (Gemmell) (aet). Att: 53,187
1971 *Wembley*: Ajax 2 (Van Dijk, o.g.), Panathinaikos 0. Att: 90,000
1972 *Rotterdam*: Ajax 2 (Cruyff 2), Internazionale 0. Att: 61,000
1973 *Belgrade*: Ajax 1 (Rep), Juventus 0. Att: 93,500
1974 *Brussels*: Bayern Munich 1 (Schwartzenbeck), Atletico Madrid 1 (Luis) (aet). Att: 65,000
Brussels (replay): Bayern Munich 4 (Hoeness 2, Müller 2), Atletico Madrid 0. Att: 23,000
1975 *Paris*: Bayern Munich 2 (Roth, Müller), Leeds United 0. Att: 48,000
1976 *Glasgow*: Bayern Munich 1 (Roth), St Etienne 0. Att: 54,684
1977 *Rome*: Liverpool 3 (McDermott, Smith, Neal), Borussia Mönchengladbach 1 (Simonsen). Att: 57,000
1978 *Wembley*: Liverpool 1 (Dalglish), Club Brugge 0. Att: 92,000
1979 *Munich*: Nottingham Forest 1 (Francis), Malmö 0. Att: 57,500
1980 *Madrid*: Nottingham Forest 1 (Robertson), Hamburg 0. Att: 51,000
1981 *Paris*: Liverpool 1 (Kennedy A.), Real Madrid 0. Att: 48,360
1982 *Rotterdam*: Aston Villa 1 (Withe), Bayern Munich 0. Att: 46,000
1983 *Athens*: Hamburg 1 (Magath), Juventus 0. Att: 80,000
1984 *Rome*: Liverpool 1 (Neal), AS Roma 1 (Pruzzo) (aet). (*Liverpool won 4–2 on penalties*). Att: 69,693
1985 *Brussels*: Juventus 1 (Platini), Liverpool 0. Att: 58,000
1986 *Seville*: Steaua Bucharest 0, Barcelona 0 (aet) .(*Steauawon 2–0 on penalties*). Att: 70,000
1987 *Vienna*: FC Porto 2 (Madjer , Juary), Bayern Munich 1 (Kogl). Att: 56,000
1988 *Stuttgart*: PSV Eindhoven 0, Benfica 0 (aet). (*PSV won 6–5 on penalties)*. Att. 55,000
1989 *Barcelona*: Milan 4 (Gullit 2, Van Basten 2), Steaua Bucharest 0. Att: 97,000
1990 *Vienna*: Milan 1 (Rijkaard), Benfica 0. Att: 56,000
1991 *Bari*: Red Star Belgrade 0, Marseille 0 (aet). (*Red Star won 5–3 on penalties*). Att: 50,000
1992 *Wembley*: Barcelona 1 (Koeman R.), Sampdoria 0 (aet). Att: 74,000
1993 *Munich*: Marseille 1 (Boli), Milan 0. Att: 72, 300 (*Marseille were later stripped of their title for alleged match fixing*)
1994 *Athens:* Milan 4 (Massaro 2, Savicevic, Desailly), Barcelona 0. Att: 76,000

seille beat Milan 1–0 in Munich, with a goal by center-back Basile Boli, but the celebrations were cut short when it emerged that Marseille officials had allegedly paid three Valenciennes players to "take it easy" in a league game shortly before the final. Chaos ensued, but in the end, Marseille was stripped of their European crown, their French title and the right to play São Paulo in the World Club Cup. Marseille's outspoken owner – socialist, millionaire and politician Tapie – threatened all sorts of lawsuits and legal actions, but in the end had to accept that Marseille's victory would be expunged from the record. So France still waits for its first European Cup, or any European trophy for that matter.

The format changed slightly again for the 1994 tournament, with the reintroduction of semifinals for the winners and runners-up of the two Champions League groups. But nothing could stop Milan, their 4–0 defeat of Barcleona was a stunning display.

If UEFA have its way, the whole nature of the tournament could change in the next few years. The increasing number of clubs entering the tournament, along with the bigger clubs' desire for a TV-bankrolled European League, has forced UEFA to consider a new approach to the tournament.

The proposals, simply, are as follows: the holders and top seven seeded teams will go through directly to the Champions League, which will be expanded to 16 teams in four groups of four; the eight other teams will come from a preliminary round involving the teams ranked eight to 23 in the seeding list, of which the rest will be off-loaded into an expanded UEFA Cup. Basically, the European Cup, as we have known and loved it for almost 40 years, will cease to exist. Champions from the "lesser" European nations will be denied entry and the lucrative matches that go with it, and we will be one step closer to a genuine European Super League.

Whether the tournament will retain its aura of glamour and prestige remains to be seen. But one thing is for sure: things will never be the same again.

EUROPEAN CUP-WINNERS' CUP

The European Cup-winners' Cup was originated by the organizing committee of the Mitropa Cup, and began in the 1960–61 season. Following the success of the European Cup, it seemed a logical step to introduce a competition for the winners of national knock-out competitions. However, many European countries did not have a knock-out competition and it was only in Britain, where the Cup dates back further than the League, that cup competitions fired the imagination of both the clubs and the public. Consequently, in many countries, new competitions were introduced, or old ones were revived.

Run along the same lines as the European Cup—home and away knock-out up to the final, which was initially a two-leg, but is now a one-off match – the first Cup-winners' Cup attracted entrants from 10 countries. Vorwärts Berlin, Red Star Brno, Ferencvaros and Rangers contested the qualifying round to decide the quarter-final line-up. Rangers, having disposed of Ferencvaros, demolished West Germany's Borussia Mönchengladbach 11–0 on aggregate in the quarterfinals, before overcoming Wolverhampton Wanderers in an all-British semifinal. Italy's Fiorentina – European Cup finalists four years previously—beat FC Luzern 9–2 in the quarterfinals, before beating Dinamo Zagreb 4–2 on aggregate in the semi-finals.

The final, played over two legs for the first and only time, saw Fiorentina at their best – defending solidly while always retaining the ability to break quickly, led by Swedish winger Kurt Hamrin. In the first leg, in Glasgow, Fiorentina frustrated the Rangers forwards, while Hamrin twice led the charge for Milani to score. In the return Hamrin again proved the match-winner, setting up Milani for the first and scoring the winner after Scott had equalized.

The success of the first tournament encouraged more clubs to get involved, and 23 entered the second in1961–62. Swansea Town and Floriana of Malta were among them, clearly attracted by the prospect of money-spinning ties with some of Europe's biggest clubs and by the outside possibility of a "giant-killings." It was not to be, though, as both went out in the preliminary round—Swansea beaten 7–3 on aggregate by Motor Jena, Floriana trounced 15–4 by Ujpest Dozsa.

Fiorentina's impressive defense took them all the way again in 1962, where they met Atletico Madrid in the final, now played as one game. The match, in Glasgow, produced a disappointing 1–1 draw, and when the replay took place—four months later —Atletico won the Cup with a straightforward 3–0 win.

In the 1963 competition the holders again reached the final, and again they lost. Atletico faced Tottenham in Rotterdam and could not contain Bill Nicholson's international-packed team, who had won the FA Cup in successive seasons. Jimmy Greaves and Terry Dyson both scored twice as Tottenham won 5–1 to become the first English winners of a European trophy.

Tottenham's reign ended in the second round in 1964, when they were unfortunate to be drawn against Manchester United, who won 4–2 on aggregate. United fell in the quarterfinals to Portugal's Sporting Lisbon, who went on to win the Cup against MTK Budapest, although they needed a 1–0 replay win after a 3–3 draw in Belgium.

The Cup-winners' Cup had now established itself on the European scene, and 30 clubs entered the 1965 tournament. West Ham United, essentially novices at the European game, emulated Tottenham's success by beating TSV Munich 1860 in front of a full house at Wembley. The match was fast and open, but two goals in two minutes by reserve

MERRY MILLER *The Aberdeen skipper leads the celebrations in 1983*

winger Tony Sealey won the Cup for the Londoners.

The following year, 1966, featured another England-West Germany final, this time involving Liverpool and Borussia Dortmund. On a rain-lashed night in Glasgow, the Germans were slightly fortunate to win in extra time when a mis-hit lob by Libuda was deflected in by Yeats. Rangers returned for the 1967 Final, also against a German club, Bayern Munich – and were strangely out of sorts. Gerd Müller was well shackled but in the 18th minute of extra time Roth fired home the winner to keep the Cup in Germany. Another German club, Hamburg, contested the 1968 final, but were no match for Milan, for whom Hamrin scored twice to win his second medal.

In 1969 the original draw was abandoned after Soviet troops entered Czechoslovakia, and a new draw, keeping East and West apart, was made. Most Eastern countries were against the idea and withdrew, but the Czechs remained . . . and with sweet irony Slovan Bratislava collected the trophy, beating the favorites Barcelona 3–2 in Basle.

For the following three years the Cup stayed in Britain as Manchester City, Chelsea and, at the third attempt, Rangers all won. Manchester City beat Poland's Gornik Zabrze 2–1 in front of a poor crowd of 8,000 in Vienna in 1970; Chelsea needed a replay the next year in Athens to overcome Real Madrid, and Rangers finally won the trophy with a 3–2 victory over Moscow Dynamo in 1972.

ON THE MARK *Hughes scores for Manchester United in the 1991 final*

The Rangers victory, however, was marred by ugly scenes in and around the Nou Camp stadium in Barcelona. The lunatic fringe of their supporters invaded the field before, during and after the match, and charged riot police outside the stadium, leaving one dead and scores injured. Rangers, having done so well to hang on for their victory, were banned for a year and were consequently unable to defend their title.

Leeds United almost made it four in a row for Britain in 1973 when they faced Milan in the Final in Salonika. Milan scored after five minutes through Chiarugi and promptly began using spoiling tactics, which were not appreciated by the Greek crowd. Leeds' frustration finally boiled over two minutes from the end, when Hunter and Sogliano were sent off for fighting.

Milan reached the final again the following year, but lost to FC Magdeburg, who became the only East German winners of a European trophy. A paltry crowd of 4,000 in Rotterdam, the smallest for a final in the competition's history, saw an own goal by Lanzi just before half-time set the East Germans on their way to a 2–0 victory

Kiev Dynamo kept the trophy behind the Iron Curtain with their first win, by beating Ferencvaros 3–0 in Basle in 1975. Belgium's Anderlecht then emerged as the competition's specialists with three successive appearances in the final – of which they won the first and the third. In 1976 they beat West Ham 4–2 in Brussels, then lost 2–0 to Hamburg in 1977, before beating FK Austria 4–0 in Paris. Dutch striker Rob Rensenbrink scored two in each of the wins.

The 1979 tournament produced the highest-scoring final in the competition's history as Barcelona beat Fortuna Düsseldorf 4–3 in Basle. Even at 2–2 after 90 minutes, Austrian striker Hans Krankl scored the clincher for the Spanish in extra time – after Rexach had made it 3–2 and Seel had equalized. Valencia retained the Cup for Spain the following season in the first European Final to be decided on penalties. A disappointing 0–0 draw in Brussels was decided when Graham Rix missed Arsenal's fifth penalty in the shoot-out, giving Valencia a 5–4 victory.

In the 1981 competition, Welsh Cup winners Newport County, then in the English Fourth Division, caused a sensation by knocking out the title holders Valencia in the second round. Newport then narrowly lost in the quarterfinals to East Germany's Carl Zeiss Jena, who went on to contest an all-Eastern final with

Winners

European Cup-winners' Cup Finals

1961 *Glasgow*: Rangers 0, Fiorentina 2 (Milani 2). Att: 80,000
Florence: Fiorentina 2 (Milani, Hamrin), Rangers 1 (Scott). Fiorentina won 4–1 on aggregate. Att: 50,000
1962 *Glasgow*: Atletico Madrid 1 (Peiro), Fiorentina 1 (Hamrin) (aet). Att: 30,000
Stuttgart (replay): Atletico Madrid 3 (Jones, Mendonca, Peiro), Fiorentina 0. Att: 39,000
1963 *Rotterdam*: Tottenham Hotspur 5 (Greaves 2, White, Dyson 2), Atletico Madrid 1 (Collar). Att: 50,000
1964 *Brussels*: Sporting Lisbon 3 (Mascaranha, Figueiredo 2), MTK Budapest 3 (Sandor 2, Kuti) (aet). Att: 4,000
Antwerp (replay): Sporting Lisbon 1 (Morais), MTK Budapest 0. Att: 14,000
1965 *Wembley*: West Ham United 2 (Sealey 2), TSV Munich 1860 0. Att: 98,000
1966 *Glasgow*: Borussia Dortmund 2 (Held, Libuda), Liverpool 1 (Hunt) (aet). Att: 42,000
1967 *Nuremberg*: Bayern Munich 1 (Roth), Rangers 0 (aet). Att: 70,000
1968 *Rotterdam*: Milan 2 (Hamrin 2), Hamburg SV 0. Att: 54,000
1969 *Basle*: Slovan Bratislava 3 (Cvetler, Hrivnak, Jan Capkovic), Barcelona 2 (Zaldua, Rexach). Att: 40,000
1970 *Vienna*: Manchester City 2 (Young, Lee), Gornik Zabrze 1 (Oslizlo). Att: 10,000
1971 *Athens*: Chelsea 1 (Osgood), Real Madrid 1 (Zoco) (aet). Att: 42,000
Athens (replay): Chelsea 2 (Dempsey, Osgood), Real Madrid 1 (Fleitas). Att: 24,000
1972 *Barcelona*: Rangers 3 (Stein, Johnston 2), Moscow Dynamo 2 (Estrekov, Makovikov). Att: 35,000
1973 *Salonika*: Milan 1 (Chiarugi), Leeds United 0. Att: 45,000
1974 *Rotterdam*: FC Magdeburg 2 (o.g., Seguin), Milan 0. Att: 5,000
1975 *Basle*: Kiev Dynamo 3 (Onischenko 2, Blokhin), Ferencvaros 0. Att: 13,000
1976 *Brussels*: Anderlecht 4 (Rensenbrink 2, Van der Elst 2), West Ham United 2 (Holland, Robson). Att: 58,000
1977 *Amsterdam*: Hamburg SV 2 (Volkert, Magath), Anderlecht 0. Att: 65,000
1978 *Paris*: Anderlecht 4 (Rensenbrink 2, Van Binst 2), FK Austria 0. Att: 48,679
1979 *Basle*: Barcelona 4 (Sanchez, Asensi, Rexach, Krankl), Fortuna Düsseldorf 3 (Allofs K., Seel 2) (aet). Att: 58,000
1980 *Brussels*: Valencia 0, Arsenal 0 (aet). (*Valencia won 5–4 on penalties.*) Att: 40,000
1981 *Düsseldorf*: Dynamo Tbilisi 2 (Gutsayev, Daraselia), Carl Zeiss Jena 1 (Hoppe). Att: 9,000
1982 *Barcelona*: Barcelona 2 (Simonsen, Quini), Standard Liège 1 (Vandermissen). Att: 100,000
1983 *Gothenburg*: Aberdeen 2 (Black , Hewitt), Real Madrid 1 (Juanito) (aet). Att: 17,804
1984 *Basle*: Juventus 2 (Vignola, Boniek), FC Porto 1 (Sousa). Att: 60,000
1985 *Rotterdam*: Everton 3 (Gray, Steven, Sheedy), Rapid Vienna 1 (Krankl). Att: 50,000
1986 *Lyons*: Kiev Dynamo 3 (Zavarov, Blokhin, Yevtushenko), Atletico Madrid 0. Att: 39,300
1987 *Athens*: Ajax 1 (Van Basten), Lokomotive Leipzig 0. Att: 35,000
1988 *Strasbourg*: Mechelen 1 (De Boer), Ajax 0. Att: 39,446
1989 *Berne*: Barcelona 2 (Salinas, Recarte), Sampdoria 0. Att: 45,000
1990 *Gothenburg*: Sampdoria 2 (Vialli 2), Anderlecht 0 (aet). Att: 20,103
1991 *Rotterdam*: Manchester United 2 (Hughes 2), Barcelona 1 (Koeman). Att: 42,000
1992 *Lisbon*: Werder Bremen 2 (Allofs K., Rufer), Monaco 0. Att: 16,000
1993 *Wembley*: Parma 3 (Minotti, Melli, Cuoghi), Antwerp 1 (Severeyns). Att: 37,393
1994 *Copenhagen*: Arsenal 1 (Smith), Parma 0. Att: 33,765

Dynamo Tbilisi, who had destroyed West Ham in the quarter-finals. Tbilisi, with several internationals in the side, won 2–1 to clinch the Soviet Union's second Cup.

Barcelona won for the second time in four years in 1982, when they beat Belgium's Standard Liège 2–1 at their own Nou Camp ground, having recovered from the shock of going a goal down after only seven minutes. Real Madrid spurned the chance to match their Catalan rivals the next year, when they lost to Aberdeen. In appalling weather in Gothenburg, both sides scored inside 15 minutes, but could not do so again until eight minutes from the end of extra time, when substitute John Hewitt scored with a header for the Scots. Juventus became the third Italian team to win the Cup when they beat FC Porto 2–1 in 1984. Everton won it for England the following season by outplaying Rapid Vienna in Rotterdam to complete a League Championship and Cup-winners' Cup double.

In 1986 Kiev Dynamo won their second title with an outstanding 3–0 win over Atletico Madrid. Kiev, at the time, was one of the top clubs in Europe and supplied the bulk of the Soviet Union's national squad, including the great Oleg Blokhin, who scored in Kiev's 1975 triumph and again against Atletico.

Ajax of Amsterdam appeared in the next two finals. In 1987 they beat Lokomotive Leipzig 1–0 in Lyon, with Marco Van Basten scoring the winner in his last game for the club before his move to Milan. The following season Ajax was expected to retain the trophy against European debutants Mechelen, but the Belgians pulled off a shock 1–0 win.

Barcelona collected their third Cup-winners' Cup in 1989, beating Italy's emerging Sampdoria 2–0 in Bern. The Italians, though, made amends the following year, beating Anderlecht 2–0 in Gothenburg, with Gianluca Vialli scoring twice in two minutes in extra time.

Barcelona was back for the 1991 series, and so were the English clubs following their ban after the Heysel tragedy in 1985. Manchester United went all the way to the final and then upset the bookmakers' forecasts by winning 2–1. The match provided Welsh striker Mark Hughes – dumped by Barcelona three years before – with sweet revenge as he scored both United's goals.

Both the 1992 and 1993 finals guaranteed to provide new winners, as the four clubs involved were all making their first appearance in European finals. Germany's Werder Bremen denied France a first European success by beating Monaco in 1992, veteran striker Klaus Allofs putting the German club on the way with the opening goal in a 2–0 win. For Allofs, the win was especially sweet because he had scored for Fortuna Düsseldorf in the 1979 Final, which they lost to Barcelona. Then Parma completed a remarkable 10-year transition from the Italian Third Division to European trophy-winners in 1993, when they beat Antwerp 3–1 at Wembley, establishing themselves as a major force in football.

The Cup-winners' Cup looks set to continue in its present format for some years to come, and, unlike the two other European competitions, is not due for major restructuring. Generally regarded as the least important of the three, the Cup-Winners Cup has nevertheless provided many highlights over the years, and has given some of Europe's smaller clubs the chance to show off their talents to a wider audience.

SPECTACULAR STYLE *Emlyn Hughes of Liverpool shoots during the the 1973 UEFA Cup final*

UEFA CUP

The UEFA Cup started life in 1955, and, unusually, was not a French idea. When UEFA was formed in 1954, FIFA vice-president Ernst Thommen, of Switzerland, thought up the idea of a European competition to give a competitive edge to friendly matches between cities holding trade fairs.

This rather dubious reason for a competition was no deterrent, as officials from 12 cities holding trade fairs approved Thommen's plans in April 1955, and the International Inter-Cities Fairs Cup, as it was originally named, was under way. The competition was to be held over two seasons to avoid disrupting domestic schedules, but because the original entrants represented cities holding trade fairs, and wherever possible games were designed to coincide with the fairs, the first tournament overran into a third year.

The Fairs Cup, as it was commonly known, was designed for representative teams, but it soon became clear that it was a competition that the clubs would dominate. In the first tournament, which ran from 1955 to 1958, 12 cities were represented by select teams. But the composition of the sides was a matter of individual choice. Thus while London chose its team from the 11 professional sides in the city, Barcelona was represented by CF Barcelona, with one token Español player, and Birmingham was represented by the entire Birmingham City side. This discrepancy clearly favored the more coherent clubs, and it was almost inevitable that two would meet in the final.

The 12 teams were organized into four groups of three, with each side to play the other two in its group at home and away. The group winners then went on to the semi-finals and ultimately the Final, which, unlike Europe's other competitions, was to be over two legs on an aggregate basis. However, the first tournament was disrupted by the withdrawals of Vienna and Cologne, leaving just two teams in Groups 1 and 3. Barcelona was too good for Copenhagen in Group 1, but things were much tighter in Group 3. Leipzig's 6–3 win over Lausanne in the first leg in Germany seemed conclusive, but the Swiss pulled off a 7–3 win in the return to go through on goal average.

Switzerland's other entrants, Basle, played a key role in Group 4, where their shock 6–2 victory against Eintracht Frankfurt allowed the London XI to qualify. England's second entrants, Birmingham, also made it to the semifinals, beating Zagreb home and away to set up a decider with Internazionale. After a hard-fought 0–0 draw in Milan, the English team won 2–1 at St Andrews to join London in the semifinals.

Birmingham met Barcelona in a

thrilling encounter that needed a third match to separate them. After Birmingham had won 4–1 at home, a late goal by Kubala in the return sent the tie to a third game. Kubala duly repeated his late-scoring trick to send Barcelona through to the final, where they met the London XI, who beat Lausanne 3–2 on aggregate.

Almost three years after the first ball had been kicked in the tournament, London and Barcelona fought out a 2–2 draw at Stamford Bridge in the first leg of the final, only for the Spaniards to win the return 6–0 – Suarez and Evaristo each scoring twice. Barcelona's win was the first of six in a row by Latin clubs in the competition, in keeping with the European Cup, which was also dominated by Latin sides in the early years of its existence.

The second tournament, 1958–60, drew 16 entrants, mostly club teams, and was played on a straight home-and-away knock-out basis. Barcelona, strengthened by the arrivals of Hungary's Sandor Kocsis and Zoltan Czibor, retained the trophy without losing a match. Their opponents were again English, but this time it was Birmingham and not London who made it to the Final. A 0–0 draw on a terrible field in Birmingham set Barcelona up for the 4–1 return win, with goals by Martinez, Czibor (two) and Coll.

NO WAY *Butcher of Ipswich tangles with Alkmaar's Tol in the 1981 final*

Barcelona's attempt to win a hat-trick of Fairs Cups ended in the second round of the 1960–61 tournament, at the unlikely hands of Scotland's Hibernian. The Edinburgh side only took part because Chelsea withdrew, but, having beaten Lausanne in the first round, they surprised everybody by beating the title holders in the next round. Birmingham again made it the final, where they faced Italy's Roma, who needed a third match to beat Hibs in the semifinals. This extended semifinal meant that the final itself was held over until the following season, by which time Roma had added to an already impressive line-up. Birmingham did well to force a 2–2 draw at home, but was beaten 2–0 in Rome in the return . . . their second successive defeat in the final.

The organizers had decided to allow three teams per country to enter the 1961–62 tournament, which had an entry of 28, and now the Spanish showed their dominance. Barcelona and Valencia reached the Final, with Valencia powering to a 7–3 aggregate victory over their countrymen. Valencia held on to the trophy the following season, beating Dinamo Zagreb 4–1 on aggregate in the final, but were thwarted in their hat trick bid by another Spanish side, Real Zaragoza. The 1964 final was played as a one-game match in

POINT BLANK *IFK Gothenburg goalkeeper Thomas Wernersson foils Billy Kirkwood of Dundee United during the 1987 final*

Barcelona, where goals by Villa and Marcelino secured a 2–1 win for Zaragoza.

The 1965 competition attracted 48 entries, and for the first time the Cup left Latin Europe, and headed east. Hungary's Ferencvaros fought their way through from the first round, with victories over Spartak Brno, Wiener Sport-Club, Roma, Athletic Bilbao and Manchester United, to face Juventus in the Final. The Italians, having safely negotiated the two opening rounds, were given a bye in the quarterfinals as the organizers sought to balance the numbers. This, coupled with the fact that the Final (again a one-game match) was in Turin, seemed to give Juve a definite advantage. But Ferencvaros produced a defensive formation that surpassed even the Italians' catenaccio, and a single goal by Fenyvesi after 74 minutes was enough.

The 1966 tournament returned to the two-game format for the final, but the earlier rounds were marked by violence. Chelsea was pelted with rubbish in Rome, Leeds and Valencia fought a battle which resulted in three dismissals, and Leeds then had Johnny Giles sent off in the semifinal against Real Zaragoza. The Spanish again emerged triumphant, as Barcelona and Real Zaragoza met in the final. A goal by Canario in the first leg at the Nou Camp gave Zaragoza the edge, but a hat trick by the teenager Pujol in the return sealed a 4–2 victory for the Catalans, who won the trophy for the third time on a 4–2 aggregate.

TOP MAN *Maradona of Napoli*

The tournament was now moving into a new era of English dominance. Leeds reached the 1967 Final, where they lost to Dinamo Zagreb, but they made amends the following season by beating Ferencvaros 1–0 on aggregate in the Final, having remained unbeaten in the previous rounds. This was the first of six consecutive victories by English clubs during the late 1960s and early 1970s.

Newcastle United picked up where Leeds left off in 1969, beating another Hungarian club, Ujpest Dozsa, 6–2 over two legs in the final. Arsenal kept the momentum going the following season with a fine win over Belgium's Anderlecht in the Final. Having lost 3–1 in Brussels, the Gunners ground Anderlecht down in the return, to win 3–0 on the night and 4–3 on aggregate.

In 1971 the Cup returned to Leeds, who beat Juventus. The first leg of the final, in Turin, was abandoned at 0–0 because of rain, and in the rearranged match Leeds forced an excellent 2–2 draw. Juve was more threatening in the return, but could only manage a 1–1 draw, which meant Leeds won on away goals. Both sides were unbeaten in the tournament, and it was most unfortunate for the Italians to play 12 matches, without defeat, and still not win the Cup!

The name of the competition changed in 1972, and the first UEFA Cup Final was between two English clubs – Tottenham and Wolverhampton Wanderers. Tottenham won 3–2 on aggregate, and Liverpool won the next tournament, beating Borussia Mönchengladbach in the Final, to complete a double hat trick

Winners

Fairs Cup Finals

1958 *London*: London Select XI 2 (Greaves, Langley), Barcelona 2 (Tejada, Martinez). Att: 45,000
Barcelona: Barcelona 6 (Suarez 2, Evaristo 2, Martinez, Verges), London Select XI 0. Att: 62,000
1960 *Birmingham*: Birmingham City 0, Barcelona 0. Att: 40,000
Barcelona: Barcelona 4 (Martinez, Czibor 2, Coll), Birmingham City 1 (Hooper). Att: 70,000
1961 *Birmingham*: Birmingham City 2 (Hellawell, Orritt), Roma 2 (Manfredini 2). Att:21,000
Rome: Roma 2 (o.g., Pestrin), Birmingham City 0. Att: 60,000
1962 *Valencia*: Valencia 6 (Yosu 2, Guillot 3, Nunez), Barcelona 2 (Kocsis 2). Att: 65,000
Barcelona: Barcelona 1 (Kocsis), Valencia 1 (Guillot). Att: 60,000
1963 *Zagreb*: Dinamo Zagreb 1 (Zambata), Valencia 2 (Waldo, Urtiaga). Att: 40,000
Valencia: Valencia 2 (Manio, Nunez), Dinamo Zagreb 0. Att: 55,000
1964 *Barcelona*: Real Zaragoza 2 (Villa , Marcelino), Valencia 1 (Urtiaga). Att: 50,000
1965 *Turin*: Ferencvaros 1 (Fenyvesi), Juventus 0. Att: 25,000.
1966 *Barcelona*: Barcelona 0, Real Zaragoza 1 (Canario). Att: 35,000
1967 *Zagreb*: Dinamo Zagreb 2 (Cercek 2), Leeds 0. Att: 40,000.
Leeds: Leeds 0, Dinamo Zagreb 0. Att: 35,000
1968 *Leeds*: Leeds 1 (Jones), Ferencvaros 0. Att: 25,000
Budapest: Ferencvaros 0, Leeds 0. Att: 76,000
1969 *Newcastle*: Newcastle 3 (Moncur 2, Scott), Ujpest Dozsa 0. Att: 60,000
Budapest: Ujpest Dozsa 2 (Bene, Gorocs), Newcastle 3 (Moncur, Arentoft, Foggon). Att: 37,000
1970 *Brussels*: Anderlecht 3 (Devrindt, Mulder 2), Arsenal 1 (Kennedy). Att: 37,000
London: Arsenal 3 (Kelly, Radford, Sammels), Anderlecht 0. Att: 51,000
1971 *Turin*: Juventus 2 (Bettega, Capello), Leeds 2 (Madeley, Bates). Att: 65,000
Leeds: Leeds 1 (Clark), Juventus 1 (Anastasi). Att: 42,000. (*Leeds won on away goals*)

UEFA Cup Finals

1972 *Wolverhampton*: Wolverhampton 1 (McCalliog), Tottenham Hotspur 2 (Chivers 2). Att: 38,000
London: Tottenham Hotspur 1 (Mullery), Wolverhampton 1 (Wagstaffe). Att: 54,000
1973 *Liverpool*: Liverpool 3 (Keegan 2, Lloyd), Borussia Mönchengladbach 0. Att: 41,000
Mönchengladbach: Borussia Mönchengladbach 2 (Heynckes 2), Liverpool 0. Att: 35,000
1974 *London*: Tottenham Hotspur 2 (England, o.g.), Feyenoord 2 (Van Hanegem, De Jong). Att: 46,000.
Rotterdam: Feyenoord 2 (Rijsbergen, Ressel), Tottenham Hotspur 0. Att: 59,000
1975 *Düsseldorf*: Borussia Mönchengladbach 0, Twente Enschede 0. Att: 42,000
Enschede: Twente Enschede 1 (Drost), Borussia Mönchengladbach 5 (Simonsen 2, Heynckes 3). Att: 21,000
1976 *Liverpool*: Liverpool 3 (Kennedy, Case, Keegan), Club Brugge 2 (Lambert, Cools). Att: 49,000
Bruges: Club Brugge 1 (Lambert), Liverpool 1 (Keegan). Att: 32,000
1977 *Turin*: Juventus 1 (Tardelli), Athletic Bilbao 0. Att: 75,000
Bilbao: Athletic Bilbao 2 (Churruca, Carlos), Juventus 1 (Bettega). Att: 43,000. (*Juventus won on away goals.*)
1978 *Corsica*: Bastia 0, PSV Eindhoven 0. Att: 15,000.
Eindhoven: PSV Eindhoven 3 (Van der Kerkhof W., Deijkers, Van der Kuijlen), Bastia 0. Att: 27,000
1979 *Belgrade*: Red Star Belgrade 1 (Sestic), Borussia Mönchengladbach 1 (o.g.). Att: 87,000
Düsseldorf: Borussia Mönchengladbach 1 (Simonsen), Red Star Belgrade 0. Att: 45,000
1980 *Mönchengladbach*: Borussia Mönchengladbach 3 (Kulik 2, Matthäus), Eintracht Frankfurt 2 (Karger, Holzenbein). Att: 25,000
Frankfurt: Eintracht Frankfurt 1 (Schaub), Borussia Mönchengladbach 0. Att: 59,000. (*Eintracht won on away goals.*)
1981 *Ipswich*: Ipswich 3 (Wark, Thijssen, Mariner), AZ 67 Alkmaar 0. Att: 27,000
Amsterdam: AZ 67 Alkmaar 4 (Welzl, Metgod, Tol, Jonker), Ipswich 2 (Thijssen, Wark). Att: 28,000
1982 *Gothenburg*: IFK Gothenburg 1 (Tord Holmgren), Hamburg SV 0. Att: 42,000
Hamburg: Hamburg SV 0, IFK Gothenburg 3 (Corneliusson, Nilsson, Fredriksson). Att: 60,000
1983 *Brussels*: Anderlecht 1 (Brylle), Benfica 0. Att: 55,000.
Lisbon: Benfica 1 (Sheu), Anderlecht 1 (Lozano). Att: 80,000
1984 *Brussels*: Anderlecht 1 (Olsen), Tottenham Hotspur 1 (Miller). Att: 35,000
London: Tottenham Hotspur 1 (Roberts), Anderlecht 1 (Czerniatynski) (aet). (*Tottenham won 4–3 on penalties*). Att: 46,000
1985 *Szekesfehervar*: Videoton 0, Real Madrid 3 (Michel, Santilana, Valdano). Att: 30,000
Madrid: Real Madrid 0, Videoton 1 (Majer). Att: 90,000.
1986 *Madrid*: Real Madrid 5 (Sanchez, Gordillo, Valdano 2, Santilana), Köln 1 (Allofs). Att. 85,000
Berlin: Köln 2 (Bein, Geilenkirchen), Real Madrid 0. Att: 15,000.
1987 *Gothenburg*: IFK Gothenburg 1 (Pettersson), Dundee United 0. Att: 50,000
Dundee: Dundee United 1 (Clark), IFK Gothenburg 1 (Nilsson L.). Att: 21,000
1988 *Barcelona*: Español 3 (Losada 2, Soler), Bayer Leverkusen 0. Att: 42,000
Leverkusen: Bayer Leverkusen 3 (Tita, Gotz, Cha-Bum-Kun), Español 0 (aet). (*Leverkusen won 3–2 on penalties*). Att: 22,000
1989 *Naples*: Napoli 2 (Maradona, Careca), Stuttgart 1 (Gaudino). Att: 83,000
Stuttgart: Stuttgart 3 (Klinsmann, o.g., Schmaler O.), Napoli 3 (Alemao, Ferrera, Careca). Att: 67,000
1990 *Turin*: Juventus 3 (Galia, Casiraghi, De Agostini), Fiorentina 1 (Buso). Att: 45,000
Avellino: Fiorentina 0, Juventus 0. Att: 32,000
1991 *Milan*: Internazionale 2 (Matthäus, Berti), Roma 0. Att: 75,000
Rome: Roma 1 (Rizzitelli), Internazionale 0. Att: 71,000
1992 *Turin*: Torino 2 (Casagrande 2), Ajax 2 (Jonk, Pettersson). Att: 65,000
Amsterdam: Ajax 0, Torino 0. Att: 42,000. (*Ajax won on away goals*)
1993 *Dortmund*: Borussia Dortmund 1 (Rummenigge), Juventus 3 (Baggio D., Baggio R. 2). Att: 37,000
Turin: Juventus 3 (Baggio D. 2, Möller), Borussia Dortmund 0. Att: 60,000
1994 *Vienna*: Salzburg 0, Internazionale 1 (Berti). Att: 43,500
Milan: Internazionale 1 (Vonk), Salzburg 0. Att: 80,326

WON BY A HEAD *Dino Baggio of Juventus in 1993*

for English clubs in the tournament. Tottenham returned for the 1974 Final, but could not cope with Holland's Feyenoord – European champions in 1970 – who won 4–2 on aggregate. The final, however, was marred by some of the worst violence in memory as both sets of supporters fought running battles with each other and the police.

Another Dutch club, Twente Enschede, reached the final the following year, but were outclassed by West Germany's Borussia Mönchengladbach. After a surprising 0–0 draw, Borussia turned on the power in the return to win 5–1, with Jupp Heynckes scoring a hat trick, and Allan Simonsen two. Liverpool won again in 1976, beating Club Brugge 4–3 on aggregate in the final. It was ironic, therefore, that this emerging Liverpool team should then go on to win two successive European Cups, in 1977 and 1978, beating Borussia and Brugge respectively in the finals.

Italy and Spain contested the 1977 UEFA Cup Final, represented by Juventus and Athletic Bilbao, with the Italians winning on away goals after a 2–2 aggregate draw. In 1978 PSV Eindhoven won the Cup for Holland again, beating France's Bastia 3–0 at home after a 0–0 draw in Corsica – the only time a European Final has been played on an island outside the British Isles.

Borussia Mönchengladbach reached their third final in 1979, and made it two wins out of three by beating Red Star Belgrade 2–1 on aggregate, although they needed an own goal and a Simonsen penalty to do it. Borussia reached the final again the following year, and faced fellow West Germans Eintracht Frankfurt in the final. After winning the home leg 3–2, Borussia went down 1–0 in the return, giving Eintracht the victory on the away goals rule.

In 1981 Ipswich Town brought the Cup back to England with a splendid 5–4 aggregate victory over the little-known Dutch side AZ 67 Alkmaar. Ipswich's John Wark scored in both legs of the Final to bring his total in that season's competition to 14 – equalling the all-time record set by Milan's José Altafini in the 1963 European Cup.

IFK Gothenburg became the first Swedish winners of a European trophy when they beat Hamburg in 1982, and they went on to win again in 1987, beating Dundee United. Between those two victories, Anderlecht and Real Madrid dominated the competition. Anderlecht beat Benfica 2–1 on aggregate to win the 1983 competition, and they returned to the final the following year against Tottenham. Both legs produced 1–1 draws, and after extra time produced no winner, Tottenham took the Cup on penalties, reserve goalkeeper Tony Parks saving the decisive kick.

Tottenham's defense of the trophy in 1985 ended in the quarter-finals, where they were narrowly and unluckily beaten 1–0 on aggregate by Real Madrid. The Spaniards, aided by the German Uli Stielike and the Argentinian Jorge Valdano, went on to beat Hungary's Videoton 3–1 in the final. Real retained the trophy the following season with a far more impressive demolition of West Germany's Köln. A 5–1 win in Madrid was followed by a 2–0 defeat in Germany, but Real kept the trophy with a 5–3 aggregate margin.

Following Gothenburg's second success in 1987, the Cup was won on penalties for the second time when Bayer Leverkusen and Español, two of Europe's lesser lights, contested the final. Español won the first leg 3–0 at home and looked all set for Spain's ninth victory, but Bayer evened the aggregate score in the second leg with a goal nine minutes from time, and then won 3–2 on penalties.

Since then the UEFA Cup has been dominated by Italian clubs who, free from import restrictions, have consistently bought up the best players in the world. In the six finals up to 1994, eight of the finalists have been Italian, two of the five have been all-Italian affairs, and the Serie A clubs have won four.

In 1989 Napoli, led by Diego Maradona, beat VfB Stuttgart; Juventus and Fiorentina contested an all-Italian final in 1990, with Juventus winning 3–1 at home and on aggregate; in 1991 Internazionale narrowly beat Roma 2–1; in 1992 Torino lost to Ajax – who were completing a hat trick of European trophy wins —but only on away goals after 2–2 and 0–0 draws; and in 1993 Juventus won the Cup again, proving themselves to be far too good for Borussia Dortmund.

And so it goes on. The system of entry into the UEFA Cup, based on past performances, insures that the more successful countries, such as Italy, Spain, Germany and – pre-Heysel – England, are guaranteed their full quota of four entrants instead of the minimum one. However, with the fragmentation of Eastern Europe, more and more clubs are entering the tournament, and UEFA is considering expanding the tournament still further to accommodate both the clubs from the "new" countries and those smaller clubs bounced out of the European Cup. What effect this will have remains to be seen, but it will certainly make an already difficult competition even harder to win.

EUROPEAN SUPER CUP

The European Super Cup is played annually between the winners of the European Cup and the European Cup-Winners' Cup. The contest is of little importance, but is a welcome revenue-generator for the clubs involved.

European Super Cup Winners

Year	Winner	Year	Winner
1972	Ajax	**1986**	Steaua Bucharest
1973	Ajax	**1987**	FC Porto
1975	Kiev Dynamo	**1988**	Mechelen
1976	Anderlecht	**1989**	Milan
1977	Liverpool	**1990**	Milan
1978	Anderlecht	**1991**	Manchester United
1979	Nottingham Forest	**1992**	Barcelona
1980	Valencia	**1993**	Parma
1982	Aston Villa		
1983	Aberdeen		
1984	Juventus		

MITROPA CUP

The Mitropa Cup was an important competition in the inter-war period, and was the forerunner of the European Cup. Created by Hugo Meisl, the Mitropa Cup (shortened form of Mittel Europa) was restricted to clubs from Austria, Italy, Hungary, Czechoslovakia, Switzerland, Romania and Yugoslavia.

To begin with, the competition involved the champions of each country, and was eventually expanded to include the top four teams from each nation. The competition was suspended between 1939 and 1950 and lost much of its status once the European Cup got under way in 1955. Since 1980 entry has been restricted to the Second Division champions of each country, and the event now receives little attention outside the towns of the participants.

Mitropa Cup Winners

1927 Sparta Prague
1928 Ferencvaros
1929 Ujpest Dozsa
1930 Rapid Vienna
1931 First Vienna
1932 Bologna
1933 FK Austria
1934 Bologna
1935 Sparta Prague
1936 FK Austria
1937 Ferencvaros
1938 Slavia Prague
1939 Ujpest Dozsa
1951 Rapid Vienna
1955 Voros Lobogo
1956 Vasas Budapest
1957 Vasas Budapest
1959 Honved
1960 Vasas Budapest
1961 Bologna
1962 Vasas Budapest
1963 MTK Budapest
1964 Spartak Sokolovo
1965 Vasas Budapest
1966 Fiorentina.
1967 Spartak Trnava
1968 Red Star Belgrade
1969 TJ Internacional
1970 Vasas Budapest
1971 Celik Zenica
1972 Celik Zenica
1973 Tatabanya
1974 Tatabanya
1975 Wacker Innsbrück
1976 Wacker Innsbrück
1977 Vojvodina
1978 Partizan Belgrade
1980 Udinese
1981 Tatran Presov
1982 Milan
1983 Vasas Budapest
1984 SC Eisenstadt
1985 Iskra Bugojno
1986 Pisa
1987 Ascoli
1988 Pisa
1989 Banik Ostrava
1990 Bari
1991 Torino

Notes:
The Mitropa Cup has now been devalued to such an extent that it no longers carries enough prestige to be considered a major tournament.

LATIN CUP

The Latin Cup replaced the Mitropa Cup as Europe's top club event in the immediate post-war years, but it also went into decline once UEFA's new competitions got under way. Played between the champions of France, Spain, Italy and Portugal, the Latin Cup was a curious event. Instead of a cup presentation, points were awarded and after four years the country with the highest total took the trophy. The tournament was discontinued in 1957.

Latin Cup Winners

1949 Barcelona
1950 Benfica
1951 Milan
1952 Barcelona
1953 Stade de Reims
1955 Real Madrid
1956 Milan
1957 Real Madrid

CONCACAF CHAMPIONS CUP

This is the premier club competition for teams from the Central American and Caribbean regions. Contested since 1962, the competition is now known as the American Airlines Cup.

CONCACAF Champions Cup Winners

1962 Guadalajara CD (Mexico)
1963 Racing Club (Haiti)
1964 Not completed
1965 Not completed.
1966 Not held
1967 Alianza (El Salvador)
1968 Toluca (Mexico)
1969 Cruz Azul (Mexico)
1970 Cruz Azul (North), Deportivo Saprissa (Central), Transvaal (Caribbean)
1971 Cruz Azul (Mexico)
1972 Olimpia (Honduras)
1973 Transvaal (Surinam)
1974 Municipal (Guatemala)
1975 Atletico Espanol (Mexico)
1976 Aguila (El Salvador)
1977 America (Mexico)
1978 Univ Guadalajara (North), Comunicaciones (Central), Defence Force (Carib.).
1979 Deportivo FAS (El Salvador)
1980 UNAM (Mexico)
1981 Transvaal (Surinam)
1982 UNAM (Mexico)
1983 Atlante (Mexico)
1984 Violette (Haiti)
1985 Defence Force (Trinidad and Tobago)
1986 LD Alajuelense (Costa Rica)
1987 America (Mexico)
1988 Olimpia (Honduras)
1989 UNAM (Mexico)
1990 America (Mexico)
1991 Puebla (Mexico)
1992 America (Mexico)
1993 Deportivo Saprissa (Costa Rica)

INTER-AMERICAN CUP

The Inter-American Cup pits the club champions of CONCACAF and South America against each other. Played over two legs, the Cup has only been won by CONCACAF clubs on three occasions, and all three were Mexican clubs.

Inter-American Cup Winners

1968 Estudiantes.(Argentina)
1971 Nacional (Uruguay)
1972 Independiente (Argentina)
1974 Independiente (Argentina)
1976 Independiente (Argentina)
1977 America (Mex)
1979 Olimpia (Paraguay)
1980 UNAM (Mexico)
1985 Argentinos Juniors (Argentina)
1986 River Plate (Argentina)
1988 Nacional (Uruguay)
1989 Atletico Nacional (Colombia)
1990 America (Mex)

AFRICAN CHAMPIONS CUP

The African Champions Cup is Africa's premier club tournament and is run along similar lines to its European equivalent, held annually with the champions of each country plus the defending champions playing on a home-and-away knock-out basis.

The early years of the competition were dominated by clubs from West and Central Africa; the 1970s belonged to Cameroon and Ghana, and the North African clubs have held the upper hand since the 1980s.

African Champions Cup Winners

1964 Oryx Douala (Cameroon)
1965 Not held
1966 Stade Abidjan (Ivory Coast)
1967 TP Englebert (Zaïre)
1968 TP Englebert (Zaïre)
1969 Al Ismaili (Egypt)
1970 Asante Kotoko (Ghana)
1971 Canon Yaounde (Cameroon)
1972 Hafia Conakry (Ghana)
1973 AS Vita Kinshasa (Zaïre)
1974 CARA Brazzaville (Congo)
1975 Hafia Conakry (Ghana)
1976 MC Algiers (Algeria)
1977 Hafia Conakry (Ghana)
1978 Canon Yaounde (Cameroon)
1979 Union Douala (Cameroon)
1980 Canon Yaounde (Cameroon)
1981 JE Tizi-Ouzou (Algeria)
1982 Al Ahly (Egypt)
1983 Asant Kotoko (Ghana)
1984 Zamalek (Egypt)
1985 FAR Rabat (Morocco)
1986 Zamalek (Egypt)
1987 Al Ahly (Egypt)
1988 EP Setif (Algeria)
1989 Raja Casablanca (Morocco)
1990 JS Kabylie (Algeria)
1991 Club Africain (Tunisia)
1992 Wydad Casablanca (Morocco)
1993 Zamalek (Egypt)

AFRICAN CUP-WINNERS' CUP

Encouraged by the success of the African Champions Cup, the CAF decided to launch a competition for each nation's Cup-winners in 1975. Again, the new event closely mirrored its European counterpart, and has been dominated by clubs from North and West Africa. Egyptian clubs have done especially well, with five victories including a hat-trick for Cairo's Al Ahly between 1984 and 1986. Clubs from the Cameroon and from Nigeria have also done well over the years

African Cup-Winners Cup Winners

1975 Tonnerre Yaounde (Cameroon)
1976 Shooting Stars (Nigeria)
1977 Enugu Rangers (Nigeria)
1978 Horoya Conakry (Guinea)
1979 Canon Yaounde (Cameron)
1980 TP Mazembe (Zaire)
1981 Union Douala (Cameroon)
1982 Al Mokaoulum (Egypt)
1983 Al Mokaoulum (Egypt)
1984 Al Ahly (Egypt)
1985 Al Ahly (Egypt)
1986 Al Ahly (Egypt)
1987 Gor Mahia (Kenya)
1988 CA Bizerte (Tunisia)
1989 Al Merreikh (Sudan)
1990 BCC Lions (Nigeria)
1991 Power Dynamos (Zambia)
1992 Africa Sports (Ivory Coast)
1993 Al Ahly (Egypt)

CAF CUP

In the light of the success of both of its continental competitions, the CAF decided, in 1992, to introduce a third tournament involving the best of the rest of those clubs not taking part in the other two Cups. The CAF Cup is essentially Africa's answer to the UEFA Cup, and is run along similar lines. The first winners of the new Cup were Nigeria's Shooting Stars – appropriately, because the gold plated trophy was donated to the CAF by a Nigerian businessman.

CAF Cup Winners

1992 Shooting Stars (Nigeria)
1993 Stella Abidjan (Ivory Coast)

THE COUNTRIES

The world governing body of Association Football boasts more than 170 members. They are grouped into six regional confederations — Europe (UEFA), South America (CONMEBOL), Central and North America (CONCACAF), Africa, Asia and Oceania. All have an equal role to play in soccer's international democracy, every member country having a single vote in the FIFA Congress.

EUROPE

Austria and Hungary in 1902 played the first international match outside Britain. In the 1920s it was the central Europeans who launched the Mitropa Cup, the predecessor of today's hugely-successful European club competitions. The French were political leaders in founding FIFA and bringing the vision of a World Cup to reality and, later, launching the European competitive structures which are so familiar, and so avidly followed, today.

Professionalism swept through western Europe in the late 1920s, engulfing Spain, Italy, France and Portugal. The big clubs of all four countries were importing star foreigners as early as the turn of the 1930s. Not until the mid-1950s did Belgium, Holland and then Germany catch up with full-time professionalism. When they did, the balance of the European game changed yet again.

The great nations spawned great clubs – Juventus, Real Madrid, then Ajax Amsterdam, Bayern Munich and Anderlecht. But the foundation remained Europe's unique framework of mixed nationalities. By the end of 1993, UEFA, the European federation, boasted a membership of 48 amid the fragmentation of the former Soviet Union and Yugoslavia and the split of Czechoslovakia.

Many of those nations are too new, as yet, to offer a note to history. They do, nevertheless, deserve a statistical starting point here for the international record.

ALBANIA

Federata Shqiptare Futbollit
Founded: 1930
FIFA: 1954

Soccer in Albania started at the beginning of the twentieth century, but progress was hampered by, first, the ruling Turks and, second, Mussolini's annexation in 1939. The Communist takeover in 1944, under Enver Hoxha, promised a new dawn – but it was a short-lived period of hope for Albanian soccer. Throughout the 1950s, Albania played the game in isolation, and between 1954 and 1963 they played only one international – against East Germany. Some progress was made in the 1960s, with Albania gaining entry to both the World Cup and the European Championship. But the cloak of Communism draped around the country has insured that its soccer prospects remain as poor as its economy.

ARMENIA

Football Federation of Armenia
Founded: 1922
FIFA: 1992

AUSTRIA

Österreicher Fussball-Bund
Founded: 1904
FIFA: 1905

Vienna arguably was the focal point of continental European soccer in the first half of the twentieth century, a situation which lasted until the 1960s. Britons living in Vienna provided Austrian soccer's early impetus and, in 1902, Austria beat Hungary 5–0 at the Prater in what has become the world's second oldest regular international game after England vs. Scotland.

The inter-war period was Austria's most successful era, when the

CONSISTENT *Germany still Europe's best*

Great Coaches

HUGO MEISL

Austria manager and general secretary 1906–37; born November 16, 1881; died February 17, 1937

Meisl was the errant son of a Viennese banking family who was too infatuated with soccer in Central Europe in the early years of the century to want to enter the business. Meisl was playing inside-forward for FK Austria when he met the English coach, Jimmy Hogan, whom he persuaded to come and work in Vienna. Later Meisl became involved with neighbors Admira and then became secretary of the Austrian federation. Simultaneously he was also national manager, and his partnership with Hogan led to the rise of the legendary Austrian "Wunderteam" of the 1920s and early 1930s. Meisl and Vittorio Pozzo were the two dominant figures in pre-war continental soccer.

"Wunderteam" – led by Matthias Sindelar ("The Man of Paper") – swept all before them. In 30 matches from spring 1931 to summer 1934, the "Wunderteam" scored 101 goals, and the 1934 World Cup seemed to be at their mercy. But defeat in the semifinal by the hosts Italy, on a quagmire of a field in Milan, ended their hopes. Austria's chances in the 1938 event were destroyed by the German occupation, and from March 1938 "Austrian" soccer ceased to exist.

A new team came together in the 1950s, led by Ernst Ocwirck and Gerhard Hanappi, which looked set for World Cup success in 1954. But the Germans again spoiled the plan, winning the semifinal, 6–1. A poor showing in 1958 in Sweden was followed by an inexorable decline, and despite qualifying for the 1978, 1982, and 1990 World Cup finals, Austria has now slipped to the lower end of the middle-ranked nations in Europe.

The low point was reached on September 12, 1991 when the Faroe Islands – playing their first ever competitive match – won 1–0 in a European Championship qualifier. The defeat caused huge embarrassment to a nation that will probably always be haunted by the ghosts of the 1930s "Wunderteam," and thoughts of what might have been, had the spectre of Fascism not engulfed Europe at the end of the decade.

BELGIUM

Union Royale Belge des Sociétés de Football-Association
Founded: 1895
FIFA: 1904

Belgian soccer has taken a long time to develop. With an association formed in 1895 and the second-oldest league outside Great Britain, it was natural for the Belgians to be a driving force behind the formation of FIFA and one of only four European teams to go to Uruguay for the first World Cup in 1930. But the strictly amateur nature of the domestic game severely hindered progress.

The yoke of amateurism was finally discarded in 1972, with the introduction of full professionalism, and the national team immediately improved. From 1972 to 1984 Belgium reached the last eight of four successive European Championships, and in 1980 they appeared in the final, where they lost to West Germany. The class of 1980 went on to represent Belgium for almost a decade and contained many of Belgium's most celebrated players, including goalkeeper Jean-Marie Pfaff, full-back Eric Gerets and forward Jan Ceulemans, their most capped player with 96 appearances.

Their finest hour came at the 1986 World Cup finals, where they reached the semifinals, only to lose to an Argentinian team inspired by Diego Maradona. The team of the 1980s have now gone, but Belgium's future seems safe in the hands of a new crop of talented players led by Enzo Scifo, one of the best midfielders in Europe. Belgium have made slow, steady progress and perhaps their best is yet to come.

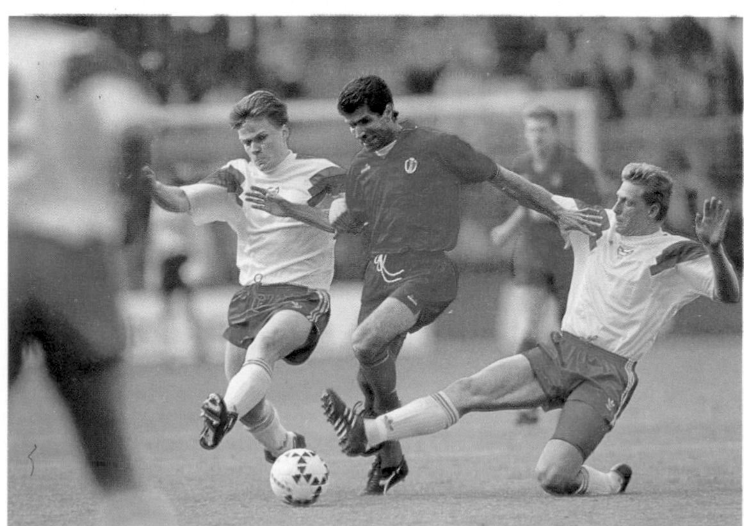
BURSTING THROUGH *Belgium's Scifo takes on two Faroe Islands defenders*

BOSNIA-HERSEGOVINA

C/o Croatian Football Federation
Founded: 1991
FIFA: 1992

BULGARIA

Bulgarski Futbolen Solus
Founded: 1923
FIFA: 1924

Bulgaria, like many Eastern Bloc countries, made little impact in international soccer until after the Communists had taken over in 1944 — and completely reorganized the domestic game. Before 1944 the game's development was hampered by the unstable political climate in the area, but matters did improve after the First World War, when many clubs were formed – especially in Varna and the capital Sofia.

The Communist reorganization, however, transformed Bulgarian soccer. A rigid style of passing play was imposed on the national team, merely requiring strong players to fit the pattern. The results were significant, making Bulgaria very difficult opponents and one of Europe's top teams during the 1960s and 1970s. However, this system discouraged individual flair and flexibility – a point illustrated by Bulgaria's astonishingly poor record in the World Cup finals. Bulgaria qualified for five of the eight World Cup finals between 1962 and 1990, playing 16 matches . . . and did not win any of them! But this period did produce arguably Bulgaria's greatest player, Georgi Asparoukhov, who scored 19 goals in 50 appearances before his untimely death in a car crash in 1971 along with teammate Nikola Kotkov.

STILL TRYING *Bulgaria in Mexico 1986*

This marked the end of an era, and a long period of decline and stagnation set in as the "state amateurs" began to look at the lucrative wages paid in the West. Since 1974 the only bright spots have been qualification for the 1986 and 1994 World Cup finals. In Mexico in 1986, Bulgaria again failed to do justice to themselves with lacklustre, unimaginative and ultimately unsuccessful performances.

The post-Communist Bulgaria allows for greater freedom of self-expression, and Bulgarian players are now much in demand in western Europe, particularly in Spain and Portugal, where Hristo Stoichkov (Barcelona) and Lubo Penev (Valencia) have been great successes. Their experience helped Bulgaria to qualify for the 1994 World Cup finals with a thrilling last-minute victory over France in Paris, a result which perhaps will herald a new era of success.

CZECH MATE *In the 1990 World Cup finals, Czechoslovakia's Tomas Skuhravy was a hat trick man against the USA*

BYELORUSSIA

Football Federation of Byelorussia
Founded: 1992
FIFA: 1992

CROATIA

Croatian Football Federation
Founded: 1991
FIFA: 1992

CYPRUS

Cyprus Football Association
Founded: 1934
FIFA: 1948

Cypriot soccer developed in the 1930s, thanks mainly to its status as a British colony. Indeed, the Cyprus FA was affiliated to the one in London in 1948, and subsequently FIFA membership was granted. But the 1974 Turkish invasion and occupation of the northern part of the island has seriously dented Cypriot hopes of progress.

They remain one of Europe's weakest nations and the 2–0 win over the Faroe Islands in 1992 was their first in a competitive international for nearly twenty years. For Cyprus, it is still a case of "United we stand, divided we are nothing."

CZECHOSLOVAKIA

Ceskoslovensky Fotbalovy Svaz
Founded: 1901
FIFA: 1906
European Championship: 1976
Olympics: 1980

When the 1994 World Cup ended, Czechoslovakia ceased to exist as a soccer nation. The Czech Republic and Slovakia went their separate ways, each setting up an new association, league and national team.

Since 1918, when Czechoslovakia came into existence, the Czechs have been at the forefront of European soccer. They were runners-up in both the 1920 and 1964 Olympic Games, before finally winning the tournament in 1980, in Moscow. They were finalists at the 1934 World Cup with a side containing Antonin Puc, still the national team's leading scorer, Frantisek Planicka, the finest pre-war goalkeeper, and Oldrich Nejedly.

The Communist takeover after the war led to the usual reorganization of the domestic game, which hindered rather than helped as clubs like Sparta and Slavia Prague had been doing very well as professional sides. The army team Dukla Prague rose to prominence and provided the basis of the 1960s Czech team which was among the best in the world. Josef Masopust, Czechoslovakia's most famous player, led the side to third place in the inaugural European Championship in 1960, and to the 1962 World Cup Final, which was lost to Brazil.

Czechoslovakia's biggest success came at the 1976 European Championship, when they beat West Germany on penalties in the final. Ivo Viktor, in goal, Anton Ondrus, in defence, Antonin Panenka, in midfield, and Zdenek Nehoda, in attack, were fine successors to the great sides of the 1930s and 1960s. Since then, results at national and club level have been poor, even though the national team did reach the quarterfinals of the 1990 World Cup, thanks to the goals of Thomas Skuhravy, who later signed for Genoa. Whether, independently, the Czech Republic and Slovakia can emulate the success they enjoyed together remains to be seen.

CZECH REPUBLIC

Football Association of the Czech Republic
Founded: 1993
FIFA: 1993

DENMARK

Dansk Boldspil-Union
Founded: 1889
*FIFA:*1904
European Championship: 1992
Olympics: 1906

Denmark was one of the first continental countries to take up soccer and has some of the oldest clubs in the world. But their rigid adherence to the principle of amateurism meant that Denmark was left behind when most of the rest of Europe adopted professionalism.

As a strong "amateur" nation, Denmark has perhaps inevitably enjoyed its greatest success at the Olympics. Winners in 1906 and runners-up in 1908 and 1912, the Danes were a force to be reckoned with at this level and produced some outstanding players — notably Nils Middelboe, who played with great distinction for Chelsea .

A period of decline occurred during the inter-war years, but qualification for the 1948 and 1960 Olympics sparked hopes of a revival. But the amateur nature of the domestic game, together with a rule which barred foreign-based players from the national team, stifled progress on both occasions. The 1970s prompted great chances for Danish soccer, though, as a flood of players — led by 1977 European Footballer of The Year Allan Simonsen — left Denmark to join clubs in Western Europe. The rule barring "exported" players such as Michael Laudrup, Preben Elkjaer, Jesper Olsen, Morten Olsen and Soren Lerby from the national team was lifted in 1976 and undoubtedly helped the national team develop. These players formed the nucleus of the 1980s "Dinamite" team which reached the semifinals of the 1984 European Championship and the second round of the 1986 World Cup.

TREBLE TOP *Geoff Hurst scores his third goal in the 1966 World Cup Final*

In the late 1980s the league was restructured, and a new generation of players emerged to propel Denmark to the dizzying heights of European Champions in 1992. That unexpected success in Sweden was all the more remarkable given that the Danes were eleventh-hour replacements for the expelled Yugoslavs.

The European success, combined with the domestic restructuring, have pushed Danish soccer into the European mainstream, with progress being made by the national side and the clubs — particularly Brondby and FC Copenhagen — who are beginning to make their presence felt in European competitions. The challenge now is to keep the momentum going.

DANISH DYNAMITE *Denmark's players celebrate their shock European Championship win in 1992*

ENGLAND

The Football Association
Founded: 1863
FIFA: 1905–1920, 1924–1928, 1946
World Cup: 1966
Olympics: 1908, 1912 (as Great Britain)

England, as every schoolboy enthusiast knows, gave soccer to the world. Developed on the playing fields of England's great public schools in the middle of the nineteenth century, the game was first codified and organized in the 1860s, when the Football Association was formed – hence the name Association Football, and the nickname "soccer," to distinguish it from Rugby Football, or "rugger." The FA Cup was introduced in 1871, both the first and now the oldest surviving tournament in the world, and was fundamental in the development of the game — pitting the established amateur sides of the south against the burgeoning professional outfits of the north.

A year later, the very first international match was played, between England and Scotland in Glasgow, and in 1888 the Football League was formed — to organize what was, by now, a largely professional game based mostly in the industrial north.

As the century closed, the British Championship, played between England, Scotland, Wales and Ireland, was the zenith of world soccer. Before the First World War, England and Scotland were well above the rest of the world and, as Great Britain, won Olympic gold in 1908 and 1912.

The inter-war period was a period of increasing isolation, though, as the rest of the world warmed to the game. The FA, which joined FIFA in 1905, always took a disdainful attitude to it and withdrew in 1920, horrified at the prospect of having to play with wartime adversaries, and again in 1928 over the definition of the word amateur. It is highly doubtful whether they would have bothered to compete in the three pre-war World Cups anyway, such was the English view of their superiority over the rest of the world.

That view was unchanged by the ignominious 1–0 defeat by the United States in the 1950 World Cup (which was dismissed as a fluke). However in 1953 Hungary's "Magic Magyars" came to Wembley . . . and destroyed English arrogance for ever.

It was not merely the 6–3 scoreline, or the fact that this was England's first defeat by a non-British side at home, which changed attitudes: it was the manner of the defeat. The Hungarians were far superior technically and tactically. Further defeats at the 1954, 1958 and 1962 World Cup finals confirmed this and forced England to face the facts of the modern game, which had left them behind in the immediate post-war years.

The challenges presented by the new order were spectacularly answered in 1966, however, when England's "wingless wonders" won the World Cup on home soil. Alf Ramsey, the stolid manager who led Ipswich to the Championship in 1962 during their first season in Division One, molded his team around the outstanding talents of goalkeeper Gordon Banks, captain Bobby Moore, and the Charlton brothers Bobby and Jack. He created a system which worked with the players at his disposal, and instilled a team spirit and an understanding which no subsequent England side has matched.

The 1966 success was the springboard from which English club sides launched an unprecedented assault on the three European competitions, winning trophy after trophy between 1964 and 1985. Conversely, as the clubs prospered the national team suffered. An unfortunate defeat by West Germany in the quarterfinal of the 1970 World Cup in Mexico marked the beginning of the end of the Ramsey era, and failure to qualify for the 1974 and 1978 finals confirmed England's worst post-war slump.

Apart from reaching the 1986 World Cup quarterfinals, and their unexpected run to the semifinal four years later, there has been little for England fans to cheer since 1966. Following England's dismal performance at the 1988 and 1992 European Championship finals and, worse, the failure to qualify for the 1994 World Cup finals, the whole structure of the English game has again been called into question. The changes forced by the appalling loss of life at Bradford (1985) and Hillsborough (1989) have led to a modernization of the country's stadiums; but many feel a restructuring of the game's organization is necessary if England is to regain the position they held at the top of the international game.

Great Coaches

ALF RAMSEY

England coach 1963–74;
born January 22, 1920

Ramsey earned a knighthood for managing England to World Cup victory over West Germany at Wembley in 1966, the peak of a double international career as both player and administrator. As a player, Ramsey was a creative and intelligent right-back with Southampton and Tottenham and an integral member of Spurs' push-and-run team which won the Second and First Division titles in successive seasons in 1950 and 1951. On retiring in 1955, Ramsey became coach of Ipswich and his success in taking the East Anglian club from the Third Division to the First Division title in just seven years earned his appointment in 1963 as England's first "proper" coach with sole responsibility for team selection. He was dismissed after the World Cup qualifying failure against Poland a decade later.

ESTONIA

Estonian Football Federation
Founded: 1921
FIFA: 1923

Estonia, like her Baltic neighbors Lithuania and Latvia, ceased to exist after 1940 when the Soviet Union took over. However, Estonia never withdrew from FIFA, their membership was merely put on ice, and in 1992 they came back into the fold. Immediately entering the qualifiers for the 1994 World Cup, Estonia even managed a 0–0 draw away to Malta.

FAROE ISLANDS

Fotboltssamband Foroya
Founded: 1979
FIFA: 1988

Soccer has been played on these tiny islands since before the Second World War, with a league starting in 1942 and a cup competition in 1967. But owing to the Faroes' remoteness and lack of grass fields, competitive matches against overseas opponents have been few and far between. Internationals against other islands (Iceland, Shetland, Orkney and Greenland) were the only exceptions, but these are not regarded as "full" internationals because the Faroes' FIFA membership dates only from as recently as 1988.

The Faroes' entry into the 1992 European Championship, however, was spectacular. A 1–0 win over Austria in their first competitive match made headlines across Europe and stimulated development of the domestic game. Funds were found for a grass field in Toftir, so that matches could be played at home, and now the clubs, too, enter European competitions. All in all, a very encouraging start.

FINLAND

Suomen Palloliito Finlands Bollofoerbund
Founded: 1907
FIFA: 1908

Soccer in the land of lakes and long winters lags well behind ice hockey, athletics, winter sports and motor rallying in terms of popularity, and that situation seems unlikely to change. Prior to the 1970s, national team outings were confined to other Nordic countries, and even though, since then, Finland has regularly entered the World Cup and European Championship, success has been scarce. However, the Finns did almost qualify for the 1980 European Championship finals and from time to time have given one of their rivals a severe fright.

FRANCE

Fédération Française de Football
Founded: 1918
FIFA: 1904
European Championship: 1984
Olympics: 1984

As England gave the game to the world, so the French organized it into a structured sport. The French were prime movers behind the creation of FIFA, UEFA, the World Cup, the European Championship and the European club cups, yet the 1984 European Championship and Olympic title are all they have to show for their skills in innovation and organization.

ALLEZ FRANCE *The 1986 World Cup side*

The FFF, formed in 1918, brought order to a chaotic domestic club scene which, at one stage, had five different bodies vying for control. Professionalism was accepted in 1932 and a league was set up. This helped the national side to improve on their previously poor results, but, despite this, the first three World Cups were disasters for the French.

In the 1950s, Stade de Reims emerged as the best club side France had produced. They twice reached the European Cup Finals, losing to Real Madrid, and the side contained Raymond Kopa and Just Fontaine — two great players and key members of the national side which finished third in the 1958 World Cup (Fontaine's 13 goals in those finals remain a record). But this success was not built on, and France qualified for only one of the next four finals

Then, in the late 1970s, Michel Platini arrived and transformed the French into the most attractive side Europe had seen since the 1950s. Platini, a midfielder with immense skill, vision and grace, had a glorious club career with Juventus in Italy, and inspired France to reach the final stages of three World Cups (1978, 1982 and 1986). They were unlucky with refereeing decisions in their match with the hosts, Argentina, in 1978, and were again unlucky when putting up their best World Cup performance in 1982 in Spain, when they were 3–1 up in the semifinal against West Germany in extra time . . . and lost on penalties, when again the referee did them no favors. Platini's finest hours came in 1984, on French soil, when his nine goals in five games earned France the European Championship and confirmed him as the greatest player in French history.

However, club success in Europe still eluded the French until May 1993, when Marseille beat Milan 1–0 to win the European Cup (Saint-Etienne had lost the final to Bayern Munich in 1976). France went wild. The European Cup, a French brainchild, had finally come home. But the joy was short-lived. Marseille became engulfed in a match-fixing scandal – perhaps the biggest scandal European soccer has ever seen – and they were stripped of the trophy.

And so the French are still waiting for that first European club success. But success in another creations, the World Cup, may be closer to hand, despite a humiliating failure to qualify for the 1994 finals. France will stage the 1998 World Cup, and if Jean-Pierre Papin, Eric Cantona and company can come up with a bit of the old Platini magic, they might just bring their ancestors' dreams alive.

GEORGIA

Football Federation of Georgia
Founded: 1992
FIFA: 1992

GERMAN GRIT *Seeler heads toward the Italian goal in Santiago, 1962*

GERMANY

Deutscher Fussball-Bund
Founded: 1900
FIFA: 1904–1946, 1950
World Cup: 1954, 1974, 1990
European Championship: 1972, 1980
Olympics: 1976 (East Germany)

Since the Second World War, Germany has enjoyed a record of success unparalleled in the history of the game. Yet Germany's pre-war record was quite poor, with third place at the 1934 World Cup the peak of their achievement. The war brought division and in 1948 East Germany, under the Soviets, formed its own association, league and national side. The East Germans, though, with their state-sponsored emphasis on individual rather than team sports, never matched the success of their countrymen on the other side of the Berlin Wall. In fact, half a century of East German soccer only produced two successes of note: Olympic gold in Montreal in 1976 and a 1–0 victory over West Germany, in the only match ever played between the two, at the 1974 World Cup finals.

But while the East floundered, the West flourished. Banished from FIFA in 1946, they were readmitted in 1950 as West Germany . . . and won the World Cup just over four years later. That victory, engineered by coach Sepp Herberger, was all the more amazing because their Final opponents were the "Magic Magyars," whose 3–2 defeat was their second loss in five years!

From that initial breakthrough, the Germans pressed on to even greater heights of achievement. In the World Cup, they were semifinalists in 1958, quarterfinalists in 1962 and runners-up in 1966. Full-time professionalism was introduced in 1963 and a decade later, the Germans were unquestionably the world's best at both national and club levels.

The 1970s seemed to belong to Bayern Munich and West Germany. Bayern, winners of a hat trick of European Cups in 1974, 1975 and 1976, provided the nucleus of the national team which won the European Championship in 1972, the World Cup in 1974, and after finishing second in 1976, the European Championship again in 1980. Goalkeeper Sepp Maier is remembered as the Germans' greatest No.1. Franz Beckenbauer single-handedly revolutionized the sweeper's role into one of attack as well as defence and was one of the finest defenders in the world; and in Gerd Müller West Germany possessed the closest thing to a scoring machine yet seen. In 62 internationals, Müller scored an incredible 68 goals, most of them coming in competitive matches, not friendlies.

And the success story continues. The 1970s sides were replaced by new stars of the world game: Karl-Heinz Rummenigge, Lothar Matthäus, Klaus Allofs, Rudi Völler, Jürgen Klinsmann and Thomas Hässler. Following the World Cup success and German reunification in 1990, they now have even more resources to call upon and more reason to feel they will continue to pile up the trophies.

Great Coaches

JOSEF "SEPP" HERBERGER

Germany coach 1936–63; born March 28, 1897; died April 28, 1977

Herberger was the founder of a German management dynasty. An inside-forward who played three times for Germany between 1921 and 1925, he became assistant national coach to Dr Otto Nerz in 1932 and then succeeded him after the disastrous defeat by Norway at the 1936 Berlin Olympics. Herberger travelled widely to keep abreast of the world game and astutely managed his players and tactics to maximum effect, above all at the 1954 World Cup. There he took the bold step of fielding his reserves for a first round match against Hungary. He was unfazed by the 8–3 defeat, knowing that his fresh "first team" could still reach the later stages and go on, as they did, to beat Hungary 3–2 in the final.

HELMUT SCHÖN

West Germany coach 1963–78; born September 15, 1915

Schön scored 17 goals in 16 internationals for Germany between 1937 and 1941 when he was a star inside-forward with the famous Dresden SC. After the war he played on in Berlin for a while and then became national coach to the briefly independent federation of the Saar. In 1955 Schön was appointed No. 2 to Sepp Herberger as manager of West Germany and succeeded him, with enormous success, in 1963. Schön took West Germany to World Cup runners-up spot in 1966, third place in 1970 and finally to victory in 1974. Under Schön, Germany was also European Champions in 1972 and runners-up in 1976. His partnership with team captain Franz Beckenbauer became very nearly unbeatable.

GREECE

Fédération Hellénique de Football
Founded: 1926
FIFA: 1927
The development of Greek soccer in the first half of the twentieth century was severely hampered by civil war and the unstable political climate in the Balkans. These factors, linked to the "Olympian" adherence to the amateur spirit of the game, meant that a national league was formed only in 1960, and full professionalism arrived as late as 1979. Consequently, success for Greek sides at national and club level has been rare.

The clubs, centered on Athens and Salonica, have spent vast amounts on players, but have so far failed to win a single European trophy. Panathinaikos went closest to breaking that duck when they reached the 1971 European Cup final, where they lost to Ajax. Similarly, the national side has consistently failed to make an impression.

Qualification for the 1980 European Championship was the first time the Greeks had qualified for any finals tournament, and it was to be another 13 years before they tasted success again. Coach Alketas Panagoulias — the man behind the 1980 success — returned to guide Greece impressively through to the 1994 World Cup finals for the first time in their history.

Greece will be hoping that this qualification will act as a catalyst for improvements at club and national level in the near future. Before that can happen, though, Greece's chronic hooligan problem needs to be addressed.

HERO RETURNS *Greece's Panagoulias*

TAKE OFF *Holland's Rep beats Argentina's Passarella and Gallego in 1978*

HOLLAND

Koninklijke Nederland Voetbalbond (KNVB)
Founded: 1889
FIFA: 1904
European Championship: 1988
The Dutch were early devotees of soccer, partly owing to the country's close proximity to Britain, and were among the continent's leading amateur sides in the early 1900s. Indeed they reached the semifinals of four consecutive Olympic Games from 1908 to 1924... but lost them all. Third place in 1908 and 1912 was their best.

The 1920s marked a move away from amateurism in other countries, and Dutch soccer entered a decline which lasted until the 1960s. Up until that decade, internationals were mostly played against European neighbors, especially Belgium, and first-round defeats in the 1934 and 1938 World Cups did little to encourage them to venture further afield.

The low point came just after the Second World War, when a dismal sequence of results, with just one victory in over five years, prompted modernization of the domestic game. So, in 1957, a national league was created and professionalism was introduced in an attempt to staunch the flow of Dutch players going abroad. The main beneficiaries of the reorganization were Ajax of Amsterdam, Feyenoord of Rotterdam and PSV Eindhoven — the "big three" who have dominated Dutch soccer ever since. The big breakthrough came in 1970, when Feyenoord won the European Cup. It was the beginning of a golden era for Dutch soccer, in which Ajax won a hat trick of European Cups (1971, 1972, 1973), Feyenoord and PSV both won the UEFA Cup, and Holland reached two consecutive World Cup finals.

The generation of Dutch players which emerged in the 1970s was among the finest the modern game has seen. Ajax led the way, providing the backbone of the national team, with hugely talented players such as Johan Neeskens, Arie Haan, Ruud Krol, Wim Suurbier and, of course, Johan Cruyff, arguably the best player of his day. Along with the Feyenoord duo of Wim Van Hanegem and Wim Jansen, they formed the nucleus of a side which was unfortunate to lose the 1974 and 1978 World Cup Finals to the host nations, West Germany and Argentina respectively. Coach Rinus Michels was the architect of the success with his "total soccer" system, which involved molding highly skilled players into a team unit, with the emphasis on interchangeability and with every player totally comfortable in possession.

As the "total soccer" side broke up, the Dutch slipped into a malaise, failing to qualify for the 1982 and 1986 World Cup finals. But a revival was soon to follow, spearheaded by a new generation of players at Ajax and PSV. Ajax won the European Cup-winners' Cup in 1987 and completed a hat trick of European successes when they won the UEFA Cup in 1992 (only the third side to complete this treble), while PSV won the European Cup in 1986. Ruud Gullit, Frank Rijkaard, Marco Van Basten and Ronald Koeman, once again under Rinus Michels' guidance, triumphed in the 1988 European Championship — Holland's only major success.

At present, the Dutch domestic game operates a sort of conveyor-belt system for developing young talent. The "big three" plunder the other clubs for the best players, and are then themselves plundered by clubs in Spain and, especially, Italy, where the Dutch axis of Rijkaard-Gullit-Van Basten propelled Milan to continental domination in the late 1980s. This process inevitably leads to stagnation at club level, where gates are low and hooliganism is rife.

At the national level, the Dutch game is handicapped by the over-inflated egos of the players, who often seem to feel that they should be running things, not the coach or Federation. This phenomenon plagued the "total soccer" side in the 1970s and wrecked Holland's 1990 World Cup bid in Italy.

HUNGARY

Magyar Labdarugo Szovetseg
Founded: 1901
FIFA: 1906
Olympics: 1952, 1964, 1968
Just as Austria will always be renowned for the "Wunderteam" of the 1930s, so Hungary will be for the "Magic Magyars" team of the 1950s. This team was the finest the world had ever seen and had lost only one international in five years before,

MAGIC MAGYARS *Hidegkuti scores Hungary's sixth goal at Wembley in 1953*

heartbreakingly, they failed in the 1954 World Cup Final. The forward line of Zoltan Czibor, Jozsef Toth, Nandor Hidegkuti, Sandor Kocsis and Ferenc Puskas — the greatest player of his era and still regarded as one of the best ever — terrorized opposition defenses and scored 173 goals in this spell. In 1953, they became the first non-British team to beat England at home, winning 6–3.

Yet this was not the first outstanding side Hungary had produced. Hungarian clubs, notably MTK Budapest, who won 10 consecutive titles (1914–25), dominated European soccer in the inter-war period, winning five Mitropa Cups in the 1930s. The national team reached the World Cup Final in 1938, where they were beaten by the Italians. The 1930s team contained such fine players as Gyorgy Sarosi and Gyula Zsengeller.

The Hungarian uprising of 1958 broke up the "Magic Magyars" team, but by the 1960s another had emerged. The new stars were Florian Albert and Ferenc Bene, who led Hungary to the 1962 and 1966 World Cup quarter-finals and Olympic gold in 1964 and 1968.

The 1970s marked the beginning of an insipid decline for the national side, despite some notable successes for the clubs, particularly Ujpest who won nine titles in eleven years. Failure to qualify for the 1970, 1974, 1990 and 1994 World Cup finals was matched by poor performances at the 1978, 1982, and 1986 tournaments, especially in Mexico in 1986 when they lost 6–0 to the Soviet Union.

The lowest point came, however, in a World Cup qualifier in June 1992 when Iceland won 2–1 . . . in Budapest!

Great Coaches

GUSZTAV SEBES

Hungary coach 1949–56; born June 21, 1906; died January 30, 1986

Sebes was a successful player in the 1920s with Vasas and MTK Budapest, but is best-known for the creation of the "Magic Magyars" of the late 1940s and 1950s. The Communist take-over allowed the Hungarian federation to transfer Hungary's top players into the two top clubs, Honved and Red Banner (formerly MTK) and Sebes fused their talents for the national team, built around the tactic of the withdrawn center-forward. Hungary won the 1952 Olympic title but lost the 1954 World Cup final, against all the odds, to West Germany. Sebes resigned following the loss of many star players who fled abroad after the 1956 Revolution.

ICELAND

Knattspyrnusamband Island
Founded: 1947
FIFA: 1929

Iceland, although definitely one of Europe's "minnow" nations, are often capable of upsetting Europe's bigger fish. In the 1994 World Cup qualifiers they beat Hungary home and away and finished five points above them in the group! They played their first international in 1946, against Denmark, and have only entered the World Cup and European Championship regularly since the 1970s.

Iceland has produced some very good players in the last few years, notably Arnor Gudjohnson and Asegir Sigurvinsson. But owing to the island's inhospitable climate and small population, the domestic game is very weak, and Iceland's top players are to be found on the continent and in Britain.

ISRAEL

Hitachdut Lekaduregel Beisrael
Founded: 1928
FIFA: 1929
Asian Championship: 1964

Although the state of Israel was not founded until 1948, a soccer association was formed, in the former Palestine, some 20 years earlier. Palestine played only a handful of international matches before the national side was revived, in 1949, as Israel.

At first only World Cup matches or friendlies were played, as Israel found itself surrounded by hostile Arab nations. All of them being members of the Asian Federation, this situation was to lead to problems as the Arab states refused to play the Israelis. In the 1958 World Cup, for instance, Israel's opponents all withdrew, forcing FIFA to order them to play-off against Wales for a finals place. Similar withdrawals disrupted the Asian Championships, which Israel hosted and won in 1964 — their only honour.

In 1976, Israel was thrown out of the Asian Confederation because their presence was disrupting the development of the game. Israel led a nomadic existence, as associate members of Oceania, until being formally accepted into UEFA in 1991. The national side and clubs now take part in European competitions, and to the benefit of the Israeli game. In 1993, Maccabi Haifa knocked Moscow Torpedo out of the European Cup-winners' Cup, and in a World Cup qualifier in Paris the national side pulled off a remarkable 3–2 win against France.

ITALY

Federazione Italiana Giuoco Calcio
Founded: 1898
FIFA: 1903
World Cup: 1934, 1938, 1982
European Championship: 1968
Olympics: 1936

The first 30 years of Italian soccer were chaotic and complicated, with various regional leagues and the industrial cities of the north — Milan and Turin — competing for power. But the Association finally settled in Rome, in 1929, and a national league was formed in 1930, providing the boost the game needed and leading Italy to unmatched success in the 1930s.

Under legendary coach Vittorio Pozzo, Italy lost only seven games during the decade, winning the World Cup in 1934 and 1938 and the 1936 Olympic title in between to confirm their superiority. The 1930s also saw the beginnings of a trend for Italian clubs to import foreign players to

Great Coaches

VITTORIO POZZO

Italy coach 1932–48; born March 12, 1886; died December 21, 1968

Pozzo was a giant figure in Italian soccer history. He "found" soccer when he came to England as a student before the First World War. His admiration for Manchester United, their center-half Charlie Roberts and soccer in general led to his refusing family orders to come home until he was sent a return ticket. In 1912 Pozzo coached Italy's team at the Olympic Games in Stockholm, where he met Hugo Meisl. He later became an admirer of Herbert Chapman. At the club level Pozzo was long associated with Torino and he was coach, dictator and psychologist of the Italian team which won the World Cup in 1934 and 1938 and the Olympic Games tournament in 1936.

AVANTI AZZURRI *Italy's hero Rossi (left) in the 1982 World Cup final*

gain an advantage in the league. The best-known stars of this era were Luisito Monti and Giuseppe Meazza.

After the war Torino were the dominant team, winning four consecutive titles, and providing virtually all of the national team. But, returning from Lisbon, their plane crashed into the Superga Hill outside Turin killing all on board, including ten internationals. Hardly surprisingly, this led to a decline for both Torino and Italy during the 1950s.

Many blamed the failure on the large number of foreign imports in the Italian game, which grew considerably in the 1950s — led by Milan with their Swedish "Gre-No-Li" trio of Gunnar Gren, Gunnar Nordahl and Nils Liedholm. Consequently, the importation of foreigners was banned in 1964. This hampered the clubs, who were making headway in Europe — Milan won the European Cup in 1963, Internazionale did so in 1964 and 1965 — but allowed a new generation of Italian players to develop, and they won the 1968 European Championship.

The 1970s, though, witnessed the rise of *catenaccio*, defensive, sterile soccer, reflecting the attitude that not losing was more important than winning. For the clubs it was a lean time in Europe, but the national team did better, reaching the 1970 World Cup Final. The import ban was lifted in the early 1980s, and it was to be a decade of great successes for the clubs, who made full use of their foreign quota. Juventus, with French midfield genius Michel Platini, dominated the first half of the decade, while the national team, skippered by 40-year-old Dino Zoff, swept to victory at the 1982 World Cup in Spain. Then Milan — with a Dutch axis of Gullit-Rijkaard-Van Basten — dominated the second half, when Napoli, Internazionale and Sampdoria also tasted European success.

Italy today has the best league in the world, with the biggest stars, huge attendances and regular success in Europe. Arrigo Sacchi's attacking Milan side of the late 1980s and early 1990s has smashed *catenaccio*, one hopes for ever. The Serie A is now a hugely exciting league with many formidable teams. Even lesser clubs such as Parma have prospered, winning the European Cup-winners' Cup in 1993. The national team failed in their bid to win the 1990 World Cup, which was held in Italy, and they failed to qualify for the 1992 European Championship. But a rebuilding program has halted the slide and, with Roberto Baggio leading the way, Italy looks set to remain one of the game's great powers.

LATVIA

Football Association of Latvia
Founded: 1921
FIFA: 1923

Latvia was the strongest of the Baltic teams before the Second World War, but still represented easy pickings for European opponents, as when France hammered them 7–0 at the 1924 Olympics. Despite this, Latvia only failed narrowly to qualify for the 1938 World Cup finals.

Occupied, and wiped off the political map of Europe by the Soviet Union in 1940, Latvia continued playing full internationals until 1949. Their return to competitive competition came on August 12, 1993, when they lost a World Cup qualifier to Lithuania. That was followed by a 0–0 draw with Denmark, and further draws in games with Spain and Lithuania and in both games against Albania. Latvia is proving to be an awkward opponent.

LIECHTENSTEIN

Liechtensteiner Fussball-Verband
Founded: 1933
FIFA: 1974

With a population of just 27,000, it is remarkable that Liechtenstein has a national team at all.

An association was formed in 1933, and they joined FIFA and UEFA in 1974, but few matches have been played. Liechtenstein made unsuccessful attempts to qualify for the 1988 and 1992 Olympic Games, and this may have prompted them to withdraw from the 1994 World Cup qualifiers before the draw was made. Liechtenstein's few teams compete in regional Swiss leagues.

LITHUANIA

Lithuanian Football Association
Founded: 1921
FIFA: 1923

Lithuania was a FIFA member between 1923 and 1940, at a time when the Baltic nations were among the weakest in Europe. Their first international was in June 1923, when they were beaten 5–0 at home by Estonia, and they made an unsuccessful bid to qualify for the Olympic tournament a year later.

The Soviets took over in 1940, but Lithuania continued playing until 1949, by which time they were the strongest of the Baltic states. Lithuania regained independence in 1991 and played its first World Cup match since 1937 on April 28, 1992, when they drew 2–2 with Northern Ireland in Belfast. Two wins and three draws from their 12 World Cup qualifiers was a fine effort.

Lithuania now has its own national league, and a pattern has yet to emerge, but while under the Soviets, Zalgiris Vilnius made the biggest impact, reaching the Supreme Division in 1982. Lithuania's most successful players are Arminas Narbekovas and Valdas Ivanauskas, who play for FK Austria.

LUXEMBOURG

Fédération Luxembourgeoise de Football
Founded: 1908
FIFA: 1910

Poor Luxembourg! After half a century of World Cup endeavor, they have yet to finish better then bottom in any of the 14 qualifying groups they have contested. Similar finishes have been recorded in the European Championship, the only exception being 1964 when they were quarterfinalists.

Being strictly amateur, Luxembourg's clubs have been equally unsuccessful in Europe. Jeunesse Esch, the best-known, remain the only Luxembourg side to have reached the second round of the European Cup, in 1964. A few players have made the grade in France and Belgium, notably Guy Hellers, who was a regular for Standard Liège.

MALTA

Malta Football Association
Founded: 1900
FIFA: 1959
Malta, as a British colony, took up soccer early. The Malta FA was affiliated with the Football Association in London until 1959, when they decided to go their own way and join FIFA. They entered the 1960 Olympic qualifiers, in the African section, but made no headway. Indeed, Malta has never qualified for the World Cup or the European Championship finals.

Maltese clubs have been regulars in European competitions since the 1960s, but consistently heavy losers. Curiously, the league has no home and away games. Since the opening of the Ta'Qali national stadium in 1980, all Premier League matches have been played there.

NORTHERN IRELAND

Irish Football Association
Founded: 1880
FIFA: 1911–20, 1924–28, 1946
Northern Ireland has the fourth oldest association and the third oldest league in the world, and has been playing internationals for 111 years. For 68 of those years the Home International Championship alone provided opposition, and it was not until 1951, when France visited Belfast, that non-British sides were engaged.

The Irish qualified for the 1958 World Cup finals, with a team led by Tottenham's skipper Danny Blanchflower, and reached the quarter-finals — better than England and Scotland could manage. In the 1960s and 1970s, despite having George Best on the team, the Irish were at a low ebb, but the 1980s marked a revival. Coached by Billy Bingham, a member of the 1958 side, the Irish reached the second round of the 1982 World Cup in Spain, and qualified again in 1986, though with less success. Those two teams contained Pat Jennings, one of the greatest goalkeepers of all time and a fine ambassador for a country torn in two by sectarian hatred.

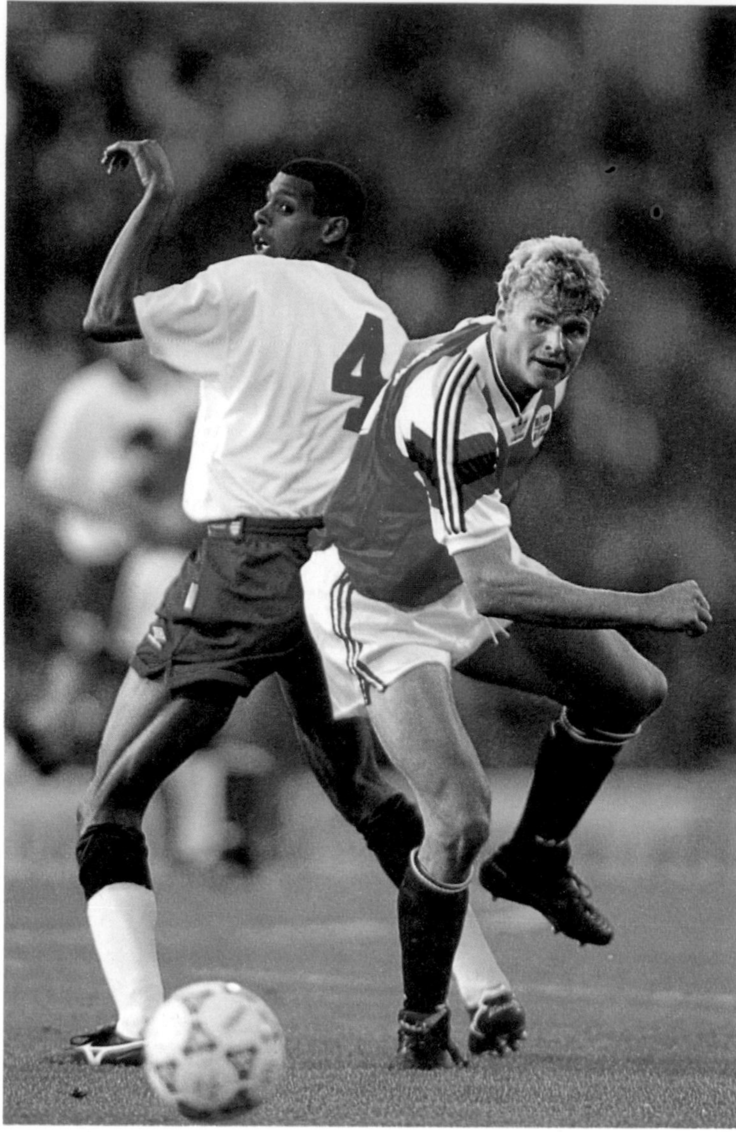

TURNING POINT *Norway's Flo turns England's Palmer inside out*

NORWAY

Norges Fotballforbun
Founded: 1902
FIFA: 1908
Norway, traditionally one of Europe's minnow nations, turned the form book upside down in the 1994 World Cup qualifiers, easily winning its group ahead of Holland, England and Poland! The current national team, unlike most of their predecessors, are largely based abroad, notably in England where Erik Thorstvedt — Norway's greatest goalkeeper — plays for Tottenham.

The qualification was Norway's first since 1938, a decade which was the national side's heyday. Having won the 1929–32 Scandinavian Championship (for the first and only time), they astonishingly finished third at the 1936 Berlin Olympics. In the quarter-finals they beat Germany 2–0, much to Hitler's annoyance, and only lost the semi-final to Italy after extra time.

POLAND

Polski Zwlazek Pilki Noznej
Founded: 1919
FIFA: 1923
Olympics: 1972
Poland's history has been turbulent to say the least, with numerous boundary changes, and between 1874 and 1918 — when continental soccer was just developing — it did not even exist! The Polish state, as it is today, was created in 1921, and the national side made its debut in December 1921 against Hungary. Despite reaching the 1938 World Cup finals (and the semifinal of the 1936 Olympics), the pre-war record was poor, but the war and subsequent Communist takeover brought great change. In familiar fashion, the Communists totally reorganized the domestic game, attaching existing clubs to government bodies and creating new ones – notably Gornik Zabrze, who dominated league soccer in the 1960s and 1970s and reached the European Cup-winners' Cup Final in 1969.

In the 1970s Poland embarked on a 15-year reign of achievement which started in 1972 with the gold medal at the Munich Olympics. This team contained Wlodzimierz Lubanski, Poland's top scorer, Kazimierz Deyna, capped 102 times, and prolific goalscorer Robert Gadocha. For the 1974 World Cup finals, this trio was joined by Gregorz Lato, Poland's most capped player (104 times), and Andrzej Szarmach in attack, with "The Clown" Jan Tomaszewski in goal and Wladislav Zmuda and Jerzy Gorgon in defence. Poland finished third and this team stayed together for most of the decade, reaching the final of the 1976 Olympics and the World Cup finals again in 1978 with arguably their best-ever team.

There was further success at the 1982 World Cup finals. With future Juventus star Zbigniew Boniek outstanding, Poland reached the semi-finals, losing to eventual winners Italy. But in the 1980s, following these successes, many top players moved abroad, weakening the domestic game. The collapse of Communism has made matters worse and, for many clubs, the only means of survival is the continual sale of players to the West . . . which simply exacerbates the problem.

PORTUGAL

Federacao Portuguesa De Futbol
Founded: 1914
FIFA: 1926
The Portuguese Football Association was founded in 1914 as the result of a merger between the associations of Lisbon and Oporto — the two cities

IN FLIGHT *Portugal's Augusto*

which have utterly dominated domestic soccer. The Lisbon duo of Benfica and Sporting Lisbon, along with their rivals FC Porto from Oporto, are among the most famous names in world club soccer. The League Championship, set up in 1935, has only ever been won by these three, except in 1948 when Belenenses broke the monopoly.

Portugal's greatest era was in the 1960s, when Benfica won the European Cup twice (1961 and 1962) and reached a further three finals. The bulk of this Benfica side formed the nucleus of the national team which was then at its peak. The most famous of them was Eusebio, a strong, Mozambique-born striker who was arguably the best player of the 1966 World Cup. Fellow Mozambican Mario Coluna and Angola-born José Aguas were other "adopted" players who augmented an impressive side which also included the Benfica quartet Costa Pereira, in goal, Germano, on defense, and Cavem and José Augusto raiding down the wings.

In those 1966 finals Eusebio scored nine goals, including four in a remarkable 5–3 win over North Korea — Portugal was three down after 22 minutes — as the Portuguese finished in third place. The national team has never again scaled such heights and the 1986 World Cup finals proved an unhappy break in the long sequence of failure.

Portuguese clubs, though, staged a revival in the 1980s. Benfica reached the UEFA Cup Final in 1983, and in 1987 FC Porto became the third club side to win in Europe — Sporting had won the European Cup-winners' Cup in 1964 — when they won the European Cup. Benfica also lost in European Cup finals in 1988 and 1990, while Portugal's youngsters won the World Youth Cup in 1989 and 1991, suggesting better times ahead.

REPUBLIC OF IRELAND

The Football Association of Ireland
Founded: 1921
FIFA: 1923

Since their first international in 1924, an Olympic qualifier against Bulgaria, the Republic of Ireland has always been on the verge of great things. With virtually all her top players playing in England and Scotland, the domestic league has always been weak, while the national team has often had gifted individuals, but never a team strong enough to qualify for the big tournaments.

All that changed in 1986 when Jack Charlton, a World Cup winner with England in 1966, was appointed manager. He utilized the Republic's physical strength, determination and skills perfected in the English League, to give the team belief in itself. In 1988 they qualified for the European Championship finals, but unfortunately Liam Brady, perhaps the greatest Republic player in history, missed the tournament and thus never displayed his exquisite passes on the big stage.

Having made the initial breakthrough, the Republic made progress and qualified for the 1990 World Cup finals in Italy. After narrowly making their way through the first round they met Romania in the second round. Goalless after extra time, the Irish won the penalty shoot-out with David O'Leary, a survivor of the pre-Charlton era, scoring the decider. No matter that Italy beat them in the quarterfinals, the Republic had arrived.

They narrowly missed out on a place in the 1992 European Championship finals in Sweden, but succeeded, where England, Scotland, Wales and Northern Ireland all failed, in claiming a place at the 1994 World Cup Finals. The trick now is for the Association to improve the quality of the club game, which is still poor.

ROMANIA

Federatia Romana de Fotbal
Founded: 1908
FIFA: 1930

Romania embraced soccer before most of her Balkan neighbors, mainly owing to the influence of the country's sovereign, King Carol, who was a soccer fanatic. He instigated the formation of a federation in 1908 and, having returned to power in 1930 after an abdication, he was determined that Romania should enter the first World Cup.

Romania duly made the long trip to Uruguay, but were beaten by the hosts in the first round. They also entered the 1934 and 1938 tournaments, but could not progress beyond the first round, despite the presence of Iuliu Bodola, their top scorer to this day.

The Communists took over in 1944 and, as usual, reorganized the domestic game. Two of the clubs created in Bucharest, Steaua, the army team, and Dinamo, the police team, have dominated Romanian soccer ever since. After the war, the national team enjoyed a brief upsurge with qualification for the 1970 World Cup finals, and a quarter-final finish in the 1977 European Championship. But, despite Anghel Iordanescu, one of the greats of Romanian soccer, it was not until 1984 that they qualified for the finals of a major tournament again, the European Championship in France.

In the 1980s, under the direct influence of the Ceaucescu regime, Steaua and Dinamo dominated even more. In 1986 Steaua became the first team from behind the Iron Curtain to win the European Cup, and not surprizingly, as they formed the nucleus of the national team, Romania now entered its most successful era. With Gheorghe Hagi, the best of his generation, on the team, they were one of the better teams at Italia '90 and won their qualifying group for the 1994 tournament. These are interesting times for Romania, with the league expected to be a far more open affair following the fall of Ceaucescu, and with many of the top players now gaining valuable experience abroad.

SHOOT-OUT SHUT-OUT *Ireland's Pat Bonner saves the decisive penalty against Romania in the 1990 World Cup*

RUSSIA

Russian Football Federation
Founded: 1922
FIFA: 1922
European Championship: 1960 (as Soviet Union)
Olympics: 1956, 1988 (as Soviet Union)

Russia's soccer playing history is inextricably entwined with that of the former Soviet Union, and it is under the banner of the latter that her greatest achievements have occurred. By the early years of the twentieth century, leagues had been formed in most of the cities of the Russian empire, notably in what was then the capital, St Petersburg.

In 1912, an all-Russian soccer union was created and a championship was introduced. In the same year "Tsarist Russia" entered the Stockholm Olympics but were beaten in the first round, by Finland, and by Germany in the consolation tournament that followed — by 16 goals to none! The First World War ended Russia's brief international career and, after the Revolution, Russia took on the guise of the Soviet Union.

The Communists reorganized soccer from top to bottom, with the emphasis on teamwork rather than individual flair. Moscow, now the Soviet capital, became the main football center with five great workers' clubs: Dynamo (electrical trades), Spartak (producers' co-operatives), Torpedo (car manufacturers), Lokomitive (railways) and CSKA (the army). The development of these clubs, and many more throughout the Union, promoted the formation of a pan-Union league in 1936, which Moscow dominated until the 1960s.

In the 1950s the national side, which had previously played few matches, began to venture out. They won a poorly-attended 1956 Olympic Games and reached the quarter-finals of the 1958 World Cup at their first attempt. This side contained some of Soviet football's greatest names, including Igor Netto, Valentin Ivanov, Nikita Simonyan and the great goalkeeper Lev Yashin.

In 1960 they entered and won the very first European Championship, beating Yugoslavia 2–1 in the final in Paris. This, however, remains the only major triumph that either the Soviet Union or Russia has ever had.

In the 1960s, the Soviets promised much, but delivered little. They lost in the final of the European Championship in 1964 and 1972 , and reached the semifinals in 1968. In the World Cup, they reached the quarter-finals in 1962 and went a stage further in 1966 in England. This gave rise, justifiably, to the notion that the Soviet "method" would always produce good sides, but never great ones.

In the 1970s Oleg Blokhin emerged as the Soviet Union's greatest-ever player at a time when the national side was in decline, failing to qualify for the 1974 and 1978 World Cup tournaments. An upturn occurred with qualification for the 1982 and 1986 finals, but on neither occasion could they progress beyond the second round. In 1988 they reached the European Championship final.

The Soviet sides of 1986 and 1988 were arguably the best since the 1960s, but were composed of mainly Kiev Dynamo players. Indeed, it is a curious fact that, despite Moscow's, and therefore Russia's, dominance of Soviet football, the only Soviet sides to win European club competitions were not Russian. Kiev, in the Ukraine, won the European Cup-winners' Cup in 1975 and 1986, and Tbilisi Dynamo, from Georgia, won the same tournament in 1981.

In September 1991, the Soviet Union began to disintegrate. The three Baltic states achieved independence and went their own way, quickly followed by the other 12 republics. The Soviets had qualified for the 1992 European Championship finals and took part under a "flag of convenience" name, the Commonwealth of Independent States. Soon afterwards the Soviet Union was swept away completely and the 15 former republics began organizing themselves into new and separate soccer playing nations.

This poses great problems for FIFA, and more so for UEFA, who has, somehow, to incorporate these new states into their competition structures. Some will join the Asian Confederation, but the bulk will have to be accommodated in Europe. Russia, picking up where the Soviet Union left off, entered the 1994 World Cup qualifying competition and qualified, with misleading ease, from a very poor group. They will undoubtedly emerge as the most powerful of the states once the initial teething problems, particularly at club level, have been overcome.

NEW BREED
Young winger Kanchelskis in action for the CIS in Sweden, 1992

TARTAN TERRIERS *Scotland's Billy Bremner and Jimmy Johnstone celebrate victory over the old enemy, England*

SAN MARINO

Federazione Sammarinese Giuoco Calcio
Founded: 1931
FIFA: 1988
Located entirely within Italy, the Most Serene Republic of San Marino, to give it its full title, is one of the smallest nations ever to enter the World Cup. A population of just 22,000 means it will never become a force in international soccer, but you cannot help admiring their pluck and persistence.

Their first taste of competition was in the 1992 European Championship qualifiers and, although they finished bottom of their group, they were not disgraced. Entry into the 1994 World Cup qualifiers followed, and things could only improve after their first match — a 10–0 defeat by Norway. However, in the return they lost by only 2–0, and on March 10, 1993, they earned their first competitive point with a 0–0 draw at home to Turkey. Even San Marino's clubs now enter European competition, but are at the same early stage of development as the national team.

SCOTLAND

Scottish Football Association
Founded: 1873
FIFA: 1910–20, 1924–28, 1946
Scotland boasts a proud soccer playing heritage and, for such a small country, it has been a remarkable story. Founded in 1873, the Scottish FA still retains a permanent seat on the international board.

Scotland was also the venue for the world's first international match when, on November 30, 1872, Scotland and England drew 0–0. The Scotland vs. England rivalry has continued ever since, sharpened by the fact that many of England's most successful club sides have contained or been managed by Scots: Bill Shankly at Liverpool, Matt Busby at Manchester United, Alex Ferguson also at Manchester United and George Graham at Arsenal have been outstanding, while the players include Hughie Gallacher (Newcastle), Alex James (Arsenal), Alex Jackson (Preston), Denis Law (Manchester United), Billy Bremner (Leeds), Kenny Dalglish (Liverpool) and literally hundreds more.

This continual draining of manpower would have withered many countries. But the Scottish League survives, thanks mainly to the two great Glasgow clubs, Celtic and Rangers. These two, representing the Catholic (Celtic) and Protestant (Rangers) halves of Scottish society, have dominated the domestic scene unlike any other country in Europe. Scottish club football was at its peak in the 1960s, with Celtic winning the European Cup in 1967 — the first British side to do so — and reaching the final again in 1970. Rangers won the 1972 European Cup-winners' Cup.

At the same time, the national team made steady progress. Having entered the World Cup for the first time in 1950, they then qualified for the finals in 1970, 1974, 1978, 1982, 1986 and 1990 — but could not progress beyond the first round on any occasion. In 1992 the Scots reached the European Championship finals for the first time, after seven attempts, and gave a good account of themselves without seriously threatening to win it, and herein lies Scotland's problem. They seem capable of reaching finals tournaments, but unable to win them, prompting one wit to comment: "No other team torments its fans quite like the Scots!"

Domestically, the Glasgow monopoly was briefly threatened in the 1980s when Aberdeen (European Cup-winners' Cup winners in 1983) and Dundee United (UEFA finalists in 1987) emerged, but today Rangers are all-powerful. With one of Europe's best stadiums and huge financial resources, they have even imported many English players!

SLOVAKIA

(*see under* Czechoslovakia)

SLOVENIA

Nogometna Zveza Slovenije
Founded: 1991
FIFA: 1992

SPAIN

Real Federation Espanola de Futbol
Founded: 1913
FIFA: 1904
European Championship: 1964
Olympics: 1992
Spain's reputation as a world power in football is based largely on the exploits of her clubs, particularly Real Madrid and Barcelona, and the successes of the national side in the 1950s and 1960s. Soccer first got a foothold in the Basque country of Northern Spain, through migrant British workers, in the 1890s. Indeed, Spain's oldest club, Athletic Bilbao, still retain its English title. The game spread rapidly and was soon popular in Madrid, Barcelona and Valencia. The various regional organizations were brought together in 1913, when the Real Federation Espanola de Futbol was formed. In 1920 the national team made its debut, with a

EUROPE'S FINEST *Real Madrid*

1–0 win over Denmark, and until the Civil War Spain's record was quite good. They reached the quarterfinals of the 1928 Olympics, and the 1934 World Cup finals — losing to Italy both times. Star of the team was goalkeeper Ricardo Zamora.

The Civil War and the Second World War halted internationals for almost a decade. But the domestic league grew stronger as the rivalry between Real Madrid, the "Royal" club, and Barcelona, the Catalan people's club, intensified. Barcelona had been a center of resistance to Franco's fascists, and for the defeated and emasculated Catalan people, became their standard-bearers. This rivalry intensified in the 1950s, as both clubs began importing foreign talent. Real had Alfredo Di Stefano and Ferenc Puskas, while Barca had the Hungarian trio of Kubala, Kocsis and Czibor.

Real Madrid won the first five European Cups (1956–60), heralding the 1960s as a decade of huge success at club and national level. Barcelona won the Fairs Cup, the former name of the UEFA Cup, in 1959, 1960 and again in 1966; Valencia won it in 1962 and 1963, Real Zaragoza in 1964. Meanwhile Atletico Madrid won the European Cup-winners' Cup in 1962, and Real Madrid won the European Cup again in 1966. There were also eight final defeats — shared among five clubs — in the three European competitions in this decade, a phenomenal record.

The national team qualified for the 1962 and 1966 World Cup finals and won the European Championship in 1964. A team containing Luis Suarez, possibly the greatest Spanish soccer player ever, and one of the few Spaniards to play in Italy (with Internazionale), beat the Soviet Union 2–1 in Madrid to clinch Spain's first major trophy. The 1970s, however, marked a decline at both levels. A ban on foreign imports, imposed in 1963, was lifted in 1973 in order to improve the national side. But it had the reverse effect. Spain failed to reach the 1970 and 1974 World Cup finals and, after Real's 1966 European Cup success, it was not until 1979 that European success returned, when Barcelona won the European Cup-winners' Cup. Spain hosted the 1982 World Cup, but failed miserably. They qualified again in 1986 and 1990 but could do no better than the quarterfinals in Mexico. But the clubs continued to do well. Real won two UEFA Cups in the 1980s, while Barcelona won the European Cup-winners' Cup in 1982 and 1989 and completed a hat trick of European trophies by winning the European Cup in 1992 – seven years after losing a final to Steaua Bucharest.

When the national side failed to qualify for the 1992 European Championship finals, the question was raised again of whether Spanish clubs' liking for foreign imports was damaging the national side's chances. When the import ban was lifted in the early 1970s, many of the world's top stars moved to Spain, including Cruyff, Neeskens, Breitner, Netzer and Rep. This influx coincided with a decline in the fortunes of the national team. Similarly, the 1980s saw top imports such as Diego Maradona, Bernd Schuster, Gary Lineker, Hugo Sanchez and Ronald Koeman playing in Spain while the national team stuttered.

However, the Under-23s success at the 1992 Barcelona Olympics and the continued successes of Barcelona and Real, domestically and in Europe, are reasons for hope. The young Olympic victors are now being integrated into the full national team, which qualified for the 1994 World Cup finals, and Spain could be heading for greatness once more.

SWEDEN

Svensk Fotbollforblundet
Founded: 1904
FIFA: 1904
Olympics: 1948

Sweden has, since the 1920s, been Scandinavia's top national side and has a deserved reputation for producing quality players. An Association was formed in 1904 and joined FIFA the same year.

Gothenburg was, and still is, the centre of Swedish domestic soccer and the National League, instituted in 1925, has been dominated by Gothenburg's clubs, Orgryte, IFK and GAIS, along with AIK and Djurgardens of Stockholm. Sweden's national team made their debut in 1908 and entered the first four Olympic tournaments — with mixed success. This era, however, produced the country's greatest striker, Sven Rydell, who scored 49 goals in 43 games. Sweden was at its best in the late 1940s when they boasted one of the most famous forward lines in history. Gunnar Gren, Gunnar Nordahl and Nils Liedholm — the "Gre-No-Li" trio — sparked Sweden to Olympic gold in 1948 and were promptly signed up by Milan, where they enjoyed great success. Swedes were regularly bought by European clubs but were then barred from the national side by the strictly-amateur rules of the association. Despite this handicap, Sweden finished third in the 1950 World Cup, with Nacka Skoglund the new star.

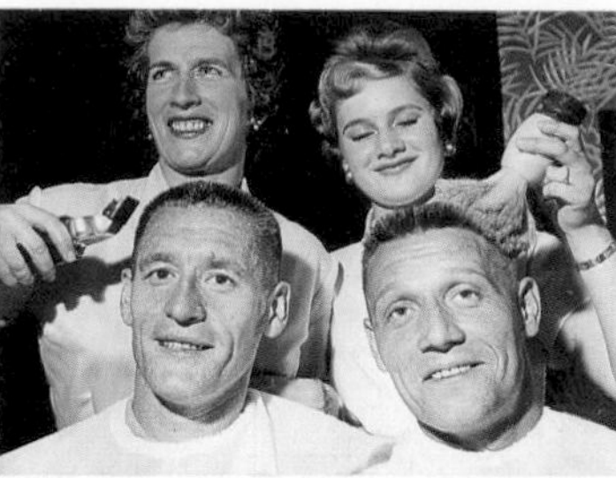

IN TRIM *Liedholm (left) and Svensson*

The import ban was lifted in time for the 1958 World Cup finals, which Sweden hosted, and with all their players available they reached the final. A decline followed in the 1960s, but Sweden qualified for all three World Cup finals in the 1970s, with Bjorn Nordqvist clocking up athen-record 115 appearances between 1963 and 1978.

The clubs too began to make an impact, and Malmo reached the European Cup Final in 1979. IFK Gothenburg enjoyed the greatest success, though, winning the UEFA Cup in 1982 and 1989 — as part-timers, because Sweden has not yet introduced full professionalism. Until it does, its top stars will continue to move abroad in droves.

Sweden's first appearance in the European Championship finals came in 1992, by virtue of being hosts, but it was beaten in the semifinal by Germany. The team surprised everybody by reaching 1994 World Cup semi-final losing narrowly to Brazil, the eventual champions; it now has a strong claim to have overtaken Denmark as the top soccer nation in Scandinavia.

SWITZERLAND

Schweizerischer Fussballverband
Founded: 1895
FIFA: 1904

Switzerland has always been at the forefront of world football without ever actually winning anything, because both FIFA and UEFA are based in the country.

The British helped develop the game in Switzerland in the late 1800s, and this can clearly be seen in the British names of two of her top clubs: Grasshopper (Zurich) and Young Boys (Bern). These two, along with Servette (Geneva), have dominated Swiss soccer without prospering in

HODGSON'S CHOICE *The Swiss celebrate a Chapuisat goal against Italy*

FINAL FLOURISH *Yugoslavia's last match, a 2–0 defeat against Holland in March 1992*

European competition.

The national team, however, has fared slightly better, particularly in the 1920s and 1930s when they were runners-up in the 1924 Olympics and quarterfinalists at both the 1934 and 1938 World Cups. The most famous names of this era were the Abegglen brothers, Max and André, who scored over 60 goals between them.

The man responsible for these successes was Karl Rappan—the father of Swiss soccer. He devised the "Swiss Bolt" system, which involved using a free man at the back as a sort of *libero*, and under Rappan the Swiss reached the finals of four of the first five World Cups played after the war. Their best performance was in 1954, when they hosted the tournament and reached the quarterfinals. After 1966 the national team suffered a reversal of fortunes and failed to qualify for six consecutive World Cups and seven European Championships. But under English coach Roy Hodgson, they have staged a remarkable comeback. They narrowly missed qualifying for the 1992 European Championship finals, but successfully claimed a place at the 1994 World Cup finals after a fine qualifying tournament that included a 1–0 win over Italy at home and an unlucky 2–2 draw in Cagliari.

TURKEY

Turkiye Futbol Federasyono
Founded: 1923
FIFA: 1933

How Turkey has failed to develop into a top European football nation is a mystery. With a population of 55 million, a fiercely competitive and well-attended league and plenty of talented players, a solitary World Cup finals appearance, in 1954, is a pretty sorry return.

The British brought soccer to Turkey in the 1890s, and by 1910 the country's top clubs — Besiktas, Galatasaray and Fenerbahce — had been founded. The clubs attract fanatical support and have done better than the national side, with Gala reaching the semi-finals of the European Cup in 1989 and dismissing Manchester United from the same competition in November 1993. Now firmly recognized as a minnow nation, and seeded as such when it comes to the World Cup and European Championship, Turkey will find it hard to improve without major organizational changes.

UKRAINE

Football Federation of Ukraine
Founded: 1992
FIFA: 1992

WALES

Football Association of Wales
Founded: 1876
FIFA: 1910–20, 1924–28, 1946

Soccer has always come second behind Rugby Union in Wales, but the tide may be turning. In 1992, for the first time, the Welsh FA set up a National League, with a place in the European Cup as an incentive for the "exile" clubs playing in England to join.

Simultaneously, the national side is at its best since the inter-war period, when Billy Meredith led them to six British Championships, and the 1950s when Wales, fortuitously, reached the quarterfinals of the 1958 World Cup with a team containing Ivor Allchurch and the legendary John Charles.

Welsh hopes of a 1994 World Cup finals appearance rested on one of world soccer's most formidable forward lines, comprizing Ian Rush, the country's top scorer, Mark Hughes, Dean Saunders and the "wonder boy" Ryan Giggs. They went very close, but sadly, it was not to be. If they could have reached the World Cup finals, it might have been just the boost the game needed to replace rugby as the top sport in the land, especially as the rugby team's form has dipped alarmingly in recent years.

YUGOSLAVIA

Fudbalski Savez Jugoslavije
Founded: 1919
FIFA: 1919
Olympic Games: 1960

Yugoslavia has often been called the "Argentina of Europe" in that, like the South Americans,it has exported hundreds of fine players and coaches over the years. Yugoslavia was World Cup semifinalists in 1930 and again in 1962, but never really achieved as much as it should have. This can be partly explained by the fact that, with so many of their players scattered across Europe, it was difficult to get a national side together.

It did win the Olympic title in 1960, though, and the outstanding player of the time was Dragoslav Sekularac. Other outstanding Yugoslav players include Stejpan Bobek, Dragan Dzajic, Milan Galic and Bora Kostic.

In 1991, however, the old nationalist tensions which have plagued the area for centuries erupted, and Yugoslavia has violently disintegrated into several independent states. Yugoπslavia's last international match was against Holland in the spring of 1992. Shortly afterwards, they were expelled from the European Championship finals and the 1994 World Cup qualifiers as part of the United Nations sanctions imposed on the country . . . a sad end to 70 years of united Yugoslav soccer.

THE AMERICAS

Wanderers and Liverpool in Uruguay, Rangers and Everton in Chile, Newells Old Boys in Argentina, Corinthians in Brazil... are all names which provide proof of the debt that the Americas owe to British soccer missionaries.

But the British were not alone in taking the round ball west. So did the French (namely Racing Club of Argentina), the Italians (Boca Juniors of Argentina and Penarol of Uruguay), the Spanish (Barcelona of Ecuador), and the Portuguese (Vasco da Gama of Brazil). Scottish exiles formed the backbone of the early United States' World Cup squads.

Many of the central American nations, in particular, may appear little more than a statistical dot in the world game's atlas. But organizations such as CONMEBOL (the South American confederation) and CONCACAF (the North and Central American confederation) are very quickly learning how to capitalize on the commercial and televisual value of soccer. The income is being used profitably for coaching schemes and administrative improvements. "American" soccer is much more now than merely those nations which have done well in the World Cup: Argentina, Brazil and Uruguay. Mexico's double staging of the World Cup finals in 1970 and 1986 proves the point. So, of course, did USA '94...

ANTIGUA AND BARBUDA

Antigua Football Association
Founded: 1928
FIFA: 1970

ARGENTINA

Asociacion del Futbol Argentino
Founded: 1893
FIFA: 1912
World Cup: 1978, 1986
South American Championship: 1910, 1921, 1925, 1927, 1929, 1937, 1941, 1945, 1946, 1947, 1955, 1957, 1991, 1993

Soccer was brought to Argentina by the British in the 1860s, and although, at first, it was exclusive to the British residents in Buenos Aires, by the turn of the century numerous clubs had been formed.

The Argentine Football Association was founded in 1891 by an Englishman, Alexander Hutton, and a league was formed the same year. Although the championship was not a truly national competition, as it contained only clubs from Buenos Aires, La Plata, Rosario and Santa Fé, the intense rivalry of the clubs in Buenos Aires ensured that Argentina had a vibrant domestic scene from the outset.

The national side also made an early start, and in 1901 a representative side played neighboring Uruguay, in the first international match to be staged outside Great Britain. The seeds were sown for a rivalry which has grown into one of the most enduring derby matches in the world.

Professionalism was adopted in 1931, and River Plate and Boca Juniors soon emerged as dominant forces in the new pro league. River's team of the 1940s was the greatest of them all, containing a forward line of Muñoz, Moreno, Pedernera, Labruna and Loustau which became known as *La Maquina* — the machine.

The national side was runners-up, to Uruguay, in the 1928 Olympics and met their deadly rivals again two years later in the 1930 World Cup final. Although they lost 4–2 the impressive Argentine team was plundered by Italian agents — starting a draining process which continues today. To avoid a repeat of this poaching, a third-rate team went to the 1934 tournament, and Argentina did not make a serious attempt on the World Cup again until the 1950s.

Indeed, the 1950s saw the birth of an exceptional team, with another famous forward line of Corbatta, Maschio, Angelillo, Sivori and Cruz. They won the South American Championship twice during the 1950s and then made an unsuccessful bid for the 1958 World Cup. Little progress was made in the 1960s and 1970s, despite Independiente and Estudiantes dominating the Libertadores Cup, and Argentina had to wait until 1978 for her first success in the World Cup.

Playing on home soil, and with a team containing only one overseas-based player, Mario Kempes, Argentina deservedly won the tournament. They did so again in Mexico in 1986, when the side was led by Diego Maradona — who ranks as one of the greatest players the world has ever seen. In fact, Argentina featured in the final of three of the four World Cups from 1978 to 1990, they won the first two South American Championships of the 1990s, and they continue to churn out gifted players.

Of all South American nations, Argentina is the most consistent, and also the most consistently successful.

ARGENTINE ACES *The 1986 World Cup-winning side*

ARUBA

Arubaanse Voetbal Bond
Founded: 1932
FIFA: 1988

BAHAMAS

Bahamas Football Association
Founded: 1967
FIFA: 1968

BARBADOS

Barbados Football Association
Founded: 1910
FIFA: 1968

BELIZE

Belize National Football Association
Founded: 1980
FIFA: 1986

BERMUDA

Bermuda Football Association
Founded: 1928
FIFA: 1962

BOLIVIA

Federacion Boliviana de Futbol
Founded: 1925
FIFA: 1926
South American Championship: 1963

Since their first international outing in 1926, Bolivia has been the perennial whipping boys of South American soccer – until now. In the 1994 World Cup qualifiers the Bolivians finished a close second in Group B to qualify for the finals for the first time in forty years, recording a notable 2–0 victory over Brazil along the way and knocking out Uruguay and Ecuador in the process. Prior to that, apart from World Cup qualification in 1930 and 1950, the 1963 South American Championship victory, played at home, was the only success of note.

SAMBA SOCCER *Vava scores Brazil's first goal in the 1958 World Cup final against Sweden, the hosts, who were beaten 5–2*

BRAZIL

Confederacao Brasileira de Futebol
Founded: 1914
FIFA: 1923
World Cup: 1958, 1962, 1970, 1994
South American Championship: 1919, 1922, 1949, 1989

Brazilian soccer has a romantic air about it that sets it apart from other nations. Between 1958 and 1970 they won the World Cup three times, with a team packed full of star players, including arguably the greatest in history – Pele. Brazil remains the only country to have played in every World Cup finals tournament.

Brazilian soccer developed at the end of the nineteenth century, prompted by migrant British workers, and leagues were established in Rio de Janeiro and São Paulo by the turn of the century. The vast size of Brazil meant that a national league was impractical and until the 1970s these leagues dominated domestic soccer. The "classic" Rio derbies between Flamengo, Fluminense, Botafogo and Vasco da Gama regularly attracted massive crowds to the 200,000-capacity Maracana Stadium.

The national team was a little slower out of the blocks, and their first real international was not played until 1914 with a visit to Buenos Aires. In 1916 they entered the South American Championship, but this event has not been a rewarding one for the Brazilians, who have won it only four times — three of them on home soil.

The World Cup, however, is another matter. The first attempt on the trophy was made in 1930, when they went out in the first round. The 1934 campaign was equally bad, despite the presence of such fine players as Leonidas da Silva and Artur Friedenreich. In 1938, however, they showed the first signs of what was to come by reaching the semifinals, where they lost to Italy.

The golden age of Brazilian soccer was between 1950 and 1970, and it is the sides of this era that stick in the memory. In 1950 they were runners-up as Uruguay pipped them for the title in the deciding match. In 1954, with Nilton and Djalma Santos established at the back and Didi running the midfield, they reached the quarterfinals in Switzerland, where it lost to an inspired Hungary's "Magic Magyars" team.

In 1958 Brazil finally won the honor the nation's fans craved. With a forward line comprising Garrincha, Vava, Zagalo and the 17-year-old Pele, they stormed to victory in Sweden, beating the hosts 5–2 in the final. In Chile in 1962, an almost identical team – minus the injured Pele – triumphed again, beating the Czechs 3–1 in Santiago.

In 1966, in England, the team was being rebuilt and Brazil fell in the first round. But the newcomers Tostao, Gerson and Jairzinho were present in Mexico four years later when Brazil clinched a hat trick of World Cups, earning them the right to keep the Jules Rimet Trophy in perpetuity. The 1970 team has been described as the best ever seen, and with some justification. The defense, marshalled by Carlos Alberto, was not all that strong, but this did not matter as the Brazilian approach at this time was all-out attack – and simply to score more goals than they conceded. This was soccer with a flourish and the global TV audience loved it. In attack, Pele was back to his best and he was superbly assisted by Jairzinho, Rivelinho and Tostao.

It was not until 1994 that Brazil returned to the World Cup winners' circle. Its path to the finals had been less than smooth, including the shock of its first ever qualifying tournament defeat, by Bolivia. But once it had qualified for the United States, Brazil became the favorites to collect the Cup. The team was generally accepted as the best at the tournament, and although the midfield may have lacked the flair of the 1970 team, the defense was more solid, and strikers Bebeto and the outstanding Romario were a dangerous presence throughout. The 1994 Championship may finally lift the burden which has weighed heavily on all Brazilian teams since 1970, and the home public's demand that the team plays what Pele once described as "the beautiful game" in the appropriate style.

Domestically, the game is in its worst ever state, with far too many meaningless competitions, too many games against mismatched opponents and continual rows between the various regional governing bodies.

CANADA

Canadian Soccer Association
Founded: 1912
FIFA: 1912
Olympics: 1904 (Galt FC of Ontario)
Soccer in Canada has struggled to establish itself for two main reasons. Firstly, the enormous size of the country makes a coherent structure difficult to implement and consequently a true, national league was only set up in 1987. Secondly, the sport trails badly in popularity behind hockey, baseball, football and basketball — the big North American sports.

Soccer took hold in Canada at the turn of the century, and in 1904 Galt FC from Ontario entered the St Louis Olympic Games. Soccer was only a demonstration sport, but Galt won the event, still Canada's only major honor. The national side made a few outings in the 1920s, but went into hibernation until the 1950s when it entered the 1958 World Cup — their first attempt. Success eluded them, however, and even when Montreal hosted the 1976 Olympics, Canada was eliminated in the first round.

During the 1970s, three Canadian clubs, from Vancouver, Toronto and Edmonton, played in the predominantly US-based North American Soccer League — just as many of Canada's hockey and baseball clubs do in their sports. Toronto won the NASL Soccer Bowl in 1976, emulated by Vancouver in 1979, and many of the Canadians playing in the NASL formed the backbone of the national team which reached the 1986 World Cup finals, their only appearance to date.

In the 1994 qualifiers Canada, with five British-based professionals in the team, reached a playoff with Oceania winners Australia, but after each side won their home matches 2-1, were beaten on penalties. The team was coached by Bobby Lenarduzzi, a member of the 1986 team and the country's best-known soccer player.

BRIEF ENCOUNTER *Canada at Mexico '86, their only World Cup appearance*

CAYMAN ISLANDS

Cayman Islands Football Association
Founded: 1992
FIFA: 1992

CHILE

Federacion de Futbol de Chile
Founded: 1895
FIFA: 1912
Until Colo Colo's Libertadores Cup triumph in 1991, no Chilean side had ever won a major honor, and Chile have often been seen as the "nearly-men" of South American soccer.

SANTIAGO STRUGGLE *Chile vs. Switzerland in the first round of the 1962 World Cup, which the South Americans won 3–1*

Chile qualified for five of the 11 postwar World Cups, but has only once progressed beyond the first round, in 1962, when they reached the semifinals on home soil. Their best performances in the South American Championship came in 1979 and 1987, when they were runners-up. Chile, like many of its neighbors, is continually drained of its best players by European clubs, and it is unlikely that the Chileans will ever be able to improve on their third place in the 1962 World Cup.

COLOMBIA

Federacion Colombiana de Futbol
Founded: 1924
FIFA: 1936
Colombia is only now emerging as a challenger to Argentina and Brazil after years of internal disputes, disruptions and turbulence. The most notorious came in 1950, shortly after professionalism was introduced, when a break-away league outside FIFA jurisdiction, the DiMayor, was formed and Colombian sides began importing players from all over South America and from Britain. The huge salaries on offer led to the four years of its existence being known as the "El Dorado" period. The bubble burst in 1954, when Colombia was readmitted to FIFA and the league collapsed, leaving many clubs in desperate financial trouble.

The national team made its debut as late as 1938, and results at first were poor. Between 1949 and 1957 no internationals were played at all, and thereafter outings were infrequent. It was a huge surprise, then, when Colombia qualified for the 1962 World Cup in Chile, although to do so they only had to beat Peru. However, the best they managed on their World Cup debut was a 4–4 draw with the USSR.

In 1965 another breakaway federation was formed and confusion reigned once more. FIFA had to intervene and effectively ran Colombian soccer up until 1971, when the present administration was installed. A new league structure was introduced in 1968, careful controls on the number of foreign imports were implemented, and the national side soon benefited.

In 1989 Nacional Medellin won the Libertadores Cup, the country's only victory, and a year later the national side, coached by Francisco Maturana — who had led Nacional to their success — qualified for the 1990 World Cup finals. But the best was yet to come. In the 1994 World Cup qualifiers, Colombia thrashed Argentina 5–0 in Buenos Aires to qualify. The current team is arguably Colombia's best ever and includes Carlos Valderrama in midfield and the new star of Italian soccer, striker Faustino Asprilla.

Sadly, the continued drugs-related violence in the country undermines this progress, highlighted by the murder of defender Andres Escobar a few days after the team returned from their disappointing performance at the finals. Escobar had scored an own goal in the 2–1 defeat by the U.S.

COSTA RICA

Federacion Costarricense de Futbol
Founded: 1921
FIFA: 1921
CONCACAF Championship: 1941, 1946, 1948, 1953, 1955, 1960, 1961, 1963, 1969, 1989
Costa Rica is one of the better teams from Central America, and between 1940 and 1970 they won an impressive nine CONCACAF Championships. Despite this, Costa Rica struggled to make an impact in the World Cup — El Salvador and Honduras both qualified before them — but in 1990 the breakthrough came. Under Yugoslav coach Bora Milutinovic, the Costa Ricans not only qualified for the finals, but also defeated both Scotland and Sweden to progress into the second round, a remarkable achievement. Costa Rica has a very healthy domestic scene too, and the country's two leading clubs, Deportivo Saprissa and LD Alajeulense, have both won the CONCACAF Club Championship.

CUBA

Asociacion de Futbol de Cuba
Founded: 1924
FIFA: 1932

DOMINICAN REPUBLIC

Federacion Dominicana de Futbol
Founded: 1953
FIFA: 1958

ECUADOR

Asociacion Ecuatoriana de Futbol
Founded: 1925
FIFA: 1926
Ecuador is one of South America's weakest nations, and they have yet to qualify for any major tournament. The closest they have gone to reaching the World Cup finals was in 1966, when they lost a playoff to Chile. Between 1938 and 1975 the national side managed only eight wins, but there are signs of improvement. In 1990, Barcelona of Guayaquil was runners-up in the Libertadores Cup, and the semifinal in which they impressively beat River Plate is surely the country's proudest moment.

KEEPER SWEEPER *Colombia's peripatetic goalkeeper Rene Higuita tangles with West Germany's Rudi Völler*

EL SALVADOR

Federacion Salvadorena de Futbol
Founded: 1935
FIFA: 1938
CONCACAF Championship: 1943
El Salvador's biggest claim to soccer fame is the 1969 "Soccer War" with Central American neighbors Honduras. The countries met in a World Cup qualifying group and rioting followed both matches, especially after the second game when El Salvador forced a play-off. El Salvador won it and, as tension mounted, the army invaded Honduras on the pretext of protecting expatriate Salvadorean citizens. The World Cup match was more an excuse than a cause for the war, but the conflict was to cost 3,000 lives before it was finally settled.

El Salvador has qualified for the World Cup finals twice, losing all three games in 1970 and again in 1982 — which included an 10–1 thrashing by Hungary.

GRENADA

Grenada Football Association
Founded: 1924
FIFA: 1976

GUATEMALA

Federacion Nacional de Futbol de Guatemala
Founded: 1926
FIFA: 1933
CONCACAF Championship: 1967

GUYANA

Guyana Football Association
Founded: 1904
FIFA: 1968

HAITI

Fédération Haitienne de Football
Founded: 1904
FIFA: 1933
CONCACAF Championship: 1957, 1973

HONDURAS

Federacion Nacional Automana de Futbol
Founded: 1935
FIFA: 1946
CONCACAF Championship: 1981
Honduras, like neighboring El Salvador, is a country which has been plagued by insurgency and guerrilla warfare. Indeed, the two went to war in 1969, over the outcome of a soccer match, as described in the entry for El Salvador.

Honduras made their sole appearance in the World Cup finals in 1982, when they drew 1–1 with hosts, Spain, and Northern Ireland, before losing 1–0 to Yugoslavia and going out of the tournament.

Honduran clubs have enjoyed some success in the CONCACAF Club Championship, notably Olimpia, who won the event in 1972 and 1988, and were runners-up in 1985.

JAMAICA

Jamaica Football Federation
Founded: 1910
FIFA: 1962

MEXICO

Federacion Mexicana de Futbol Asociacion
Founded: 1927
FIFA: 1929

CONCACAF Championship: 1963, 1971, 1977, 1993
Mexico utterly dominate their Central American region, but this has hindered rather than helped their game. With no decent, local opposition for the national side or the clubs, Mexico has enjoyed their greatest moments in the World Cup.

The federation was formed in 1927, and a trip to the Amsterdam Olympics a year later ended after just one match. Two years later they entered the World Cup and have qualified for 10 of the 15 finals tournaments, a record which includes 1990, when they were barred by FIFA for breaches of age regulations in a youth tournament. Mexico's best World Cups were those of 1970 and 1986, when they were hosts. They reached the quarter-finals of both and were unlucky to lose on penalties to West Germany in the 1986 event.

Star of the 1986 side was Hugo Sanchez, an agile forward who led Real Madrid to many honors in the 1980s. Famous for his exuberant, cartwheeling celebrations when he scores, Sanchez is Mexico's greatest player since Antonio Carbajal, the goalkeeper who created a record by playing in all five World Cup finals tournaments from 1950 to 1966. Mexico won the CONCACAF Championship four times, but were shocked in 1991 when the United States beat them in the semifinals and won the tournament, though Mexico regained the upper hand in 1993.

Many believe Mexico would benefit from joining the South Americans, and in 1993 they, and the United States, were invited to take part in the South American Championship as guests.

The Mexicans embarrassed their hosts by reaching the final, where they narrowly lost to Argentina. Mexico then qualified for the 1994 World Cup finals from among the 23 contenders in the CONCACAF group with comparative ease, but until they are forced to face tougher opposition more often, it is unlikely that their results in the finals will improve greatly.

BALL CONTROL *Mexican star Hugo Sanchez*

NETHERLANDS ANTILLES

Nederlands Antiliaanse Voetbal Unie
Founded: 1921
FIFA: 1932

NICARAGUA

Federacion Nicaraguense de Futbol
Founded: 1931
FIFA: 1950

PANAMA

Federacion Nacional de Futbol de Panama
Founded: 1937
FIFA: 1938
CONCACAF Championship: 1951

PARAGUAY

Liga Paraguaya de Futbol
Founded: 1906
FIFA: 1921
South American Championship: 1953, 1979
Asuncion dominates Paraguayan soccer, and Olimpia dominates Asuncion. They are the country's most successful side and have won the Libertadores Cup twice, in 1979 and 1990, and have been runners-up three times.

The national team has also done well, for such a small and impoverished country. They won the South American Championship in 1953 and again in 1979—a year in which Paraguayan teams won every trophy available to them. Paraguay has reached the World Cup

CONCENTRATION *Paraguay's Mendoza holds off England's Reid*

finals four times, most lately in 1986, but in the search for honors, Olimpia will continue to lead the way.

PERU

Federacion Peruana de Futbol
Founded: 1922
FIFA: 1924
South American Championship: 1939, 1975.

Lima has always dominated Peruvian soccer, and it was there that the association was founded in 1922. The local Lima League was the strongest in the country and, until a national championship was introduced in 1966, the winners were considered national champions. The Lima clubs Alianza, Universitario and Sporting Cristal have dominated Peruvian soccer, but have never achieved success in the Libertadores Cup. Sadly, the eyes of the world were nevertheless focused on Peru in 1964, when 300 spectators died in a riot, and in 1988, when the Alianza team was wiped out in a plane crash.

The national side made their debut in 1927, in the South American Championship, and won the event on home soil in 1939. The World Cup record was initially poor, however, a first-round exit in 1930 their best effort in four attempts. It all changed in the 1970s, when a generation of notable players came together and made the decade the country's most successful ever.

Stars of the 1970s side were the highly eccentric and entertaining goalkeeper Ramon "El Loco" Quiroga, Hector Chumpitaz and midfield maestro Teofilo Cubillas, the greatest Peruvian player of all time. Coached by Brazilian World Cup winner Didi, this side reached the quarter-finals of the 1970 World Cup, won the 1975 South American Championship, and qualified for the 1978 World Cup, where they fell — some said "suspiciously" heavily — to Argentina in the second round.

Peru qualified for the World Cup again in 1982, but the team was past its best and went out in the first round. Since then, Peru has slipped back into its familiar role of the "middlemen" of South American soccer. The spiralling political violence in the country has hardly helped matters, and it may be some time before we see Peru in the World Cup finals again.

PUERTO RICO

Federacion Puertorriquena de Futbol
Founded: 1940
FIFA: 1960

SAINT KITTS AND NEVIS

St Kitts and Nevis Football Association
Founded: 1992
FIFA: 1992

SAINT LUCIA

St Lucia National Football Association
Founded: 1988
FIFA: 1988

SAINT VINCENT & THE GRENADINES

St Vincent and the Grenadines Football Federation
Founded: 1988
FIFA: 1988

SURINAM

Surinaamse Voetbal Bond
Founded: 1920
FIFA: 1929

TRINIDAD AND TOBAGO

Trinidad and Tobago Football Association
Founded: 1906
FIFA: 1963

UNITED STATES

United States Soccer Federation
Founded: 1913
FIFA: 1913
CONCACAF Championship: 1991

The United States is viewed by many as a non-soccer country, yet US soccer has a long and interesting history (*for a more comprehensive review, see pages 226–47*). For example, the Oneida club of Boston was founded in 1862, making it the oldest outside England.

The national team, containing five former Scottish professionals, entered the 1924 and 1928 Olympics and then traveled to Uruguay for the first World Cup in 1930 — where they reached the semifinals. Four years later they were represented at the finals again, but lost

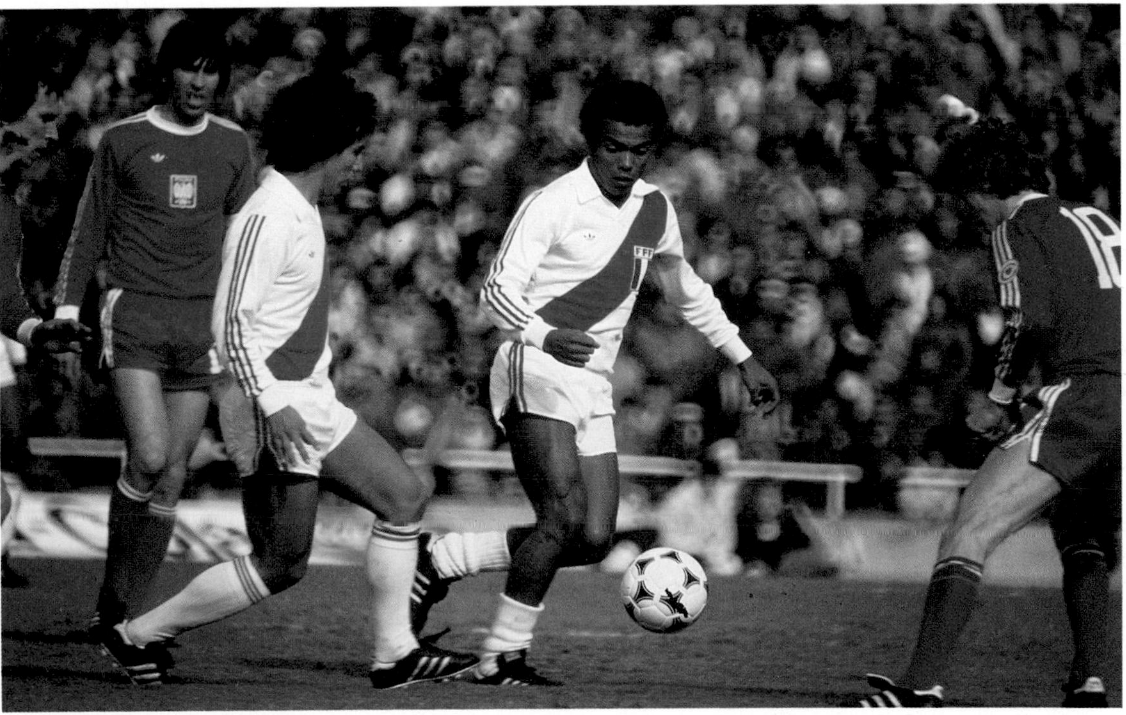

MIDFIELD MAESTRO *Teofilo Cubillas, Peru's greatest ever player*

to hosts Italy in the first round. In 1950 the U.S. caused one of the biggest World Cup shocks ever when they beat England 1–0, with Haiti-born Joe Gaetjens scoring the winning goal.

Subsequent efforts to qualify for the World Cup ended in failure until 1990, by which time FIFA, bidding to promote the game worldwide, had selected the U.S. to host the 1994 finals. The hosts faced a huge task if they were to improve on their first-round exit last time round, but they did, beating highly-favored Colombia en route a second-round defeat by Brazil. But the U.S. is improving all the time, as evidenced by the growing number of players gaining experience in Europe. In 1991 they won the CONCACAF Championship — their only major honor to date.

Apart from the 1950 victory over England, U.S. soccer is famed for one other reason — the North American Soccer League. Founded in 1967, the NASL featured corporate-backed teams which enabled the clubs to pay huge wages and attract top foreign stars. Pele, Franz Beckenbauer, Johan Cruyff and George Best were among numerous veterans who played in the League in its heyday in the 1970s. But the reliance on foreign stars ultimately proved the NASL's undoing, and it folded in 1984. Since then numerous other professional leagues have come and gone, but none with the appeal or impact of the NASL, and the U.S. is still without a true national league.

UNCLE SAM'S GLORY *The U.S.A.'s greatest victory came against England in 1950*

URUGUAY

Asociacion Uruguaya de Futbol
Founded: 1900
FIFA: 1923
World Cup: 1930, 1950
South American Championship: 1916, 1917, 1920, 1923, 1924, 1926, 1935, 1942, 1956, 1959, 1967, 1983, 1987.
Olympics: 1924, 1928

Before the Second World War, Uruguay was undoubtedly the best team in the world, effectively winning three world championships. Today they are no longer a world power, but they have a proud history and can still be dangerous opponents. Montevideo dominates the domestic scene and, as it is located just across the River Plate estuary from Buenos Aires, the two cities can justifiably claim to be the center of South American soccer. Montevideo's two great clubs, Penarol and Nacional, have dominated Uruguayan soccer, winning more than 80 championships between them. The clubs are fierce rivals and have both enjoyed great success in the Libertadores Cup; Penarol winning it five times, Nacional three times. Both clubs have also won the World Club Cup.

The national team dominated world soccer in the first half of the twentieth century, but have faded badly since the 1950s. Early successes in the South American Championship were followed by a stunning victory in the 1924 Olympics in Amsterdam, at a time when the Olympic winners could justifiably claim to be world champions. Having amazed Europe with their skill at the 1924 Olympics, Uruguay repeated the trick in 1928 and two years later, as the host nation, swept to victory in the first World Cup. The team of the 1920s and 1930s contained many of Uruguay's all-time greats: skipper Jose Nasazzi, the midfield "Iron Curtain" of Jose Andrade, Lorenzo Fernandez and Alvarez Gestido, and outstanding forwards Hector Castro, Pedro Cea and Hector Scarone. In 1950 Uruguay pulled off one of the biggest World Cup finals shocks in history, coming from a goal down to beat Brazil 2–1 in the deciding match... in Brazil. The team contained striker Juan Schiaffino, Uruguay's greatest player, Victor Andrade, nephew of the great Jose, Roque Maspoli in goal, Obdulio Varela on defense and Omar Miguez up front. Four years later, in Switzerland, the defense of their crown ended with a 4–2 semifinal defeat by Hungary in one of the best World Cup games ever. Since the 1950s Uruguay have enjoyed regular success in the South American Championship, but in the World Cup they have earned an unsavory reputation as "hard men," and have never matched the feats of the 1930s and 1950s sides. They did finish fourth in the 1970 World Cup, but elimination by Bolivia in the 1994 qualifiers shows just how far they have slipped.

INITIAL SUCCESS *Uruguay open the scoring in the 1930 World Cup Final*

Uruguay still produces outstanding players, like Enzo Francescoli and Carlos Aguilera, but they usually move to Europe to further their careers. With so many foreign-based players, Uruguay has developed a schizophrenic approach to the World Cup and South American Championship, often entering wildly different teams for tournaments staged less than a year apart. Until Uruguay can overcome this problem they are likely to be seen as a team of the past, and not considered prospects for the future.

VENEZUELA

Federacion Venezolana de Futbol
Founded: 1926
FIFA: 1952

Venezuela is the weakest of the ten South American countries, which is hardly surprising because the national sport is baseball. Originally members of CONCACAF, they made their international debut in 1938 and switched to CONMEBOL in 1958. The national record is downright awful, with just one match won in the South American Championship and three in the World Cup qualifiers, even though they have entered both regularly from the 1960s onwards.

The clubs are weak too, and three Libertadores Cup semifinals are the best they have managed. A professional league was finally set up in 1956, but Venezuela have a long way to go if they are even to catch up with the other South American minnows.

THE REST OF THE WORLD

MOVING AHEAD *Algeria's Assad leaves a Chilean defender trailing*

FIFA's family worldwide has grown from the seven original members of 1904 through 73 in 1950 to around 170 nations. The majority are small but ambitious. They all share a love of soccer, and all share the same right within FIFA of an equal single vote in the international body's congress.

In the past 20 years FIFA has concentrated millions of dollars in educational programmes for coaches, referees, administrators and players in the developing world. Progress has been measured by World Cup finals entry: three African nations were present, for the first time, at USA'94. The next World Cup, in France in 1998, may well see Asian representation extended from two nations to three.

Communications technology may have made the world smaller but the soccer world goes on growing.

AFGHANISTAN

The Football Federation of the National Olympic Committee
Founded: 1922
FIFA: 1948

ALGERIA

Fédération Algérienne de Football
Founded: 1962
FIFA: 1963
African Nations Cup: 1990

The French brought soccer to Algeria in the late 1900s, and by the 1930s several Muslim Algerian clubs had been formed. The earliest was Mouloudia Challia (1920), and they won the African Champions Cup in 1976 at the first attempt.

Algeria gained independence in 1962, and since then the national side has improved considerably. In 1980 they reached the final of the African Nations Cup, where they lost 3–0 to hosts Nigeria, and two years later qualified for the World Cup finals in Spain. At the 1982 finals the Algerians pulled off one of the biggest World Cup shocks when they beat West Germany 2–1, and had it not been for a contrived result between the Germans and Austria, Algeria would have reached the second round. Rabah Madjer and Lakhdar Belloumi were the goal scorers against West Germany and they remain Algeria's greatest players. Madjer won a European Cup-winners' Cup medal with FC Porto in 1987, when he was also voted African Footballer of the Year.

Algeria was a semifinalist in the African Nations Cup in 1984 and 1988, and in between qualified for the 1986 World Cup finals in Mexico, where they again fell at the first round. Then, in 1990 they won the African Nations Cup for the first time. In 1993 they again qualified for the African Nations Cup finals, but were later barred for fielding an ineligible player in a qualifying match. Their 1994 World Cup hopes ended in the second African round.

Algerian clubs have done well in African competitions, with MC Algiers (1976), JS Kabylie (1981 and 1990) and ES Setif (1988), all winning the African Champions Cup.

ANGOLA

Federacao Angolana de Futebol
Founded: 1977
FIFA: 1980

AUSTRALIA

Australia Soccer Federation
Founded: 1961
FIFA: 1963

Soccer has struggled to gain a foothold in Australia, where cricket, Australian Rules football, rugby union and rugby league are the nation's most popular sports. The domestic league, introduced in 1977, is populated with ethnically-linked clubs, as the names of Sydney City Hakoah, St George Budapest, South Melbourne Hellas and Adelaide City Juventus amply indicate.

Australia qualified for the 1974 World Cup finals, via the Asian qualifiers, but their performances in the finals were poor. Oceania now has its own World Cup qualifying groups, but not automatic entry to the finals. In the 1994 qualifiers Australia, having won their group, had to beat New Zealand in a play-off for the right to meet CONCACAF runners-up Canada in another play-off. Having won that, the "Socceroos" then failed to beat the South American Group A runners-up, Argentina, for a finals berth.

BAHRAIN

Bahrain Football Association
Founded: 1951
FIFA: 1966

BANGLADESH

Bangladesh Football Federation
Founded: 1972
FIFA: 1974

BENIN

Fédération Beninoise de Football
Founded: 1968
FIFA: 1969

OCEANS APART *Argentina's Simone and Australia's Farina*

BOTSWANA

Botswana Football Association
Founded: 1970
FIFA: 1976

BRUNEI

Brunei Amateur Football Association
Founded: 1959
FIFA: 1969

BURKINA FASO

Fédération Burkinabe de Football
Founded: 1960
FIFA: 1964

BURUNDI

Fédération de Football du Burundi
Founded: 1948
FIFA: 1972

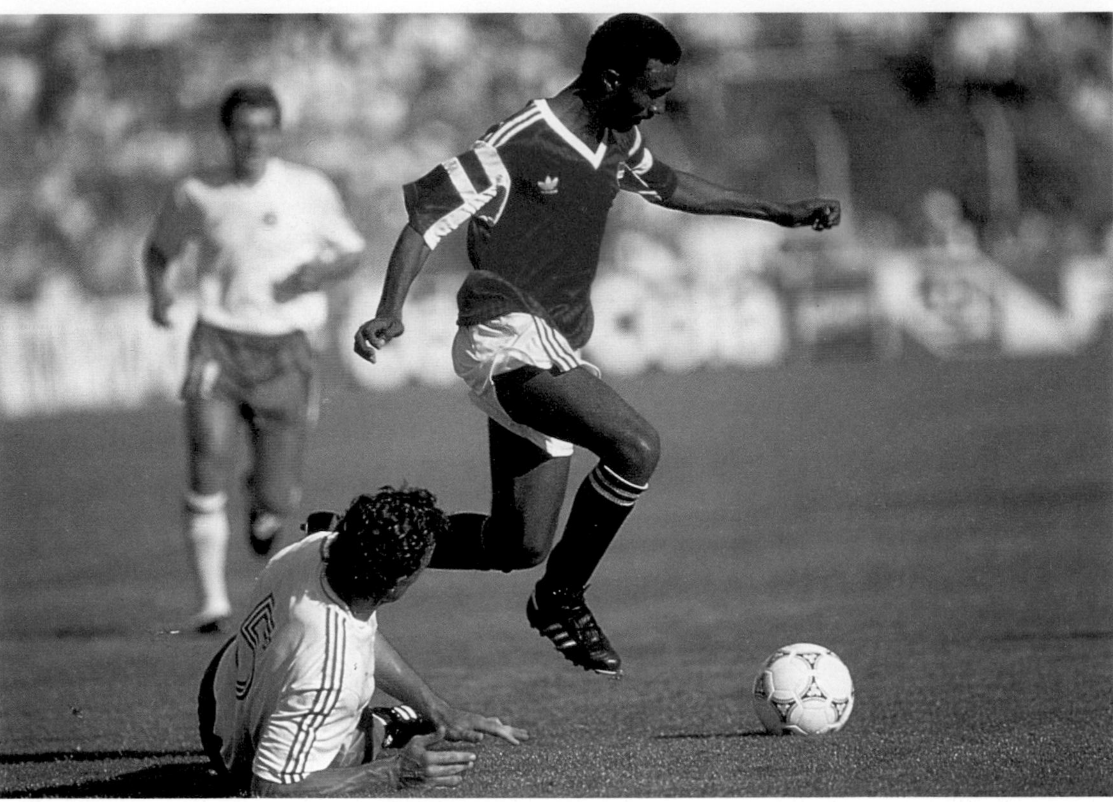

DOWN AND OUT *Ireland's Moran is left grounded by Egypt's El Kass*

CAMEROON

Fédération Camerounaise de Football
Founded: 1960
FIFA: 1962
African Nations Cup: 1984, 1988.

Of all the African nations to have reached the World Cup finals, Cameroon has made by far the biggest impact. In 1982, in Spain, they drew all three of their first round games — against Italy (eventual winners), Poland (third) and Peru — but were unfortunately eliminated at that stage. They qualified again in 1990 and beat reigning champions Argentina in the opening match. They went on to reach the quarter-finals, where they narrowly lost to England, and as a result of these outstanding performances FIFA agreed to grant Africa a third berth at the 1994 finals. And the "Indomitable Lions" won a decisive match with Zimbabwe 3–1 to qualify for a record-equalling third time.

Cameroon's greatest player is undoubtedly Roger Milla, who played in the 1982 and 1990 World Cup teams. Milla was voted African Footballer of the Year in 1976 and again in 1990, and delighted fans at Italia '90 with his goals and his celebratory wiggle which usually followed. Other Cameroon players to have won the award include Theophile Abega (1984), Thomas N'Kono (1979 and 1982) and Jean Onguene (1980). N'Kono is one of the greatest goalkeepers Africa has produced, and enjoyed a fine club career in Spain.

Cameroon also won the African Nations Cup twice (1984 and 1988) to confirm their status as Africa's top side of the decade. Cameroon clubs have also enjoyed great success in African competitions: the Champions Cup has been won five times, the Cup Winners' Cup three times.

CAPE VERDE

Federacao Cabo-Verdiana de Futebol
Founded: 1982
FIFA: 1986

CENTRAL AFRICAN REPUBLIC

Fédération Centrafricaine de Football
Founded: 1937
FIFA: 1963

CHINA

Football Association of the People's Republic of China
Founded: 1924
FIFA: 1931–58, 1979

China took part in the first international match played on Asian soil, when they met the Philippines, in Manila, in February 1913, in the Far Eastern Games. But progress was thwarted because of the Taiwan issue. A side containing only Hong Kong players took part in the 1954 Asian Games, calling themselves China. The Chinese Association protested that they were the controlling body and subsequently withdrew from FIFA in 1958.

Despite being the most populous country on earth, success has utterly eluded China. Their greatest achievement to date is a runners-up spot in the 1984 Asian Cup.

Efforts to improve the game are now being made, with more emphasis on coaching, but China is still some way short of their Asian rivals — as a disappointing first-round exit in the 1994 World Cup qualifiers illustrates. However, the Chinese are now considering a bid to host the 2002 World Cup finals. FIFA's desire to spread the game globally may give the Chinese an advantage here, and staging the game's premier event would provide a massive boost.

CONGO

Fédération Congolaise de Football
Founded: 1962
FIFA: 1962
African Nations Cup: 1972

EGYPT

All Ettihad el Masri Li Korat el Kadam
Founded: 1921
FIFA: 1923
African Nations Cup: 1957, 1959, 1986

Egypt was one of the four founder members of the Confédération Africaine de Football and were the first Africans to join FIFA, in 1923. Given this 20-year start on most of her neighbors, it is no surprise that Egypt became one of the great powers of the continent, winning the first two African Nations Cups in 1957 and 1959.

Egypt finished fourth in the 1928 Olympics and then entered the 1934 World Cup. Having beaten Palestine in a qualifying play-off, they lost 4–2 to Hungary in the first round. They were Olympic semi-finalists again in 1964, but entered only one of the World Cups played between 1938 and 1970.

A revival in the 1970s saw them finish third in the African Nations Cup in 1970 and 1974, fourth in 1976 and reach the Olympic quarterfinals in 1984. Two years later, as hosts, they won the African Nations Cup for the third time, and then qualified for the 1990 World Cup finals, where they did well to hold Holland and the Republic of Ireland to draws.

Allied to this success at national level, Egyptian clubs are among the most powerful in Africa. Well organized, well-financed and well supported, Egypt's clubs have won the Champions Cup and the Cup Winners' Cup ten times. Al Ahly, the most successful, have won the former twice and the latter three times — in consecutive years: 1984, 1985 and 1986.

Al-Titsh, who played for Al Ahly in the 1920s, was one of Egypt's finest players, and Ahly's stadium still bears his name. Other great Egyptian players include Mahmoud Al Khatib (African Footballer of the Year 1983), Ibrahim Youssef and Abu Zeid, Egypt's best striker during the 1980s.

EQUATORIAL GUINEA

Federacion Equatoguineana de Futbol
Founded: 1976
FIFA: 1986

ETHIOPIA

Yeithiopia Football Federechin
Founded: 1943
FIFA: 1953
African Nations Cup: 1962

FIJI

Fiji Football Association
Founded: 1938
FIFA: 1963

GABON

Fédération Gabonaise de Football
Founded: 1962
FIFA: 1963

GAMBIA

Gambia Football Association
Founded: 1952
FIFA: 1966

GHANA

Ghana Football Association
Founded: 1957
FIFA: 1958
African Nations Cup: 1963, 1965, 1978, 1982
Ghana achieved independence in 1957 and soon the "Black Stars," as they are known, had established themselves as a powerful force in African soccer. They won the African Nations Cup in 1963, in their first attempt, and retained the trophy two years later. In the following two events, 1968 and 1970, they were beaten finalists, but victories in 1978 and 1982 made them the only nation to have won the trophy four times.

In club football, Asante Kotoko have won the African Champions Cup twice and Ghana have produced some outstanding players. Mohamed Ahmed Polo and Adolf Armah were stars in the 1970s; Ibrahim Sunday, African footballer of the year in 1971, played for Werder Bremen in the German League; Abedi Pele won many trophies with Marseille in the 1980s; and Nii Lamptey, of PSV Eindhoven, led Ghana's young side to victory in the 1991 World Youth Championship. Yet, despite all this success, Ghana have never qualified for the World Cup finals.

GUINEA-BISSAU

Federacao de Football da Guinea-Bissau
Founded: 1974
FIFA: 1986

GUINEA

Fédération Guinéenne de Football
Founded: 1959
FIFA: 1961

HONG KONG

Hong Kong Football Association
Founded: 1914
FIFA: 1954

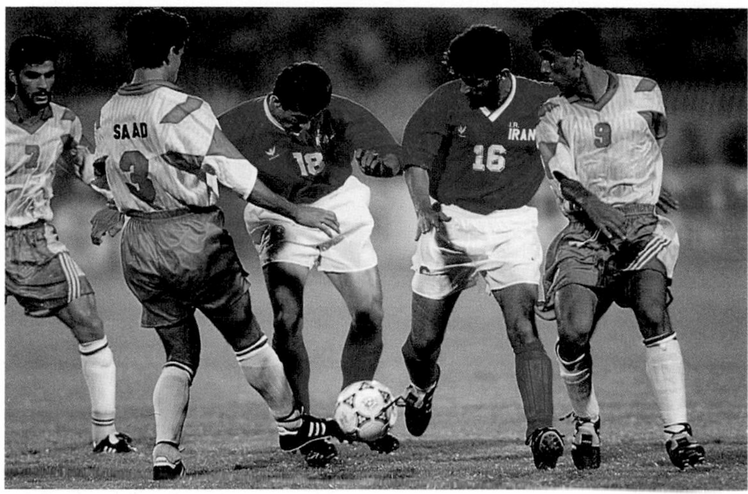

COMPETITIVE NEIGHBORS *Iran (red shirts) and Iraq in World Cup action*

INDIA

All India Football Federation
Founded: 1937
FIFA: 1948
India's only successes at international level have come in the Asian Games, which they won in 1951 and 1962. They also finished third at the 1956 Olympic Games, but since then the national team's record has been poor, despite the massive enthusiasm for soccer in this huge heavily-populated country.

The annual Nehru Cup tournament, featuring guest European and South American national sides or selections, is a popular event, though India has never won it. The Calcutta League — the best in the country — is dominated by India's most famous clubs, Mohammedan Sporting, East Bengal and Mohun Bagan. Originally brought to India by the British in the late 1800s (the Gloucestershire Regiment were the first Calcutta champions), soccer is now rapidly gaining popularity in a country where cricket and field hockey have always been the top sports.

INDONESIA

All Indonesia Football Federation
Founded: 1930
FIFA: 1952

IRAN

Football Federation of the Islamic Republic of Iran
Founded: 1920
FIFA: 1948
Asian Championship: 1968, 1972, 1976
Iran emerged as a major Asian power in the 1960s, and in the 1970s they were the continent's most successful team. They took a hat trick of Asian Championships, in 1968, 1972 and 1976, won the gold medal at the 1974 Asian Games and then qualified for the 1978 World Cup finals in Argentina. There, they pulled off a massive shock by holding Scotland to a 1–1 draw, and even the Scots' goal was an own goal!

The Asian Championship hat trick was even more remarkable because Iran won every game they played in the tournament between 1968 and 1976. Since then, they have reached the semifinals in each of the three subsequent tournaments that have been played, and almost qualified for the 1994 World Cup finals in the United States.

Iranian teams have twice won the Asian Champions Cup – Taj Club in 1970 and Esteghlal SC in 1990.

IRAQ

Iraqi Football Association
Founded: 1948
FIFA: 1951
The 1970s witnessed a shift in the balance of power in Asian football towards the Arab states, and Iraq has been at the forefront of this movement. They won the Asian Games gold medal in 1982 and four years later qualified for the World Cup finals in Mexico, where they gave creditable performances.

Iraq has huge resources at its disposal, and this should insure that the national team will remain strong for many years to come. Iraq was thrown out of FIFA and suspended from international football in 1991 because of the invasion of Kuwait, but has since been re-admitted to the international fold. They almost qualified for the 1994 World Cup finals in the United States, which could have caused problems for the hosts . . . Saddam Hussein threatened to attend! Iraq's most noted player of the past is striker Ahmed Radhi.

IVORY COAST

Fédération Ivoirienne de Football
Founded: 1960
FIFA: 1960
African Nations Cup: 1992

The Ivory Coast is one of Africa's great soccer enigmas. They have a stable government, a healthy economy and a well-organized league — advantages which many African countries do not enjoy — and yet success at international level eluded them until 1992. In that year "The Elephants" won the African Nations Cup in Senegal, defeating Ghana 11–10 on penalties after a 0–0 draw in the final. They had previously been semifinalists three times without going further.

The 1992 success confirmed the Ivorians as favorites to qualify for the 1994 World Cup finals for the first time ever, but they faded badly in the final round and finished second behind Nigeria.

JAPAN

The Football Association of Japan
Founded: 1921
FIFA: 1929–45, 1950

Japan has never won a major tournament, but that could soon change – their soccer authorities have begun an ambitious program to put the country firmly on the international soccer map.

In 1993 a professional league, the J. League, was introduced, and the corporate-backed teams have used their wealth to attract numerous star veterans including England's Gary Lineker, Brazil's Zico and Germany's Pierre Littbarski.

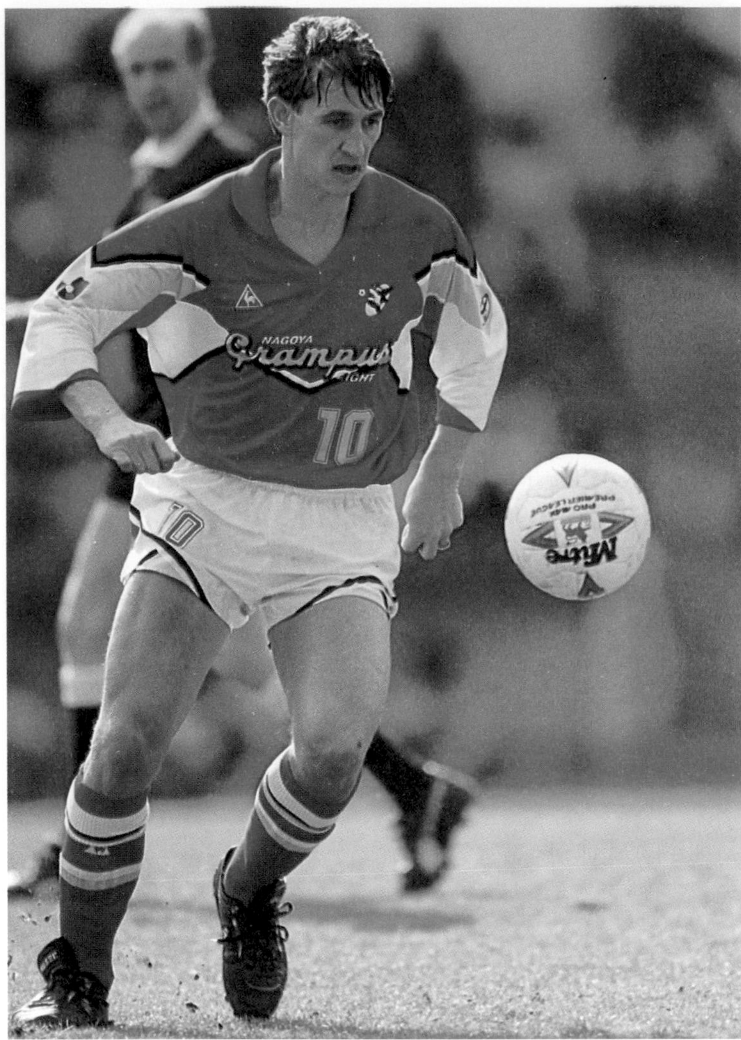

JAPANESE IMPORT *England's Lineker, one of the J. League's foreign stars*

Simultaneously, the Japanese have put together an impressive bid for the hosting rights to the 2002 World Cup. Japan undoubtedly has the stadiums, communications and facilities to host the event, but the national team's failure in the 1994 qualifiers could cost them dearly. Needing a win to qualify from their final game against Iraq, Japan gave away a soft equalizer in the last minute and their World Cup hopes had gone. Several Japanese players are beginning to make an impact alongside the imported stars in the J. League, notably national team striker Kazuyoshi Miura, affectionately known as "Kazu."

JORDAN

Jordan Football Association
Founded: 1949
FIFA: 1958

KAMPUCHEA

Fédération Khmère de Football Association
Founded: 1933
FIFA: 1953

KENYA

Kenya Football Federation
Founded: 1932
FIFA: 1960

KUWAIT

Kuwait Football Association
Founded: 1952
FIFA: 1962
Asian Championship: 1980

LAOS

Fédération de Foot-Ball Lao
Founded: 1951
FIFA: 1952

LEBANON

Fédération Libanaise de Football
Founded: 1933
FIFA: 1935

LESOTHO

Lesotho Sports Council
Founded: 1932
FIFA: 1964

LIBERIA

Liberia Football Association
Founded: 1936
FIFA: 1962

LIBYA

Libyan Arab Jamahiriya Football Federation
Founded: 1962
FIFA: 1963

MACAO

Associacao de Futebol de Macau
Founded: 1939
FIFA: 1976

MADAGASCAR

Fédération Malagasy de Football
Founded: 1961
FIFA: 1962

MALAWI

Football Association of Malawi
Founded: 1966
FIFA: 1967

MALAYSIA

Persuatuan Bolasepak Malaysia
Founded: 1933
FIFA: 1956

MALDIVES

Football Association of Maldives
Founded: 1983
FIFA: 1986

MALI

Fédération Malienne de Football
Founded: 1960
FIFA: 1962

MAURITANIA

Fédération de Football de la République de Mauritanie
Founded: 1961
FIFA: 1964

MAURITIUS

Mauritius Football Association
Founded: 1952
FIFA: 1962

MOROCCO

Fédération Royale Marocaine de Football
Founded: 1955
FIFA: 1956
African Nations Cup: 1976

Morocco qualified for the World Cup finals in 1970—the first African team to do so — and has made steady progress since, even applying to host the finals in 1984 and 1998. In those 1970 finals they held Bulgaria to a draw and gave West Germany a terrible fright before losing 2–1. They qualified again in 1986 and won their first round group ahead of England, Poland and Portugal. In the second round they lost to the Germans again, but only through an unfortunate free kick in the last minute. The side contained an outstanding goalkeeper, Zaki, and Mohammed Timoumi and Aziz Bouderbala were fine ball players in midfield. In 1976 they won the African Nations Cup for the only time and their qualification for their third World Cup finals in 1994 confirmed them, along with Cameroon, as one of the powers of the African continent.

Moroccan domestic football is untypical of Africa, inasmuch as the clubs are well spread throughout the country, rather than concentrated in one city. They have also been highly successful. FAR Rabat won the

SWERVING *Morocco's Lamriss*

SHEER DELIGHT *Nigeria celebrates reaching their first World Cup finals*

Champions Cup in 1985, Raja Casablanca repeated the trick in 1989, and Wydad Casablanca completed a hat-trick of titles in 1992.

Morocco has also provided several stars of French soccer. Probably the greatest was Larbi Ben Barek, the "Black Pearl," who won 17 French caps and had a distinguished career with Marseille and Stade Français in the inter-war years. Another French star born in Morocco was Just Fontaine, whose 13 goals in the 1958 World Cup finals remains a record.

MOZAMBIQUE

Federacao Moçambicana de Futebol
Founded: 1975
FIFA: 1978

MYANMAR

Myanmar Football Federation
Founded: 1947
FIFA: 1947

NAMIBIA

Namibia Football Federation
Founded: 1992
FIFA: 1992

NEPAL

All Nepal Football Association
Founded: 1951
FIFA: 1970

NEW ZEALAND

New Zealand Football Association
Founded: 1938 *FIFA:* 1963

New Zealand suffers from the same problems as their great rivals, Australia. Football faces stiff competition from other sports, and the astonishingly complicated, and some would say unfair, World Cup qualifying process inhibits the development of the game there, and in Oceania as a whole.

New Zealand's only World Cup finals appearance was in 1982 in Spain, when they were eliminated in the first round. Wynton Rufer was a member of that team, and won a German Championship medal with Werder Bremen in 1992–93 to establish himself as New Zealand's greatest-ever player.

NIGER

Fédération Nigérienne de Football
Founded: 1967
FIFA: 1967

NIGERIA

Nigeria Football Association
Founded: 1945
FIFA: 1959
African Nations Cup: 1980, 1994

Nigeria, with a huge population and over 500 registered clubs, should be one of the most powerful nations in Africa. But the international record of the "Green Eagles" is very poor, with the 1980 and 1994 African Nations Cup victories their only major successes. However, Nigeria's youngsters have proved more capable than their elders when it comes to winning trophies, and this bodes well for the future of the national team.

In 1985 Nigeria won the World Under-17 Championship in China, becoming the first African side to win a FIFA world tournament at any level, beating West Germany 2–0 in the final; in 1989, Nigeria was runners-up in the World Under-20 Youth Championship; and in 1993 the "Green Eaglets" won the Under-17 title again, their second triumph in only its fifth staging.

With so many talented young players, and with many older players gaining experience in Europe, a World Cup breakthrough simply had to come . . . and in the 1994 qualifiers it did. Nigeria finished ahead of the reigning African champions, Ivory Coast, and the disappointing Algerians to book their place in America, along with Cameroon and Morocco, representing Africa's strongest World Cup challenge to date.

Nigerian clubs have yet to win the African Champions Cup, but they have done well in the Cup Winners Cup. Shooting Stars won in 1976, Enugu Rangers in 1977, and BCC Lions in 1990.

One of Nigeria's most successful exports is Stephen Keshi, a strong center-back in the Anderlecht team of the late 1980s in Belgium.

NORTH KOREA

Football Association of the Democratic People's Republic of Korea
Founded: 1945
FIFA: 1958

North Korea's national side has consistently lived in the shadow of more successful neighbors from the South, but in 1966 the North made headlines around the world. At the 1966 World Cup finals in England, the North Koreans delighted the neutral spectators with their energetic, if disorganized, brand of soccer and then stunned Italy in the first round, winning 1–0. Pak Do Ik will be remembered forever as the man who scored the most famous goal in North Korean soccer history. Then, in an incredible quarter-final against Portugal, the Koreans went 3–0 ahead after just 22 minutes before Eusebio inspired an amazing comeback — scoring four goals as the Portuguese won 5–3. The two Koreas are now considering a joint bid to host the 2002 World Cup finals.

OMAN

Oman Football Association
Founded: 1978
FIFA: 1980

PAKISTAN

Pakistan Football Federation
Founded: 1948
FIFA: 1948

PAPUA NEW GUINEA

Papua New Guinea Football Association
Founded: 1962
FIFA: 1963

PHILIPPINES

Philippine Football Federation
Founded: 1907
FIFA: 1928

QATAR

Qatar Football Association
Founded: 1960
FIFA: 1970

RWANDA

Fédération Rwandaise de Football Amateur
Founded: 1972
FIFA: 1976

SAO TOME AND PRINCIPE

Federacion Santomense de Futebol
Founded: 1975
FIFA: 1986

SAUDI ARABIA

Saudi Arabian Football Federation
Founded: 1959
FIFA: 1959
Asian Championship: 1984, 1988
Saudi Arabia is one of the emergent nations of Asian football, and with untold oil-based wealth at their disposal, they could come to dominate the region's soccer as the Koreans and the Iranians have.

Saudi's first honors came in the 1980s, when they won the 1984 and 1988 Asian Championships. The progress continued with qualification for the 1994 World Cup finals.

The Saudis are also developing their infrastructure and organization. Many foreign coaches have been employed and the magnificent King Fahd stadium in Riyadh is one of the best in the world. The Saudis hosted the first Intercontinental Cup in 1993 (a competition for the five continental champions), and the event is to become a regular feature of the FIFA calendar. Playing against the best nations in the world will further strengthen Saudi Arabia's already impressive hand.

SENEGAL

Fédération Sénégalaise de Football
Founded: 1960
FIFA: 1962

SEYCHELLES

Seychelles Football Federation
Founded: 1976
FIFA: 1986

SIERRA LEONE

Sierra Leone Amateur Football Association
Founded: 1923
FIFA: 1967

ASIAN POWER *South Korea's 1986 World Cup finals team*

SINGAPORE

Football Association of Singapore
Founded: 1892
FIFA: 1952

SOLOMON ISLANDS

Solomon Islands Football Federation
Founded: 1988
FIFA: 1988

SOMALIA

Somalia Football Federation
Founded: 1951
FIFA: 1961

SOUTH AFRICA

South African Football Association
Founded: 1892
FIFA: 1952–76 (suspended 1964–76), 1992

SOUTH KOREA

Korea Football Association
Founded: 1928
FIFA: 1948
Asian Championship: 1956, 1960
South Korea has always been the strongest nation in Asian soccer, and they won the first two Asian Championship tournaments, in 1956 and 1960. Their World Cup record is the best in Asia, qualifying in 1954, 1986, 1990 and 1994.

In the qualifiers for the 1994 tournament they were undefeated in the first round, and scraped through from the second round group — thanks to Japan's last-minute slip against Iraq.

Cha Bum Kun is probably South Korea's best-known player, having enjoyed a lengthy career in Germany's Bundesliga. In 1988 he helped Bayer Leverkusen win the UEFA Cup, scoring the crucial aggregate-levelling goal in the second leg of the final against Spain's Español.

South Korea, with or without their neighbors from the North, is bidding to host the 2002 World Cup finals. With their pedigree, and having successfully hosted the 1988 Olympics in Seoul, they stand a good chance of winning the battle against Japan and China.

SRI LANKA

Football Federation of Sri Lanka
Founded: 1939
FIFA: 1950

SUDAN

Sudan Football Federation
Founded: 1936
FIFA: 1948
African Nations Cup: 1970

SWAZILAND

National Football Association of Swaziland
Founded: 1964
FIFA: 1976

SYRIA

Association Arabe Syrienne de Football
Founded: 1936
FIFA: 1937

TAHITI

Fédération Tahitienne de Football
Founded: 1938
FIFA: 1990

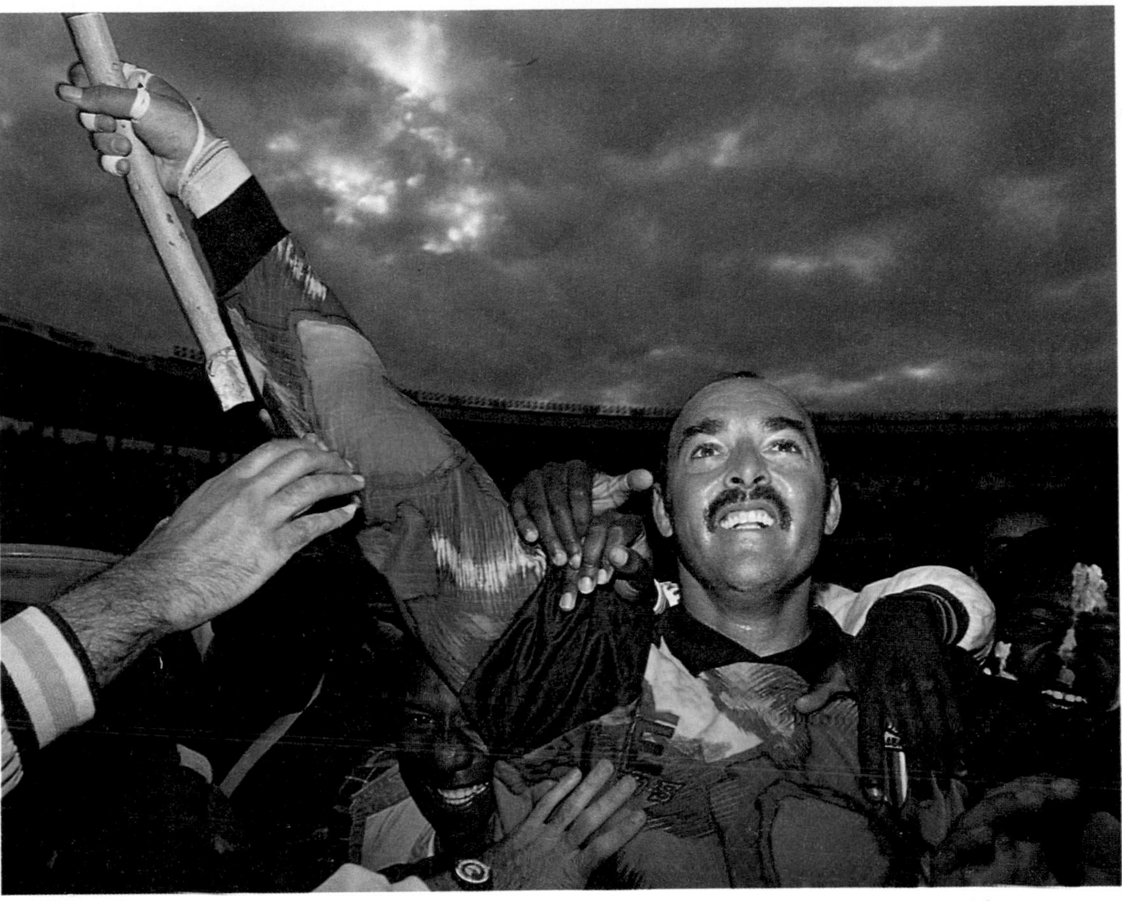

HARARE'S HERO *Goalkeeper Bruce Grobbelaar savors victory, but Zimbabwe just missed World Cup qualification*

TAIWAN

Chinese Taipei Football Association
Founded: 1936
FIFA: 1954

TANZANIA

Football Association of Tanzania
Founded: 1930
FIFA: 1964

THAILAND

Football Association of Thailand
Founded: 1916
FIFA: 1925

TOGO

Fédération Togolaise de Football
Founded: 1960
FIFA: 1962

TUNISIA

Fédération Tunisienne de Football
Founded: 1956
FIFA: 1960

UGANDA

Federation of Uganda Football Associations
Founded: 1924
FIFA: 1959

UNITED ARAB EMIRATES

United Arab Emirates Football Association
Founded: 1971
FIFA: 1972
With only 25 registered clubs and 3,400 players, the UAE caused a big surprise when they qualified for the 1990 World Cup finals. Brazilian coach Mario Zagalo led them in qualifying, but he was fired prior to the tournament, and a Pole, Bernard Blaut, took over in Italy, where they lost all three first-round matches.

VANUATU

Vanuatu Football Federation
Founded: 1934
FIFA: 1988

VIETNAM

Association de Football de la République du Vietnam
Founded: 1962
FIFA: 1964

WESTERN SAMOA

Western Samoa Football Association
Founded: 1968
FIFA: 1986

YEMEN

Republic of Yemen Football Association
Founded: 1940 (South), 1976 (North)
FIFA: 1967 (South), 1980 (North)

ZAIRE

Fédération Zaïreoise de Football-Association
Founded: 1919
FIFA: 1964
African Nations Cup: 1968, 1974
Zaïre won their second African Nations Cup in 1974, the year in which they also became the first black African side to qualify for the World Cup finals. But the gulf in experience between the "Leopards" and their European and South American opponents was cruelly exposed. Since then, their best performances have been in the African Nations Cup.

ZAMBIA

Football Association of Zambia
Founded: 1929
FIFA: 1964
Zambia's national team has been semi-finalists in the African Nations Cup three times since 1974, and pulled off a remarkable victory over Italy in the 1988 Olympics in Seoul. The star was Kalusha Bwalya, who became a top professional with PSV Eindhoven in Holland.

Sadly, Zambia will always now be remembered for the plane crash in April 1993 which wiped out the entire national squad—except for the five overseas-based professionals who were not travelling with the rest to a World Cup qualifier in Senegal. Astonishingly, the Zambians rebuilt their squad around their five exports, and went on to reach the 1994 African Nations Cup Final. They also managed to reach the second round of the African World Cup qualifiers and agonizingly missed clinching a place in the finals when they lost their last match 1–0 in Morocco.

Zambian clubs are also beginning to do well in the African club competitions. Nkana Red Devils was runners-up in the 1990 Champions Cup, and Power Dynamos won the 1991 Cup-winners' Cup.

ZIMBABWE

Zimbabwe Football Association
Founded: 1950
FIFA: 1965
Zimbabwe won independence in 1983 and has been making steady progress ever since. They went within one game of reaching the 1994 World Cup finals, but lost the last group match 3–1 in Cameroon. Their emergence owes much Liverpool goalkeeper Bruce Grobbelaar, and more recently to another English based player, Peter Ndlovu.

THE GREAT CLUBS

Professionalism swept through western Europe in the late 1920s. The big clubs of Spain, Italy, France and Portugal were importing star foreigners by the turn of the 1930s. Not until the mid-1950s did Belgium, Holland and then Germany catch up with full-time professionalism. When they did, the balance of the European game changed yet again.

The great traditions of soccer are kept alive, week in, week out, by the clubs. From Ajax in Holland to Vasco da Gama in Brazil, from Barcelona in Spain to Liverpool in England, they provide the first call of loyalty on the public. People who may never have attended a match in years still look out for the result of "their" club each week. Evidence of the depths of loyalty which certain clubs can inspire is widely available — from the way Real Madrid's fans came up with the money to fund the building of the Estadio Bernabeu in the 1940s to the proud boast from Portugal's Benfica of 122,000 members. Every club has its tales of the great days and great players, great coaches and great victories. Some, like Manchester United, have been touched by tragedy, others, like Marseille, with controversy. The greatest, clearly, are those who have repeatedly proved their power and strength by lifting the continental club competitions in Europe and South America. Some of them are described here.

AJAX AMSTERDAM
HOLLAND

Founded: 1900
Stadium: De Meer (19,500)
Colors: Red and white broad stripes/white
League: 24
Cup: 12
World Club Cup: 1972
European Cup: 1971, 1972, 1973
European Cup-winners' Cup: 1987
UEFA Cup: 1992
Supercup: 1972, 1973

Ajax, on beating Torino in the 1992 UEFA Cup Final, became only the second team after Italy's Juventus to have won all three European trophies and a full house of all seven titles eligible for clubs. The achievement was a popular one, bearing in mind the entertainment and style the Amsterdam club had consistently provided. The first hints of glory to come were in evidence in 1966–67 when, under former Dutch international Rinus Michels, Ajax thrashed Liverpool 5–1 in a European Cup match. Two years later Ajax became the first Dutch side to reach the European Cup Final, though they lost 4–1 to Milan. In 1971 Ajax were back as winners, beating Panathinaikos 2–0 at Wembley. In the next two Finals, they beat Internazionale 2–0, then Juventus 1–0. Johan Cruyff was their inspiration.

Ajax's trademark was the "total soccer" system, which involved taking full advantage of a generation of skilled all-round players whose versatility and soccer intelligence allowed bewildering changes of position. It was "The Whirl," as envisaged early in the 1950s by that soccer prophet, Willi Meisl. After the sale of Cruyff to Barcelona in 1973, Ajax fell away and it took his return, a decade later, as technical director, to propel them back to the peaks of the European game. Under Cruyff, the new Ajax generation won the

DENNIS BERGKAMP *The new generation*

Coaches

Marinus "Rinus" Michels

Coach of Ajax Amsterdam (Holland), Barcelona (Spain), Los Angeles Aztecs (US), Bayer Leverkusen (Germany); also Holland national team (born February 9, 1928)

Michels, a Dutch international center-forward in the early 1950s, led a revolution in the late 1960s when he developed the "total soccer" philosophy at Ajax. Much of Michels's coaching career with Ajax was linked with the presence, as leader on the field, of Johan Cruyff. Michels went to Barcelona after winning the European Cup with Ajax in 1971, went back to Ajax to sign Cruyff and the pair were partners again when Holland finished runners-up at the 1974 World Cup. "Iron Rinus" was never afraid to take tactical risks, such as when he guided Holland to European Championship success in 1988 by using Ruud Gullit as a static, right-side attacker. Nor was Michels ever afraid of stating his opinions, however blunt.

Cup-winners' Cup in 1987 — his friend and pupil Marco Van Basten scoring the goal which beat Lokomotive Leipzig in the final in Athens. Cruyff's successor Louis Van Gaal then secured the UEFA Cup five years later. Ajax maintained their high standards of both achievement and entertaining soccer despite regularly selling their young star players — such as Bryan Roy, Wim Jonk and, the best of all, Dennis Bergkamp — to Italian clubs.

ANDERLECHT BRUSSELS, BELGIUM

Founded: 1908
Stadium: Constant Vanden Stock/Parc Astrid (29,000)
Colors: White with mauve/white
League: 22
Cup: 7
European Cup-winners' Cup: 1976, 1978
UEFA Cup: 1983
Supercup: 1976, 1978

Anderlecht's international debut was not a happy one: they crashed 10–0 and 12–0 on aggregate to Manchester United in an early European Cup. Since then, however, the Royal Sporting Club has earned respect far and wide for their domestic domination and an international outlook which has brought success in both the European Cup-winners' Cup and the UEFA Cup. Much credit reflects on the coaching work of Englishman Bill Gormlie, a former Blackburn goalkeeper, who helped lay the foundations for success in the late 1940s and early 1950s. Equally important was the financial power of the millionaire brewer, Constant Vanden Stock. Before his takeover Anderlecht relied mainly on home-grown talent likePaul Van Himst, the greatest Belgian soccer player of all time.

As Anderlecht's prestige grew, particularly thanks to the European Cup competitions, they were able to compete in the international transfer market. A significant coaching influence, in the early 1960s, was Frenchman Pierre Sinibaldi, who perfected a tactical formation which relied on a flat back four, the offside trap, and possession soccer in midfield. It worked well against almost all opposition except British clubs, whose more direct style constantly caught the defenders on the turn. Thus, the first time Anderlecht reached a European final — in the Fairs Cup in 1970 — they were beaten by Arsenal. European success did come, in the Cup-winners' Cup in 1976 and 1978, but this was after the arrival of the more pragmatic coaching approach of Dutchman Wiel Corver and Belgium's Raymond Goethals. Later, with Van Himst having returned as coach, Anderlecht won the UEFA Cup and in Enzo Scifo produced the finest Belgian player since Van Himst himself.

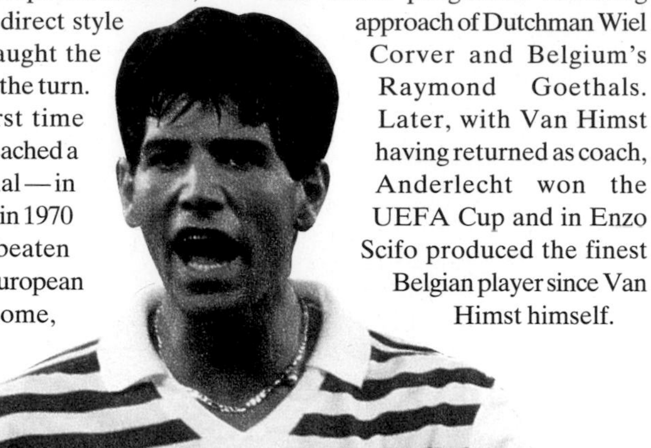

ENZO SCIFO *Anderlecht discovery, and the finest Belgian player of recent years*

GLORY GOAL *Arsenal's 1989 title-clincher*

ARSENAL LONDON, ENGLAND

Founded: 1886
Stadium: Highbury (38,000)
Colors: Red/white
League: 10
Cup: 6
European Cup-winners's Cup: 1994
Fairs Cup: 1970

Arsenal, today a North London club, had their origins south of the Thames, at the Woolwich Arsenal. The club turned professional in 1891 and entered the Football League a year later, reaching the First Division in 1904 and the FA Cup semifinals in 1906. After the First World War they moved to Highbury, and appointed the legendary Herbert Chapman as coach in 1925.

Chapman had a flair for publicity, an innovative approach to tactics and a talent for motivation. He spent heavily but wisely on the likes of first Charlie Buchan and Alex James, introduced the stopper center-half and created the all-conquering outfit which won the League five times in the 1930s and the FA Cup twice. Arsenal won the League twice more and the FA Cup once in the eight years after the war. A 17-year hiatus then followed before the Gunners ended their longest trophy drought by winning the Fairs Cup.

Suddenly, the jinx was broken. A year later coach Bertie Mee was celebrating a historic league and cup "double." His team mixed the volatile flair of Charlie George, determined leadership of Frank McLintock, rugged tackling of Peter Storey and creative class of George Graham. He later returned as coach, masterminding two league titles, in 1989, thanks to a dramatic last-minute winner against Liverpool at Anfield, and 1991; the 1993 League Cup and FA Cup; and the 1994 European Cup-winners' Cup.

ATLETICO MADRID
SPAIN

Founded: 1903
Stadium: Vicente Calderon/Manzanares (62,000)
Colors: Red and white stripes/blue
League: 8
Cup: 8
World Club Cup: 1974
European Cup-winners' Cup: 1962

Atletico Madrid has always existed in the shadow of neighbors Real, but they still rank among the Big Three of Spanish soccer and boast a proud record at the international level. Not that life has always been easy. In the late 1930s, after the Spanish Civil War, it took a merger with the Air Force club to keep Atletico in business; in 1959, they just failed to reach the European Cup Final when Real beat them in a semifinal playoff; in the early 1960s they had to share Real's Estadio Bernabeu, because Atletico's Metropolitano had been sold to developers before the club's new stadium could be completed. European glory did come to Atletico in the shape of the Cup-winners' Cup in 1962 and was a well-deserved prize for players such as inside-left Joaquin Peiro and his wing partner Enrique Collar. But it was not until the early 1970s that Atletico put together a comparable team, thanks to the purchases of Argentines Ruben Hugo Ayala and Ramon Heredia. In 1974, Atletico secured that elusive place in the European Cup Final. But, after taking the lead against Bayern Munich in extra time, Atletico conceded a last-kick equalizer.

Consolation for their 4–0 defeat in the replay came with the opportunity to substitute for reluctant Bayern in the World Club Cup against Independiente of Argentina. By the time the tie came around Atletico had appointed as coach Luis Aragones, the midfielder who had scored their goal in the European Cup Final against Bayern. Atletico duly beat Independiente 1–0 and were, for a year at least, on top of the world. In the late 1980s the club was taken over by the extrovert builder Jesus Gil. He pumped millions of dollars into the club, signed major personalities such as the Argentine coach César Luis Menotti and Portuguese forward Paulo Futre, but generated more publicity and controversy than success.

PAULO FUTRE *Atletico Madrid's skipper in the controversial Jesus Gil years*

ATLETICO NACIONAL
MEDELLIN, COLOMBIA

Founded: 1938
Stadium: Atanasio Giradot (35,000)
Colors: Green and white stripes/white
League: 4
South American Club Cup: 1989
Inter-American Cup: 1989

Atletico Nacional of Medellin is not the most famous club to come out of Colombia. That honor will always belong to Millonarios, who led the professional, pirate revolution in the early 1950s. But Nacional earned a place in history by becoming the first club to take the Copa Libertadores, the South American Club Cup, across the Andes to the western side of the continent. Nacional, which provided the base of the Colombian World Cup team in 1990, became in 1954 the first champions of Colombia after the rapprochement with FIFA. Yet it was not until 1971 that they made their debut in the South American Club Cup under Argentine coach Osvaldo Zubeldia. He had earned a fearsome reputation as boss of the rugged Estudiantes de La Plata team which had dominated Argentine and South American club soccer in the late 1960s. However, without resorting to the cynicism which made Estudiantes hated, he turned Nacional into Colombian champions three times in the mid-1970s and early 1980s. Zubeldia was followed by Luis Cubilla, at whose suggestion, in 1986, Nacional appointed a former stalwart central defender, Francisco Maturana, as boss. In 1987 and 1988 they finished championship runners-up and then, in 1989, seized the South American club crown. Unfortunately, their preparations for the world club showdown with Milan were wrecked when the government halted the league season because of the increasing violence being engendered on the fringes of the game by the drug and betting cartels. Nacional did not emerge with their reputation unscathed. It was not only that Medellin was the center of the drugs trade; several Nacional players were friends of the notorious drugs baron Pablo Escobar. Indeed, when Escobar was eventually killed in 1993 by security forces, at his funeral the coffin was draped in a Nacional flag.

BARCELONA
SPAIN

Founded: 1899
Stadium: Nou Camp (115,000)
Colors: Blue and red stripes/blue
League: 14
Cup: 22
European Cup: 1992
European Cup-winners' Cup: 1979, 1982, 1989
Fairs Cup: 1958, 1960, 1966
Supercup: 1992

Barcelona finally ended a duel with destiny when, in 1992, they beat Sampdoria 1–0 at Wembley to win the European Cup. It was a case of third time lucky, for the greatest prize in the European club game had twice eluded them at the final hurdle. Barcelona had been the first winners of the Inter-Cities Fairs Cup and had won the Cup-winners' Cup three times. But their European Cup campaigns seemed to have been jinxed. First, in 1961, when Barcelona had apparently achieved the hard part by eliminating the title-holders and their bitter rivals Real Madrid, they lost to Benfica in the Final in Berne. Barcelona hit the woodwork three times, yet lost 3–2 against the run of play. Great players such as Luis Suarez, Ladislav Kubala, Sandor Kocsis and Zoltan Czibor had everything on their side except luck.

Coaches

HELENIO HERRERA

Coach of Red Star Paris, Stade Francais (France), Atletico Madrid, Valladolid, Sevilla (Spain), Belenenses (Portugal), Barcelona (Spain), Internazionale and Roma (Italy); also Spanish and Italian national teams (born April 17, 1916)

One of the world's most innovative and single-minded coaches. Herrera, born in Argentina, brought up in Morocco and a player in France, experimented at Barcelona in the 1950s by using inside-forwards at wing-half to turn "easy" matches into goal sprees. His attacking tactics proved ineffective at Inter so Herrera developed, instead, the most ruthlessly disciplined catenaccio. Herrera demanded total obedience, insisting that his players place their hands on the ball and swear loyalty to each other before going out for a match. Stars who baulked at such rituals were sold, however popular or successful. Inter won the World and European Cups twice each before Herrera's career went into decline at Roma.

History repeated itself in even more galling circumstances in 1986. Barcelona, coached by Terry Venables and gambling on the fitness of long-time injured Steve Archibald, faced Steaua Bucharest in Seville. Barcelona lost in a penalty shoot-out after a goal-less draw.

It took the return of 1970s inspiration Johan Cruyff, this time as coach, to steer a new generation of international stars — including Ronald Koeman, Hristo Stoichkov and Michael Laudrup — to victory long overdue for one of the world's biggest clubs. Barcelona's 1994 league title was their fourth in a row, the last three of them achieved in the closing moments of the final day, twice at the expense of great rivals Real Madrid.

Barcelona enjoy the support of more than 100,000 members and, in the Nou Camp, have a quite breathtaking stadium.

BAYERN MUNICH
GERMANY

Founded: 1900
Stadium: Olimpiastadion (69,261)
Colors: All red
League: 13
Cup: 8
World Club Cup: 1976
European Cup: 1974, 1975, 1976
European Cup-winners' Cup: 1967

Bayern is Germany's most glamorous club, even though high tax rates mean they have never been able to hold stars tempted by the rich pickings of Italy. In the 1980s Bayern became almost an Italian nursery as they lost Karl-Heinz Rummenigge, Andy Brehme and Lothar Matthäus to Internazionale and Stefan Reuter and Jurgen Kohler to Juventus. All this transfer activity underlined the fact that the Bayern success story is — with the exception of one championship in 1932 and one cup in 1957 — a relatively recent affair. The identities of the men who secured all the glittering titles read like a Who's Who of the world game: Franz Beckenbauer, Gerd Müller, Sepp Maier, Paul Breitner, Rummenigge and Matthäus. The German championship was originally organized in regional leagues, with the winners playing off at the end of each season for the title: only once in the pre-war years did Bayern win all the way through. That was in 1932, when they defeated Eintracht Frankfurt 2–0. Not until 1957, and a 1–0 win over Fortuna Düsseldorf in the cup final, did Bayern have anything more to celebrate. Indeed their record was so mediocre that they were not included in the inaugural Bundesliga in 1963–64. But, a year later, Bayern won promotion; in 1966 they won the cup, and in 1967 they secured the European Cup-winners' Cup, thanks to an extra-time victory over Rangers. That was the team led and inspired by Beckenbauer in the role of attacking sweeper, with Maier in goal and Müller up front. All three stars

HRISTO STOICHKOV *Barcelona's Bulgarian striker is denied for once in a 1993 Spanish league match against Real Zaragoza. Stoichkov, his country's Player of the Year four times, has been a consistent scorer throughout a career liberally rewarded with money and medals*

shone even more brightly as Bayern landed a European Cup hat-trick in the mid-1970s. In the 1980s Bayern were twice European Cup runners-up, but complacency set in and it was not until Beckenbauer returned, first as executive vice president and then as coach, that Bayern regained their pre-eminence.

BENFICA
LISBON, PORTUGAL

Founded: 1904
Stadium: Estadio do Benfica/Da Luz (130,000)
Colors: Red/white
League: 29
Cup: 25
European Cup: 1961, 1962

Benfica is a national institution with their 130,000-capacity stadium and 122,000 membership. Living up to the standards of history is what Benfica believe they owe Cosme Damiao who, on February 28, 1904, organized the first recorded local game of futebol on a patch of Lisbon wasteland. The next day he formed his "team" into a club named Sport Lisboa and, two years later was instrumental in arranging a merger with neighbors Sport Clube de Benfica. In the early years it was cycling which brought the club its first prizes. But from the launch of a unified Portuguese championship in the late 1920s, Benfica lorded it over Portuguese sport. In due course, Benfica set their sights on international glory and, in 1950, won the Latin Cup — one of the forerunners of the European Cup. English coach Ted Smith laid the foundations of a team which would dominate not only Portugal but then Europe.

In 1954 Benfica followed the example being set in Spain and built a vast new stadium. An exiled Hungarian named Bela Guttman became coach, and his team filled the new stadium as Benfica twice swept to success in the European Cup in 1961 and 1962. First they beat Barcelona, amid intense drama, by 3–2 in Berne, then Real Madrid 5–3 in Amsterdam. On both occasions Benfica was captained by their veteran center-forward, José Aguas. They also introduced one of the most famous Portuguese soccer players of all time in Eusebio, greatest of the many fine players Benfica had discovered in the Portuguese colonies of Angola and Mozambique. Benfica's boast of only "Portuguese" (including colonial) players was scrapped in the mid-1970s, when the African colonies were cast adrift. Now they hunt Brazilians, Slavs and Danes with the rest.

BOCA JUNIORS
BUENOS AIRES, ARGENTINA

Founded: 1905
Stadium: Bombonera (58,740)
Colors: Blue with yellow hoop/blue
League: 19
World Club Cup: 1977
South American Club Cup: 1977, 1978
South American Supercup: 1989
Inter-American Cup: 1989

Boca is one of the two great clubs in the Argentine capital of Buenos Aires, along with old rivals River Plate. They were founded by an Irish man named Patrick MacCarthy and a group of newly-arrived Italian immigrants. They joined the league in 1913 and were immediately caught up in a domestic soccer "war" which saw two championships being organized for most of the 1920s and early 1930s. Boca bestrode the two eras. They won the last Argentine amateur championship in 1930 and the first unified professional one the following year. Two more titles followed in the next four years, thanks to some fine players, including the great Brazilian defender, Domingos da Guia. In the 1940s and 1950s Boca slipped into River Plate's shadow, re-emerging in 1963 when a team fired by the goals of José Sanfilippo reached the Final of the South American Club Cup.

Winning the title, however, would have to wait until the late 1970s. Then they reached the Final three years in a row — beating Brazil's Cruzeiro in 1977 and Deportivo Cali of Colombia in 1978 before losing to Olimpia of Paraguay in 1979. Boca's rugged style, under Juan Carlos Lorenzo, proved controversial. Not one Boca player figured in the squad which won the 1978 World Cup. But Boca had already secured their own world crown, beating West Germany's Borussia Mönchengladbach in the World Club Cup in 1977. Boca rebuilt their team around Diego Maradona in 1981, but wasted the record $5million fee they received from Barcelona for him a year later.

THE OLD FIRM *Celtic's Paul McStay tangles with Rangers' Iain Durrant*

CELTIC
GLASGOW, SCOTLAND

Founded: 1888
Stadium: Celtic Park (51,709)
Colors: Green and white hoops/white
League: 35
Cup: 29
European Cup: 1967

Celtic and old rivals Rangers are Scottish soccer's greatest clubs, but it was Celtic who first extended that hunger for success into Europe when, in 1967, they became the first British club to win the European Cup. It was a measure of the way they swept all before them that season that they won every domestic competition as well: the League, the Cup and League Cup. No other team in Europe had, until then, ended the season with a 100 per cent record in four major competitions. In winning the European Cup Celtic refuted accusations — mostly from England — that their Scottish honors owed more to a lack of solid opposition than their own abilities. Celtic's 1967 team was shrewdly put together by coach Jock Stein, a former Celtic player. As well as new Scottish stars he included veterans such as goalkeeper Ronnie Simpson and scheming inside-left Bertie Auld. In the Lisbon final. after going behind to an early penalty, they beat former holders Internazionale 2–1 with goals from fullback Gemmell and center-forward Chalmers.

Sadly, Celtic's golden touch did not survive long. A few months later they were beaten by Kiev Dynamo right at the start of their European Cup defence, and were then dragged down to defeat and fisticuffs in the infamous World Club Cup battle with Racing of Argentina. In 1970 Celtic returned to the European Cup Final, only to lose to Feyenoord in Milan; and, two years later, they lost only on penalties after two goal-less draws in the semifinals against Inter. More trouble lay ahead as Celtic proved unable to match Rangers' commercial and playing revolution in the late 1980s and slipped to the brink of bankruptcy and a boardroom revolution.

COLO COLO
SANTIAGO, CHILE

Founded: 1925
Stadium: Colo Colo (50,000)
Colors: White/black
League: 18
South American Recopa: 1991

Colo Colo, Chilean nickname for a wildcat, were founded by five angry members of the old Magallanes FC. Even though Chilean soccer is generally held to lag far behind that of traditional giants Brazil, Argentina and Uruguay, Colo Colo has an enviable reputation throughout the continent. The club's vision has always stretched beyond the Andes. Such a tradition was laid down by David Orellano. He was a founder member of Colo Colo and one of the five Magallanes rebels who disagreed over the choice of a new club captain. The choice of the five fell upon Orellano and, within two years of Colo Colo's foundation, they had sent a team off to tour Spain and Portugal. In 1933 Colo Colo was among the founders of a professional league; in 1941 they set another pioneering trend by introducing a foreign coach in the Hungarian, Ferenc Platko; and in 1948 they organized a South American club tournament which can now be seen as a forerunner of the Copa Libertadores, the official South American Club Cup launched in 1960. Record league winners in Chile and the supreme transfer destination for most domestic players, Colo Colo's greatest achievement was in reaching the 1973 South American Club Cup Final. The teams drew 1–1 in Avellaneda and 0–0 in Santiago, and thus went on to a play-off in Montevideo, which Independiente won 2–1 in extra time. Colo Colo's consolation goal was scored by their most famous and popular player of the modern era, Carlos Caszely.

EINTRACHT FRANKFURT
GERMANY

Founded: 1899
Stadium: Waldstadion (61,146)
Colors: Black and red stripes/black
League: 1
Cup: 4
UEFA Cup: 1980

Eintracht Frankfurt occupies a very special place in soccer legend as the team Real Madrid beat in the European Cup final at Hampden back in 1960. The score was 7–3 to Madrid, but Frankfurt was far from crushed and had proved their class by putting six goals past Glasgow Rangers — both home and away — in the semifinals. Frankfurt's team was built on the midfield strength of Dieter Stinka and Jurgen Lindner, plus the creative talents of veteran inside-left Alfred Pfaff and right-winger Richard Kress. It may sound odd to suggest that everything after a defeat was an anti-climax, but though Frankfurt was a founding member of the West German Bundesliga in 1963 and has never been relegated, it has achieved comparatively little. The mid-1980s were taken up with a three-year struggle against relegation — Frankfurt once saving themselves only in the relegation/promotion play-off. Boardroom problems also dogged the club until the businessman Matthias Ohms took over and appointed Bernd Holzenbein, a World Cup winner in 1974 and an old Frankfurt favorite, as his executive vice-president. Holzenbein put Frankfurt back on a sound financial footing and bought stars such as midfielder Andy Möller (later sold to Juventus) and the brilliant Ghanaian striker, Anthony Yeboah. In 1992–93 Frankfurt was just beaten for the league title after the controversial mid-season departure of their charismatic Yugoslav coach, Dragoslav Stepanovic.

Frankfurt's one European success over the years was in winning the UEFA Cup in 1980. Frankfurt beat their fellow Germans, Borussia Mönchengladbach, on the away goals rule in the final, losing 3–2 away and then winning 1–0 back in the Waldstadion. Holzenbein had himself scored the all-important second away goal in the first leg.

FEYENOORD
ROTTERDAM, HOLLAND

Founded: 1908
Stadium: De Kuyp (63,910)
Colors: Red and white halves/black
League: 13
Cup: 9
World Club Cup: 1970
European Cup: 1970
UEFA Cup: 1974

Feyenoord was founded by mining entrepreneur C. R. J. Kieboom. Their star player in the successful pre-war years was left-half Puck Van Heel, who appeared in the final tournaments of both the 1934 and 1938 World Cups and set what was for many years a Dutch record of 64 international appearances. The post-war years were bleak until after the introduction of professionalism in the late 1950s. Then Feyenoord entered their most glorious domestic era, winning the league title six times in 13 years. Indeed, their 1965 and 1969 successes brought them league and cup "doubles." Stars included goalkeeper Eddie Pieters-Graafland, a then record signing from Ajax, half-backs Reinier Kreyermaat, Hans Kraay and Jan Klaasens and, above all, outside-left Coen Moulijn. He was still a key figure when they won the European Cup in 1970, along with Swedish striker Ove Kindvall and burly midfield general Wim Van Hanegem. Feyenoord's coach, for their extra time victory over Celtic in Milan, was Ernst Happel, the former Austrian international. Feyenoord — and not Ajax — was thus the first Dutch club to break through to European success, and they went on to defeat Estudiantes de La Plata of Argentina in the World Club Cup Final.

In 1974, with Van Hanegem pulling the strings in midfield, Feyenoord added the UEFA Cup to their trophy room. But, as time went on, they lost their grip on the Dutch game. Star players had to be sold to balance the books, among them Ruud Gullit, whom Feyenoord had discovered with Haarlem. He was sold to PSV Eindhoven and, later, of course, moved on to Milan. Not until the arrival as general manager of

RUUD HEUS *One of the men who spearheaded Feyenoord's revival in the early 1990s takes on a Vitesse opponent*

Wim Jansen, a former Feyenoord star who starred with Holland at the 1974 World Cup, did Feyenoord pull themselves back together and regain the league title in 1993.

FK AUSTRIA
VIENNA, AUSTRIA

Founded: 1911
Stadium: Horr (10,500) / Prater (62,270)
Colors: White with mauve/white
League: 21
Cup: 21

The history of the Fussball Klub Austria-Memphis began with a game of cricket. Just as the English exported their industrial know-how and educational skills around the world in the latter half of the nineteenth century, they also took with them their newly codified games and sports. Thus the Vienna Cricket and Football Club was founded by the expatriate community in the 1890s. Cricket did not gain universal acceptance, but soccer was another matter, and November 15, 1894 saw the first proper soccer match ever staged in Austria. The Vienna Cricket and Football Club beat 1st Vienna FC by 4–0 — and they have been winning matches and titles ever since.

Changing their name in 1925, FKA notched up many domestic honors in a list which includes runners-up spot in the European Cupwinners' Cup in 1978, when a team inspired by midfield general Herbert Prohaska became the first Austrian side to reach a modern-day European final. That was long overdue since, in the late 1920s, FK Austria was one of the pioneers of European international club soccer when the Mitropa Cup drew clubs from Austria, Czechoslovakia, Hungary, Yugoslavia, Switzerland and Italy. FK Austria was triumphant in 1933 and 1936, inspired by the legendary center-forward Matthias Sindelar. Their delicate style of play, known as the "Vienna School," was modeled on the old Scottish close-passing game and had been taught them by Englishman Jimmy Hogan. His coaching genius contributed mightily to the development of the so-called "Wunderteam" which lost unluckily to England, by 4–3, at

Stamford Bridge in 1932 and then reached the semifinals of the 1934 World Cup. The backbone of the Wunderteam was provided by FK Austria. That tradition has been maintained ever since. Thus no fewer than six FKA stars traveled with the national squad to the 1990 World Cup Finals in Italy.

FLAMENGO RIO DE JANEIRO, BRAZIL

Founded: 1895 as sailing club; 1911 as football club
Stadium: Gavea (20,000) and Maracana (130,000)
Colors: Black and red hoops/white
Rio state league: 22
Brazil championship (incl. Torneo Rio-São Paulo): 5
World Club Cup: 1981
South American Club Cup: 1981

Flamengo is the most popular club in Brazil, having been formed by dissident members of the Fluminense club but under the umbrella of the Flamengo sailing club — which now boasts more than 70,000 members. They first competed in the Rio league in 1912, winning the title two years later. In 1915 they regained the crown without having lost a game. A string of great names have graced the red-and-black hoops over the years, among them defenders Domingos Da Guia and the legendary center-forward Leonidas da Silva. Known as the "Black Diamond," Leonidas played for Flamengo from 1936 to 1942, inspiring two state championship triumphs and earning a worldwide reputation through his brilliance in the 1938 World Cup finals in France.

Flamengo ran up a Rio state hat-trick in the mid-1950s with their team nicknamed the "Steamroller," but had to wait until 1981 for their greatest success. Then, riding high on the goals of a new hero, Zico — the so-called "White Pele" — they won both the South American and World Club Cups. The South American Club Cup campaign was one of the most hostile in memory. Flamengo won a first round play-off against Atletico Mineiro after their rival Brazilians had five players sent off, provoking referee José Roberto Wright to abandon the game. In the final, Flamengo beat Cobreloa of Chile in a play-off in Montevideo which saw the expulsion of five players. Fears about the outcome of Flamengo's world showdown against Liverpool proved unfounded. Zico was in a class of his own. Liverpool could not touch him as he created all of Flamengo's goals in a 3–0 win. The players dedicated their success to the memory of Claudio Coutinho, their former coach who had died in a skin-diving accident. Like old rivals Fluminense, Flamengo play all their big matches in the Maracana.

FLUMINENSE RIO DE JANEIRO, BRAZIL

Founded: 1902
Stadium: Laranjeira (20,000) and Maracana (130,000)
Colors: Red, green and white stripes/white
Rio state league: 27
Brazil championship (incl. Torneo Rio-São Paulo): 4

Fluminense has yet to win an international trophy, but that does not alter their status as one of South America's great clubs. "Flu" were founded in 1902 by an Englishman named Arthur Cox, and many of their first players were British residents. The club's wealth and upper-class clientele resulted in the nickname "Po de Arroz" ("Face Powder," after the fashion of the time at the turn of the century). Today the club's fans wear white powder on their faces as a sign of loyalty. In 1905 Flu was a founding member of the Rio de Janeiro league and of the Brazilian confederation; they won the first four Rio (Carioca) championships in 1906–09; and, in 1932, Flu became the first Brazilian club to go professional.

By this time the "Flu-Fla" rivalry (Fluminense-Flamengo) had been flourishing for 20 years, the first meeting between the clubs having taken place in 1912. In 1963 their clash drew an official crowd of 177,656 to the Maracana stadium in Rio, which remains a world record for a club game. By 1930 Flu's stadium was the home of the national team and the club had launched a weekly newspaper, among other schemes. A few years later and Flu were ruling the roost with five Rio titles between 1936 and 1941. Star players were forwards Romeu, Carreiro and Tim — who coached Peru at the 1978 World Cup finals. In the early 1950s Fluminense's star was the World Cup winning midfield general Didi. In the late 1960s and early 1970s the key player was another World Cup winner, Brazil's 1970 captain and right-back, Carlos Alberto Torres. In the 1980s the mantle of inspiration-in-chief passed to the Paraguayan Romerito (Julio César Romero). Fluminense won a hat-trick of Rio titles in 1983, 1984 and 1985 with Romero their guiding light. He was rewarded by being nominated as South American Footballer of the Year in 1985 and later starred at the 1986 World Cup finals.

HAMBURG GERMANY

Founded: 1887
Stadium: Volksparkstadion (61,234)
Colors: White/red
League: 6
Cup: 3
European Cup: 1983
European Cup-winners' Cup: 1977

Hamburg can be considered by many to be the oldest league club in Germany, if one takes as their foundation date that of SC Germania, the oldest of three clubs which later amalgamated. The other two were Hamburger FC (1888) and FC Falke (1905). Hamburg's tradition, from that day to this, has been one of attacking soccer. The first major trophy

ROMERITO *Fluminense's midfield general scoring for Paraguay against Chile in a World Cup qualifying match in Santiago*

KEVIN KEEGAN *European Footballer of the Year with Hamburg in 1978 and 1979*

could have been theirs in 1922. But when the championship playoff was abandoned because injury-hit Nürnberg had only seven men left on the field, Hamburg sportingly declined to accept the title. A year later Hamburg did win the championship, and again in 1928.

They did not win it again until 1960, by which time they were being led by the greatest soccer player in the club's history. Center-forward Uwe Seeler, son of a former Hamburg player, turned down a string of lucrative offers from Spain and Italy to stay loyal throughout his career to Hamburg, for whom brother Dieter also played at left-half. Uwe Seeler was four times Hamburg's top scorer in the old regional league system, and after the creation of the Bundesliga was on one occasion the country's leading marksman. He also spearheaded Hamburg's thrilling 1960–61 European Cup campaign, in which they lost to Barcelona only in a playoff in the semifinals. Seeler went on to captain West Germany in their brave World Cup efforts of 1966 and 1970, but he had retired by the time Hamburg achieved a European breakthrough and won the Cup-winners' Cup in 1977. Hamburg beat defending cup-holders Anderlecht of Belgium 2–0 in a final which was the big-occasion debuts of two long-serving internationals, defender Manni Kaltz and midfield general Felix Magath.

Both were stalwarts of the side beaten by Nottingham Forest in the 1980 European Cup Final, when Englishman Kevin Keegan tried in vain to stimulate the Hamburg attack. Keegan had returned to England by the time Hamburg beat Juventus in Athens three years later.

INDEPENDIENTE
AVELLANEDA, ARGENTINA

Founded: 1904
Stadium: Cordero (55,000)
Colors: Red/blue
League: 11
World Club Cup: 1973, 1984
South American Club Cup: 1964, 1965, 1972, 1973, 1974, 1975, 1984
Inter-American Cup: 1973, 1974, 1976

Independiente is perhaps the least familiar of international club soccer's great achievers, outside Argentina at least. This is because, despite two lengthy periods of command in South American club soccer, they won the world title only twice in five attempts, and that at a time when the competition's image was tarnished.

Also, Independiente has always relied on team soccer rather than superstar inspiration. One outstanding player who made his name with the club, however, was Raimundo Orsi. He was the left-winger who played for Argentina in the 1928 Olympics, signed for Juventus, and then scored Italy's vital equalizer on their way to victory over Czechoslovakia in the 1934 World Cup final. Later, the Independiente fans had the great Paraguayan center-forward, Arsenio Erico, to idolize. Erico had been the boyhood hero of Alfredo Di Stefano and, in 1937, set an Argentine First Division goal scoring record of 37 in a season.

Independiente did not regain prominence until the early 1960s, when coach Manuel Giudice imported an Italian-style catenaccio defence which secured the South American Club Cup in both 1964 and 1965. Independiente was the first Argentine team to win the continent's top club prize. But in the World Club Cup Final they fell both years to the high priests of catenaccio, Internazionale of Italy.

In the 1970s Independiente's Red Devils won the South American Club Cup four times in a row and collected the World Club Cup. It was an odd victory: European champions Hamburg declined to compete, so runners-up Juventus took their place — on the condition that the final was a single-game match in Italy. Independiente not only agreed, they won it with a single goal from midfield general Ricardo Bochini.

INTERNAZIONALE
MILAN, ITALY

Founded: 1908
Stadium: Meazza (85,847)
Colors: Blue and black stripes/black
League: 13
Cup: 3
World Club Cup: 1964, 1965
European Cup: 1964, 1965
UEFA Cup: 1991, 1994

MATTHÄUS *Internazionale's driving force and Germany's World Cup captain in 1990*

Internazionale was founded out of an argument within the Milan club in the early years of the century. Some 45 members, led by committee man Giovanni Paramithiotti, broke away in protest at the authoritarian way the powerful Camperio brothers were running the club. That was not the end of the politics, however. In the 1930s, fascist laws forced Internazionale into a name change to rid the club of the foreign associations of their title. So they took the name of the city of Milan's patron saint and became Ambrosiana. Under this title they led the way in continental club competition — being one of the leading lights in the pre-war Mitropa Cup.

After the war, the club reverted to the Internazionale name and pioneered a tactical revolution. First coach Alfredo Foni, who had been a World Cup-winning full-back before the war, won the league title twice by withdrawing outside-right Gino Armani into midfield; then Helenio Herrera conquered Italy, Europe and the world with catenaccio. Goalkeeper Giuliano Sarti, sweeper Armando Picchi and man-marking backs Tarcisio Burgnich, Aristide Guarneri and Giacinto Facchetti were as near watertight as possible. They were

the foundation on which Spanish general Luis Suarez constructed the counter-attacking raids carried forward by Brazil's Jair da Costa, Spain's Joaquim Peiro and Italy's own Sandro Mazzola. Inter won the European and World Club Cups in both 1964 and 1965 — beating Real Madrid and Benfica in Europe, and Argentina's Independiente twice for the world crown. But even they could not soak up pressure indefinitely. In 1966 Real Madrid toppled Inter in the European Cup semi-finals, Celtic repeated the trick a year later in a memorable Lisbon final, and Herrera was lured away to Roma. Not until the late 1980s could Inter recapture their international and domestic allure, when West German midfielder Lothar Matthäus drove them to the 1989 league title, following up with success in the 1991 UEFA Cup.

JUVENTUS
TURIN, ITALY

Founded: 1897
Stadium: Delle Alpi (71,012)
Colors: Black and white stripes/white
League: 22
Cup: 8
World Club Cup: 1985
European Cup: 1985
European Cup-winners' Cup: 1984
UEFA Cup: 1977, 1990, 1993
Supercup: 1984

Juventus was founded by a group of Italian students who decided to adopt red as the color for their shirts. In 1903, however, when the club was six years old, one of the committee members was so impressed on a trip to England by Notts County's black-and-white stripes that he bought a set of shirts to take home to Turin. In the 1930s Juventus laid the foundations for their legend, winning the Italian league championship five times in a row. Simultaneously they also reached the semifinals of the Mitropa Cup on four occasions and supplied Italy's World Cup-winning teams with five players in 1934 and three in 1938. Goalkeeper Gianpiero Combi, from Juventus, was Italy's victorious captain in 1934, just as another Juventus goalkeeper, Dino Zoff, would be in 1982.

After the war, the Zebras (after the colors of their shirts) scoured the world for talent to match their imported rivals. First came the Danes, John and Karl Hansen, then the Argentine favorite Omar Sivori and the Gentle Giant from Wales, John Charles, followed by Spanish inside-forward Luis Del Sol and French inspiration Michel Platini. In 1971 they lost the Fairs Cup Final to Leeds United on the away goals rule but, six years later, it was the same regulation which brought Juventus victory over Bilbao in the UEFA Cup Final.

In 1982 no fewer than six Juventus players featured in Italy's World Cup winning line-up, and Cabrini, Tardelli, Scirea, Gentile and Paolo Rossi helped Juve win the 1984 European Cup-winners' Cup and the 1985 European Cup. Seeking new magic in the 1990s, Juventus paid huge fees for Italy's Roberto Baggio and Gianluca Vialli. Baggio soon began repaying his world record $13 million fee with outstanding displays, but Vialli had two injury-filled seasons.

DINO ZOFF *Juventus record-breaker*

Coaches

GIOVANNI TRAPATTONI

Coach of Milan, Juventus, Internazionale, Bayern Munich (born March 17, 1939)

Trapattoni was a wing-half in the late 1950s and early 1960s whose sure tackling and soccer brain earned him a reputation as the only man who could play Pele out of a game by fair means rather than foul. After winning two European Cups with Milan, Trapattoni retired to a post on the youth coaching staff. In time he became first-team caretaker before moving to Juventus with whom he became the most successful club coach of all time. Inside eight years, Trapattoni guided Juve to the World Club Cup, European Cup, European Cup-winners' Cup, UEFA Cup, European Supercup, seven Italian championships and two national cups. Nothing further in his career, either at Internazionale or after returning controversially to Juventus, matched that golden decade. He became coach of Bayern Munich for the 1994–95 season.

IGOR BELANOV *Kiev's European Footballer of the Year in 1986*

KIEV DYNAMO
UKRAINE

Founded: 1927
Stadium: Republic (100,100)
Colors: White/blue
League: 1 Ukraine, 13 Soviet
Cup: 1 Ukraine, 9 Soviet
European Cup-winners' Cup: 1975, 1986
Supercup: 1975

Kiev was the finest exponent of Soviet soccer from the late 1960s to the early 1990s, before the collapse of the USSR led to their seceding to become the first, though financially rickety, champions of the new, independent Ukraine. The club's history, though, must be read in the context of Soviet soccer. It was a founding member of the Soviet top division, yet had to wait until 1961 before they became the first club outside Moscow to land the title. Soon they were dominating the Soviet scene. They achieved the league and cup "double" five years later and went on to a record-equaling hat trick of league titles. Key players were midfielders Iosif Sabo and Viktor Serebryanikov and forwards Valeri Porkuyan and Anatoli Bishovets. Porkuyan starredat the 1966 World Cup finals in England, and Bishovets four years later in Mexico.

In 1975 Kiev became the first Soviet team to win a European trophy when they beat Ferencvaros of Hungary by 3–0 in the Cup-winners' Cup. Later that year they clinched the league title for the seventh time in 14 seasons. It was then that the Soviet federation grew too demanding, saddling the Ukraine club en bloc with all the national team matches and, when the Olympic qualifying team began to falter, with their schedule as well. It all proved too much. But that did not deter Kiev coach Valeri Lobanovsky from going back to square one and painstakingly developing another formidable team around record goal-scorer Oleg Blokhin. In 1985, the renewed Kiev stormed to another league and cup "double." A year later, Kiev charmed their way to the European Cup-winners' Cup as well, defeating Atletico Madrid 3–0 in the final. Igor Belanov earned the accolade of European Footballer of the Year.

LIVERPOOL
ENGLAND

Founded: 1892
Stadium: Anfield (45,000)
Colors: All red
League: 18
FA Cup: 5
League Cup: 4
European Cup: 1977, 1978, 1981, 1984
UEFA Cup: 1973, 1976
Supercup: 1977

Liverpool: a name which says so much, in pop music, in sport — specifically, in soccer. The Beatles may have moved on, split up, become part of the memorabilia of a major industrial center in the north-west of England. But the soccer club goes on, purveyor of dreams not only for the thousands who fill the seats and the condemned terracing but for the millions on Merseyside who achieved international acclaim through their soccer players.

For years the proud boast of English soccer's hierarchy had been that such was the depth of talent that no one club would ever dominate the championship in the manner of Juventus in Italy, Real Madrid in Spain or Benfica in Portugal. Then, along came Bill Shankly. He was appointed coach of shabby, run-down, half-forgotten Liverpool FC in December, 1959. In two-and-a-half years he won promotion; the purchases of left-half Billy Stevenson and outside-left Peter Thompson, both for small sums, secured the League Championship in 1964; and a year later they had won the FA Cup. Those years and the succeeding 20 brought success on the greatest scale at home and abroad.

The secret was continuity. Shankly was succeeded in the coach's tracksuit by his former assistant coaches, Bob Paisley and Joe Fagan. A new player would be bought young and cheap, consigned to the reserves for a year to learn "the Liverpool way," and then slotted in to replace one of the fading heroes whose game had lost its edge. Thus the generation of Emlyn Hughes, Ian St John, Roger Hunt and Ron Yeats gave way to the likes of Kevin Keegan and John Toshack, who were followed in turn by Alan Hansen, Kenny Dalglish and Graeme Souness, the last two of whom also later succeeded to Anfield coachship. Under Dalglish Liverpool became in 1986 only the third English club to achieve the League and Cup "double" this century — a wonderful achievement on the field which was tarnished by the disasters off it, first at the Heysel stadium in 1985 and then at Hillsborough in 1989.

MANCHESTER UNITED
ENGLAND

Founded: 1878
Stadium: Old Trafford (46,000)
Colors: Red/white
League: 9
Cup: 8
European Cup: 1968
European Cup-winners' Cup: 1991
Supercup: 1991

Manchester United was an appropriate leader of English re-entry into Europe in 1990, after the five-year Heysel disaster ban, since United had been the first English club to play in Europe in the mid-1950s. Chelsea had been barred from entering the inaugural European Cup by the FA and League. The Establishment also tried to prevent Matt Busby's United entering it in 1956–57, but they ignored the ban and reached the semifinals of the European Cup in both 1957 (losing to eventual winners Real Madrid) and in 1958. On the latter occasion they lost to Milan with a somewhat makeshift team which had been hastily pulled together in the wake of the Munich air disaster in which eight players, including skipper Roger Byrne and the inspirational young Duncan Edwards, had been killed.

It took United ten years to recover, in international terms. Thus it was in May 1968 that Busby's European quest was rewarded as United defeated Benfica 4–1 in extra time at Wembley. Bobby Charlton, a Munich survivor along with defender Bill Foulkes and coach Busby, scored twice to secure the club's most emotional triumph. Busby had been a Scotland international wing-half with Manchester City in the 1930s and took over United when war damage to Old Trafford meant playing home games at Maine Road. Yet within three years Busby had constructed a team that scored a superb FA Cup Final victory over Blackpool and created the entertaining, attacking style which has been mandatory for the club ever since. In the 1960s United boasted not only Charlton but great crowd-pullers such as Scotland's Denis Law and Northern Ireland's George Best. Later came England's long-serving skipper Bryan Robson, who was still in harness in 1993 when United, under Alex Ferguson, regained the English League title for the first time in 26 years.

Robson retired in 1994, but not before United became the fourth team this century to complete the Double of League and FA Cup, the latter a 4–0 defeat of Chelsea.

Coaches

Bill Shankly

Manager of Carlisle, Grimsby, Workington, Huddersfield and Liverpool (born September 2, 1913; died September 29, 1981)

Shankly played for Carlisle, Preston and Scotland in the 1930s and returned to Carlisle to begin his coaching career. He took over a faded Liverpool in the Second Division in December, 1959, and there was no stopping either him or the club once promotion had been achieved in 1962. Shankly's dry humor struck a chord with Anfield fans. He brought them League, FA Cup and League successes in consecutive seasons, signed some of the club's greatest servants and laid foundations for further success both on and off the field. Shankly had an eye for youthful talent — which he squirreled away in the reserves until they were ready — and for coaching expertise. Later coaches Bob Paisley, Joe Fagan and Roy Evans came out of Shankly's fabled "boot-room".

Coaches

Matt Busby

Manager of Manchester United (born May 26, 1909; died January 20, 1994)

Busby was a Scottish international wing-half who played before the Second World War for Liverpool and Manchester City and took over as coach at Manchester United in 1945 when air raid damage had reduced Old Trafford to near-rubble. Such was his gift for coaching that, within three years, he had created the first of three memorable teams. His 1948 side won the FA Cup, his Busby Babes of the mid-1950s went twice to the European Cup semifinals before being wrecked by the Munich air disaster, and his third team completed the European quest with victory over Benfica in 1968's European Cup final. Busby's love of entertaining soccer inspired some of British soccer's greatest talents —from Johnny Carey and Duncan Edwards to Bobby Charlton, Denis Law and George Best.

DOOMED *Marseille's Basile Boli, scorer of the only goal, robs Milan's Marco Van Basten in the French club's ill-fated 1993 European Cup final triumph*

MARSEILLE
FRANCE

Founded: 1898
Stadium: Vélodrome (46,000)
Colors: All white
League: 9 (1993 title revoked)
Cup: 10
European Cup: 1993 (but revoked)

No French club had ever won the European Cup before Marseille; and no one will ever forget what happened when they did. Millionaire entrepreneur Bernard Tapie, the club's high-profile president, had invested millions of dollars in pursuit of European glory. Unfortunately, some of Marseille's money had been used to try to fix matches along the road — if not in Europe then in the French championship. Barely had Marseille finished celebrating their Cup-winning 1–0 victory over Milan in Munich in May, 1993, than it emerged that midfielder Jean-Jacques Eydelie had offered cash to three players from Valenciennes to "go easy" on Marseille in a league fixture a week earlier. Marseille was duly banned from their European defense in 1993–94, the French federation revoked their league championship title and they were subsequently further penalized with enforced relegation.

Marseille's first championship had been celebrated back in 1929. Personalities in those days included Emmanuel Aznar (scorer of eight goals in a 20–2 league win over Avignon) and three English coaches in Peter Farmer, Victor Gibson and Charlie Bell. After the war Marseille soon won the championship in 1948, but heavy expenditure on big-name foreigners such as Yugoslavia's Josip Skoblar, Sweden's Roger Magnusson and Brazil's Jairzinho and Paulo César drew only sporadic rewards, and Marseille had slipped into the Second Division by the time ambitious businessman-turned-politician Tapie took over the helm in 1985. Marseille immediately gained promotion and then, thanks to the attacking genius of Jean-Pierre Papin, Enzo Francescoli and Chris Waddle, swept to four league titles in a row. They also suffered the agony of a penalty shoot-out defeat by Red Star Belgrade in the 1991 European Cup Final.

MILAN
ITALY

Founded: 1899
Stadium: Meazza (85,847)
Colors: Red and black stripes/white
League: 14
Cup: 4
World Club Cup: 1969, 1989, 1990
European Cup: 1963, 1969, 1989, 1990, 1994
European Cup-winners' Cup: 1968, 1973
Supercup: 1989, 1990

Milan's domination of the European club game in the late 1980s and the early 1990s was achieved on a unique stage which would appear to represent the pattern of the future for a sport increasingly controlled by the intertwined commercial interests and demands of big business and television. In Milan's case, all these strands were in the hands of a puppet-master supreme in media magnate and now Prime Minister of Italy, Silvio Berlusconi. He had come to the rescue in 1986, investing $30 million to save Milan from bankruptcy and turn the club into a key player in his commercial empire. Milan had been one of the founders of the Italian championship back in 1898, but until the Second World War they tended to be in the shadow of neighbors Inter. After the war Milan achieved spectacular success, largely thanks to the Swedish inside-forward trio of Gunnar Gren, Gunnar Nordahl and Nils Liedholm. They also paid a then world record fee for Uruguay's Juan Schiaffino. They were dangerous rivals to Real Madrid in the new European Cup — losing narrowly to the Span-

SAFETY FIRST *Milan's Alessandro Costacurta (right) clears his lines in the 1993 European Cup final*

ish club in the semi-finals in 1956 and then only in extra time in the final of 1958. That was the year Milan's scouts first saw the teenage "Golden Boy" Gianni Rivera, whose cultured inside-forward play and partnership with José Altafini inspired Milan to a European Cup victory in 1963 over Benfica. Rivera was Milan's figurehead as they won the European Cup again in 1969 and the European Cup-winners' Cup in 1968 and 1973. But even his charisma could not save the club from the scandals and financial disasters inflicted by a string of disastrous presidents. That was where Berlusconi came in, providing the money and the men — coach Arrigo Sacchi, superstars Ruud Gullit, Marco Van Basten, Frank Rijkaard and Franco Baresi — who turned Milan into a world-beating millionaires' club.

MILLONARIOS
BOGOTA, COLOMBIA

Founded: 1938
Stadium: El Campin — Estadio Distrital Nemesio Camacho (57,000)
Colors: Blue/white
League: 13

Millonarios remains a legendary name, if only because of the manner in which they led Colombia's fledgeling professional clubs into the El Dorado rebellion which lured star players from all over the world in the late 1940s and the early 1950s. Many famous names in the game made their reputations there. The then club president, Alfonso Senior, later became president of the Colombian federation and a highly-respected FIFA delegate. Star player Alfredo Di Stefano used Millonarios as a springboard to greatness with Real Madrid.

Taking massive advantage of an Argentine players' strike, Millonarios led the flight from FIFA and the chase for great players — not only Di Stefano but the acrobatic goalkeeper Julio Cozzi, attacking center-half Nestor Rossi and attacking general Adolfo Pedernera. Nicknamed the "Blue Ballet," they dominated the pirate league and, when an amnesty was negotiated with FIFA, made lucrative "farewell" tours in Europe. Credit for the club's name goes to a journalist, Camacho Montayo. The club had been founded as an amateur side, Deportivo Municipal, in 1938. But as they pushed for a professional league, so Montayo wrote: "The Municipalistas have become the Millonarios." The name stuck. Millonarios remain a leading club but, despite appearing frequently in the South American Club Cup, the glory days have never been repeated.

MOSCOW DYNAMO
RUSSIA

Founded: 1923
Stadium: Dynamo (51,000)
Colors: White/blue
League: 11 Soviet
Cup: 6 Soviet

Dynamo is probably the most famous of all Russian clubs, having been the first Soviet side to venture out beyond the Iron Curtain in the 1940s and 1950s. Also, they were fortunate enough to possess, in goalkeeper Lev Yashin, one of the greatest personalities in the modern game — a show-stopper wherever he went.

Dynamo's origins go back to the start of soccer in Russia, introduced by the Charnock brothers at their cotton mills towards the end of the last century. The team won successive Moscow championships under the name Morozovsti and, after the Russian Revolution, was taken over first by the electrical trades union and then by the police. Thus the 1923 date marks the formal setting-up of Moscow Dynamo rather than the foundation of the original club. Immediately after the end of the Second World War, Dynamo became a legend as a result of a four-match British tour in the winter of 1945. They drew 3–3 with Chelsea and 2–2 with Rangers, thrashed Cardiff 10–1 and beat a reinforced Arsenal 4–3 in thick fog. Inside-forward Constantin Beskov later became national coach, but it was goalkeeper Alexei "Tiger" Khomich whose reputation lasted long after he had retired to become a sports press photographer. He was succeeded in the team by an even greater goalkeeper in Yashin, who was to become the first Soviet player to be nominated as European Footballer of the Year. Given Dynamo's leadership, it was appropriate that, in 1972, they became the first Soviet team to reach a European final. But their 3–2 defeat by Rangers in Barcelona also stands as the high point of their modern achievement. Back home, Dynamo were pushed back down the ranks by neighbors Moscow Spartak and the fast-rising Kiev Dynamo.

MOSCOW SPARTAK
RUSSIA

Founded: 1922
Stadium: Olympic-Lenin/Luzhniki (102,000)
Colors: Red and white/white
League: 2 Russia; 12 Soviet
Cup: 10 Soviet

Moscow Spartak, champions of Russia for both the first two seasons after the collapse of the Soviet Union, faces an enormous challenge in the years ahead. Spartak was a power in the land under the old system, but those were the days when players were not allowed to move abroad. Now Spartak must maintain their domestic command and compete effectively in Europe in an "open" transfer society. This is all the more challenging because Spartak had, for years, represented the Party line. They play their home matches in the Olympic-Lenin stadium in the

Luzhniki suburb of Moscow, and their past heroes included such officially-approved characters as 1950s' top scorer Nikita Simonian (a club record-holder with 133 goals) and left-half Igor Netto (another club record-holder with 367 appearances). Spartak's best season in European competitions was 1990–91, when they beat both Napoli and Real Madrid to reach the semi-finals of the European Cup, before falling 5–1 on aggregate to Marseille.

For years the club had been ruled by the most respected members of the managerial old guard in veteran administrator Nikolai Starostin and former national coach Constantin Beskov. Starostin, a Spartak player in the club's early days, stayed on after the political upheaval, but Beskov handed over the coaching mantle to his former pupil and international full-back, Oleg Romantsev. Despite the loss of sweeper Vasili Kulkov and midfielders Igor Shalimov and Alexander Mostovoi, Romantsev kept Spartak on top of the table. New heroes were left-back and captain Viktor Onopko, versatile Igor Lediakhov and the young forward Mikhail Beschastnikh. Not only did Spartak win the 1992 and 1993 Russian league titles; they also won — in both 1993 and 1994 — the pre-season CIS Cup, contested by the champions of all the former Soviet states.

NACIONAL
MONTEVIDEO, URUGUAY

Founded: 1899
Stadium: Parque Central (20,000) and Centenario (73,609)
Colors: White/blue
League: 35
World Club Cup: 1971, 1980, 1988
South American Club Cup: 1971, 1980, 1988
South American Recopa: 1988
Inter-American Cup: 1971

Nacional and Penarol are the two great clubs of Uruguay and bitter rivals on both the domestic and international stages. Nacional was formed from a merger of the Montevideo Football Club and the Uruguay Athletic Club, and in 1903 was chosen to line up as Uruguay's national team against Argentina in Buenos Aires. Nacional won 3–2 and has enjoyed the international limelight ever since.

Penarol won the first South American Club Cup in 1960, but Nacional soon set about catching up: runners-up three times in the 1960s, they first won the cup by defeating Estudiantes de La Plata in 1971. That led Nacional on to the World Club Cup, where they beat Panathinaikos of Greece (European title-holders Ajax having refused to compete). The two decisive goals in Montevideo were scored by Nacional's former Argentine World Cup spearhead, Luis Artime. It was nine years before Nacional regained those crowds. This time they had a new center-forward in Waldemar Victorino, who scored the only goal in the 1980 South American Club Cup triumph over Internacional of Brazil, and then the lone strike which decided the world final against Nottingham Forest in Tokyo. By the time Nacional regained the crown in 1988 Victorino had left for Italy, just as so many Uruguayan stars before and since.

VICTOR ONOPKO *New hero of Moscow Spartak in the post-Communist era*

Back in the 1930s Nacional sold center-half Michele Andreolo to Italy, with whom he won the 1938 World Cup. But Nacional quickly replaced him and, from 1939 to 1943, achieved what is nostalgically recalled as their Quinquenio de Oro: their golden five years. Nacional won the league in each of those seasons with a legendary forward line built around the prolific Argentine marksman Atilio Garcia. He was Uruguay's top scorer eight times and ended his career with a record of 464 goals in 435 games. Under Scottish coach William Reasdale, Nacional also celebrated an 8–0 thrashing of the old enemy from Penarol.

PENAROL
MONTEVIDEO, URUGUAY

Founded: 1891
Stadium: Las Acacias (15,000) and Centenario (73,609)
Colors: Black and yellow stripes/black
League: 40
World Club Cup: 1961, 1966, 1982
South American Club Cup: 1960, 1961, 1966, 1982, 1987
Inter-American Cup: 1969

Penarol was the first club to win the World Club Cup three times, but their success is no modern phenomenon. Penarol has been the pre-eminent power in Uruguayan soccer since its earliest days, providing a host of outstanding players for Uruguay's 1930 and 1950 World Cup-winning teams. Their own international awakening came in 1960, when Penarol won the inaugural South American Club Cup (the Copa Libertadores). They were thrashed by Real Madrid in the

World Club Cup, but made amends the next year with victory over Benfica. It was no less than the talents of players such as William Martinez, center-half Nestor Goncalves and striker Alberto Spencer deserved. Penarol regained the world club crown in 1966, at the expense of Real Madrid, and then again in 1982 when they beat Aston Villa in Tokyo. By now Penarol had unearthed another superstar in center-forward Fernando Morena. He was the latest in a long line of great players, which included the nucleus of the Uruguayan national team who shocked Brazil by winning the 1950 World Cup. Goalkeeper Roque Maspoli — later World Club Cup-winning coach in 1966 — captain and center-half Obdulio Varela, right-winger Alcide Ghiggia, center-forward Oscar Miguez, right-half Rodriguez Andrade and inside-right Juan Schiaffino all came from Penarol. Schiaffino was the greatest of all.

Penarol had been founded as the Central Uruguayan Railway Cricket Club in 1891, and changed their name in 1913 as the British influence waned. The railways sidings and offices were near the Italian Pignarolo district — named after the landowner Pedro Pignarolo — and so the Spanish style of the name was adopted for the club.

FC PORTO OPORTO, PORTUGAL

Founded: 1893
Stadium: Das Antas (76,000)
Colors: Blue and white stripes/white
League: 13
Cup: 11
World Club Cup: 1987
European Cup: 1987
Supercup: 1987

Porto was always considered to be No. 3 in the Portuguese soccer hierarchy until their thrilling European Cup victory over Bayern Munich in Vienna in 1987. Events then and since have insured that, while their trophy count may not yet match those of Benfica and Sporting, Porto are clearly seen as an alternative center of power

PINTO *Porto's European Cup-winner*

in the domestic game. Porto beat Bayern with the Polish goalkeeper Mlynarczyk, Brazilians Celso and Juary, and Algerian winger Rabah Madjer supporting Portugal's own wonderboy, Paulo Futre. But that was entirely appropriate since, in the early 1930s, Porto had been pioneers in the international transfer market.

They began by bringing in two Yugoslavs, and that ambition was reflected in Porto's initial championship successes in 1938 and 1939. In those days Porto's home was the old, rundown Campo da Constituciao. Now, as befits a club with European Cup-winning pedigree, home is the impressive, 76,000-capacity Estadio das Antas.

Not only has Porto won the Champions' Cup; they also finished runners-up to Juventus in the European Cup-winners' Cup in 1984. The creative force behind the club's progress in the 1980s was the late José Maria Pedroto. He led Porto to the cup in 1977 and league title in 1978 and 1979. After a brief interregnum under Austrian Hermann Stessl, Pedroto was recalled in January 1982. Later his work was carried on by his pupil, former national team center-forward Artur Jorge, who coached Porto to their 1987 European title. Later, under Brazilian Carlos Alberto da Silva, later succeeded by Bobby Robson, Porto enhanced their standing as members of the European establishment when they competed in the inaugural Champions League in 1992–93.

PHILIPS SV EINDHOVEN, HOLLAND

Founded: 1913
Stadium: Philips (28,000)
Colors: Red and white stripes/white
League: 13
Cup: 6
European Cup: 1988
UEFA Cup: 1978

PSV equalled the achievements of Celtic (in 1967) and Ajax Amsterdam (in 1972) when they defeated Benfica in a penalty shoot-out to win the 1988 European Cup. Only those other two clubs had previously secured the treble of European Cup and domestic league and cup all in the same season. Remarkably, PSV achieved all they did despite having sold their finest player, Ruud Gullit, to Milan at the start of the season for a world record $9 million. The money was, however, invested wisely to secure the best players from Holland, Denmark and Belgium.

Such success was the reward for a long wait since PSV had been one of the invited entrants in the inaugural European Cup in 1955–56, when they crashed 1–0, 1–6 to Rapid Vienna in the first round. Surprisingly, considering PSV's position as the sports club of the giant Philips electrics corporation, they were long outshone by Ajax and Feyenoord. For years the Philips company took comparatively little interest in PSV, even though an estimated 40,000 of the 200,000 urban population of Eindhoven work directly or indirectly for Philips. Only in the past decade has Philips become seriously involved with club policy and finance.

PSV had won the 1976 UEFA Cup without much fanfare. But ten years later, realising the potential to be reaped from soccer sponsorship, the company came up with the funds, and was duly rewarded two years later with the European Cup. In 1992, taking the process a stage further, the club changed its name in order to promote itself outside Holland as Philips SV (while Dutch sponsorship regulations required it to stick with the PSV abbreviation in Holland).

RANGERS GLASGOW, SCOTLAND

Founded: 1873
Stadium: Ibrox Park (44,500)
Colors: Blue/white
League: 43
Cup: 26
League cup: 18
European Cup-winners' Cup: 1972

Rangers is one half of the "Old Firm" — its rivalry with Celtic having dominated Scottish soccer for a century. Yet Rangers has never extended that power into Europe, their only prize from virtual non-stop international competition being the 1972 Cup-winners' Cup Final victory over Moscow Dynamo. Not that Rangers' history is short on proud moments. One particularly glorious era was the 1920s, when Rangers' heroes included the legendary "Wee Blue Devil," Alan Morton. His career overlapped with that of Bob McPhail, whose 233 goals in 354 league matches remains a club record. After the Second World War Rangers' success was built on the so-called "Iron Curtain" defense, starring George Young and Willie Woodburn, with the goals created by Willie Waddell for Willie Thornton.

In the 1960s, Rangers endured heavy European defeats at the hands of Eintracht Frankfurt, Tottenham and Real Madrid. The start of the 1970s was a time of mixed emotions: 1971 saw the Ibrox disaster, when 66 fans died in a stairway crush at the end of a game against Celtic. Then, a year later, Rangers' European Cup-winners' Cup triumph was immediately followed by a European ban because of the way their celebrating fans ran amok in Barcelona. The upturn began in November, 1985, when Lawrence Marlboro bought control of the club. He brought in Graeme Souness as player-coach. In 1988 steel magnate David Murray bought Rangers, and Souness revolutionized their image by buying 18 English players and smashing the club's traditional Protestants-only ethic with his $2.25 million capture of Catholic Mo Johnston.

BOTH SIDES NOW *Mo Johnston*

UNDER PRESSURE *Rapid's Kurt Garger clears the ball from Graeme Sharp of Everton during the Austrians's 1985 European Cup-winners' Cup final defeat*

RAPID VIENNA
AUSTRIA

Founded: 1899
Stadium: Hanappi (19,600)
Colors: Green and white/green
League: 29
Cup: 13

Rapid was founded as the 1st Arbeiter-Fussballklub (First Workers Football Club) but, on changing their name, also set about refining the short-passing style of the "Vienna School" to such good effect that they won the championship eight times between 1912 and 1923. The success story did not end there. In 1930 Rapid became the first Austrian club to win the Mitropa Cup, defeating powerful Sparta Prague 2–0, 2–3 in the final. Several of Rapid's key players were members of the "Wunderteam," the national side who finished fourth in the 1934 World Cup under the captaincy of Rapid center-half Pepe Smistik.

Four years later Austria was swallowed up into Greater Germany, and the Austrian league was incorporated into the Greater German championship. To the mischievous delight of their fans, Rapid not only won the German Cup in 1938 (3–2 against FSV Frankfurt in the final) but also the German championship in 1941. On a day which has entered soccer legend Rapid hit back from 3–0 down to defeat an outstanding Schalke side 4–3 before a 90,000 crowd in the Olympic stadium in Berlin. Their hero was center-forward Franz "Bimbo" Binder, whose hat-trick was crowned by the winning goal when he hammered a free kick through the defensive wall. Binder ended a great career with 1,006 goals and later became club coach.

Many of Rapid's old heroes returned as coaches, among them Karl Rappan (who developed the Swiss Bolt system), Edi Fruhwirth and Karl Decker. Great players in the post-war years included wing-half Gerhard Hanappi — an architect by profession, who laid out the designs for the club stadium — tough-tackling defender Ernst Happel and another prolific goal-scoring center-forward in Hans Krankl. He led Rapid's attack on their one appearance in a European final, the 3–1 defeat by Everton in the 1985 Cup-winners' Cup decider in Rotterdam.

REAL MADRID
SPAIN

Founded: 1902
Stadium: Santiago Bernabeu (105,000)
Colors: All white
League: 25
Cup: 17
World Club Cup: 1966
European Cup: 1956, 1957, 1958, 1959, 1960, 1966
UEFA Cup: 1985, 1986

What else is there left to say about Real Madrid? Six times champions of Europe, 25 times champions of Spain — both record achievements. They have also won the World Club Cup, two UEFA Cups and 16 Spanish cups, which add up to a soccer honors degree for the club founded by students as Madrid FC. (The Real prefix, meaning Royal, was a title bestowed on the club later by King Alfonso XIII.) Madrid was not only among the founders of the Spanish cup and league competitions: it was also the Madrid president, Carlos Padros, who attended on Spain's behalf the inaugural meeting of FIFA in Paris in 1904. In the late 1920s Madrid launched a policy of buying big. They paid a then Spanish record fee for Ricardo Zamora, still revered as the greatest Spanish goalkeeper of all time.

The Spanish Civil War left Madrid's Chamartin stadium in ruins. At the time the club had no money, but boasted one of the greatest visionaries in European soccer history. He was Santiago Bernabeu, a lawyer who had been, in turn, player, team coach and secretary, and was now club president. Bernabeu launched an audacious public appeal which raised the cash to build the wonderful stadium which now bears his name. The huge crowds which flocked in provided the cash to build the team who dominated the first five years of the European Cup. Argentine-born center-forward Alfredo Di Stefano was the star of stars, though Bernabeu surrounded him with illustrious teammates such as Hungary's Ferenc Puskas, France's Ramond Kopa, Uruguay's José Santamaria and Brazil's Didi. They set impossibly high standards for all the players and teams who followed. Madrid won the European Cup again in 1966 and the UEFA Cup twice in the 1980s, but even later superstars such as Pirri, Santillana, Juanito, Hugo Sanchez and Emilio Butragueño would occasionally complain that nothing they achieved would ever be quite enough. The 1960 team had been, if anything, too good.

RED STAR BELGRADE YUGOSLAVIA

Founded: 1945
Stadium: Crvena Zvezda (Red Star) (97,422)
Colors: Red and white stripes/white
League: 19
Cup: 13
World Club Cup: 1991
European Cup: 1991

This may be the most schizophrenic club in the world. In Germany they are known as Roter Stern; in France as Etoile Rouge; in Spain as Estrella Roja; in Italy as Stella Rossa; in Serbo-Croat it's Fudbalski Klub Crvena Zvezda; in English, of course, Red Star Belgrade. Under whichever name, the 1991 European and world club champions stood revered as one of the pillars of the worldwide establishment until civil strife in the former Yugoslavia led to international suspension for both country and clubs. The consequences for Red Star threatened to be disastrous, since millions of dollars paid in transfer fees for their star players were suddenly frozen in banks around Europe.

But Red Star is no stranger to disaster, having been the last team to play Manchester United's "Busby Babes" before the Munich air disaster. Red Star fought back from 3–0 down to draw 3–3, but lost on aggregate despite all the efforts of balletic goalkeeper Vladimir Beara, gypsy midfielder Dragoslav Sekularac and dynamic striker Bora Kostic (scorer of a club record 157 goals in 256 league games). All three men later moved abroad, members of an ongoing exodus of more than 40 players including stars like Dragan Dzajic (to Bastia), Dragan Stojkovic (to Marseille), Robert Prosinecki (to Real Madrid) and Darko Pancev (to Internazionale). This explains, perhaps, why Red Star, for all their talent, boast only one victory in the European Cup (the 1991 penalty shoot-out victory over Marseille in Bari) and one runners-up spot in the UEFA Cup (beaten on away goals by Borussia Mönchengladbach in 1979).

Red Star was formally set up by students of Belgrade University after the war. They play their home matches in the so-called "Marakana," which was the first stadium in eastern Europe to host a mainstream European final, when Ajax beat Juventus in the 1973 European Cup.

ROBERT PROSINECKI *Outstanding graduate of the Red Star soccer "university"*

RIVER PLATE BUENOS AIRES, ARGENTINA

Founded: 1901
Stadium: Antonio Liberti/Monumental (76,000)
Colors: White with red sash/black
League: 21
World Club Cup: 1986
South American Club Cup: 1986
Inter-American Cup: 1986

River Plate is one of the two giants of Argentine soccer, Boca Juniors being the other. Traditionally the club from the rich side of Buenos Aires, River was a founding member of the first division in 1908, then took a leading role in the "war" which accompanied the introduction of professional soccer in the 1920s. Over the years River has fielded some wonderful teams. In the 1930s they boasted Bernabe Ferreyra, a legendary figure in Argentine soccer; in the late 1940s their high-scoring forward line was so feared and admired they were nicknamed "La Maquina" (The Machine). The names of Muñoz, Moreno, Peder-nera, Labruna and Loustau mean little outside Argentina today, but there they inspire awe like Real Madrid in Europe.

Later River produced more great players: Alfredo Di Stefano, who would one day turn Real Madrid into possibly the greatest team of all time; Omar Sivori, who would form a wonderful partnership with John Charles after joining Juventus; and then 1978 World Cup winners Ubaldo Fillol, Daniel Passarella, Leopoldo Luque and Mario Kempes. In 1986 they were joined in River's Hall of Fame by the likes of goalkeeper Nery Pumpido, center-back Oscar Ruggeri and schemer Norberto Alonso, after victory in the South American Club Cup provided River with formal confirmation of their lofty status. River really should have succeeded to the crown years earlier, but was unlucky runner-up in 1966 to Penarol of Uruguay and in 1976 to Cruzeiro of Brazil. In 1986 they made no mistake, beating America of Colombia, then adding the World Club Cup by defeating Steaua of Romania 1–0 in Tokyo.

SANTOS
SÃO PAULO, BRAZIL

Founded: 1912
Stadium: Vila Belmiro (20,000)
Colors: All white
São Paulo state league: 15
Brazil championship (incl. Torneo Rio-São Paulo): 5
World Club Cup: 1962, 1963
South American Club Cup: 1962, 1963

The name of Santos will always be synonymous with that of Pele, who played all his mainstream career with the club and returned as a director at the end of 1993 to try to help lift his old club out of the depths of a severe financial and administrative crisis.

Santos had been founded by three members of the Americano club, who stayed home in the port of Santos when their club moved to São Paulo. Santos joined the São Paulo state championship in 1916, became only the second Brazilian club to embrace professionalism in 1933, but did not hit the headlines until the mid-1950s. Then, to organize a host of talented youngsters, they signed the 1950 World Cup veteran, Jair da Rosa Pinto, and discovered the 15-year-old Pele.

To say that Santos was a one-man team, as it often appeared from the publicity, would be unfair. Santos harvested millions of dollars from whistle-stop friendly match tours around the world and reinvested heavily in surrounding Pele with fine players: World Cup winners in goalkeeper Gilmar, center-back Mauro and wing-half Zito; an outside-left with a ferocious shot in Pepe; and the precocious young talents of right-winger Dorval, schemer Mengalvio and center-forward Coutinho, Pele's so-called "twin" with whom he established an almost telepathic relationship on the field. Santos was more than a soccer team; they were a touring circus.

Sadly, the constant touring and playing burned out many young players before they had a chance to establish their talent. But not before Santos had scaled the competitive heights as

PELE *The man who "made" Santos*

Pele inspired their victories in the South American Club Cup and the World Club Cup in both 1962 and 1963.

One more year and it was all over. Independiente beat Santos in the 1964 South American Club Cup semi-finals, and the spell had been broken. Santos went on touring and raking in cash, capitalizing on Pele's name, for as long as they could. But further competitive achievement was rare and, by the early 1970s, much of the money appeared to have vanished as well.

SÃO PAULO
BRAZIL

Founded: 1935
Stadium: Morumbi (150,000)
Colors: White with a red and black hoop/white
São Paulo state league: 17
Brazil championship (incl. Torneo Rio-São Paulo): 4
World Club Cup: 1992, 1993
South American Club Cup: 1992, 1993

São Paulo's victories over Barcelona and Milan in the 1992 and 1993 World Club Cups in Tokyo left no doubt about which was the finest club team in the world — for all the European hype which had surrounded the Italian champions. Those victories also underlined the depth of talent available to São Paulo, since their key midfielder, Rai (younger brother of 1986 World Cup star Socrates), had been sold to French club Paris Saint-Germain in the summer of 1993. Dual success also enhanced the reputation of coach Tele Santana, Brazil's World Cup manager in 1982 and 1986 and one of the most eloquent and down-to-earth of soccer coaches and analysts.

São Paulo is, even so, a comparative newcomer — having been founded in 1935, at a time when the likes of River Plate, Penarol and the rest were already well-established powers in their own lands. The club was formed from a merger between CA Paulistano and AA Palmeiras. A leading light was Paulo Machado de Carvalho, who would later, as a senior administrator, contribute behind the scenes to Brazil's World Cup hat trick.

Within a decade of being founded, São Paulo developed into the strongest team in the country, winning the state title five times in the 1940s. They imported Argentine inside-forward Antonio Sastre, and the continuing pressure of success led to the construction of the 150,000-capacity Morumbi stadium — the world's largest club-owned sports arena.

In the 1960s São Paulo had to take a back seat to Santos. In 1974 they reached their first South American Club Cup Final (losing to Argentina's Independiente), but it was not until the arrival of Santana, in the late 1980s, that São Paulo emerged from the doldrums. Despite the continuing sale of star players — key defender Ricardo Rocha went to Real Madrid — São Paulo secured three state league titles in four years, used the cash to strengthen their squad and was duly rewarded at the highest level.

São Paulo's World Club Cup victory over the highly rated European giants Milan in Tokyo in 1993 was very impressive, with Cafu and Massaro the outstanding players. São Paulo became the first team to register consecutive wins in the Tokyo final.

Coaches

TELE SANTANA

Coach of Atletico Mineiro, Gremio, Flamengo, Fluminense, Palmeiras (Brazil), Al Ahly (Saudi Arabia), São Paulo FC (Brazil); also Brazil national team (born July 26, 1933)

Santana was an outside-right with Fluminense in the early 1950s but never good enough to challenge Julinho or Garrincha in Brazil's World Cup teams. Instead, he reached the World Cup finals in both 1982 and 1986 as coach of Brazil. Santana's insistence on attacking soccer was criticized as naive after Brazil's failures in, respectively, the second round and quarterfinals. But Santana had the last laugh when he won the World Club Cup twice as coach of São Paulo in 1992 and 1993. Simultaneously, Santana was not afraid to pinpoint high levels of corruption in the Brazilian game as well as poor refereeing for the failure to regain World Cup primacy in the 1980s and early 1990s.

JAN STEJSKAL *Maintaining Sparta's great traditions*

SPARTA PRAGUE
CZECH REPUBLIC

Founded: 1893
Stadium: Letna (36,000)
Colors: All red
League: 20
Cup: 8

Sparta is the most popular club in what is now the Czech Republic, as well as one of the oldest. They were founded as King's Vineyard in 1893, and took the name of Sparta, from one of the states of Ancient Greece, a year later. They were one Europe's great teams preceding the Second World War, winning the Mitropa Cup in the inaugural final in 1927 against Rapid Vienna. Victory over Ferencvaros of Hungary followed in 1935, and they were runners-up in 1936. Sparta's team then included the great inside-left, Oldrich Nejedly. He was a star in the 1934 World Cup, when Czechoslovakia finished runners-up. Again in 1962, when the Czechs next reached the World Cup Final, there were key places in the team for Sparta men such as right-winger Tomas Pospichal and schemer Andrzej Kvasnak.

Sparta suffered after the last war, and was forced to alter their name to Sparta Bratrstvi and then Spartak Sokolovo. But their loyal fans never called them anything but Sparta, and reality was recognized when the club's present title was adopted in 1965. That same year they celebrated their first league title in more than a decade. Memories of the glory days of the Mitropa Cup were revived by the club's run to the European Cup-winners' Cup semi-finals in 1973 and by the impressive 1983–84 UEFA Cup campaign, during which they scored notable victories over Real Madrid and Widzew Lodz. Sparta's continuing domination of the domestic game in the early 1990s was remarkable because, immediately after the World Cup finals, they lost a string of senior internationals, such as goalkeeper Jan Stejskal, defenders Julius Bielik and Michal Bilek, midfield general Ivan Hasek and striker Tomas Skuhravy, the second-top scorer at Italia '90 with five goals.

SPORTING CLUBE
LISBON, PORTUGAL

Founded: 1906
Stadium: José Alvalade (70,000)
Colors: Green and white hoops/white
League: 16
Cup: 15
European Cup-winners' Cup: 1964

Sporting Clube do Portugal last reached a European final back in 1964, when they won the Cup-winners' Cup. Now Benfica's deadly rivals — the grounds are barely a mile apart — dream of the day when they can bring those old heroes out of retirement obscurity to celebrate a European revival. The late 1980s and early 1990s brought Sporting the worst era in their history, an empty decade following the heady 1981–82 season in which they won the league and cup "double" under Englishman Malcolm Allison.

In 1992 the new president, José Sousa Cintra, brought in ex-England coach Bobby Robson to try to recapture the Allison magic. Robson was given only 18 months, however, before former Portugal national coach Carlos Queiros, instead, was given the task of reviving the glories of the 1950s, when Sporting rivaled Benfica as the country's top club and took the championship seven times in eight years.

En route to Sporting's sole European trophy, they beat APOEL Nicosia in the second round first leg by a European record 16–1.In the Final against MTK Budapest, an entertaining match saw Sporting go 1–0 down, recover to lead 2–1 then go 3–2 behind before securing a 3–3 draw and a replay. In Antwerp a single 20th-minute goal from winger Morais, direct from a corner, was enough to win the cup. Their back four of Morais, Batista, José Carlos and Hilario starred on the Portugal team which finished third in the 1966 World Cup finals in England.

The nearest Sporting has since come to European success was in 1990–91, when they reached the UEFA Cup semifinal before falling 0–0, 0–2 to eventual winners Internazionale.

STEAUA
BUCHAREST, ROMANIA

Founded: 1947
Stadium: Steaua (30,000)
Colors: Red/blue
League: 16
Cup: 17
European Cup: 1986

Steaua — the word means "Star" — was one of the army clubs created in eastern Europe after the Communist takeovers of political power. Originally Steaua was known as CCA Bucharest, under which title they won the championship three times in a row in the early 1950s. Later, renamed Steaua, they won the cup five times in six seasons in the late 1960s and early 1970s.

In 1986 Steaua became the first eastern European team to win the European Cup when the beat Barcelona on penalties in Seville. Their penalty stopping hero in the climactic minutes was Helmut Ducadam, whose career ended prematurely by illness soon after. Steaua's power — including the right to sign any player they liked from any other Romanian club — was significantly reduced after the overthrow of the Communist dicatorship of the Ceausescu family.

VASCO DA GAMA
RIO DE JANEIRO, BRAZIL

Founded: 1898 as sailing club, 1915 as football club
Stadium: São Januario (50,000) and Maracana (130,000)
Colors: All white with black sash
Rio state league: 17
Brazil championship (incl. Torneo Rio-São Paulo): 4

Like Flamengo, one of their long-time Rio de Janeiro rivals, Vasco grew from a sailing club — the impetus for soccer coming from former members of a club called Luzitania FC, who had been refused entry into the early Rio de Janeiro state championship because of their "Portuguese-only" policy. Transformed into Vasco da Gama, however, they were elected to the championship in 1915 and had progressed to the top tier by 1923. Support, both vocal and financial, has come to the club over the years from the city's Portuguese community. In spite of their original policies, Vasco quickly became noted for their inclusion of mixed-race players at a time, early in Brazilian soccer's development, when the game was riven by race and class divisions. Vasco led the way, too, by creating the São Januario stadium, which was the first national stadium in Brazil and hosted all major club and national team matches before the building of the Maracana in 1950.

In 1958 Vasco supplied Brazil's World Cup-winning team with center-back Luiz Bellini, the captain, and center-forward Vava. They earned a long-awaited consolation for events eight years earlier when no fewer than eight Vasco players had figured in the Brazilian squad which was just beaten to the World Cup by Uruguay. In the 1960s and 1970s Vasco figured, as ever, among the most powerful of challengers to Fluminense and Flamengo — from whom they controversially signed the popular striker, Bebeto.

LEGENDS

In soccer, as in other sports, the word "great" is over-used and devalued, having been applied to almost any and every fleeting moment of drama or high skill. Thousands of players have been described in terms of ultimate praise. But at the highest echelon of the game there is a small elite group acknowledged by millions of fans as the truly great.

BECKENBAUER
WEST GERMANY

"Kaiser Franz" can boast that he has lifted the World Cup as both captain, in 1974, and coach, in 1990. But his achievements are not the only measure of his true greatness. Beckenbauer's innovative strength was through the revolutionary role of attacking sweeper which, with majestic calm and precision, he introduced in the late 1960s.

CHARLTON
ENGLAND

Bobby Charlton, throughout the world, is probably the most famous English soccer player who has ever thrilled a crowd. He won 106 caps, and his name is synonymous with some of the greatest moments of the modern English game, but also with the highest traditions of sportsmanship, modesty and integrity.

CRUYFF
HOLLAND

Johan Cruyff stands out as not merely the greatest Dutch footballer but one of the greatest players of all time. He made his first-team debut at 17, his goal-scoring international debut at 19 and went on to inspire Ajax and Holland through most of their golden 1970s.

DI STEFANO
SPAIN

Alfredo Di Stefano is reckoned by many to be the greatest soccer player of all. Although Pele's admirers may consider that sacrilege, the millions who wondered at Di Stefano's awesome majesty as he dominated European football in the 1950s and early 1960s will happily concur.

EUSEBIO
PORTUGAL

Eusebio, the greatest Portuguese soccer player in history, did not come from Portugal at all. Born and brought up in Mozambique, then still one of Portugal's African colonies, Eusebio was the first African soccer player to earn a worldwide reputation. Fans around the world took Eusebio to their hearts not only for his ability but for the sportsmanlike way he played.

MARADONA
ARGENTINA

Diego Maradona was not only the world's greatest soccer player throughout the 1980s and early 1990s. He was also the most controversial and the most enigmatic player, unable to appear in public or on a soccer field without arousing the most contrasting of emotions.

MATTHEWS
ENGLAND

Stanley Matthews was the first great soccer player of the modern era. There will be cases made for Billy Wright, Bobby Charlton, Bobby Moore and others but none dominated his particular era as long as the barber's son from Hanley in the Potteries area of the English Midlands.

PELE
BRAZIL

Pele remains one of those great examples and inspirations of world sport: a poor boy taking the world stage at 17, whose talent lifted him to the peaks of achievement, fame and fortune ... yet who, amidst all that, retained his innate sense of sportsmanship, his love of his calling, the desire to entertain fans and the respect of fellow players.

PUSKAS
HUNGARY

Ferenc Puskas remains one of the greatest players of all time — a symbol of the legendary "Magical Magyars" who dominated European soccer in the early 1950s and stand as perhaps the greatest team never to have won the World Cup. He very rarely used his right foot (except to stand on, as they say) but his left was so lethal that he hardly ever needed it.

YASHIN
USSR

In South America they called Lev Yashin the "Black Spider"; in Europe the "Black Panther." Eusebio described him as "the peerless goalkeeper of the century." Yashin's fame spread throughout the world, not merely for his ability as a goalkeeper to stop shots that no one else could reach, but as a great sportsman and ambassador for the game.

BECKENBAUER

"KAISER FRANZ" AND A UNIQUE DOUBLE

Franz Beckenbauer has always been accompanied by the sort of luck which only a player of his genius deserves.

The smile of fate was on him through an illustrious playing career and on into coaching when – in his first appointment at any level – he took West Germany to the Final of the World Cup in Mexico in 1986 and four years later went one better with victory in Italy.

Thus only "Kaiser Franz" can boast that he has lifted the World Cup as both captain, in 1974, and manager, in 1990.

No other soccer player has ever had a career which reached such tangible heights. He was the first German to reach a century of international appearances before leaving Bayern Munich for spells with New York Cosmos and then with Hamburg, where he wound down his playing career.

His honors include the World Cup in 1974 (runner-up in 1966), the European Championship in 1972 (runner-up 1976), the World Club Cup (1976), the European Cup (1974, 1975, 1976), the European Cup-winners' Cup (1967), as well as the West German league and cup. He was also a runner-up in the UEFA Cup with Hamburg and a runner-up in the SuperCup with Bayern. With New York Cosmos, Beckenbauer also won the NASL Soccer Bowl in 1977, 1978 and 1980.

But achievement is not the only measure of true greatness. Beckenbauer's innovative strength was through the revolutionary role of attacking sweeper which, with the encouragement of Bayern Munich coach Tschik Cajkovski, he introduced in the late 1960s.

The boy Beckenbauer took his first steps on the football ladder with local club Munich 1906, before he switched to Bayern and was first recognized by West Germany at youth level. Within a year of making his league debut with Bayern, as an outside-left, Beckenbauer was promoted to the senior national team.

BECKENBAUER *Attacking sweeper*

The occasion was one to test the nerve of the most experienced player, never mind a fledgling newcomer: West Germany were away to Sweden in a decisive qualifier for the 1966 World Cup. The odds were against them. Yet they won 2–1. West Germany's place in the World Cup finals was all but secured as was Beckenbauer's place on the national team for almost a decade.

In due course he was voted German Footballer of the Year and European Footballer of the Year. Out on the pitch he was grace and elegance personified, combining an athlete's physique with a computer-like brain for the game which saw gaps before they had opened and goal opportunities — for himself and his teammates — for which the opposing defense had not prepared.

> **"He's converted football into an art form."**
>
> *Willi Schulz, 1966 World Cup teammate*

The Elegant Manipulator

Beckenbauer spent almost all his senior career with Bayern Munich as attacking sweeper. Many critics said he was wasting his talent. But Beckenbauer, in an increasingly crowded modern game, found that the sweeper role provided him with time and space in which to work his magical influence on a match. He was the puppet master, standing back and pulling the strings which earned West Germany and Bayern Munich every major prize.

Not that Beckenbauer shied away from the attacking opportunity when it presented itself. He scored the goal which inspired West Germany's revival against England in the 1970 World Cup quarterfinal.

During his four years with Cosmos Beckenbauer made many friends and admirers in the United States and was expected to take a central role in their 1994 World Cup buildup before other interests distracted him.

On retiring, Beckenbauer was much in demand as a newspaper and television columnist. Then he was invited to put his words into deeds when offered the post of national coach in succession to Jupp Derwall after the disappointing 1984 European Championship.

The Germans had always promoted coaches from within their system. Beckenbauer was an outsider with no coaching experience: his appointment represented a huge gamble. It paid off. Such was Beckenbauer's Midas touch that "his" West Germany was crowned world champions in Rome and he earned his unique place in history.

Career facts

1945 *Born on September 11 in Munich*
1955 *Began playing for the schoolboy team, FC 1906 Munich*
1959 *Joined Bayern Munich youth section*
1962 *Gave up a job as a trainee insurance salesman to sign full-time with Bayern*
1964 *Made his Bayern debut in a 4–0 win away to St Pauli in Hamburg*
1965 *Made his national team debut in a 2–1 World Cup qualifying win in Sweden*
1966 *Starred in midfield, on the losing side, for West Germany in the 4–2 World Cup final defeat by England at Wembley*
1967 *Captained Bayern Munich, from sweeper, to victory over Rangers in the European Cup-winners' Cup final*
1972 *Captained West Germany to European Championship victory over the Soviet Union in Brussels*
1974 *Captained Bayern Munich to victory in the European Cup final and then West Germany to victory in the World Cup final against Holland*
1976 *Completed a record 103 appearances for West Germany before transferring to the New York Cosmos in the North American Soccer League*
1984 *Appointed national coach of West Germany, succeeding Jupp Derwall*
1986 *Guided an average side to the World Cup final, where they lost 3–2 to Argentina*
1990 *Became the first man to captain and then coach a World Cup-winning team when West Germany beat Argentina 1–0 in Rome*
1993 *After a short spell coaching French club Olympique Marseille, Beckenbauer returned to Bayern Munich as executive vice president*

CHARLTON

ENGLAND'S AMBASSADOR

THUNDERBOLT SHOOTING *Charlton on target against West Ham*

Bobby Charlton, throughout the world, is probably the most famous English soccer player who has ever thrilled a crowd. His name is synonymous with some of the greatest moments of the English game, but also with the highest traditions of sportsmanship and integrity.

Long after he had finished playing Charlton's reputation worked wonders in breaking down the tightest security at World Cups and European Championships. It only needed a player or coach to glance out and see Charlton arriving for barred doors and gates to be flung open. Today's heroes may possess a string of fan clubs and millions in Swiss banks, but they still recognize magic.

The delight which much of the English public took in Manchester United's success in the inaugural Premier League in 1992–93 is at least partly explained by the respect in which Bobby Charlton is held for reasons which transcend "mere" soccer.

Soccer was always in the blood. The Charltons — Bobby and World Cup-winning brother Jackie — were nephews of that great Newcastle United hero of the 1950s, Jackie Milburn. They began in the back streets of Ashington in the northeast of England, and Charlton fulfilled every schoolboy's dream when, at 17, he was signed by Manchester United.

Busby Babe and United Captain

Matt Busby had invested more time and determination than any other coach in seeking out the finest young talents in the country. Not only Charlton, but Duncan Edwards, Eddie Colman, David Pegg and many more had been singled out for the Old Trafford treatment: turned from boys into young soccer playing men under the tutelage of assistant Jimmy Murphy, and then released to explode into the League.

This was the philosophy behind the Busby Babes, the team of youngsters who took the League by storm in the mid-1950s and brought a breath of optimistic fresh air into an austere postwar England. The sense of that spirit of a new generation being lost added to the nation's grief when United's plane crashed in the snow and ice at the end of a runway in Munich on their way home from a European Cup quarterfinal in Belgrade in February 1958.

Charlton had established his first-team potential the previous season. He was initially an inside-right, later switched to outside-left with England, and finally settled as a deep-lying center-forward, using his pace out of midfield and thunderous shot to score some of the most spectacular goals English soccer has ever seen. One such goal marked his England debut against Scotland, another broke the deadlock against Mexico in the 1966 World Cup finals, and dozens of them inspired Manchester United's post-Munich revival.

The European Cup victory at Wembley in 1968, when he captained United and scored twice, was a highly emotional moment.

Then, as now, he was soccer's perfect ambassador for the game.

Career facts

1937 *Born on October 11 in Ashington, County Durham*
1957 *Played in the FA Cup Final at 19*
1958 *Survived the Munich air crash to play in another FA Cup Final*
1963 *Played in his third FA Cup final, and was at last on the winning side as United beat Leicester City 3–1*
1966 *Starred for England in the World Cup victory, scoring goals against Mexico and Portugal along the way to help earn him the European Footballer of the Year award*
1968 *Scored two of the goals as Manchester United finally won the European Cup, defeating Benfica 4–1 after extra time at Wembley*
1970 *Played his record 106th and last international for England in the 3–2 defeat by West Germany at the World Cup finals in Mexico*
1973 *Moved to neighboring Preston for a two-year spell as player-coach before becoming a director back at Old Trafford*

"It's difficult enough replacing him as a monument in the team without having to replace him as a person as well."

Tommy Docherty, then Manchester United coach, after Charlton's retirement

CRUYFF

CLOSE CONTROL *Cruyff tantalizes Argentine defender Pedro Sa at the 1974 World Cup*

'TOTAL' SOCCER PLAYER

Johan Cruyff stands out as not merely the greatest Dutch soccer player but one of the greatest players of all time, a status which owes much to the persistence of his mother.

She worked as a cleaner in the offices of the Ajax club and persuaded the club coaching staff to take Johan into their youth teams when he was still only 12 years old. The rest is history and a virtually unbroken 25-year succession of trophies and awards on the highest plane as first player and then coach.

Cruyff made his first-team debut at 17, his goal-scoring international debut at 19 and went on to inspire Ajax and Holland through most of their golden 1970s. This was the era of "total soccer," a concept of the game first described as "The Whirl" in the early 1950s by the Austrian expert Willy Meisl. He saw the day when every player in a team would possess comparable technical and physical ability and would be able to interchange roles at will.

Cruyff was The Whirl in action. Nominally he played centre-forward. But Cruyff's perception of center-forward was as orthodox as the squad No. 14 he wore on his back for most of his career with Ajax.

“Johan’s secret is that he loves football, seeking out new ways of trying to achieve perfection.”

Stefan Kovacs, former Ajax coach

FINAL SHOWDOWN *Cruyff’s face-to-face with Berti Vogts*

Cruyff did turn up at the apex of the attack: but he was also to be found meandering through midfield and out on the wings, using his nimble, coltish pace to unhinge defenses from a variety of angles and positions.

Single-handed he not only pulled Internazionale of Italy apart in the 1972 European Cup final but scored both goals in Ajax’s 2–0 win. The next year, in Belgrade, he inspired one of the greatest 20-minute spells of soccer ever seen as Ajax overcame another strong Italian outfit, Juventus.

Already the vultures were gathering. Spain had reopened their borders to foreign players and Cruyff was an obvious target. Eventually Barcelona won the transfer race — but after the close of the Spanish federation’s autumn deadline. However, such was the magnitude of the transfer that the federation bent their own regulations so that Cruyff could play immediately.

When Cruyff arrived in Barcelona, the Catalans were struggling down the standings. By the season’s end they were champions, Cruyff’s triumphant progress having included a spectacular 5–0 victory away over deadly rivals Real Madrid. Surprisingly, apart from that league title, Barcelona won little else, though Cruyff himself completed the first ever hat trick of European Footballer of the Year awards.

RED ALERT *Cruyff created panic when he had the ball.*

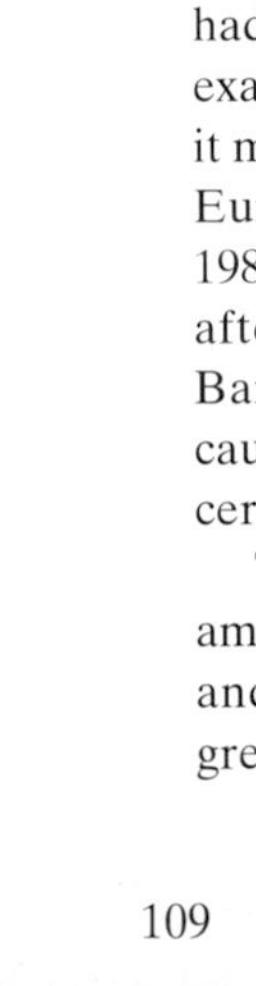

It was at the end of his first season with Barcelona that Cruyff’s career reached its international zenith. At the 1974 World Cup finals Holland took their total soccer through round after round. No one could withstand them. Above all, no one could handle the mercurial Cruyff, who inspired victories over Uruguay and Bulgaria in the first round, then provided two goals to lead the way against Argentina in the second. The last group match — in effect the semifinal — was against Brazil: the old masters against the new. Cruyff scored Holland’s decisive second goal in a 2–0 victory which signaled a new era.

The Final, of course, ended in defeat at the hands of West Germany and, though Holland reached the final again in 1978, Cruyff, by then, had retired from the national team and was about to head west.

First he joined the Los Angeles Aztecs in the NASL. He won the Most Valuable Player award that year, moved to the Washington Diplomats in 1980 and, late in 1981, returned to Holland to win the championship twice more with Ajax and once, mischievously, with old rivals Feyenoord.

Retracing his steps as a Coach

Cruyff’s move into coaching, typically, aroused new controversy as he had never obtained the necessary examination qualifications. Not that it mattered. He guided Ajax to the European Cup- winners’ Cup in 1987, and repeated the trick in 1989 after retracing his steps to Barcelona. His innovations now cause as much fuss as the total soccer of his playing days.

Thus Cruyff ranks not only among the game’s greatest players and personalities but among its greatest innovators as well.

Career facts

1947 *Born on April 25 in Amsterdam*

1959 *Enrolled by his mother in the Ajax youth teams*

1963 *Signed his first Ajax contract at 16 on the recommendation of English coach Vic Buckingham, then marked his debut with a goal*

1966 *Made his debut for Holland in a 2–2 draw against Hungary and scored a last-minute equalizer in the first of his 48 internationals*

1969 *Made his first European Cup final appearance with Ajax, but Milan won 4–1 in Madrid*

1971 *Won the first of three successive European Cups, helping Ajax defeat Panathinaikos of Greece at Wembley. He was also voted European Footballer of the Year, the first of three such accolades*

1973 *Sold by Ajax to Barcelona of Spain for a then world record transfer fee of $1.85 million*

1974 *Captained and inspired Holland to reach the 1974 World Cup final in Munich, where they lost 2–1 to hosts West Germany*

1978 *Retired from the national team before the World Cup finals in Argentina, and left Barcelona to play in America with Los Angeles Aztecs and Washington Diplomats*

1981 *Returned to Europe to play for minor club Levante in Spain, then to Holland with Ajax and, finally, Feyenoord*

1984 *Went back to Ajax, this time as technical director*

1987 *Guided Ajax to victory in the European Cup-winners’ Cup as a parting gift before being appointed coach of Barcelona*

1992 *Managed Barcelona to their long-awaited victory in the European Cup final, where they beat Sampdoria 1–0 at Wembley*

1994 *Led Barcelona to their fourth successive Spanish championship*

DI STEFANO

FIFA'S AMBASSADOR *Di Stefano leads the rest of the world by example against England at Wembley in 1963*

WORLD-CLASS ALL-ROUNDER

Alfredo Di Stefano is reckoned by many to be the greatest soccer player of all. While Pele's admirers consider it sacrilege, the millions who wondered at Di Stefano's majestic domination of European football in the 1950s and 1960s may concur.

Di Stefano's greatness lay not only in his achievement in leading Madrid to victory in the first five consecutive European Cup finals — and inspiring a great breakthrough in international soccer — but also because no other soccer player so effectively combined individual expertise with an all-embracing ability to organize a team to play to his command.

Today he is a wealthy elder statesman of soccer. Yet he was born in Barracas, a poor suburb of the Argentine capital of Buenos Aires, and learned his soccer first in the tough streets of the city, then out on the family farm. This was where he built up the stamina which would become legendary across the world in later years.

Di Stefano's grandfather had emigrated to Argentina from Capri. His father had played for the leading Buenos Aires club, River Plate, but abruptly ended his career when professionalism was introduced. To Di Stefano senior football was a recreation, not a means to earn a living. Thus he was not particularly pleased when his sons Alfredo and Tulio launched their own teenage careers with local teams.

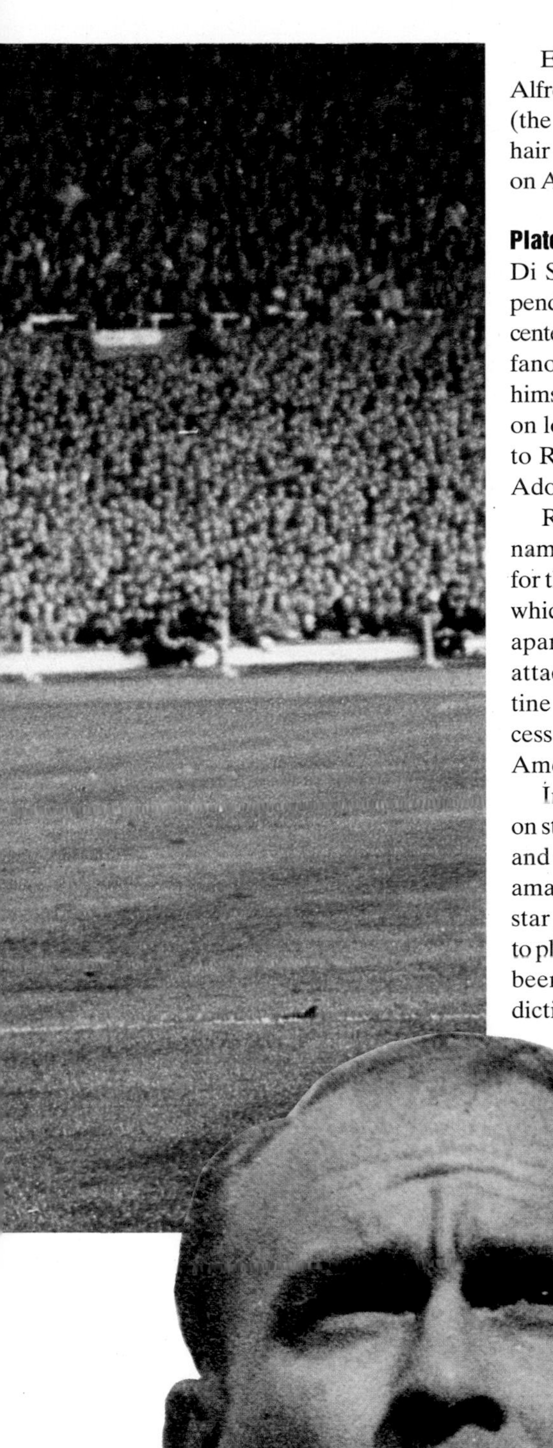

Eventually, he relented and young Alfredo — nicknamed "El Aleman" (the German), because of his blond hair — made his River Plate debut on August 18, 1944, at outside-right.

Plate left on Shelf

Di Stefano's hero had been Independiente's free-scoring Paraguayan center-forward, Arsenio Erico. Di Stefano wanted to be a center-forward himself. He learned his trade while on loan to Huracan, then returned to River Plate to replace the great Adolfo Pedernera.

River's forward line was nicknamed *La Maquina* (the Machine), for the remorseless consistency with which they took opposing defences apart. Di Stefano transferred his attacking prowess into the Argentine national team with equal success when they won the 1947 South American championship.

In 1949 Argentine players went on strike. The clubs locked them out and completed their schedule with amateur players. Meanwhile, the star professionals were lured away to play in the pirate league which had been set up, outside FIFA's jurisdiction, in Colombia.

Di Stefano was the star of stars there, playing for Millonarios of Bogota, the so-called "Blue Ballet." When Colombia was reintegrated in FIFA, Millonarios went on one last world tour . . . where Di Stefano was spotted by Real Madrid after starring in the Spanish club's fiftieth anniversary tournament.

Madrid agreed a fee with Millonarios and thus nearly outflanked rivals Barcelona, who had sealed a deal with Di Stefano's old club, River Plate. A Spanish soccer court ruled that Di Stefano should play one season for Madrid, one season for Barcelona. But after he made a quiet start to the season, Barcelona, unimpressed, sold out their share in Di Stefano to Madrid.

Four days later he scored a hat-trick in a 5–0 win against . . . Barcelona. A legend had been born.

"Two Players in every Position"

Madrid was Spanish champion in Di Stefano's first two seasons and European Cup winners in his next five. He scored in each of Madrid's European Cup finals, including a hat trick against Frankfurt in 1960 in a 90-minute spectacular which has become one of the most-admired soccer matches of all time.

Di Stefano was "total soccer" personified before the term had been invented. One moment he was defending in his own penalty area, the next organizing his midfield, the next scoring from the edge of the opponents' six-yard box. As Miguel Muñoz, long-time Madrid colleague as player and then coach, once said: "The greatness of Di Stefano was that, with him in your side, you had two players in every position."

THE BLOND ARROW *of Real Madrid and Spain*

> **"Di Stefano is the greatest player I have ever seen. The things he does in a match will never be equaled."**
>
> *Luis Del Sol, 1960 European Cup-winning team-mate*

Career facts

1926 *Born Alfredo Stefano Di Stefano Lauhle on July 4 in Barracas, a poor suburb of Buenos Aires, Argentina*

1940 *Hinted at things to come by scoring a hat trick in 20 minutes for his first youth team, Los Cardales*

1942 *Left Los Cardales after a fight with the coach, to join his father's old club, River Plate*

1943 *Made his debut for River Plate, playing as a right-winger, aged 17, against Buenos Aires rivals San Lorenzo*

1944 *Transferred on loan to Huracan, for whom he scored the winner in a league game against River Plate*

1946 *Returned to River Plate to succeed the great Adolfo Pedernera at center-forward in an attack nicknamed* La Maquina *(the Machine)*

1947 *Already an international, won the South American Championship with Argentina*

1949 *Lured away, during the famous Argentine players' strike, to play in a pirate league outside of FIFA's jurisdiction in Colombia for Millonarios of Bogota*

1953 *Moved to Spain where he joined Real Madrid*

1956 *Inspired Madrid to the first of five successive European Cup victories and made his national team debut for Spain*

1960 *Scored a hat trick in Real's legendary 7–3 victory over Eintracht Frankfurt in the European Cup final at Hampden Park, Glasgow*

1963 *Kidnapped — and later released unharmed — by urban guerrillas while on tour with Real Madrid in Venezuela*

1964 *Left Madrid for one last season as a player with Espanol of Barcelona, before becoming a coach in both Argentina and Spain*

EUSEBIO

FRIENDLY INTENT *Eusebio outpaces Arsenal's admiring George Graham at Highbury*

HIS MAJESTY KING SOCCER

Eusebio, the greatest Portuguese soccer player in history, did not, in fact, come from Portugal at all. Born and brought up in Mozambique, then still one of Portugal's African colonies, Eusebio was the first African soccer player to earn a worldwide reputation.

The big Portuguese clubs such as Benfica, Sporting and Porto financed nursery teams in Mozambique and Angola and unearthed a wealth of talent which they then transported into not only Portuguese soccer but the Portuguese national team.

The young Eusebio, ironically, was a nursery product not of Benfica but of their great Lisbon rivals, Sporting. But when Sporting summoned him to Lisbon for a trial in 1961, he was virtually kidnapped off the airplane by Benfica officials and hidden away until the fuss had died down and Sporting, having all but forgotten about him, lost interest.

Hijacked by Benfica

Bela Guttmann, a veteran Hungarian, was coach of Benfica at the time. He had a high regard for the potential offered by Mozambique and Angola. The nucleus of the Benfica team which Guttmann had guided to European Cup victory over Barcelona that year came from Africa: goalkeeper Costa Pereira, center-forward and captain Jose Aguas, and the two inside-forwards

Joaquim Santana and Mario Coluna. But Eusebio would prove the greatest of all.

Guttmann introduced him to the first team at the end of the 1960–61 season. He was a reserve when Benfica went to France to face Santos of Brazil — inspired by Pele — in the famous Paris Tournament. At half-time Benfica were losing 3–0. Guttmann, with nothing to lose, sent on Eusebio. Benfica still lost, but Eusebio scored a spectacular hat trick and outshone even Pele. He was still only 19.

A year later Eusebio scored two cannonball goals in the 5–3 victory Benfica ran up against Real Madrid in the European Cup Final in Amsterdam. In 13 seasons he helped Benfica win the League seven times and the Cup twice; he was European Footballer of the Year in 1965; top scorer with nine goals in the 1966 World Cup finals; scorer of 38 goals in 46 internationals and the league's leading scorer seven times before knee trouble forced a halt at 32.

But soccer was Eusebio's life. When the fledgeling North American Soccer League offered him the chance of a lucrative extension to his career, he flew west to play for the Boston Minutemen (alongside old Benfica teammate Antonio Simoes), then for the Toronto Metros-Croatia, and then for the Las Vegas Quicksilver.

Benfica's faithful had mixed feelings about his self-imposed exile in North America. But controversy was soon forgotten when he returned to Lisbon to take up various appointments as television analyst, as assistant coach and as the most honored public face of Benfica.

A Majestic Sportsman

Fans around the world took Eusebio to their hearts not only because of his ability but because of the sportsmanlike way he played the people's game. At Wembley in 1968 Eusebio very nearly won the European Cup final for Benfica against Manchester United in the closing minutes of normal time, being foiled only by the intuition of Alex Stepney. Eusebio's reaction? He patted Stepney on the back, applauding a worthy opponent.

UNSTOPPABLE *against Milan*

Wembley Stadium played a major role in Eusebio's career. It was at Wembley, in a 2–0 World Cup qualifying defeat by England in 1961, that his youthful power first made the international game sit up; it was at Wembley, in 1963, that he scored one of his finest individual goals as consolation in a 2–1 European Cup final defeat by Milan; and it was at Wembley again, in 1966, that Eusebio led Portugal to their best-ever third place in the World Cup. The semi-final, in which Portugal lost 2–1 to England, will long be remembered as as exemplary exhibition of sportsmanship under pressure.

Appropriately, a statue of Eusebio in action now dominates the entrance to the Estadio da Luz. Appropriately, also, a film made about his life was subtitled *Sua Majestade o Rei* ... His Majesty the

“Everywhere I go, Eusebio is the name people mention.”

Mario Soares, President of Portugal

Career facts

1942 *Born Eusebio Da Silva Ferreira on January 25 in Lourenço Marques, Mozambique*

1952 *Joined the youth teams of Sporting (Lourenço Marques), a nursery team for the Portuguese giants of the same name*

1961 *Sporting tried to bring Eusebio to Lisbon, but he was "kidnapped" on arrival by Benfica. In the autumn, with barely a dozen league games to his name, he made his debut for Portugal*

1962 *Scored two thundering goals as Benfica beat Real Madrid 5–3 in a classic European Cup final in Amsterdam*

1965 *Voted European Footballer of the Year*

1966 *Crowned top scorer with nine goals as Portugal finished third in the World Cup finals in England, where he was nicknamed the "new Pele" and the "Black Panther"*

1969 *Won Portuguese championship medal for the seventh and last time with Benfica before winding down his career in Mexico and Canada*

1992 *A statue in his honour was unveiled at the entrance to Benfica's Estadio da Luz in Lisbon*

HOLD-UP *Yashin foils Eusebio in the 1966 World Cup third place game*

MARADONA

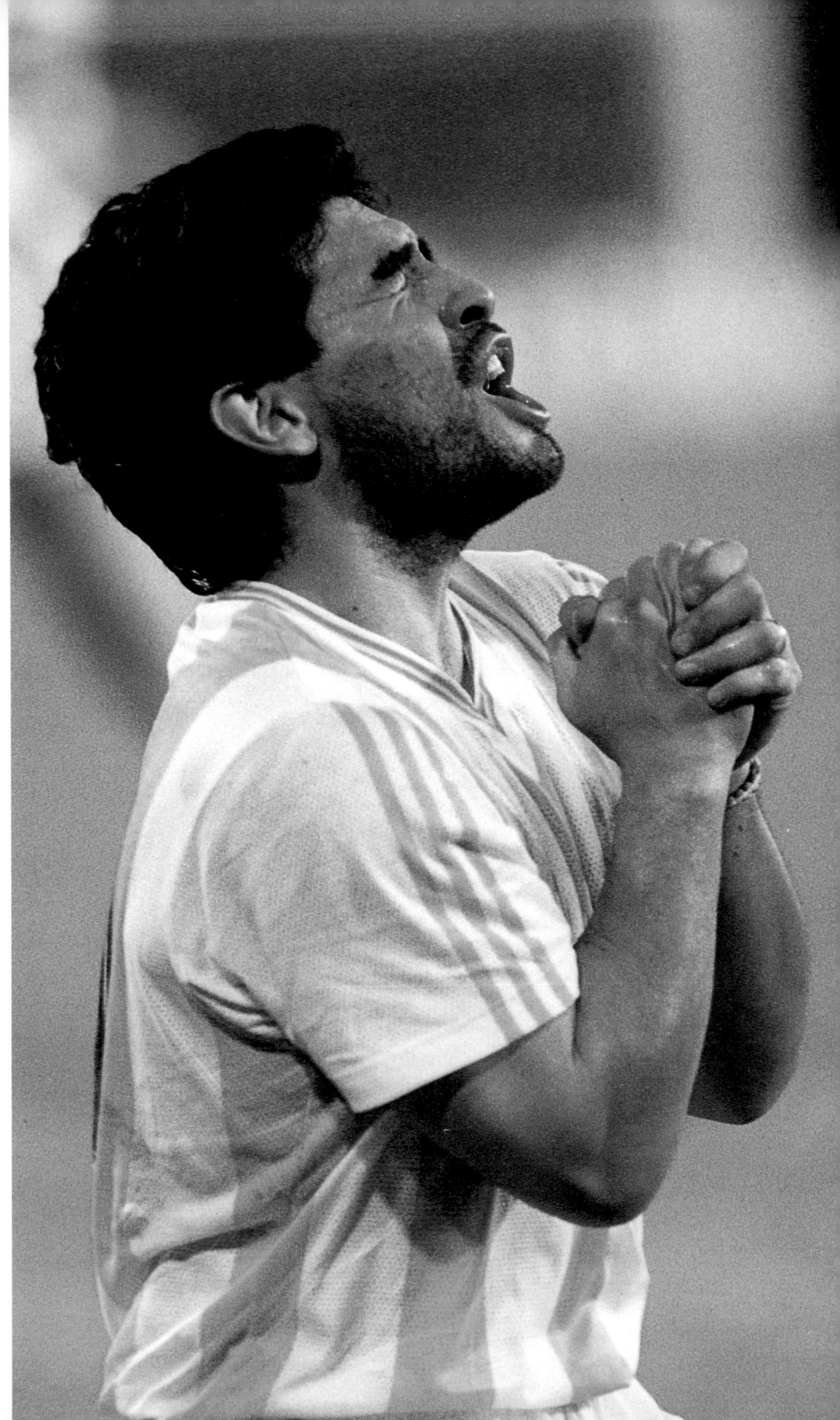

IDOL OF TWO CONTINENTS

CROWD-PULLER, CROWD-PLEASER *Maradona, the inspiration of Napoli*

Diego Maradona was not only the world's greatest soccer player throughout the 1980s and early 1990s. He was also the most controversial and the most enigmatic.

His admirers in Argentina, where he knew the early glory days with Argentinos Juniors and Boca Juniors, considered him little less than a god, and the *tifosi* in Italy, where he triumphed with Napoli, worshipped his shoelaces. So did all of Argentina after Maradona reached the zenith of his career, captaining his country to victory in the 1986 World Cup finals in Mexico.

English fans still rage over his "Hand of God" goal in the quarter-final in Mexico City. But Argentine fans remember most clearly his other goal in that game when he collected the ball inside his own half and outwitted five defenders and goalkeeper Peter Shilton before gliding home one of the greatest goals in the history of the World Cup.

Maradona provided a repeat against Belgium in the semifinals: another brilliant slalom through the defense but from the left, not the right. Then, in the final against West Germany, his slide-rule pass sent Jorge Burruchaga away to score the dramatic winner.

Maradona's great ability made his subsequent fall all the greater. His love affair with Italian soccer went sour after the 1990 World Cup, when Maradona's Argentina defeated their hosts on penalties in the semifinal in Maradona's adopted home of Naples. The following spring a dope test showed cocaine traces. He was banned from Italian and then world football for 15 months, returned to Argentina and was arrested there for cocaine possession.

Released on probation, he sought to revive his playing career in Spain, but half a season at Sevilla proved a disaster. Only after Maradona returned home once more to Argentina and attempted another new start, with Newell's Old Boys in Rosario, did glimpses emerge of the great soccer player he had once been.

> **"Pele was the supreme player of his era; Maradona is the pre-eminent player of his time. You cannot compare them. Such greatness does not submit to comparison."**
> *Cesar Luis Menotti, former coach of Argentina*

A Roller-Coaster Career

It all began in the working-class Fiorito suburb of Lanus in the province of Buenos Aires where Maradona began playing for a kids' team named Estrella Roja (Red Star) at the age of nine. Later he and his friends founded a team known as Los Cebollitas (The Little Onions) who were so promising that the team was signed up en bloc by Argentinos Juniors as one of the club's youth sides.

On October 20, 1976, Maradona (wearing No. 16) made his league debut as a 15-year-old substitute against Talleres of Cordoba, and a week later he played his first full match against Newells Old Boys from Rosario. In February 1977 he made his international debut.

It appeared certain that Maradona would be at least a member of the squad with which coach Cesar Luis Menotti planned to win the World Cup for Argentina for the first time in front of their own fanatical fans in 1978, but he was one of the three players dropped on the eve of the finals.

It was months before he would speak to Menotti again, but their eventual peace talk paved the way for the first international success of Maradona's career at the 1979 World Youth Cup in Japan.

Boca Juniors bought him for a world record $1.5 million and resold him two years later to Barcelona for $4.5 million, another record. Before joining the Catalans he succumbed to the pressures of the World Cup, in Spain in 1982, where he was sent off for an awful lunge at Batista of Brazil. It was the recurring theme of his career: a unique talent for soccer shadowed by a similarly unique aptitude for arousing controversy.

It says much for the magical technique of his left foot that, despite all the negative vibes, Maradona continued to entrance the game. In 1984 Napoli paid another world record, this time $7.5 million, to end Maradona's injury-battered two-year stay with Barcelona. Within weeks Napoli sold a staggering 70,000 season tickets. Two Italian League championships and one UEFA Cup success were the reward for the fans.

Seven glorious, roller-coaster years went by before the partnership was dissolved. Soccer in Naples will never be the same again.

Career facts

1960 *Born on October 30 in Lanus, Buenos Aires*
1976 *Made his league debut at 15 for Argentinos Juniors*
1977 *Made his international debut at 16 for Argentina in a friendly against Hungary*
1980 *Sold to Boca Juniors for a world record $1.5 million*
1982 *Sold to Barcelona for another world record $4.5 million, then out of the game for four months after a reckless tackle by Bilbao's notorious defender Andoni Goicoechea*
1984 *Sold to Napoli for a third world record, this time $7.5 m*
1986 *Inspired Argentina to victory at the World Cup finals in Mexico and was the unanimous choice as Player of the Tournament*
1987 *Led Napoli to their first ever Italian league title plus victory in the Italian cup*
1988 *Won his only European prize as Napoli beat Stuttgart in the UEFA Cup final*
1990 *Despite a collection of injuries, Maradona led Argentina back to the World Cup final, where they were defeated 1–0 by West Germany*
1991 *Failed a dope test and was banned for 15 months*
1992 *Made a disappointing comeback with Sevilla in Spain*
1993 *Sacked by Sevilla, Maradona began a second comeback in Argentina with Newells Old Boys and was restored as national captain for the World Cup play-offs against Australia*
1994 *Banned from World Cup finals after failing drug test*

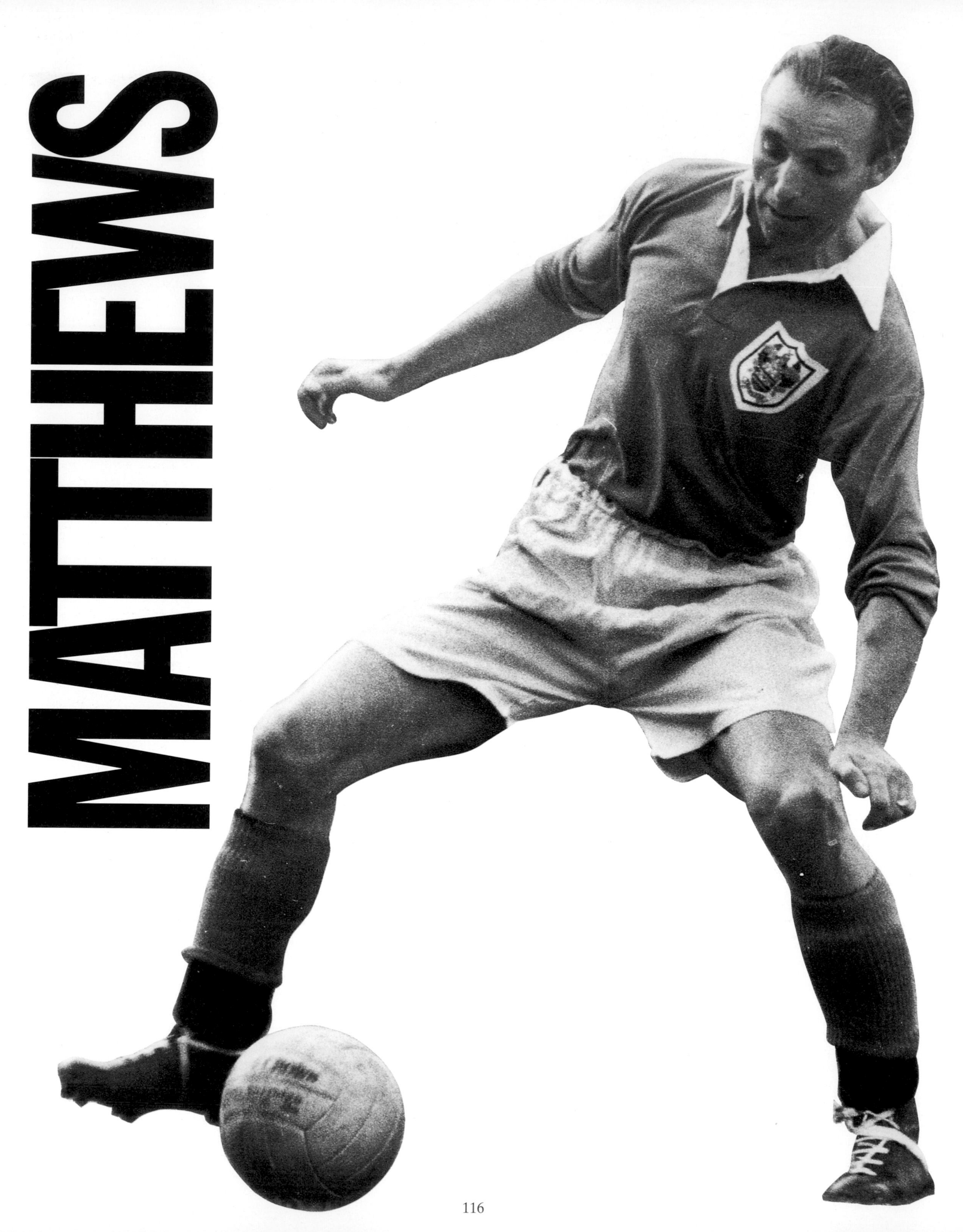
MATTHEWS

A LEFT-BACK'S NIGHTMARE

CHEERS! *Matthews is carried off by his Cup-winning teammates in 1953*

Stanley Matthews was the first great soccer player of the modern era. There will be cases made for Billy Wright, Bobby Charlton, Bobby Moore and others but none dominated his particular era as long as the barber's son from Hanley in the Potteries area of the English Midlands.

Matthews was nicknamed the Wizard of Dribble and the magic of his talent and reputation survived right through to the closing days of his career when he returned to his original club, Stoke City, and inspired them to win promotion out of the Second Division doldrums. That achieved, at the climax of the longest first-class career of any player, he decided to retire, at the age of 50. Later, however, Matthews insisted that he could — and should — have played for several more years.

Matthews went out in a style befitting one of the legends of the game. Among the other great players who turned out for his testimonial match at Stoke were Di Stefano, Puskas and Yashin. Always keen to put back into soccer as much, if not more, than he had taken out in terms of fame and glory, Matthews became general manager of another Potteries club, Port Vale. But the role was too restrictive for a man who had painted his soccer on a grand canvas, and Matthews left after 18 months to take coaching and exhibition courses around the world, in particular to Africa. Later he lived for many years in Malta before returning to settle again in England.

> **"The greatest tribute to Stanley Matthews is that he can go to any ground and make a monkey of a fullback and still be loved by the crowd."**
>
> *Leslie Edwards,* Liverpool Echo

In the 1930s and 1940s Matthews was without rival as the greatest outside-right in the world. Opposing left-backs feared their duels with him as Matthews brought the ball towards them, feinted one way and accelerated clear another. His adoring public desperately wanted to see him crown his career with an FA Cup winners' medal. That dream was denied by Manchester United in 1948 and Newcastle in 1951. But in 1953 — a remarkable year for English sport with England reclaiming cricket's "Ashes" trophy from Australia and the veteran jockey Sir Gordon Richards winning the Derby — the 38-year-old Matthews tried again.

When Blackpool was 3–1 down to Bolton with time running out, it seemed Matthews was destined never to claim that elusive prize. But Matthews took over, ripping the Bolton defense to shreds and providing not only the inspiration for Blackpool's climb back to equality, but also the cross from which Bill Perry shot the winning goal. Blackpool scored twice in the last three minutes.

An Artist and a Gentleman

Like any soccer player, Matthews knew his share of defeats. One of the most remarkable was England's 1–0 upset by the United States at the 1950 World Cup finals in Belo Horizonte, Brazil, when he had to watch in embarrassment after being omitted from the team. But England might have found more consistency if controversy had not been raised now and again over whether Matthews or Preston's Tom Finney was the more effective right-winger. Eventually the problem was solved by switching the versatile Finney to outside-left.

Matthews, by contrast, was always and only an outside-right, demonstrating supreme artistry in a position which was later declared redundant when work-rate mechanics took over the game in the mid-1960s. Only much later, when coaches suddenly understood the value of breaking down massed defenses by going downthe wings, was old-fashioned wing play revived.

But Matthews was, like many of the game's greatest players, a personality and an inspiring example for all youngsters. His knighthood was appropriate recognition for a 33-year career, completed without a single booking, in which he had graced the game as the First Gentleman of Soccer.

Career facts

1915 *Born on February 1 in Hanley, Stoke-on-Trent.*

1932 *Turned professional with local club Stoke City*

1934 *Made his debut for England in a 4–0 win over Wales in Cardiff*

1946 *Sold to Blackpool to the dismay of the local fans*

1948 *Played a key role in one of England's greatest victories, by 4–0 over Italy in Turin, and was voted Footballer of the Year*

1953 *Sealed his place among soccer's legends by inspiring Blackpool's FA Cup final comeback against Bolton*

1955 *One of his many summer exhibition tours took him to Mozambique, where among the ball boys mesmerized at a match in Lourenço Marques was Eusebio*

1957 *Played the last of 84 games for England (including wartime internationals) in a 4–1 World Cup qualifying victory over Denmark in Copenhagen*

1961 *Returned to Stoke for a paltry transfer fee and, despite his 46 years, inspired their successful campaign to get back into the First Division*

1965 *Retired after a star-spangled Farewell Match at Stoke's Victoria Ground featuring the likes of Di Stefano, Puskas and Yashin*

PELE

THE MASTER SHOWMAN

Pele remains one of those great examples and inspirations of world sport: a poor boy whose talent lifted him to the peaks of achievement, fame and fortune ... yet who, amidst all that, retained his innate sense of sportsmanship, his love of his calling and the respect of team-mates and opponents alike.

His father Dondinho had been a respectable soccer player in the 1940s, but his career had been ended prematurely by injury. He was his son's first coach and his first supporter.

Most Brazilian footballers are known by nicknames. Pele does not know the origin of his own tag. He recalled only that he did not like it and was in trouble at school for fighting with classmates who called him Pele. Later, of course, it became the most familiar name in world sport.

World Cup Triumph

Pele's teenage exploits as a player with his local club, Bauru, earned him a transfer to Santos at the age of 15. Rapidly he earned national and then international recognition. At 16 he was playing for Brazil; at 17 he was winning the World Cup. Yet it took pressure from his teammates to persuade national coach Vicente Feola to throw him into the action in Sweden in 1958.

Santos was not slow to recognize the potential offered their club by Pele. The directors created a sort of circus, touring the world, playing two and three times a week for lucrative match fees. The income from this gave the club the financial leverage to buy a supporting cast which helped turn Santos into World Club Champions in 1962 and 1963.

“Pele is to Brazilian football what Shakespeare is to English literature.”

Joao Saldanha, former manager of Brazil

Mexico Makes up for Everything

The pressure on Pele was reflected in injuries, one of which restricted him to only a peripheral role at the 1962 World Cup finals. He scored a marvelous solo goal against Mexico in the first round, but pulled a muscle and missed the rest of the tournament. Brazil, even without him, went on to retain the Jules Rimet Trophy.

In 1966 Pele led Brazil in England. But referees were unprepared to give players of skill and creativity the necessary protection. One of the saddest images of the tournament was Pele, a raincoat around his shoulders, leaving the pitch after being forced out of the tournament by Portugal. Brazil, this time, did not possess the same strength in depth as in 1962, and crashed out.

Four years later Pele took his revenge in the most glorious way. As long as the game is played, the 1970 World Cup finals will be revered as the apotheosis of a great player, not only at his very best, but achieving the rewards his talent deserved.

As a 17-year-old Pele had scored one of the unforgettable World Cup goals in the final against Sweden — in 1970 he twice nearly surpassed it. First, against Czechoslovakia, he just missed scoring with a shot from his own half of the field, and against Uruguay he sold an outrageous dummy to the goalkeeper and just missed again.

It says everything about Pele's transcending genius that he was the one man able to set light to soccer in the United States in the 1970s. Although the North American Soccer League eventually collapsed amid financial confusion, soccer was by that stage firmly established as a grassroots American sport. Without Pele's original allure that could never have happened and the capture of host rights for the 1994 finals would never have been possible.

MUTUAL RESPECT *With Bobby Moore*

O REI *Pele, king of Brazilian soccer from the late 1950s to the early 1970s*

Career facts

1940 *Born Edson Arantes do Nascimento on October 21 in Tres Coracoes*

1950 *Began playing with local club Bauru, where his father was a coach*

1956 *Transferred to big-city club Santos and made his league debut at 15*

1957 *Made his debut for Brazil, at 16, against Argentina*

1958 *Became the youngest-ever World Cup winner, scoring two goals in the final as Brazil beat Sweden 5–2 in Stockholm*

1962 *Missed the 1962 World Cup win because of injury in the first round ... but compensated by winning the World Club Cup with Santos*

1970 *Inspired Brazil to complete their historic World Cup hat trick in Mexico*

1975 *Ended an 18-month retirement to play for Cosmos of New York in the dramatic, short-lived North American Soccer League*

1977 *Retired again after lifting Cosmos to their third NASL championship*

1982 *Presented with FIFA's Gold Medal Award for outstanding service to the world-wide game*

PUSKAS

THE MAGICAL LEFT FOOT

Ferenc Puskas remains one of the greatest players of all time — a symbol of the legendary "Magic Magyars" who dominated European football in the early 1950s and stand as perhaps the greatest team never to have won the World Cup.

Puskas's father was a player and later coach with the local club, Kispest. At 16 Ferenc was a regular at inside-left, terrorizing opposing goalkeepers with the power of his shooting. He rarely used his right foot but then his left was so lethal that he seldom needed it.

At 18 he was in the national team, too. His brilliance had much to do with the decision to convert Kispest into a new army sports club named Honved, that formed the basis of the national team.

For four years Hungary, built around goalkeeper Gyula Grosics, right-half Jozsef Bozsik and the inside-forward trio of Sandor Kocsis, Nandor Hidegkuti and Puskas, crushed all opposition. They also introduced a new tactical concept. The inside-forwards, Kocsis and Puskas, formed the spearhead of the attack, with Hidegkuti a revolutionary deep-lying center-forward. Hungary won the 1952 Olympic title before ending England's record of invincibility against continental opposition with a stunning 6–3 triumph at Wembley.

Early the following year, Hungary thrashed England again, 7–1 in Budapest. No wonder they were overwhelming favorites to win the 1954 World Cup in Switzerland. But Puskas presented a problem. He had been injured in an early round game against West Germany and was a hobbling spectator at training before the final, against these same West Germans, in Berne. Could his great left foot withstand the strain? Puskas thought so and decided to play, thus taking one of the most controversial gambles in the game's history. After only 12 minutes the gamble appeared to be paying off when Hungary led 2–0. However, they lost 3–2, their dominance finally ended in the one match which mattered most.

The Toast of Spain

It was eight long years before Puskas would return to the World Cup finals. Then, in Chile in 1962, his trusty left foot was doing duty for Spain, because Puskas had, in the meantime, defected to the West, joining Real Madrid. Honved had been abroad when the Hungarian Revolution of 1956 erupted. Puskas and several teammates decided to stay in the West. He made an attempt to sign with several Italian clubs, but they thought him too old. How wrong they were was underlined when Puskas developed, at Madrid, a new career to emulate his first in brilliance.

Four times Puskas was the Spanish league's top scorer and his partnership with the Argentine center-forward, Alfredo Di Stefano, was one of the greatest of all time. They hit perfection together on the famous night when Madrid thrashed Eintracht Frankfurt 7–3 in the European Cup final before a record 135,000 crowd at Hampden.

Di Stefano scored three goals, Puskas four. The Spanish fans loved him. In his Hungarian army club days at Honved, Puskas had been known as the Galloping Major. Now they called him *Cañoncito* — the little cannon.

In 1966 he finally retired. His future was secure, thanks to business investments which included a sausage factory near Madrid. He tried his hand at coaching without a great deal of success — save for the remarkable 1970–71 season when he took Panathinaikos of Athens to the European Cup final.

In the course of time he was able to visit his native Hungary, where he was celebrated once more as a national hero. Hardly surprising. After all, how many can boast 83 goals in 84 games for their country?

> **"His was a name fit for any sporting hall of fame, worthy of any and every superlative."**
> *Billy Wright, England captain against Hungary in 1953*

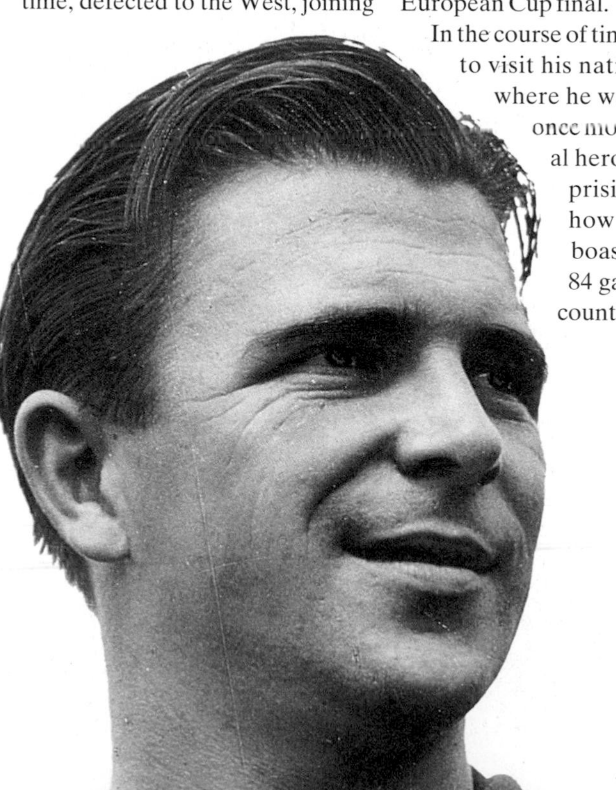

Career facts

1927 *Born on April 2 in Budapest*

1943 *Made his debut for his father's old club, Kispest*

1945 *Played his first international for Hungary against Austria*

1948 *Transferred with the entire Kispest playing staff to the new army club, Honved, and top-scored with 50 goals in the League championship*

1952 *Captained Hungary to victory over Yugoslavia in the final of the Olympic Games soccer tournament in Helsinki*

1953 *Earned a place in history by inspiring Hungary's historic 6–3 victory over England at Wembley*

1954 *Played despite injury, amid controversy, in the World Cup final which Hungary lost 3–2 to West Germany in Berne — their first defeat for four years*

1956 *Stayed in western Europe when the Hungarian Revolution broke out while Honved were abroad to play a European Cup tie against Bilbao*

1958 *Signed for Real Madrid by his old coach at Honved, Emil Oestreicher*

1960 *Scored four goals for Madrid in their famous 7–3 demolition of Eintracht Frankfurt in the European Cup final at Hampden Park, Glasgow*

1962 *Played in the World Cup finals in Chile, this time for his adopted country of Spain*

1966 *Retired and turned to coaching*

1971 *Achieved his greatest success as a trainer, guiding outsiders Panathinaikos of Athens to the European Cup final (they lost 2–0 to Ajax at Wembley)*

1993 *Appointed, briefly, as caretaker-coach of Hungary during the 1994 World Cup qualifiers*

YASHIN

INTUITION PERSONIFIED *Yashin in action in his last active World Cup finals in 1966*

"BLACK PANTHER" WAS THE SUPREME SOVIET

In South America they called Lev Yashin the "Black Spider;" in Europe the "Black Panther." Portugal's Eusebio described him as "the peerless goalkeeper of the century." It says everything about his ability and his personality that the likes of Pele, Eusebio and Franz Beckenbauer made the journey to Moscow for his farewell match.

Yet Yashin very nearly gave up soccer altogether in favor of ice hockey. That was in 1953. He was tiring of standing in as reserve at Moscow Dynamo to the legendary Alexei "Tiger" Khomich. He was 23, after all, and Dynamo's ice hockey coaches were begging him to commit himself to their cause.

Then Khomich was injured. Dynamo coach Arkady Chereny-

"Yashin was the peerless goalkeeper of the century."

Eusebio

shev called on the impatient reserve, and Yashin took over to such outstanding effect that, a year later, he was making his debut for the Soviet Union in a 3–2 win over Sweden. Two years later, in 1956, Yashin kept goal for the Soviet side who won the Olympic title in Melbourne, Australia. In 1960 he was goalkeeper for the Soviet team that won the inaugural European Championship, then called the Nations Cup.

After that first summons in 1953, Yashin had never looked back. In the first seven years after his debut for the Soviet Union he missed only two internationals, ending his career with a then Soviet record 78 caps to his name. For Dynamo, Yashin played 326 Supreme League matches and won the league title six times and the Soviet cup twice. On his death in 1990, the official news agency, Tass, described him as "the most famous Soviet sportsman ever."

First Goalkeeper and First Soviet

Yashin's fame had quickly spread throughout the world, not merely for his ability as a goalkeeper, to stop shots that no one else could reach, but as an outstanding sportsman and ambassador for the game. Appropriately, in 1963 he became the first Soviet player to be nominated as European Footballer of the Year by the French magazine, *France Football*. To this day, he remains the only goalkeeper to have received the award. In South America, when the magazine *El Grafico* ran a readers' poll to determine the Greatest Team of All Time, Yashin was virtually unchallenged as goalkeeper.

The World Cups of 1958, 1962 and 1966 saw Yashin at work, and he was also in Mexico in 1970 though only as a reserve because of the value of his experience behind the scenes and in the dressing-rooms. In 1965, Yashin was outstanding in the Stanley Matthews Retirement Match at Stoke when a British eleven lost narrowly to a World eleven featuring not only Yashin but Di Stefano, Puskas, the other great exiled Hungarian Ladislav Kubala, and Yashin's immediate predecessor as European Footballer of the Year, Czechoslovakia's Josef Masopust.

One of Yashin's saves that night — diving full length across the face of his goal to grip a shot from Jimmy Greaves which few goalkeepers would even have got a finger to — will live for ever in the memory of those who were present.

Yashin was said to have saved more than 150 penalties during his career. One of the few which got past him was struck by Eusebio in the third place play-off at the 1966 World Cup finals at Wembley. The Soviets finished fourth, but that remains their best finish in the game's greatest competition.

Grand Testimonial

When Yashin retired in 1970, a testimonial match was arranged and stars from all over the world turned out in honor of the great sportsman. The match at Lenin stadium, before 100,000 fans, was an unforgettable event in Soviet soccer history.

Yashin remained in sport after his retirement, not as a coach or trainer but as head of the Ministry of Sport's soccer department and then as a vice-president of the national association. His film archive, compiled from shots he had taken all round the world, was an object of admiration, as was his modern jazz record collection. Towards the end of his career, Yashin was honored by the Soviet government with its ultimate honour, the Order of Lenin. In recent years Lenin's reputation has gone into steep decline: something that could never be said of Lev Yashin.

Career facts

1929 *Born Lev Ivanovich Yashin on October 22 in Moscow*
1946 *Joined Moscow Dynamo as an ice hockey goaltender*
1951 *Made his first-team debut for Moscow Dynamo*
1953 *Finally took over as Dynamo's first-choice keeper*
1954 *Made his debut for the Soviet Union in a 3–2 win over Sweden*
1956 *Won Olympic gold with the Soviet Union at the Melbourne Games*
1958 *Appeared in his first World Cup and helped the Soviet Union reach the quarterfinals*
1960 *Won the first European championship with the Soviet Union against Yugoslavia in Paris*
1963 *Voted European Footballer of the Year and played for FIFA's World eleven at Wembley in a match to mark the centenary of the Football Association*
1968 *Awarded the Order of Lenin by the Soviet government*

SEMI-FINALISTS *The Soviet Union's 1966 World Cup team*

YASHIN *The "Black Panther"*

THE GREAT PLAYERS

Every country produces great players. These are the men who have delighted fans over the years not merely with their achievements but with their personalities. They drew spectators who may have had no previous attachment to their clubs but who were simply attracted by their skills. The advent of TV has widened their fame.

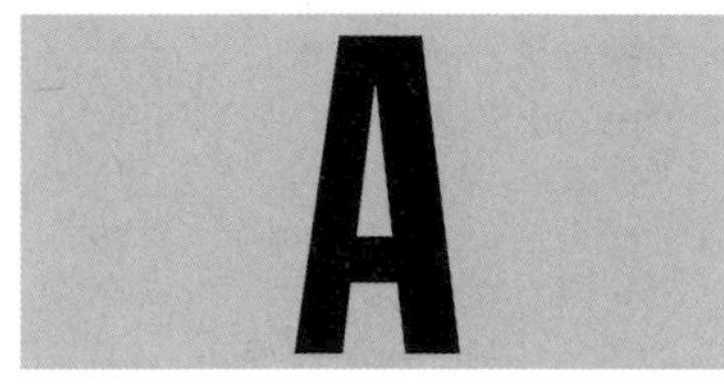

Andre "Trello" Abegglen

Born: March 7, 1909, Switzerland.
Clubs: Etoile Rouge, Cantonal, Grasshoppers (Swz), Sochaux (Fr), Servette, La Chaux-de-Fonds (Swz).

Abegglen was the first great Swiss player to make his mark on the world stage. He and brother Max, nicknamed Xam, were inside-forward stalwarts together at the Grasshoppers club of Zurich. Trello scored 30 goals in 52 internationals for Switzerland between 1927 and 1943. He starred at the 1934 and 1938 World Cup finals and won three Swiss championships, two while with Grasshoppers and one after moving on to Servette of Geneva. Brother Max played 68 times for Switzerland and was top scorer at the 1924 Olympic Games.

Ademir Marques de Menezes

Born: November 8, 1922, Brazil.
Clubs: FC Recife, Vasco da Gama, Fluminense, Vasco da Gama.

Ademir was the seven-goal leading scorer at the 1950 World Cup finals when he played center-forward for Brazil. The inside-forward trio of Ademir, Zizinho and Jair da Rosa was considered one of the greatest in Brazil's history. Ademir scored 32 goals in 37 internationals after beginning his career as an outside-left. He had a powerful shot in both feet and was six times a Rio state league champion, five times with Vasco da Gama and once with Fluminense. It was said that Brazilian coaches created 4–2–4 because Ademir's ability forced opposing teams to play with an extra central defender.

José Pinto Carvalho dos Santos Aguas

Born: c. 1930, Portugal.
Clubs: Benfica (Port), FK Austria.

Aguas was captain and center-forward of the Benfica side which succeeded Real Madrid as European champions in 1961. In his native Angola, legend has it, he was a famed local lion-hunter when Benfica persuaded him he could enjoy a more lucrative existence hunting goals. He flew to Portugal in 1950 and scored more than 250 goals for Benfica as well as finishing top league scorer five times. In 1960–61 he was also top scorer, with 11 goals, in the European Cup and collected the trophy as captain after the final victory over Barcelona. In 1963 he transferred to FK Austria but later returned to Portugal to work as a coach.

Florian Albert

Born: September 15, 1941, Hungary.
Club: Ferencvaros.

Albert was the first outstanding player to emerge in Hungary after the dissolution of the

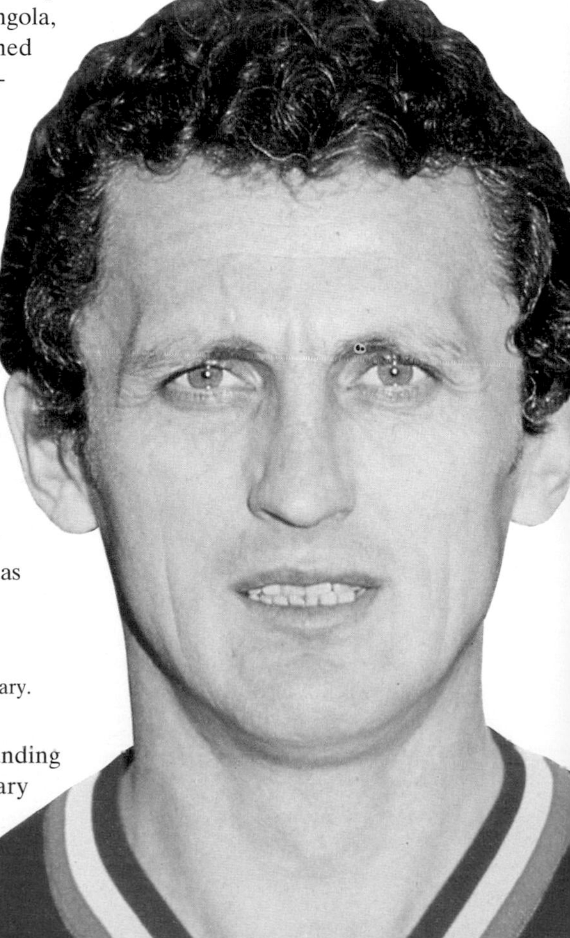

great team of the early 1950s. Albert was a farmer's son whose family moved to Budapest while he was still a boy. His talent was quickly recognized by the youth coaches of Ferencvaros, and he made his international debut at 17, in a 3–2 win over Sweden in Budapest, a few days after passing his major school examinations. Center-forward Albert was three times the leading scorer in the Hungarian league and four times a league championship winner with Ferencvaros. His most memorable display was as the inspiration of Hungary's 3–1 win over Brazil at the 1966 World Cup finals, and he was voted European Footballer of the Year the following year.

Ivor Allchurch

Born: October 16, 1919, Wales.
Clubs: Swansea (Wales), Newcastle (Eng), Cardiff, Swansea (Wales).

Slim, elegant, creative and a natural scorer: Ivor the Golden Boy had just about everything an inside-forward needed in the first quarter-century after the Second World War, except luck. He was fated to play in mediocre club teams throughout his long career, and even his excellent work for his country went largely to waste, except in the 1958 World Cup. He won 68 caps, spread over 16 years, and scored 23 goals – records which stood until the 1990s. His 251 League goals in nearly 700 appearances emphasized his excellent finishing.

Luigi Allemandi

Born: November 18, 1903, Italy.
Clubs: Juventus, Internazionale, Roma.

Allemandi was a left-back and one of the outstanding personalities in *Calcio* in the inter-war years. He played 25 times for his country and would have made more appearances but for a match-fixing scandal. Allemandi was accused of having accepted a bribe from a director of Torino to fix a match while playing for Juventus in 1927. The matter did not emerge until a year later when Allemandi, despite reports identifying him as one of the best players on the field, was found guilty and suspended for life. By now he was playing for Internazionale, who challenged the ban on his behalf and had it quashed. In 1929 Allemandi returned to Italy's team for a match against Czechoslovakia, and he went on to win a World Cup medal in 1934.

(LEFT) ALBERT *National debut at 17*

José Altafini

Born: August 27, 1938, Brazil.
Clubs: Palmeiras, São Paulo FC (Br), Milan, Napoli, Juventus (It), Chiasso (Swz).

Altafini was a subject of both confusion and admiration throughout his career. A direct, aggressive center-forward, he began with Palmeiras of São Paulo, where he was known by the nickname of Mazzola because of his resemblance to the Italian star of the late 1940s. He played at the 1958 World Cup and was immediately signed by Milan. The Italians insisted on reverting to Altafini's own name and he played for his "new" country at the 1962 World Cup finals. A year later Altafini scored a record 14 goals in Milan's European Cup success, including two goals in the final victory over Benfica at Wembley. After falling out with Milan he joined Omar Sivori in inspiring a Napoli revival, then became a "super substitute" with Juventus. Altafini is now a TV soccer analyst in Italy.

AMANCIO *10 times a champion*

Amancio Amaro Varela

Born: October 12, 1939, Spain.
Clubs: La Coruña, Real Madrid.

In 1962 Real Madrid, seeking a replacement for Italy-bound Luis Del Sol, bought outside-right Amancio from his home-town club, Real Deportivo de La Coruña. Coach Miguel Muñoz switched him to inside-right, playing him first in midfield and then as a striker. His outstanding technique and acceleration brought him a string of honors. He played 42 times for Spain between 1964 and 1971, was 10 times a Spanish league champion with Madrid and four times a cup-winner. In 1968 he was honored with selection for a World eleven against Brazil, but the highlight of his career was winning the European Nations Championship with Spain in 1964 on his home ground, the Estadio Bernabeu in Madrid.

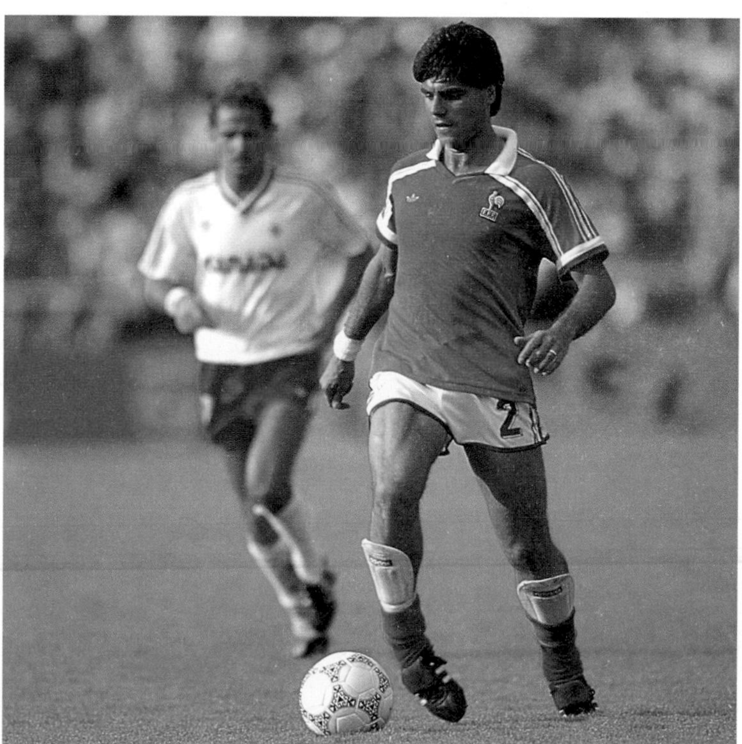

AMOROS *Set a French record of 82 international caps*

Amarildo Tavares Silveira

Born: June 29, 1939, Brazil.
Clubs: Botafogo (Br), Milan, Fiorentina (It).

Amarildo, an attacking inside-left whose slight appearance disguised a wiry frame, burst on to the international scene at the 1962 World Cup finals after Pele was injured. He had not expected to play when he was called in to deputize for O Rei in a decisive group match against Spain. Brazil recovered from a goal down to win 2–1 thanks to two late strikes from Amarildo, and in the final against Czechoslovakia he proved decisive once more – scoring with a snapshot which deceived the goalkeeper on the near post. A year later Amarildo was bought by Milan, and he enjoyed a successful career in Italy with Milan and Fiorentina, with whom he won the championship in 1969. Amarildo stayed in Italy after retiring and joined Fiorentina's youth coaching staff.

Manuel Amoros

Born: February 1, 1961, France.
Clubs: Monaco, Marseille.

Amoros played both right- and left-back in the outstanding French national team of the 1980s. Born in Nimes of Spanish parents, Amoros was an outstanding teenage exponent of both soccer and rugby. Monaco persuaded him to concentrate on soccer, and he played for France at youth and Under-21 levels before a surprise, and highly successful, promotion to the senior national team at the 1982 World Cup finals, in which France finished fourth. Amoros won a European Championship medal in 1984, despite missing most of the tournament after being sent off in the opening match against Denmark. During his career, most of which he spent with Monaco before joining Marseille, he set a French record of 82 caps.

José Leandro Andrade

Born: November 20, 1898, Uruguay.
Clubs: Bella Vista, Nacional.

Andrade was an old-fashioned wing-half in the 2–3–5 tactical system which served much of the world for the first half of the century. He was a stalwart of the great Uruguayan teams of the 1920s and 1930s, winning gold medals at the Olympic Games soccer tournaments of both 1924 and 1928. Injury then threatened to end his career but Andrade was recalled, because of his vast experience, for the inaugural World Cup finals which Uruguay won on home ground in 1930. He played 41 times for his country before retiring in 1933. Andrade's nephew, Victor Rodriguez Andrade, won the World Cup in 1950 and was never once booked or sent off.

Giancarlo Antognoni

Born: April 1, 1954, Italy.
Club: Fiorentina.

In the 1970s and early 1980s Antognoni was considered by Italian fans to be the successor to Milan's Gianni Rivera as their Golden Boy of Italian soccer. A graceful, wonderfully intuitive midfield general, Antognoni cost Fiorentina a large transfer fee as a teenager from Fourth Division Astimacombi in 1972. He went straight into the Fiorentina team and made the first of his 73 appearances for Italy in the autumn of 1974. Antognoni was a regular transfer target for Italy's richest clubs but remained faithful to Fiorentina until he eventually wound down his career in Switzerland. Sadly, Antognoni missed Italy's victory over West Germany in the 1982 World Cup final after suffering a gashed ankle in the semi-final defeat of Poland.

ANTONIONI *Italian soccer's golden boy of the 1970s*

Osvaldo Ardiles

Born: August 3, 1952, Argentina.
Clubs: Huracan (Arg), Tottenham (Eng), Paris S-G (Fr), Tottenham, Queen's Park Rangers (Eng).

Ardiles combined legal and soccer studies in the mid-1970s when he earned his initial reputation as midfield general of Argentina under the coaching of Cesar Luis Menotti. Hardly had Ardiles collected his winners' medal at the 1978 World Cup when he and national team-mate Ricardo Villa were together subjects of a remarkable transfer to Tottenham Hotspur. Ardiles cost Spurs $500,000, which made him one of the greatest bargains of modern soccer history. He completed his outstanding playing career which included Tottenham's FA Cup success of 1981 and their UEFA Cup triumph of 1984. He returned to White Hart Lane as coach in the summer of 1993.

ARDILES *success on two continents*

Luis Artime

Born: 1939, Argentina.
Clubs: Atlanta, River Plate, Independiente (Arg), Palmeiras (Br), Nacional (Uru), Fluminense (Br).

Artime was a center-forward in the traditional Argentine mold: powerful, aggressive and prolific. He scored 47 goals in two teenage seasons with minor Buenos Aires club Atlanta to earn a move in 1961 to River Plate, with whom he will always be most closely linked. He climaxed a three-year spell, including 66 league goals, by leading Argentina's attack at the 1966 World Cup finals. Artime then joined Independiente, scoring 44 goals in 18 months before moving on to Palmeiras and then to Nacional of Montevideo, with whom he was top Uruguayan league marksman three years in a row. He also scored 24 goals for Argentina.

Georgi Asparoukhov

Born: May 4, 1943, Bulgaria.
Clubs: Botev Plovdiv, Spartak Sofia, Levski Sofia.

"Gundi" Asparoukhov remains one of the most outstanding yet tragic players in Bulgaria's history. A tall, direct center-forward, he had scored 19 goals in 49 internationals when he died in a car crash, aged 28, in 1971. Asparoukhov led Bulgaria's attack in the World Cup finals of 1962, 1966 and 1970 and scored 150 goals in 245 league games for his only senior club, Levski Sofia. Portuguese club Benfica tried to sign him in 1966 after he impressed in a European Cup match. But Asparoukhov did not want to move because he had all he wanted in Bulgaria . . . including his favorite Alfa Romeo sports car which, ultimately, proved the death of him.

José Augusto

Born: April 13, 1937, Portugal.
Clubs: Barreirense, Benfica.

Augusto was originally a center-forward, and had already made his debut for Portugal in this position when Benfica bought him from local club Barreirense in 1959 on coach Bela Guttmann's recommendation. He then succesfully converted him into an outside-right. Augusto was considered, after Frenchman Raymond Kopa, as the best "thinking" player in Europe and appeared in five European Cup finals. He was a winner in 1961 and 1962 and a loser in 1963, 1965 and finally in 1968 against Manchester United, by which time he had been transformed again into an attacking midfield player. Augusto was a key member of the Portugal side which finished third at the 1966 World Cup, and later coached both Benfica and Portugal.

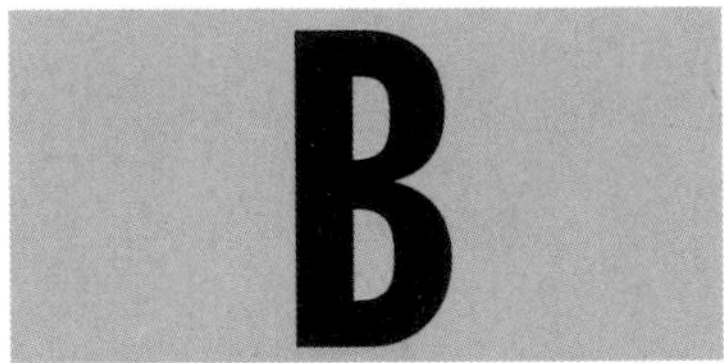

Roberto Baggio

Born: February 18, 1967, Italy.
Clubs: Fiorentina, Juventus.

Roberto Baggio became the world's most expensive soccer player when Juventus bought him from Fiorentina in the summer of 1990, on the eve of the World Cup finals. In those finals he showed why he was worth $13 million by scoring a marvelous solo goal against Czechoslovakia. His transfer provoked three days of riots by angry fans in the streets of Florence. Juventus saw Baggio as the successor to Michel Platini as the inspiration of their attack. The Italian league title continued to elude them but at least, in 1993, Baggio led Juventus to victory in the UEFA Cup. In the autumn he guided Italy's World Cup qualifying campaign, topped a century of league goals and was voted World and European Footballer of the Year.

Gordon Banks

Born: December 20, 1937, England.
Clubs: Leicester, Stoke.

A product of the prolific Chesterfield "goalkeeper academy," Banks went on to undying fame with England. He set all kinds of keeping records, including 73 caps, 23 consecutive

ROBERTO BAGGIO *Cost Juventus a world record fee of $12 million in 1990*

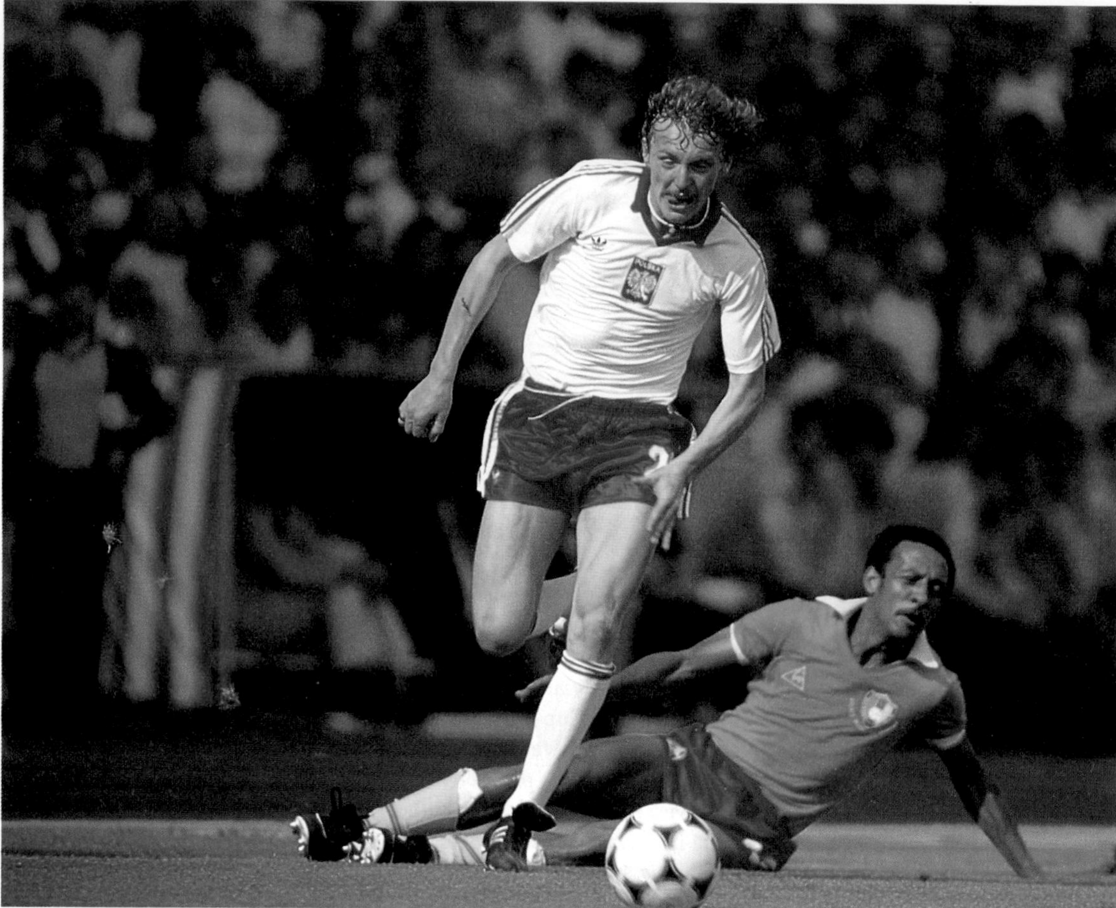

BONIEK *The greatest Polish player of all time thanks to his feats with Juventus*

the final against Liverpool in the shadow of the Heysel disaster. Boniek scored 24 goals in 80 internationals.

Giampiero Boniperti

Born: July 4, 1928, Italy.
Club: Juventus.

Boniperti was the original Golden Boy of Italian soccer. He enjoyed a meteoric rise: within a few months of being signed by Juventus from minor club Momo, in July 1946, he was promoted to the Italian national team and made his debut in a 5–1 defeat by Austria in Vienna. Originally a center-forward, Boniperti later switched to inside-forward and played on the right wing for FIFA's World eleven against England in 1953 (scoring twice in a 4–4 draw). Boniperti won five Italian league titles with Juventus, for whom he played a record 444 league games. He was a "father figure" in the Charles/Sivori team of the late 1950s and scored eight goals in 38 internationals. On retiring from the game he took up a business career which eventually turned full circle when he became a hugely successful president of Juventus in the 1970s and early 1980s under the Agnelli family patronage.

Jozsef Bozsik

Born: September 28, 1929, Hungary.
Clubs: Kispest, Honved.

Bozsik will always be remembered as right-half of the wonderful Hungarian national team of the early 1950s. A teammate of Ferenc Puskas with Kispest and then Honved, Bozsik was the midfield brains but could also score spectacular goals, including one from 30 yards in the historic 6–3 win over England at Wembley in 1953. Bozsik made his debut for Hungary against Bulgaria in 1947, returned home – unlike teammates Puskas, Kocsis and Czibor – after the 1956 Revolution and combined a career as a soccer player with that of a Member of Parliament. In 1962 he scored a goal against Uruguay in a friendly to mark his 100th and last game for his country. Bozsik had been a member of Hungary's victorious side at the 1952 Helsinki Olympics.

Raymond Braine

Born: April 28, 1907, Belgium.
Clubs: Beerschot (Bel), Sparta Prague (Cz), Beerschot (Bel).

Braine was considered the greatest Belgian soccer player until the advent of Paul Van Himst in the 1960s. In 1922 he made his league debut for Beerschot at the age of 15 and was chosen, that same year, for a Belgian eleven against Holland. Clapton Orient of London tried to sign Braine in 1928 but could not obtain a work permit for him to come to England, so instead he turned professional in Czechoslovakia with the great Sparta Prague club. The Czechs wanted him to get citizenship and play for them in the 1934 World Cup, but Braine preferred to represent Belgium – and did so at the 1938 World Cup after returning home to Beerschot. Braine's center-forward talents earned him selection for Western Europe against Central Europe in 1938, and then for Europe against England that same year. He won 54 caps for Belgium.

Paul Breitner

Born: September 5, 1951, West Germany.
Clubs: Bayern Munich (W Ger), Real Madrid (Sp), Eintracht Braunschweig, Bayern Munich (W Ger).

Breitner was a flamboyant virtuoso of a left-back when Helmut Schön brought him onto the West German national team in 1971–72. He was a key member of a the new, Bayern-dominated side which also featured Franz Beckenbauer, Sepp Maier, Uli Hoeness and Gerd Müller. Breitner demonstrated his big-match temperament by nervelessly converting the penalty which brought West Germany even in the 1974 World Cup final against Holland. A soccer playing intellectual, he felt he was being stifled at Bayern and moved forward to midfield on transferring to Real Madrid. A falling-out with the West German soccer authorities caused him to miss the 1978 World Cup, but he returned in 1982 and again scored in the final — this time only the Germans' consolation goal in their defeat by Italy on his old home field in Madrid. Breitner is one of only four players to have scored in two World Cup finals.

BREITNER *Soccer intellectual*

Billy Bremner

Born: December 9, 1942, Scotland.
Clubs: Leeds United, Hull, Doncaster (Eng).

Bremner made his debut for Leeds at 17, as a winger partnered by Don Revie, a man nearly twice his age. Later midfielder Bremner and coach Revie were outstanding figures as Leeds emerged from decades of mediocrity to be a force feared throughout the game. Bremner's fierce tackling, competitive spirit and selfless example made him a worthy winner of various medals, though the list of second places was much longer. He was not a prolific scorer, but a useful one, providing the winner in each of three FA Cup semifinals. He also won 55 caps, including three at the 1974 World Cup, when Scotland were eliminated after three matches without defeat.

Tomas Brolin

Born: November 29, 1969, Sweden.
Clubs: GIF Sundsvall (Swe), Parma (It).

Brolin had long been considered one of Sweden's outstanding attacking prospects before proving the point by scoring twice in his debut for the senior team in the 4–2 win over Wales in the spring of 1990. Brolin followed up with two more against Finland to earn a late call to Sweden's World Cup team. At Italia '90, although the rest of the team was disappointing and Sweden was quickly eliminated, Brolin's outstanding displays alerted Italian clubs and Parma immediately bought him. He starred for Sweden at the 1992 European Championship – scoring a marvelous solo goal against England – and then helped Parma to their first European success in the 1993 European Cup-winners' Cup.

Emilio Butragueño

Born: July 22, 1963, Spain.
Clubs: Castilla, Real Madrid.

Butragueño, nicknamed "the Vulture," was once considered not good enough by Real Madrid's youth coaches. Fortunately, Real's nursery club Castilla had second thoughts and Butragueño became "leader" of Madrid throughout the 1980s. His close control and talent as a marksman helped Madrid win the UEFA Cup in 1985 and 1986, and in both years Butragueño won the Prix Bravo as Europe's best young player. He made his scoring debut for Spain in 1984 in a World Cup qualifying victory over Wales, and in 1986 became a World Cup sensation when he scored four times for Spain in a five-goal thrashing of the well-respected Denmark in the second round of the finals in Mexico.

TOMAS BROLIN *Rocketed from nowhere to world star in six months in 1990*

C

Antonio Cabrini

Born: October 8, 1957, Italy.
Clubs: Atalanta, Juventus.

Antonio Cabrini had played only 22 games at left-back for Juventus when he was promoted to stardom by national coach Enzo Bearzot at the 1978 World Cup finals in Argentina. Overnight he was hailed as the "new Facchetti." Four years later Cabrini made a luckless piece of history when, against West Germany, he became the first man to miss a penalty in a World Cup final. But he deserves to be remembered for his all-round abilities which established him as both an outstanding defender and tackler as well as counter-puncher. During a decade of service with Juventus Cabrini won almost every honor in the game.

Rodion Camataru

Born: June 22, 1958, Romania.
Clubs: Universitatea Craiova, Dinamo Bucharest (Rom), Charleroi (Bel).

Camataru was a bluff, determined center-forward who scored more than 300 goals in Romanian league soccer before transferring to Belgium towards the end of his career. In 1986–87 he won the Golden Boot awarded to Europe's top league marksman, albeit amid controversial circumstances. Camataru totalled 44 goals but many of them were scored in a string of "easy" matches towards the end of the season and revelations after the collapse of the Communist regime cast doubt on

CAMATARU *Golden Boot-winner*

the integrity of the matches. Not that this detracted from Camataru's abilities which were rewarded, even in the twilight of his career, with selection for the 1990 World Cup finals.

Eric Cantona

Born: May 24, 1966, France.
Clubs: Martigues, Auxerre, Marseille, Bordeaux, Montpellier (Fr), Leeds, Manchester United (Eng).

Eric Cantona is one of the great paradoxes of European soccer; his career a mixture of glorious success and disciplinary muddle. Cantona, born in Marseille, was discovered by Auxerre and sold to Marseille for $3 million in 1988. Two months later he scored in his international debut against West Germany. Later he was banned for a year from the national team for insulting coach Henri Michel, then bounced controversially to Bordeaux, Montpellier and Nimes before quitting the game after a shouting match with yet another disciplinary commission. Sheffield Wednesday offered him a trial, but it was Leeds United whom he joined. He played a crucial role in their 1992 championship win, then repeated the magic in the next two years for Manchester United.

Antonio Carbajal

Born: June 7, 1929, Mexico.
Clubs: España, Leon.

Carbajal set a record, at the 1966 World Cup in England, as the only man to have appeared in no fewer than five finals tournaments. A tall, agile goalkeeper, he played for Mexico in Brazil in the 1950 finals, in Switzerland in 1954, in Sweden in 1958 and in Chile in 1962. The 1966 finals provided an appropriate retirement point, since Carbajal had made his international debut at the 1948 London Olympic Games. On his return to Mexico that year he turned professional with Leon and played for them until his retirement in 1966. Later he became a respected and popular coach and was presented with FIFA's gold award for services to the world game.

Careca

Born: October 5, 1960, Brazil.
Clubs: Guarani, São Paulo (Br), Napoli (It), Hitachi (Jap).

Careca was one of the outstanding spearheads in the world game throughout the 1980s and early 1990s. Born in Brazil's Campinas state, he helped unrated Guarani win the 1987–88 national championship and was later sold to São Paulo. Careca missed the 1982 World Cup after being injured in training on the eve of the finals. He made superb amends with five goals in Mexico in 1986, was voted Brazil's Sportsman of the Year and was subsequently transferred to Italy's Napoli. His attacking partnership with Diego Maradona lifted Napoli to the 1989 UEFA Cup and 1990 Italian league championship. Careca quit Brazil's World Cup squad in the spring of 1993 to start a new career in Japan.

Johnny Carey

Born: February 23, 1919, Rep. of Ireland.
Club. Manchester United (Eng).

Johnny Carey was one of the early all-purpose players, at home as full-back, wing-half, inside-forward, even as back-up goalkeeper. He was a calming influence, short on pace but long on perception. Traded from a Dublin junior club he was one of the transfer bargains of all time. He captained the fine Manchester United team of the early post-war years, winning League and Cup once each and narrowly missing several more, earned 37 caps, and led the Rest of Europe selection against Great Britain in 1946. Carey later coached Blackburn (twice), Everton – until he was fired in the back of a taxi when they were lying fifth in the table – Orient and Nottingham Forest.

CAREY *One of the great captains*

Amadeo Carrizo

Born: June 12, 1926, Argentina.
Clubs: River Plate (Arg), Alianza (Peru), Millonarios (Col).

Carrizo set a string of longevity records in a goalkeeping career which lasted from the mid-1940s to the mid-1960s. A dominant character with great personality, Carrizo played 520 Argentine league matches over 21 seasons until he was 44. He won five league championships with River Plate in the early 1950s and played in the 1958 World Cup finals in Sweden. Carrizo was blamed for Argentina's 6–1 defeat by Czechoslovakia but was recalled two years later with great success when Argentina beat England and Brazil to win the 1960 "Little World Cup" in Brazil. After parting company with River Plate he played on in Peru and Colombia before returning home to coach youth teams.

Carlos Caszely

Born: July 5, 1950, Chile.
Clubs: Colo Colo (Chile), Levante (Sp), Colo Colo (Chile).

Caszely was outstanding as a goal-scoring inside-forward in the early 1970s when Colo Colo became the first Chilean club to reach a final of the South American club cup (Copa Libertadores). However, his loudly-proclaimed left-wing political beliefs placed him at risk after the revolution which overthrew President Allende in 1973, and he moved to Spain with Levante. Caszely played for Chile in the 1974 World Cup finals in West Germany and then again eight years later in Spain. By this time, the political situation had eased back home and he had returned to Colo Colo to end his playing days there.

Jan Ceulemans

Born: February 28, 1957, Belgium.
Clubs: Lierse, Club Brugge.

Ceulemans was the central pillar of Belgium's national team throughout the 1980s, first as a striker and then as a midfield general. He began with Lierse and cost Brugge a then record

JAN CEULEMANS *The pillar of Belgium's recent World Cup success*

STÉPHANE CHAPUISAT *Even more famous son of a famous father*

domestic fee of $500,000 in the summer of 1978. In 1980 he scored 29 of their 76 goals in a league title win and was voted Footballer of the Year for the first time. A year later Ceulemans was poised to join Milan but his mother persuaded him to stay in Belgium, a decision which he never regretted. Ceulemans played with distinction in the Belgian team which finished fourth at the 1986 World Cup finals in Mexico. In 96 internationals – a Belgian record – he scored 26 goals.

Cha Bum Kun

Born: May 21, 1953, South Korea.
Clubs: Darmstadt, Eintracht Frankfurt, Bayer Leverkusen (W Ger).

Thanks to his record at the peak of the European game in West Germany's Bundesliga, Cha ranks as South Korea's finest player. He was a popular fixture from 1978, when he arrived at Darmstadt, until his retirement in 1986 after appearing at his first and only World Cup finals. Cha, who won the UEFA Cup with Eintracht Frankfurt in 1980, was ignored by his country after moving to Germany, and recalling him for those World Cup finals in 1986 demanded a major diplomatic exercise. Original South Korean records claimed an astonishing 141 international appearances for Cha, but on further scrutiny this was later reduced to the more probable total of 41.

Stéphane Chapuisat

Born: June 28, 1969, Switzerland.
Clubs: FC Malley, Red Star Zurich, Lausanne (Swz), Bayer Uerdingen, Borussia Dortmund (Ger).

Chapuisat, the finest current Swiss striker, is son of a former international, Pierre-Albert Chapuisat, who earned notoriety in his day as a sharp-tempered defender. Son Stéphane, by contrast, not only plays his soccer at the other end of the field but has the most even temperament, which has helped him lead Dortmund's revival in goal-scoring partnership with Denmark's Flemming Povlsen. Chapuisat moved to Germany in 1991 with Uerdingen and transferred to Dortmund a year later, helping them reach the 1993 UEFA Cup final.

John Charles

Born: December 27, 1931, Wales.
Clubs: Leeds (Eng), Juventus (It), Leeds (Eng), Roma (It), Cardiff (Wales).

Known as the Gentle Giant, John Charles allied great skill to an awesome physique, and was good enough to set a Leeds record of 42 goals in one season as a centre-forward, while also playing as a dominant central defender for his country. He was one of the first British exports to Italy, in 1957, and probably the best. The record fee for a British player bought Juventus a man who became a legend and helped to win the Serie A title three times in five years, scoring 93 times in 155 games. After some unhappy final seasons he became a non-league coach, bar owner and shopkeeper.

Bobby Charlton

see Legends (pages 106–07)

Igor Chislenko

Born: January 4, 1939, Soviet Union.
Clubs: Moscow Torpedo, Moscow Dynamo.

Chislenko was one of Europe's most incisive outside- or inside-rights in the 1960s, despite standing only 5–7. He began with the Moscow Torpedo youth section but transferred to Dynamo at 17 and played 300 league games, winning two league titles, with the club. Chislenko, also a good ice hockey player, appeared at the World Cups of 1962 and 1966 as well as in the European Nations Championship in between. He was the best Soviet forward in the 1966 World Cup, and their prospects of reaching the final disappeared when he was sent off during the semifinal against West Germany.

Hector Chumpitaz

Born: April 12, 1944, Peru.
Club: Sporting Cristal.

Chumpitaz, a powerful, inspirational center-back, starred for Peru in the World Cup finals of both 1970 and 1978. On the first occasion he was a promising youngster, on the second an experienced, resilient organizer of an otherwise fragile defence. Chumpitaz played all his senior career with Sporting Cristal of Lima and appeared around 100 times for his country between his debut in 1966 and the six-goal thrashing by Argentina which controversially ended Peru's 1978 World Cup campaign. Earlier claims that he played 147 full internationals have been discounted, Peru having played "only" 110 matches in that time.

Mario Esteves Coluna

Born: August 6, 1935, Mozambique.
Clubs: Deportivo Lourenço Marques (Mozambique), Benfica (Port).

Coluna was midfield general of Benfica's outstanding club team in the 1960s as well as commander of the Portuguese national team which reached the World Cup semifinals in 1966. Born in Mozambique, Coluna was the local long-jump record-holder when he was lured away by Benfica to play soccer in 1954. Originally a center-forward, he was converted to inside-left and then midfield by Benfica and won 73 caps for Portugal. In both of Benfica's European Cup final victories of 1961 and 1962, he scored with typically spectacular long-range efforts. Coluna later turned to coaching and became Sports Minister in Mozambique.

Gianpiero Combi

Born: December 18, 1902, Italy.
Club: Juventus.

Combi was goalkeeper and captain of the Italian team which won the 1934 World Cup, thus pre-dating Dino Zoff in that dual role by nearly 50 years. Combi was considered Italy's best goalkeeper until Zoff came along. He started unpromisingly, beaten seven times by Hungary in Budapest in his first international in 1924, and did not gain a regular place in Italy's team until the Paris Olympics of 1928. He was goalkeeper in Juventus's four consecutive league title successes of 1931 to 1934, the year when he retired – immediately after captaining Italy to victory over Czechoslovakia in the World Cup final in Rome. That was Combi's 47th international.

CONTI *Outwits West Germany's Uli Stielike in the 1982 World Cup final*

Bruno Conti

Born: March 13, 1955, Italy.
Clubs: Roma, Genoa, Roma.

Wingers made a comeback on the tactical scene thanks to the displays of Bruno Conti at the 1982 World Cup. Italy's right-winger proved a crucial influence in increasing the momentum of their campaign, which took them past Argentina and Brazil and on via Poland to victory over West Germany in the final. Conti had struggled to make an impression in the early years of his career but was rescued by Swedish coach Nils Liedholm, who brought Conti back from a loan spell with Genoa and turned him into one of the most consistently effective creative players in *Calcio*. Conti scored five goals in 47 internationals between his debut against Luxembourg in 1980 and the second round defeat by France at the 1986 World Cup.

Henri "Rik" Coppens

Born: April 29, 1930, Belgium.
Clubs: Beerschot, Charleroi, Crossing Molenbeek, Berchem, Tubantia.

Coppens was the *enfant terrible* of Belgian soccer in the 1950s: a center-forward or occasional outside-left of great goal-scoring talent, but one who carried his aggression over into his dealings with teammates, clubs and other officials. Coppens began with Beerschot as a 10-year-old, and on his debut at 16 in a crucial relegation match he scored twice and made Beerschot's two other goals. Three times he was the league's leading scorer and ended his career with a then record total of 217 goals. He once scored six goals in a game against Tilleur. Coppens altogether played 47 times for Belgium.

Alberto da Costa Pereira

Born: 1929, Portuguese East Africa.
Club: Benfica.

Costa Pereira was another of Portugal's great discoveries in the African colonies. He was born in Nacala, Portuguese East Africa, and joined Benfica in 1954. He was a tower of strength in their biggest triumphs, though prone to the odd unpredictable error when the pressure was off. Costa Pereira won seven league titles with Benfica and played in four European Cup finals – the victories of 1961 and 1962 and the defeats of 1963 and 1965. In the latter game, against Internazionale on a quagmire of a field in Milan, Costa Pereira was injured early in the game and had to leave the field. He retired soon after to take up coaching. Costa Pereira played 24 times for Portugal, but is not to be confused with the José Pereira who kept goal at the 1966 World Cup.

Johan Cruyff

see Legends (pages 108–09)

Teofilo Cubillas

Born: March 8, 1949, Peru.
Clubs: Alianza (Peru), Basel (Swz), FC Porto (Port), Alianza (Peru), Fort Lauderdale Strikers (US).

Cubillas was a key figure in Peru's greatest international successes, their appearances at the 1970 and 1978 World Cup finals, in which he scored a total of 10 goals. A powerfully-built inside left, he forged an ideal partnership with the more nimble Hugo Sotil in 1970 then, in 1978, emerged as an attacking director. Cubillas also packed a powerful shot, scoring

CUBILLAS *Attacking director*

a memorable goal against Scotland in the 1978 finals. He was not particularly successful in Europe, where he grew homesick. But in Peru he remained a legend after 38 goals in 88 internationals and an appearance for the World eleven in a 1978 UNICEF charity match.

Zoltan Czibor

Born: 1929, Hungary.
Clubs: Ferencvaros, Csepel, Honved (Hun), Barcelona, Español (Sp).

Czibor was outside-left in the great Hungarian team of the early 1950s. He had pace and a powerful shot, which he used to great effect in 43 internationals before he moved to Spain following the Hungarian Revolution of 1956. Czibor and teammate Sandor Kocsis were persuaded to sign for Barcelona by Ladislav Kubala and enjoyed five more years in the international spotlight, reaching a climax when Barcelona, most unluckily, lost to Benfica in the 1961 European Cup Final. Czibor had a short spell with neighbors Español before he retired and eventually returned home to live in Hungary.

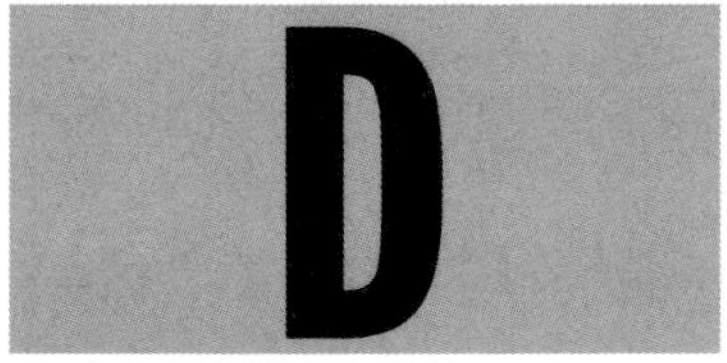

DALGLISH *A winner as player and manager*

Kenny Dalglish

Born: March 4, 1951, Scotland.
Clubs: Celtic (Scot), Liverpool (Eng).

Kenny Dalglish is the most "decorated" man in senior British soccer, having won 25 major trophies as player and coach, in addition to 102 caps (a record for Scotland) and 30 goals (another record, held jointly with Denis Law). Dalglish's signing for Celtic was their other coup – aside from their European Cup triumph – in 1967. He went on to inspire the club to more great deeds before joining Liverpool for $600,000 in 1977, to replace Kevin Keegan. Already a very good player, he became legendary at Anfield, thanks to initial pace, excellent control, an eye for a chance and the priceless gift that so few have, of appearing to exist in his own cocoon of time and space. He also won many new friends for his dignified bearing after the two disasters of Heysel and Hillsborough.

Bill "Dixie" Dean

Born: January 22, 1907, England.
Clubs: Tranmere, Everton, Notts Co.

Anybody who begins his international career by scoring 2, 3, 2, 2, 3 – even in days of lax defense and five forwards – deserves a place in the Hall of Fame. Curly-topped Bill Dean was 20 at the time, and still only 21 when he scored his record 60 League goals in one season for Everton, finishing 2, 4, 3 to overhaul George Camsell's 59 for Middlesbrough. Overall, he scored 18 goals in 16 England appearances, 47 in 18 of the other representative matches which were so popular in pre-television days, 28 in 33 Cup ties (one in the 1933 Wembley win), and 379 in 438 League games. All this despite, as a teenager, fracturing his skull.

Luis Del Sol Miramontes

Born: 1938, Spain.
Clubs: Betis Seville, Real Madrid (Sp), Juventus (It).

Del Sol was inside-right on the legendary Real Madrid forward line which won the 1960 European Cup against Eintracht Frankfurt at Hampden. A neat, aggressive midfielder, he had been a wing-half at his hometown club, Betis of Seville, when the Madrid management decided that the great Brazilian, Didi, was not fitting in well enough alongside Alfredo Di Stefano. Del Sol was hurriedly bought in the middle of the 1959–60 season and ran his legs off in support of veterans Di Stefano and Puskas. In 1962 Madrid sold Del Sol to Juventus to raise the cash for a vain attempt to buy Pele from Santos. Del Sol was a pillar of the Italian league, consistently reliable and inspirational through eight seasons with Juventus and two with Roma, before his retirement and return to Spain in 1972.

Kazimierz Deyna

Born: October 23, 1947, Poland. *Clubs:* Starogard, Sportowy Lodz, Legia Warsaw (Pol), Manchester City (Eng), San Diego (US).

Poland's emergence as a world power in the early 1970s owed a huge debt to the skilled grace of Deyna, their midfield fulcrum. Deyna played center midfield, supported by workers such as Maszczyk and Kasperczak, and was constantly creating openings for strikers Lato and Gadocha. He earned a domestic reputation in helping army club Legia win the league in 1969 and was promoted to the national squads when the Legia coach, Kazimierz Gorski, was appointed coach of Poland. Deyna won an Olympic gold medal with Poland in Munich in 1972 then returned to the Olympiastadion two

DIDI *Making the ball "talk" in the 1958 World Cup finals*

years later to celebrate Poland's best-ever third-place finish at the World Cup. He was never quite the same player after moving abroad, first to England and then to the United States, where he died in a car crash. Deyna scored 38 goals in 102 internationals.

Didi (full name: Waldyr Pereira)

Born: October 8, 1928, Brazil.
Clubs: FC Rio Branco, FC Lencoes, Madureiro, Fluminense, Botafogo (Br), Real Madrid, Valencia (Sp), Botafogo. (Br).

The success of Brazil's 4–2–4 system, revealed in all its glory internationally at the 1958 World Cup, rested heavily on the creative talent of Didi, one of the greatest of midfield generals. Didi's technique was extraordinary. Team-mates said he could "make the ball talk," and drop it on a coin from any distance, any angle. Didi was the first to perfect the "dead leaf" free kick, with which he scored a dozen of his 31 goals in 85 appearances for Brazil. He won the World Cup in 1958 and 1962 and counted as the only failure of his career a spell in between with Real Madrid, where he failed to settle in alongside Di Stefano and Puskas.

Alfredo Di Stefano

see Legends (pages 110–11)

Domingos Antonio da Guia

Born: November 19, 1912, Brazil.
Clubs: Bangu, Vasco da Gama (Br), Nacional (Uru), Boca Juniors (Arg), Flamengo, Corinthians, Bangu (Br).

Domingos was a full-back of the old school, as much a pivoting central defender as a marker in the old-fashioned 2–3–5 tactical scheme of things. His talents earned him transfers all around South America, and he remains less of a legend in Uruguay and Argentina than he is in Brazil. The Uruguayans nicknamed him the Divine Master. Domingos made his debut for Brazil in 1931, was a key member of the team which reached the 1938 World Cup semifinals, and did not retire until 1948. By this time he had returned to his original club, Bangu. His contemporary, center-forward Leonidas da Silva, once said no defender ever "read a game" better than Domingos.

Hans-Jürgen Dorner

Born: January 25, 1951, East Germany.
Club: Dynamo Dresden.

East Germany produced a handful of outstanding individual players in that state's independent soccer existence between 1950 and 1990. Joachim Streich was a fine center-forward, Jurgen Sparwasser a dangerous fellow striker, Hans-Jurgen Kreische the most creative inside-forward. Dorner was by far the greatest defender, a stopper then a sweeper who commanded the edge of his penalty area with security and respect. He played his entire career with Dynamo Dresden and totaled exactly 100 internationals between 1969 and 1985, scoring nine goals and winning an Olympic gold medal in 1976. Dorner was three times Footballer of the Year, five times East German champion and four times a cup-winner. After the reunification of Germany he was appointed on to the coaching staff of the German federation.

Dragan Dzajic

Born: May 30, 1956, Yugoslavia.
Clubs: Red Star Belgrade (Yug), Bastia (Fr), Red Star (Yug).

The British press baptized Dzajic the "magic Dragan" after his left-wing skills helped take England apart in the semifinals of the 1968 European Nations Championship. Dzajic had pace, skill and intelligence and was perhaps the greatest soccer hero to have emerged in post-war Yugoslavia. He was five times a national champion, four times a cup-winner and earned selection for a variety of World and European elevens on five occasions. Dzajic remained an outside-left throughout a career which brought him 23 goals in 85 internationals, never needing to fade back into midfield like so many wingers who lose the edge of their talent. He retired in 1978 and became general manager of his original club, Red Star.

E

Duncan Edwards

Born: October 1, 1936, England.
Club: Manchester United.

Duncan Edwards was a giant who is still revered by generations who never saw him play. Comparatively few did, for his career was brief, but his awesome power and genuine all-round skill, as creator as well as destroyer, made him a man apart. His death in the 1958 Munich air disaster robbed England of possibly its most-capped player of all time, after 18 appearances in under three years. He remains England's youngest international this century. At club level, Edwards was the outstanding discovery among Manchester United's many fine Busby Babes. Sometimes he seemed to be a team in himself, as at Wembley in 1958, when ten men fought so bravely in a vain effort against an Aston Villa side set on depriving United of a merited cup and league "double."

Arsenio Erico

Born: 1915, Paraguay.
Clubs: FC Asuncion (Par), Independiente, Huracan (Arg).

The quality of Erico as a center-forward can best be illustrated by the fact that he was the boyhood hero of none other than Alfredo Di Stefano. Born in Paraguay, Erico went to Buenos Aires at 17 to play for a fund-raising team organized by the Paraguay Red Cross during the war with Bolivia. Directors of Independiente

EDWARDS *Epitome of the Busby Babes*

in the crowd were so impressed that immediately after the match they obtained his signature – in exchange for a donation to the Red Cross. Erico started badly, twice breaking an arm, but once he was fully fit he scored goals at a prolific rate and set a record with 47 goals in the 1936–37 league season. Several times he scored five goals in a game before going home to Paraguay in 1941 after squabbling over terms with Independiente. The club persuaded him to return, but knee cartilage trouble forced his premature retirement in 1944.

Eusebio

see Legends (pages 112–13)

Giacinto Facchetti

Born: July 18, 1942, Italy.
Clubs: Trevigliese, Internazionale.

Fullback was never a romantic role until the revolutionary emergence of Facchetti in the early 1960s. He had been a big, strapping center-forward with his local club in Treviso when he was signed by Inter and converted into a left-back by master coach Helenio Herrera. The rigid man-to-man marking system perfected by Herrera permitted Facchetti the freedom, when Inter attacked, to stride upfield in support of his own forwards. Facchetti scored 60 league goals, a record for a fullback in Italy, including 10 in the 1965–66 season. But his most important goal was reserved for the 1965 European Cup semifinals when he burst through in the inside-right position to score a decisive winning goal against Liverpool. Later Facchetti switched to sweeper, from which position he captained Italy against Brazil in the 1970 World Cup final. He would surely have taken his total of 94 caps to 100 but for an injury before the 1978 World Cup finals.

FACCHETTI *Great attacking fullback*

TOM FINNEY *Preston plumber equally skilled at dismantling defences*

Giovanni Ferrari

Born: December 6, 1907, Italy.
Clubs: Alessandria, Juventus, Internazionale, Bologna.

"Gioanin" Ferrari was inside-left of the Italian team who won the 1934 World Cup and was one of only two team members – the other was Giuseppe Meazza – retained for the 1938 triumph in France. Appropriately, both men made their international debut in the same game against Switzerland in Rome in 1930. Ferrari played then for Alessandria but soon moved to Juventus, with whom he won a record five consecutive league titles. He won further championship honours with Ambrosiana-Inter in 1940 and with Bologna in 1941. He scored 14 goals in 44 internationals and managed Italy at the 1962 World Cup finals in Chile.

Bernabe Ferreyra

Born: 1909, Argentina.
Clubs: Tigre, River Plate.

Nicknamed "the Mortar" for his ferocious shooting, Ferreyra was the first great hero of Argentine soccer. He scored more than 200 goals for Tigre and then River Plate in the 1930s, having joined River in one of the first formal transfers in Argentina after the establishment of professionalism. In his first season with River, 1932–33, Ferreyra scored a league record 43 goals and was such a regular feature of the weekly score sheets that one Buenos Aires newspaper offered a gold medal to any goalkeeper who could defy him. Ferreyra played only four internationals before retiring in 1939 and going back to his home town of Rufino. In 1943 he returned to River's front office and in 1956 was honored with a testimonial match in recognition of his loyalty and service to one of Argentina's great club institutions.

Tom Finney

Born: April 5, 1922, England.
Club: Preston.

Moderate in height, thin and fair, Finney was nondescript in appearance, but a player whose versatility was matched by his skill. "Grizzly strong" was the description applied to him by Bill Shankly, who played wing-half behind winger Finney at Preston – "Grizzly" in the sense of bear-like power rather than miserable attitude, for he always had a generous word for opponents as well as a rock-like solidity that belied his frame. Finney was genuinely two-footed, brave as they come, and in his later years a deep-lying center-forward similar to Hidegkuti. Lack of support left him bereft of honors at club level, but a 12-year England career, with 76 caps and a then-record 30 goals, established him at the highest peak.

Just Fontaine

Born: August 18, 1933, France.
Clubs: AC Marrakesh, USM Casablanca (Mor), Nice, Reims (Fr).

Fontaine secured a place in the history books when he scored a record 13 goals in the 1958 World Cup finals. Yet he was a surprising hero. Born in Morocco, he was a quick, direct center-forward who had played only twice for France before 1958. He had been discovered by Nice, then bought by Reims as replacement for Raymond Kopa, who had joined Real Madrid in 1956. He expected to be reserve to Reims teammate René Bliard at the 1958 World Cup, but Bliard was injured on the eve of the finals and Fontaine took his opportunity in record-breaking style. He owed most of his goals to Kopa's creative work alongside him and the partnership was renewed when Kopa returned to Reims in 1959. Sadly Fontaine had to retire in 1961 owing to two double fractures of a leg. He was twice top league scorer and totalled 27 goals in 20 internationals. Later he was president of the French players' union and, briefly, national coach.

FONTAINE *World Cup record*

ENZO FRANCESCOLI *Sends Melgar of Bolivia (No. 7) the wrong way in a World Cup qualifier*

Enzo Francescoli

Born: November 12, 1961, Uruguay.
Clubs: Wanderers (Uru), River Plate (Arg), Matra Racing, Marseille (Fr), Cagliari, Torino (It).

Francescoli is one of the latest in a long line of Uruguayan superstars, starting with the heroes of the 1920s and 1930s and continuing through Schiaffino, Goncalves and Rocha. He began with a small club, Wanderers, and then both Uruguayan giants, Penarol and Nacional, were outbid by River Plate of Argentina. Francescoli was top scorer in the Argentine league and voted South American Footballer of the Year before transferring to France with Racing in 1986. Even Francescoli's 32 goals in three seasons were not enough to save Racing from financial collapse. He scored 11 goals in 28 games in Marseille's championship season of 1989–90 before moving, first, to Italy with Cagliari, then in 1993 to Torino.

Arthur Friedenreich

Born: 1892, Brazil.
Clubs: Germania, Ipiranga, Americao, Paulistano, São Paulo FC, Flamengo.

Friedenreich was the first great Brazilian soccer player and the first player officially credited with more than 1,000 goals. His overall total was 1,329. The son of a German father and a Brazilian mother, Friedenreich was also significant as the first black player to break through the early racial/cultural barriers in Brazilian soccer. Nicknamed "the Tiger," Friedenreich began playing senior soccer at 17 and did not retire until 1935, when he was 43. He scored eight goals in 17 internationals for Brazil between 1914 and 1930. His first appearance for Brazil was in a 2–0 win against the English club Exeter City on July 21, 1914, when he lost two teeth in a collision with a defender.

Paulo Futre

Born: February 28, 1966, Portugal.
Clubs: Sporting, FC Porto (Port), Atletico Madrid (Sp), Benfica (Port), Marseille (France), Reggiana (Italy).

Futre was only 17 when he made his international debut and his star continued to shine brightly after FC Porto snatched him away from Sporting to inspire their European Cup victory of 1987. A few weeks later Futre was signed by Atletico Madrid as the first major coup in the controversial presidency of Jesus Gil. Futre survived all the tempests at Atletico until the start of 1993, when he forced his sale home to Benfica. However, financing the deal proved beyond even Benfica. They sold him to Marseille, who also had to sell him after only a few months to resolve their own cash crisis. Reggiana of Italy paid $12 million to become Futre's fourth club in a year – only to see him tear knee ligaments after scoring in his Italian league debut.

PAULO FUTRE *skipping over a tackle from Switzerland's Bregy*

G

Robert Gadocha

Born: January 10, 1946, Poland.
Clubs: Legia Warsaw (Pol), Nantes (Fr).

Poland's outstanding team of the early 1970s depended on Deyna in midfield, Tomaszewski and Gorgon in defence and Gadocha and Lato in attack. Gadocha was an unorthodox left-winger, not particularly quick but intelligent in his use of the ball and an outstanding finisher. He scored 17 goals in 65 internationals between 1967 and 1976. He won a gold medal at the Munich Olympics in 1972 and then achieved a third-place finish at the World Cup back in Germany two years later. Gadocha was twice Polish champion with Legia in 1969 and 1970, as well as a cup-winner when he was still a 20-year-old newcomer in 1966. He wound down his career in France with Nantes in the late 1970s.

Garrincha (full name: Manoel Francisco dos Santos)

Born: October 28, 1933, Brazil.
Clubs: Pau Grande, Botafogo, Corinthians (Br), AJ Barranquilla (Col), Flamengo (Br), Red Star Paris (Fr).

Garrincha was up there alongside Pele in Brazilian soccer in the 1960s. Born in poverty, childhood illness left his legs badly twisted and the surgeons who carried out corrective surgery thought he would do well merely to walk, let along turn out to be one of the quickest and most dangerous right-wingers of all time. Garrincha was a great practical joker, a trait which nearly cost him his place on

GARRINCHA *Team-mates' favourite*

Brazil's team. It took a players' deputation to persuade manager Vicente Feola to include him in the 1958 World Cup side in Sweden. Once in, Garrincha was there to stay and was the dominant personality at the 1962 finals after the early injury to Pele. Sadly, his private life was chaotic and he died prematurely of alcoholic poisoning.

Tommy Gemmell

Born: October 16, 1943, Scotland.
Clubs: Celtic (Scot), Nottingham Forest (Eng).

A big and sometimes clumsy full-back who became a folk hero because of his goals. He scored eight in European matches for his club, a remarkable record for a so-called defender, and two of them were in European Cup finals. Gemmell crashed one past Internazionale to equalize when Celtic won in 1967, and another against Feyenoord when they lost three years later. His extroverted style of play was well suited to upsetting foreign defenses during Celtic's greatest years, but he also collected a large haul of domestic honors before a final fling at Forest.

Francisco Gento

Born: October 22, 1933, Spain.
Clubs: Santander, Real Madrid.

Real Madrid's great team of the 1950s and 1960s was more than "only" Di Stefano and Puskas. Tearing great holes in opposing defences was outside-left Gento, whose pace earned him the nickname of "El Supersonico." Gento began with Santander and was considered a player with pace but little else when Madrid signed him in 1953. Fortunately, he found a marvelous inside-left partner in José Hector Rial, who tutored Gento in the arts of the game. Gento is the only man to have won six European Cup medals. He scored 256 goals in 800 games for Madrid, with whom he won Spanish championship medals on 12 occasions. He played 43 times for Spain despite the challenging rivalry of Enrique Collar, an outstanding left-winger with city neighbors Atletico Madrid.

TOMMY GEMMELL *Historic goal in the 1967 European Cup final*

Sergio Javier Goycochea

Born: October 17, 1963, Argentina.
Clubs: River Plate (Arg), Millonarios (Col), Racing (Arg), Brest (Fr), Cerro Porteno (Par), River Plate (Arg).

Goycochea earned fame at the 1990 World Cup finals when he stepped into the action during Argentina's match against the Soviet Union after Nery Pumpido had broken a leg. Goycochea's heroics in the penalty shoot-out victories over Yugoslavia and Italy subsequently took Argentina to the final. Yet he had not played a competitive game over the previous six months because of the domestic unrest in Colombia, where he had been contracted to Millonarios of Bogota. After the 1990 World Cup finals Goycochea signed for the ambitious French provincial club, Brest. They soon went bankrupt, however, and he returned to Argentina.

GOYCOCHEA *Magic touch in World Cup penalty shoot-outs*

Jimmy Greaves

Born: February 20, 1940, England.
Clubs: Chelsea (Eng), Milan (It), Tottenham, West Ham (Eng).

Greaves was an instinctive goal scorer, whose speed in thought and deed made up for lack of size and power. His 44 goals in 57 full internationals included two hauls of four goals and four threes, and his 357 in League games (all First Division) included three fives. An unhappy interlude in Italy did little to mar his scoring ability, and he gave wonderful value for money until his closing chapter with West Ham. By then drink had taken its grip, and his overcoming that blight to become a popular television pundit set an inspiring example to others in the same position.

Harry Gregg

Born: October 25, 1932, Northern Ireland.
Clubs: Dundalk (Rep. of Ire.), Doncaster, Manchester United, Stoke (Eng).

Genial, popular Gregg won his first cap after only nine Football League games for Second Division Doncaster, and had established himself as Ireland's first choice before the fateful 1957–58 season. Hardly had he left Yorkshire for Manchester United when, as a survivor of the Munich air crash, he became a hero by helping to rescue some of the injured. Later that year he performed well in helping his club to the FA Cup final, where they lost 2–0 to Bolton, and the Irish to the quarterfinal of the World Cup in Sweden. Injury kept him out of United's FA Cup-winning side in 1963.

John Greig

Born: September 11, 1942, Scotland.
Club: Rangers.

A 16-year spell of hard labor in defense and midfield brought Greig a record 496 League appearances for Rangers and a considerable number of honors, although Celtic were the dominant team in Scotland for a large part of that time. He was Footballer

KNVB

of the Year in 1966, the season in which he scored a spectacular goal against Italy in a World Cup qualifier, and won 44 caps, often as captain. Greig also played in two European Cup-winners' Cup finals, losing in 1967 and winning in 1972. Later, he spent a spell as coach at Ibrox.

Gunnar Gren

Born: October 31, 1920, Sweden.
Clubs: IFK Gothenburg (Swe), Milan, Fiorentina (It), Orgryte, GAIS Gothenburg (Sw).

Gren, nicknamed "the Professor," claimed Italian attention when on the Olympic Games winning team in London in 1948. His nickname stemmed both from his premature baldness and his astute inside-forward play. Milan won the transfer race and Gren forged, with fellow Swedes Nordahl and Liedholm, the legendary "Grenoli" trio which took Italian soccer by storm. In 1955, after a spell with Fiorentina, he returned home to Sweden and, at 37, helped the hosts to the final of the 1958 World Cup. That was the last of Gren's 57 internationals. Later he returned to IFK Gothenburg – with whom he had won the Swedish championship in 1942 – as manager of the souvenir shop.

Ruud Gullit

Born: September 1, 1962, Holland.
Clubs: Haarlem, Feyenoord, PSV Eindhoven (Hol), Milan, Sampdoria (It).

It was not merely his distinctive dreadlocks hairstyle which made Gullit stand out from European soccer in the late 1980s and early 1990s: he was the outstanding player on the continent. Early in his career his soccer intelligence helped him play at sweeper. With PSV Eindhoven he moved forward and after his world record $10 million sale to Milan in 1987 he became an out-and-out attacker. A year later Gullit captained Holland to victory in the European Championship and won the European Cup with Milan. The next few years were marred by serious knee problems and Milan, perhaps prematurely, released him on virtually a free transfer to Sampdoria.

RUUD GULLIT *Showing off the 1988 European Championship trophy*

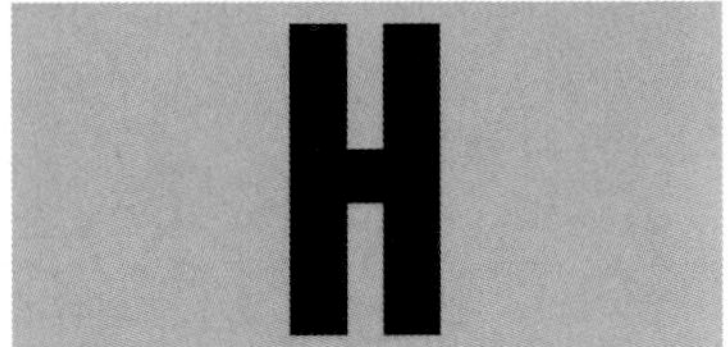

Gheorghe Hagi

Born: February 5, 1965, Romania.
Clubs: FC Constanta, Sportul Studentesc, Steaua Bucharest (Rom), Real Madrid (Sp), Brescia (It).

Hagi was always destined for stardom. He played for Romania's youth team at 15, was a top-flight league player at 17, an international at 18, and a year later, in 1984, was taking part in the finals of the European Championship. One year more and Hagi was 20-goal top league marksman, as he was again in 1986 when he totaled 31 goals after scoring six in one match. Steaua Bucharest virtually kidnapped Hagi from neighbors Sportul without a transfer fee – an escapade approved by the ruling Ceaucescu family, who were Steaua supporters and directors. After the 1990 World Cup Real Madrid paid $3.2 million for Hagi, but while he delighted their fans, his individualism was not so popular with teammates and he was duly sold on to Brescia.

Helmut Haller

Born: July 21, 1939, Germany.
Clubs: BC Augsburg (W Ger), Bologna, Juventus (It), Augsburg (W Ger).

Haller earned a teenage reputation as an inside-forward in West Germany in the late 1950s, before the advent of full-time professionalism and the Bundesliga. Italian club Bologna gambled on his youth and was superbly rewarded: in 1963 Haller's partnership with the Dane Harald Nielsen brought Bologna their first league title in more than 20 years. Later Haller played with success for Juventus before returning to Augsburg. He will be remembered above all for his outstanding contribution to West Germany's 1966 World Cup campaign.

HAMRIN (LEFT) *Goes for goal*

HAGI *Accelerates away from Irish defender Paul McGrath*

Kurt Hamrin

Born: November 19, 1934, Sweden.
Clubs: AIK Sola (Swe), Juventus, Padova, Fiorentina, Milan, Napoli, Caserta (It).

Hamrin ranks close behind Matthews and Garrincha among the great outside-rights of the modern game. He was a quick, darting attacker who was not only nimble and clever but one of the most successful goal-grabbers in Italian league history. Hamrin disappointed Juventus and they sold him off after only one year. Once he had adjusted, however, Hamrin proved an irresistible one-man strike force with Fiorentina, with whom he scored 150 goals in nine seasons and won the European Cup-winners' Cup in 1961. At 34, while with Milan, he added a European Cup winners' medal to his collection.

Gerhard Hanappi

Born: July 9, 1929, Austria.
Clubs: Wacker, Rapid Vienna.

Hanappi was one of the most versatile soccer players to be found anywhere in the world in the 1950s. He played mainly wing-half or occasionally inside-forward for his long-time club, Rapid, but also lined up at center-forward and at fullback in the course of winning 93 caps for Austria. He would have topped a century had it not been for a fight with officialdom. Hanappi, an architect by profession, designed a new stadium for Rapid which was, after his premature death, named in honor of his memory. Hanappi was Austrian champion and a cup-winner once each with Wacker then national champion six times and cup-winner once again with Rapid. He played for FIFA's World XI against England at Wembley in 1953.

Eddie Hapgood

Born: September 27, 1908, England.
Club: Arsenal.

Hapgood was small for a left-back, but as tough as teak. He was an inspiring captain who led England in 21 of his 30 games during the 1930s, with 13 more during the war. In his teens he was an amateur with Bristol Rovers, but was allowed to leave and was with non-league Kettering when Arsenal recruited him. He went on to earn five championship medals and played in three FA Cup finals, winning two. His first international was against Italy in Rome; his first as captain was also against Italy but on his club ground in the infamous "Battle of Highbury" – when he returned to play on after an opponent's elbow had smashed his nose.

After retirement he coached Blackburn and Watford, but with little success.

Ernst Happel

Born: June 29, 1925, Austria.
Clubs: Rapid Vienna, 1st FC Vienna (Aus), Racing Club Paris (Fr).

Happel was a redoubtable center-back with Rapid and Austria in the 1950s, his 51-cap playing career reaching a climax at the 1958 World Cup finals. He possessed a powerful shot and once scored a hat trick, with free kicks and a penalty, in an early European Cup tie against Real Madrid. After retiring, Happel became one of Europe's most successful coaches, taking Feyenoord to the World Club Cup and European Cup in 1970. In Argentina in 1978, he was manager of Holland when they reached the World Cup final, and he had further success in the 1983 European Cup with Hamburg.

HURST *World Cup legend*

Johnny Haynes

Born: October 17, 1934, England.
Clubs: Fulham (Eng), Durban City (SA).

Like Tom Finney, Haynes won precisely nothing in nearly two decades with one club. However, he was the hub of many an England team in a 56-cap career, hitting long passes through a needle's eye and scoring a surprising number of goals with an incredibly powerful shot that belied his comparatively slight frame. As England's first $250-a-week player he often was unjustly criticized, but he earned every penny in the service of Fulham (generally struggling) and England (frequently rampant). He was England captain from 1960 till a serious car accident in 1962, in a period when, in successive games, England won 5–2, 9–0, 4–2, 5–1, 9–3 and 8–0. The 9–3 result was a slaughter of Scotland, perhaps the best performance of his era. His career might have added up differently if Milan had persisted in their bid for him, or if, after his accident, a record-breaking bid from Tottenham Hotspur had succeeded. He ended his playing career in South Africa, winning a championship medal with Durban City.

Willie Henderson

Born: January 24, 1944, Scotland.
Clubs: Rangers (Scot), Sheffield Wednesday (Eng).

If "Wee Willie" had performed throughout his career as he did in his first few years, he would have been perhaps the best Scottish player ever. Despite persistent foot trouble and far from perfect eyesight, he had won all four domestic honors – league, cup, League Cup and cap – before his 20th birthday. By then Rangers had sold international winger Alex Scott to Everton in order to make room for the kid. Henderson went on to play in 29 internationals and captivate fans with his wizardry, but his career was marred by discontent, and gradually petered out in disappointment.

Geoff Hurst

Born: December 8, 1941, England.
Club: West Ham, Stoke.

A big man who was made for the big occasion, Hurst, strong and deceptively fast, was frequently mundane in West Ham's toils through their League schedules. But when needed in the big events, he was out of the shoot like a greyhound. He scored the remarkable total of 46 goals in the League Cup, 23 in the FA Cup (including a fluke in the 1964 final) and three in the 1966 World Cup final, when he appeared virtually from nowhere to put the trophy on the nation's sideboard with his hat trick against West Germany. Like so many big name players, he became a mundane coach, at Chelsea. Memories of him as a player will last much longer.

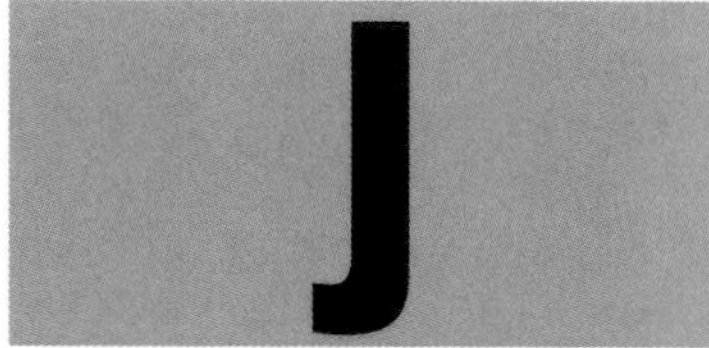

J

JAIRZINHO *Unique World Cup feat*

Jairzinho (full name: Jair Ventura Filho)

Born: December 25, 1944, Brazil.
Clubs: Botafogo (Br), Marseilles (Fr), Cruzeiro (Br), Portuguesa (Ven).

Jairzinho was the heir to Garrincha's glory, both with Botafogo and with Brazil. He moved from his home town of Caxias to sign professional with Botafogo at 15, and played in the same Brazil squad as his hero at the 1966 World Cup. Four years later Jairzinho made history by scoring in every game in every round of the World Cup on the way to victory. He scored seven goals, including two in Brazil's opening win over Czechoslovakia and one in the defeat of Italy in the final. He tried his luck in Europe with Marseille but returned home after disciplinary problems to win yet another trophy, the South American club cup, with Cruzeiro at the age of 32.

Alex James

Born: September 14, 1901, Scotland.
Clubs: Raith (Scot), Preston, Arsenal (Eng).

Eight caps were a meager reward for the outstanding inside-forward of the 1930s. James began as a fiery attacking player (sent off twice in successive matches at Raith) but changed his style to fit Arsenal coach Herbert Chapman's "W" formation. He scored only 26 League goals in eight years at Highbury, but made countless others with his astute passing from deep to the flying wingers or through the middle. Despite his superb display in the 5–1 rout of England by the "Wembley Wizards," James was often thought too clever by the selectors, though not by fans: at the club level he won six major medals and undying fame.

Pat Jennings

Born: June 12, 1945, Northern Ireland.
Clubs: Newry Town (NI), Watford, Tottenham, Arsenal (Eng).

A goalkeeper with character and charm to match his size, Jennings even bowed out of soccer in a big way by winning his 119th cap on his 41st birthday – and in a World Cup, too. Only defeat, by Brazil, marred the occasion. By then Jennings had played well over 1,000 senior matches in a 24-year career, four of them in FA Cup finals. He won with Spurs

PAT JENNINGS *Veteran of more than 1,000 first-class matches*

in 1967 and Arsenal in 1979, lost with Arsenal in 1978 and 1980. Jennings also scored a goal with a clearance from his hand during the 1967 Charity Shield against Manchester United. He remains one of the finest British goalkeepers ever seen.

Jimmy Johnstone

Born: September 30, 1944, Scotland.
Clubs: Celtic (Scot), San José (US), Sheffield United (Eng), Dundee (Scot), Shelbourne (Ire).

Johnstone was a remarkably talented winger, but infuriatingly inconsistent, as shown by the fact that his 23 caps were spread over 12 years. Small and nippy, he was an old-style "ball-tied-to-the-shoelaces dribbler" and nicknamed The Flea. He won 16 medals with his club – one European Cup, eight league, three Scottish cup, four League Cup. Johnstone also earned a reputation for occasional wayward behavior, on the field and off, but his courage was never in doubt, as many a far bigger opponent found to his dismay. He was particularly effective in the 1966–67 season, when Celtic won every competition they entered, culminating in their defeat of Internazionale in Lisbon.

Julinho (full name: Julio Botelho)

Born: August 3, 1929, Brazil.
Clubs: Portuguesa (Br), Fiorentina (It), Palmeiras (Br).

Brazil's production line of brilliant right-wingers began with Julinho in the 1950s. He was playing for Portuguesa of São Paulo when he starred in the Brazilian side which fell to Hungary in the quarter-finals of the 1954 World Cup. A year later he was in Italy with Fiorentina of Florence, where he enjoyed three wonderful seasons. Julinho made a keynote contribution to Fiorentina's league title win in 1956, when they lost only once – the last match of the season. Playing in Italy cost Julinho a chance of playing for Brazil in the 1958 World Cup. A year later he returned home with Palmeiras but, despite one match-winning display against England, failed to regain his place from Garrincha.

K

Jack Kelsey

Born: November 19, 1929, Wales.
Club: Arsenal (Eng).

Big Jack was beaten five times on his debut for Arsenal in 1951, but he went on to be first-choice keeper for 11 years until a spinal injury, sustained in a collision with Vava of Brazil, forced him to retire. He remained a familiar figure at Highbury as manager of the club shop. He was powerful enough to withstand the challenges of an age when keepers were not well protected, and agile enough to make many remarkable stops, helped by rubbing chewing gum into his palms. Kelsey won 43 caps for Wales and played for Britain against the Rest of Europe in 1955.

Mario Alberto Kempes

Born: July 15, 1952, Argentina.
Clubs: Instituto Cordoba, Rosario Central (Arg), Valencia (Sp), River Plate (Arg), Hercules (Sp), Vienna, Austria Salzburg (Austria).

MARIO KEMPES
Argentina's World Cup hammer in 1978

Kempes, an aggressive young striker with legs like tree trunks, had a first taste of World Cup soccer in West Germany in 1974. He swiftly earned a transfer to Spain with Valencia, where he developed into such a devastating hammer of opposing defenses that he was the only foreign-based player recalled to join the hosts' World Cup squad under Cesar Luis Menotti in 1978. His addition proved decisive: Kempes was the event's top scorer with six goals, including two in the 3–1 defeat of Holland in the final. Strangely, he was never able to scale those heights again, despite playing once more for Argentina in the 1982 finals in Spain, where he should have felt at home.

Jürgen Klinsmann

Born: July 30, 1964, Germany.
Clubs: Stuttgart Kickers, VfB Stuttgart (Ger), Internazionale (It), Monaco (Fr).

The retirement from international soccer of Rudi Völler in the autumn of 1992 left Klinsmann to shoulder the responsibility of being Germany's top striker. However, he had done more than enough to prove his readiness for the role. Klinsmann was German league top scorer and Footballer of the Year during his first Bundesliga spell with VfB Stuttgart, whom he also led to the UEFA Cup final in 1989. Stuttgart lost to Napoli and, shortly afterwards, Klinsmann moved south himself to join Internazionale. Three successful years included the 1990 World Cup final victory over Argentina in Rome. When Inter decided to replace their German foundation with Dutchmen, Klinsmann moved to France with Monaco and, after Marseille's disgrace, found himself appearing in the international spotlight of the European Champions League.

Ivan Kolev

Born: November 1, 1930, Bulgaria.
Club: CDNA/CSKA Sofia.

Kolev was the first great Bulgarian soccer player. He was often compared for control and vision with Hungary's Ferenc Puskas, with whom he was a contemporary. Kolev, who could play outside- or inside-left, spent all his career with the Bulgarian army club, variously known as CDNA and then CSKA Sofia. He scored 25 goals in 75 internationals and led Bulgaria on their first appearance at a major soccer tournament in the 1952 Helsinki Olympic Games. With CDNA/CSKA he was champion of Bulgaria on 11 occasions and won the cup four times.

Sandor Kocsis

Born: September 30, 1929, Hungary.
Clubs: Ferencvaros, Honved (Hun), Young Fellows (Swz), Barcelona (Sp).

Kocsis was an attacking inside-right in the Honved and Hungary line-ups of the early 1950s. He and fellow inside-forward Puskas pushed forward while the nominal center-forward withdrew towards midfield, creating gaps for the others to exploit. Kocsis did so to the extent of 75 goals in 68 internationals. He was three times the Hungarian league's top scorer, as well as the leading marksman, with 11 goals, at the 1954 World Cup finals. After the Hungarian Revolution of 1956 Kocsis decided to stay abroad and joined Barcelona with further success, winning the Fairs Cup in 1960. A year later Kocsis was on the losing side with Barcelona at the European Cup final against Benfica in Bern.

JÜRGEN KLINSMANN *Never slow to communicate with referees*

Kalman Konrad

Born: 1895, Hungary.
Clubs: MTK Budapest (Hun), FK Austria (Aus).

Konrad was one of the early greats of central European soccer, first capped at inside-forward for Hungary in 1914, the same year MTK began a decade-long domination of the domestic game. His skills were hailed as the example followed by successive early stars such Alfred Schaffer – the original "Football King" – and Gyorgy Orth. Konrad was persuaded to move to FK Austria in the mid-1920s, returned to Hungary to play again for the national team in 1928 and later coached in Sweden.

Raymond Kopa

Born: October 13, 1931, France.
Clubs: Angers, Reims (Fr), Real Madrid (Sp), Reims (Fr).

Born Kopaszewski, the son of an emigrant Polish miner, Kopa gained an added incentive to escape from a mining future when he damaged a hand in a pit accident as a teenager. He was spotted with the local club in Noeux-les-Mines by Angers and then sold on to Reims in 1950. Originally a right-winger, Kopa soon switched to a creative center- or inside-forward role. He led Reims to the first European Cup final in 1956, being transferred afterwards to their conquerors on the day, Real Madrid. Kopa starred in midfield for third-placed France at the 1958 World Cup, and returned to Reims a year later as European Footballer of the Year. He played 45 times for France but his playing career ended amid controversy over his outspoken espousal of the cause of freedom of contract.

Johannes "Hans" Krankl

Born: February 14, 1953, Austria.
Clubs: Rapid Vienna (Austria), Barcelona (Sp), 1st FC Vienna (Austria), Barcelona (Sp), Rapid, Wiener Sportclub (Austria).

For Krankl, son of a Viennese tram driver, everything happened in 1978. He scored 41 goals for Rapid Vienna, to win the Golden Boot as the leading league marksman in Europe, and starred for Austria at the World Cup finals in Argentina. Then Barcelona beat Valencia to his signature and he inspired their victory over Fortuna Dusseldorf in the 1979 European Cup-winners' Cup. Serious injury in a car crash interrupted Krankl's career in Spain and he went home to Austria briefly. Later he returned to Rapid, with whom he became general manager after retiring. Krankl scored 34 goals in 69 internationals and was top league scorer four times in Austria and once in Spain.

Ladislav Kubala

Born: June 10, 1927, Hungary.
Clubs: Ferencvaros (Hun), Bratislava (Cz), Vasas Budapest (Hun), Barcelona, Español (Sp), FC Zurich (Swz), Toronto Falcons (Can).

One of the ironies of 1950s soccer was that Hungary created a great team without one of their very greatest players. Centre- or inside-forward Kubala had escaped to the West after having played international soccer for both Czechoslovakia and Hungary in the late 1940s. In exile in Italy, Kubala formed a refugees' team called Pro Patria which played exhibition tours and provided him with the springboard to join Spain's Barcelona. There Kubala was Spanish champion five times and twice won the Fairs Cup. He also gained international recognition with a third country, winning 19 caps for Spain to add to his seven for Czechoslovakia and three for Hungary. He left Barcelona after the 1961 European Cup final defeat by Benfica, but later returned to coach both Barcelona and the Spanish national team.

Angel Amadeo Labruna

Born: September 26, 1918, Argentina.
Clubs: River Plate, Platense (Arg), Green Cross (Chile), Rampla Juniors (Uru).

Labruna remains one of the greatest Argentine soccer personalities of all time. Not only was he a great inside-left, but he earned longevity records by playing with River Plate for 29 years and won a reputation as a South American Stanley Matthews by playing on until he was 41. At the 1958 World Cup finals in Sweden, Labruna was recalled at the age of 40 to complete an international career which brought him 17 goals in 36 games for Argentina. Labruna began with River Plate when he was 12 and won nine league championships. In the late 1940s he was a member of the legendary "Maquina," or "Machine," forward line. In 1986 Labruna was coach when River at last won the South American club cup.

Marius Lacatus

Born: April 5, 1964, Romania.
Clubs: Steaua Bucharest (Rom), Fiorentina (It), Oviedo (Sp), Steaua.

Tall, slim and sharp in front of goal, Lacatus was a key figure in the Romanian upsurge of the 1980s. Playing nominally as outside-right, he used his pace to great effect to help shoot his country to the 1990 World Cup finals. After the finals, he stayed on in Italy with Fiorentina, and the Romanian federation allocated much of the fee to the redevelopment of sports facilities in the country. Lacatus found it hard to adjust to Italian soccer and later moved on to Spain before returning home in the autumn of 1993.

DENIS LAW *The promising youngster in Huddersfield days*

LAUDRUP *Brilliant elder brother*

Grzegorz Lato

Born: April 8, 1950, Poland.
Clubs: Stal Mielec (Pol), Lokeren (Bel), Atlante (Mex).

Lato was a Polish phenomenon, an outstanding striker who later proved equally influential when he moved back into midfield. At the 1974 World Cup finals, Lato was top scorer with seven goals. He had made his debut for Poland against Spain in 1971 and was a member of the squad which won the Olympic gold medal in Munich a year later. Lato became a fixture in the senior national team in 1973, after impressing manager Kazimierz Gorski on a tour of the United States and Canada, and he went on to score 46 goals in 104 internationals, a Polish record. After leading Poland's attack at the 1978 World Cup finals in Argentina, Lato was permitted the "reward" of a transfer to Lokeren in Belgium, and he ended his career in Mexico with Atlante.

Michael Laudrup

Born: June 15, 1964, Denmark.
Clubs: Brondbyernes (Den), Lazio, Juventus (It), Barcelona (Sp).

Michael and younger brother Brian are sons of a former Danish international, Finn Laudrup, who closely guided their early careers. Michael, as a teenager, attracted scouts from all Europe's top clubs but finally chose Juventus, who loaned him to Lazio before recalling him to replace Poland's Zbigniew Boniek. With Juventus Laudrup won the World Club Cup before becoming disillusioned with *Calcio* and moving on to win the European Cup with Barcelona. He starred at the 1986 World Cup finals before falling out with Denmark's national coach Richard Moller Nielsen and thus missing the 1992 European Championship triumph – where younger brother Brian stepped into his boots as their nation's attacking inspiration.

Denis Law

Born: February 22, 1940, Scotland.
Clubs: Huddersfield, Manchester City (Eng), Torino (It), Manchester United, Manchester City (Eng).

Denis Law and Jimmy Greaves were born within four days of each other, and spent several years as rival scorers and supreme entertainers. Law, of only medium height and slim in build, had a lion's heart and a salmon's leap, scoring many spectacular goals with headers and acrobatic shots. He was also an incisive passer of the ball, and a fierce competitor. Suspensions and injury cost him many more goals. He was European Footballer of the Year in 1964, won two league titles and the 1963 FA Cup, and scored 30 goals in 55 internationals, but missed United's European Cup victory in 1968 with knee trouble.

Tommy Lawton

Born: October 6, 1919, England.
Clubs: Burnley, Everton, Chelsea, Notts County, Brentford, Arsenal.

One of the first soccer players to realize what his market value was, and to work at getting it. Lawton made frequent moves, at a time when there rarely was any percentage for a transferred player. Lawton was a star from his grease-smothered toe-caps to his glistening center-parted hair. He got a hat trick on his senior debut aged 16, was the First Division top scorer two years in a row, won a title medal aged 19, scored 23 goals in 22 full internationals, and goals by the dozen during the Second World War. Lawton was still frightening foes deep into his 30s and pulling in fans everywhere he went.

Leonidas da Silva

Born: November 11, 1910, Brazil.
Clubs: Havanesa, Barroso, Sul Americano, Sirio Libanes, Bomsucesso (Br), Nacional (Uru), Vasco da Gama, Botafogo, Flamengo, São Paulo (Br).

Leonidas was Brazil's 1930s superstar although he played only 23 times for his country. He was the inventor of the overhead bicycle kick, which was unveiled to the international game when he scored twice on his international debut against Uruguay in 1932. The Uruguayans were so impressed he was immediately signed by the top club, Nacional. Later he returned home with Vasco da Gama and was top scorer at the 1938 World Cup with eight goals, including four in a 6–5 victory over Poland. Unfortunately, an overconfident coaching staff rested Leonidas from the semifinal against Italy, wanting to keep him fresh for the final . . . and they lost.

Billy Liddell

Born January 10, 1922, Scotland.
Club: Liverpool (Eng).

An accountant, Justice of the Peace and youth worker, Liddell allied all these activities to soccer. He is still revered as one of the greatest players in Liverpool's history, which is saying a great deal. Liddell missed six years with war service and spent all his career with one club. Apart from the championship in 1947 and a Cup final defeat three years later, Liverpool achieved little during his 15 years, but he set club records with 492 league appearances and 216 goals, as well as representing Scotland 28 times and Great Britain in two games against the Rest of Europe.

Nils Liedholm

Born: October 8, 1922, Sweden.
Clubs: Norrköping (Swe), Milan (It).

Liedholm played originally at inside-forward, later moved back to wing-half and finally became one of the best of sweepers in his veteran years. He began with Norrköping, winning two championship medals and playing 18 times for his country. After helping Sweden win, from outside-left, the 1948 Olympic title, he moved to Italy. There Liedholm formed Milan's celebrated trio with Gunnar Gren and Gunnar Nordahl and he scored 60 goals in 367 league games. At the end of his career Liedholm captained hosts Sweden to runners-up spot at the 1958 World Cup finals. After retiring as a player, he stayed with Milan as a youth coach and later took charge of the senior team in 1964. He also coached Fiorentina and Roma.

LITTBARSKI *Testing the resolve of Italian defender Claudio Gentile*

Gary Lineker

Born: November 30, 1960, England.
Clubs: Leicester, Everton (Eng), Barcelona (Sp), Tottenham (Eng), Nagoya Grampus Eight (Jap).

All sorts of records fell to this unassuming son of a market trader, who accepted good and bad with the

GARY LINEKER *Scoring, against the Irish Republic in the 1990 World Cup, one of his 48 international goals*

smiling sincerity that, allied to his skill, made him such a popular figure. This was never more evident than in the desperate days when serious illness struck his first-born son. He went within one goal of England's 49-goal scoring record, ten coming in World Cup final stages, led the First Division marksmen with three different clubs, scored a hat trick for Barcelona against Real Madrid, and won the FA Cup after missing a penalty, having scored in an earlier final and lost.

Pierre Littbarski

Born: April 16, 1960, Germany.
Clubs: Hertha Zehlendorf, Köln (Ger), Racing Paris (Fr), Köln (Ger), JEF United (Japan).

Littbarski, an outside right who later took his dribbling skills back into midfield, shot to prominence by hitting two goals in his debut for West Germany in a World Cup qualifier against Austria in 1981. He joined Köln, the club with which he is most associated, in 1978, played in the 1982 and 1986 World Cup finals and finally achieved victory in Italy in 1990. Before heading out to Japan to wind down his career, Littbarski described his career ambition as "scoring a goal after beating all 10 outfield players, dribbling round the goalkeeper and putting the ball in the net with a back-heel."

Wlodzimierz Lubanski

Born: February 28, 1947, Poland.
Clubs: GKS Gliwice, Gornik Zabrze (Pol), Lokeren (Bel), Valenciennes, Quimper (Fr), Lokeren (Bel).

Lubanski ranks among Poland's finest players even though injuries were not kind to him. He emerged with the miners' club, Gornik, in the mid-1960s taking over the mantle of inspiration with both club and country from Ernest Pol. Lubanski was four times top league marksman in Poland and captained his country to the 1972 Olympic Games victory in Munich. The following year he suffered a serious thigh injury in a World Cup qualifier against England and missed the finals in which Poland finished third. He returned to national team duty at the 1978 finals in Argentina, before winding down his career in Belgium and France.

M

Ally McCoist

Born: September 24, 1962, Scotland.
Clubs: St. Johnstone (Scot), Sunderland (Eng), Rangers (Scot).

A powerful striker who survived a disastrous spell in England to become a hugely successful and popular player back in his homeland. McCoist was born in Bellshill, home town of Alex James and Matt Busby, and St Johnstone earned a club record $600,000 when selling him to Sunderland in 1981. After two unsettled seasons, 56 games and a mere eight goals, he was sold to Rangers, and began a decade of almost constant medal-collecting as the club dominated the Scottish game. He won the Golden Boot as Europe's leading league marksman before a broken leg, suffered against Portugal in a World Cup qualifier in 1993, interrupted a prolific career.

Paul McGrath

Born: December 4, 1959, England.
Clubs: Manchester United, Aston Villa.

McGrath is a fine player whose career has been dogged by ill-luck and – on occasions – lack of self-discipline. Born in Middlesex of Irish parentage, McGrath had a troubled progress through Manchester United's junior ranks and on into the senior squad, with injuries and authority combining to hinder him. But coach Ron Atkinson kept faith, and took McGrath with him when he moved to Villa. As a club player, one FA Cup win in 1985 – he performed heroically for ten-man United – was poor reward. As an international for the Republic of Ireland, his skill and commitment have made him a folk hero among the Irish fans during European Championship and World Cup campaigns.

McGRATH *Defied knee injuries*

Jimmy McIlroy

Born: October 25, 1931, Northern Ireland.
Clubs: Glentoran (NI), Burnley, Stoke, Oldham (Eng).

If Blanchflower was the key man of the Irish World Cup campaign in 1958, Jimmy McIlroy was only a little way behind him. His unhurried, elegant work at inside-forward proved ideal for the tactics devised by team coach Peter Doherty. Altogether McIlroy played 55 games for his country, to go with more than 600 at the club level, earning a championship medal with the attractive young Burnley squad in 1960, and a runners-up medal in the FA Cup two years later – against Blanchflower's Spurs. He later enjoyed a brief but brilliant combination with Stanley Matthews at Stoke.

McCOIST *Crowned his goal-grabbing career with the Golden Boot*

Sammy McIlroy

Born: August 1, 1954, Northern Ireland.
Clubs: Manchester United, Stoke, Manchester City (Eng).

Another valuable midfielder, like his namesake, but of a totally different type. Sammy McIlroy's all-action style was in complete contrast to Jimmy's deliberate method, but was ideally suited to the hurly-burly of the modern game. It earned him 88 games for his country, spread over 15 years, but only five goals. He also played in three FA Cup finals with United, losing to Southampton in 1976 and Arsenal in 1979, beating Liverpool in 1977. McIlroy's late equalizer in the 1979 final seemed sure to take the game to extra time, but Arsenal went downfield to snatch the winner straight from the restart.

BILLY McNEILL *Celtic's captain in the glorious 1960s*

Billy McNeill

Born: March 2, 1940, Scotland.
Club: Celtic.

The nickname Caesar suited McNeill. In both size and style he was a big man, and was the hub of the Celtic defense during their great days of the 1960s.He won a host of domestic medals and, in 1967, became the first Briton to lift the European Cup, the most coveted prize in club soccer. He was a soldier's son and educated at a rugby-playing school, but made up for a late introduction to soccer with years of splendid service and a club record number of appearances. His international debut was in the 9–3 mauling by England in 1961, but he recovered to gain 28 more caps. McNeill was later manager of his old club (twice), as well as Aston Villa and Manchester City.

Paul McStay

Born: October 22, 1964, Scotland.
Club: Celtic.

This product of Hamilton played for his country as a schoolboy and at the youth level before graduating to the Under-21 team and then to the full national squad. He made his senior debut against Uruguay in 1983 and has plied his creative midfield trade to such good effect that Kenny Dalglish's record of 102 caps might possibly be within his reach. McStay's loyalty to Celtic has been a welcome change in the modern climate of frequent transfers, and he has given good value for his high earnings in a period when his club have been very much overshadowed by Rangers. He is an elegant, classy play-maker with the necessary touch of steel.

Josef "Sepp" Maier

Born: February 28, 1944, West Germany.
Clubs: TSV Haar, Bayern Munich.

Maier reached the pinnacle of his career in 1974 when he first won the European Cup with Bayern Munich and then, a few weeks later, the World Cup with West Germany on his home ground of the Olympic stadium in the Bavarian capital. He was noted, apart from his goalkeeping talent, for his trademark long shorts and his love of tennis. Maier even opened a tennis school thanks to the money he earned in a 19-year career with Bayern from 1960 to 1979. Maier played 473 league matches, including a run of 422 consecutive games. He made his international debut in 1966, when he was No. 3 goalkeeper in West Germany's World Cup squad in England, and was a member of the European Championship-winning side against the Soviet Union in Brussels in 1972. Maier won the European Cup three times with Bayern as well as the World Club Cup against Atletico Mineiro of Brazil in 1976.

Paolo Maldini

Born: June 26, 1968, Italy.
Club: Milan.

Soccer runs in the family for the fast raiding left-back of Italy and Milan. Paolo's father, Cesare, was a sweeper who captained Milan to their first European Cup success in 1963, played 16 times for his country and was later boss of Italy's Olympic and Under-21 teams. Paolo began with Milan's youth section and made his first-team debut at 17. He followed in father's footsteps by winning the European Cup in 1989 and 1990 and was soon acclaimed as one of the finest all-round soccer players in the world when he helped Italy reach third place in the World Cup finals. Many experts consider Maldini the heir apparent to Franco Baresi as sweeper and commander of Milan and Italy's defenses. If he stays clear of injury he could set remarkable international appearance records, having topped 50 caps before the age of 26.

Diego Armando Maradona

see Legends (pages 114–15)

Silvio Marzolini

Born: 1940, Argentina.
Clubs: Ferro Carril Oeste, Boca Juniors.

To many experts, and not only Argentines, Marzolini is the finest full-back of the modern era. He was a left-back who could tackle and intercept with the best of them but also displayed the technique and virtuoso skill of a forward when he had the opportunity to go on attack. At only 13 Marzolini won the Buenos Aires youth title with Ferro Carril Oeste and became a first division regular at 19. In 1960 he was bought by Boca Juniors, winning the league title in 1962, 1964 and 1965. He played in the World Cup finals of 1962 and 1966 – where he rose above all the unpleasant mayhem of the quarterfinal defeat by England at Wembley. Marzolini, after retirement, enjoyed some success as a TV and film actor before he returned to Boca as coach and took them to the league title in 1981. He was forced to retire because of a heart condition.

MALDINI *Emulated his father*

Josef Masopust

Born: February 9, 1931, Czechoslovakia.
Clubs: Union Teplice, Dukla Prague (Cz), Crossing Molenbeek (Bel).

Masopust is the only Czechoslovak player to have won the European Footballer of the Year award, which he collected in 1962 after an outstanding World Cup campaign in Chile. Czechoslovakia finished runners-up to Brazil, and Masopust scored the opening goal in the final, which they ultimately lost 3–1. Originally an inside-forward, Masopust made his name as a left-half but was, to all intents and purposes, more of an old-fashioned center-half. He preferred to dominate games from a central position in midfield both for Czechoslovakia and the army club Dukla. His intuitive understanding with left-back Ladislav Novak and defensive wing-half Svatopluk Pluskal was renowned throughout the world.

Lothar Matthäus

Born: March 21, 1961, Germany.
Clubs: Borussia Mönchengladbach, Bayern Munich (Ger), Internazionale (It), Bayern Munich (Ger).

Matthäus has been Germany's outstanding leader from midfield – and, lately, sweeper – since the early 1980s. His career reached its zenith in 1990 when he was not only West Germany's World Cup-winning captain in Rome, but was also voted Player of the Tournament by the world's media. Matthäus was a substitute on the West German side that won the 1980 European Championship and established himself only in 1986, when he scored a magnificent winner against Morocco in the World Cup second round on the way to defeat by Argentina in the final. He began with Borussia, joined Bayern for a then domestic record of $1 million in 1984 and moved to Italy with Inter in 1988 for $3.6 million. Injury kept Matthäus out of the 1992 European Championship finals and he was still convalescing when he agreed to go home to Bayern Munich.

Stanley Matthews

see Legends (pages 116–17)

Alessandro "Sandro" Mazzola

Born: November 7, 1942, Italy.
Club: Internazionale.

Sandro is the son of Valentino, the captain of Torino and Italy who was killed in the 1949 Superga air disaster when Sandro was six. To escape comparisons, he launched his soccer career with Inter rather than Torino, and made his debut in a 9–1 defeat by Juventus – when Inter fielded their youth team in protest at the Italian federation's decision to order an earlier game to be replayed. In 1962–63 Mazzola, a striking inside-forward, scored 10 goals in 23 games as Inter won the league title. In both 1964 and 1965 he won the European Cup and World Club Cup, scoring in the victories over Real Madrid and Benfica. Mazzola reverted to midfield to help Italy win the 1968 European Championship and was outstanding when Italy reached the World Cup final in Mexico in 1970.

Valentino Mazzola

Born: January 26, 1919, Italy.
Clubs: Venezia, Torino.

Mazzola was an inside-left who was born in Milan, where he played for Tresoldi and then the Alfa Romeo works team. In 1939 he was bought by Venezia, where he struck up a remarkable inside-forward partnership with Ezio Loik – with whom he moved to Torino in 1942. Mazzola captained and inspired Torino to five consecutive league championship victories in 1943 and 1946–49.

Before he could celebrate the fifth title, however, Mazzola and 17 of his Torino colleagues had been killed in the 1949 Superga air disaster. Mazzola was the league's top scorer in 1947, and made his Italy debut against Croatia in Genoa in 1942. He scored four goals in 12 internationals and would certainly have captained Italy's World Cup defence in Brazil in 1950.

MATTHÄUS *Proud World Cup-winning captain of West Germany in Italy in 1990*

Giuseppe Meazza

Born: August 23, 1910, Italy.
Clubs: Internazionale, Milan, Juventus, Varese, Atalanta.

Only two Italian players won the World Cup in both 1934 and 1938: Giovanni Ferrari was one, inside-forward partner Meazza was the other. Meazza was considered the most complete inside-forward of his generation, able both to score goals and create them. Born in Milan, Meazza made his debut with Inter at 17 and scored a then league record 33 goals in 1928–29. Meazza spent a decade with Inter before switching to Milan in 1938, playing wartime soccer with Juventus and Varese and retiring in 1947 after two seasons with Atalanta.

Meazza marked his international debut by scoring twice in a 4–2 win over Switzerland in Rome in 1930 and, later the same year, scored a hat-trick in a 5–0 defeat of Hungary.

MEAZZA *Double World Cup-winner*

In all, he scored 33 goals in 53 internationals.

Joe Mercer

Born: August 9, 1914, England.
Clubs: Everton, Arsenal.

"Your legs wouldn't last a postman his morning round" was Dixie Dean's description of Mercer's spindly shanks. But Joe played for a quarter of a century on his odd-shaped pins before breaking one of them and going into coaching. He won a league title with Everton and two with Arsenal after they had gambled on his durability when he was 32 and had two dodgy knees. He also won a cup final with the Gunners in 1950 and lost one two years later, when he captained a ten-man team (Arsenal had a player carried off injured and no substitues were allowed at the time) to a narrow defeat. Mercer repeated his league and cup success as manager of Manchester City, and had a brief spell as England caretaker coach between Alf Ramsey and Don Revie.

Billy Meredith

Born: July 30, 1874, Wales.
Clubs: Manchester City, Manchester United, Manchester City (Eng).

Meredith won his first medal, for a dribbling contest, at the age of ten, and played his last senior game – a losing FA Cup semifinal – when nearly 50. He was a rugged individual, originally a miner, and a strong union man, often involved in off-field rows with officialdom. On the field he was rarely in trouble, plying his trade down the right wing with enviable skill and consistency. He won 48 caps (scoring 11 goals) spread over 25 years, with five lost to the First World War, and played around 1,000 first-team matches, in spite of missing a complete season after being involved in a match-fixing scandal.

MICHEL *Grounds Northern Ireland's Kingsley Black with his skill*

Michel (full name: José Miguel Gonzalez Maria del Campo)

Born: March 23, 1963, Spain.
Clubs: Castilla, Real Madrid.

Michel was one of European soccer's classic midfield operators throughout the 1980s and early 1990s. He made his debut with Castilla, the nursery team of Real Madrid, and was promoted to the senior outfit in 1984. A year later he starred in the UEFA Cup final defeat of Videoton, scoring Madrid's first goal and making the other two in their 3–0 win in the first leg in Hungary. Michel made his Spain debut in 1985. He was unlucky to be denied a goal at the 1986 World Cup finals when his shot was cleared from behind the line against Brazil, but in 1990 in Italy he claimed a hat-trick against South Korea.

Roger Milla

Born: May 20, 1952, Cameroon.
Clubs: Leopard Douala, Tonnerre Yaounde (Cameroon), Valenciennes, Monaco, Bastia, Saint-Etienne, Montpellier (France).

Center-forward Milla – real name Miller – delighted crowds at the 1990 World Cup with his celebratory dances around the corner flags. His goals, especially the winner against Colombia, made him the first player to become African Footballer of the Year for a second time. Milla played most of his club soccer in France, winning the cup there in 1980 with Monaco and in 1981 with Bastia. Milla scored six goals in the qualifiers to lead Cameroon to the World Cup finals for the first time in 1982. He was first voted African Footballer of the Year in 1976.

Milos Milutinovic

Born: February 5, 1933, Yugoslavia.
Clubs: FK Bor, Partizan, OFK Belgrade (Yug), Bayern Munich (Ger), Racing Paris, Stade Français (Fr).

Milutinovic, a powerful, aggressive center-forward, was head of a famous dynasty of soccer players which has included Bora Milutinovic, coach to the United States' 1994 World Cup side. Milos began with FK Bor, made his debut for Yugoslavia in 1951 and, the same year, transferred to Belgrade with army club Partizan. He scored 183 goals in 192 games before moving controversially to neighbors OFK, then to Germany with Bayern Munich and finally settling in France. Milutinovic proved a huge success with Racing Paris before injury forced his retirement in 1965. He scored 16 goals in 33 internationals between 1953 and 1958.

Severino Minelli

Born: September 6, 1909, Switzerland.
Clubs: Kussnacht, Servette, Grasshoppers.

Minelli was a steady, reliable right-back with great positional sense who played a then record 79 times for Switzerland during the inter-war years. In 1930 he made his national team debut while simultaneously winning his first league championship medal with Servette of Geneva. In the next 13 years he won another five league medals as well as eight cup finals with Grasshoppers of Zurich. Minelli was a key figure in the "*verrou*" or "bolt" defense introduced by fellow-countryman Karl Rappan, and played to great effect for Switzerland in the World Cups of both 1934 and 1938. One of his finest games was Switzerland's 2–1 defeat of England in Zurich in May 1938.

Luisito Monti

Born: January 15, 1901, Argentina.
Clubs: Boca Juniors (Arg), Juventus (It).

Monti was an old-style attacking center-half in the late 1920s and early 1930s. He was notable for a rugged, ruthless style but was also one of the great achievers of the inter-war years. Monti won an Olympic Games silver medal in 1928 when Argentina lost to Uruguay in Amsterdam and was again on the losing side against the same opponents at the first World Cup final two years later. In 1931 Juventus brought Monti to Italy. At first he looked slow and vastly overweight, but a month's lone training brought him back to fitness and, little more than a year later, he made his debut for Italy in a 4–2 win over Hungary in Milan. Monti was not only a key figure in the Juventus side which won four successive league titles in the 1930s but he also played for Italy when they first won the World Cup, defeating Czechoslovakia in Rome in 1934.

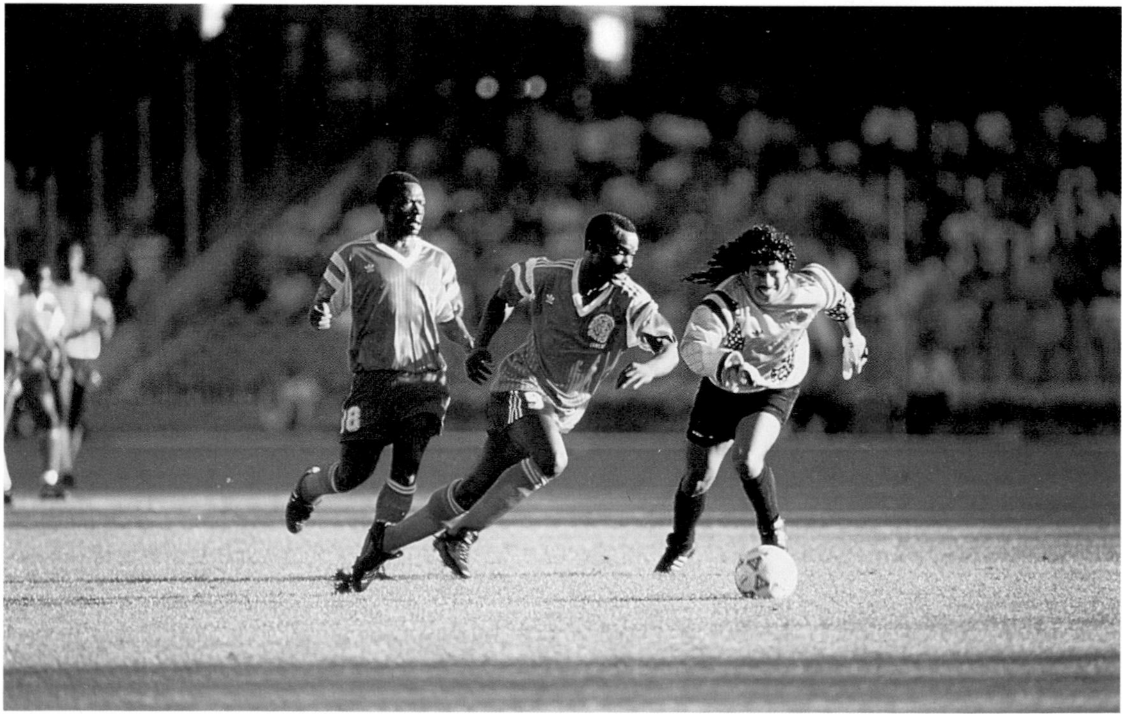

MILLA *Runs away from Colombian goalkeeper Higuita to score the winner in the 1990 World Cup second round*

MOORE *Leadership by example*

Bobby Moore

Born: April 17, 1941, England.
Clubs: West Ham United, Fulham (Eng), San Antonio Thunder, Seattle Sounders (US).

Bobby Moore was the inspirational, ice-cool captain of England's victorious 1966 World Cup side. Yet an FA Cup, one European Cup-winners' Cup, the 1966 World Cup and 108 England caps (100 of them under Sir Alf Ramsey) represent only part of his value to West Ham and England. Even at 34 he went back to Wembley, for Fulham against his old club, but by then fate was no longer smiling on him. He is likely to remain the only English captain to receive the World Cup trophy. Cruelly he developed cancer, from which he died in 1993, but which he defied with the utmost bravery to the end.

Juan Manuel Moreno

Born: August 3, 1916, Argentina.
Clubs: River Plate (Arg), España (Mex), River Plate (Arg), Universidad Catolia (Chile), Boca Juniors (Arg), Defensor (Uru), FC Oeste (Arg), Medellin (Col).

Many Argentines consider Moreno to have been the greatest soccer player of all time. An inside-right for most of his career, Moreno began with River Plate's youth teams and was a league championship winner in 1936. He won four league titles with River and was a member of the legendary forward line of the late 1940s, together with Muñoz, Pedernera, Labruna and Loustau. Moreno played for España in Mexico between 1944 and 1946, returned to River for two more years, then wandered off again to Chile, Uruguay and Colombia. He scored an impressive 20 goals in 33 internationals.

Stan Mortensen

Born: May 26, 1921, England.
Clubs: Blackpool, Hull, Southport.

As fast over ten yards as any English forward, with finishing skill to round off the openings his pace created, Mortensen scored four times in a 10–0 win over Portugal (away!) in his first international, and his goal in his last England game was his 23rd in 25 appearances. That was against the 1953 Hungarians, a few months after he had become the first man to score a hat trick in a Wembley Cup final: his third, after two defeats. Morty loved the FA Cup, scoring in each of Blackpool's first 12 post-war rounds in the tournament and finishing with 28 Cup goals as well as 225 in the league.

Alan Morton

Born: April 24, 1893, Scotland.
Clubs: Queen's Park, Rangers.

"The Wee Blue Devil" was a left-winger with elusive dribbling skill and a waspish shot who had a 20-year career and gained nine championship medals and three for the Scottish Cup. He was a mining engineer who spent several seasons with the amateurs at Queen's Park, before becoming the first signing for Rangers by the then new coach, William Struth, who was to remain in charge for 34 years. Morton played well over 500 games for Rangers and is reputed never to have appeared as a reserve. He was always very much the gentleman, often appearing for matches in a bowler hat and carrying an umbrella.

Coen Moulijn

Born: February 15, 1937, Holland.
Clubs: Xerxes, Feyenoord.

Moulijn was perhaps Holland's first post-war superstar. A brilliant outside-left, he played 38 times for Holland between his debut in a 1–0 defeat by Belgium in Antwerp in 1956 and his last game, a 1–1 World Cup draw against Bulgaria, in October 1969. That may have been Moulijn's last international, but his final and greatest achievement came the following May when Feyenoord beat Celtic in the European Cup final in 1970. Moulijn helped Feyenoord go on to beat Estudiantes de La Plata in the World Club Cup and retired in 1972 with five league championships to his name. At the insistence of the Dutch federation, Feyenoord had inserted a clause in Moulijn's contract that he should never be sold abroad.

Gerd Müller

Born: November 3, 1945, Germany.
Clubs: TSV Nordlingen, Bayern Munich.

Coach Tschik Cajkovski was not impressed when Bayern bought a stocky new center-forward in 1964. "I can't put that little elephant in among my string of thoroughbreds," said Cajkovski. But once he had done so, Bayern never looked back. Müller not only had the opportunist's eye for goal, but he was a powerful header of the ball. His goals shot Bayern out of the regional league to victory in the European Cup-winners' Cup in little more than three years. He went on to score well over 600 goals, including a record 365 in the Bundesliga and an astonishing 68 in 62 internationals for West Germany. Müller once scored four goals in a victory over Switzerland, but his most famous goal was his last, the one with which the Germans beat Holland in the 1974 World Cup final. Müller won the European Cup three times and was also a European Championship winner in 1972.

MÜLLER *Volleys the dramatic winner against England in 1970 in Leon*

José Nasazzi

Born: May 24, 1901, Uruguay.
Clubs: Lito, Roland Moor, Nacional, Bella Vista.

Nasazzi was one of the great captains in soccer history. He led Uruguay to their victories in the 1924 and 1928 Olympic Games and then to the 1930 World Cup. Nasazzi was nicknamed "The Marshal" for his organizational ability at the heart of defense from right-back, though he also played occasionally at center-half and at inside-forward. Nasazzi was also a South American champion on four occasions in his 15-year, 64-game international career and was a key member of the Nacional team which so dominated the league championship in 1934 that it became nicknamed "The Machine."

Zdenek Nehoda

Born: May 9, 1952, Czechoslovakia.
Clubs: TJ Hulin, TJ Gottwaldov, Dukla Prague (Cz), SV Darmstadt (W Ger), Standard Liège (Bel), FC Grenoble (Swz).

Nehoda, a skilled, mobile general of a center-forward was the first – and last – Czechoslovak player to get anywhere close to a century of caps. He scored 31 goals in 90 internationals, of which the highlight was the European Championship victory over West Germany in Belgrade in 1976. Nehoda was three times a champion of Czechoslovakia with the army club, Dukla Prague, twice a domestic cup-winner and was twice voted his country's Footballer of the Year, in 1978 and 1979. Nehoda's international reputation also earned him selection for a Europe eleven against Italy in 1981.

Johan Neeskens

Born: September 15, 1951, Holland.
Clubs: Haarlem, Ajax (Hol), Barcelona (Sp), New York Cosmos (US).

Neeskens was an aggressive, sharp-tackling midfielder who fitted perfectly into the "total soccer" pattern set by Ajax and Holland in the early

NEESKENS *Goes past Argentina's Ardiles in the 1978 World Cup final*

1970s. Neeskens provided the steel which supported the more technical gifts of team-mates Cruyff, Keizer and Van Hanegem. He scored 17 goals in 49 internationals and earned a place in history by converting the first-ever World Cup final penalty against West Germany in Munich in 1974. With Ajax, Neeskens won hat tricks of victories in the European Cup, the Dutch league and the Dutch cup. In 1974 he moved to Barcelona, with whom he won the Spanish cup in 1978 and the European Cup-winners' Cup in 1979. After a spell in the North American Soccer League he attempted a comeback, in vain, in Switzerland.

Oldrich Nejedly

Born: December 13, 1909, Czechoslovakia.
Clubs: Zebrak, Rakovnik, Sparta Prague.

Nejedly was inside-left for the Sparta club which dominated the Mitropa Cup for much of the 1930s and for the Czechoslovak national team which reached the 1934 World Cup final. His skills were described as "pure as Bohemian crystal," and his partnership with outside-left Antonin Puc was one of the best of its kind in Europe in the inter-war years. Nejedly scored twice in the 3–1 defeat of Germany in the semi-finals but could make no headway against Italy in the final. Nevertheless he was the World Cup's top scorer with five goals. A broken leg against Brazil in 1938 ended Nejedly's dream of revenge over Italy. He scored 28 goals in 44 internationals and was chosen for Central Europe against Western Europe in 1937.

Igor Netto

Born: September 4, 1930, Soviet Union.
Club: Moscow Spartak.

Netto was a left-half in the 1950s who captained the Soviet Union from 1954 to 1963, leading by example and winning what was then a

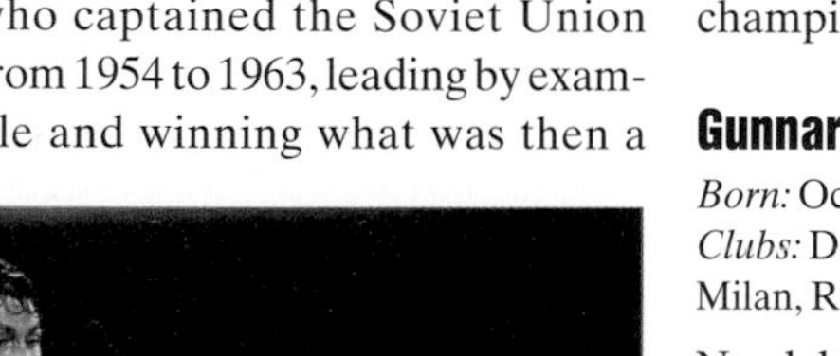

NEHODA *Provokes unorthodox attention from Italian defender Collovati*

record 57 caps with four goals. Netto led the Soviets to victory in the 1956 Olympic Games in Melbourne, but injury kept him out of all but one match at the 1958 World Cup finals. In 1962 he played in all four games when the Soviets reached the quarter-finals in Chile. Altogether he scored 37 goals in 367 league games for Spartak, with whom he stayed throughout his playing career, winning five Soviet championships.

Gunter Netzer

Born: September 14, 1944, West Germany.
Clubs: Borussia Mönchengladbach (Ger), Real Madrid (Sp), Grasshoppers (Swz).

In the late 1960s and 1970s, West Germany had a surfeit of outstanding midfield generals. Netzer was at his best in the West German side which won the 1972 European Championship, forging a marvelously refined partnership with sweeper Beckenbauer behind him. He lost his place in the national team to Wolfgang Overath after transferring to Spain with Real Madrid, and never regained it on a permanent basis, although he made an occasional appearance. He was twice West German champion with Borussia, twice Spanish champion with Real Madrid, and a cup-winner once in each country. Netzer was also once West German Footballer of the Year before, as coach, masterminding Hamburg's 1989 German championship.

Gunnar Nordahl

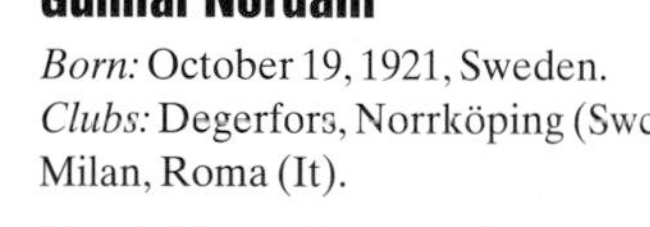

Born: October 19, 1921, Sweden.
Clubs: Degerfors, Norrköping (Swe), Milan, Roma (It).

Nordahl was the most famous of five first division brothers. He was born in Hornefors in northern Sweden and scored 77 goals in 58 games with local Degerfors. Next came 93 goals in 92 games which brought Norrköping four championships in a row. A fireman by training, Nordahl gave that up in 1948 when, after Sweden's Olympic Games victory in London, he was lured away to Milan. There Nordahl formed the central spearhead of the "Grenoli" trio (with Gunnar Gren and Nils Liedholm). Five times he was the Italian league's leading scorer, and by the time he retired in 1957 he had totaled 225 goals in 257 Italian league matches.

Bjorn Nordqvist

Born: October 6, 1942, Sweden.
Clubs: IFK Hallsberg, Norrköping (Swe), PSV Eindhoven (Hol), IFK Gothenburg (Swe), Minnesota Kicks (US), Orgryte (Swe).

For some time in the mid-1980s, Nordqvist was the world's longest serving international with 115 caps. He played in three World Cups, in 1970, 1974 and 1978, and, with Norrköping, was twice champion of Sweden and once a cup-winner. Having taken the plunge to turn full-time professional in 1974, Nordqvist immediately won the Dutch league championship with PSV Eindhoven and later tried his luck briefly with Minnesota in the North American Soccer League. Surprisingly, considering his century of caps, Nordqvist had to wait a year between his first cap in 1963 and the second.

Ernst Ocwirk

Born: March 7, 1926, Austria.
Clubs: FK Austria (Austria), Sampdoria (It).

Ocwirk, nicknamed "Clockwork" by the British for his consistent creativity in midfield, was the last of the old-fashioned attacking center-halves – a role for which he was ideally suited, with both technical and physical strengths. Ocwirk began with FK Austria of Vienna, made his debut for his country in 1947 and appeared at the 1948 Olympic Games in London. Three years later he was back at Wembley, captaining an Austrian side which thoroughly deserved a 2–2 draw against England. In 1953 the stopper center-back had taken over throughout Europe and Ocwirk was selected at wing-half in the Rest of the World team which drew 4–4 with England in a match played to celebrate the 90th anniversary of the Football Association. In 1956, at the advanced age of 30, he undertook the Italian adventure with Sampdoria with whom he spent five seasons before returning for one last campaign with FK Austria. Later he coached FKA to league titles in 1969 and 1970.

Raimundo Orsi

Born: December 2, 1901, Argentina.
Clubs: Independiente (Arg), Juventus (It).

Vittorio Pozzo, Italy's manager in the 1920s and 1930s, had no hesitation in picking imported South Americans such as Orsi for his team. "If they can die for Italy," said Pozzo, "they can play soccer for Italy." Orsi played outside-left for Argentina in the 1928 Olympic final against Uruguay before switching, amid controversy, to Juventus. He spent six months kicking his heels before finally making his Juventus debut. Within four months he was playing for Italy and scoring twice on his debut in a 6–1 win over Portugal in November 1929. Orsi was one of the exceptional players who won five successive league titles with Juventus in the early 1930s. For good measure, he scored Italy's all-important equalizer on the way to an extra-time victory over Czechoslovakia in the 1934 World Cup final.

Wolfgang Overath

Born: September 29, 1943, Germany.
Club: Köln.

Overath, an old-style inside-left and then a left-footed midfield general, was one of the most admired members of the West German sides which featured in starring roles at the World Cups of 1966, 1970 and 1974. Overath played all his senior club career for Köln and scored 17 goals in 81 internationals between 1963 and 1974. He was a World Cup runner-up in 1966, scored the goal against Uruguay which earned West Germany third place in 1970, and won a personal duel to oust Gunter Netzer as midfield commander for the World Cup victory of 1974. Overath then retired from the national team, though he was selected for the World eleven which played Brazil in Rio de Janeiro in 1968. The latter years of Overath's Köln career were sadly marred by disagreements with opinionated coach Hennes Weisweiler.

PAPIN *French goal scoring ace*

Antonin Panenka

Born: December 2, 1948, Czechoslovakia.
Clubs: Bohemians Prague (Cz), Rapid Vienna (Austria).

Panenka was a throw-back in style, a languid, skilled, dreamer of a midfield general who might have appeared more at home in the central European game of the 1930s than in the increasing hurly-burly of international soccer in the 1970s. He spent most of his career in the Czech shadows with Bohemians, from which the national manager, Vaclav Jezek, rescued him for the 1976 European Championship finals. Panenka was influential in midfield and struck the decisive blow in the final when his penalty shot, stroked so deliberately past Sepp Maier, brought Czechoslovakia their shoot-out triumph. Later he spent several successful years in Austria with Rapid Vienna. Panenka's 65 caps including helping Czechoslovakia finish third, this time after a penalty shoot-out against Italy, in the 1980 European Championship.

Jean-Pierre Papin

Born: November 5, 1963, France.
Clubs: Valenciennes (Fr), Club Brugge (Bel), Marseille (Fr), Milan (It).

Papin is one of the outstanding strikers of the modern game. He began his career with

Valenciennes and played in Belgium with Brugge before returning to France to become captain and the attacking inspiration of Marseille. Papin was the top scorer in the French league for four successive seasons before joining Milan in the summer of 1992. A year later he found himself appearing as a substitute for Milan against Marseille in the final of the European Cup, which the French club won 1–0. That was Papin's second European Cup final defeat, for he had been on the losing side in a penalty shoot-out when Red Star Belgrade beat Marseille in Bari in 1991. Papin was voted European Footballer of the Year later that year to give him at least some consolation.

Daniel Passarella

Born: May 25, 1953, Argentina.
Clubs: Sarmiento, River Plate (Arg), Fiorentina, Internazionale (It).

Passarella belongs to that select band of heroes who can claim to have received the World Cup as winning captain. His moment of triumph came in the River Plate stadium – his own home stadium – in 1978. Passarella thoroughly deserved the honor of holding the cup aloft, since he had guided, controlled and commanded Argentina from central defense. Time and again Passarella powered up into midfield to serve Ardiles and Kempes, while his vicious free-kicks and strength in the air at corners added to the pressure on opposing defenses. He seemed like three players in one, and later enjoyed outstanding success as a goal-grabbing defender with Fiorentina and Inter in Italy, before returning home to River Plate as coach.

PASSARELLA *Argentina's inspiration*

Adolfo Pedernera

Born: 1918, Argentina.
Clubs: River Plate, Atlanta, Huracan (Arg), Millonarios (Col).

Pedernera was a great center-forward turned rebel. He made his debut for River Plate in 1936 and won five league championships in 11 years. In the late 1940s Pedernera led the legendary "Maquina," or "Machine," attack with Munoz, Moreno, Labruna and Loustau. River sold him, perhaps prematurely, to Atlanta and he joined Huracan just before the Argentine soccer players' strike of 1948. Millonarios of Bogota, from the pirate Colombian league, signed up Pedernera not merely as a player but as "liaison officer" to lure away other top Argentines, including his center-forward successor at River Plate, Alfredo Di Stefano. Later Pedernera returned to Argentina as coach of Gimnasia y Esgrima, Boca Juniors, Huracan and Independiente. He played 21 times for Argentina.

Pele

see Legends (pages 118–19)

Roger Piantoni

Born: December 26, 1931, France.
Clubs: Nancy, Reims.

Piantoni was one of the last great European inside-forwards, before the "old" positions were wiped out by the advent of the 4–2–4 and 4–3–3 formations, with their new roles and terminology. Piantoni, who was born at Etain, in the Meuse, built his reputation with Nancy and transferred to Reims in 1957. He played in the World Cup finals of 1958 – when France finished third – and in the European Cup final of 1959 (which Reims lost to Real Madrid). Piantoni played 38 times for France, having made a scoring debut in a 1–1 draw against the Irish Republic in Dublin in 1952. He also scored in his last international, nine years later, against Finland. Piantoni's left-wing partnership, for Reims and France, with outside-left Jean Vincent was famed throughout the continent.

PIRRI *From striker to captain to club doctor with Real Madrid*

Silvio Piola

Born: September 29, 1913, Italy.
Clubs: Pro Vercelli, Lazio, Torino, Juventus, Novara.

Piola was a tall, strong, athletic, aggressive center-forward who scored 30 goals in 24 internationals between his debut against Austria in 1935 – when Piola scored both Italy's goals in a 2–0 win – and his last game, a 1–1 draw against England in 1952. Piola, a World Cup-winner in 1938 when he scored twice in the 4–2 final defeat of Hungary, would have collected even more goals and won more caps had it not been for the war years. As it was he played on until he was 43 in a prolific career which included his fair share of controversy – such as the goal he later admitted he punched against England, nearly 50 years before Maradona's Hand of God repetition. Piola scored six goals in Pro Vercelli's 7–2 win over Fiorentina in 1933–34.

Pirri (full name: Jose Martinez Sanchez)

Born: March 11, 1945, Spain.
Club: Real Madrid.

Pirri epitomized the spirit of Spanish soccer during his 15 extraordinary years with Real Madrid between 1964 and 1979. He began as a goal-grabbing inside-forward, then shifted back successively to midfielder and central defender in a glittering career which brought honors flooding in – eight Spanish championships, three Spanish cups and the European Cup in 1966. Pirri played 44 times for Spain between 1966 and 1978 and was twice selected for Europe elevens, first against Benfica in 1970, then against South America in 1973. After retiring, Pirri completed his studies to qualify as a doctor and was appointed to the Real Madrid medical staff.

Frantisek Planicka

Born: June 2, 1904, Czechoslovakia.
Clubs: Slovan Prague, Bubenec, Slavia Prague.

Planicka was Central Europe's finest goalkeeper of the 1930s, a great personality as well as an outstanding and courageous player in the World Cups of both 1934 – when Czechoslovakia lost the final 2–1 to Italy – and 1938. In the latter competition, long before the days of substitutes, Planicka played the last half of the quarter-final draw against Brazil despite the pain of a broken arm. Planicka won more honors than almost anyone in the history of the Czechoslovak game. He was a domestic league champion nine times with the great Slavia club, and won the cup six times and the Mitropa Cup – forerunner of today's European club competitions – in 1938. Planicka played 74 times for his country between 1925 and 1938.

Michel Platini

Born: June 21, 1955, France.
Clubs: Nancy-Lorraine, Saint-Etienne (Fr), Juventus (It).

Platini was the greatest achiever in world soccer in the early 1980s. He first appeared on the international stage at the 1976 Olympic Games in Montreal, and two years later, at his first World Cup in Argentina, gave an indication of the great things to come. In 1982 Platini inspired France to fourth place at the World Cup when he was man of the match in the dramatic semifinal defeat by West Germany in Seville. After the finals Platini was sold to Juventus, with whom he was three times the Italian league's top scorer. He also converted the penalty kick which brought "Juve" their long-awaited European Cup victory in 1985 (albeit overshadowed by the Heysel tragedy). After retiring, Platini concentrated on commercial interests and TV work until he was persuaded to become national coach and took France to the finals of the 1992 European Championship. France disappointed, and Platini left the job to become joint head of the team set up by the French federation to organize the 1998 World Cup.

Ernst Pol

Born: November 3, 1932, Poland.
Clubs: Legia Warsaw, Gornik Zabrze.

Pol was the first great Polish soccer player of the post-war era. He played center- or inside-forward and scored 40 goals in 49 internationals – then a Polish record – between 1950 and 1966. He was a complete player, with ball-control, good passing and tactical ability and an accurate shot. Pol won the Polish championship twice with the army club Legia, then five times with Gornik, the Silesian miners' club. He once scored five goals in an international against Tunisia in 1960, and had the consolation of scoring a marvelous individual strike for Gornik in their 8–1 thrashing by Tottenham in the European Cup in 1961. It was Pol's ill fortune that eastern European players were not allowed transfers to the professional west. His total of 186 Polish league goals stood as a record for 20 years.

MICHEL PLATINI *More successful as France's captain than coach*

Ferenc Puskas

see Legends (pages 120-1)

Helmut Rahn

Born: August 16, 1929, West Germany.
Clubs: Altenessen, Olde 09, Sportfreunde Katernberg, Rot-Weiss Essen, Köln (W Ger), Enschede (Hol), Meiderich SV Duisburg (W Ger).

Rahn was anything but a typical outside-right, being heavily built and tall, but his power carried him through many a defense and his right-foot shot was ferocious. Hungary discovered this to their chagrin in the 1954 World Cup final, when Rahn struck the equalizer at 2–2 and then the winner with only eight minutes remaining. Yet Rahn, enfant terrible of the German game, might not have even been in Europe: shortly before the finals he had been on a South American tour with Rot-Weiss and was in negotiations with Nacional of Uruguay when national coach Sepp Herberger sent a telegram to summon him home. In 1958 Rahn was far from either his best form or his best playing weight, and could not repeat his World Cup feats. Altogether he scored 21 goals in 40 internationals.

Antonio Ubaldo Rattin

Born: May 16, 1937, Argentina.
Club: Boca Juniors.

Rattin was a midfield pillar with club and country in the 1950s and 1960s. He made his league debut in 1956 and played 14 inspiring seasons with Boca Juniors, setting a club record of 357 league appearances and winning five championships. Rattin was also a key figure in the Boca side – along with Silvio Marzolini and Angel Rojas – which lost narrowly to Pele's Santos in the final of the South American club cup in 1963. Born in the Tigre delta outside Buenos Aires, Rattin played 37 times for Argentina. His most unfortunate game is, however, the one for which he is best remembered. This was the 1966 World Cup quarterfinal against England at Wembley, when Rattin's refusal to accept expulsion by German referee Kreitlein very nearly provoked a walk-off by the entire Argentine team. Rattin always insisted he was an innocent victim of dark circumstances.

Thomas Ravelli

Born: August 13, 1959, Sweden.
Clubs: Oster Vaxjo, IFK Gothenburg.

Ravelli and twin brother Andreas, a midfielder, are both internationals, but Thomas has been by far the most successful – with a record number of caps for a Swedish goalkeeper. Ravelli's parents emigrated to Sweden from Austria, and Thomas made his initial reputation with Oster Vaxjo. In the spring of 1989 he stepped up to join IFK Gothenburg, Sweden's leading and most popular club, as successor to Tottenham Hotspur-bound Erik Thorstvedt. Early in his career, Ravelli's temperament was considered suspect: for example, he was sent off for dissent during a 2–0 defeat in Mexico in November 1983. By the time the 1992 European Championships came around, however, Ravelli's calming influence was a key factor in host Sweden reaching the semifinals. He failed to achieve an ambition to play abroad but continued to do well as Sweden reached the 1994 World Cup finals.

Frank Rijkaard

Born: September 30, 1962, Holland.
Clubs: Ajax Amsterdam (Hol), Sporting (Port), Zaragoza (Sp), Milan (It), Ajax (Hol).

Rijkaard has been one of the most universally-admired and versatile players in evidence over the past decade at both the club and international levels. He turned professional under Johan Cruyff at Ajax in 1979 and made his Holland debut at 19 despite Ajax protests that he was "too young." In 1987 Rijkaard fell out with Cruyff and had brief spells in Portugal and Spain before committing the key years of his career to Milan with whom he won the World Club Cup and the European Cup twice each. Rijkaard played in midfield for Milan, but usually in central defense for Holland, with whom he won the 1988 European Championship. After Milan's defeat by Marseille in the 1993 European Cup final he returned to Ajax.

Luigi "Gigi" Riva

Born: November 7, 1944, Italy.
Club: Cagliari.

Riva is remembered as one of the finest strikers in the history of Italian soccer. Orphaned in early childhood, he made a teenage reputation with Third Division Legnano as a left winger and was signed by Second Division Sardinian club Cagliari in 1963. Riva's formidable left foot and nose for the goal sent Cagliari rocketing out of the shadows and to ultimate league championship success in 1970. Riva was top league marksman three times, including the 1969–70 season when he scored 21 goals in 28 games. His 35 goals in 42 internationals meant Riva shouldered much of the responsibility for Italy's World Cup challenge in 1970. He scored three times in the quarter- and semi-final victories over Mexico and West Germany before Italy's defeat in the final. Complications stemming from two broken legs ultimately forced a premature retirement.

RAVELLI *Sweden's calming influence*

Roberto Rivelino

Born: January 1, 1946, Brazil.
Clubs: Corinthians, Fluminense.

Rivelino was originally the deep-lying left-winger who filled the Zagalo role in Brazil's 1970 World Cup-winning team. He was not particularly quick, but was possessed of a superb technique which made him a perpetual danger with his banana-bending of free kicks and corners. Rivelino later moved into center midfield as Brazil's general in succes-

RIJKAARD *Great all-rounder*

sion to Gerson and was influential in the third-place finish of 1978.

Rivelino is credited unofficially with the fastest goal in soccer history: scored in three seconds with a shot from the starting pass after he noticed the opposing goalkeeper still concentrating on his pre-match prayers.

Gianni Rivera

Born: August 18, 1943, Italy.
Clubs: Alessandria, Milan.

The "Bambino d'Oro," the Golden Boy: that was Rivera in the early 1960s. As a creative inside-forward, he had everything: skill, pace and a deft shot, plus the rare natural gift of grace. Rivera in full flight was soccer poetry in motion. Milan paid Alessandria $200,000 for a half-share in the 15-year-old Rivera and signed him "for real" in 1960. In 16 years with the "Rossoneri" he was twice a winner of the World Club Cup, the European Cup and the Italian league, as well as three times an Italian cup-winner and once European Footballer of the Year, in 1969. Rivera became a controversial figure, however, as successive national coaches struggled to build teams around him. Thus he played only the last six minutes of the 1970 World Cup final – although his Italy career produced 14 goals in 60 games. On retiring Rivera turned to politics and became a member of the Italian parliament.

Bryan Robson

Born: January 11, 1957, England.
Clubs: West Bromwich, Manchester United.

A considerable part of English soccer in the 1980s was played to the accompaniment of breaking bones, many of them Bryan Robson's. Despite his season ticket to the hospital he won an impressive list of honors, with 90 caps (often as captain), three FA Cup medals, European Cup-winners' Cup in 1991, and the inaugural Premier League championship in 1992-93. Robson was an inspiring, driving force in midfield, with a good scoring record as well, and a believer in the value of an early strike: three of his England goals were in the first minute. He broke a leg twice as a teenager with West Bromwich, and then broke the transfer fee record when Manchester United bought him for $2.2 million.

LUIGI RIVA *Shoots for goal before an Israeli defender can get in a tackle*

BRYAN ROBSON *Manchester United and England's oft-injured captain*

Pedro Rocha

Born: December 3, 1942, Uruguay.
Clubs: Penarol (Uru), São Paulo (Br).

Rocha was far removed from the typical image of angry, temperamental Uruguayans. A statuesque inside left of great skill to match his height, he was surprisingly quick and soon became a local hero after joining mighty Penarol of Montevideo at 17. Seven times in the next nine seasons Rocha was a champion of Uruguay, and he inspired Penarol to victory both home and away over Real Madrid in the 1966 World Club Cup final. He captained Uruguay into the 1970 World Cup finals but was injured in the first match. Fit again, he moved to Brazil and led São Paulo to victory in the Paulista state championship in his debut season. Rocha won 62 caps for Uruguay.

Romario da Souza Faria

Born: 29 January, 1966, Brazil.
Clubs: Vasco da Gama (Br), PSV Eindhoven (Hol), Barcelona (Sp).

Romario has been arguably the finest attacker in the world game in the 1990s. Discovered by Vasco da Gama, he was still a teenager when he began to establish a reputation for controversy after being banished from Brazil's World Youth Cup squad for flouting a hotel curfew. After starring at the 1988 Seoul Olympics, he transferred to PSV Eindhoven. There he clashed with coaches and teammates, yet still totaled 98 league goals in five seasons to earn a $4.5 million sale to Barcelona in the summer of 1993. Simultaneously, he was recalled by Brazil after almost a year in the wilderness and scored the two goals which beat Uruguay and sent Brazil to the 1994 World Cup finals.

PAOLO ROSSI *Stranger than fiction*

Paolo Rossi

Born: September 23, 1956, Italy.
Clubs: Prato, Juventus, Como, Lanerossi Vicenza, Perugia, Juventus, Milan.

The true story of Paolo Rossi is more fantastic than fiction. As a teenager Rossi was given away by Juventus because of knee trouble. Later, when they tried to buy him back, they were outbid by provincial Perugia, who paid a world record $5 million. Rossi, a star already at the 1978 World Cup, was then banned for two years for alleged involvement in a massive betting-and-bribes scandal. Juventus finally got him back, but he was only three matches out of his ban when Italy took him to the 1982 World Cup finals, where he led all scoring with six goals and collected a winner's medal from the final victory over West Germany. In the end, his earlier injuries caught up with him. Rossi was only 29 when he retired into legend.

Karl-Heinz Rummenigge

Born: September 25, 1955, West Germany.
Clubs: Lippstadt, Bayern Munich (W Ger), Internazionale (It), Servette (Swz).

Rummenigge was one of the great bargains of German soccer. Bayern Munich paid Lippstadt a small fee for their young, blond right-winger in 1974 and sold him to Italy a decade later for more than $3 million. In between Rummenigge had won the World Club championship and the European Cup and had twice been hailed as European Footballer of the Year. The former bank clerk, who first impressed Internazionale officials with a World Cup hat trick against Mexico in 1978, developed into a central striker, as his career progressed. Injuries reduced his effectiveness in the early 1980s, and controversy lingered over whether national coach Jupp Derwall was right to play his injured captain from the start in the 1982 World Cup final when West Germany lost to Italy in Madrid.

RUMMENIGGE *Twice best in Europe*

Ian Rush

Born October 20, 1961, Wales.
Clubs: Chester, Liverpool (Eng), Juventus (It), Liverpool (Eng).

Rush is the goal-scorer supreme in modern British soccer, but he would have been a great player even if he had never hit a net. His off-the-ball running and excellent passing are bonuses to go with his acutely developed finishing ability. The youngest of seven brothers, Rush was only 18 when Liverpool had to pay $450,000 to get him, but the fee has been repaid many times over. In two spells at Anfield, interrupted by a none-too-happy Italian adventure, he broke scoring records for club, country and FA Cup finals (five goals in three winning appearances), with medals for five league titles and three League Cups as well.

IAN RUSH *One of the great bargains, at $450,000 from Chester*

S

Hugo Sanchez

Born: June 11, 1958, Mexico.
Clubs: UNAM (Mex), Atletico Madrid, Real Madrid (Sp), America (Mex), Rayo Vallecano (Sp).

Hugo Sanchez was top league goal scorer in Spain five seasons in a row in the late 1980s and early 1990s. His 230-plus goals in Spain left him second overall behind Bilbao's Telmo Zarra and underlined his claim to be considered one of the great strikers of the modern game. Each one of Sanchez's goals was followed by a celebratory somersault, taught him originally by a sister who was a gymnast on Mexico's team for the 1976 Olympics on Montreal – at which Hugo made his soccer debut on the international stage. Despite a World Cup finals debut as far back as 1978, Sanchez totaled only around 50 games for Mexico – his many absences caused either by club commitments in Spain or by disputes with Mexican soccer bureaucracy.

Leonel Sanchez

Born: April 25, 1936, Chile.
Club: Universidad de Chile.

Leonel Sanchez was the outstanding left-winger in South America in the late 1950s and early 1960s – perhaps not as fast as Pepe of Brazil or as intelligent a player as Zagalo of Brazil, but far more forceful when it came to making his presence felt in the penalty box. Sanchez was a star of the Chilean team which finished third as hosts in the 1962 World Cup, but he also featured in controversy: earlier in the tournament he somehow escaped punishment from the match referee for a punch which flattened Humberto Maschio in the so-called Battle of Santiago against Italy. Sanchez played 106 times for Chile, though only 62 of those appearances may be counted as full internationals. He was seven times national champion with "U," his only club.

PETER SCHMEICHEL *In winning command of defense for Denmark*

José Emilio Santamaria

Born: July 31, 1929, Uruguay
Clubs: Nacional (Uru), Real Madrid (Sp).

Santamaria was a ruthless center-back whose finest years were spent at Real Madrid in the 1950s and early 1960s, closing down the defensive gaps left by great attacking colleagues such as Di Stefano, Puskas and Gento. Santamaria was first called up at 20 by Uruguay but missed the 1950 World Cup finals because his club, Nacional, refused to let him accept the inside-forward spot allocated to him on the squad bound for Brazil. Four years later Santamaria was one of the stars of the 1954 World Cup, this time in his traditional place in the center of defense. Madrid brought him to Europe in 1957 and, having played 35 times for Uruguay, he collected another 17 caps in the service of Spain, including the 1962 World Cup. He was a World Club championship and triple European Cup winner with Real Madrid and later managed hosts Spain at the 1982 World Cup finals.

Djalma Santos

Born: February 27, 1929, Brazil.
Clubs: Portuguesa, Palmeiras, Atletico Curitiba.

Djalma Santos is considered a cornerstone of the Brazil team which won the World Cup in 1958 and 1962 and lost it in 1966. Yet, in Sweden in 1958, he was brought in only for the

DJALMA SANTOS *A great survivor*

1
hummel

GAETANO SCIREA *Skilled contrast to the rugged sweepers before him*

final because coach Vicente Feola considered his acute soccer brain and positional sense would make him more effective against Swedish left-winger Skoglund than regular right-back Nilton Di Sordi. In due course he became the first Brazilian player to reach an official century of international appearances, though he was well past his best when – to his own surprise – he was recalled by Feola for the 1966 World Cup finals in England. He played for the World eleven against England in 1963 in the match which celebrated the 100th anniversary of the FA.

Nilton Santos

Born: May 16, 1927, Brazil.
Club: Botafogo.

Nilton Santos was a left-back and, though no relation to Brazil partner Djalma Santos, equally outstanding. Nilton Santos played 83 times for his country between 1949 and 1963, having made his Brazil debut just a year after signing for his only club, Botafogo of Rio. He loved nothing more than powering forward in support of attack, a tactic which surprised the opposition and owed everything to the new freedom afforded "wing backs" by the advent of 4–2–4. Santos was a World Cup-winner in 1958 and 1962 and was immensely respected by teammates and officials. He led the player delegation which, in Sweden in 1958, crucially persuaded coach Vicente Feola to call up his Botafogo teammate, the match-winning right-winger Garrincha.

Gyorgy Sarosi

Born: September 12, 1912, Hungary.
Club: Ferencvaros TC (Hun).

Sarosi, one of the world's greatest soccer players between the wars, died in 1993 in his adopted home of Genoa, Italy, aged 81. Sarosi was born in Budapest, where he duly played both at center-forward and center-half for FTC (Ferencvaros), scoring 349 goals in 383 games. He won the Hungarian championship eight times, the cup once and the Mitropa Cup once. In internationals Sarosi scored 42 goals in 75 appearances, and captained Hungary to the 1938 World Cup final. Doctor, lawyer and magistrate, he made his debut for Hungary in a 3–2 defeat by Italy in Turin in November, 1931. When the Communists took over in Hungary in 1947, Sarosi fled to Italy, where he coached Padova, Lucchese, Bari, Juventus (winners of the 1952 championship), Genoa, Roma, Bologna and Brescia. He also coached Lugano in Switzerland.

Hector Scarone

Born: June 21, 1898, Uruguay.
Clubs: Sportsman, Nacional (Uru), Barcelona(Sp), Ambrosiana-Internazionale, Palermo (It).

Scarone was Uruguay's inspiring inside-forward in their greatest era of the 1920s and early 1930s. He won the Olympic gold medals in Paris in 1924 and in Amsterdam in 1928 – in between playing in Spain for Barcelona – and was top scorer at both the 1926 and 1927 South American Championships. He then led Uruguay to victory at the inaugural World Cup finals on home soil in Montevideo in 1930. Inevitably, his talents drew more offers from Europe, but he insisted on waiting until after that World Cup before returning, this time to Italy with Ambrosiana-Inter. Later he went back to Spain in the early 1950s as coach to Real Madrid before making a playing comeback in Uruguay with Nacional and retiring finally at 55 – a South American and probably a world record.

Juan Alberto Schiaffino

Born: July 28, 1925, Uruguay.
Clubs: Penarol (Uru), Milan, Roma (It).

"Pepe" Schiaffino always wanted, as a boy, to play center-forward, but youth coaches with Penarol of Montevideo, his first club, considered him too thin and fragile. They switched him to inside-forward and, at 20, he was playing for Uruguay at the South American Championship and leading scorer with 19 goals in Penarol's league-winning side. In World Cup terms, Schiaffino peaked in 1950 when he scored Uruguay's equalizer at 1–1 on the way to their shock victory over Brazil. After starring again at the finals in 1954, he was sold to Milan for a world record fee, and is regarded as one of the great-

DARTING IN *Two Uruguayans can't stop Uwe Seeler getting in a header*

ENZO SCIFO *A mixture of loyalties between soccer in Belgium, Italy and France*

est players ever to have graced *Calcio*. He wound down his career with Roma, after narrowly failing to lead Milan to victory over Real Madrid in the 1958 European Cup final, when, despite Schiaffino's fine solo goal, they lost 3–2.

Peter Schmeichel

Born November 18, 1963, Denmark.
Clubs: Hvidovre, Brondbyerenes (Den), Manchester United (Eng).

Schmeichel very nearly came to England in 1987, after Newcastle sent spies to watch him. Although he was then considered too inexperienced for the English First Division, Manchester United certainly landed a bargain when they bought Schmeichel for $1.2 million in 1991. By then he had starred for Denmark in the 1988 Olympic qualifiers, ousted Troels Rasmussen from the No. 1 spot at the 1988 European Championship finals in West Germany and then starred in Denmark's astonishing triumph at the 1992 finals in Sweden. Schmeichel's saves at crucial moments against Holland in the semifinal and Germany in the final helped secure him the accolade of being voted the world's Best Goalkeeper of 1992.

Karl-Heinz Schnellinger

Born: March 31, 1939, West Germany.
Clubs: Duren, Köln (W Ger), Mantova, Roma, Milan (It).

Schnellinger, a left-back who later played in most other defensive positions, was to be found at the heart of the international action throughout the 1960s. He stood out not merely for his blond hair and bulky frame but for his power, pace and will to win. He made his World Cup finals debut at 19 in Sweden and was a key member of the West German teams which reached the quarterfinals (1962), the final (1966) and third place (1970) over the next 12 years. His injury-time goal in the 1970 semifinal with Italy, which forced extra time, typified his fighting spirit.Roma took him to Italy but had to sell him to Milan to overcome a cash crisis. Their loss was Milan's gain as Schnellinger's steel lifted them to victory in the 1969 European Cup. This was the peak of a career which also earned success in the German and Italian championships and the Italian cup, three selections for World elevens and four for Europe selects. He was West German Footballer of the Year in 1962.

Vincenzo "Enzo" Scifo

Born: February 19, 1966, Belgium.
Clubs: Anderlecht (Bel), Internazionale (It), Bordeaux, Auxerre (Fr), Torino (It), Monaco (Fr).

Born in Belgium of Italian parents, Scifo joined Anderlecht as a teenager after scoring hatfuls of goals at junior level for La Louvière. In 1984 he chose to take up Belgian citizenship just in time to play for his country at the finals of the European Championship in France. His Latin technique and vision earned an almost instant transfer to Italy, but he was really too inexperienced to cope with the challenge of running Inter's midfield. A spell in France and appearances at the 1986 and 1990 World Cups revived Italian interest and he joined Torino but, after Scifo schemed them to the 1992 UEFA Cup final, the club told him – to Monaco – to stave off creditors.

Gaetano Scirea

Born: May 25, 1953, Italy.
Clubs: Atalanta, Juventus.

Scirea was "the sweeper with charm," a skilled, graceful performer very different from the sort of ruthless "killers" employed by many Italian clubs in the 1960s and 1970s. Scirea began with Atalanta as an inside-forward and later became the defensive cornerstone of the all-conquering Juventus side of the 1980s. His central defensive partnership with rugged Claudio Gentile was one of the most effective in the international game, as they proved at the heart of Italy's World Cup-winning defense in Spain in 1982. Scirea's sustained brilliance – he was seven times Italian champion with Juventus in 11 years – long thwarted the international ambitions of Milan's Franco Baresi. Sadly, soon after retiring, he was killed in a car crash in Poland while on a scouting mission for Juventus.

Uwe Seeler

Born: November 5, 1936, West Germany.
Club: Hamburg.

Seeler, son of a former Hamburg player, was so much the central figure in West German soccer in the 1960s and early 1970s that the fans used his name – "Uwe, Uwe" – as their chant at international matches. He made his full senior debut in a 3–1 defeat by England at Wembley in 1954 when still only 18. Seeler captained West Germany in their World Cup final defeat at Wembley in 1966, but gained a measure of revenge by scoring a remarkable back-headed goal when Germany won 3–2 in extra time in the dramatic 1970 quarterfinal. He scored 43 goals in 72 internationals: he and Pele are the only men to score in four World Cups. Seeler played for Hamburg throughout his career from 1952 to 1971, loyally rejecting a string of offers from Italy and Spain.

Dragoslav Sekularac

Born: November 10, 1937, Yugoslavia.
Clubs: Red Star Belgrade (Yug), TSV 1860 Munich, Karlsruhe (W Ger), St. Louis (US), OFK Belgrade (Yug).

"Sekki" was one of the creative geniuses of European soccer in the late 1950s and early 1960s. His dribbling talents and eye-of-the-needle passing created goal upon goal for attacking partners such as Bora Kostic, and he was an outstanding member of the Red Star side which jousted so memorably with Manchester United on the eve of the Munich air disaster.

Sekularac's Achilles' heel was a quick temper which brought him into repeated conflict with match officials, administrators and teammates. After a spell with St. Louis in the United States he turned to coaching, first in Yugoslavia and later in Central and South America.

Peter Shilton

Born: September 18, 1949, England.
Clubs: Leicester, Stoke, Nottingham Forest, Southampton, Derby, Plymouth.

Shilton was only 20 when first capped, and nearly 41 when he made his 125th and last appearance for England, during the 1990 World Cup. That was his 17th game in such competitions, a record for a Briton. He conceded only 80 international goals, every one of them a dreadful blow to such a perfectionist. Shilton's awesome pursuit of personal fitness and elimination of error were renowned throughout the game. He played in an FA Cup final with Leicester, which lost (and was relegated as well), when he was 19, but never appeared in another. Only with his move to Forest, and their brief dominance of England and Europe, did club honors flow. He still played on, well into his 40s, after entering coaching with Plymouth.

Nikita Simonian

Born: October 12, 1926, Soviet Union.
Clubs: Kirilia Sovietov, Moscow Spartak.

Simonian, one of the few Armenian soccer players to have succeeded in the Soviet game, was small for a center-forward but skilful and quick – talents which brought him a then record 142 goals in 265 league matches in the 1950s. Three times he was leading scorer in the Soviet Supreme league, and his 1950 haul of 34 goals set a record that was not overtaken until the emergence of Oleg Protasov in the 1980s. Simonian began his career on Georgia's Black Sea coast, moved to Moscow with Kirilia Sovietov, or "Wings of the Soviet," and, three years later in 1949, joined Spartak. He won the league four times and the cup twice, and scored 12 goals in 23 internationals before retiring. Later he was coach to Spartak, then joint coach of the Soviet national team at the 1982 World Cup finals in Spain.

SKUHRAVY *Outpaces Austrian defender Pecl in the 1990 World Cup*

Agne Simonsson

Born: October 19, 1935, Sweden.
Clubs: Orgryte (Swe), Real Madrid, Real Sociedad (Sp), Orgryte (Swe).

The Swedish team which reached the 1958 World Cup final on home soil leaned heavily on foreign-based veterans but they, in turn, depended for the injection of a decisive attacking edge on Simonsson, the splendid center-forward from the Gothenburg club of Orgryte. Simonsson enhanced his reputation by leading Sweden to victory over England at Wembley in 1959 and was signed the following summer by Real Madrid. They envisaged Simonsson becoming the successor to the ageing Alfredo Di Stefano, but Simonsson failed to adjust to life and soccer in Spain and, in any case, Di Stefano was not ready to go. After a spell with Real Sociedad, Simonsson returned to Orgryte and played again for Sweden, but never quite recovered his earlier spark.

SHILTON *European Cup-winner*

Matthias Sindelar

Born: February 18, 1903, Austria.
Clubs: FC Hertha Vienna, FK Austria.

Nicknamed "the Man of Paper," for his slim build, Sindelar was the very spirit of the Austrian "Wunderteam" of the 1930s as well as their center-forward and attacking leader. Born and brought up in Kozlau, in Czechoslovakia, he was discovered by a minor Viennese club, Hertha, in 1920, and joined neighboring giants FK Austria a year later. Twice he won the Mitropa Cup – the inter-war forerunner of the European Cup – with FK Austria in the 1930s and added 27 goals in 43 internationals to his list of honours. Those 27 included two hat tricks against old rivals Hungary in 1928 and the two goals which beat Italy in the newly-built Prater Stadium in Vienna in 1932. Sindelar scored in both Austria's classic matches against England in 1932 and 1936 and led Austria to the World Cup semifinals of 1934. Depressed by the 1938 Anschluss, when Austria was swallowed up into Hilter's Greater Germany, he and his girlfriend committed suicide together in January, 1939.

Omar Enrique Sivori

Born: October 2, 1935, Argentina.
Clubs: River Plate (Arg), Juventus, Napoli (It).

Sivori was nicknamed "Cabezon" – Big Head – by his admirers in Argentina and Italy, because his technical virtuosity prompted him to humiliate and embarrass opposing defenders in the most outrageous ways. An inside-left with great talent and a quick temper, Sivori put fire into the Juventus attack of the late 1950s alongside the coolness of John Charles and the experience of veteran Giampiero Boniperti. He cost Juventus a world record fee and repaid them with 144 goals in eight seasons before falling out with Paraguayan coach Heriberto Herrera and sulking off to Napoli, where his partnership with Milan outcast José Altafini produced the sort of fervour seen in the 1980s for Maradona. Sivori played 18 times for Argentina, as well as nine times for Italy, and was European Footballer of the Year in 1961.

Tomas Skuhravy

Born: September 7, 1965, Czechoslovakia.
Clubs: Sparta Prague (Cz), Genoa (It).

Tall, gangling Skuhravy earned instant acclaim when he opened up his 1990 World Cup finals campaign by scoring a hat trick in the Czechoslovaks' 5–1 defeat of the United States. He finished the tournament as second leading scorer, with five goals, behind Toto Schillaci and with a lucrative new contract from Genoa in his pocket. Skuhravy's partnership there with the Uruguayan, Carlos Aguilera, brought Genoa some measure of success in the league and the UEFA Cup before a succession of injuries took their toll. Skuhravy, who invested his money in an old prince's castle in Italy, always insisted that he would have preferred to star in Formula One motor racing than in soccer.

Graeme Souness

Born: May 6, 1953, Scotland.
Clubs: Tottenham, Middlesbrough, Liverpool (Eng), Sampdoria (It), Rangers (Scot).

Souness walked away from Spurs without playing in the first team in a League game, though he did appear for them in a European match in Iceland. Even as a teenager, he was a player who knew his own value. He developed into a world-class midfielder, winning 54 caps and a string of honors with Liverpool, where he was an influential player and captain. Despite his abrasive style, he then became a great favorite with Sampdoria in Italy, but returned to become player-coach of Rangers. His huge spending ensured a string of titles for the club in the small arena of Scottish soccer, but he was less successful after his return to Anfield, where he succeeded his old friend Kenny Dalglish as Liverpool coach, and he lasted less than three seasons.

Neville Southall

Born: September 16, 1958, Wales.
Clubs: Bury, Everton, Port Vale (on loan), Everton (Eng).

A fiery character, Southall played Welsh League soccer at 14 and worked as a dish-washer, hod-carrier and garbageman before joining Bury. He was then 21, and shortly afterwards was signed by Everton. A moderate start and a brief loan period were forgotten after his return, when he suddenly hit the form that established him as one of the world's top goalkeepers. He won two championship medals, one FA Cup, and one European Cup-winners' Cup medal, and was voted Footballer of the Year in 1985. After passing the Welsh record of 73 caps, ironically he made an expensive error in the defeat that prevented his country from qualifying for the 1994 World Cup.

STOICHKOV *Specially recommended to Barcelona by Johan Cruyff*

Jürgen Sparwasser

Born: June 14, 1948, East Germany.
Club: Magdeburg.

Sparwasser was one of the few outstanding soccer players produced by East Germany in its 40 years of independent soccer existence. Sweeper Hans-Jürgen Dorner and center-forward Joachim Streich both earned a century of caps, but the most memorable achievement fell to Sparwasser at the 1974 World Cup finals.

An excellent attacking midfield player, Sparwasser scored the historic goal in Hamburg which beat World Cup hosts West Germany in the first and last meeting between the two states at the international level. Sparwasser's career featured 15 goals in 77 internationals and a European Cup-winners' Cup medal after Magdeburg's victory over Milan in Rotterdam in 1974. Later he fled East Germany by taking advantage of his selection for a veterans' tournament in West Germany.

SOUNESS *Commitment personified*

Pedro Alberto Spencer

Born: 1937, Ecuador.
Clubs: Everest (Ecu), Penarol (Uru), Barcelona Guayaquil (Ecu).

Spencer is probably the greatest Ecuadorian player of all time. He scored a record 50-plus goals in the South American club cup (Copa Libertadores), though all in the service of the Uruguayan club, Penarol, who dominated the event's early years in the 1960s. Spencer helped Penarol win the World Club Cup in 1961 and 1966 and earned such status on the field that, with his business interests, he was created Ecuadorian consul in Montevideo. Uruguayan officials so coveted Spencer's talents that he was called up to lead Uruguay's attack against England at Wembley in 1964, and scored their only goal in a 2–1 defeat. But protests from Ecuador and other South American nations ensured that this remained his one and only appearance for the "Celeste."

Hristo Stoichkov

Born: August 2, 1966, Bulgaria.
Clubs: CSKA Sofia (Bul), Barcelona (Sp).

Stoichkov built a reputation as one of Europe's finest marksmen since being reprieved from a life suspension after a controversial Bulgarian cup final between his army team, CSKA, and old Sofia rivals Levski-Spartak in 1985. Stoichkov spent only six months sidelined before being recalled for club and country and then so impressed Barcelona they bought him for a Bulgarian record $3.5million in 1990. Stoichkov rewarded coach Johan Cruyff's personal recommendation by scoring more than 60 goals for Barcelona in his first three seasons in league and European competition for the Catalan giants. He also led Barcelona to their long-awaited European Cup victory when they overcame Sampdoria in the final at Wembley in 1992 and then played well as Bulgaria won a surprise place in the 1994 World Cup finals with a last-gasp victory in France.

Luis Suarez

Born: May 2, 1935, Spain.
Clubs: Deportivo de La Coruna, Barcelona (Sp), Internazionale, Sampdoria (It).

Suarez was born and brought up in La Coruña, where he was discovered by Barcelona. The Catalans insisted on buying him immediately after he had earned a standing ovation in their own Nou Camp stadium, playing against them at 18 in 1953. Suarez was hailed as the greatest Spanish player of all time, a world-class midfield general who was later the fulcrum of the Internazionale team which dominated world club soccer in the mid-1960s. Suarez's ability to turn defense into attack with one pinpoint pass suited Inter's hit-and-hold tactics admirably. It did not go unnoticed, outside Scotland, that injury prevented Suarez lining up against Celtic when Inter lost the 1967 European Cup final in Lisbon. Later Suarez was twice coach of Inter and coached Spain at the 1990 World Cup finals.

Frank Swift

Born: December 26, 1913, England.
Club: Manchester City.

Big Frank was a personality among goalkeepers, who enjoyed a joke with opponents and referees, but was deadly serious at stopping shots.

He stood in the crowd and watched Manchester City lose the 1933 FA Cup final, then played for them when they won a year later, fainting at the finish as nervous exhaustion overcame him. During the war his entertainment value became even greater, and he won 19 caps while in his 30s – only twice on the losing side. After his retirement he became a journalist, and was one of those killed in the Munich air crash in 1958.

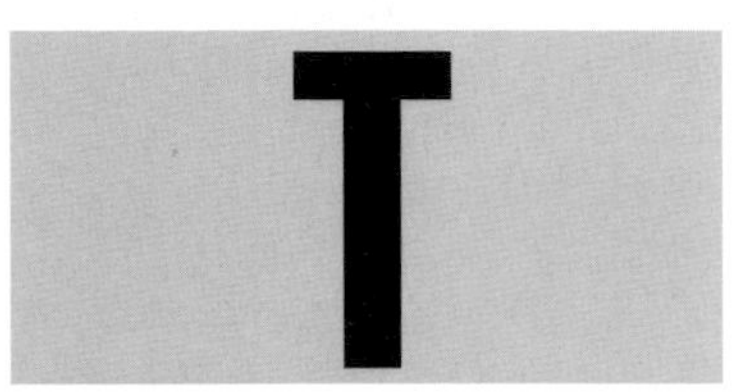

Marco Tardelli

Born: September 24, 1954, Italy.
Clubs: Pisa, Como, Juventus, Internazionale.

Tardelli was a utility defender or midfielder who was seen to best effect playing for Juventus and Italy in the first half of the 1980s. With both club and country Tardelli succeeded the more physical Romeo Benetti in midfield, though his Azzurri debut, against Portugal in Turin in 1976, was at right back. Tardelli is one of the very few players to have won every major prize in the modern domestic and European game, from the World Cup to the 1985 European Cup with Juventus. He scored six goals in 81 appearances for Italy and was voted official Man of the Match in the 1982 World Cup final defeat of West Germany in Madrid.

Tostao (full name: Eduardo Goncalves Andrade)

Born: January 25, 1947, Brazil.
Clubs: Cruzeiro, Vasco da Gama.

Tostao, a small, nimble, center-forward, was already nicknamed "the White Pele" when he made his World Cup debut for Brazil at the 1966 finals in England. He scored Brazil's consolation goal in their 3–1 defeat by Hungary. It nearly became his only World Cup appearance when, in 1969, he suffered a detached retina during a South American cup tie against Millonarios in Bogota. Tostao underwent special surgery in Houston and recovered to become one of the heroes of Brazil's World Cup victory in Mexico a year later. However Tostao, a qualified doctor, recognized that the longer he played on, the greater the risk of permanent injury, and retired at 26 in 1973... to become an eye specialist.

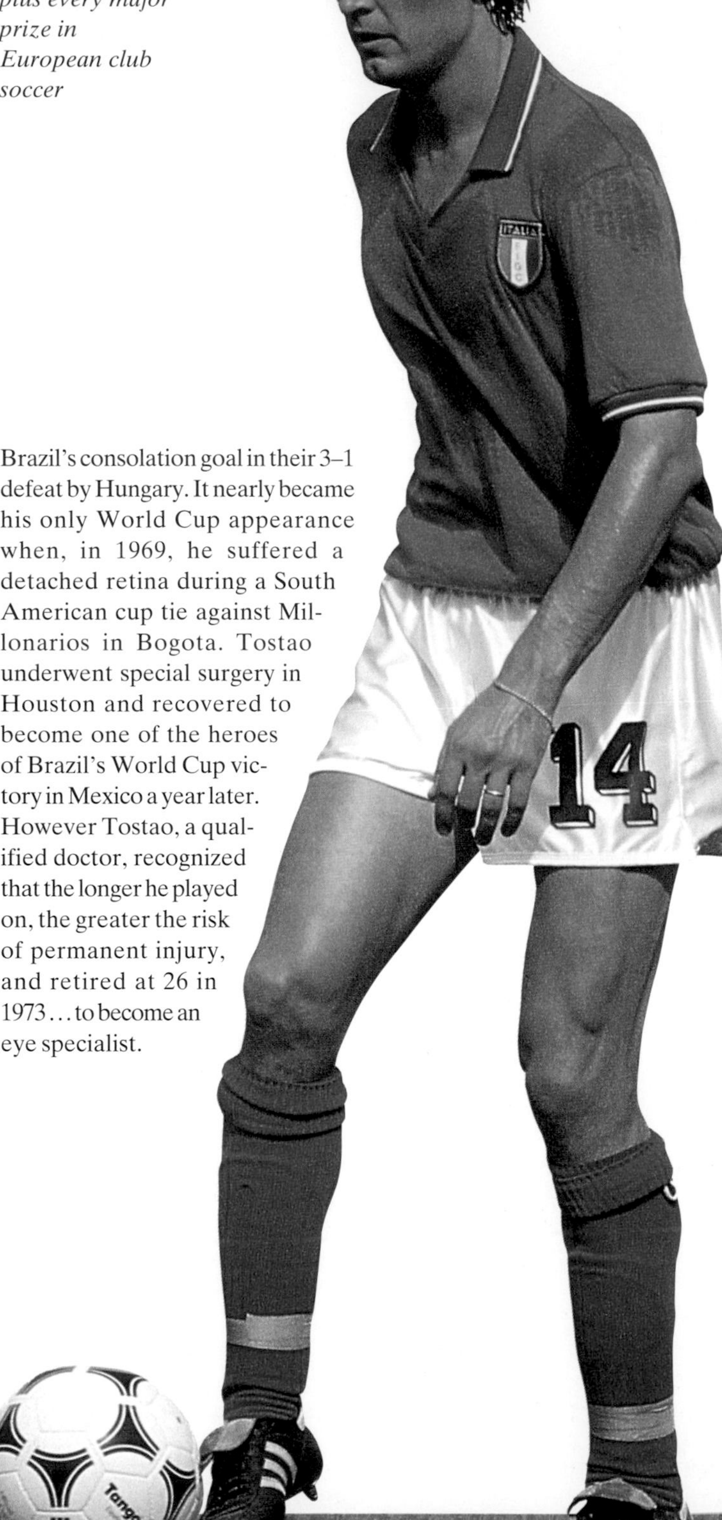

MARCO TARDELLI
One of the elite few who have won a World Cup winner's medal plus every major prize in European club soccer

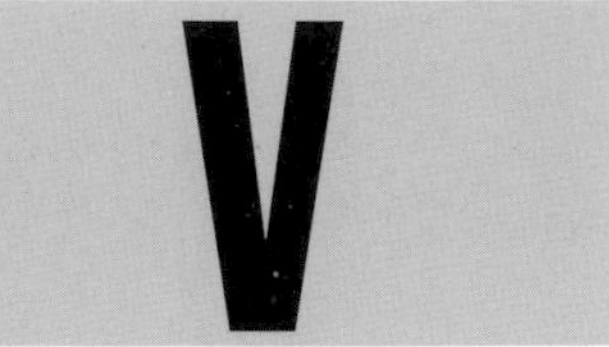

Jorge Valdano

Born: October 4, 1955, Argentina.
Clubs: Newell's Old Boys (Arg), Alaves, Zaragoza, Real Madrid (Sp).

Valdano has proved a rare personality in the world game: an author, poet, polemicist, coach and World Cup-winning player. Born in Las Parejas, he left Argentina for political reasons as a teenager and built his playing career in Spain. His success in winning the UEFA Cup twice in the mid-1980s with Real Madrid earned him selection for Argentina, and his positional and tactical skills were massive influences in the 1986 World Cup victory in Mexico. Originally an outside-left, Valdano was converted by Argentine coach Carlos Bilardo into a roving link between midfield and attack. He was later struck down by hepatitis, struggled in vain to make a World Cup comeback in 1990 and retired to become a journalist, an analyst and a successful coach with Tenerife before going back to Real as coach.

Carlos Valderrama

Born: September 2, 1961, Colombia.
Clubs: Santa Marta, Millonarios, Atletico Nacional (Col), Montpellier (Fr), Valladolid (Sp), Medellin, Atletico Junior Barranquilla (Col).

Carlos Valderrama was voted South American Footballer of the Year in 1987 after guiding surprise team Colombia to a fine third place at the Copa America. The combination of frizzy hairstyle and all-around skill earned him the nickname of "the South American Gullit," and he shared South American Cup glory with Atletico Nacional before trying his luck in Europe with Montpellier of France and Valladolid of Spain. In

VALDERRAMA *Compared to Gullit for both hairstyle and talent, Valderrama dances past a Bolivian opponent*

neither country could he reproduce his earlier fine form, although he played well as Colombia reached the second round of the 1990 World Cup finals. He rediscovered his touch completely after returning to Colombia in 1992. Then, the manner in which he masterminded Colombia's sensational 1994 World Cup qualifying campaign, notably the 5–0 rout of Argentina, earned him a second award as South American Footballer of the Year.

VAN BASTEN *Cruyff's protégé*

Marco Van Basten

Born: October 31, 1964, Holland.
Clubs: Ajax Amsterdam (Hol), Milan (It).

Marco Van Basten contributed one of the all-time great international goals when he volleyed home a long, looping cross in the 1988 European Championship final in Munich. That was Van Basten just reaching his peak, one year after graduating from Ajax Amsterdam to Milan. Tall and angular, Van Basten made his international debut at the 1983 World Youth Cup and scored 128 league goals for Ajax before joining Milan for a mere $2.2 million in 1987. With Ajax he had won the European Golden Boot (37 goals in 1985–86) and the European Cup-winners' Cup, but with Milan he added even more honors – including FIFA, World and European Player of the Year awards plus World Club and European Cup medals. Sadly, ankle trouble wrecked the latter years of his career.

Paul Van Himst

Born: October 2, 1943, Belgium.
Clubs: Anderlecht, RWD Molenbeek, Eendracht Aalst.

Van Himst, the coach who guided Belgium to the 1994 World Cup finals, is still regarded as his country's greatest player. He joined the Brussels club Anderlecht at the age of nine and, at 16, was playing center-forward in the first team. He was to be Belgian champion eight times, a cup-winner four times, league top scorer three times and was four times Footballer of the Year. Van Himst scored 31 goals in 81 internationals between 1960 and 1979, which included the 1970 World Cup finals and a third-place finish as hosts at the 1972 European Championship. Later he coached Anderlecht to victory in the UEFA Cup before being appointed coach of Belgium after the qualifying failure in the 1992 European Championship in Sweden.

Odbulio Varela

Born: September 20, 1917, Uruguay.
Clubs: Wanderers, Penarol.

Varela was captain of the Uruguayan team which shocked Brazil by beating their hosts in Rio's Maracana stadium in the 1950 World Cup "final" (the deciding match of the final pool). Varela was an old-style attacking center-half and a captain who led by example. He had made his league debut with Wanderers at 21 and had already played for Uruguay before joining local giants Penarol in 1942. Twice he won the South American Championship with Uruguay but the 1950 World Cup saw him at his zenith, driving his team forward with every confidence even after Uruguay went down 1–0 early on. Varela was outstanding again, even at 37, in the 1954 World Cup finals in Switzerland. He retired immediately afterwards and was briefly coach of Penarol.

Vava (full name: Edvaldo Izidio Neto)

Born: November 12, 1934, Brazil.
Clubs: Recife, Vasco da Gama (Br), Atletico Madrid (Sp), Palmeiras, Botafogo (Br).

Vava may not have been one of the most refined center-forwards in soccer history, but he was one of the most effective when it mattered. Originally an inside-left, Vava was switched to the center of attack by Brazil at the 1958 World Cup to allow Pele into the line-up. He scored twice in the 5–2 final victory over Sweden to earn a transfer to Spain with Atletico Madrid. The hawk-nosed Vava was successful and hugely popular in Spain, but his family grew homesick. Returning home in time to regain his Brazil place for the World Cup defence in Chile in 1962, he scored another of his typically vital goals in the 3–1 final victory over Czechoslovakia. In all, Vava scored 15 goals in 22 internationals spread over 12 years between 1952 and 1964.

VALDANO *Sprinting into the clear*

Fritz Walter

Born: October 31, 1920, Germany.
Club: Kaiserslautern.

Fritz Walter and center-forward brother Ottmar starred with Kaiserslautern in the late 1940s and early 1950s and were World Cup-winners together against hot favorites Hungary in the 1954 final in Bern, Switzerland. Yet that triumph came late in a career which was cut in two by the war. Walter scored a hat trick on his Germany debut in his favorite position of inside-left in a 9–2 thrashing of Romania in July 1940. After soccer was halted Walter was called up as a paratrooper, but his wartime flying experiences led him to refuse to fly to games in later, peacetime years. On the resumption of international soccer, Walter was restored as captain by long-time admirer and coach Sepp Herberger with success in the 1954 World Cup. Walter retired from the national team but was persuaded by Herberger to return in 1958 when, now 37, he led his team to the semifinals. Walter, who scored 33 goals in his 61 internationals, later wrote successful soccer books.

Norman Whiteside

Born: May 7, 1965, Northern Ireland.
Clubs: Manchester United, Everton (Eng).

At the age of 17, Whiteside became the youngest World Cup player in history in 1982, when he made his debut after only two League appearances, one as a substitute. He later became the youngest-ever FA Cup final and League Cup final scorer, against Brighton (won) and Liverpool (lost), and curled a splendid winner into the Everton net to earn another FA Cup medal in 1985. By then his muscular work in attack had altered to a more painstaking approach through midfield, partially brought about by the amount of damage he had sustained up front. Everton bought him, but more injuries sadly ended his career before he was 30.

WALTER *1954 World Cup-winner*

Ernst Wilimowski

Born: June 23, 1916, Poland.
Clubs: Ruch Chorzow (Pol), PSV Chemnitz, TSV 1860 Munich, Hameln 07, BC Augsburg, Singen 04, VfR Kaiserslautern (Ger).

Wilimowski wrote his name into World Cup history when he scored four goals against Brazil in a first-round tie in France in 1938 – yet still finished on the losing side after a 6–5, extra-time defeat. He totaled 21 goals in 22 games for Poland, where he won five league titles with Ruch Chorzow. Yet, for years, his name was omitted from Polish sports records – because Wilimowski, after the German invasion, continued his career with German clubs and scored a further 13 goals in eight internationals for Greater Germany. In 1942 he scored 1860 Munich's first goal in their 2–0 defeat of Schalke in the Greater German cup final. After the war he played on in Germany with a string of regional league clubs before retiring at 37 in 1953. Ironically, Wilimowski, born in Katowice, made his Poland debut playing against Germany in 1934.

Billy Wright

Born: February 6, 1924, England.
Club: Wolverhampton Wanderers.

A lively wing-half who moved into the center of defense and – by reading play superbly, timing tackles well and leaping to remarkable heights for a smallish man – he extended his career for years and years. Two League titles and one FA Cup went his way, plus the little matter of 105 caps (the majority as captain) in 13 seasons (out of a possible 108). He was the first in the world to reach a century of caps, and might have had more, even at 35, but for ending his career at virtually a moment's notice, in response to being left out of his club side for a lesser player. Later he coached Arsenal with little success, and then became a TV executive.

BILLY WRIGHT *First Englishman to win 100 international caps*

Lev Yashin

see Legends (pages 122–3)

George Young

Born: October 27, 1922, Scotland.
Club: Rangers.

Young was a dominant figure in the 1940s and 1950s – nearly 210 pounds of muscle, and a sharp brain as well. He was equally adept at right-back and center-half, and played in 53 of Scotland's first 62 post-war internationals. Young was remarkably clever on the ball for such a huge man, an inspiring captain, and a dead shot with a penalty. He scored twice from the spot in the 1949 Scottish Cup final, and acted as emergency goalkeeper in the 1953 match, helping to insure a replay that Rangers won to give him his fourth medal. Young also gained six championship medals and two for the League Cup, and had a spell as Scotland national coach before he left soccer to go into business.

Ricardo Zamora

Born: January 21, 1901, Spain.
Clubs: Español, Real Madrid (Sp), Nice (Fr).

Zamora was a legendary goalkeeper and Spain's first great soccer hero. He was a member of the Spanish team which became the first foreign side to beat England when they triumphed by 4–3 in Madrid in 1929. Conversely, one of the worst moments in Zamora's career was Spain's seven-goal thrashing in the revenge match at Highbury, London, two years later. In the 1934 World Cup quarterfinals, Zamora brilliantly and courageously defied a rugged Italian attack as Spain clung on for a 1–1 overtime draw in Florence. Unfortunately, Zamora took such a battering that he was not fit enough to play in the replay, which Spain lost. In 1936, when Spanish soccer was shut down by the civil war, Zamora moved to France to play for two further years with Nice before returning home to coach. He played 46 times for Spain and his transfer fee on moving from Español to Real Madrid in 1929 set a then Spanish record.

ZICO *Eludes the lunge of Poland's Roman Wojcicki in the 1986 World Cup*

ZOFF *Goalkeeper who captained Italy to World Cup success in 1982*

Zico (full name: Artur Antunes Coimbra)

Born: March 3, 1953, Brazil.
Clubs: Flamengo (Br), Udinese (It), Flamengo (Br), Kashima Antlers (Jap).

The youngest of three professional football brothers, Zico was at first considered too lightweight by Flamengo. Special diets and weight training turned him into the wiry attacker who scored with one of his speciality free kicks in his Brazil debut against Uruguay in 1975. Injury and tactical disagreements spoiled the 1978 and 1986 World Cups for Zico, and he was thus seen at his best only in Spain in 1982. At the club level he inspired Flamengo's victory in the 1981 South American club cup and their subsequent demolition of Liverpool in Tokyo in the World Club Cup final. That was the start of Zico's mutual love affair with Japan which was resumed when, after a spell as Brazil's Minister of Sport, he joined Kashima Antlers to lead the launch of the professional J.League in the spring of 1993.

Dino Zoff

Born: February 28, 1942, Italy.
Clubs: Udinese, Mantova, Napoli, Juventus.

Zoff is Italy's longest-serving international, with 112 appearances to his credit, of which the 106th was the World Cup final defeat of West Germany in Madrid in 1982. He secured a remarkable double that day, becoming the second Juventus goalkeeper to receive the World Cup, following in the footsteps of 1934 skipper Gianpiero Combi. Zoff played his way steadily up the *Calcio* hierarchy. After spells with Udinese and Mantova, his transfer to Napoli provided him with the springboard to national team recognition in time to help Italy win the 1968 European Nations Championship. In 1973–74 Zoff set a world record of 1,143 international minutes without conceding a goal. By then he had moved to Juventus, with whom he won league, cup and European Cup-winners' Cup honors. After his retirement, Zoff remained as cool and undemonstrative under pressure when coaching Juventus to UEFA Cup success in 1990.

THE GREAT

Even before film, television and videos brought soccer to a much certain matches became legendary. This section presents a number

April 28, 1923

THE WHITE HORSE FINAL

Wembley, London, FA Cup Final
Bolton Wanderers 2 (Jack 3, Smith, J.R., 55) West Ham United 0
HT: 1–0. Att: 126,047 (officially, though many thousands more forced their way in).
Ref: D. D. H. Asson (West Bromwich)
Bolton: Pym, Haworth, Finney, Nuttall, Seddon, Jennings, Butler, Jack, Smith, J.R., Smith, J., Vizard.
West Ham: Hufton, Henderson, Young, Bishop, Kay, Tresadern, Richards, Brown, Watson, Moore, Ruffell.

King George V was there, and somehow a match was laid on for him which, through good fortune and the crowd's good sense, was not the tragedy it might have turned into. Otherwise, the first event staged at the now historic Wembley Stadium might well have been the last. Such was the overcrowding that there could have been a disaster beyond even the awful proportions of Heysel or Hillsborough. Thanks to the self-discipline of the fans in a less impatient age, and to the police – led by Constable George Scorey on his legendary white horse, Billy – the Cup final took place, starting almost an hour late. The match was not ticket-only, and nobody had anticipated such an enormous turnout at the new stadium, built as part of the complex to house the Empire Exhibition. The stadium was estimated to have a capacity of 125,000, but the combination of a fine spring day, the new arena and the appearance of a London club in the final (even if a Second Division club) led to an estimated 250,000 trying to gain admittance — and mostly succeeding.

Many who had bought seats were unable to claim them in the crush. Some of the Bolton directors, traveling separately from the team, did not see a ball kicked, but the match went on and soccer entered the mass consciousness.

The first goal, by David Jack, came as an opponent was trying to climb back out of the crowd next to the touchline; and the second, by the Scot, J. R. Smith, was thought by some to have rebounded from a post: instead, it had hit spectators standing on the goal netting.

July 30, 1930

THE FIRST WORLD CHAMPIONS

Centenary Stadium, Montevideo
World Cup Final
Uruguay 4 (Dorado 12, Cea 57, Iriarte 68, Castro 90)
Argentina 2 (Peucelle 20, Stabile 37)
HT: 1–2. Att: 93,000. Ref: J. Langenus (Belgium)
Uruguay: Ballesteros, Nassazzi, Mascharoni, Andrade, Fernandez, Gestido, Dorado, Scarone, Castro, Cea, Iriarte.
Argentina: Botasso, Della Torre, Paternoster, Evaristo, Monti, Suarez, Peucelle, Varallo, Stabile, Ferreira, Evaristo.

Few papers outside South America and Central Europe bothered to report the match. The referee wore a tie and plus-fours, and several players covered their heads with handkerchiefs to keep the sun at bay. What film survives shows a near laughable standard of goalkeeping and defensive technique. Yet this game went into history simply because it could not be repeated. The first World Cup was over, and international soccer now had a standard to surpass.

Soccer statesmen Guérin from France and Hirschman from Holland had developed the idea of a World Cup and brought it to fruition, even if only 13 nations turned up, including a mere four from Europe. Uruguay, celebrating 100 years of independence, guaranteed to refund all expenses to the visitors, just managed to get a new stadium built in time, and fittingly reached the final. There were no seeds, just four groups, each of which sent one team to the semi-final, where Yugoslavia and the United States both lost 6–1. So the final pitted hosts against neighbors, with thousands crossing the River Plate to play their part in a deafening climax to the fledgling tournament.

UNREPEATABLE *The first World Cup final goal, by Uruguay's Dorado*

The Uruguayans took the lead, fell behind, then went ahead again at 3–2 before Stabile, top scorer in the competition with eight goals, hit their bar. Castro, who had lost part of an arm in childhood, then headed the goal which clinched Uruguay's victory, to be greeted by a national holiday in his country . . . and bricks through the windows of the Uruguayan Embassy in Buenos Aires.

MATCHES

wider audience than could sit in the stands or stand on the terraces, of games that will continue to live on in soccer's folklore.

May 14, 1938

SHAMED ENGLAND HIT SIX

Olympic Stadium, Berlin
Friendly international
Germany 3 (Gauchel 20, Gellesch 42, Pesser 70)
England 6 (Bastin 12, Robinson 26, 50, Broome 36, Matthews 39, Goulden 72)
HT: 2–4. Att: 103,000. Ref: J. Langenus (Belgium)
Germany: Jakob, Janes, Muenzenberg, Kupfer, Goldbrunner, Kitzinger, Lehner, Gellesch, Gauchel, Szepan, Pesser.
England: Woodley, Sproston, Hapgood, Willingham, Young, Welsh, Matthews, Robinson, Broome, Goulden, Bastin.

One of England's most effective displays followed a shameful incident brought about by political pressures of the era. In an effort to placate Hitler, still furious at the way the majority of his athletes had been humbled in the same stadium at the 1936 Olympics, the England team was ordered to join the Germans in giving the Nazi salute as the German national anthem was played. The instruction came from the British Ambassador, Sir Neville Henderson, supported by Stanley Rous (later Sir Stanley), then FA secretary. The players, unwilling to make a fuss, reluctantly did it, then showed their feelings by beating a very good German team out of sight. Don Welsh, one of two men making their England debut, was to say later: "You couldn't have asked for a greater team performance than this. Only when the heat got to us in the second half did we have to slow down a bit. I honestly thought we could have scored ten."

MOMENT OF INFAMY *England salutes*

Jackie Robinson, only 20, was a perfect partner for Stan Matthews, and little Len Goulden hit a tremendous 30-yard goal to add to his all-round industry. The other debut player, Frank Broome, also scored.

July 16, 1950

BRAZIL FAIL AT THE FINISH

Maracana, Rio de Janeiro
World Cup final pool
Brazil 1 (Friaca 47)
Uruguay 2 (Schiaffino 66, Ghiggia 79)
HT: 0–0. Att: 199,000. Ref: G. Reader (England)
Brazil: Barbosa, Da Costa, Juvenal, Bauer, Alvim, Bigode, Friaca, Zizinho, Ademir, Jair, Chico.
Uruguay: Maspoli, Gonzales, Tejera, Gambetta, Varela, Andrade, Ghiggia, Perez, Miguez, Schiaffino, Moran.

Figures for the attendance vary from source to source, but this was certainly the highest at any soccer match since Wembley 1923. The first post-war World Cup, played without a knockout final stage, provided what was in effect a final and established the tournament as the leading worldwide soccer competition. Even England was in it this time, having snubbed the three pre-war events. They failed miserably, however, struggling to beat Chile, then losing to the United States and to Spain. So the Spaniards went through to the final pool, with Brazil, Uruguay and Sweden, and the schedule worked out perfectly.

FOILED *Goalkeeper Maspoli stops a Brazilian attack*

Brazil, overwhelming favorites, won their first two games, scoring 13 goals to two. Uruguay trailed both Spain and Sweden 2–1, but drew the first game and won the second. So they had to beat Brazil at the enormous newly-built Maracana, while Brazil needed only to draw. Coach Flavio Costa seemed the only Brazilian unsure of victory, but his warnings about previous encounters in which Uruguay had disturbed Brazil went unheeded. Even after Friaca hit their 22nd goal in six games, Brazil kept pressing forward: Costa later protested that he had ordered men back into defense, but his words had gone either unheard or unheeded. Uruguay, remarkably calm amid the crescendo, equalized through Schiaffino. Then Ghiggia slipped through on the right and shot between Barbosa and his near, left-hand post: not a great goal, but an historic one.

EUPHORIC *Bill Perry (right) scores the seventh and last goal of Wembley's most dramatic Cup final, as Ball lunges in vain*

May 2, 1953

STANLEY AND STANLEY

Wembley, London, FA Cup Final
Blackpool 4 (Mortensen 35, 68, 89, Perry 90)
Bolton 3 (Lofthouse 2, Moir 41, Bell 55)
HT: 1–2. Att: 100,000. Ref: M. Griffiths (Wales)
Blackpool: Farm, Shimwell, Garrett, Fenton, Johnston, Robinson, Matthews, Taylor, Mortensen, Mudie, Perry.
Bolton: Hanson, Ball, Banks, Wheeler, Barrass, Bell, Holden, Moir, Lofthouse, Hassall, Langton.

Stanley Matthews, at 38, stood soccer on its head. He gained a Cup-winners' medal after being on the losing side twice, he played a barely credible part in his team's rally from three down (the first of only two such recoveries in Wembley history) and he persuaded the hidebound FA to add him to their party to go to South America a few days later, after they had left him out because of his age. Blackpool's victory now seems to have been achieved by fate as much as by soccer: England was basking in the glow of Queen Elizabeth's Coronation and Mount Everest had been conquered by a British-led expedition. How, then, could unheralded Bolton have won the Cup?

But they very nearly did, in a game of remarkable drama, poor goalkeeping – goals 1, 3, 5 and 6 ought to have been stopped – and tactical naivete. In the last half-hour, with goalscorer Bell limping badly from a first-half injury and Banks limping not quite so badly, Bolton still kept both on their left (this was 13 years before substitutes). That was also Blackpool's right, the flank that Fenton and Taylor insured was stuffed full of passes for the shuffling, mesmerizing genius named Matthews. In the incredible final moments, after the other Stanley, Mortensen, completed his hat trick (still the only one in a Wembley FA Cup final) with a free kick, and Matthews had assisted on the winner for Perry, the scoreboard momentarily showed the score as 4–4. Even today, when the talk is of Cup finals, 1953 is usually No. 1.

November 25, 1953

THE MATCH THAT CHANGED THE GAME

Wembley, London
Friendly international
England 3 (Sewell 15, Mortensen 37, Ramsey 62 pen)
Hungary 6 (Hidegkuti 1, 20, 56, Puskas 22, 29, Bozsik 65)
HT: 2–4. Att: 100,000. Ref: L. Horn (Holland)
England: Merrick, Ramsey, Eckersley, Wright, Johnston, Dickinson, Matthews, Taylor, Mortensen, Sewell, Robb.
Hungary: Grosics (Geller 74), Buzansky, Lantos, Bozsik, Lorant, Zakarias, Budai, Kocsis, Hidegkuti, Puskas, Czibor.

Why was England so confident? Did they not know that Hungary went to Wembley having won 25 and drawn six of their previous 32 games, and having scored in every match they had played for six seasons? Yet England, fielding two first-time national team players in a team averaging over 30 years of age, still looked on the match as something of a training camp, fooled by a xenophobic press which had little or no direct knowledge of Ferenc Puskas and his colleagues. "This will be easy," said one England player as the teams walked out, "they've all got carpet slippers on." Indeed, Hungary's footwear did look like slippers compared with England's thunderous shoes, but they could smack the ball pretty hard when they had to. As Hidegkuti did in the opening seconds, from 20 angled yards, arrow-straight past Gil Merrick. The Hungarians played in tight little triangles, then suddenly opened up with a slicing pass of 30, 40, 50 yards or more to a sprinting colleague. They gave the impression that they could always score a goal if they really needed one.

The defeat, clear and unequivocal, was England's first by a continental invader. That was not in itself important, but the manner and the margin of the massacre forced a furious tactical rethinking in succeeding seasons. So great a rethinking that it is fair to consider whether, without the shock treatment administered by Puskas and Co, England would have won the World Cup 13 years later.

HISTORIC *Ference Puskas (left) and Billy Wright lead the teams out*

June 27, 1954

THE BATTLE OF BERNE

Wankdorf Stadium, Berne
World Cup quarter-final
Brazil 2 (D. Santos 18 pen, Julinho 65)
Hungary 4 (Hidegkuti 4, Kocsis 7, 90, Lantos 55 pen)
HT: 1–2. Att: 40,000. Ref: A. Ellis (England)
Brazil: Castilho, Santos, D., Santos, N., Brandaozinho, Bauer, Pinheiro, Julino, Didi, Humberto, Indio, Maurinho.
Hungary: Grosics, Buzansky, Lantos, Bozsik, Lorant, Zakarias, Toth, M., Kocsis, Hidegkuti, Czibor, Toth, J.

This violent clash between two outstanding teams had a cleansing effect on soccer, for a time. The appalling scenes and continuing controversy served to warn players and officials that soccer could go close to anarchy unless all concerned showed some respect for the traditions of the game as well as for its rules.

DISGRACE *Nilton Santos and Bozsik*

Hungary's part in this disgrace made a lot of people glad when they eventually lost the final, although victory in the world championship would have been a fitting reward for a team of majestic power. Some of the blame must attach to referee Ellis, who sent off three players but never had the match under control.

Hungary, 2–0 up early on, showed unseemly arrogance, and a wild tackle cost them a penalty, halving their lead. When another penalty enabled them to go two up again, after most people felt that Kocsis had committed the foul, Brazil lost their heads. Offense followed offense on both sides of Julinho's goal, until Ellis at last sent off Bozsik (a Member of the Hungarian Parliament) and Nilton Santos for fighting, followed by Humberto for a deliberate kick. Kocsis headed a clinching goal in the last seconds, but the violence continued in the locker room, and Ellis needed an armed guard. FIFA abstained from punitive action, but the Hungarian authorities threatened all sorts of sanctions if there was any repetition. In the semifinal, three days later, Hungary – with nine of their quarterfinalists in action again – played superbly, and cleanly, to beat Uruguay 4–2. The lesson had been learned.

July 4, 1954

HUNGARY FAIL AT LAST

Wankdorf Stadium, Berne
World Cup Final
West Germany 3 (Morlock 10, Rahn 18, 82)
Hungary 2 (Puskas 6, Czibor 8)
HT: 2–2. Att: 60,000. Ref: W. Ling (England)
West Germany: Turek, Posipal, Kohlmeyer, Eckel, Liebrich, Mai, Rahn, Morlock, Walter, O., Walter, F., Schafer.
Hungary: Grosics, Buzansky, Lantos, Bozsik, Lorant, Zakarias, Czibor, Kocsis, Hidegkuti, Puskas, Toth, J.

German fortitude overtook Hungarian class in a thrilling final, played with great speed and skill despite steady rain. The match was perhaps the first major indication that West Germany's well-organized methods could prove too much for technically superior opposition. Germany has been a force in virtually every World Cup since, whereas Hungary has rarely approached the heights of the Puskas era.

The game also showed the benefit of tactical awareness. German coach Sepp Herberger had fielded only six of his eventual finalists in an earlier group game, which Hungary won 8–3, gambling on doing well in the playoff against Turkey that this defeat would bring. Sure enough, the Turks were beaten 7–2, and Germany went into the quarterfinals and then on to eventual victory. Ironically, Puskas could be held responsible for his team's defeat. He had been injured in the qualifying game against the Germans a fortnight earlier and had not played since. Although he said he was fit, and scored the first goal, he was nowhere near 100 per cent. The offside decision by linesman Mervyn Griffith that prevented what would have been his late equalizer was another decisive blow. Two early goals took Hungary's total for the tournament to 27, still the record for all finals, but two defensive errors enabled Germany to draw even with only 18 minutes gone. More than another hour passed before the powerful Rahn – a late addition to the squad after his international career had seemed over – scored Germany's third. Hungary had lost for the first time in 32 games, and the Germans had outsmarted the rest.

DELIGHT *Czibor (right) celebrates as Kohlmeyer and goalkeeper Turek are powerless to intervene*

May 13, 1956

REAL KINGS OF EUROPE

Parc des Princes, Paris
European Cup Final
Real Madrid 4 (Di Stefano 15, Rial 30, 80, Marquitos 72)
Reims 3 (Leblond 4, Templin 11, Hidalgo 63)
HT: 2–2. Att: 38,238. Ref: A. Ellis (England)
Real Madrid: Alonso, Atienza, Lesmes, Muñoz, Marquitos, Zarraga, Joseito, Marsal, Di Stefano, Rial, Gento.
Reims: Jacquet, Zimny, Giraudo, Leblond, Jonquet, Siatka, Hidalgo, Glovacki, Kopa, Bliard, Templin.

The European Champions Club Cup at last came struggling into life, having been conceived and forced through a difficult birth by a Frenchman, Gabriel Hanot, a former French international fullback and by now the editor of the influential daily newspaper, *L'Equipe*. Only 16 clubs were invited to compete – not all of them national champions: Hibernian, who reached the semifinals, had finished only fifth in Scotland in the previous season.

England, still insular, did not take part, Chelsea meekly complying with a Football League ruling that a European tournament would complicate the schedule. Now, of course, there are three of them, and many clubs would be destitute without the receipts these games bring in. Attack was the order of the day, or night, in those earlier, more innocent times. The 29 games contained 127 goals (an average of 4.37 per match), with Real Madrid scoring 20 and Reims 18, while attendances averaged 31,000. The tournament was a winner, beyond any shadow of doubt.

So too were Real, inspired off the field by far-seeing president Santiago Bernabeu and on it by Alfredo Di Stefano, arriving from Argentina via a brief stop in Colombia's rebel, unrecognized league. Real's exploits over this and the next few seasons established the club at the top of both the Spanish and European competition, proving the wisdom of Bernabeu's expenditure on a ground capable of holding 125,000.

His team can seldom have rallied better than against Reims, who scored two easy early goals and under Raymond Kopa's direction – Real had already arranged to sign him immediately afterwards – looked capable of more. But Real battled on to earn the first of their five successive European victories. A great team had arrived.

SUPERB *Pele (left) scores his first goal after a ball-juggling act that mesmerized the Swedish defense and the spectators*

June 29, 1958

FIRE IN THE FRIENDLY FINALS

Rasunda Stadium, Stockholm
World Cup Final
Brazil 5 (Vava 9, 30, Pele 55, 90, Zagalo 68)
Sweden 2 (Liedholm 4, Simonsson 80)
HT: 2–1. Att: 49,737. Ref: M. Guigue (France)
Brazil: Gilmar, Santos, D., Santos, N., Zito, Bellini, Orlando, Garrincha, Didi, Vava, Pele, Zagalo.
Sweden: Svensson, Bergmark, Axbom, Borjesson, Gustavsson, Parling, Hamrin, Gren, Simonsson, Liedholm, Skoglund.

Brazil's victory over the host nation in Stockholm proved to a vast audience – thanks to the spread of television – that South Americans can, after all, travel well.The team deservedly went into history as one of the greatest ever, after wonderful performances in the semifinal (5–2 against France) and the final, when they overcame an early deficit with unstoppable power. Coach Vicente Feola had restored Didi, thought by some to be too old at 30, and preferred Vava to 19-year-old Mazzola as striker. These changes worked well, as did Feola's decision to bring back Djalma Santos in defense after Di Sordi had played all the previous games in the final stages. But perhaps the most crucial decision was made by the players, who demanded a place for Garrincha on the right wing. Feola somewhat reluctantly agreed – and Garrincha, often tantalizingly inconsistent, responded superbly.

His speed left the Swedes for dead to make two goals for Vava, and Pele conjured a magical third, controlling a pass on one thigh, flicking the ball over his head, whirling and shooting, all in milliseconds. After adding the final goal, the boy dissolved in tears of joy. Pele, perhaps the greatest player ever, had made a worldwide mark.

May 18, 1960

GLASGOW SEES THE GREATEST

Hampden Park, Glasgow
European Cup Final
Real Madrid 7 (Di Stefano 27, 30, 73, Puskas 36, 48 pen, 58, 63)
Eintracht Frankfurt 3 (Kress 18, Stein 72, 80)
HT: 3–1. Att: 127,621. Ref: A. Mowat (Scotland)
Real Madrid: Dominguez, Marquitos, Pachin, Vidal, Santamaria, Zarraga, Canario, Del Sol, Di Stefano, Puskas, Gento.
Eintracht: Loy, Lutz, Hofer, Weilbacher, Eigenbrodt, Stinka, Kress, Lindner, Stein, Pfaff, Meier.

LAP OF HONOR *Real players show off the European Cup after the final*

Real Madrid's fifth successive European Cup was achieved by their greatest performance in front of yet another great crowd. In their seven matches they scored 31 goals and were watched by 524,097 people – an average of nearly 75,000 per game. In the semifinal Real beat Barcelona 3–1 home and away, after Barça had crushed Wolves, the English champions, 9–2 on aggregate. In the other semifinal, Eintracht performed the barely credible feat of twice scoring six goals against Rangers, but in the final they conceded hat tricks to both Di Stefano and Puskas in a wonderful performance watched by a crowd so big that only one larger attendance has been recorded in Britain since. Hardly any left early, even though the Germans were a beaten team well before the end. The fans stayed to bay a seemingly never-ending roar of tribute to one of the finest displays ever put on by any team, anywhere. The Scots were quick to appreciate their good fortune.

Real was now under their fourth coach in five years, wing-half Miguel Muñoz from their 1956 team having taken over. His two signings, Del Sol and Pachin, augmented an already illustrious squad, with the Uruguayan Santamaria a rock in defense, Gento a rapier on the left, and – towering above all – Di Stefano and Puskas, creators and finishers of a standard rarely seen before or since. Yet not even Real could win everything. Although they went on to beat Penarol 5–1 in the first (unofficial) club championship, they were runners-up in both their domestic league and cup.

May 31, 1961

BENFICA BETTER THAN BARÇA

Wankdorf Stadium, Berne
European Cup Final
Benfica 3 (Aguas 30, Ramallets 31 (o.g.), Coluna 55)
Barcelona 2 (Kocsis 20, Czibor 79)
HT: 2–1. Att: 33,000. Ref: G. Dienst (Switzerland)
Benfica: Costa Pereira, Mario Joao, Angelo, Neto, Germano, Cruz, José Augusto, Santana, Aguas, Coluna, Cavem.
Barcelona: Ramallets, Foncho, Gracia, Verges, Garay, Gensana, Kubala, Kocsis, Evaristo, Suarez, Czibor.

A curious match that showed a corporate rise and some individual falls. Benfica, little known outside Portugal and rank outsiders before the kickoff, took the European Cup and began a parade of domestic success that brought them 12 championships in the next 16 seasons, all in bunches of three: 1963–64–65, 1967–68–69, 1971–72–73 and 1975–76–77. And the Hungarian link with European Cup finals was now almost severed. Kocsis and Czibor, who both scored for Barcelona, had been on the losing side – beaten by the same score on the same field – in the 1954 World Cup final. They were virtually the last link with the marvelous Magyar team, although Puskas was to have the final word with a hat-trick for Real in the European Cup final a year later. Another Hungarian, Kubala – who played for three countries – was a third key figure in the Barça side, but their downfall was due mainly to a home-bred player.

Their international keeper Ramallets missed a cross and let in Aguas for Benfica's equalizer. A minute later he fumbled a back-header by Gensana and allowed the ball to cross the line before knocking it back again. Even Coluna's thunderous, long-range third might have been saved had Ramallets reacted more quickly.

Not surprisingly, these errors sapped a lot of Barca's confidence, but they kept battling. They hit the woodwork three times, four if Kubala's shot that came out after striking both posts is counted as doubly unlucky. Benfica, however fortunate with their goals, was a good, adventurous team. They held out calmly even after conceding a late second, and Kocsis and Czibor left the field in tears.

May 25, 1967

LISBON'S LIONS

National Stadium, Lisbon
European Cup Final
Celtic 2 (Gemmell 73, Chalmers 85)
Internazionale 1 (Mazzola 8 pen)
HT: 0–1. Att: 45,000.
Ref: H. Tschenscher (W Germany)
Celtic: Simpson, Craig, Gemmell, Murdoch, McNeill, Clark, Johnstone, Wallace, Chalmers, Auld, Lennox.
Internazionale: Sarti, Burgnich, Facchetti, Bedin, Guarneri, Picchi, Domenghini, Mazzola, Cappellini, Bicicli, Corso.

Celtic, one of Scotland's big two clubs, were minnows in the mainstream of Europe, despite frequent forays. Only two of their team on this balmy night in Portugal, before a frenzied crowd of adoring travellers, had any experience of the game outside their native land. Auld spent a none-too-productive spell at Birmingham, and Simpson had left Newcastle over a decade earlier (and now, at 37, was Scottish Footballer of the Year). The rest were a mixture of Glasgow lads and small-fee bargains recruited by Jock Stein, a coach wondrously adept at making the whole much greater than the sum of the parts – nowadays he would have a degree in human resources.

Inter, European champions in 1965, returned to the final with the help of a "deal" that would not now be allowed: after two draws with CSKA, Inter won the right to stage a vital home play-off in Bologna simply by promising the impoverished Bulgarians of CSKA 75 per cent of the takings. When Inter won through by a lone goal, many neutrals turned against them: certainly Celtic had incredible support in a comparatively small crowd at Lisbon, where they won the right to be called Lions.

Even though they trailed for more than an hour, their faith in hard work and uncomplicated, attacking soccer paid off with two goals. So bargain-basement Celtic won every tournament they contested that season, while big-money Inter did not win a thing. Delightful irony!

May 29, 1968

BUSBY'S BELATED REWARD

Wembley, London
European Cup Final
Manchester United 4 (Charlton 53, 104, Best 91, Kidd 95)
Benfica 1 (Graça 85). After extra time.
HT: 0–0. 90 minutes: 1–1. Att: 100,000.
Ref: C. Lo Bello (Italy)
Manchester United: Stepney, Brennan, Dunne, Crerand, Foulkes, Stiles, Best, Kidd, Charlton, Sadler, Aston.
Benfica: Henrique, Adolfo, Cruz, Graça, Humberto, Jacinto, José Augusto, Eusebio, Torres, Coluna, Simoes.

One shot, one save . . . so much glorious English soccer history might never have happened. Eusebio, the mainspring of a fine Benfica side, had a chance to win the game, moments after Graça's late equalizer of a rare Bobby Charlton headed goal had sent United reeling. A thunderous right-foot shot from 18 yards after he had been put through the middle brought an instinctive save from Stepney and a rueful hand clap from Eusebio: did he realize, even then, that a more delicate placing could have won the Cup for his own team?

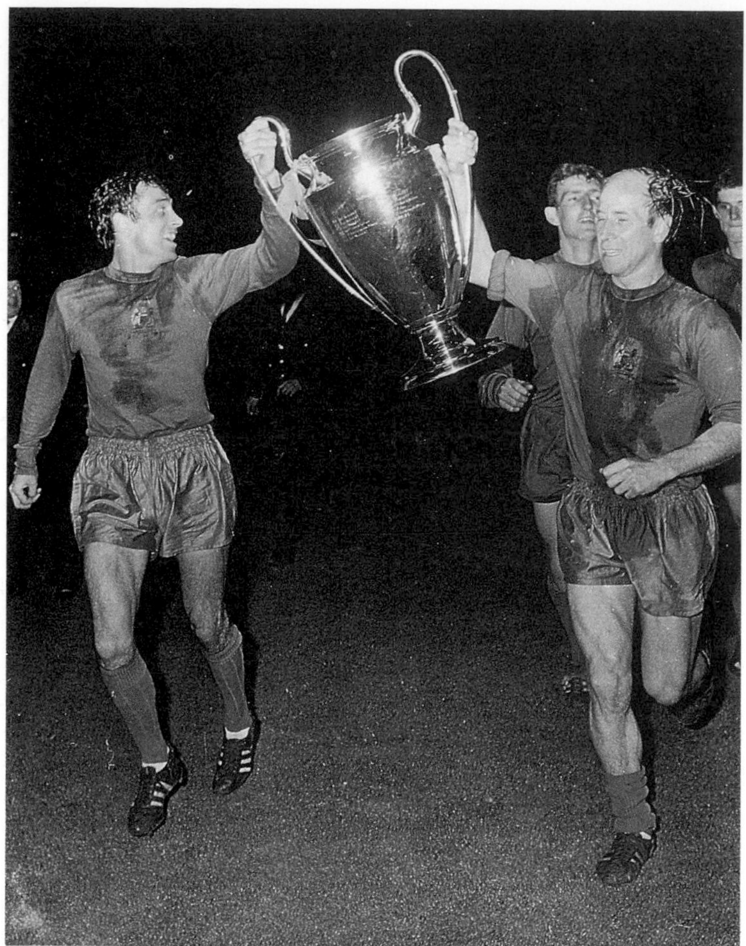

INSPIRED *Charlton (right) and Brennan lead the lap of honor*

In extra time, United regained their poise and power, with a glorious solo goal by Best being followed by two others, one from Kidd, on his 19th birthday, who headed the ball in on his second attempt after the goalkeeper had parried his first header, pushing it back out to him, and the other by captain Charlton, one of the World Cup winners on the same field two years earlier.

So United, the third fine team assembled by coach Matt Busby in 20 years, became the first English club to annex Europe's leading trophy.The early postwar United was too soon for Europe: the mid-1950s Busby Babes reached the semi-finals in 1957, losing to Real Madrid, and the patched-up, post-Munich side went down to inevitable defeat against Milan in 1958.

Thus a decade passed after Munich before Busby's third great team swept to their majestic triumph. Charlton and Foulkes were Munich survivors in the team. In so doing, they gave extra heart to other English clubs who had faltered on Europe's threshold: in the next decade, nine English clubs reached various finals on the Continent.

June 17, 1970

LOSERS AT THE LAST GASP

Azteca Stadium, Mexico City
World Cup semi-final
Italy 4 (Boninsegna 7, Burgnich 97, Riva 103, Rivera 111)
West Germany 3 (Schnellinger 90, Müller 95, 110). After extra time.
HT: 1–0. 90 minutes: 1–1. Att: 80,000.
Ref: A. Yamasaki (Mexico)
Italy: Albertosi, Burgnich, Cera, Bertini, Facchetti, Rosato (Poletti), Domenghini, Mazzola (Rivera), De Sisti, Boninsegna, Riva.
West Germany: Maier, Vogts, Beckenbauer, Schulz, Schnellinger, Grabowski, Patzke (Held), Overath, Seeler, Müller, Löhr (Libuda).

Six goals in 21 minutes made this one of the most exciting matches in the history of the World Cup or any other competition. Sadly, such are the demands of modern tournament structures, both teams ended up as losers. Three days earlier, in a thrilling quarterfinal, Germany had played extra time before beating England 3–2, and coach Helmut Schön blamed defeat by Italy on the draining effects of that match. Four days later, an unchanged Italian side crashed 4–1 in the final, and although there was no mistaking Brazil's right to the Jules Rimet Trophy, equally there was no doubting the fact that the Italians, in turn, had not fully recovered from their exertions against the Germans.

INSUFFICIENT *Gerd Müller scores, but the Italians rally to win*

Players, no matter how fit, need ample time to recuperate from two tense, testing hours in the Mexican sun. Schön, usually a master at tactical substitution, was caught out this time and forced to leave Beckenbauer on the field after dislocating a shoulder – bravery unquestioned but ability impaired. The gallant Beckenbauer played for an hour, including extra time, with the damaged shoulder strapped.

Germany could not afford such luxuries. Italy led for nearly all normal time, after Boninsegna's early snap shot, but Schnellinger, playing in his fourth World Cup, equalized for West Germany in injury time – only seconds from defeat. That began a remarkable scoring burst, with Germany leading 2–1, Italy levelling then leading 3–2, Germany getting even again – Müller's tenth goal of the tournament – and Rivera carefully rolling in what proved to be the decider, straight from the restart.

July 5, 1982

ROSSI'S TIMELY RETURN

Sarria Stadium, Barcelona
World Cup Group C
Italy 3 (Rossi 5, 25, 75)
Brazil 2 (Socrates 12, Falcao 68)
HT: 2–1. Att: 44,000. Ref: A. Klein (Israel)
Italy: Zoff, Gentile, Collovati (Bergomi), Scirea, Cabrini, Tardelli (Marini), Antognoni, Oriali, Graziani, Conti, Rossi.
Brazil: Waldir Peres, Leandro, Oscar, Luisinho, Junior, Toninho Cerezo, Socrates, Zico, Falcao, Serginho (Paulo Isidoro), Eder.

BRILLIANT *Rossi scores for Italy in Barcelona, and two great Brazilian goals are still two too few*

On the morning of April 29, 1982, Paolo Rossi returned from suspension, having been banned for three years – later reduced to two – for allegedly accepting a bribe and helping "fix" a match in the Italian league. Some 11 weeks later Rossi was the hero of all Italy. He scored three goals in this vital group qualifying match to eliminate the favorites, Brazil, two in the semi-final against Poland, and one in the final, when Italy beat West Germany 3–1. His six goals made him the tournament's leading marksman and completed a remarkable comeback for one of the most effective strikers of his generation.

Rossi was still only 24, and Juventus had such faith in him that they paid Perugia $900,000 to buy him while he had a year of the ban left. He had always protested his innocence – and his demonic efforts to regain match fitness, plus his finishing, took Italy to a merited success after they had managed only three draws in their initial qualifying group.

Brazil began against Italy needing only a draw to reach the semi-finals, and should have achieved it with some ease. But their two brilliant goals encouraged them to keep on attacking and their over-stretched defense made too many errors against a forward in such inspired mood as Rossi, the man who came back.

July 8, 1982

THE MAN WHO STAYED ON

Sanchez Pizjuan Stadium, Seville
World Cup semi-final
West Germany 3 (Littbarski 18, Rummenigge 102, Fischer 107)
France 3 (Platini 27 pen, Trésor 92, Giresse 98). After extra time. West Germany won 5–4 on penalties
HT: 1–1. 90 minutes: 1–1. Att: 63,000. Ref: C. Corver (Holland)
West Germany: Schumacher, Kaltz, Forster, K.-H., Stielike, Briegel (Rummenigge), Forster, B., Dremmler, Breitner, Littbarski, Magath (Hrubesch), Fischer.
France: Ettori, Amoros, Janvion, Bossis, Tigana, Trésor, Genghini (Battiston, Lopez), Giresse, Platini, Rocheteau, Six.

The first World Cup finals match to be decided on penalties was resolved because indomitable German spirit proved just too much for French skill. But West Germany was lucky to go through after an appalling foul by goalkeeper Harald Schumacher on French substitute Patrick Battiston. Schumacher's headlong charge left Battiston unconscious for several minutes. A penalty? A sending-off? Not even a card. The referee, in his wisdom, allowed Schumacher to remain, staring cold-eyed as Battiston was carried away.

BATTERED *For the semi-conscious Patrick Battiston, the semifinal is over*

France recovered so well after a poor opening that they might well have won inside 90 minutes. Then two quick goals in extra time seemed to have made them safe, and delighted all neutrals. Yet the Germans, again showing remarkable spirit in adversity, turned the game around. Rummenigge, the captain, went on as a substitute, although far from fit, and scored almost at once. Then an overhead hook from Fischer leveled the scores.

Even then France should have won. They were given the first penalty of the shoot-out, which usually proves a mental advantage, and when Stielike missed Germany's third attempt, France led 3–2. But Six failed with his and, after West Germany had evened things at 4–4, Schumacher made himself even less popular with the world at large by parrying a weak effort from Bossis. Hrubesch promptly hit the winner, deciding a soccer thriller.

June 21, 1986

THE CARNIVAL IS OVER

Jalisco Stadium, Guadalajara
World Cup quarter-final
France 1 (Platini 40)
Brazil 1 (Careca 18). After extra time.
France won 4–3 on penalties.
HT: 1–1. 90 minutes: 1–1. Att: 65,777.
Ref: I. Igna (Romania)
France: Bats, Battiston, Amoros, Bossis, Tousseau, Giresse (Ferreri), Tigana, Platini, Fernandez, Stopyra, Rocheteau (Bellone).
Brazil: Carlos, Josimar, Julio César, Edinho, Branco, Alemao, Socrates, Junior (Silas), Elzo, Muller (Zico), Careca.

Seven French survivors from Seville four years earlier had to go through another penalty shoot-out after a classic two-hour struggle ended in a draw. This time, French nerves held better than they had done in 1982, even though the captain and midfield inspiration, Michel Platini, failed with his shot when the score was 3–3. Julio César missed with the next Brazilian effort, and Luis Fernandez scored with his to put France into the semifinal . . . where West Germany, Schumacher included, was waiting to beat them 2–0.

Although the Brazil team could not compare with some of their predecessors, they were still a strongly-knit outfit, unusually so in defense. When Platini's shot from the brilliant Rocheteau's center beat Carlos, this was the first goal the Brazilians had conceded for 401 minutes. More importantly, it wiped out the advantage Careca had given them with a typically fluent opening score. Manager Tele Santana kept half-fit Zico on the bench for most of the 90 minutes, before responding to the crowd's chants and sending him on. Almost at once goalkeeper Bats fouled Branco to concede a penalty, only to make amends by saving Zico's shot.

So France survived into extra time, when they looked slightly the better side as the midday heat drained the pace from tired legs. Eventually, a classic battle ended all square, and penalties were needed. The normally majestic Socrates missed the first shot, and France managed to stop the Brazilian carnival.

EQUAL *Tigana, Tousseau, the goal scorer Platini and Fernandez (9) celebrate after the French had drawn even against Brazil*

June 24, 1990

A STRIKING SUCCESS

Stadio Meazza, Milan
World Cup second round
West Germany 2 (Klinsmann 50, Brehme 84)
Holland 1 (Koeman 86 pen)
HT: 0–0. Att: 74,559. Ref: J. C. Loustau (Argentina)
West Germany: Illgner, Reuter, Brehme, Kohler, Augenthaler, Buchwald, Berthold, Littbarski, Völler, Matthäus, Klinsmann (Reidle).
Holland: Van Breukelen, Van Aerle (Kieft), Rijkaard, Koeman, Van Tiggelen, Wouters, Witschge (Gillhaus), Winter, Van't Schip, Gullit, Van Basten.

Teamwork has become more and more important as soccer has developed. Organization, discipline and fitness now frequently obscure flair. But there is still no substitute for an outstanding individual, one who can win a game virtually single-handed.

SHADOWS *Van Basten and Kohler*

The audience in Milan and the millions watching on TV were privileged to see such a display in this match, when the German striker, Jurgen Klinsmann, played the game of his life to knock out the Dutch. Klinsmann was left as the only man up front after a disgusting incident in the 20th minute, when Voller was harshly sent off for a foul and Rijkaard went too after twice spitting at him. The versatile Holland team seemed better equipped to handle the loss but even their several outstanding defenders could not cope adequately with Klinsmann.

Helped by the tireless running of Matthäus and Littbarski, he kept up a remarkable degree of pressure on the Dutch, so that they were rarely able to launch their own renowned attacking force of Gullit and Van Basten. Early in the second half Klinsmann controlled an awkward pass, beat a marker and shot into the far side of the net to put Germany ahead. This led to the tightening of an already fierce grip, and a curling shot by Brehme left Holland with an impossible task. A controversial penalty after Van Basten went falling was too late. The night belonged to Germany, and especially Klinsmann, substituted near time to an ovation to end all ovations.

July 4, 1990

UNFORTUNATE END TO A CLASSIC

July 4, 1990. Stadio Delle Alpi, Turin
World Cup semi-final
West Germany 1 (Brehme 59)
England 1 (Lineker 80). After extra time. Germany won 4–3 on penalties.
HT: 0–0. Att: 62,628. Ref: J. R. Wright (Brazil).
West Germany: Illgner, Brehme, Kohler, Augenthaler, Buchwald, Berthold, Matthaus, Hässler (Reuter), Thom, Völler (Riedle), Klinsmann.
England: Shilton, Wright, Parker, Butcher (Steven), Walker, Peace, Beardsley, Platt, Gascoigne, Waddle, Lineker.

FAILURE *Chris Waddle hits his penalty high and wide, so England goes out of the World Cup*

Two of soccer's oldest rivals served up a magnificent match, sadly decided by what seems to be FIFA's only solution to draws after 120 minutes: penalties. England went so very, very close to reaching the final for only the second time. Despite all the trials and tribulations besetting their manager, Bobby Robson, and despite the lack of class players – in the English game at large, let alone in the squad – there was only the merest fraction between the teams at the end. The splendid spirit in which the match was contested was another bonus. So, on a more personal level, was the flood of tears released by the England enigma, Paul Gascoigne, which made him a media and public darling overnight and earned him a wallet of gold to go with his later-revealed feet of clay. This was a night with many heroes, perhaps none more so than the referee, José Roberto Wright, who let the game run without the nit-picking fussiness of so many other officials. The Germans, so often wanting to referee as well as to play, were none too happy with Wright's firm hand, but that suited England perfectly and helped them to play above themselves. Only a freak goal by Brehme, deflected high over Shilton by Parker's attempted interception, put Germany in front. The indomitable Lineker pounced on a half-chance to even the game, and from then on penalties seemed inevitable. The Germans scored all the four they needed to take whereas Stuart Pearce and Chris Waddle missed England's last two. No arguing with that – only with the system.

June 26, 1992

HANS ANDERSEN FAIRY TALE

Ullevi Stadium, Gothenburg
European Championship Final
Denmark 2 (Jensen 18, Vilfort 78)
Germany 0
HT: 1–0. Att: 37,800. Ref: B. Galler (Switzerland)
Denmark: Schmeichel, Piechnik, Olsen, Nielsen, Sivebaek (Christiansen 68), Vilfort, Jensen, Larsen, Christofte, Laudrup, B., Povlsen.
Germany: Illgner, Reuter, Kohler, Helmer, Buchwald, Brehme, Hässler, Effenberg (Thom 80), Sammer (Doll 46), Klinsmann, Riedle.

Germany or Holland seemed the likely winners of the ninth European Championship. France and perhaps even England looked likely to have a good run. As for Denmark, they had not even qualified for the final stages, and only got in when poor, war-ravaged Yugoslavia had to withdraw after topping their qualifying group, a point ahead of the Danes. When Denmark began by drawing with England and losing to Sweden, they seemed lost beyond retrieval. And why not? Many of the players had been on vacation and out of training when the call came for them to sweat off the pounds and make the short trip to neighboring Sweden. The coach, Richard Moller Nielsen, was just about to start decorating his kitchen.

Apart from that, most of the fine team from the 1980s was no longer in the reckoning, and several of the squad was injured as the tournament went on. But despite all that, the Danes showed remarkable spirit and considerable skill. A late goal against France made them second in their group and meant a semifinal against the Dutch, who snatched a late equalizer but then lost on penalties – the decisive kick being wasted by Marco Van Basten, of all people.

So Denmark went through to meet Germany in a what was expected to be a one-sided final, except that nobody had told the Danes. From Schmeichel to Povlsen, they all played their parts to perfection on an evening when little the Germans did went right. Vilfort, who scored the deciding goal (did he handle the ball first?) had just returned to the squad after going home because of his daughter's illness. Hans Christian Andersen could not have written a finer fairytale.

SUCCESS *The Danish team celebrates their European Championship win*

THE STADIUMS

The role of the stadium is simple: to organize spectators so that as many as possible can watch the action. Many stadiums enjoy a fame which equals that of the clubs and individuals: permanent witnesses to the game's twin impostors of triumph and disaster.

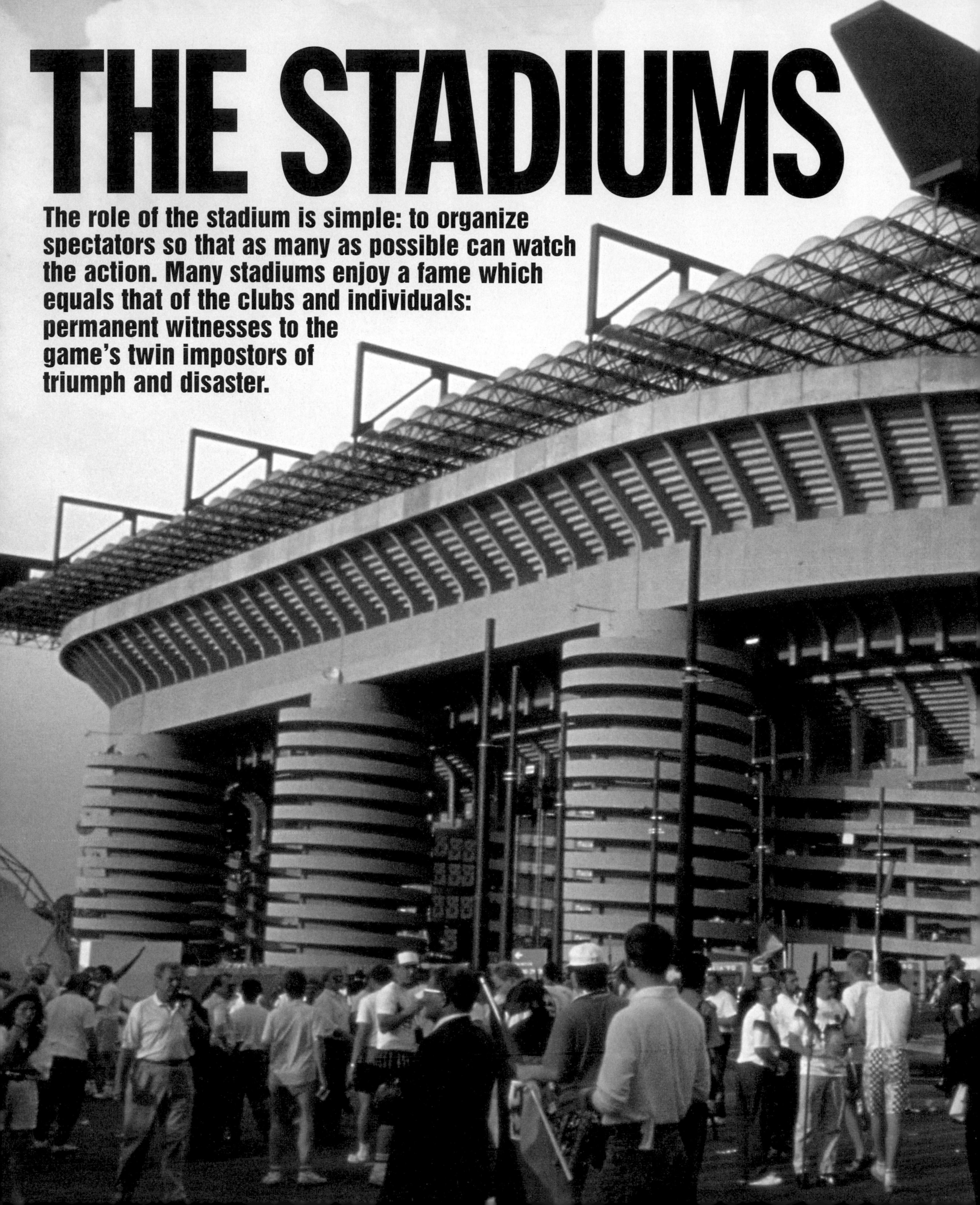

NOU CAMP BARCELONA, SPAIN

Capacity: 130,000
Opened: 1957
Club: FC Barcelona
Hosted: 1982 World Cup Opening Match (Belgium 1, Argentina 0); 1992 Olympic final (Spain 3, Poland 2); 1989 European Cup final (Milan 4, Steaua Bucharest 0); 1982 European Cup-winners' Cup final (Barcelona 2, Standard Liège 1)

PRIDE OF CATALONIA *Barcelona's 130,000 capacity Nou Camp stadium*

Higher and higher, bigger and better could be the motto of Barcelona's towering and breathtaking Nou Camp, "the new ground," which opened its doors on September 24, 1957 and was massively financed by club members. In Europe today only Benfica's Estadio da Luz can claim to be larger. Sport, it has been said, is the acceptable substitute for war, and Barcelona has always been a vehicle for the fervent nationalism of Catalonia. The rivalry with Madrid is intense, and the Nou Camp's continual improvements and expansion have much to do with the desire to outdo Real's Bernabeu stadium.

Barcelona, formed in 1899, outgrew their old Les Corts field in the 1940s and moved to the new stadium, built in an area of gardens to the west, in 1957. When Nou Camp was inaugurated with a match against Legia Warsaw, plans had already been laid to extend facilities and increase capacity to 150,000.

An indoor sports hall, connected to Nou Camp by a concourse, was opened in 1971 and houses the club's basketball, handball and volleyball teams. Ice hockey is held in the adjacent Ice Palace. Even more remarkably, there is a walkway over a road leading to another soccer stadium, the 16,500 capacity Mini-Estad, opened in 1982 and used by Barcelona's reserve team in the Spanish Second Division as well as by the club's top amateur side.

The first major redevelopment of the main stadium was in the early 1980s, when the addition of a third tier increased capacity to 120,000 in time for Nou Camp to host the opening ceremony of the 1982 World Cup, after which a crowd of 85,000 saw Belgium upset the holders Argentina 1–0.

When the old Les Corts field was opened in 1922, "Barca" had a membership of 5,000. When Pope John Paul II visited the Nou Camp in World Cup year he was enrolled as member No. 108,000. Since then membership has passed 110,000, making Barcelona the largest club in the world.

The work never stops. For the 1992 Olympic Games in Barcelona, two more tiers holding 10,000 seats were installed above the previous roof line, with a suspended cantilevered roof soaring overhead.

OLYMPIASTADION BERLIN, GERMANY

Capacity: 76,006
Opened: 1936
Clubs: Hertha BSC, Blau-Weiss 90
Hosted: 1936 Olympic final (Italy 2, Austria 1); 1974 World Cup group matches

LEGACY OF THE GREAT DICTATOR *Berlin's Olympiastadion was originally a stage for Adolf Hitler and his Nazis*

Berlin's historic – or notorious – stadium may be considered not so much a theatre of dreams, more a monument to the nightmarish world of Adolf Hitler and his national socialism. It was here that Hitler opened the 1936 Olympics, a giant propaganda exercise, to Wagnerian strains before an ecstatic 100,000 crowd. It was here, much to his chagrin, that the black American athlete Jesse Owens won four gold medals to challenge the myth of Aryan superiority. It was here two years later that the England team played Germany and avenged the politically-engineered demand that they give the Nazi salute by winning 6–3.

The Olympiapark, of which the Olympiastadion is the neo-classical centerpiece, had its origins before the First World War since Germany had been chosen to stage the Games in 1916. The unused facilities, adjacent to the Grunewald racecourse, were taken over when Hitler came to power in 1933. His grand plan involved the 86,000 capacity stadium on a 324-acre sports field which also included hockey, riding and swimming stadia plus an open-air amphitheatre. These were all linked to the vast Maifeld, used by the Nazis for mass rallies.

The stadium suffered from Allied bombing but was repaired by the mid-1960s, when Hertha Berlin drew 70,000 crowds in the early years of the Bundesliga, the new national championship of West Germany. The stadium was renovated for the 1974 World Cup when it staged three group matches. The use of the Olympiastadion in the first place had caused political tension between East and West, and its incorporation in the World Cup program at all was a triumph for German soccer chief Hermann Neuberger.

The unique political problems of Berlin meant that the stadium was underused for years. It was the home of both Hertha and Blau-Weiss Berlin but that meant mainly Second Division soccer. Now, since reunification, the Olympiastadion has regained its status as a focal point for German soccer and it is once again the permanent home of the German Cup final.

HAMPDEN PARK
GLASGOW, SCOTLAND

Capacity: 50,000
Club: Queen's Park
Hosted: 1960 European Cup final (Real Madrid 7, Eintracht Frankfurt 3), 1976 (Bayern Munich 1, Saint-Etienne 0); 1961 European Cup-winners' Cup fina; (Fiorentina 2, Rangers 0), 1962 (Atletico Madrid 1, Fiorentina 1, replay in Stuttgart), 1966 (Borussia Dortmund 2, Liverpool 1); 1989 World Under-17 Championship final (Saudi Arabia 1, Scotland 1 aet: Saudi Arabia 5–4 on pens).

GIANT OF THE PAST *In its heyday Hampden Park attracted record crowds*

As early as 1908, Glasgow had three of the largest fields in the world: Ibrox, home of protestant Rangers, Celtic Park, home of Catholic Celtic, and Hampden, owned by the amateurs of Queen's Park. Hampden was already the national stadium, never more vibrant than when hosting games against the old enemy England, whom Scotland had met in the first-ever international in 1872. Hampden was the largest stadium in the world until Maracana opened in 1950 and still holds several attendance records. On April 17, 1937, 149,415 paid to see the Scots beat England 3–1, a record for a match in Europe. Seven days later, 147,365 witnessed Celtic's 2–1 Scottish Cup win over Aberdeen, a European club record. In 1960, a crowd of 135,000 watched a dazzling Real Madrid trounce Eintracht Frankfurt 7–3 in the European Cup final, and that record was only bettered five years later by one of their own, when 136,505 paid to see to see Celtic play Leeds in a semifinal. But by this time the stadium had deteriorated and, although it was spruced up by a $4.5 million refurbishment in 1975, it closed its doors after the 1992 Scottish Cup final for a $18 million facelift designed to transform it into a 50,000 all-seat facility by the end of 1994.

ESTADIO DA LUZ
LISBON, PORTUGAL

Capacity: 130,000
Opened: 1954
Club: Benfica
Hosted: 1991 World Youth Cup final (Portugal 0, Brazil 0: Portugal 4–2 on pens); 1967 European Cup final (Celtic 2, Internazionale 1); 1992 European Cup-winners' Cup final (Werder Bremen 2, Monaco 0)

Although the "Stadium of Light" is one of the most evocatively named arenas in the world, it takes its name not from the power of its floodlighting but from the nearby Lisbon district of Luz. Yet one of the most dazzling players in history, the "Black Pearl" Eusebio, led Benfica to unparalleled heights here during the 1960s and 1970s when 14 league titles, two European Cup wins (1960 and 1961) and three more final appearances established Benfica among the aristocracy of European soccer. In 1992, a statue of their greatest son was unveiled to celebrate his fiftieth birthday, before a match with old rivals Manchester United, and this now greets visitors as they arrive at the entrance.

Benfica, or Sport Lisboa e Benfica as they are officially named, was formed in 1908, and by the 1950s had long outgrown their fifth field at Campo Grande. Plans for the 60,000 capacity Estadio da Luz were drawn up by a former Benfica athlete in 1951 and the two-tiered stadium was opened in 1954. Porto won the first game 3–0, and Portugal's first floodlit game, again won by Porto, took place four years later. By 1960 a third tier increased capacity to 75,000, and by the late 1970s the Estadio Da Luz, all white and bright, seated 130,000, and was a legend in Europe.

SANTIAGO BERNABEU
MADRID, SPAIN

Capacity: 105,000
Opened: 1947
Club: Real Madrid
Hosted: 1982 World Cup final (Italy 3, West Germany 2); 1964 European Championship final (Spain 2, Soviet Union 1); 1957 European Cup final (Real Madrid 2, Fiorentina 0), 1969 (Milan 4, Ajax 1), 1980 (Nottingham Forest 1, Hamburg 0).

It is thanks to the visionary foresight of long-time president Santiago Bernabeu that Real Madrid boast an imposing edifice on Madrid's most prestigious street, the Castellana, housing one of the world's foremost clubs and a trophy room bulging with silverware and displaying more than 5,000 items. The stadium, which began life as the Nuevo Chamartin Stadium in 1944 on 12 acres of prime land, was Bernabeu's brainchild. He was a lawyer who had been, in turn, player, captain, club secretary, coach and then, from 1942, president. The old stadium had been ravaged during the Spanish Civil War and Bernabeu decided that a super new stadium was needed if the club were to raise the funds needed to build a super new team. Real, who now include the King and Queen of Spain and President of the International Olympic Committee Juan Antonio Samaranch among their members, raised an astonishing $3 million by public subscription to finance the land purchase and first stage of building. The stadium was opened, with a 75,000 capacity, for a testimonial match for veteran player Jesus Alonso against Belenenses of Lisbon in December, 1947.

MONUMENT TO A VISIONARY *The Bernabeu stadium is a most exclusive venue*

In the 1950s the finance raised by Real's dominance of the fledgeling European Cup enabled capacity within the distinctive white towers to be extended to 125,000. The name Estadio Santiago Bernabeu was adopted in 1955 and the floodlights were switched on in 1957 for the European Cup Final.

Bernabeu, who died in 1978, had plans for a new stadium north of the city but for once did not get his way and, instead, Spain's hosting of the 1982 World Cup led to more improvements. A total of 345,000 people watched three group matches and an outstanding final in a stadium offering 30,200 seats and standing room for 60,000. Ten years on, the improvements continue. A third tier has been completed and further remodelling has increased the seating to 65,000 within a total capacity of 105,000.

STADIO GUISEPPE MEAZZA
MILAN, ITALY

Capacity: 83,107
Opened: 1926
Clubs: Milan, Internazionale
Hosted: 1965 European Cup final (Internazionale 1, Benfica 0), 1970 (Feyenoord 2, Celtic 1 aet); 1992 World Cup opening and group matches.

Fantastic is a much misused word but it seems appropriate to describe the home of two of Europe's leading clubs in the city which can claim to be the continent's premier soccer center. The cylindrical towers which allowed builders to construct a third tier and roof in advance of the 1992 World Cup have become just as much a trademark as the ramp system which gave access to the original two tiers of what used to be known as the San Siro. The cost of the remodeling came close to $75 million – even before the extra expense of sorting out problems with the field caused by shutting out both light and breeze.

San Siro, named after the suburb, was originally the home of Milan, formed in 1899 by the Englishman Alfred Edwards. They outgrew their original field in the mid-1920s, and the site of their new stadium was bought by their wealthy president,

MAGNIFICO *Inter and Milan's home*

Piero Pirelli of tire fame. It was Inter of all teams who ruined the opening party at the 35,000 capacity Stadio Calcistico San Siro by winning 6–3 in September 1926. The stadium was bought from Milan by the local council and was gradually enlarged until a 65,000 crowd was able to watch Italy play their Axis partners Germany in 1940. Inter had outgrown their own Stadio Arena by 1947; but the proposed sharing of facilities needed an even larger stadium. The San Siro reopened in 1955 with an increased capacity of 82,000 as the home ground for two teams who have been bettered in domestic soccer by Juventus and Torino but are second to none in European success. The San Siro was renamed Stadio Giuseppe Meazza in 1979 to honor the memory of one of the only two players to appear in both Italy's 1934 and 1938 World Cup-winning sides. The inside-forward had been hero-worshipped while playing for both Milan clubs.

LUZHNIKI STADION
MOSCOW, RUSSIA

Capacity: 100,000
Opened: 1956
Club: Spartak Moscow
Hosted: 1980 Olympic final (Czechoslovakia 1, East Germany 0)

A statue of Vladimir Ilyich Lenin, the now discredited father of the Russian Revolution, for years welcomed visitors to the Centralny Stadion Lenina on the banks of the Moscow River, which is the site of possibly the largest and most popular sports complex in the world. There are 140 separate sports centers, including a Palace of Sports, an open-air swimming center, a multi-purpose hall, 22 smaller halls, 11 soccer fields, four tracks, three skating rinks and 55 tennis courts. Many countries cannot offer as much! The all-seater soccer stadium plays host to the capital's most popular club, Spartak, and internationals. It is built on the site of the old Red Stadium where Spartak, then Moscow Sports Club, was founded in 1922. They adopted the present name in 1935 after affiliating with the trade unions for producers' co-operatives. The new stadium opened in 1956 with the first All Union Spartakia, which brought together 34,000 athletes to celebrate Communist sport. But the history of the Luzhinski is darkened by one of soccer's major disasters, which was kept hidden from the Russian people and the outside world for many years. In 1982, Spartak was playing Haarlem of Holland in a UEFA Cup match. Most of the crowd were leaving just before the end when Spartak scored a late goal. As fans tried to get back up the icy steps a fatal crush occurred. The Soviet people only learned of the tragedy seven years later, and then the official death toll was way below the 300 estimated by observers at the time.

OLYMPIASTADION
MUNICH, GERMANY

Capacity: 74,000
Opened: 1972
Club: Bayern Munich
Hosted: 1972 Olympic final (Poland 2, Hungary 1); 1974 World Cup final (West Germany 2, Holland 1); 1988 European Championship final (Holland 2, Soviet Union 0); 1979 European Cup final (Nottingham Forest 1, Malmo 0), 1993 (Marseille 1, Milan 0)

Descriptions of the individualistic Olympiastadion vary from a futuristic Bedouin tent to a steel and glass spider's web – although the desert analogy can feel rather tenuous in the depths of a Bavarian winter on the site of the airfield to which Neville Chamberlain flew in 1938 for his infamous ("Peace in our time") meeting with Hitler. The tragic

NOTHING QUITE LIKE IT *Munich's futuristic Olympiastadion*

shadow of history fell across the stadium again at the end of the 1972 Olympics for which it had been built, when Arab terrorists took hostage and murdered Israeli athletes competing at the Games.

The bill for Behnisch and Otto's staggering creation at the center of the green and pleasant Olympiapark came to $85 million. It was money well spent. The Park has become Germany's leading tourist attraction and a stunning venue for major events.

Bayern Munich, about to establish themselves as European giants with players such as Franz Beckenbauer, Paul Breitner and Gerd Müller, moved into the new stadium in 1972, two seasons before they lifted the first of their three successive European Champions Cups. Müller had helped to celebrate the opening by scoring all four goals in West Germany's 4–1 win over the Soviet Union in 1972. Two years later the stocky striker's place in soccer's hall of fame was assured by his winning goal against Holland in the 1974 World Cup final in front of his home fans.

The Dutch took happier memories away from the 1988 European Championship final when they overcame the Soviets 2–0. Most recently Marseille became the first French club to win a European trophy by defeating Milan 1–0 there ... only to become embroiled in a major bribery scandal at home.

SAN PAULO
NAPLES, ITALY

Capacity: 85,102
Opened: 1960
Club: Napoli
Hosted: 1968 European Championship semifinal (Italy 2, Soviet Union 1); 1980 European Championship finals venue; 1992 World Cup semifinal (Italy 1, Argentina 1 aet: Argentina 4–3 on pens)

UNRIVALLED ATMOSPHERE *Napoli's colorful fans turn a match in the Sao Paolo into an unforgettable experience*

Regarded purely as a stadium, the concrete bowl of San Paulo, complete with roof since the 1992 World Cup, is unremarkable. But on match days it is transformed into a vibrant, uninhibited place by the local *tifosi*, some of the most colourful, eccentric and volatile fans (hence the moat and fences) in the world.

San Paulo represents the third home for Napoli, a club formed in 1904 with the help of English sailors and looked upon with some disdain by the more sophisticated clubs of Turin and Milan, though one of them, Juventus, deigned to come south to play the first match in the new stadium in the Olympic year of 1960.

Napoli, despite the largesse of millionaire president and shipping owner Achille Lauro, had little success until the arrival of the Argentine superstar Diego Maradona in the mid-1980s. He filled San Paolo as it had never been filled before. The size of the stadium enabled Napoli to sell 70,000 season tickets, an Italian record, and thus not only pay Barcelona the then world record transfer fee of $7.5 million for Maradona but afford his wages and bring in other superstars, such as Brazil's Careca, into the bargain.

Sadly, the club has recently been embroiled in controversy, first over links with the Camorra (the local version of the Mafia) and then over the misuse and misappropriation of funds set aside for development work in and around the stadium for the 1990 World Cup.

A THING OF BEAUTY *France's national stadium, but soon to be superseded*

PARC DES PRINCES
PARIS, FRANCE

Capacity: 49,700
Opened: 1897 (rebuilt 1932, 1972)
Clubs: Paris Saint-Germain, Racing Club
Hosted: 1984 European Championship final (France 2, Spain 0); 1956 European Cup final (Real Madrid 4, Reims 3), 1975 (Bayern Munich 2, Leeds 0), 1981 (Liverpool 1, Real Madrid 0); 1978 European Cup-winners' Cup final (Anderlecht 4, FK Austria 0)

The award of the 1998 World Cup to France has spelled the beginning of the end of the checkered career of the national stadium as a major soccer venue. The all-concrete near-50,000 capacity stadium designed by Roger Taillibert for soccer and rugby union in the early 1970s fails to meet FIFA's minimum capacity of 80,000 for a final, and the French government announced in October 1993 that $450 million is to be spent on a new stadium in the northern suburb of St Denis.

The Parc des Princes lies in the southwest and, as the name suggests, before the Revolution it was a pleasure ground for royalty. The stadium began life as a velodrome at the end of the last century and, until 1967, was the finish for the Tour de France.

When professional soccer was introduced in 1932 it became home to Racing Club de France, but they enjoyed only limited success and the Stade Colombes remained the favorite ground for internationals and the 1938 World Cup. Until the current stadium was built, one of the biggest soccer matches staged was the first European Cup final in 1956, when a sell-out 38,000 crowd saw Real Madrid beat Stade Reims 4–3. Paris, sad to say, is the great capital underachiever in soccer terms.

The creation of the Périphérique, the Paris ring road, led to the new two-tiered state-of-the-art stadium being built. It was the first in Europe with integral floodlighting and closed-circuit television. Problems with the field dogged its early years, but these ills were cured by the time the Parc was needed to host three group matches and the final of the 1984 European Championship, won in style by France's finest ever team, led by Michel Platini.

Racing Club went out of the professional soccer business in 1964, and Paris Saint-Germain, an amalgamation of Paris FC and Saint-Germain, moved into the new stadium in 1973. They drew 20,000 crowds, became only the second Paris club to win the Championship (1986) and won the Cup twice. In 1982, a new club Racing de Paris – unconnected with the old one – began to share the Parc des Princes. For better or, more probably, worse, they will have exclusive use after 1998.

OLIMPICO
ROME, ITALY

Capacity: 80,000
Opened: 1953
Clubs: Roma, Lazio
Hosted: 1960 Olympic final (Yugoslavia 3, Denmark 1); 1990 World Cup final (West Germany 1, Argentina 0); 1968 European Championships final (Italy 1, Yugoslavia 1; replay, Italy 2, Yugoslavia 0), 1980 (West Germany 2, Belgium 1); 1977 European Cup final (Liverpool 3, Borussia Mönchengladbach 1), 1984 (Liverpool 1, Roma 1: Liverpool 4–2 on pens)

Benito Mussolini was bad news for Italy. But allegedly he did make the trains run on time, and he also left the beautiful Foro Italico sports complex at the foot of Monte Mario as a legacy. His original plan was to stage the 1944 Olympics there, much as Hitler used Berlin for propaganda purposes in 1936. Then the Second World War intervened. The stadium was originally called Stadio dei Cipressi, but was inaugurated in 1953 as the Olimpico by the legendary Hungarian team who beat Italy 3–0 in front of an 80,000 crowd. The stadium became the focal point of the 1960 Olympic Games, a home to both Roma and Lazio, and the scene of a home triumph in the 1968 European Championship when Italy overcame Yugoslavia in a replay.

All roads led to Rome for Liverpool in 1977, when they turned the stadium into a sea of red celebrating the first of their four European Cup triumphs. They returned for the 1984 final to beat Roma, playing on their own ground but unable to take advantage. Liverpool eventually won on penalties.

BELLA *Rome's Olympic Stadium*

To allow the stadium to stage the 1990 World Cup, individual seating had to be increased to 80,000 and a roof added to give two-thirds cover. Only in Italy could the wrangling and talking have gone on until May 1988. A year later the roof design was ditched, costs had risen to $112 million, and the odds shifted against the stadium being ready.

FIFA's threat to move the final to Milan eventually saw to it that this beautiful venue was ready for West Germany's revenge over Argentina: a gracious setting for what proved to be an uninspiring contest.

PRATER
VIENNA, AUSTRIA

Capacity: 62,958
Opened: 1931
Club: None as permanent
Hosted: 1964 European Cup final (Internazionale 3, Real Madrid 1), 1987 (Porto 2, Bayern Munich 1), 1990 (Milan 1, Benfica 0); 1970 European Cup-winners' Cup final (Manchester City 2, Gornik Zarbrze 1)

The Wienerstadion, more commonly known as the Prater, fringes the pleasure grounds forever linked abroad with Orson Welles and The Third Man. Austrian soccer fans, however, associate it more with the Hugo Meisl "Wunderteam" of the 1930s, who counted England among their victims in 1936. The Wiener, Viennese, Stadium has been transformed in recent years into one of Europe's leading venues, the original open two-tiered amphitheatre topped by a remarkable roof which was erected in 10 months during 1985 at a cost of $26 million. The original 60,000-capacity stadium, a legacy of the socialist-controlled city administration, opened in July 1931 with a match appropriately between two workers' teams, and hosted athletics championships and the long-forgotten Workers Olympiad.

After the Anschluss, the stadium became an army barracks and, unnervingly, still staged wartime internationals while serving as a staging post for Austrian Jews on their way to concentration camps. Although badly damaged by Allied bombers, the stadium was quickly restored after the war. Rapid Vienna played Real Madrid under the first floodlights in 1955; later a third tier was added and a record crowd of 90,593 watched Austria play Spain in 1960. During the 1970s, the building of an all-weather track reduced capacity to 72,000.

No club has used it permanently since FK Austria moved out in 1982. Austrian soccer attendances have sunk so low – around an average 3,000 – that none need it.

WEMBLEY
LONDON, ENGLAND

Capacity: 80,000
Opened: 1923
Club: None
Hosted: 1948 Olympic final (Sweden 3, Yugoslavia 1); 1966 World Cup final (England 4, West Germany 2 aet); 1963 European Cup final (Milan 2, Benfica 1), 1968 (Manchester United 4, Benfica 1 aet), 1971 (Ajax 2, Panathinaikos 0), 1978 (Liverpool 1, Brugge 0), 1992 (Barcelona 1, Sampdoria 0 aet); 1965 Cup-Winners Cup final (West Ham 2, Munich 1860 0); 1993 (Parma 3, Antwerp 1)

Wembley may be the aging *grande dame* of stadia but, steeped in history and with its distinctive twin towers, it remains the Mecca of English soccer and is revered by players and fans throughout the world. Wembley is synonymous with England internationals, the FA Cup final and the epic World Cup final of 1966.

WEMBLEY *England's soccer home*

Unusually for a major stadium, Wembley is privately owned and financed by its staging of major soccer, greyhound racing, rugby league, showpiece football games, and ancillary sporting activities at the nearby 9,000-seat Arena.

In the 1920s the green fields of Wembley Park were chosen as the site for the 1923 Empire Exhibition. The then Empire Stadium was built between January 22 and April 23. It was hailed as the largest monumental building of reinforced concrete in the world, and a troop of soldiers marched up and down the terracing in a unique safety check.

Since a crowd of "only" 53,000 had turned up for the 1922 FA Cup final at Stamford Bridge, the authorities were concerned that Bolton and West Ham might not fill the new 126,000 capacity ground the following year. But on April 28 more than 200,000 people besieged Wembley, and that Bolton were eventually able to defeat West Ham 2–0 was due in no small part to the good nature of the crowd in the presence of King George V and a celebrated policeman on his white horse. The Wembley legend was born.

The watersheds of English soccer followed: the Cup was taken out of England for the only time by Cardiff in 1927; a year later Scotland destroyed England 5–1 with their famous forward line, dubbed the Wembley Wizards; Stanley Matthews had the 1953 final "named" after him, when he inspired Blackpool to beat Bolton 4–3 from 3–1 down. Later that year, Hungary changed world soccer by crushing England 6–3 there.

England held their heads high again in 1966, and when Manchester United became the first club to win the European Cup on a memorable June night two years later they could not have triumphed on more appropriate turf.

Wembley, like soccer itself, has had to move with the times. The surrounding exhibition center was redeveloped while the stadium was being remodeled in the late 1980s through a $90 million refurbishment. Capacity was necessarily reduced through turning Wembley into an all-seat venue, but the addition of the Olympic Gallery around the stadium under the roof edge maintained it at 80,000.

ROSE BOWL
PASADENA, CALIFORNIA, USA

Capacity: 102,083
*Opened:*1922. *Club:* None
Hosted: 1984 Olympic f inal (France 2, Brazil 0) 1994 World Cup final (Brazil 0, Italy 0 aet: Brazil 3–2 on pens)

The Rose Bowl, synonymous with football, came into its own as a soccer venue at the 1994 World Cup when it served as a home from home for the United States, then hosted second round matches, a semifinal, the third place match and the final itself.

The rose-covered stadium, based in the leafy city of Pasadena seven miles north of downtown Los Angeles, cut its teeth on soccer in the 1984 Olympics, when the tournament drew massive crowds. Yugoslavia versus Italy drew 100,374, France's semifinal against Yugoslavia 97,451, and 101,799 watched France defeat Brazil in the final. That topped the record attendance for football's Super Bowl XVII in 1983, when 101,063 watched the Washington Redskins defeat the Miami Dolphins.

The Rose Bowl has hosted five Super Bowls but is best known as the home of UCLA and the annual Rose Bowl game on New Year's Day.

NAME OF THE GAME *The Rose Bowl in Pasadena has long been synoymous with football but played a major part in the 1994 World Cup*

NATIONAL OLYMPIC STADIUM
TOKYO, JAPAN

Capacity: 62,000
Opened: 1972
Club: None
Hosted: 1979 World Youth Cup final (Argentina 3, Soviet Union 1); World Club Cup finals (every year since 1980)

Soccer is the 1990s growth sport in Japan, and it was natural that the stadium built to host the 1964 Olympics should serve as the home of the national team and launch the successful professional J-League in 1993. Japan's appetite for big-time soccer was whetted in 1980 when Tokyo became the permanent home of the World Club Cup final sponsored by Toyota. This previously two-leg affair between the European and South American Club Champions had become progressively discredited since its inception in 1960, often degenerating into violence. But the decision to change the format to a single game in front of an excitable but well-behaved Japanese crowd, beginning with Nacional of Uruguay's 1–0 defeat of Nottingham Forest in 1980, has transformed it into a popular match on the international calendar on the second Sunday each December. There is currently doubt about the stadium as a major venue following the Japanese bid to stage the 2002 World Cup. The capacity is well below the 80,000 required by FIFA, and the city of Tokyo and the Japanese government have yet to agree how a replacement venue should be funded. There is no room to expand the current stadium, and officials may decide to project the exciting new stadium in the port of Yokohama as a replacement to play prospective host to a Japanese World Cup final.

GROWING PAINS *Surging crowds may make the Olympic stadium obsolete*

AZTECA
MEXICO CITY, MEXICO

Capacity: 110,000
Opened: 1960
Club: America (but others for big matches)
Hosted: 1968 Olympic final (Hungary 4, Bulgaria 1); 1970 World Cup final (Brazil 4, Italy 1); 1986 World Cup final (Argentina 3, West Germany 2)

PRIDE AND JOY *Azteca stadium, home of two World Cup finals, and an amazing experience for spectators*

The Azteca, pride and joy of Mexican soccer, has been the venue for some of the most memorable World Cup matches in history. It is also one of the most enjoyable, passionate and colorful stadiums in which to watch a game since its lower tier is only thirty feet from the pitch, thus providing fans there with a sense of immediacy while those in the upper tier benefit from the steep, cliff-like design. The Azteca was the first stadium to have staged two World Cup final matches and the 1970 tournament also produced an incredible semifinal between West Germany and Italy. The drama was won 4–3 by the talented Italians who were, in turn, swept aside 4–1 in the final by a Brazilian team, rated as the finest to take the field in the history of the competition.

Some 16 years later Mexico stepped in on short notice to beat the United States and Canada for the right to host the finals after Colombia pulled out. Argentina, led by Diego Maradona at the height of his powers, lifted the crown for a second time against West Germany. The stadium, built on scrubland to the south-west of the sprawling mass which is Mexico City, required 100,000 tons of concrete, four times more than was used to build Wembley. It was planned for the 1968 Olympics and opened in June 1966 with a match betweeen Mexico and Turin, but the first major internationals came during the 1968 Games. Since then, America, Atlante, Necaxa and Cruz Azul have all used the the three-tiered Azteca for important games.

MARIO FILHO/MARACANA
RIO DE JANEIRO, BRAZIL

Capacity: 120,000
Opened: 1950
Clubs: Botofago, Vasco da Gama, Flamengo, Fluminense
Hosted: 1950 World Cup final (Uruguay 2, Brazil 1); 1989 South American Championship

What Wembley is to the old world, Maracana is to the new. This architectural marvel is the largest stadium in the world and the spiritual home to Brazil's second religion, soccer. However, it has spent much of the last few years out of commission while work has been carried out to renovate a bowl which had started, literally, to fall apart.

Maracana, which quite simply takes its name from the little river that runs close by, was begun outside the city in 1948 in preparation for the 1950 World Cup, but was not completed until 1965. What has become Brazil's national stadium was originally intended to replace Vasco da Gama's club field and was built and is still owned by the city, being formally named after the mayor, Mario Filho, who carried the project through. It was officially opened in June 1950 with a game beween Rio and São Paulo, the first goal being scored by Didi.

The first great matches were staged in the fourth World Cup, which culminated in the hosts losing to old rivals Uruguay before a world record crowd of 199,850. Like Hampden Park in Glasgow, Maracana sets and holds attendance records. In 1963, 177,656 watched a league match between Flamengo and and Fluminense, a world club record attendance. Internationals have drawn crowds of 180,000, and league matches in the 1980s were watched regularly by 130,000. Santos even flew north to use Maracana for their World Club Cup final games against Benfica and Milan in 1962 and 1963.

The stadium is oval in shape and topped by a breathtaking cantilevered roof while a moat separates the fans from the field. Like Wembley and the Olympiastadion in Munich, Maracana has become a major tourist attraction and is held in such esteem that several smaller versions have been built throughout Brazil. Next to the stadium is the Maracanazinho, a scaled down indoor version which stages boxing, tennis, festivals and concerts.

A FADING GIANT *Maracana still conjures up magic visions*

MONUMENTAL BUENOS AIRES, ARGENTINA

Capacity: 76,000
Opened: 1938
Club: River Plate
Hosted: 1978 World Cup final (Argentina 3, Holland 1 aet); 1946, 1959 and 1987 South American Championships

A MONUMENTAL VICTORY *Home advantage held for Argentina in 1978*

There were many misgivings about holding the 1978 World Cup in Argentina, not the least of which concerned the political climate. Ultimately, the ruling military junta invested huge sums in the renovation of the Monumental, which had been the home of the national team and of one of the world's great clubs, River Plate. Several of River's own players – skipper Daniel Passarella, goalkeeper Ubaldo Fillol and forwards Leopoldo Luque and Oscar Ortiz – played on the team which defeated Holland 3–1 in the final amid a paper snowstorm which tumbled down their "own" Monumental. Work had begun on the Monumental on September 27, 1936 and it was ready for River to move in by May 1938. The locker rooms and offices were of a standard then unique in South America, while the three-sided horseshoe boasted an original capacity of 100,000, with the potential of a third tier which would lift it to 150,000. Needless to say, it was never needed.

The opening game, a 3–1 win over the Uruguayan champions Penarol, was watched by a crowd of 70,000. But the stadium itself was not completed, even in its initial phase, until 1957, when River invested much of the world record fee they had received from Italy's Juventus for inside-forward Omar Sivori.

Apart from the 1978 World Cup, the Monumental has played host to many internationals and South American club matches, as well as key games when Argentina has taken their turn to host the Copa America (the South American Championship).

CENTENARIO MONTEVIDEO, URUGUAY

Capacity: 76,609)
Opened: 1930
Clubs: Penarol, Nacional
Hosted: 1930 World Cup final (Uruguay 4, Argentina 2); 1942, 1956, 1967 and 1983 South American Championships

HISTORY MAKER *The Centenario staged the first World Cup final*

The Centenario holds a special place in soccer history, having been the stage for the first World Cup final in 1930 when Uruguay, then Olympic champions and enjoying their golden age in international soccer, defeated Argentina, their old rivals from across the River Plate, by 4–2 after being 2–1 down at half-time. But it was a close call for Montevideo's magnificent new stadium, which was being built especially for the fledgling world championship and to celebrate one hundred years of the country's independence. Work continued throughout the first days of the tournament to have it ready for the final.

It has since become the regular venue for internationals, the South American Championship (the world's longest running international competition since the demise of the British Home Championship in 1984), the World Club Championship, the South American club championship (Copa Libertadores), Supercopa and Recopa. Uruguay's last real international successs came in the 1983 South American Championship, when Brazil was beaten 2–0 in the Centenario before being held 1–1 in Rio.

Soccer in Uruguay is really all about soccer in Montevideo and the Centenario is home to two of the leading clubs, Penarol and Nacional, who dominated the Copa Libertadores, in its early years. From 1960, when Penarol defeated Olimpia of Paraguay 1–0 in the Centenario and 2–1 on aggregate, they and Nacional were involved in 10 of the first 11 finals, and in 1968 the stadium was full to see Estudiantes beat Palmeiras 2–0 in a final playoff. Penarol entertained Real Madrid in the first World Club Championship in 1960, but was held to a goalless draw and lost 5–0 away. They took their revenge by beating Benfica the next season in a playoff, and Real, by 2–0 both home and away, in 1966.

MORUMBI SÃO PAULO, BRAZIL

Capacity: 150,000
Opened: 1978
Clubs: São Paulo FC, Corinthians
Hosted: 1992 Copa Libertadores (South American club championship) final 2nd leg (São Paulo 1, Newells Old Boys 0: agg 2–1)

The rivalry between Rio de Janeiro and São Paulo provides much of the dynamic which fires domestic soccer within Brazil. Fans from the respective cities consider "their" state championships – the Carioca and the Paulista – as the best and most important, and fail to understand why players from the other city should ever be preferred to any of their favorites for the national team.

They are equally partisan about their stadia. Just as Rio de Janeiro boasts Maracana, so São Paulo soccer centers on the magnificent Morumbi. The name, in fact, is that of the local suburb of São Paulo, and the stadium is formally entitled the Estadio Cicero Pompeu de Toledo – explaining, perhaps, why it is generally known by the much shorter name "barrio."

São Paulo FC and Corinthians both play all their big games in the Morumbi, though Corinthians did have to move out briefly for a South American club match last year when the date clashed with a pop concert.

THE BUSINESS OF SOCCER

Professional soccer is a multi-million dollar business in which 22 highly-trained, highly-paid, highly-valued athletes chase a ball around a potentially priceless development site. But it wasn't always so. . .

Before the 1970s, British soccer was run simply as a game and not as a business. While other European countries, notably Italy, Spain and Germany, were investigating and exploiting the new commercial opportunities available to the game, the British were still steeped in the amateur traditions of the last century. Clubs which had been set up almost a century ago were still run in the same way, with little thought given to the opportunities presented by the new technological age.

Since organized soccer began in Britain in the middle of the nineteenth century, the main source of income has come from gate receipts. From the 1970s on, however, other sources of revenue opened up. Advertising, sponsorship, and the money paid by television companies to screen soccer became increasingly important.

Nevertheless the gate money, although providing an ever-reducing percentage of overall income, remained the foundation of the average professional soccer club's balance sheet.

BOOM TIME *Arsenal vs. Sunderland in 1937 attracted a massive crowd*

THE CLUBS

In 1991 Manchester United — one of the most famous clubs in world soccer — were floated on the London Stock Exchange. Net assets were estimated at $£60 million, with each share offered at $5.55 with a guaranteed first dividend of 26 cents per share in the first year. All this is a far cry from the way United, in common with the rest of British soccer, used to be run. By 1991 gate receipts accounted for less than half United's income, with television, sponsorship, advertising and food concessions making up the greater part. This is a situation which is now becoming more and more common in British soccer.

One of the main sources of new revenue is sponsorship. Between 1976 and 1990 the sponsorship money spent in Britain rocketed from $3 million to $345 million. The High Street bank, Barclays, paid $17.5 million for the right to sponsor the Football League for six years from 1987; and brewers Bass took up sponsorship of the FA Premier League in 1993 at a cost of $18 million over four years, to add to its patronage of the Scottish League and the Charity Shield. The attractions for the sponsors are obvious. Soccer is a huge market-place attracting all socio-economic groups. Television coverage provides nation-wide exposure, encourages brand loyalty and is virtually a form of free advertising.

Licensing the logos of clubs, national teams and competitions is another moneyspinner. The Football Association estimates that licens-

KITTED UP *England's uniform 1993-style*

UMBRO

ON THE FRINGE *Perimeter advertising seen here at a stadium during the 1993–94 European Champions League has become a lucrative business*

ing the logos of the England national team and the FA Cup alone could generate $37.5 million for the game.

Merchandising is also an area of expansion — and controversy. Clubs have, for years, sold replica uniforms, but in recent times there has been an explosion of "official" club memorabilia. Tottenham Hotspur produces a lavish catalogue containing hundreds of items ranging from pens to pillow cases. But uniform sales have attracted the most controversy. Many clubs have been accused of ripping off younger fans by constantly changing the design of their uniform, knowing that fans will always want to wear the latest style. With junior uniforms costing anything up to $60, and with many clubs now having three uniforms — Manchester United in 1993–94 had four — there was a growing feeling that clubs were taking financial advantage of the loyalty of their supporters.

In the spring of 1994 Manchester United signed what was touted as the most lucrative uniform deal in British soccer. The four-year deal negotiated with manufacturers Umbro will earn United $37.5 million, eclipsing the previous records — Umbro's $24 million four-year package with the England team, and Arsenal's $2 million a year arrangement with Nike.

Britain's betting companies also provide valuable income for the game, but without having any direct influence on it. It is thanks to the monies generated from betting revenue and channeled through the Football Trust that so many clubs have been able to meet the capital costs incurred by redeveloping their stadiums in the wake of the Taylor Report into the Hillsborough disaster.

More than 30 years earlier, the advent of floodlighting in the early 1950s had opened up another, perhaps less obvious, route to riches. The ability to play matches under

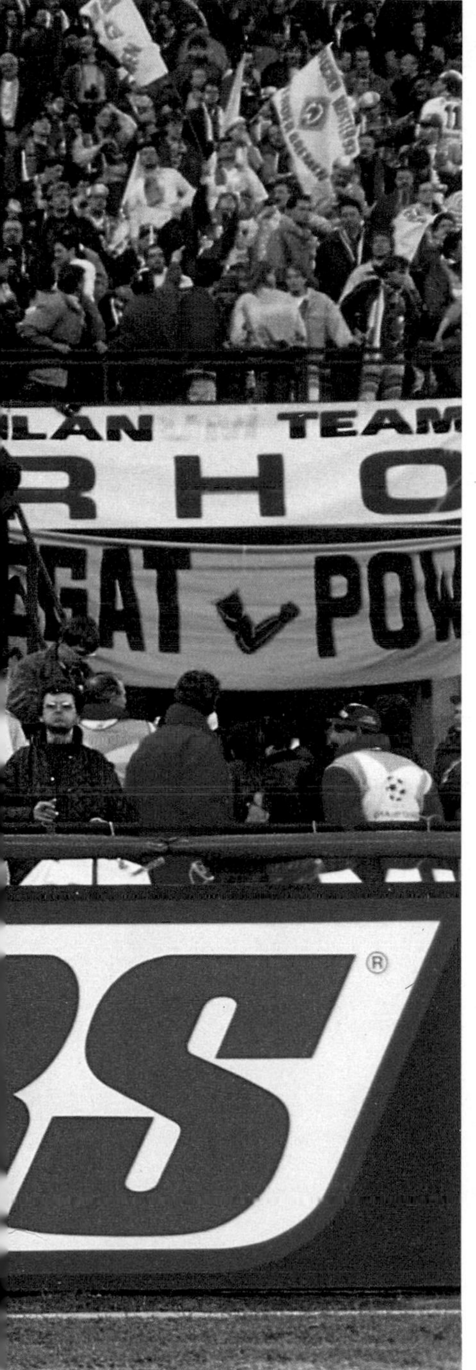

lights in the evenings brought in midweek European competitive soccer and the switching of Football League Cup and even international matches from the weekend to midweek. Thus clubs — and national teams — were able to lure the paying public to more matches . . . and bind them still further and deeper into the commercial fabric of the game.

Closely allied to the development of sponsorship is advertising. Important income for many clubs comes from advertising on stadium perimeter boards around their pitches. In general terms, clubs in the top divisions tend to attract national — and often international — advertisers, while those lower down the scale attract advertising from local concerns, producing smaller financial returns.

CHAMPIONS' LEAGUE

The importance of and correlation between sponsorship, advertising and television is clearly displayed in the thinking behind the European Champions League. By binding all three together to create a high-prestige "product," UEFA has effectively driven the cost of sponsorship upwards. Originally, the Champions League had four sponsors who were guaranteed sole category rights covering all advertising within the stadia.

The clubs taking part were not even allowed to display the name of their own domestic sponsors on their shirts — a rule which fell after two seasons of controversy when the new, expanded Champions' League came into effect at the start of 1994–95. Nevertheless UEFA's thinking, it seems, is that exclusivity equals maximum returns.

The new Champions' League involved restricting the number of entries to 24 with the overspill of league title-winners being diverted into the UEFA Cup. A preliminary knockout round was followed by a series comprising four mini-leagues of four clubs each, with the top two in each group entering the revived knockout quarterfinals.

Average European Top Division League Attendances (to 1 January 1994)

Country	*Average attendance*
Belgium	8,147
England	21,125
France	14,062
Germany	27,041
Holland	9,698
Italy	31,118
Portugal	16,884
Spain	24,331

THE PLAYERS

A soccer club's most versatile and liquid assets are the players. For clubs everywhere, particularly those in the lower divisions, selling their best players to clubs further up the League is often the key to survival. One big sale can bring in more money than a season's gate receipts and help keep a struggling club afloat for another season.

For the clubs at the top end of the league, the need — some would say pressure — to buy players is twofold. First, clubs must have the best players available if they are to compete for survival in the FA Premiership — the top priority — and then for the prizes. Secondly, many clubs feel obliged to make big-name, big-money purchases during the summer months to help boost season ticket sales and maintain interest in the team. There are, after all, only three domestic trophies to be won, and with 22 teams in the Premiership, 19 are bound to go empty-handed each season — 20 if two trophies are won by the same club, as happened in 1993 when Arsenal won the FA Cup and the Coca-Cola-sponsored League Cup, and 1994, when Manchester United won the Premiership and the FA Cup. There are other, less obvious reasons for buying players. For example, if a club is coming to the end of its financial year and has too much cash sitting in the bank, the directors may well buy to reduce the tax liabilities.

Given that players are the most valuable asset, it follows that they are likely to be highly rewarded for agreeing to sign with a new club. A new player can add thousands to attendances and, with so many clubs competing for relatively few top-class players, transfer fees, signing-on fees and salaries have spiraled much faster than the rate of inflation.

In Britain, the average weekly salary for a player in the Premiership is $3,750. In the First Division, the figure falls to $1,365; in the Second Division it is $685; in the Third Division $500. For those players at the top of their profession, the rewards are immense. When John Barnes was at his Liverpool peak he was reputed to earn $15,000 a week. Even this seemingly unjustifiable salary is paltry compared with what players may earn in Italy. England's Paul Gascoigne was signed by Lazio to a contract worth $27,000 a week; David Platt earned even more on transferring to Sampdoria in the summer of 1993; and Des Walker's year with Sampdoria in 1992–93 earned him a staggering $42,000 a week.

Even these vast figures pale into insignificance, however, when compared with the monumental sums lavished on top sportsmen in America. In 1993 Michael Jordan, of the Chicago Bulls basketball team, earned an estimated $36 million . . . $692,300 a week!

The salary gap between the Premiership and the First Division is widening — partly owing to Sky TV's $455 million, five-year deal with the Premiership — and this in itself causes problems. Some reserves would rather be highly paid in the Premiership than move down to the First Division, where regular soccer would be accompanied by a salary cut. This denies other clubs and their supporters a "dead" pool of talent.

Another reason for the increase in players' salaries, particularly in the top two divisions, is the activity of agents. Although technically operating outside the laws of soccer (agents are barred from transfer negotiations by Section 6, Rule 76 of the Football League Rules), they are having an increasingly large influence on transfer deals, salaries and the game in general.

Arguments for and against agents are plentiful. Those in favor claim that as players are effectively entertainers, they are entitled to have an agent to handle their affairs, just like actors, pop stars and comedians. The pro-agent lobby would also point out that a professional soccer player's career is a short and risky one, and that he therefore needs all the help available to maximize his earnings while it lasts. Opponents of the all-pervading influence of agents argue that they simply encourage greed and take money out of the game.

The PFA, most club officials and many managers are publicly suspicious of agents, whom they view as interfering, grasping sharks. Brian Clough, the former Nottingham Forest manager, spoke for many when he said: "If Bill Shankly had offered a player a deal and the player had told him to speak to his agent about it, Bill would have hit him. And I would have held him so Bill could hit him."

Privately, however, many managers use the services of outside "advisers" to facilitate their transfer activities. Even the Football Association employed agents such as Harry Swales and then Jon Smith to try to ensure that the rulers of the domestic game were not trapped in a commercial minefield. For several years, FIFA has been trying to compute a formula by which agents could be licensed for work in the transfer market and in match arrangement. It appears doubtful, however, whether men who, by the very nature of their business, act in soccer's shadow lands, can be brought within formal regulations.

During the 1992–93 season in England $120 million changed hands in transfer fees, all during a time of recession. The "Big Five" clubs, Manchester United, Liverpool, Everton, Tottenham and Arsenal, are traditionally the "buying" clubs of English soccer. They have, however, been joined in recent seasons by clubs with wealthy benefactors, such as Blackburn Rovers, Wolves and Derby County.

WORLD RECORD TRANSFERS

Amount $	Player	Clubs involved	Year
1,500	*Alf Common*	*Sunderland to Middlesbrough*	1905
16,335	*David Jack*	*Bolton to Arsenal*	1929
34,500	*Bernabe Ferreyra*	*Tigre BA to River Plate*	1932
40,500	*Ruben Bravo*	*Rosario Central to Racing Avellaneda*	1946
60,000	*Juan Ferraro*	*Velez Sarsfield to Boca Juniors*	1949
108,000	*Juan Alberto Schiaffino*	*Penarol to Milan*	1954
139,500	*Enrique Omar Sivori*	*River Plate to Juventus*	1957
213,000	*Luis Suarez*	*Barcelona to Internazionale*	1961
375,000	*Angelo Sormani*	*Mantova to Roma*	1963
750,000	*Pietro Anastasi*	*Varese to Juventus*	1968
1.38m	*Johan Cruyff*	*Ajax Amsterdam to Barcelona*	1973
1.80m	*Giuseppe Savoldi*	*Bologna to Napoli*	1975
2.55m	*Paolo Rossi*	*Juventus to L R Vicenza*	1978
4.50m	*Diego Maradona*	*Boca Juniors to Barcelona*	1982
7.50m	*Diego Maradona*	*Barcelona to Napoli*	1984
9.00m	*Ruud Gullit*	*PSV Eindhoven to Milan*	1987
12.00m	*Roberto Baggio*	*Fiorentina to Juventus*	1990
15.00m	*Jean-Pierre Papin*	*Marseille to Milan*	1992
18.00m	*Gianluca Vialli*	*Sampdoria to Juventus*	1992
19.50m	*Gianluigi Lentini*	*Torino to Milan*	1992

Note: As exchange rates fluctuate from country to country and era to era, a standard rate is quoted throughout.

Blackburn's involvement in the transfer market has been expensive, effective and dramatic. With the backing of steel multi-millionaire Jack Walker, coach Kenny Dalglish spent more than $30 million in taking the team from the First Division to the Premiership and then European soccer. Blackburn broke the British record for a transfer in July 1992 when they paid $4.8 million to Southampton for striker Alan Shearer, and has continually challenged to purchase the best players Britain has to offer.

With more and more clubs competing for the top players, and, crucially, more of them able to afford such huge transfer fees and wages, the price of a top player has continued to rise. In 1993 Rangers broke the British transfer record by paying $6 million to Dundee United for forward Duncan Ferguson, and Manchester United equaled the English record with their $5.4 million signing of Nottingham Forest midfielder Roy Keane. The outcome of all this can only be the widening of the gap between the Super Rich of the Premiership and the rest of the field. Perhaps the much-touted Super League is here already.

SIGNING ON *Roy Keane puts pen to Manchester United paper*

POLITICS

KING OF THE HILL *FIFA's Brazilian President Joao Havelenge*

From its humble beginnings at London's Freemasons Tavern in 1863, Association Football has developed into a truly global game. Almost every country on earth plays the game and its smooth running requires the authority of an international body. This has been provided since 1904 by the Fédération Internationale de Football Association, or FIFA for short.

In that year, representatives from France, Belgium, Holland, Denmark, Switzerland, Sweden and Spain met in Paris to discuss the possibility of founding an international governing body. An initial setback was the refusal of the four British associations to join, but by 1910 all four had entered the fold. In 1920, however, they withdrew over the continued membership of Germany and the Central Powers following the First World War, and, having rejoined four years later, they withdrew again in 1928 over the broken-time (amateurism) dispute which arose during the 1928 Amsterdam Olympics. The British associations stayed out for nearly twenty years, thus denying themselves the chance to enter the World Cup until after the Second World War.

Membership of FIFA is restricted solely to national associations, one per country, and these associations must represent either a sovereign nation, a dominion or a protectorate. Each national association has one vote at the FIFA Congress held every two years. FIFA is responsible for reviewing the Laws of the Game, organizing and administering international competitions, regulating the international movement of players in order to protect clubs from "poaching," administering standards for referees, coordinating developments in sports medicine, settling disputes over questions involving amateurism and professionalism, aiding in the development of soccer in underdeveloped countries, disciplining clubs or individuals in violation of the regulations and managing the game's finances.

Disputes between countries are supposed to be resolved internally and without bias. The essential aim of the organization is to promote the good of the game as a whole, rather than the interests of one member over another. Although FIFA may occasionally seem to lean in one ideological direction or another, it strives to maintain the integrity of its statutes, and succeeds, for the most part, in remaining politically neutral.

In 1953, to further assist the administration and organization of a growing sport, FIFA authorized the formation of continental confederations. Europe and Asia established confederations in 1954, Africa in 1956, North and Central America in 1961, and Oceania in 1966. The South American confederation, founded in 1916, also became an affiliate of FIFA. The six continental confederations — UEFA (Europe), AFC (Asia), CAF (Africa), CONCACAF (North/Central America and the Caribbean), OFC (Oceania) and CONMEBOL (South America) — are affiliated with FIFA, and each in turn controls its own geographic region. Meanwhile the national associations in each continent are affiliated with their respective confederations, and the various national and regional leagues are in turn affiliated to the national associations. In this way, every soccer club in the world has access to FIFA through its league, national association and continental confederation.

NO MORE MR MARSEILLE *Bernard Tapie*

From its modern headquarters overlooking Lake Zurich, FIFA controls everything in world soccer. Its statutes give it wide enforcement powers over 200 million players and more than one million teams worldwide. Recent crackdowns on doping and match-fixing serve to demonstrate the wide-ranging power within FIFA's mandate.

The organization is not shy about flexing its muscles. Marseille felt FIFA's wrath after their 1993 European Cup success was tainted by allegations that the club had paid opposing players to throw a French league match. FIFA pushed its European affiliate UEFA to ban Marseille from defending their title, even though no court had ruled on the bribery charges. When Marseille's owner, politician-businessman Bernard Tapie, challenged the ban in court, FIFA threatened to suspend France from international soccer, and Tapie was forced to back down.

Above all, FIFA's control of participation in the game's golden egg, the World Cup, provides it with the ultimate weapon for bringing recalcitrant countries, clubs and individuals to heel. This was illustrated, in 1989, when the Chilean goalkeeper Roberto Rojas faked injury — claiming he had been struck by a flare thrown from the crowd — during a vital World Cup qualifier against Brazil at the Maracana. Chile's team, losing at the time, walked off the pitch in mid-match in protest at the inadequate security, and claimed victory by default. In vain. FIFA's response was to ban Chile from the 1990 World Cup.

The major challenge of the 1990s was to develop a significant consciousness about soccer in the United States, following the successful U.S.

SKY
SPORTS

bid to host the 1994 World Cup finals. This also proved to be a catalyst in attempts — particularly dear to the heart of long-serving general secretary Sepp Blatter — to review dispassionately the true effectiveness of each and every Law of the Game. Proposals for, at the most, change and, at the least, experiment, were drawn up by the ad hoc Football 2000 commission which was set up with a personality panel — including former French captain Michel Platini and UEFA president Lennart Johansson — after the 1990 finals. Certainly, the Football 2000 commission functioned at first with one eye on concern for law changes emanating from the United States in an attempt to "assist" their staging of the 1994 World Cup in advancing the cause of the game there (suggestions included "real" time, kick-ins, offside "zones," etc.).

The success can at least be measured in financial terms. Thus the 1994 World Cup was forecast to yield income of about $200 million from ticket sales, television rights and advertising contracts. A percentage of the profits was divided among the 24 participating teams — depending on how far they progressed in the finals — and another portion of cash allocated to FIFA's development programs for emerging countries. By the mid-1990s these included many of the central and eastern European states created by the collapse of both the Soviet Union and Yugoslavia.

Joao Havelange of Brazil, who secured the FIFA presidency at the expense of England's incumbent Sir Stanley Rous in 1974, proved a pragmatic visionary, and has done much to spread the global commercialization of the game — not least by his controversial promise (in return for securing presidential votes from Africa and Asia in 1974) to expand the World Cup finals from 16 to 24 nations. Further evidence of the game's international evolution was available at the 1994 World Cup finals, in which three African nations (Cameroon, Morocco and Nigeria) competed for the first time.

THE MEDIA

MILAN MAN *Silvio Berlusconi*

The success of soccer around the world has generated massive interest in the professional game, a fact not lost on the world's media, which eagerly exploits the sport. The relationship, generally, is mutually beneficial, and in the case of television, particularly, the direct financial benefits are obvious. But while television could survive without soccer, it is becoming increasingly true that soccer in many countries could not survive without television and its huge investment in the game. The dangerous day ahead is the one on which TV moguls discover superior weapons in the ratings war.

To understand the relationship, it is necessary first to understand why television is so eager to show soccer. The entertainment value of soccer is not consistently high enough to merit its purchase alone, although televised soccer in Europe does attract large audiences. To the TV companies, the value of televised soccer comes not from the game itself, but from the access it provides advertisers to those who follow it. In televising soccer, they are not so much paying for the right to show the match, as they are buying the right to sell advertising space during it. Soccer fans, and by logical extension, those who watch soccer on TV, are generally young males, with high disposable incomes. What better time, then, to advertise products such as cars, toiletries, electronics, alcohol and financial services than during a soccer game?

Perhaps the best example of this intertwining of soccer and television comes from Italy. Silvio Berlusconi is owner of the Fininvest group which owns, among many other things, Milan soccer club, a string of local commercial TV stations including the flagship Canale 5, a supermarket chain and dozens of other non-related companies. Berlusconi has pumped millions of pounds into Milan to make them the best club team in Europe, if not the world. And, by showing soccer on his various TV channels, Berlusconi has a captive audience at which to aim his advertisements. It would seem to be the perfect relationship. Not only that, but Berlusconi hijacked Italy's soccer slogan — Forza Italia — for his political party when he won the General Election in March, 1994.

Press coverage of soccer varies. Italy, France, Portugal, Spain, Hungary, Poland, Slovakia, Romania and Bulgaria all sustain at least one daily sports newspaper. Yet Britain, such a sports-loving nation, is unable to do so. Or rather, it does not need to. In Britain the national press has always given far greater priority to soccer coverage than "general" daily newspapers on the continent — thus removing the need for a sports daily. Indeed the importance of soccer to the British newspaper industry can be gauged from the fact that *Today* newspaper sponsored the Football League during the 1986–87 season.

In Europe the situation is different, creating a need for daily newspapers such as the seven-day-a-week *Gazzetta dello Sport*, *Tuttosport* and *Corriere dello Sport/Stadio* (Italy), *A Bola* (Portugal), *Marca*, *AS* and *Mundo Deportivo* (Spain) and *L'Equipe* (France). These soccer papers devote wide coverage to the game and feature in-depth investigations, interviews and opinion as well as results and statistics. Britain does have many weekly and monthly soccer magazines, but these are mostly aimed at the younger reader and are often little more than glorified posters. In Europe, soccer magazines tend to be aimed at older teenagers and adults, and there can be little doubt that *France Football*, *Kicker* (Germany), *Voetbal International* (Holland) and *Guerin Sportivo* (Italy) are "serious" soccer magazines.

Soccer is, it seems, an endless source of fascination to book publishers. Every year hundreds of soccer books are published worldwide, covering every conceivable angle. Many are straightforward statistical logs and yearbooks; others explore the wider influences of soccer on society. Britain has a tradition for the "kick and tell" book in which a famous player tells his life/career story in autobiographical terms with the help of a friendly journalist, who acts as a ghostwriter. Such books would not, generally, be commercially viable without a few controversial chapters which can be sold for serialization in one of the popular (usually Sunday) newspapers for a fee which helps underwrite the book publisher's capital costs.

Radio has an important role to play too. In Britain, for example, BBC Radio 5 currently broadcasts, on average, five live matches a week on Saturday, Sunday, Monday, Tuesday and Wednesday. The station also provides regular news bulletins and score checks — its output and style having been revolutionized in the 1990s to compete with the plethora of commercial local radio stations which have sprung up around the country.

Managers and players can be notoriously sensitive to bad publicity. But, in commercial terms, no general business, no single company could afford to buy the acres of print and technological space being filled hour by hour, day by day, by soccer. All free publicity. The media, as ever, will always have the last word.

EXCLUSIVELY LIVE *Sky Sports' slogan for their coverage of top-flight English soccer*

THE LAWS AND TACTICS

The first Laws of soccer were drawn up at Cambridge University in 1848, and since then they have been considerably rewritten and amended. As the game changed, so tactics, too, have developed as teams try to outwit each other with bolts, liberos, 4–2–4 and the like.

THE LAWS OF SOCCER

The Laws (not the rules) of soccer have been honed down to 17 in number, with numerous sub-clauses. This evolutionary process began in the mid-nineteenth century and continued through to the 1930s, when Stanley Rous recodified the Laws. Nowadays there is an annual review by FIFA, and on any proposed law change eight votes are cast, four of them from the Home Countries of England, Scotland, Wales and Northern Ireland, and four from FIFA. It takes a three-quarter majority to alter a Law.

What follows is a summary of the Laws, as published by FIFA, simplified for general use.

THE OBJECT OF THE GAME

The game is played by two teams, each consisting of 11 players, one of whom must be a goalkeeper. The goalkeeper must wear clothing that distinguishes him from his team-mates and does not clash with the colors worn by his opponents or the referee. Substitutes are allowed on each team, but once a player has been replaced that player may not re-enter the game. Each competition has its own rules which dictate how many substitutes per side are permitted. In international soccer it is usually two, selected from five named before the match, but this does vary. Most domestic competitions allow either two or three, the third being a goalkeeper, all of whom have to be named beforehand.

On the field the game is regulated in senior soccer by a referee and two linesmen, whereas in junior soccer it is permitted simply to have a referee.

The object of the game is to propel a ball by foot or any part of the body other than the hands or arms into your opponents' goal. At each end of the field there is a goal consisting of two uprights placed eight yards apart (the inside measurement between the two posts), and joined at the top by a cross-bar eight feet in height (to the lower part of the bar) above the ground. The uprights and cross-bars should not exceed five inches in width and must be the same width. Normally these are made of wood or tubular steel. In senior soccer a net is is attached to the uprights and cross-bar or free-standing supports, to indicate clearly when a goal has been scored.

THE FIELD OF PLAY

The game is played on a field the surface of which is usually grass, although some competitions allow artificial surfaces of different types. The field of play is rectangular and measures between 100 to 130 yards in length and 50 to 100 yards in width. Under no circumstances can the field be square. The field of play is bounded by painted lines. Those down the longer side are known as the touch lines, and those across the shorter side, on which the goals are positioned, as the goal lines. All such boundary lines and other field markings, which should be no more than five inches wide, form part of the field of play.

Other field markings consist of a center-line drawn across the field at a point midway between the two goallines. In the middle of this is placed a center spot, from which play commences at the start of each

THE FIELD OF PLAY *The dimensions and markings of a soccer field*

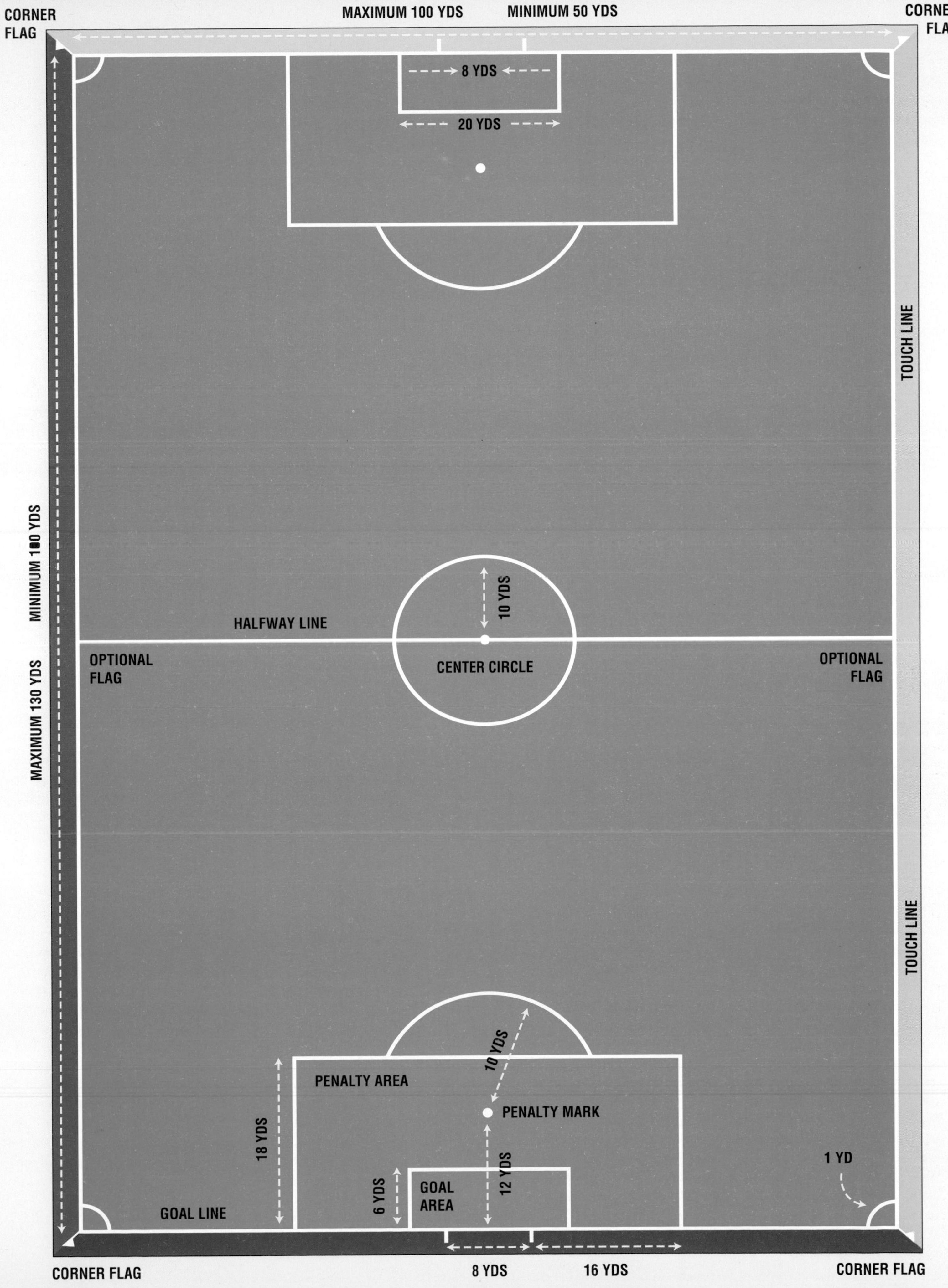

CORNER FLAG
MAXIMUM 100 YDS
MINIMUM 50 YDS
CORNER FLAG
8 YDS
20 YDS
TOUCH LINE
MINIMUM 100 YDS
MAXIMUM 130 YDS
10 YDS
HALFWAY LINE
OPTIONAL FLAG
CENTER CIRCLE
OPTIONAL FLAG
TOUCH LINE
10 YDS
PENALTY AREA
PENALTY MARK
18 YDS
1 YD
6 YDS
GOAL AREA
12 YDS
GOAL LINE
CORNER FLAG
8 YDS
16 YDS
CORNER FLAG

half and after a goal is scored. A circle is drawn, with a ten-yard radius from the center spot, within which no opponent is allowed to encroach until the ball is kicked into play. In each corner of the field, where the goal line and touch line meet, is a corner flag with a minimum height of five feet. A quadrant with a one-yard radius is drawn at each corner of the field. As an optional extra, flags may be placed opposite the center line but must be at least one yard behind the touch lines.

The goals are placed at the center of each goal line, and two lines are drawn at right angles to the goal line six yards from the goal posts. They extend into the field of play for a distance of six yards and are joined by a line of 20 yards parallel to the goal line. This section defines the goal area. The goal area is enclosed within the larger penalty area, which is created by drawing two lines at right angles to the goal line, 18 yards from each goal post, which extend into the field of play a distance of 18 yards and are joined by a line of 44 yards parallel to the goal line.

The penalty mark from where penalty kicks must be taken is marked twelve yards from the goal line and facing the mid-point of the goal. The Laws decree that there must be no encroachment when a penalty kick is taken. In order to insure that all players apart from the kicker stand 10 yards from the ball until such a kick is taken, an arc with a radius of ten yards, using the penalty spot as its center, is drawn outside the penalty area, and the players must stand outisde the penalty area and outside this arc.

The game is played with a ball which must be round and made of leather or any other approved material, its circumference being between 27 and 28 inches and its weight between 14 and 16 ounces.

The object of the game is to score more goals than the opposition. In order to score a goal the whole of the ball must pass between the goal posts, under the crossbar and across the goal line. The whole of the ball must cross the whole of the line. If no goals are scored, or the teams have an equal number of goals, the match is termed a tie.

THE DURATION OF PLAY

The match starts with a kickoff, with the ball placed on the center spot and kicked forward by one of the attackers. Prior to that, the captains of the two teams meet the referee to toss a coin for choice of ends or kick-off. The winning captain generally selects for the first half, since the teams change ends to start the second half. Every time a kick-off occurs the teams are positioned in their respective halves of the field and cannot move until the ball is kicked into play. The ball is in play once it has traveled its own circumference in the opponents' half of the field. The player taking the kickoff may not play the ball again until it has been touched by another player.

Play is divided into two equal halves, and in senior soccer a half lasts 45 minutes (although this can be reduced either by the rules of the competition or by agreement between the teams), and there is a half-time interval lasting a minimum of five minutes. To decide cup matches which are tied after 90 minutes, extra time, usually of 15 minutes each way, is played. Some competitions allow for a penalty kick decider to occur to ascertain the winner.

EQUIPMENT

A player's equipment consists of a jersey or shirt, shorts, socks, shinguards and footwear. The teams must wear colors that do not clash with each other or the referee. A player shall not wear anything that is dangerous to another player.

IN PLAY AND OUT OF PLAY

The ball is in play at all times from the start of the match to the finish, including where an infringement of the Laws occurs (until a decision is given and the game is stopped by the referee). It is still in play when it rebounds inside the boundaries of the field from a goal post, crossbar or corner flag. The ball only goes out of play when it wholly crosses the boundaries of the field, whether on the ground or in the air.

When the ball leaves the field of play over the touch line it re-enters the field by means of a throw-in. The throw is taken by a member of the team opposing that of the player who put it out of play. The throw must be taken from as close as possible to the point at which the ball left the field. If not taken from there it is described as a foul throw and the throw-in given to the other team. The thrower takes the ball in both hands and throws it from behind and over his head. He must face the field with both feet on the ground on or behind the touch line at the moment he delivers the throw.

When the ball leaves the field of play over the goal line it is returned into play either by means of a goal kick, if last touched by an attacker, or a corner kick, if last touched by a defender. At a goal kick the defending side (usually the goalkeeper) restarts the game by kicking the ball from either half of his goal area, and the ball is not deemed to be in play until it has passed out of the penalty area. Any infringement of this procedure results in the kick being retaken.

At a corner kick the ball is played from the quadrant, which is a quarter circle with a radius of one yard situated in the corner of the field. The ball must be within the quadrant, and the kick must be taken at the end of the defending side's goal line nearest to where the ball went out of play. Again the player taking the corner kick may not play the ball a second time until it has been touched by another player, and defenders must remain at a distance of ten yards until the ball has been kicked.

Where there is no other method of restarting the game, following an injury, interference by spectators or for any other accidental reason, the restart is achieved by dropping the ball at the point where it was when play was suspended. The ball is deemed to be in play the moment it touches the ground, and no player may kick or attempt to kick the ball until that moment. In the event of a breach of this procedure the drop is retaken.

OFFSIDE

Arguably the most complex of the 17 Laws is Law 11, relating to "offside."

THE PENALTY KICK

This is for the serious offenses mentioned. Taken from the penalty mark, it can be awarded irrespective of where the ball is at the time the offense is committed, provided that the ball is in play and the offense takes place in the penalty area. A goal may be scored directly from a penalty and the only players allowed in the penalty area until the ball has been kicked are the one taking the kick and the goalkeeper. If either team infringes these regulations, the kick will be retaken, except in the case of an infringement by the defending team where a goal has been scored. In that event the goal will normally be awarded, because to do otherwise would be to allow the offending team to gain an advantage from the infringement. Examples of when a retake is ordered are: where the goalkeeper saves the ball or the kick is missed, but the goalkeeper has moved his feet before the kick is taken or there is encroachment by the defending side; where a goal is scored and there is encroachment by the attacking side; and, finally, where the kick is taken, whether or not a goal is scored, and there is encroachment by both sides. A match shall be extended at half-time or full-time to allow the penalty kick to be taken or retaken, but the extension shall last only until the moment that the penalty kick has been completed, whether it results in a goal, a miss or a save. Different rules apply in cup competitions when the teams are even at the end of regulation time and the game is to be decided by the taking of an initial five penalties by each side.

Even the wording is difficult, which pronounces that "a player is offside if he is nearer his opponents' goalline than the ball and interfering with play or an opponent at the moment the ball is last played unless . . ." Then follow four exceptions: (l) from restarts, namely goal kicks, corner-kicks and throw-ins, but not free kicks; (2) if a player is in his own half of the field; (3) if the ball was last played to him by an opponent; (4) if he is not nearer to the goal line than at least two defenders, even if one is the goalkeeper. In these cases he is not offside. The main problems come in deciding when the ball was last "played," and whether or not an attacker is "interfering." If the referee deems that an attacking player, albeit in an "offside position," is not interfering with play or with an opponent or seeking to gain an advantage by being in that offside position, he shall refrain from penalizing him and stopping play. It is to be noted that a player who is even with a defender is not nearer to the goal line than that defender. Therefore, provided the goalkeeper is between him and the goal line, and another defender is level with him, he is not in an offside position.

INFRINGEMENTS OF THE LAWS

As soccer is a physical contact sport, infringements of the Laws will inevitably occur, giving rise to punishment by the referee in the form of "free kicks." These free kicks may be either "direct" or "indirect." The difference is that a goal may be scored directly from a direct free kick but not from an indirect free kick. At an indirect free kick a second player must play the ball after the kicker before a goal can be scored. A direct free kick is awarded for more serious offences, and if these occur in the penalty area a penalty is awarded. All free kicks (except penalties) are taken from the place where the infringement occurred unless they take place in the goal area. Then the attacking side take this indirect free kick from that place on the goal area line which is parallel to the goal line

SEEING RED *Tony Gale of West Ham receives a red card and is sent off for stopping a likely scoring opportunity*

and is nearest the infringement. For the defending side, the free kick can be taken from anywhere inside the goal area. Although opponents must be at least 10 yards from the ball at the moment the free kick is taken, the attacking side has the option of waiving this rule should they consider that they would obtain greater advantage from taking the kick quickly. The referee may play what is known as the "advantage clause" and not award a free kick if he considers that to play on is advantageous to the attacking team.

The more serious offenses, for which a direct free kick can be awarded, are intentional fouls or misconduct and are divided into nine categories, of which six are fouls against an opponent, two are against either an opponent or a teammate, and one is technical. The six are: (a) tripping or hitting an opponent; (b) jumping at an opponent; (c) charging an opponent from behind (unless he is obstructing); (d) holding an opponent; (e) pushing an opponent; (f) charging an opponent in a violent or dangerous manner. The two more serious offenses are kicking or attempting to kick another player and striking or attempting to strike or spit at another player — or indeed the referee. The final offense is deliberately handling the ball which is defined as "carrying, propelling or striking the ball with the hand or arm." If any of these nine offenses is committed by the defending side in their own penalty area, the referee will award a penalty, which is taken from the penalty mark.

Indirect free kicks are awarded for eight main offenses, which are: (a) dangerous (rather than violent) play;

THE GOALKEEPER

The goalkeeper is the only player entitled to handle the ball, but he is only allowed to do this within his own penalty area. When he leaves his penalty area he becomes an ordinary player. He wears clothing which distinguishes him from all other members of his team, his opponents and the referee, and if he fails to do so he can be sent from the field until he complies with this ruling.

The goalkeeper is the only other player apart from the striker of the kick to be in the penalty area at the time a penalty is taken. He must stand on his own goal line and must not move his feet until the ball is struck.

The goalkeeper is king in his own goal area and may not be charged except when he is holding the ball or obstructing an opponent in that particular area.

However, he is capable of being penalized more than any other player on the field. He may be penalized for taking more than four steps in any direction while in possession of the ball, whether holding or bouncing the ball or throwing it in the air and catching it again without releasing it into play; or if, having released the ball into play before, during or after the four steps, he touches it again with his hands before it has been touched or played by another player of the same team outside the penalty area, or by a player of the opposing team inside or outside the penalty area. Similarly, where a defending player deliberately kicks the ball to him, he is not permitted to touch it with his hands, and if he does he is penalized by the award of an indirect free kick against him.

Finally, the goalkeeper is the only player to suffer the wrath of the Laws if he indulges in tactics which in the opinion of the referee are designed merely to hold up the game and thus waste time, giving an unfair advantage to his own team. These disadvantages are intended to balance out the advantage of being the only one who can legitimately handle the ball.

He is able to score a goal with a kick from his hands from his own penalty area, provided the ball is in play; and if he chooses to be just another player he can come out of his penalty area to score at the other end.

THE REFEREE *The wisdom of Solomon and the patience of Job*

BLOWING THE WHISTLE *The appropriate punishment for a foul is administered*

(b) charging fairly but at a time when the opponent does not have the ball within playing distance; (c) obstruction; (d) charging the goalkeeper except when he is holding the ball or is obstructing an opponent or has passed outside his goal area; (e) time-wasting by the goalkeeper; (f) the goalkeeper taking more than four steps while in possession of the ball; (g) any occasion when a player deliberately kicks the ball to his goalkeeper and the goalkeeper then touches it with his hand or hands, or when the goalkeeper deliberately handles the ball twice without an opponent touching it if he is not attempting to save the ball; (h) indulging in anything which the referee considers to be ungentlemanly conduct, including trying to circumvent the Laws — particularly the deliberate kick to the goalkeeper rule. In addition, an indirect free kick is also awarded for the technical offense of offside.

The referee has power to punish these offenses further if they are considered serious enough. A player shall be cautioned and shown a yellow card by the referee if he (a) enters or leaves the field of play without receiving a signal from the referee to do so; (b) persistently infringes the Laws of the Game; (c) shows, by word or actions, dissent from any decision given by the referee, or (d) is guilty of any act of ungentlemanly conduct, with particular reference to kicking the ball away after the award of a free kick, encroaching from a "defensive wall" or standing in front of the ball to stop a free kick being taken.

For even more serious offenses a player shall be shown a red card and sent off the field if (a) in the opinion of the referee a defending player intentionally impedes an opponent through unlawful means when that opponent has an obvious goalscoring opportunity; (b) any player is guilty of violent conduct or serious foul play, including spitting; (c) a defending player other than the goalkeeper in his own penalty area intentionally handles the ball to deny his opponents a goal or goal scoring opportunity; (d) any player uses foul or abusive language to anyone on the field of play; (e) a player after already having received a caution persists in misconduct. FIFA has also instructed referees to issue a red card to a player who tackles an opponent from behind if he does so recklessly. Play is restarted by an indirect free kick, except where the stoppage was caused by an offense which would normally result in a direct free kick.

THE OFFICIALS

Originally soccer was played with an umpire and a referee rather like the game of tennis. Gradually it was necessary to introduce sideline judges with the umpire's role transformed into that of the modern day referee who is assisted by two linesmen. The linesmen are qualified referees who specifically indicate ball in and out of play at throw-ins, corner kicks and goal kicks; who mainly are given the responsibility of deciding offside; who are required to attract the attention of the referee at substitutions and are generally there to aid and assist the referee.

The referee is the sole timekeeper and enforcer of the Laws. He therefore in order to carry these obligations into effect takes on to the field with him a stop watch, a whistle to start and stop the game, a pencil so as to write in all weather conditions, a note book or paper and a red and yellow card to administer punishment. In senior soccer he is usually entrusted with one match ball to take on to the field although he is required to inspect all match balls before the match starts to ensure they comply with the Laws.

The referee must report all misconduct to the appropriate body governing the game; he may refrain from punishing to play the advantage in favour of the attacking team and he can reverse his decision so long as the game has not been re-started. He should only accept the intervention of a linesman if the linesman is better placed to see the incident.

Referees are encouraged to absorb and administer the unwritten eighteenth Law shortly known as "common sense" and therefore he should indicate by means of approved signals various decisions. The referee will decide how to administer the game with his linesmen and advise them where to stand. The usual system is known as the "diagonal system" and involves the referee being in the middle with each of the linesmen being on either the right or left diagonal so that they are always in vision of each other. He will also discuss with them what positions to take up at penalties and corners and who shall be the senior one in case of need. The three officials all compare watches before the start of the game.

Over a period of years the referees' outfit evolved from a jacket top and plus-fours trousers into a blazer and shorts, followed by a tunic top, which ultimately became an all-black outfit with white trimmings and socks to match. In recent years experiments have taken place with different color outfits but FIFA generally requires referees to wear predominantly black in international competitions of all varieties.

THREE WISE MEN *A referee flanked by two linesmen before the kickoff*

THE HISTORY OF TACTICS

Tactics can be divided into three main categories:

(1) Team formations
(2) Team tactics involving the whole or part of the team, whether for (a) attack or (b) defense
(3) Restarts or setpieces

For coaches and players it is important to identify the roles of the players within the team framework and how they dovetail to achieve the object of the game — which is to score goals and to prevent your opponents from scoring (i.e. score more goals than the opposition). The objective here is to deal with tactics under the three categories mentioned above, and to follow the evolution of the game as a whole.

TEAM FORMATIONS

Team formations basically set out where players are positioned on the field, on the general principle of keeping to a "shape." Although all soccer should ideally be free-flowing and full of innovation, nonetheless all successful teams have had in common a large measure of discipline, enabling the players to maintain the formation devised by the manager or coach.

As time has gone on, more and more systems have evolved since the game was first organized in the nineteenth century. In those days there was little or no method employed to bring players into the game in intricate playing formations because there were no clearly defined positions. Just as children who are not conditioned to play "small-sided" games, or to stick to positions, will follow the ball all over the field in great numbers, so the game was played in its earliest days. Individual skills, particularly the art of dribbling, tended to predominate.

Gradually, as the game became more sophisticated, greater use was made of the offside Law. This was borrowed from rugby soccer and stemmed from the influence of the private schools, where most soccer was played. At that time the offside provision applied whenever the ball was passed to a player who was in front of the ball, irrespective of how many opponents he had in front of him. It was not uncommon for eight of the team to attack the opposition goal, leaving the goalkeeper with two down field, one of whom would be a defender and the other a "half-back," so named because he was half attacker, half defender. At that point the first real formation was created — in effect 1–1–1–8 — but within a short space of time one of the forwards was pulled back to a wing-half position, thus making it 1–1–2–7.

Soon, however, the influence of Scottish soccer started to make itself felt. Because their game had a set of Laws which were commonly adhered to, they were able to vary their methods of play and evolve a system of passing to supplement the dribbling. Their leading club, Queens Park, promoted the passing game to such an extent that instead of the mad scramble upfield, the ball was spread across and along the whole of the field.

Owing to this new method of play it was necessary to pull another attacker back and spread the game a little wider, thus creating a 1–2–2–6 formation; and once it was established that the ball could be moved across field and from one side to

The "2–3–5" formation, used at the turn of the century.

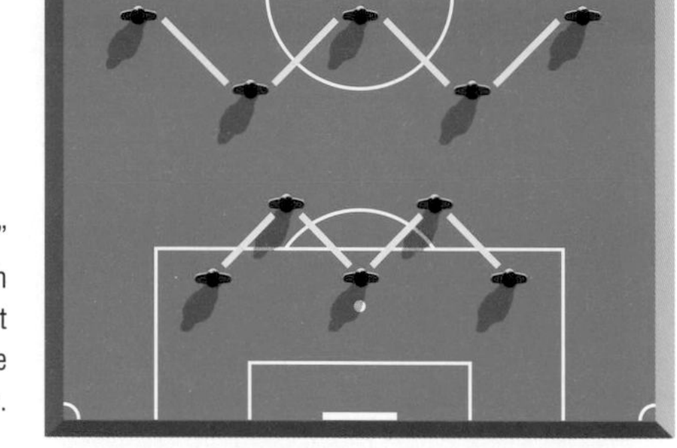

The "WM" formation, which developed out of the 1925 change in the offside law.

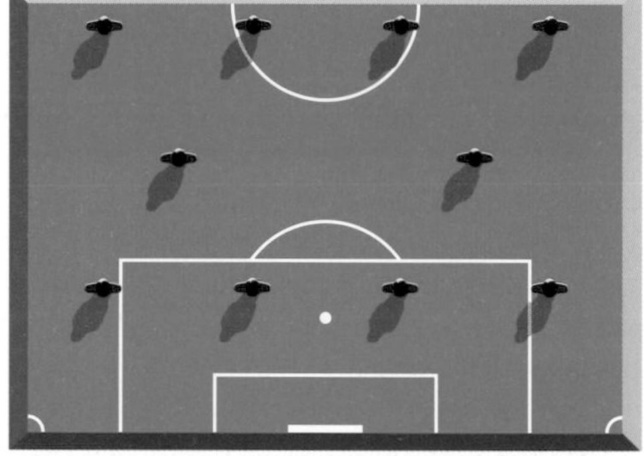

Brazil's 1958 World Cup winning "4–2–4" system.

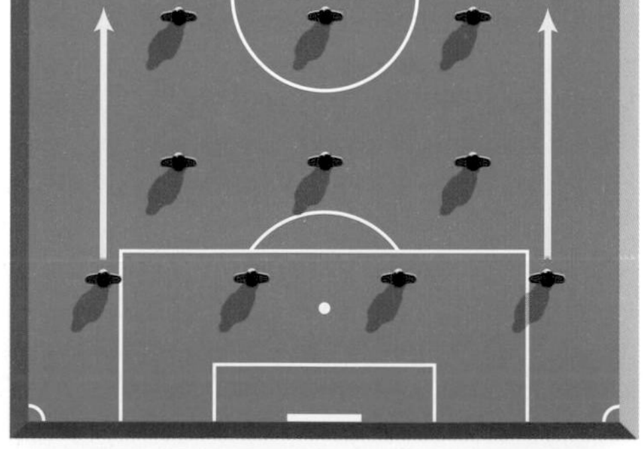

The "4–3–3" stystem, used by Brazil in the 1970 World Cup.

Italy's *catenaccio* defensive formation with the introduction of the "sweeper" or *libero*.

another, radical changes took place until eventually the "WM" formation was evolved, as hereafter mentioned.

In 1866 the offside law was modified to stipulate that a player was now onside if he had at least three opponents (one of whom could be the goalkeeper) between himself and the opposing goal line at the time the ball was passed. Thus it was now possible to pass the ball forward instead of always worrying about trying to pass it back. The use of a system based loosely on a 1–2–3–5 formation, with a combination of dribbling and passing, brought a spate of goals. However, in the early twentieth century the Newcastle defender Bill McCracken organized his defense in such a way that everyone moved up at his given signal to create a trap into which the opposition attackers readily fell. Attacks were therefore killed off at the half way line and some games were even stopped as often as every two minutes. Like every successful tactic it was copied slavishly by other teams, and as a result pressure grew for a change in the Laws to stop the game being destroyed as a spectacle.

In 1925 the law-making International Board put forward and passed proposals to change the offside law so that the number of opponents required to be between the attacker and the goal line was reduced from three to two. The effect was dramatic: whereas in the previous season a total of 4,700 goals had been scored across the board in the Football League, the total now rose to 6,373. By judicious use of the attacking center-half and astute wing play with crosses for the striking center-forward, goals abounded. In the 1926–27 season George Camsell scored 59, which was then a record, bettered immediately the following season by Dixie Dean, who scored 60 goals (a record which incidentally still stands). The ability of the center-forwards in the air and the massive number of goals they were scoring soon caused consternation amongst defenders, but it was not long before the best combination of captain and manager found a remedy.

Charlie Buchan, once the most expensive player in soccer, got together with his Arsenal coach, Herbert Chapman, to devise a system whereby the center-half, who had previously lined up alongside the other two half-backs, was taken out of that midfield line and put into the back line between the fullbacks. Although initially Jack Butler was drafted into the position, it was not until Herbie Roberts became the regular center-half (or really center-back) that the "stopper" position was cemented into place. Having achieved that success, Chapman then withdrew two of his attackers into more midfield positions and, with a system of 1–3–2–2–3, the "WM" formation was now complete. It was so named because if you looked from the back it formed a W and if you looked from the front it formed an M. That was a system adopted not only in Britain but in much of Europe. This owed much to Arsenal's achievements, as they rapidly became the most successful team in English soccer, winning five First Division titles and two FA Cups during the 1930s. Additionally, with English coaches and English teams traveling abroad, the system became universally recognized, although in a number of European countries it was not adopted. Hungary, Austria and Switzerland had other ideas.

TEAM TACTICS

In Austria, led by Hugo Meisl, the national team continued to play with the attacking center-half. In Italy Vittorio Pozzo encouraged his teams to attack with mobility, using long passing and an adaptation of the attacking center-half. Switzerland developed a system known as "Le Verrou," meaning "the bolt." This was based on the attacking center-half and the fullbacks defending the center, and the wing halves defending the wings. One of the inside-forwards was pulled back to play alongside the center-half, but one of the fullbacks played behind the other in a role similar to that of the sweeper, as we know it today. Because center-forwards were so revered, the aim was to double mark the opposition's No. 9. As with many sweeper systems, utilized correctly it enabled other members of the team to attack more readily and with freedom.

Just prior to a spate of innovations, the Italians moved from their attacking center-half system to a similar but more restrictive bolt system. Coaches such as Alfredo Foni, Nereo Rocco and — above all — Helenio Herrera perfected a catenaccio system in which the sweeper was placed behind the line of three or four defenders, with no serious attacking pretensions. His job was merely to stop anyone who got through the line of defenders in front of him. Whereas the Swiss bolt system lined up 1–1–3–2–4, the Italian system's line-up was 1–1–3–3–3 or 1–1–3–4–2 or 1–1–4–3–2.

One of the coaches who had left England and created enormous changes abroad was Jimmy Hogan. As time went on, he moved his soccer bandwagon from Austria through Italy to Hungary, and in the 1950s the Hungarian side was vastly effective. They became the first foreign team to win on English soil and in the process revolutionized soccer in Britain. Whereas with the cult of the center-forward the man in the No.9 shirt was regarded as the all-important striker, the Hungarians changed the system completely. They withdrew their No.9, Nandor Hidegkuti, towards the midfield, and played with two wingers and two strikers wearing traditional inside-forward numbers. In addition, they withdrew one of the wing-halves to a central defensive position and created a 1–4–2–4 system.

Although the Hungarians' only international prize was the 1952 Olympic gold medal, they dominated European playing and thinking. Meanwhile, their "4–2–4" system was being simultaneously — and independently — refined by the magnificent Brazilians, who won three out of four World Cups between 1958 and 1970. Later they cautiously revised it by pulling left-winger Mario Zagalo back into midfield, thus creating a 1–4–3–3 formation.

In between the Brazilians' successes in the World Cup Sir Alf Ramsey devised a new English system which relied heavily on strong midfield running, with "overlapping" by the fullbacks since the wingers had been subsumed into midfield. While most sides in England, after the revolutionary examples of Hungary and Brazil, played a 4–2–4 system, Ramsey withdrew his wingers into a tactical formation that read 1–4–4–2. His club team Ipswich won the First Division title and subsequently England went on to win the World Cup. Ever since, English teams and a good many Continental teams have adopted his 4–4–2 system, and wing play has suffered as a result, almost to the point of extinction. There have been calls for the return of the WM formation, which effectively was a 3–3–4 system, but many teams are unwilling to attempt it, preferring to restrict themselves to 4–3–3 or 4–4–2.

One country who almost won the World Cup twice with what they termed "total soccer" were Holland. They attempted to attack from all departments of the field. When their defenders were attacking it was the job of the attackers to defend. Unfortunately this, more than any other system, relies upon having a squad of exceptionally intelligent and technically gifted players who can both attack and defend. It could be said that Holland's ultimate failure resulted not from any weakness of their defenders in attack but from their attackers' weakness in defense. As a result very few club teams or countries have ever dared follow the spectacular Dutch experiment.

In modern soccer the English spectator is likely to see any number of combinations. While 4–4–2 and 4–3–3 predominate, Arsenal, in winning its last two League Championships, experimented with three defenders at the back, with the fullbacks pushed into midfield. In South America team formations vary considerably, but in Europe almost every side plays with a sweeper. A notable exception is Arrigo Sacchi's Milan who, in recent seasons, reverted to a flat back four and a zonal defense. After the earlier Italians developed the catenaccio with man-to-man marking, a further refinement was pioneered in Germany, as the sweeper became a libero (or "free man") with power to attack from the back. Both the Germans and the Dutch use this system extensively and to great effect, and it is an irony that the attacking center-half has returned, albeit from a more defensive situation on the field.

Experiments with other modern formations include the Soviet national side in the 1986 World Cup, who played with one front man and five in midfield, thus making a 1–4–5–1 formation. This method was copied by Tottenham in the Football League under manager David Pleat, for whom Clive Allen scored 40 goals in one season as a lone front player. The Soviet Union, at both club and international level, once played with two sweepers in a formation which looked very much like 1–2–3–3–2. Meanwhile, many sides in England adopted what is known as the "front screen," where one sweeper plays in front of a line of four, making a 1–4–1–3–2 formation.

Latterly several teams have used a "diamond formation," whereby the four midfield players arrange themselves so as to effect a diamond shape, making a strange configuration of 1–4–1–2–1–2. Clearly managers can go on altering all the systems, but whatever formation is stipulated, a set pattern for certain players will always be the central theme, while the other players will have a more fluid role within the team framework. It is obviously easier to produce defensive tactics than attacking ones, and every attempt to score goals by a new formula provokes new methods to defeat it.

The stopper center-back in England produced a defensive formation of a diagonal/dogleg system. This involved the three backs always keeping in a line, so that, if the right-back went to meet the left-winger, the center-back — or pivot — tucked in directly behind him and the far fullback tucked in behind him, but slightly straighter to form a shape like a dog's hind leg. When teams played four at the back and the flat back four became prevalent, this encouraged the use of the offside trap, with defenders squeezing up to the halfway line to compress the play into their opponents' half. In this way anyone getting in behind them too quickly would be offside. Modifications of this have seen the two central defenders drop slightly behind the two fullbacks, while in the defensive sweeper system one player will line up behind four others and will then try to pick up the pieces of any ball or player getting through that line of four.

Frequently the defensive choice is between, on the one hand, playing with a sweeper and adopting a man-to-man approach (catenaccio, in which each defender is allocated an attacker, whom he follows all over the pitch) and, on the other, the "zonal" system. In the latter, a player is allocated an area of the field and marks anyone who comes into that area. This technique requires a high degree of teamwork, which in turn requires defenders to "pass on" opponents to one another.

RE-STARTS OR SET-PIECES:
CORNERS

Corners are one of three basic set-pieces, the others being free kicks and throw-ins. It is estimated that more than 50 per cent of all goals come from such dead ball situations.

Corners divide into three types. The one hit to the far post; the one swung into the near post; and the short corner.

For many years the English game favored the long ball to the far post, where an attacker would attempt to head home — a somewhat basic ploy. In the 1960s, Spurs dominated with the short corner, with Danny Blanchflower passing to Tommy Harmer, who would run forward and either draw defenders or chip the ball long or short.

Finally there was the inswinging corner kick adopted by Wimbledon in their rise from non-League soccer to the Premier League. Arsenal has also used this tactic, particularly in their 1989 Championship success. Brian Marwood would swing the ball into the near-post area, where Steve Bould would flick it on, and again a teammate coming in late would score from directly in front of goal or at the far post. This tactic can also be used without the flick-on, as when Jackie Milburn headed home for New-

The near-post corner is one of the hardest of set plays to defend against. Here, in the 1994 European Cup-winners' Cup semifinal, the Paris St. Germain corner-taker (1) is aiming at David Ginola (2). Two Arsenal defenders, Paul Merson (in front) and Lee Dixon (formerly guarding post) are trying to cut off the danger. However, Merson goes to the edge of the goal area and the ball is hit over him to Ginola, now unmarked. Dixon rushes out to cover the danger, but is not quick enough. Ginola heads the ball just inside the near post as goalkeeper David Seaman, trying to cover the spot Dixon left, helps the ball over the line and PSG score their equalizer.

As was proved at the 1990 World Cup in Italy, direct free kicks around the edge of the opponents' penalty area always pose a threat. Michel's second goal in his hat trick for Spain against South Korea was a fine example of the dead ball kicker's art. Faced with a free kick about 22 yards out, just to the left of the goal, the South Koreans lined up the standard defensive wall (1). With a swerving shot, Michel (2) curved the ball over the wall — aided by a ducking teammate (3) — into the top corner of the net.

castle against Manchester City in the 1955 FA Cup Final.

FREE KICKS

The opportunity of scoring from free kicks depends on their distance from goal and whether they are direct or indirect. West Ham, in particular, developed the near-post free kick, and it worked with great success in the 1966 World Cup final, when Bobby Moore curled a near-post kick for Geoff Hurst to head the equaliser against West Germany. The Brazilians have always been noted for their long-range shooting and deliberate attempts at goal from free kicks. Pele, Garrincha and Rivileno used them to score spectacular goals in the 1966 and 1970 World Cup competitions. Lately Ronald Koeman scored for Holland against England in a World Cup qualifier with a clever chip from a twice-taken free kick from just outside the area, and has scored regularly with tremendous long-range efforts for the Spanish club, Barcelona, including the winner in the 1992 European Cup final.

THROW-INS

Throw-ins which carry into the penalty area can be designed either to create a "flick-on" or a direct header or shot at goal. A move used by the 1961 "double"-winning Spurs side involved Dave Mackay throwing the ball to the head of Bobby Smith, who stood on the goal line. Smith would then head sideways for a colleague to score. If a defender reached the ball first, Spurs usually won at least a corner, but quite often they created a goal. Some of the most spectacular long throws involved Cliff Holton of Arsenal throwing the ball almost to the penalty spot for Doug Lishman to head past keeper Bobby Brown in a prestigious friendly match in 1951, Simon Stainrod throwing to Bob Hazell for Terry Fenwick's equalizer for Queen's Park Rangers against Tottenham in the 1982 FA Cup Final, and Ian Hutchinson's long throw, inadvertently headed on by Jack Charlton, which led to David Webb's 1970 FA Cup winning goal for Chelsea against Leeds.

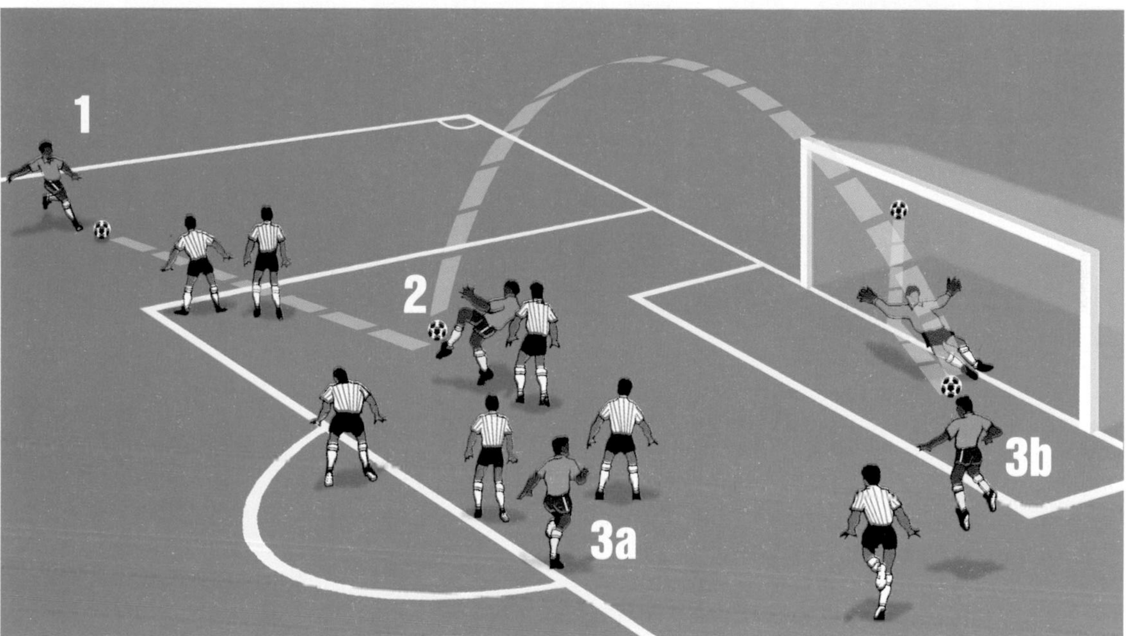

This diagram, of the only goal in the Cameroon vs. Argentina 1990 World Cup game, illustrates the importance of heading the ball downwards. Argentina concedes a free kick on Cameroon's left wing and the kick (1) is driven hard across goal. Makanaky (2) sticks out a boot and deflects the ball high toward the far post. François Omam Biyik (3a), covered by two defenders sprints to the far post and leaps brilliantly to actually get his header at goal (3b). The defender at the far post plays Omam Bikik onside and makes no attempt to go for the ball, it being too high for him. Omam Biyik's header is not particularly powerful, but because he heads the ball down Nery Pumpido in the Argentina goal is surprised and cannot make the easy save.

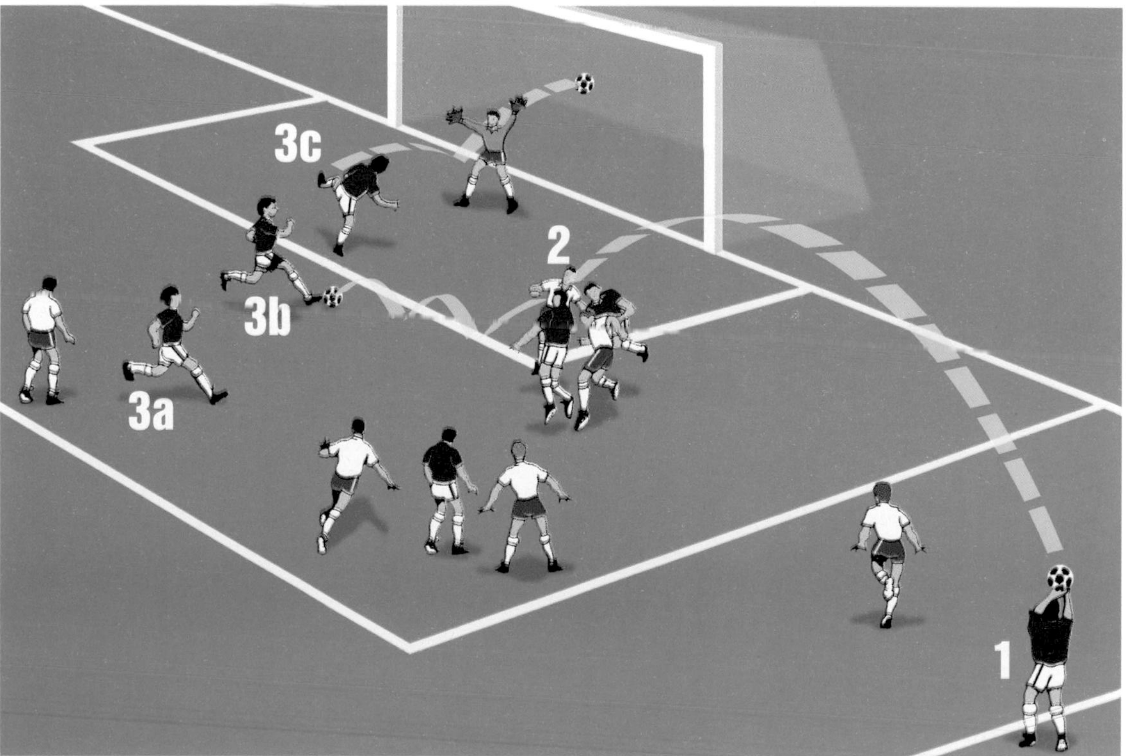

England's goal after 27 seconds of their 1982 World Cup match with France came as a result of three important factors. First, the throw-in taken by Steve Coppell (1) is long. Second,Terry Butcher rises above the two French defenders and teammate Paul Mariner all contesting the ball level with the goal area eight yards from goal (2) and he heads the ball behind him. Third, and most important, Bryan Robson (3A, 3B and 3C) makes a late run into the penalty area. Robson gambles that Butcher (who is a little taller than the three players with whom he is jumping) will win the ball, and it pays off as he is alone (3C) when flick-on reaches him five yards from goal. Robson acrobatically scores with the goalkeeper coming off his line too late in stop the shot. The defender just inside the penalty area starts to follow Robson's run (3a), but stops as he does not think Robson will reach the ball, so the England captain's chance is easier than it should have been.

EQUIPMENT

When soccer first took root in England during the 1870s, it was a game for the upper classes, played by gentlemen to a strict amateur code. Early photographs of teams such as Old Harrovians and Hampstead Heathens show players dressed more like Little Lord Fauntleroy than serious sportsmen. But with the advent of professionalism a decade or so later, working-class teams from the north of England soon started to dominate the game, bringing with them a demand for cheap, basic clothing. Even in today's highly commercialized game, a complete soccer uniform remains relatively inexpensive when compared to other sports, explaining the huge appeal and rapid growth of football in Third World countries.

Today, well over a hundred years after the beginning of professional football, many aspects of the football uniform still look remarkably familiar in basic design. The materials may have changed, but the function remains the same — as the following pages will demonstrate.

1994
The shirt worn by modern Swedish internationals demonstrates the influence of commercialism on design. The three stripes have little to do with aesthetics, nothing to do with tradition and everything to do with the manufacturers' branding.

One of soccer's greatest appeals is its simplicity. Law IV of the Laws of the Game merely states: "the basic compulsory equipment of a player shall consist of a jersey or shirt, shorts, stockings, shinguards and footwear. A player shall not wear anything which is dangerous to another player. The goalkeeper shall wear colors which will distinguish him from the other players and the referee."

1909
The first soccer shirts were made of thick wool, but cotton soon proved to be cheaper and more practical. This shirt, worn by Manchester United right-back George Stacey in the FA Cup final, shows the original lace-up collar design which briefly resurfaced in recent seasons.

1911
Two years later and buttons have replaced laces in this England shirt. The original England uniform for the 1872 game against Scotland was white jerseys, dark blue caps and white knickerbockers.

1948
The shirt worn by Charlie Mitten for Manchester United against Blackpool in the FA Cup Final bears a remarkable resemblance to modern day rugby shirts, with thick cuffs and button-up collars.

1960
Thick woolen goalkeeper's jersey as worn by Dominguez of Real Madrid. It wasn't until 1913 that goalkeepers had to wear distinctive colors. Until then they wore the same shirt as their team-mates and were distinguished by a cap.

1982
The development of synthetics from the 1960s signaled the end of cotton. This Brazilian shirt of light nylon is specially designed for maximum ventilation to cope with the heat and altitude of South American soccer.

1992
Multi-colored, synthetic goalkeeper's shirt, worn by Denmark's Peter Schmeichel in the 1992 European Championship final. Less than ten years previously the rules stated that goalkeepers could wear only green, yellow or white. How times change!

1958
(Top right) *The arrival of the modern soccer shoe. Superior quality leather was used in a design cut under the ankles in these boots belonging to Manchester United's David Pegg. The specially designed leather soles allowed for screw-in molded nylon studs.*

1936
(Below) *Arsenal socks, made of thick wool and weighing a couple of pounds each when wet! During the Second World War, in Britain such items of soccer equipment were available only with clothing coupons allocated by the Board of Trade.*

1994
(Bottom right) *Millions are spent on the research and manufacture of shoes, and the results are plain to see. Today's top quality shoes are usually made of kangaroo leather with aluminum studs and molded plastic soles.*

The changing face of soccer is demonstrated by the way shoes have developed. Manufacturing is now a huge industry, generating millions of dollars on the back of improved scientific and technical developments.

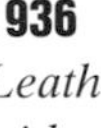

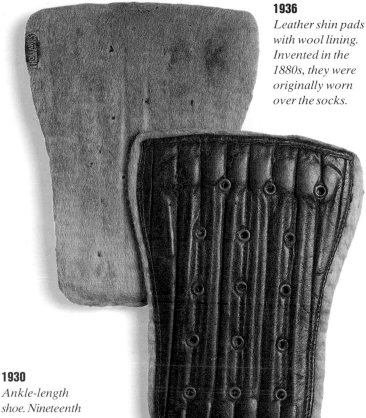

1936
Leather shin pads with wool lining. Invented in the 1880s, they were originally worn over the socks.

1972
Stylo Matchmaker shoes as worn by George Best. Possibly seeking to reflect the image of the wearer rather than provide solid protection, these look more like a pair of slippers than soccer shoes.

1930
Ankle-length shoe. Nineteenth century soccer players nailed studs into their ordinary working shoes for matches.

1936
Stud making kit. Using the hand stamp, three circles were removed from a 2 inches thick strip of leather and nailed together to make one stud.

Even ordinary items like soccer balls and goalkeeper's gloves have changed over the years. Medals and caps change, too, though only the lucky few who win them

1992
Modern day goalkeeper's gloves. Like so many other areas of soccer equipment, these now represent a lucrative market for the manufacturers. Until the mid-1970s, keepers were more than happy with simple cotton gloves.

1968
Captain's armband, as worn by Manchester United's Bobby Charlton during his side's European Cup campaign. They were once worn only in European games to help the referees identify captains.

1990
Official World Cup ball. Modern balls actually weigh an ounce more than pre-War soccer balls but seem lighter due to the plastic coating and superior manufacturing techniques that mean virtually no water retention.

ETRUSCO
UNICO
OFFICIAL BALL OF THE FIFA WORLD CUP 1990
adidas

1948
FA Cup final ball with laces. During the previous two finals the ball had burst due to the inferior quality leather that was used shortly after the Second World War.

1063
A pennant presented to Manchester United in a friendly played at Old Trafford. It is customary for teams to exchange souvenirs before international matches.

1961
This cap was won by Dennis Viollet, in a 4–1 victory.

1930
FA Cup winner's medal, won by Arsenal's Jack Lambert in the 2–0 defeat of Huddersfield Town.

1913
One of the seven England caps awarded to Manchester United's George Wall. This earlier cap is a different color and lacks the embroidery and tassel.

1958
Although the white ball had come into official use in 1951, the brown ball continued to dominate for another 20 years. The lacing had now been replaced by stitched panels, saving dedicated headers of the ball too many headaches.

1931
Championship winners' medal awarded to Arsenal forward Jack Lambert. Players no longer have to appear in a specific number of games to win one.

SOCCER CULTURE

Soccer supporters are as much a part of soccer as the players themselves. Without them, there would be no professional game. It would cease to exist. Soccer needs its supporters in order to survive.

Despite the money professional soccer clubs now make from television coverage, corporate hospitality, merchandising and advertising, their single biggest revenue is still generated by fans flooding through the turnstiles.

From the very beginnings of the formal sport, way back in the nineteenth century, people have watched soccer. Over the years, the increase in that vicarious interest has made it the biggest spectator sport in the world. Supporters come in all shapes and sizes, from all walks of life, united in their love for the game — a common bond between nations whose social and political ideologies may be diametrically opposed.

This chapter examines the culture of soccer supporters and considers how the game has catered to them over the years. From the early days of standing on vast open terraces to the modern game, with executive boxes and satellite television, soccer has held a unique appeal.

Vast crowds now travel long distances to watch their teams in action and, belatedly, clubs are starting to appreciate their importance. In the United Kingdom, facilities are being improved in keeping with the demands of the twenty-first century, and watching is now becoming a more pleasant experience. This is because fans will no longer accept second-rate conditions while being asked to pay ever larger sums of money for the privilege of watching their team.

The authorities' realization of the supporters' value is leading to a far better relationship between the corridors of power and the stadium ramps. Only as that relationship improves can the game expect to continue to grow and prosper.

A WORKING-CLASS GAME

Soccer, for much of the century, was considered the game of the working classes. Once the game had been codified by the universities and public schools in the middle of the last century it was quickly popularized among the common man because it did not discriminate between the haves and have-nots. It was a recreational and spectator pursuit which was readily accessible to all, not merely the well-off. And it was that welcoming outlook which attracted so many people.

As the game grew in the early 1900s, men would spend all week working in blue-collar jobs, and then either play themselves or congregate on the terraces on a Saturday afternoon. The development of Wednesday half-day closing for shops

SAMBA SOCCER *Brazilian fans celebrate a victory during the 1986 World Cup*

1903
ROMÃO

LIVERPOOL F.C.

and offices led to the proliferation of many popular Wednesday league competitions for amateurs to contest and support at amateur levels up and down the country.

Soon Saturday on the terraces became the traditional meeting place where men could lose themselves for 90 minutes and escape the pressures of everyday life. Soccer was a man's game then, both on and off the field.

But what was it really like for the soccer supporter of those times? Not for those hardy souls the luxury of all-seater, covered stadiums with excellent bathroom and refreshment facilities. Times were hard and the conditions reflected those times. Huge wide open terraces were the norm and biting winds and rain often made watching decidedly unpleasant. There was none of the protection that fans today take for granted, but the public still turned up in their thousands as the game developed into the biggest spectator sport in the world.

For a few old pennies, a man could enjoy an afternoon's entertainment with his friends and they flocked to fields all over the country.

It is estimated that 250,000 people crammed into Wembley to try to watch the 1923 FA Cup final between Bolton and West Ham. Perhaps it was unfortunate for the FA, who had switched the game from Stamford Bridge when the construction of Wembley finished a year earlier than planned, that West Ham was one of the finalists. The authorities, used to the smaller crowds who had attended finals at Chelsea's home, clearly felt that Wembley's capacity would be sufficient. But the Hammers — as events would prove — were one of the biggest draws of those times and practically the whole of the East End wanted to see the game.

Huge attendances were not unusual in the years between the wars. On February 12, 1938, 75,031 people crammed into The Valley to watch Charlton take on Aston Villa in an FA Cup fifth-round match. Never again will British soccer see a crowd like that at a domestic game, other than for cup finals at Wembley. Indeed, when The Valley re-opened in December 1991 after being closed for nearly seven years, it was with a capacity of just 7,600 all-seated, which will eventually rise to around 16,000.

Not only were the stadiums different, so were the people. It was common to see fathers entering grounds with their young sons, a feature that is now, thankfully, beginning to return. But it was easy, then. Soccer stadiums were considered safe places, far removed from the ugly violence which beset the British and European game in the 1970s and 1980s. Fans supported their local teams and that was all. Fighting for its own sake would not have occurred to them and the sights and sounds of the stadiums were far removed from those we know today.

Community singing, brass bands and rattles were once the norm where now crude chanting reflects a change in society which has left soccer the poorer. Clubs had their "wags" on the terraces — jokers who were the forerunners of today's fanzine wits. The humor was sharp but not usually malicious, and visiting teams were treated sportingly.

Perhaps the best time to be a soccer fan was in the 1960s. Certainly those who grew up in those times speak fondly of the era. Britain as a whole was optimistic and the mood of the people reflected that. Nowhere was it more evident than on Merseyside. The area boasted The Beatles, the biggest thing ever to hit the music scene, and it also boasted Liverpool, about to be the biggest thing ever to hit domestic soccer. Liverpool Football Club was set for a period of unprecedented success and there was no better place to watch soccer than on the Kop.

Television pictures of the day have captured forever the unique atmosphere that was generated by those fans on that particular block of concrete. Tens of thousands of fans singing as one was truly a sight and sound to behold . . . and which the imposition of all-seat stadiums has denied the game's next generation.

THE KOP *A last glance at the Anfield terrace stronghold demolished in May 1994*

INVADERS *England fans earned a reputation for violence at home and abroad, but they were also a soft target for hooligans of other nations*

SOCCER TRIBES

Supporters may be the lifeblood of the game but their presence and involvement brings problems of their own. And those problems in recent years have threatened to tear the game apart.

As a competitive sport played between two teams, soccer will always generate rival opinions and loyalties. And rival opinions and loyalties can lead to trouble.

Soccer will always create that special kind of rivalry because it is a tribalistic game. Not in a malevolent or evil way, but by its very nature. Supporters of one particular team become their own tribe, with their own identity, and repel anyone who threatens it. When supporters travel away to watch their team, they are bonded together even more closely. It's as simple as that. There's no malice intended — or at least, not usually, not among the real fans.

Most of the time the banter between rival fans is good-natured and limited to exchanging chants from opposing ends of the stadium. Sadly though, particularly during the 1970s and 1980s, this rivalry occasionally spilled over into mindless violence. There was no excuse for some of the sickening behavior witnessed at grounds around the world, but it took a long time for the authorities to bring the problem under control.

The disease has been seen worldwide but English fans developed the worst hooligan reputation for the manner in which they exported their terrace and street violence. Partly this was because the culture of the traveling fan is much more widely accepted in a comparatively small country such as England than in, say, Spain, Italy or France.

When European soccer arrived with increasingly easy foreign travel facilities, so the disease traveled too and the problem has not been confined to English soccer followers alone. The 1988 European Championship finals in Germany, and those in Sweden in 1992, were marred by violent clashes between rival supporters. English fans were sometimes caught in the middle and there was a feeling that they had become victims of their own reputation. Certainly gangs among the Dutch and Germans took great delight in trying to prove that they had the "toughest fans in soccer."

Sadly the disease has sometimes led to tragedy. The 1985 European Cup final in Brussels will always be remembered as the Heysel Disaster, the night 39 Juventus fans lost their lives trying to escape a terrace charge by Liverpool supporters. No one who was present or saw those pictures will ever forget the terror that was wreaked on that fateful night in Belgium. No sporting event can be worth such a price and the scenes shocked and sickened the world.

As a result of that shameful night, English teams spent five years in European exile, first withdrawn and then banned from international club competition — as much to protect innocent citizens in continental towns and cities as punishment.

The situation provoked calls in Parliament for drastic measures of control. The Government threatened to ban the England national team and moves were made to introduce an ID card scheme which would make it easy to spot — and do something about — the hooligans. The proposal caused uproar among genuine fans who considered it an infringement of civil liberties.

The move eventually proved unworkable and was quietly forgotten though many clubs did undertake tighter control of membership and season ticket arrangements in an effort to combat hooliganism.

The result was the turning of a corner: the game is no longer blighted in such measure by the terrace thugs and, for the first time, soccer is beginning to think in terms of full-family entertainment — catering to female as well as male spectators — so more genuine fans may return to the game, safe in the knowledge that violence at stadiums has been restricted to isolated incidents.

Better control of the hooligan threat does not mean the problem has been eradicated, as the notorious Millwall hangers-on proved in 1994 with another outbreak.

PROGRAMS AND FANZINES

One of the biggest changes down the years has been in the development of club programs. In dim and distant days gone by, they consisted of nothing more than a single sheet of paper containing the team lineups and a few advertisements. At the turn of the century, they would sell at around one old penny. Nowadays, they are glossy brochures which retail at up to $2 just for a normal League game. As for the "brochures" which accompany major internationals and Cup finals, the cost goes spiraling up to $7. That was how much supporters of Chelsea and Manchester United were asked for the program at the 1994 FA Cup Final.

As programs became, more and more, vehicles for the soccer establishment's commercial, promotional face, so the arrival of the fanzine became inevitable. Fans had become increasingly disillusioned by the "everything in the garden is rosy" outlook of club programs and their growing demand for their own voice within the game led to a nationwide movement to secure outlets for independent comment. Generally witty and irreverent, the fanzines became a vehicle in which the fans could express their honest — frequently caustic — opinions of the people running "their" clubs and "their" game. The days of supporters accepting everything their clubs told them are long gone and fanzines have played an important role in the mobilization of terrace opinion on issues such as bond schemes and the redevelopment of stadia.

TERRACE SOUNDS

Viewing the old newsreel television pictures of supporters in the 1930s and 1940s, it is hard to associate them with today's modern game. Cloth caps and overcoats as far as the eye could see with wooden rattles providing the most distinguishable sounds of the games gone by. Wooden and heavy, they would be twirled around the air to make that distinctive, ratchet sound that was unique to soccer grounds. There are modern equivalents, such as the klaxon horn, but the daddy of all soccer instruments was that old wooden rattle.

Not that the boys and men who twirled them would recognize today's terrace sounds as a development of the same culture. The community singing, which now lives on only through the moving relic of "Abide With Me" before the FA Cup final, has been replaced by repetitive chants with no more stirring lyrics than "Here we go! Here we go! Here we go!"

Some clubs' fans have kept their link with past traditions alive. Bristol Rovers fans sing "Goodnight, Irene," Birmingham City supporters still persist with "Keep right on to the end of the road," but the street culture of the 1960s and 1970s led to many clubs replacing their traditional songs with pop-led creations, few of which lasted more than a season or two.

Of course, "You'll never walk alone," has surged and inspired several generations of players at Liverpool and served the community anew in sad circumstances in 1989, when a new recording by the Merseyside singer, Gerry Marsden, raised thousands of dollars for the Hillsborough disaster fund.

Many of the other modern terrace sounds, however, have done the game a disservice. "Industrial language" echoed through the traditional shouts of encouragement and criticism and the increasing influence of black players met volleys of racial abuse, often quite illogically aimed by fans whose own teams included black players.

In the early 1990s, as part of English soccer's drive to clean up its act and raise the class profile of the game, stringent attempts were launched to police bad language and eject the louts whose foul-mouth abuse hindered the drive to attract a family audience.

Rattles may have been banned but fans found other ways of making their presence noticed, such as with the giant inflatables (hammers at West Ham, fish at Grimsby, canaries at Norwich, etc.).

The message of the mid-1990s is that attending a match should be an enjoyment and that the traditional humor can still flourish.

SCARVES AND COLORS

Wearing your club colors is a trait which is, largely, unique to soccer. It's become a tradition to go to games wearing replica shirts, scarves and badges to let everyone know who you support. Cricket has lately tried to copy the trend with the "Sunday pajamas." The downside is the increasing criticism heaped upon clubs and the uniform industry, which has been accused of exploiting younger fans (not to mention their parents!) with the frequent changes of colors and styles.

ROLIGANS *Danish fans, so-called because of the derivation from a word meaning "peace"*

FACE IN THE CROWD *Courtesy of a giant screen, video technology brings the teams to the fans at Arsenal's Highbury stadium*

CHANGING FACE OF SOCCER

In the approach to the year 2000, professional soccer is changing radically. Money talks. Soccer is big business which needs to generate serious income and is targeting the "middle class" as a more lucrative audience.

That shift in emphasis has brought increasing demands on the game; people want better value for their money. Thus clubs are learning to listen to supporters' views and act on them — particularly now that many more leisure interests are competing for the public's support and cash.

For too long, soccer's rulers remained oblivious to the reasons why the public might prefer to spend its time and money watching other sports in a civilized atmosphere rather than huddling together on a cold terrace in the pouring rain. Clubs now realize that their facilities must be improved if they expect to continue to attract the crowds their budgets demand.

Europe has led the way — proof is to be seen in the superb stadiums in Italy, Germany and Spain — but it took the pressure of disaster and legislation before English soccer finally got the message.

After the Hillsborough Disaster in 1989, in which 95 Liverpool fans died at an FA Cup semifinal against Nottingham Forest, the Taylor Report deemed that all higher-division clubs must make their grounds all-seat.

This was obviously going to take time, as well as vast sums of money, but it was a development which was long overdue. Many fans felt, initially, that the removal of the terraces would take something away from the game and lead to a muted atmosphere. That has not happened. People have realized that it is just as easy to sing and chant sitting down as it is standing up. And watching soccer, certainly in the top divisions all around the world, has now become a more comfortable experience.

A significant by-product is that, with so many all-seat stadiums available, England could once more compete to host major international events — starting in 1996 with the European Championship finals which, if successful, could lead to an application to host the World Cup finals in 2006.

EXECUTIVE BOXES

Despite initial terrace resistance, executive boxes generate huge revenue to help keep prices down elsewhere within stadiums. Perhaps the image of supporters in pin-stripe suits smoking cigars behind glass panels is alien to the soccer tradition, but soccer today is a branch of the entertainment industry and needs its high-income supporters. Corporate entertainment is a thriving business and companies are prepared to pay substantial sums of money to wine and dine potential clients at top sporting events.

INDOOR STADIUMS

When England played Germany in the Pontiac Silverdome near Detroit in the U.S. Cup in June 1992, it represented a revolutionary new move in world soccer. For the first time, a major international was being played on artificially-grown grass in an indoor stadium. With science and technology becoming more and more advanced in the cause of sport, the numbers of fully-covered stadiums will increase. If it is possible to recreate the same playing conditions as outdoors, then it must be a logical step forward. The indoor stadiums would mean no more games falling victim to extreme weather conditions, and no more tedious midfield battles played out on mud-bath fields in the middle of winter. So-called "plastic pitches" were tried, without conspicuous success, but the fully-covered stadium is something the elements cannot touch.

VIDEO SCREENS

For years, clubs have been seeking ways to encourage supporters to arrive early for matches and one solution is the "entertainment package." Pre-match entertainment, in various guises, has been tried by just about everybody, with varying degrees of success. What better way to keep fans happy before kickoff than by showing action on giant video screens? Arsenal was the first club in Britain to get in on the act and their huge screen has been a popular addition to the redeveloped Highbury. They also managed to obtain permission to show replays of match incidents, an option which had been taken up successfully in Germany, Spain and Italy over the preceding years.

FAMILY AUDIENCES

Clubs are now beginning to cater to the whole family on matchdays. With ideas ranging from family stands to the introduction of nurseries, the English game is doing its best to appeal to a brand new audience. Clubs have realized — not before time — that if a father can sit with his wife and son or daughter in an area just for them, then he is more likely to take them along.

Family stands boast a two-fold attraction: they offer reduced admission prices compared with other areas of the ground, and they are safe places from where to watch. The youngsters who now take their place in those stands are the fans of tomorrow. Clubs should do everything possible to keep them.

COMMITMENT *Brazilian fans bringing colorful support — literally — to their cause*

SAMBA SOCCER

Pele once described soccer as "the beautiful game." And that sums up Samba Soccer. The Brazilians are the best exponents of it, both on the pitch and off it. The fans who play their part in Samba Soccer certainly know how to enjoy themselves.

Whether their team is winning or losing, you can rely on the Brazilians to give you a show. The Samba beat of the lone drummer is always heard from the terraces, where the fans treat the event as a carnival. Brightly colored clothing and frantic dance routines are all part of the culture of Samba Soccer.

That culture has been adapted by the rest of the world as fans seek to reap maximum enjoyment from sporting events. A world away from the snarling and intimidating attitude of the hooligans, it's a practice which should be encouraged. Thus Spain's national team was accompanied all over the world in the 1980s and 1990s by the familiar figure of the drummer known only as Manolo; thus Holland's total soccer was played out to the vibrant, strident tones of a brass band; and the medium of television allowed fans of different countries to swap their favorite tune chants.

The Danish fans added to the fun not only with their enthusiasm for their nation's cause but by introducing the practice of face-painting. Now the sight is commonplace at football grounds around the world, even in the exciting new J–League in Japan.

It seems that everyone, from the youngest fan to the oldest, has been caught up in the craze of decorating themselves in the colors of club and country. The World Cup and European Championship have now become a pageant of facial color as thousands of fans take their places proudly colored in their country's flag for the whole world to see. Some have even gone as far as to dye their hair in the appropriate colors in order to demonstrate their allegiance.

"Soccer watching" around the world can be very different to watching in Britain. Even the English love of the game pales in comparison with the demonstrations of passion to be seen in, say, Italy.

In Italy, soccer is a religion. Everyone it seems is a supporter, right across the social and financial divides, and that has helped establish the Italian league championship as the world's No 1. Supporters of the top Italian clubs have the best of everything. The stadiums are magnificent and so are the facilities. So, too, are the prices. That is why the Italian clubs compete regularly to sign the game's greatest players: they learned long ago that their passionate fans demand value for money. The fact that Italy has, for years, boasted the highest average top division attendances in the world — around 30,000-plus on average — proves that such a philosophy works.

SCANDALS & DISASTERS

Soccer has always had its seamy side and its tragic side. With so much money involved there was bound to be financial crookedness, and with such large and passionate crowds there were bound to be disasters.

SOCCER BABYLON

Ever since professionalism transformed an English private school pastime towards the end of the last century, the game's underworld has been hard at work refining its activities. For years, the little tax-free extras or inducements took the form of "boot money" — a few notes left surreptitiously in a player's boot — but in the era of the multi-million pound transfer, corruption, feeding on ambition and greed, has embroiled leading chairmen, players and referees, and the new breed of shadowy middlemen, the agents, have devised ever more sophisticated ways of keeping a cut for themselves and their clients, even to the extent of using off-shore tax havens.

In 1993 alone European champions Marseille, Italian giants Torino, and leading English club Tottenham Hotspur were shown to have been entangled in the seamy side of the game. At the same time, the growing curse of drug-taking has reduced Diego Maradona, one of the greatest players the game has ever seen, to a pathetic figure in the twilight of his career.

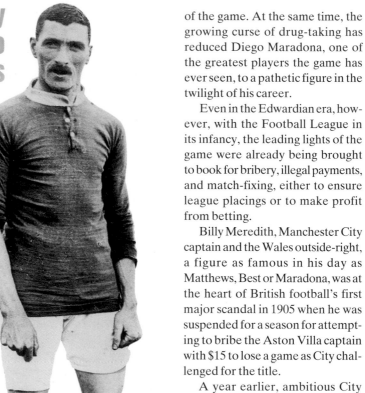

BILLY MEREDITH *Banned for a season for an attempted bribe*

Even in the Edwardian era, however, with the Football League in its infancy, the leading lights of the game were already being brought to book for bribery, illegal payments, and match-fixing, either to ensure league placings or to make profit from betting.

Billy Meredith, Manchester City captain and the Wales outside-right, a figure as famous in his day as Matthews, Best or Maradona, was at the heart of British football's first major scandal in 1905 when he was suspended for a season for attempting to bribe the Aston Villa captain with $15 to lose a game as City challenged for the title.

A year earlier, ambitious City had been found guilty of illegal payments to players, but the Meredith case eventually proved catastrophic for the club when he fell out with his employers and informed the FA of widespread financial corruption in the club's affairs. In 1906, seventeen current or former City players were fined, suspended for a year and forbidden to play for the club again

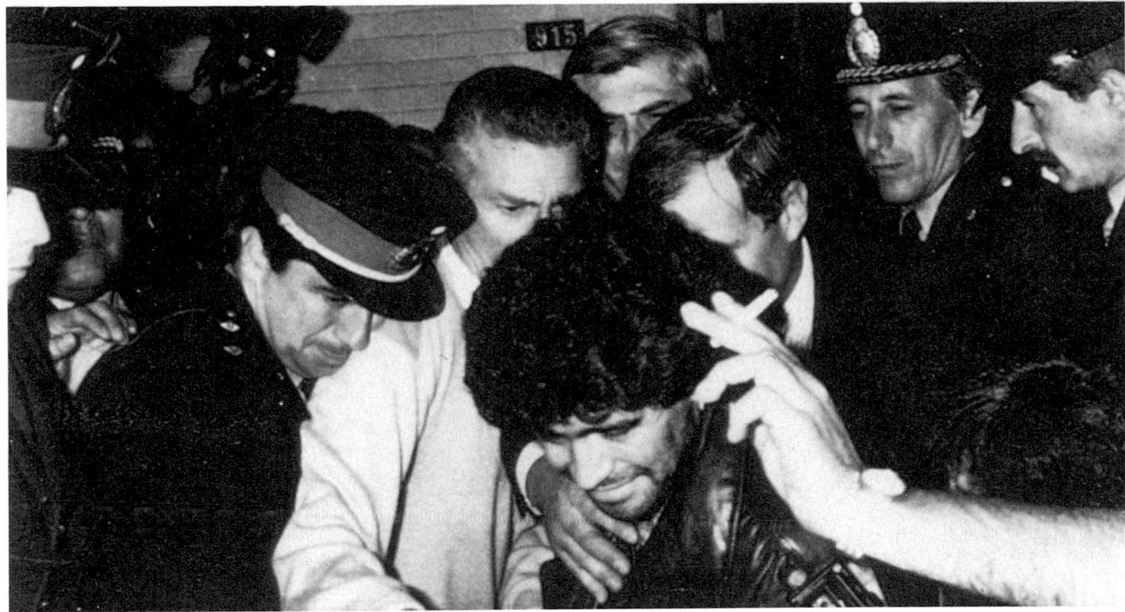

MARADONA *His soccer was sublime but drugs were his downfall and he was arrested for possession in Argentina*

because they had accepted illegal payments.

The whole issue of these payments stemmed from the attempt by the English football authorities to impose limits on salaries and signing-on fees. In Meredith's day salaries were $6, and the maximum salary rising to $30, survived until 1961. Within months of its abolition, Fulham was paying England international Johnny Haynes $150 per week. Incredibly, the $15 signing-on fee was abolished in Britain only in 1958, a year after John Charles is reputed to have received $15,000 for joining Juventus.

The system was abused by the majority for years, involving even such famous names as Herbert Chapman, coach of Leeds City when they were thrown out of the League in 1919, and Stanley Matthews, manager of Port Vale when they were expelled, then re-elected in the 1960s. The clubs used all types of ruses to cover payments. Sunderland, the first club to take the FA to law and win, included expenditure of $4,500 in their annual accounts for straw — enough to protect their Roker Park field for 25 seasons!

Meredith exposed the hypocrisy which still survives when he said: "Clubs are not punished for breaking the laws. They are punished for being found out." But the end of the maximum salary did not bring an end to under-the-counter payments in England, which are still widespread and have become an integral part of the transfer system.

Today it is not just the soccer mandarins clubs and officials have to fear, but an increasingly vigilant taxman. The English can of worms was opened when Swindon Town was raided in 1990 and manager Lou Macari, the former Scotland and Manchester United player, and chairman Brian Hillier were arrested. The inquiry uncovered illegal payments, petty cash being paid to club officials as perks, and the understating of gate receipts. Macari was acquitted, Hillier jailed for tax fraud.

But the tip of an English iceberg pales into insignificance beside the bribery and match-fixing scandals affecting Italy and France, as the European club competitions have grown in stature since the 1950s and begun to attract television deals capable of financing some Third World countries. Italy, a country where corruption in public life is little short of endemic, has suffered post-war match-fixing and bribery scandals involving Lazio, Milan, Roma and now Torino, while France's league boom in the 1980s led to problems with the taxman over illegal payments. In 1993 French football was rocked to the core when their first European champions, Marseille, were accused of trying to buy a match to insure they retained the championship and with it the automatic passport to more riches in the European Cup.

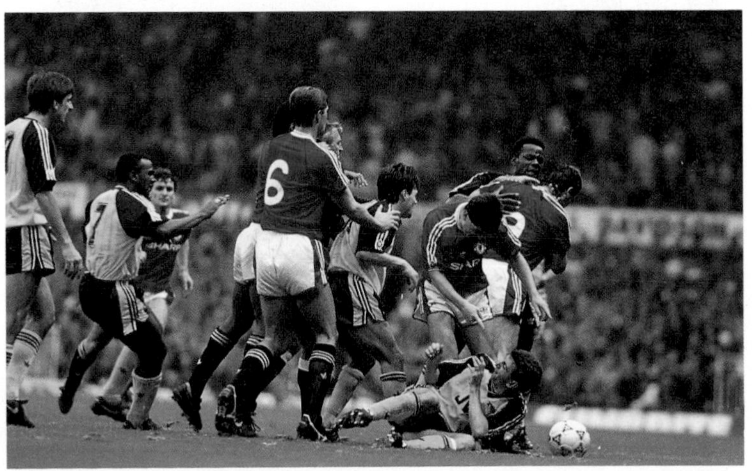

FLASHPOINT *Arsenal and Manchester United were heavily penalized for this brawl*

CASH AND CORRUPTION

1891 Maximum $15 signing-on fee introduced.

1900 Maximum wage of $6 introduced in England, but not Scotland.

1900 Burnley goalkeeper Jack Hillman banned for one year for trying to bribe Nottingham Forest to lose. It was not a roaring success. Forest won 4–0, Burnley was relegated!

1904 Second Division Glossop fined $375 for wholesale mismanagement and deception. Four directors suspended for three seasons, secretary censured, six players suspended for three months.

1904 Sunderland fined $375 and directors and secretary suspended for one to three seasons for illegal payments.

1904 Manchester City found to have broken transfer rules involving Glossop players Irvine Thornley and Frank Norgrove. Clubs fined $375, Hyde Road stadium shut for two games, five directors suspended and Thornley banned for a season.

1905 Billy Meredith, Manchester City's captain and Welsh international outside-right, banned for a season after attempting to bribe Aston Villa captain Alec Leake towards end of 1904–05 season when City was making a challenge for the championship.

1905 Middlesbrough, who had just paid the first $1,500 transfer fee for Alf Common from Sunderland (three times the previous record), fined $375, 11 of 12 directors suspended until 1908 for illegal payments.

1906 Seventeen current and former Manchester City players fined a total of $1,350, suspended for six months and banned from playing for the club again after accepting illegal payments. Chairman W. Forrest and manager Tom Maley banned sine die, directors suspended. Players later auctioned by League for $4,000.

1909 George Parsonage of Fulham banned for life after requesting $75 signing-on fee from Chesterfield.

1911 Middlesbrough's respected manager Andy Walker and chairman Thomas Gibson Poole, a prospective MP, banned from soccer

for trying to fix home game against local rivals Sunderland. Boro won 1–0.
1919 An example is made. Leeds City expelled from League for making illegal payments.
1924 John Browning, former Scotland player, and Archibald Kyle of Rangers, Blackburn and Airdrie, given 60 days' hard labor for offering Bo'Ness players $45 to fix Second Division match with Lochgelly.
1932 Former Montrose captain Gavin Hamilton given 60 days' jail for offering $60-$75 to Montrose player David Mooney to fix home match against Edinburgh City.
1957 Sunderland fined record $7,500 by Football League for illegal payments to players.
1958 Leyton Orient fined $3,000 for irregularities in accounts.
1965 Everton alleged to have been involved in match-fixing during their 1962–63 championship. No proof.
1965 England's most sensational match-fixing scandal. Ten League professionals found guilty at Nottingham Assizes of match-fixing. Jimmy Gauld, an inside-forward for Charlton, Everton, Plymouth, Swindon and Mansfield between 1955 and 1960, was jailed for four years, the others for terms between four and 15 months. After years of rumors, Gauld had told all for $10,500. Although Gauld was the ringleader, the three most celebrated players among the ten were England players Peter Swan (Sheffield Wednesday) and Tony Kay (Everton, but previously with Wednesday) and their Sheffield Wednesday colleague David Layne.
1965 Kay, Layne and Swan banned from soccer for life, although after many campaigns the bans were lifted in 1972.
1967 Peterborough United fined $750 and demoted from Third to Fourth Division for illegal payments.
1967 Millwall fined $1,500 for attack on referee by spectators at The Den.
1968 Port Vale fined $6,000 and expelled from League for illegal payments, but re-elected for following season.
1969 Manchester United fined $10,500 for certain administrative irregularities.
1970 Derby fined $15,000 and barred from Fairs Cup for a year for administrative irregularities.
1971 Officials of Arminia Bielefeld found guilty of putting up $135,000 to fix four West German League games.
1973 Wolverhampton Wanderers player Bernard Shaw alleged he was approached to sell a championship deciding game against Leeds in 1972.
1974 The Solti-Lobo Case. Juventus accused of using a go-between, Deszo Solti, to try to bribe Portuguese referee Francisco Marques Lobo, the official for their European Cup semifinal against Derby in 1973.
1974 Italian players accused by Polish opponents of offering money to them on the field to lose a World Cup match in Stuttgart. Italy, needing a draw to stay in the finals, is beaten 2–1.
1978 Millwall fined $2,250 and have their stadium closed for two weeks after crowd trouble during FA Cup tie against Ipswich. Millwall's notorious fans had also caused The Den to be closed in 1934, 1947 and 1950.
1978 Fulham fined $22,500 for illegal payments.
1978 Scotland's top referee John Gordon and linesmen Rollo Kyle and David McCartney suspended by Scottish FA after admitting they accepted presents worth $1,500 from Milan before a UEFA Cup match with Levski Spartak. Milan, fined $12,000 by UEFA, had drawn 1–1 in Bulgaria and won 3–0 at home.
1980 The world's highest paid player, Italian striker Paolo Rossi,is one of more than 30 banned for their part in widespread Italian match-fixing on behalf of an illegal betting ring. Milan and Lazio relegated. Rossi's ban ended just in time for him to lead Italy to their 1982 World Cup victory in Spain.
1983 Derby fined $15,000 by the Football League for poaching coach Roy McFarland from Bradford City.
1983 Tottenham fined $12,000 for illegal payments to Argentine World Cup stars Osvaldo Ardiles and Ricky Villa.
1985 Celtic fined $25,500 by UEFA for crowd trouble at a European Cup-winners' Cup replay against

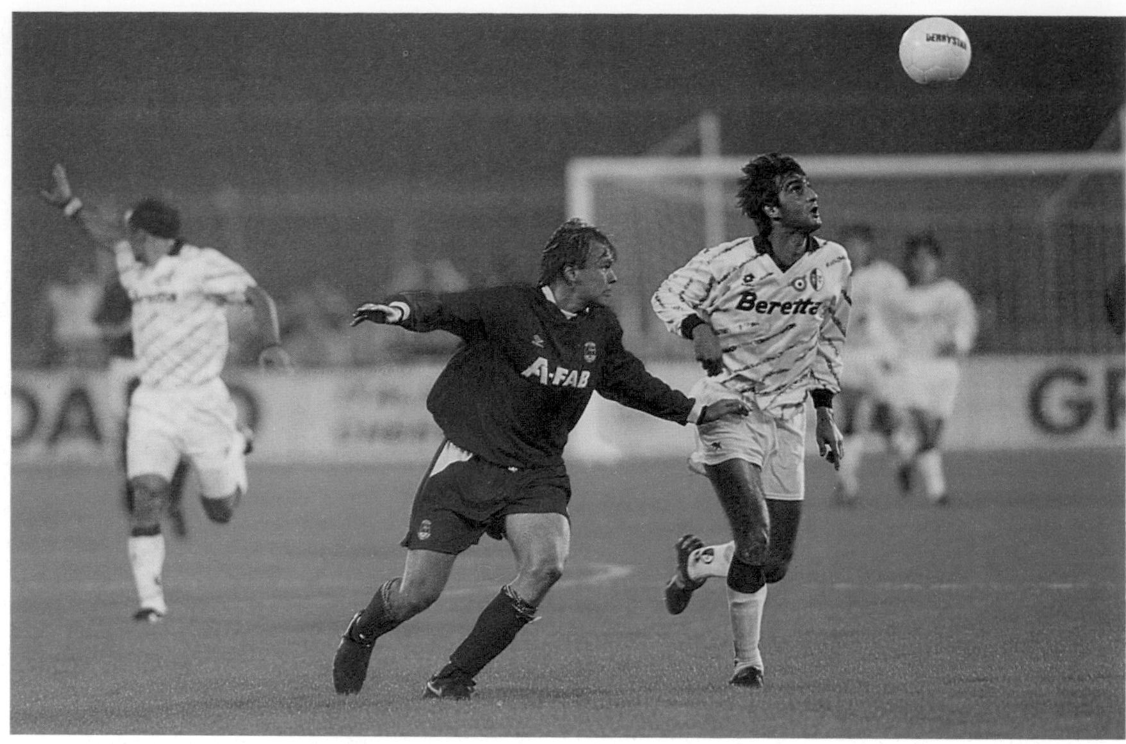

CLOUD OVER TORINO *A bribery scandal erupted over Torino's (in white vs. Aberdeen) 1991–92 UEFA Cup campaign*

FALLEN IDOLS *Peter Swan (left) and Tony Kay were jailed for match-fixing*

Rapid Vienna at Old Trafford.

1986 UEFA bars Roma from their competitions for a season and president Dino Viola from UEFA activities for four years after he tried to bribe a European Cup referee in a semi-final game against Dundee United in 1982. Roma won 3–0, and 3–2 on aggregate, before losing to Liverpool in the Final.

1988 Peterborough fined $3,750 for transfer irregularity.

1988 Hungarian full-back Sandor Sallai and former national team coach Kalman Meszoly are among more than 40 players and officials arrested in match-fixing investigation.

1988 Chelsea fined record $112,500 by FA for serious crowd trouble in play-off against Middlesbrough.

1989 Nottingham Forest manager, Brian Clough, fined $7,500 by FA and banned from sidelines for a season for striking a spectator at League Cup tie against QPR.

1989 Wimbledon fined $15,000 for making unauthorized loans to their players.

1989 Bradford City fined $15,000 for poaching coach Terry Yorath from Swansea.

1990 Swindon Town fined $11,000 by FA, former coach Lou Macari $1,500 and censured, chairman Brian Hillier suspended from soccer for three years after breaching rules by betting on Newcastle vs. Swindon FA Cup tie in January 1988.

1990 Swindon, having been promoted to Division One via play-offs, demoted to Division Three (Division Two on appeal), for irregular payments to players over four years.

1990 FA deducts two points from Arsenal, one from Manchester United and fine both clubs $75,000 after players involved in mass brawl.

1991 League fines Chelsea record $157,000 for illegal payments to three players. A company linked to Chelsea was found to have paid $150,000 over market price for the Scottish home of England defender Graham Roberts, who signed from Rangers.

1991 Diego Maradona arrested in Argentina for possession of drugs. He had just left Italy where he was banned from playing for 15 months after taking cocaine before a Napoli match. He is also given a 14-month suspended sentence by a Naples court for possessing cocaine.

1992 FA fines Vinnie Jones of Wimbledon $30,000 — a record for an individual — for bringing game into disrepute by narrating the Soccer Hard Men video.

1993 League newcomers Barnet fined $37,000 for making irregular payments and warned that any further indiscretion could cost them their League status.

1993 Jean-Jacques Eydelie, Marseille midfielder, arrested and accused of trying to bribe three Valenciennes players to lose league match, six days before the French champions beat Milan to win the European Cup. General coach Jean-Pierre Bernes also charged. An envelope containing $45,000 is dug up in the garden of the mother-in-law of Valenciennes player Christophe Robert.

1993: In the High Court battle over Tottenham Hotspur between Terry Venables and Alan Sugar, evidence is offered suggesting that some coaches accept illegal cash payments as part of transfer deals.

1993 UEFA bars Marseille from defending the European Cup over the Valenciennes bribery scandal.

1994 Four directors and five referees accused by federal police of fraud for their alleged involvement in Brazilian match-fixing. The directors included Eduardo Viana, president of the Rio de Janeiro federation, and Eurico Miranda, a director of leading club Vasco da Gama. Former referee Reginaldo Mathias claims match-fixing had been common since 1985.

1994 Bernard Tapie is charged with corruption and ordered to quit as president of Marseille.

1994 Torino is placed under investigation by the Italian fraud squad after being accused of providing prostitutes for match officials in their attempt to win the 1992 UEFA Cup. The club are also alleged to have siphoned off under-the-counter cash from transfers, including $698,000 for the "phantom transfer" of Alessandro Palestro, son of a club secretary and not registered with the club but studying at college.

1994 Maradona expelled after the second round of the World Cup finals for failing a random drug test.

SOCCER DISASTERS

DISASTER AT IBROX *25 people died at the Scotland vs. England international in 1902*

Drama and excitement have attracted huge crowds to soccer stadiums around the world, just as ambition and the explosion of international competition have kept the world's airlines busy with teams crisscrossing the oceans and continents. Sadly, but inevitably, the game could not avoid the accompanying disasters which turned sporting events into national and international tragedies. From the Superga air disaster of 1949 to the Zambian air crash in 1993, from the first Ibrox Park disaster in 1902 to the Corsica tragedy more than 90 years later... sad shadows have been cast over the game.

STADIUM DISASTERS AND PLANE CRASHES

1902 Scotland plays out a 1–1 draw with England, largely unaware that 25 fans have been killed and hundreds more injured after wooden planking, 40 feet above the ground, collapses in Ibrox Park's new 20,000-capacity West Stand.

1946 The Burnden Park gates are closed on 65,000 fans before Bolton meet Stoke in a sixth round FA Cup tie, but another 20,000 are milling

1931

JOHN THOMPSON

Tragedy struck in the Old Firm derby between Rangers and Celtic on September 5, 1931 when Celtic's 23-year-old goalkeeper John Thomson dove at the feet of Rangers' Sam English.

Thomson, who had joined Celtic as a 17-year-old and had already established himself in the Scotland team, was renowned for his dashes off the line to thwart opposing forwards. This time, Thomson did not get up, having fractured his skull. He died five hours later in the local hospital.

Such was his popularity that 30,000 mourners saw his coffin off at Glasgow's Queen Street Station, and 3,000 attended his funeral.

around outside. Many force their way in and two barriers collapse under sheer weight of numbers. Thirty-three die from crush injuries and more than 500 are injured. The match is eventually completed, scoreless and without a halftime, Bolton winning 2–0 over the two legs.

1949 The cream of Italian soccer is wiped out when the plane carrying the Torino team back from a match in Portugal crashes into a hillside at Superga just outside Turin. Eighteen players die, including the bulk of Italy's team led by captain Valentino Mazzola. Journalists, officials and English coach Leslie Lievesley raise the death toll to 31. Torino had won four successive League titles and was four points ahead at the top on the day of the crash. The Torino youth team completes the season and receives the championship trophy.

1958 Manchester United's plane crashes on take-off at snowy Munich airport, killing eight of the famous Busby Babes, three club officials and eight journalists. United is returning from a 3–3 draw with Red Star Belgrade which had earned them a place in the European Cup semi-finals.

BUSBY'S TRAGIC BABES *Manchester United's team in 1957; in February 1958 seven of this team perished at Munich*

1961 A plane crashes into the Las Lastimas mountain, killing 24 members of the Green Cross team on their way from Santiago to Osorno for the Chile Cup play-offs.

1962 In Libreville, Gabon, an international between Congo-Brazzaville and Gabon is halted when a landslide hits the stadium. Nine spectators die and 30 are injured.

1964 The world's worst soccer disaster. In Lima, Peru, 318 people die and another 500 are injured during rioting sparked by a last-minute Peruvian goal being disallowed in an Olympic match against Argentina. The goal would have sent Peru to the Tokyo Games. Martial law was in force for 30 days after the game.

1967 Another disallowed goal sparks rioting during a Turkish championship game, and 41 people die with a further 600 injured, many being trampled as they flee the stadium.

Jun 23, 1968 In Buenos Aires at the Monumental Stadium, venue ten years later for the World Cup Final, 74 people die and another 113 are injured when Boca Juniors supporters drop lighted torches on their arch rivals from River Plate and panic ensues.

1969 Nineteen players and officials of The Strongest, Bolivia's most popular team, die when their plane crashes in the Andes, 72 miles from their destination La Paz.

1969 El Salvador and Honduras go to war over a World Cup tie played in Mexico and won 3–2 by the Salvadorians. Hundreds of Hondurans launch attacks on Salvadorians living in their country, causing deaths, and the Salvadorian govern-ment retaliates with an armed attack lasting a week. The conflict is stopped eventually by the intervention of the Organization of American States.

1971 Sixty-six people die and 150 are injured when they tumble down a stairway while leaving a Rangers vs. Celtic match. A last-minute Rangers equalizer has led to departing fans

1934 HERBERT CHAPMAN

If ever a man died in harness, it was the great Arsenal coach Herbert Chapman. On New Year's Day, 1934, Arsenal was dominating English soccer and the envy of the world. They had won the League twice and the Cup once in the previous four seasons under the innovative and tactically astute Chapman, and was top of the league again.

Chapman caught a chill watching a game at Bury, but still decided to go and watch Arsenal's next opponents Sheffield Wednesday the following day. Against doctor's advice, he also traveled to Guildford to see Arsenal's reserves. When he eventually took to his bed it was too late, pneumonia had set in, and he died at 3 a.m. on Saturday, January 6.

Stunned Arsenal fans learned the news from newspaper billboards on their way to Highbury for the game against Wednesday.

1953 DEREK DOOLEY

Derek Dooley was 23 and on the brink of a great career as a prolific goalscorer with Sheffield Wednesday. The big center-forward had earned a reputation for scoring from apparently impossible situations, with 46 goals in 30 games as Wednesday won promotion, and 16 in 29 First Division games up to St Valentine's Day, 1953.

On that day, he broke his right leg challenging the Preston goalkeeper for a 50–50 ball. A few days later, when he was about to be discharged from hospital, it was discovered that gangrene had set in and there was no alternative but to have it amputated.

Dooley stayed in soccer, eventually coaching Wednesday and being fired by them, and later joining rivals Sheffield United as commercial manager.

attempting to get back in the ground, with horrific results.

1979 Seventeen players of Pakhtakor Tashkent of the Soviet Union are killed in a plane crash on their way to a league match.

1981 Eighteen fans die and a further 45 are injured when a wall collapses during a match between Deportes Tolima and Deportivo Cali in Ibague, Colombia.

1982 In Cali, Colombia, drunken youths urinate from the upper deck of the Pascual Geurrero stadium, causing a stampede in which 22 die and more than 100 are injured.

1982 More than 300 Soviet fans die at a UEFA Cup match between Spartak Moscow and Haarlem of Holland. As revealed seven years later by the authorities, a last-minute Spartak goal sent departing fans surging back into the Lenin Stadium, causing a horrific crush.

1985 A day of celebration turns to tragedy. Fifty-six people are burned to death and more than 200 taken to the hospital when Bradford City's 77-year-old wooden main stand is engulfed by flames within five minutes just before half-time in the last match of the season against Lincoln City. Before the game City had been presented with the Third Division championship.

1985 Thirty-nine people die and more than 400 are injured when a wall collapses during rioting started by English fans an hour before the European Cup Final between Liverpool and Juventus in the the Heysel Stadium, Brussels. Live TV pictures relay the tragedy around the world.

STEPS TO DISASTER *66 died at Ibrox Park when fans tried to return to the terraces*

The game is eventually played, Juventus winning 1–0, but as a result English club teams are banned from European competition.

1987 Forty-three players, officials' wives and supporters of Alianza Lima die while returning from a league game, their plane crashing into the sea six miles north of the Peruvian capital.

1988 A stand collapses just before half-time at an international between Libya and Malta in Tripoli, causing 30 deaths and many injuries. A man runs amok brandishing a gun among the 65,000 crowd, causing a stampede for the exits, and the weight of numbers breaks a retaining wall.

1988 Between 70 and 100 fans die in Katmandu when a violent hailstorm causes a stampede among the 25,000 fans at a game between Janakpur of Nepal and Mukti Jodha of Bangladesh.

1989 In Britain's worst sports disaster, 95 Liverpool supporters are crushed to death and almost 200 injured at Hillsborough, Sheffield, before an FA Cup semifinal against Nottingham Forest. Crowds anxious to see the start surge into the Leppings Lane End and pin fans against the security fences designed to keep people off the pitch. The tragedy leads to the dismantling of security fences and to requirements for all-seater stadiums.

1989 Twelve people in Lagos, Nigeria, are trampled to death, and a player dies on the field during a World Cup qualifier between Nigeria and Angola. Nigerian winger Sam Okwaraji collapses with exhaustion in the 82nd minute and cannot be revived.

1991 Forty people are killed and more than 50 injured in South Africa's worst sports disaster at a match in the gold mining town of Orkney, 80 miles from Johannesburg. Most of the victims are trampled as they try to escape fighting between fans, following the referee's decision to allow Kaizer Chiefs a disputed goal against arch rivals Orlando Pirates.

1982 Disaster strikes before a French Cup semi-final in the Corsican town of Bastia, whose team are due to play Marseille. Fifteen spectators die and 1,300 are injured when a temporary metal stand collapses. The whole competition is canceled by the authorities at the insistence of the clubs.

1993 Eighteen members of the Zambian national team are killed when their plane crashes into the sea off Gabon after a refueling stop on their way to a World Cup qualifying tie against Senegal. There were no survivors.

1964 JOHN WHITE

John White, the Scotland and Spurs player who, with Danny Blanchflower, was at the heart of the London club's great "double" side in 1961, was struck by lightning and killed while golfing on July 21, 1964.

The 27-year-old inside-forward had just driven off the first tee at Crews Hill club in Enfield when it started raining. He took shelter under a line of oak trees, and was seen sitting under one of them by other golfers running for the clubhouse. There was a single flash of lightning and White's body was found later by groundskeepers. White was a frail-looking figure on the field and, although best known for his passing, possessed a fierce shot. He had earned the nickname "The Ghost of White Hart Lane" for his ability to drift into dangerous positions.

1985 JOCK STEIN

Moments after watching his Scotland side snatch a late equalizer against Wales in a World Cup qualifier at Ninian Park in September, 1985, manager Jock Stein collapsed and died. He was 62.

Stein made his name as a player with Celtic, helping them win the league and cup double in 1954 before injury cut short his career a year later. He went into coaching.

Stein was a giant of British soccer and the most successful club manager. After he joined Celtic in 1965, they won the Scottish League 10 times, the Cup seven times and League Cup six. They competed in Europe for nine seasons and in 1967 became the first British club to win the European Cup, beating Internazionale 2–1 in Lisbon. He became Scottish coach in 1978.

SOCCER IN AMERICA

Most of the world looks upon the United States as a soccer Johnny-come-lately. In truth, the game has a long and storied American history. The sport dates back to colonial times; it includes an upset or two on the international scene – and its growth has now been spurred by the very successful 1994 World Cup.

THE EARLY YEARS

Contrary to the beliefs of much of the world – Americans included – soccer did not suddenly land in the U.S. the day the 1994 World Cup began. Nor did it arrive 19 years earlier, when Pele leaped out of retirement to join the New York Cosmos and jolt the North American Soccer League into the big time. In fact, soccer's history in the United States is at least as old as the rest of the planet.

Legend has it that the Pilgrims who landed at Plymouth Rock in Massachusetts found Native Americans playing a ball-and-goal game remarkably similar to what later evolved into soccer. By 1820 many American universities were playing "football," though – as in England – they lacked a standardized set of rules. The first organized soccer club in the United States was formed in 1862. The Oneidas were undefeated from 1862–65, a feat commemorated by a plaque in Boston Common, where they played their home matches.

American football traces its origins to 1869, though in fact that first game (between two college teams) had much more in common with soccer and rugby than with gridiron. But as American football branched off and developed in one form during the latter part of the nineteenth century, soccer evolved too. Spurred by thousands of European immigrants, the game flourished in Eastern, Midwestern and Pacific Coast cities. As was happening throughout the industrial world, working-class communities based on mills, factories or mines supported soccer as an inexpensive, enjoyable and much-needed form of recreation.

The American Football Association was organized in 1884 in Newark, N.J., as a means of uniting the many soccer clubs springing up throughout the Eastern U.S. Twenty years later FIFA was formed; but the U.S. Football Association (USFA) was not granted full membership until 10 years after that. In 1916 an "All-American" team traveled to Norway and Sweden; the Americans' first European foray ended with a record of 3 wins, 2 losses and 1 tie.

Organized soccer boomed in the carefree 1920s. Virtually every East Coast city boasted thriving ethnic leagues filled with players from England, Scotland, Germany, Poland, Italy and points beyond; as early as 1921 the top teams united in an American Professional Soccer League (APSL). That league played continuously, in various shapes and forms and with differing degrees of success, through 1984. The U.S. even organized the world's first indoor soccer league with 11-man teams; they played on a full-sized field during the winter at a Boston armory.

The First World Cup

But it was not until 1930 that the Americans made their first mark in the international soccer arena. That year, the U.S. was one of 13 nations to compete in the first FIFA World Cup competition in Uruguay. Ironically, though Britain's row with FIFA made them ineligible for the games, six American players were ex-English professionals who had emigrated to the States in search of better jobs. The Americans were nicknamed "the shot putters" by the French, because of their (relatively) enormous size, but they proved to be far more than large men relying solely on physique to power them through.

Seeded in Group 4, the U.S. won their first two matches handily, by 3–0 scores over Belgium and Paraguay. That qualified them for the semifinals, and a sudden introduction to new levels of both skill and physical prowess. Argentina struck for five second-half goals en route to a 6–1 pasting, and the U.S. had its first rude World Cup awakening.

Fast forward to 1950. The intervening two decades had been the most eventful in the nation's history – a cataclysmic Depression, followed by an equally catastrophic world war – and, of necessity, soccer's growth was slowed.

FLYING THE FLAG *The U.S. team heads onto the field prior to their dismal showing in the 1934 World Cup*

The major event of the 1930s and 1940s was the formation, in 1941, of the National Soccer Coaches Association of America (NSCAA) by 10 coaches. The organization became, by the end of the century, one of the most powerful in American soccer; 10,000 members strong, it was emblematic of the influential role high schools and colleges play in the sport.

But all that scholastic development lay ahead when the 1950 World Cup – the first in 12 years – got underway in Brazil. For the first time the competition included England; its long, petty dispute with FIFA was finally over, and the English were favorites to capture the first post-war championship.

The Americans kindled memories of 1930 in their first match, grabbing a 1–0 lead against Spain. They held it until 10 minutes from time, finally falling 3–1. But that was just a preview of things to come.

England Shocked

Four days later, on June 29, 1950, before 10,000 fans gathered under a cloudy sky in the dusty, bumpy Belo Horizonte stadium, came a shot that was soon heard 'round the world. As in 1930, the U.S. fielded a hybrid side – captain Eddie McIlvenny was a Scot – and the Americans knew what they were up against. "The only question was how big (the English) were going to win," recalled U.S. star Harry Keough.

But goalkeeper Frank Borghi (an undertaker in real life) kept the English out of the American net and – aided by two shots that beat him but caromed off the post – as the game wore on, the upstarts' confidence grew.

In the 37th minute the incredible happened: Joe Gaetjens – a native of Haiti – scored off what appeared to be a header. Debate still rages today whether Gaetjens was trying to shoot or if the ball simply struck his head, but it really doesn't matter. The goal counted, the Americans stood fast, and an hour later the lowly, ragtag upstarts had fashioned an incredible 1–0 upset over the World Cup favorites.

The news, transmitted by wire from South America, was so stunning that newspaper editors in England refused to believe it. One man simply amended it to read England 10, United States 1.

Though the editor was powerless to change the actual scoreline, the effect of the American win was less powerful than it might seem. The victory, so enormous in the rest of the world, was reported in tiny type in most U.S. newspapers – if it was mentioned at all. The Yanks went on to lose their next match, 5–2 to Chile, and were eliminated from further competition; it was to be their last

World Cup match for 40 years. Soccer failed to advance from its status as a sport played primarily in city parks on Sunday afternoons by recent immigrants.

Even poor Joe Gaetjens did not gain anything from his historic strike. In the 1960s he returned to his native Haiti, where it is believed he was murdered by the Tontons Macoutes.

The 1950s saw fitful efforts to advance the cause of soccer in the United States. College soccer grew in popularity, culminating in the first championship tournament in 1959 (won by St. Louis University, a team from the Midwestern city that was perhaps the only place where native-born Americans embraced the game as their own). A fledgling International Soccer League (ISL) was formed in 1960, under the sponsorship of the American Soccer League. ISL teams were actually top-class European and South American sides, such as Everton from the English league, which visited the U.S. to play American hosts.

Fans and – equally importantly – television showed a bit of interest (some crowds exceeded 20,000) in the ISL, but as the bandwagon began rolling it attracted, inevitably, too much attention. In 1965 three separate groups of businessmen attempted to start what each claimed would be the best pro soccer league. The result, of course, was cannibalism and chaos, and by 1967 the three leagues dwindled into one: the North American Soccer League (NASL).

For eight years the NASL – along with the smaller American Soccer League – puttered along. Games were played before small but appreciative crowds; press coverage was minimal, but everyone involved – owners, players and fans – loved soccer, and had fun. A ripple of excitement rolled through in 1973, when Kyle Rote Jr. – son of a famous American football player – became the first rookie and first American to win the NASL scoring title (10 goals, 10 assists), and a year later captured the first of three victories in a televised "Superstars" competition.

But that was nothing compared to the excitement that would erupt in the NASL in 1975.

PELE AND THE NASL

The New York Cosmos ended the 1974 season as they had their three previous North American Soccer League seasons: playing in front of tiny crowds in unattractive stadiums. Randalls Island, a decrepit spot underneath a busy bridge, held about 20,000 fans, but only 3,600 were showing up to watch a team whose "stars" bore names like Siggy Stritzl, Mordecai Shpigler and Joey Fink. The New York media – whose attention to a story could ignite an entire nation, or whose disinterest was akin to a pronouncement of death – cared not one whit about the Cosmos, the NASL or, for that matter, the entire sport of soccer.

All that changed in 1975. If Stritzl, Shpigler and Fink were not household names, Pele was. Though retired for a year, he remained the most famous athlete – perhaps the most famous human being, period – on the globe. He was the only soccer player most Americans had ever heard of. And suddenly he was coming to play in the United States, bringing to the last soccer frontier his brilliant skills, graceful elegance and joyful personality.

The bizarre turn of events actually began in 1969, when Pele was mentioned as the one man able to provide instant credibility for American soccer. Six years later Clive Toye, who had run the Cosmos since their inception, found himself pursuing Yugoslav national team player Dragan Dzajic. Told that the Yugoslavs wanted $1 million for their star, he said that if the Cosmos had that kind of money to spend, they'd go after Pele. This time it proved not to be mere idle speculation. The team indeed had that much money; they were owned by corporate giant Warner Communications. In fact, the company was looking to add yet another superstar to its roster of recognizable names, which ranged from rock stars and movie starlets to Bugs Bunny.

Pele Boosts the NASL

The Brazilian legend was flown by helicopter to Randalls Island, where he watched the Cosmos lose 1–0 to the Vancouver Whitecaps and was given a rousing ovation by the 7,331 fans. After intense negotiations that – finally – garnered the Cosmos headlines (in the sports pages, although it was Page One news in the rest of the world), 34-year-old Pele signed a three-year, $4.5 million contract.

The reality of the world's most famous athlete signing with one of the sport's least glamorous teams rocked New York as no other news could. His first press conference resembled the mob scene that was *de rigueur* in every other country; photographers scuffled while competing for the best camera angles. The Cosmos office, a cramped, nondescript suite in midtown Manhattan, was besieged by requests from people who had never before exhibited the slightest interest in soccer. Reporters demanded credentials; fans needed tickets; President Nixon

SHINING STAR *Pele brought his magic to America in 1975*

EVER POPULAR *Rodney Marsh hoists Tampa Bay's Soccer Bowl trophy*

wanted a visit at the White House. Best of all, CBS-TV hoped to televise Pele's first NASL game.

An exhibition match with the Dallas Tornado was hastily arranged. Randalls Island was filled beyond capacity; the heat that Sunday afternoon was searing, but the electricity in the air more than made up for any inconvenience. The 21,278 fans, and a viewing audience in the millions, knew they were watching history. The 2–2 result was meaningless – what could be more inconsequential than an exhibition game draw, even if the tying goal came on a spectacular header by Pele? – but the match transcended the final score. Soccer had finally arrived in America.

It continued to arrive throughout 1975. The mere name "Pele" guaranteed sellout crowds in Boston, Seattle and St. Louis; in Washington, D.C., 35,620 gathered to watch the same two teams that a year before had attracted one-tenth that number of fans. That was good news for soccer, good news for the NASL, and especially good news for the Cosmos, who earned half the gate receipts above the average of each opposing team. The richest team in the NASL – the only club that could afford to lure Pele out of retirement – was getting richer by the day.

Pele's arrival did not help the Cosmos' less-than-stellar play on the field, although his presence did lend a bit of poise to a group that had not previously been noted for passing or ball control. The team finished third in their division, with a 10–12 record (Tampa Bay copped the "Soccer Bowl" championship) – but that hardly mattered. They did exceptionally well at the gate, and in the off-season embarked on the first of their global tours. Fans as far away as China wanted to see the Cosmos, who were quickly becoming the world's most famous team, in soccer or any other sport.

More Big Names

Nineteen-seventy-six began as 1975 ended, with a couple of exceptions: The Cosmos had a new home (baseball's famed Yankee Stadium) and another superstar (controversial Italian striker Giorgio Chinaglia). Meanwhile, other teams tried to emulate their free-spending ways. The Tampa Bay Rowdies signed English crowd favorite Rodney Marsh; fellow U.K. soccer star – and equally aging – George Best went to the Los Angeles Aztecs. The Boston Minutemen snagged fading Portuguese superstar Eusebio, while the San Antonio Thunder inked the old English World Cup star Bobby Moore. A rule mandating a minimum number of Americans (two) on the field at all times was in effect, but clearly the North American Soccer League was a place for Europeans and South American names. Seemingly, age mattered far less than reputation.

For the first time the league surpassed total attendance of two million, quintuple the number five years earlier. An exhibition game in Seattle drew 58,128, shattering all previous U.S. records. The Cosmos improved on the field, winning 16 of 24 matches and finishing second in their division; at the same time, their rivalry with the Tampa Bay Rowdies was developing into a sports classic. The Floridians stunned the Cosmos 5–1 in a nationally televised game in June; a month later the Rowdies traveled north and, in a contest that laid all gibes about defensive soccer to rest, blew a large lead before falling 5–4 to the Cosmos, who by that time were feeling intense corporate pressure from Warner Communications to win, win, win – or else. As early as 1976, the heads of executives and players alike began to roll at the slightest hint of losing. In late summer the Rowdies booted the Cosmos out of the playoffs, 3–1, and ultimately it was Toronto that captured the somewhat-prestigious Soccer Bowl title.

AZTEC GOLD *Los Angeles' George Best*

No matter. In 1977, for the second straight season the Cosmos unveiled a new home: sparkling Giants Stadium in New Jersey's Meadowlands across the Hudson River from New York City, a 77,000-seat football stadium that nonetheless offered three tiers of fabulous sightlines, new-fangled luxury boxes for corporate honchos – and artificial grass. For the third year in a row they signed a new superstar: Franz Beckenbauer, captain of reigning World Cup champion West Germany. Joining the high-powered (and high-priced) trio were the likes of Dave Clements, Northern Ireland's 1976 captain; Ramon Mifflin of Peru; Terry Garbett, Steve Hunt and Tony Field from England; Nelsi Morais of Brazil, and South Africa's Jomo Sono. The Cosmos were truly an international aggregation – and by the end of the season, all 77,000 seats in Giants Stadium were filled, every Wednesday night and each Sunday afternoon, by a rabid congregation of ethnic and native New Yorkers.

The North American soccer attendance record was set on August 14, when 77,691 fans watched the Cosmos take an 8–3 playoff decision from the Fort Lauderdale Strikers. The Cosmos went on to reach the elusive Soccer Bowl championship match, played in Portland, Oregon against the Seattle Sounders. The New Yorkers won 2–1, the winning tally coming off a header by Chinaglia, and Pele had another championship to go along with his already-announced retirement. Six weeks later, on October 1, another sellout crowd braved a chill rain to turn out for the King's farewell game. He led the faithful in a chant of "Love! Love! Love!"; he played one half of the game for the Cosmos, the other half for his original club team, Santos (the teams drew 1–1, the same result as in his first U.S. game), and then he and his magnetic personality were gone. American soccer would never be the same – for better, and for worse.

The game was booming, especially among young boys and girls. Youth leagues were blooming all across the country, in places one would never expect: the football country of Texas and Oklahoma; the hockey-mad states of Minnesota and Michigan; the suburbs of Atlanta. Youngsters were kicking soccer balls, attending soccer camps, shanghai-ing their mothers and fathers – who knew nothing about the game – into serving as coaches.

NASL executives, business leaders and civic boosters saw the soccer surge, and reacted to it. Figuring that young players were the same as young fans – not an unwise assumption, based on recent spectator figures – they pressed the league to expand. In 1978 there were 24 teams, in cities as varied as San Diego, Houston and Memphis. Attendance remained high – the championship game at Giants Stadium, won for the second year in a row by the Cosmos, 3–1 over Tampa Bay, drew 74,901 – but cracks in the game's bright face were already starting to appear. Rodney Marsh was injured; no new "name" player had arrived to replace Pele, and though 1979 marked another big year at the turnstile (the average attendance of 14,000 represented a nine percent increase over 1978), the final years of the 1970s proved to be not the start of something big for professional soccer in the United States, but rather the beginning of the end.

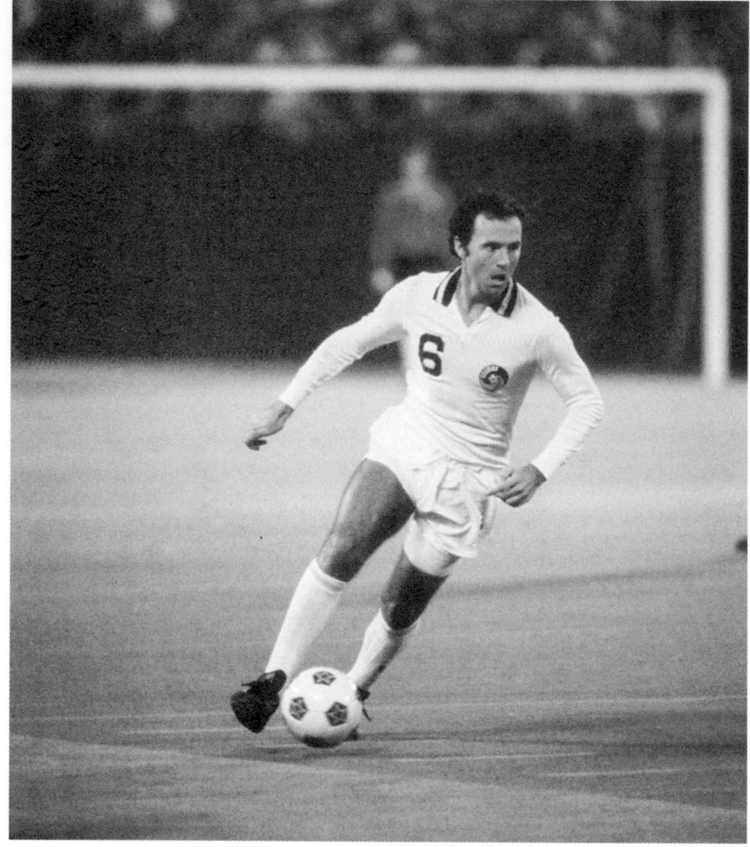

FRANZ BECKENBAUER *World Cup captain, coach – and New York Cosmo*

Decline Begins

The European and South American stars were growing older; names like Beckenbauer and the great Brazilian sweeper Carlos Alberto still held magic, but the Cosmos were the only team that could afford them. Several of them, it was said, earned more than the entire payroll of other teams. Yet, feeling the need to compete, clubs continued to import aging, fading foreigners; at the same time, most teams did little to stimulate the growth of American players, even in their own backyards. Few offered contracts to graduates of local colleges; even the Cosmos, who were pushing Californian Ricky Davis as the first American superstar, went clear across the country again to draft a 17-year-old defender, Jeff Durgan, known more for his physical style of play than for any great skill. It was their only draft choice; they traded the rest away, opting to buy existing talent rather than attempt to develop it on their own.

The strategy proved workable in the short run, disastrous in the long term. Americans, brought up on American sports played by players from American towns, soon wearied of watching teams (which swooped into, then abandoned, cities with alarming frequency) fill their roster with unknown athletes with unpronounceable names. Youngsters enjoyed playing soccer but, as ticket prices rose (a function of the high prices clubs were paying their foreign imports), they found it increasingly difficult to drag their ticket-buying parents to games.

As the 1980s dawned another danger loomed: indoor soccer. Though played in Europe and South America for decades, it was always seen there as a training-type adjunct of the outdoor game. In the U.S., however, a group of entrepreneurs – intrigued, ironically, by a series of NASL indoor exhibition games – launched the Major Indoor Soccer League (MISL) in 1978. There were six original franchises, 10 the next year, and more in the years to come. Indoor soccer was marketed as a "better," more American version of outdoor soccer. With substitutions on the fly, a penalty box and higher scoring, it was supposed to appeal to Americans' insatiable thirst for constant action, plenty of goals and – ultimately – lucrative timeouts for television commercials.

The MISL thrived through the first half of the 1980s, even eclipsing the NASL in some cities in attendance and press coverage. The competition – though seen by some as unwarranted, for it involved two completely different games, played at different times of the year – proved to be the undoing of both leagues. Americans were ready for only so much soccer; the MISL and NASL were too much (especially when the NASL launched an indoor season itself, in an attempt to destroy the rival league). In 1984 four NASL teams jumped to the MISL; the following year the North American Soccer League was history, and several years later the MISL (now calling itself the Major Soccer League) was too.

That was not, of course, the death knell for professional soccer in the United States. Smaller, less ambitious leagues soon sprouted, including the Western Soccer Alliance; a reconstituted American Soccer League (the two merged in 1990 to form the American Professional Soccer League), and the United States Interregional Soccer League. Crowds today average 2,000 to 5,000; spectators watch teams comprised primarily of American players, in venues smaller than Giants Stadium. It isn't the North American Soccer League – but then again, nearly two decades later, many new American soccer fans scarcely remember the NASL at all.

ENTERING THE FRAY *Tampa Bay and Vancouver at Soccer Bowl '79*

THE SUPERSTARS OF U.S. SOCCER

While the phrase "American soccer superstars" may still be regarded as an oxymoron, a number of more-than-adequate U.S.-born or -bred athletes nevertheless dot the rosters of soccer teams worldwide. Joined by those who, by virtue of ancestry, are eligible to compete for the U.S. national team, they form a player pool already making its presence felt in upper levels of the sport – as their presence on top teams in places like England and Germany attests.

TOM DOOLEY *U.S. Soccer Male Athlete of the Year in 1993 and an important member of the American World Cup team in 1994*

Tom Dooley

Perhaps the best known of the lot is Tom Dooley. Though he shares a name with a popular American folk song, until 1991 he had no stateside connection beyond his father, a U.S. army sergeant who abandoned his German wife when Thomas was just 1. Dooley grew up with a fondness for anything American, but he was as German as one can be – including carving out a professional soccer career spent primarily with FC Homburg, where he earned a reputation as one of the Bundesliga's top defenders.

The U.S. Soccer Federation discovered Dooley's American connection in 1991; because he had never played for a German national team, all he needed for U.S. eligibility was an American passport. He made his international debut in 1992, a 2–1 win over Ireland in which he surged forward constantly and helped create both goals.

Dooley adapted quickly to his American teammates, though learning English took longer. By mid-1993 he was an integral part of the team, scoring the first goal in the historic 2–0 U.S. Cup upset of England. He was named U.S. Soccer Male Athlete of the Year in 1993, and hopes were high that he would lead his side to an impressive World Cup showing. He had a quiet Cup, however, and has now returned to Germany, where he plays for Bayer Leverkusen.

John Harkes

Nearly as well known as Dooley is John Harkes. One of three national team players from the small New Jersey town of Kearny (Tab Ramos and Tony Meola are the other two), the midfielder earned soccer headlines several times. In his first English League season, 1990–91, he helped Sheffield Wednesday win promotion from the Second Division to the top tier of English soccer, while also winning the League Cup. His amazing 35-yard shot past Peter Shilton in an earlier round Cup match was dubbed one of the "Goals of the Season."

Two years later, he played in not one but two Wembley Cup finals. His goal in the 2–1 loss to Arsenal in the League Cup final was the first scored by an American in a cup final at the hallowed ground. He also set up the tying tally to force a replay of the FA Cup final, again against Arsenal. Despite another assist in the replay, Wednesday fell 2–1. Harkes, who contributed an effective World Cup effort, now plays with Derby County of the English First Division.

Alexi Lalas

One American who proved more than effective in the World Cup – in fact, he was downright dominant – has seen his efforts pay off with an Italian League contract. Alexi Lalas first gained notice with his looks (wild red hair and a scruffy red goatee), his height (6–3) and his off-field activities (he's a guitarist in a rock band). But his crunching tackles and on-target heading – both defensive and offensive – earned the rugged, aggressive defender enough praise to be named one of nine alternates to the All-World Cup team, and selected by the German weekly *Kicker* to its all-Cup side.

Lalas also caught the attention of a number of European clubs. Padova, a Serie A side, won out by offering a $200,000 transfer fee,

GOATEE POWER *Alexi Lalas and Brazil's Bebeto duel in World Cup USA '94*

making the Michigan native the first American-born player to sign with an Italian club.

Tab Ramos

Dooley, Harkes and Lalas are hardly alone in Europe. Tab Ramos remains in Spain with Real Betis of the Second Division, where he transferred in 1992 for $350,000 after two years with UE Figueras. The Uruguayan-born midfielder, who moved to New Jersey at an early age, scored a spectacular 161 goals in high school, taking time out as a 16-year-old to compete in the Under-20 world championship. He started all three games for the U.S. in the first round of World Cup 1990 in Italy, and was expected to be a dominant factor for the Americans when they hosted the 1994 World Cup.

He was relatively quiet in the opening round, but was the man of the hour for the U.S. in their July Fourth round of 16 encounter with Brazil. Suddenly, just before halftime, a wicked elbow from defender Leonardo fractured a bone in his skull. The Brazilian was shown the red card – but the Americans ended up losing more when Ramos was hauled off on a stretcher. All semblance of attack vanished in the second half, and Brazil rolled to victory en route to their fourth world title.

Eric Wynalda

Also playing in Europe is Eric Wynalda, who in August of 1992 became the first U.S. product to breach the Bundesliga barrier when he signed with FC Saarbruecken – at that point a First Division club. Even more remarkable, the Southern California native did it not in the traditional American role of goalkeeper or defender, but as a striker.

Wynalda, who played in the 1990 World Cup at the tender age of 21 (and was given a red card in the very first match, against Czechoslovakia) was the second leading scorer in the German League halfway through his rookie season, netting nine goals in his first 10 matches. He was soon named U.S. Male Player of the Year. But as often happens with newly promoted teams, Saarbruecken was unable to sustain its momentum. Wynalda found himself moved into a depleted midfield; his scoring chances waned (he tallied just once in the second half of the season), and the team was relegated.

However, his European experience has helped make Wynalda perhaps the U.S.' first true striker. He is high on the list of the nation's all-time goal scorers, and his value has increased on the European market. After the '94 Cup, he signed with VfB Bochum.

Marcelo Balboa

Marcelo Balboa recovered sufficiently from a severe, complete tear of the anterior cruciate ligament of his right knee to recapture, less than eight months later, his spot in the U.S. defense. Balboa, equally at home shutting down opponents like Switzerland's Stephane Chapuisat, Colombia's Faustino Asprilla and Romania's Florin Raducioiu (as he did in the 1994 World Cup) or surging forward to attempt a bicycle kick (as he did successfully to win a 1991 CONCACAF Gold Cup match against Trinidad and Tobago, and nearly replicated against Colombia in the '94 World Cup), was the only American named to *France Football*'s all-World Cup team, based on its game rankings.

ERIC WYNALDA *High-scoring striker*

ERNIE STEWART *Dutch recruit*

Roy Wegerle

Two other European-based field players are, like Dooley, American by happenstance more than home town. Roy Wegerle boasts a pedigree and passport that would make Marco Polo proud. A South African native with a German father and Scottish mother, the midfielder/forward played for Blackburn, Queen's Park Rangers, Luton Town and Chelsea before landing with his current club, Coventry City. But he also has experience in the States, setting a school record for goals in a season (21) at the University of South Florida and becoming the first player selected in the entire 1984 North American Soccer League draft (by the nearby Tampa Bay Rowdies). He married an American woman and received his U.S. citizenship in 1991. Having never played for another national team, Wegerle was eligible to compete for the U.S. – an opportunity he quickly seized.

KASEY KELLER *Tends goal for Millwall*

Ernie Stewart

Ernie Stewart's story parallels Dooley's more than Wegerle's does. The speedy, skillful front-runner has a Dutch mother and American father (a retired U.S. Air Force veteran and former American football player). He lived in the U.S. from ages to 2 to 7, but played no soccer – it was not until he returned to The Netherlands that he picked up the game.

And learn it he did. With Willem II in 1991 he finished third in the Dutch First Division in scoring, netting 17 goals in 33 games. His American heritage was discovered that year, and in 1992 he played in all three matches en route to the U.S.' inaugural U.S. Cup championship.

Tony Meola

Yet despite the success of Dooley, Harkes et al, the most international attention of all has been focused on America's goalkeepers. Tony Meola has been the center of much of that notice, by virtue of his starter's status in both the 1990 and '94 World Cups. But many observers believe that two England-based keepers are actually better than the chunky New Jerseyan who, following World Cup '94, abandoned plans to play overseas in order to sign on as a kicking specialist with the New York Jets football team.

Kasey Keller

Playing with Millwall, Kasey Keller established himself as one of the top keepers in the English First Division. In 1992–93 he started 51 consecutive matches, earning 16 shutouts while conceding just 53 goals, and Millwall fans named him the team's Most Valuable Player. Not selected for the World Cup '94 final roster – a decision for which U.S. coach Bora Milutinovic was roundly criticized – Keller continues his heroics with Millwall today.

Juergen Sommer

Juergen Sommer, who stands 6–5 and boasts an equally impressive wingspan, signed with First Division Luton Town in 1990 following a stellar collegiate career. He appeared at Wembley in the FA Cup semifinals in the spring of '94, and today vies with Keller for honors as one of the top keepers in England.

Brad Friedel

Another fine U.S. keeper, Brad Friedel, is just 23 years old. At 6–4, he too is a commanding presence. The winner of the Hermann Trophy as college soccer's top male player in 1992, Friedel is also set to challenge for the top spot now that Meola has announced his retirement from international soccer.

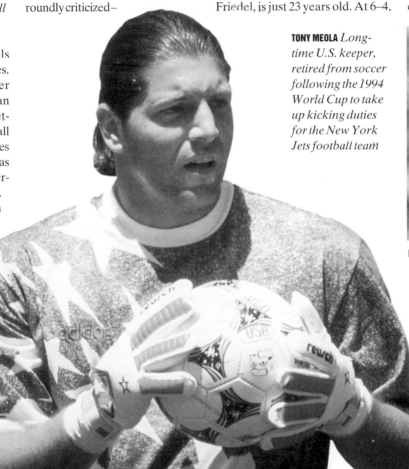

TONY MEOLA *Long-time U.S. keeper, retired from soccer following the 1994 World Cup to take up kicking duties for the New York Jets football team*

Claudio Reyna

Arguably the most promising American player of all never set foot on the field during World Cup '94 – and perhaps if he had, the results for the Yanks might have been different. Claudio Reyna was a mere 20 years old during the Cup, but U.S. fans eagerly anticipated his play. A skillful, creative midfielder whose magic had sparked the Under-17, Under-20 and 1992 Olympic teams (and helped lead the University of Virginia to an unprecedented three straight national college championships), Reyna was felled by torn hamstring just a few days before the Cup began, and missed the entire tournament.

BRAD FRIEDEL *Aiming for the top spot*

He's playing now for Bayer Leverkusen in the Bundesliga, alongside Tom Dooley. He chose the German club over Barcelona, opting for a team where he knew he stood a good chance of playing. If he continues to develop as rapidly as he has – and, based on the experience of his U.S. teammates, there is no reason to think he cannot – the entire world could be talking about an American player, 24-year-old Claudio Reyna, after World Cup '98.

CELEBRATE GOOD TIMES *Tom Dooley and Mike Sorber in joyful mood after America's upset 2–1 win over Colombia at World Cup '94*

THE 1994 WORLD CUP

See pages 26–7 for a general report on the 1994 tournament.

Some trace the history of American soccer to one specific date: November 6, 1876, the day Princeton and Rutgers Universities engaged in the first intercollegiate match in New Brunswick, New Jersey (now, ironically, claimed to be the birth of gridiron football). Others say American soccer came of age on June 29, 1950, the afternoon the U.S. shocked England 1–0 in a World Cup match in Brazil. A good argument comes from those who cite June 10, 1975, the day Pele inked his legendary New York Cosmos contract.

But perhaps the most important date in U.S. soccer history, is, significantly, July 4. On that day in 1988 – the country's 212th birthday – FIFA senior vice president Harry Cavan made official in Zurich what soccer fans the world over both anticipated and feared: The 1994 World Cup would be played for the first time in the United States. The last soccer wilderness in the world was about to be conquered – or FIFA would go down trying.

Although the international organizing body tried to paint the decision (10 executive committee votes for the U.S., seven for Morocco and two for Brazil) in altruistic terms – that it was their duty as the sport's governing body to try to bring the world's most popular game to a so-far-uncomprehending American public – in fact many people suspected the truth lay closer to the bottom line. If soccer could gain a foothold in the corporate-rich, media-crazed United States, who knew how many dollars would flow across the Atlantic to FIFA headquarters in Switzerland? Whatever the reason, the Americans set about organizing an event only a tiny percentage of its population knew anything about. A World Cup USA 1994 committee was named; bid packages were sent out to dozens of interested cities; television networks and many corporate sponsors were approached, and slowly but surely the 15th World Cup began to take its peculiarly American shape.

Italia '90

First, however, there was the matter of the 14th World Cup, set for 1990 in Italy. For the American public to take any interest in '94, they first had to be primed four years ahead of time. And though the U.S. was assured, as host nation, of playing in 1994, they had to qualify for 1990 the same way virtually every other nation, from Argentina to Zambia, tried: by playing soccer matches.

Incredibly, the United States almost did not make it. It took a 35-yard dipping shot by Paul Caligiuri in the late minutes of a second match against tiny Trinidad and Tobago – a Caribbean nation with 0.4 percent of the population of the States – to assure the U.S. of one of two World Cup berths from the none-too-rugged CONCACAF region. The 1–0 win on November 19, 1989, achieved in front of 35,000 red-clad and roaring Trinidadians, clinched America's first World Cup appearance in 40 years.

Their performance in Italy was hardly the stuff to make their countrymen salivate over the prospect of '94. Three stinging defeats – 5–1 to Czechoslovakia, 1–0 to Italy and 2–1 to Austria – brought home a brutal reality: Hosting a World Cup is one thing; performing in it is quite another. And if the Americans could not do well in the event they themselves were hosting, all of FIFA's hopes could well go for naught.

So the U.S. Soccer Federation, which in 1991 relocated to Chicago, had two difficult tasks ahead of itself prior to 1994: To prepare nine stadiums, dozens of sponsors, 500 full-time employees, over 10,000 volunteers, millions of tickets and billions of other details for the event itself, and to prepare a team that would play at least adequately in that competition. After all, no World Cup host had ever failed to qualify for at least the second round.

The Build-Up

The off-the-field preparations, while time-consuming and complicated, proved to be the easier part. Twenty-seven American communities formally bid to serve as host venues; after numerous visits from scores of dignitaries, nine were chosen and announced at a New York news conference on March 23, 1992. Selected were Boston, Chicago, Dallas, Detroit (where the Silverdome was to become the site of the first indoor World Cup games ever), Los Angeles, New York (where the Meadowlands would, like the Silverdome, need to be converted from artificial turf to natural grass), Orlando, San Francisco and Washington. Out were such places as New Orleans, Las Vegas and Honolulu.

"BORA" *Appointed American soccer coach for the 1994 World Cup – the Serbian proved to be an inspired choice*

Gradually the other pieces fell into place too. Dallas was awarded the International Broadcast Center; a television contract was announced (along with a most un-American twist: no commercial interruptions during games); the official mascot (a dog-like creature named "Striker") was introduced by Pele, Bobby Charlton and U.S. women's team star Shannon Higgins.

The on-the-field task was a bit more difficult. Bob Gansler, the amiable yet somewhat ineffective American coach who had never tasted real international success, was let go; in his place came Bora Milutinovic, the charismatic, energetic, Serbian-born legend who had worked wonders in two previous World Cups. In 1986 "Bora," as he was universally known, led Mexico as far as the quarterfinals in the World Cup they hosted; four years later, with just three months' preparation time, he coached Costa Rica into the second round.

Bora spoke four languages, none of them English. That was not a problem, he and his patron, U.S. Soccer Federation president and World Cup '94 chief executive officer Alan Rothenberg, insisted; Bora spoke soccer, the international tongue.

American soccer officials put their money where their mouths were. They were

JUMP UP *Colombia's Antony De Avila evades Tom Dooley during World Cup '94*

quick to establish a first-ever permanent training site in Mission Viejo, an hour outside of Los Angeles. They signed a host of players to full-time contracts; others, playing in Europe, were brought home for key matches. And they embarked on an ambitious exhibition schedule, mixing games against minnows like Iceland, Moldova and Estonia with big-time events such as the two U.S. Cups. The Americans won the inaugural one in 1992, defeating Ireland 3–1 and Portugal 1–0, and tying three-time world champion Italy 1–1. The following year they surrendered their title, but earned headlines (and a bit of credibility) with a 2–0 defeat of England. Attendance and media interest were growing; nearly 300,000 fans attended the tournament's six games, and the U.S.–Germany match was broadcast nationwide.

The Tournament Begins

By June 17, 1994 the Americans were ready to host the world. Germany and Bolivia kicked off the Cup before an enormous crowd, including President Clinton, with an afternoon match played in sweltering Chicago heat. Those themes – high temperatures and humidity, countered by high interest and media attention – quickly became two centerpieces of World Cup '94.

Another theme – perhaps the most important, from the American point of view – was the performance of the U.S. side. If this Cup were to serve its purpose – to galvanize the interest of the largest untapped territory on earth, and awaken this sleeping giant to the pleasures and possibilities of the world's beautiful game – then the Yanks would have to do more than what they'd done four years earlier in Italy: show up, lose and go home. At the very least, they would have to earn their way into the second round, the round of 16.

Their first test came the day after the Cup began. If Chicago's Soldier Field was hot, the Silverdome an hour outside of Detroit was positively stifling. Built expressly for American football, which is played in the fall, it had no air conditioning – and because it was domed, the torrid air had nowhere to go to escape.

The sweltering conditions favored neither the U.S. nor the Swiss; both teams were relatively fit, yet nervous and anxious to get out of the opening game with a minimum of damage. FIFA's new method of encouraging goal-oriented play – three points for a win, one for a tie – took some of the incentive out of the once-popular tactic of sitting back looking for an opening game draw. An added motivation for the Americans was the schedule: Switzerland seemed, on paper, to be the "easiest" opponent in a rather difficult Group A draw that included pre-tournament darling Colombia, and dangerously underrated Romania. If the Americans were going to advance – and a minimum of four points was what most experts believed it was going to take – they figured they needed to pick up three there.

Wynalda Makes a Point

Over 73,000 fans packed the Silverdome, and if they lacked the experience of cheering raucously or cleverly (their quiet chants of "USA! USA!" were quite pallid compared with "Ole-ole-ole-ole" or the rhymes of English-influenced spectators), they made up for it with earnestness. And the game they were treated to lacked nothing in the way of excitement or style.

This Swiss, making their first World Cup appearance since 1966, controlled the early going. The Europeans belted long balls into the middle of a retreating U.S. defense right from the start, and earned several dangerous free kicks by following them up well. Goalkeeper Tony Meola saved the Americans once, touching away a powerful header by Dominique Herr, but he was not as fortunate in the 39th minute. He lined up poorly on Georges Bregy's 20-yard free kick, and the 36-year-old midfielder bent a shot over Meola's left shoulder. It landed well inside the far post – certainly a savable ball.

But moments before intermission, the Americans staved off disaster. Against the flow of play, John Harkes made a run and was decked 10 yards outside the penalty area. Eric Wynalda, suffering from hives and an allergic reaction, took the kick. He bent it sharply with the inside of his right foot, slicing it beyond the defensive wall and squeezing it through a tiny gap between goalkeeper Marco Pascolo's right hand and the crossbar.

The revived Americans held on well into the second half, thanks especially to the defensive pressure Alexi Lalas and Marcelo Balboa applied on Stephane Chapuisat. The match ended 1–1. The U.S. had one point – two less than the three they'd hoped for, but one more than they'd registered in three games in Italy. They were still in contention for a second round spot.

However, the next match would be played against Colombia, and everyone agreed that the crafty, speedy South Americans would be much more formidable foes than the stolid Swiss. Worse yet, the Colombians – everyone's dark horse to win the tournament before the first ball was ever kicked – had just dropped a 3-1 decision to Romania. They were starved for three points.

1950 Revisited

The matchup drew 93,194 people to California's Rose Bowl – not surprising, since virtually every World Cup game was turning out to be a sellout – and they certainly got their money's worth. The North Americans pulled off one of the biggest upsets in their entire soccer history, downing Colombia 2–1 and precipitating one of the most tragic footnotes in World Cup annals, the murder of a player who scored an own goal.

True to form, the South Americans applied terrific pressure early. Playing without midfielder Gabriel Gomez (a fax sent to the team's hotel threatened his home would be bombed, and coach Francisco Maturana would be killed, if he played), Colombia nonetheless used their skill and experience to bedevil their foes.

But for 35 minutes they could not score – at least, not in their own net. Midfielder John Harkes dribbled deep down the left wing and lofted a cross into the penalty area for Ernie Stewart, who was making all kinds of mischief in Colombia's end. Perhaps the pass was on target; no one will ever know. Before it got there the ball bounced off the shin of Andres Escobar, as the popular defender lunged to clear. It deflected goalward; keeper Oscar Cordoba was unable to react in time, and suddenly the U.S. led Colombia.

There was plenty of time for the South Americans to come back – but then, five minutes into the second half, Stewart scored a second goal. Ramos chipped him a lead ball; he out-legged the rattled Colombia defense, as he had been doing incessantly the entire match, and beat the already shaken Cordoba. Suddenly the upstart North Americans were up by two – and in command of the play as well. The defenders conceded the wings, but in the middle Lalas, Balboa, Caligiuri and Fernando Calvijo clogged things as thickly as the traffic on the nearby Los Angeles freeways.

Suddenly, near the end of the match, Balboa found himself forward. He launched a backward-somersaulting bicycle kick that caught everyone – Cordoba included – by surprise. The shot sailed wide left by inches, but it provided yet another video clip for the news highlights. It showed too that the Americans now not only knew how to win, but could even play the game with a bit of flair and innovation.

A last minute tally by Adolfo Valencia made the final margin respectable for Colombia, but for the Americans the score line hardly mattered. Forty years after their last big World Cup upset, they once again made their mark on the soccer universe. And this time they'd done it in their very own home.

Front Page News

The U.S. public responded immediately, and fervently. The match was the lead story on virtually every television and radio sports report; it made Page One headlines throughout the land. Suddenly every American, it seemed, was talking not only about the World Cup, but about the home team's chances. With surging confidence, the U.S. players looked forward to Romania.

The match, played in the Rose Bowl on Sunday, June 26, was hardly the U.S.' finest hour. An entire nation, primed by three days of unprecedented media coverage, forswore its usual viewing habits of baseball, golf and Wimbledon tennis to watch the battle against Romania, a country many Americans scarcely knew existed.

When the game was over, the U.S. knew all about the Eastern Europeans. Perhaps it was the heat (120 degrees F. on the field), the excitement of being in such a novel position, or perhaps the pressure the opposition applied. Whatever the reason, the Americans put on

DANCING IN THE STREETS *For Brazilian fans, the 1994 World Cup was one long party*

their poorest performance of the tournament. Although the U.S. controlled the tempo, and with it the attack, from the outset (with the Romanians' blessing), the magic of the previous game did not last long. Harkes hit the post – in hindsight, the best effort the day – and Romania sat back, absorbed what the U.S. offered (although the crisp passing they displayed against Colombia was lacking), and then counterattacked. The goal came quickly. In the 17th minute Dan Petrescu slotted in a near-side ball, as a flat-footed Meola looked for a cross, and after that the Americans appeared at a loss for how to recover.

The defeat deflated their rapidly rising balloon of confidence, but it did nothing to lessen the media's coverage of the team, or the entire Cup. In fact, interest rose: By finishing the first round as they did, the U.S. garnered a July 4th Rose Bowl round of 16 date – with tourney favorite Brazil.

Newspaper, television and radio reporting crescendoed as Independence Day neared. Everyone wanted to know: Could the home team – playing without Harkes (suspended with two yellow cards) – pull off the biggest miracle of all, at their own World Cup, on their country's birthday?

End of the Dream

A raucous crowd of 84,147 packed aging Stanford Stadium an hour south of San Francisco to find out. Ironically, the Brazilians had been based just minutes away, in Los Gatos, and over the previous month had won the hearts of American fans throughout that city. But on July 4th there was no time for sentimentality: The Americans had not only not beaten Brazil in 64 years, they had not even scored a goal on them in that span.

Alexi Lalas, the red-haired defender who'd earned so much respect in his play the first three games, tried to explain that all the pressure was on the other side: "If we lose, nobody cares. That's what we're supposed to do. But if Brazil loses...." However, that was not exactly true. If America lost, a country newly crazy about soccer would care – and

SICKENING BLOW *Brazil's Leonardo decks Tab Ramos during the Independence Day encounter at World Cup '94*

if they won, a new era in soccer would be ushered in.

The unthinkable nearly happened just 12 minutes into the match. Dooley missed the net by inches. There were other close calls too – but mostly they were Brazil's: Aldair, Bebeto and Romario twice, the latter two proving the most dangerous (one rocket off the post, another cleared brilliantly off the line by an off-balance Dooley).

The most important event of the first half, however, occurred not far from midfield. Leonardo's elbow caught Tab Ramos in the temple, fracturing a bone in his skull and shattering the U.S.' already-weak attack. Leonardo was ejected, but Ramos' loss was far more significant. It disrupted whatever rhythm the Americans had been attempting to build, and from the start of the second half on the game clearly belonged to Brazil.

Bebeto's goal in the 74th minute, set up by Romario, was a long time coming – too long, to the suspiciously quiet green-and-yellow-clad fans who filled a significant number of Stanford's seats – but it was also inevitable. The final 16 minutes were all Brazil; Bora's hopes for 120 minutes of scoreless soccer, followed by an up-for-grabs penalty kick shootout, vanished, and with it America's hopes for the biggest soccer miracle of all. Brazil, of course, went on to play in, and win, a penalty kick match of its own – the first-ever World Cup championship determined from the spot – and the U.S. team went home, a moral victor but, in reality, a round of 16 loser.

Heroes in Defeat

However, they did not have far to go – they were, after all, home already – and they hardly vanished without a trace. Television talk show hosts clamored for Lalas; newspaper columnists who never before bothered with Bora began debating the efficacy of his defensive tactics (which Sweden had employed successfully in a 1–1 first round draw) were right or wrong; even President Clinton called to invite the entire team to the White House.

And the elimination of the host team from the World Cup was hardly the end of America's infatuation with the event. Their interest whetted by their up-close-and-personal encounter with the samba-dancing, soccer-loving South Americans and their crisp, clever and creative team, Americans by the millions embraced the final three rounds with a fervor that surprised even the most optimistic U.S. Soccer officials. Television audiences continued to surge, with viewing records shattered game after game; merchandise kept selling well, and the casual conversation in bars, elevators and around the office water cooler continued to be about soccer, not baseball or politics or movie stars.

By July 17, the date of the final match at the Rose Bowl, it was clear that World Cup '94 would be wildly successful, by any measure anyone cared to use. The total attendance for 52 games was a record 3,567,415; the average of 68,102 torpedoed the 1990 mark of 48,411. The Brazil–Italy final drew 94,194 fans, netting gate receipts of $43.5 million – reportedly a record for any single sporting event. The streets of Pasadena were filled, before the game and after, with partying fans, just like every World Cup final that had ever been played in Europe or South America. The championship match itself was far from classic, but no matter: The party ended happily (especially for the many partisans of Brazil), and all agreed that the hosts had done a magnificent job.

"I think this is the most beautiful World Cup I have seen in terms of the participation of the public. The stadiums are always full, and full with Americans," said Carlos Maranhao, executive editor of *Vega*, a weekly news magazine in São Paulo, Brazil, who attended his first Cup in 1974.

"The atmosphere in the stadiums has been fantastic," concurred Paul Gardner, an Englishman who has lived in New York for over three decades, covered six World Cups, and sometimes doubted whether the U.S. could produce a proper Cup. "Going into one of the stadiums, you could be in Rio or Milan or anywhere. There's been a lot of cheering, a lot of flavor, a lot of excitement and passion inside the stadiums and around them. The party atmosphere has been terrific."

Yet when the crowds dispersed, the bunting was taken down and the world's media disappeared, what, in the final analysis, did it all mean?

THE FUTURE OF SOCCER IN AMERICA

July 18, 1994. Brazil returned home, their tetra trophy in hand, with fond memories of their month-long adventure in the United States; the 23 other final teams already were setting their sights on France '98. Six long, contentious, often worrisome years preparing for the first World Cup ever held in the United States were over; the event represented the climax of more than a hundred years of American soccer history.

What next? FIFA's announcement that the '94 World Cup would be held in the U.S. elicited shock, anger and criticism throughout the rest of the world. For such a prestigious event to be played in such a soccer wilderness was illogical, unfair and heretical, purists screamed; we're only trying to help develop the sport in the last virgin territory on earth, FIFA patiently replied.

Now that the financial bills have been paid by the World Cup Organizing Committee (and as they tally the millions they earned), the intangible bills have come due. FIFA gave the World Cup to the U.S. not for altruistic reasons, but for mercenary ones: If soccer booms in the States, the international governing body will make money – even more money than it already does.

FIFA originally believed that the World Cup would lead to the formation of a full-fledged, first-class American professional league. Seamlessly, it was thought, the tournament would flow into the league's first (hopefully lucrative) season. That was the quid pro quo given in exchange for the Cup.

But as 1988 stretched into the 1990s, and on into 1994, it became clear that there would be no professional league in place the day the World Cup ended. The best the U.S. Soccer Federation could do was plan for Major League Soccer (MLS) to debut in the spring of 1995.

Major League Soccer

Establishing Major League Soccer has not been without its problems. Organizers of the league – who are, by and large, the same men who led the World Cup '94 committee, and who fill the top posts in the U.S. Soccer Federation – hoped to announce all 12 cities to the international press gathered in Chicago two days before the Cup began. But lagging season ticket sales (the initial demand that cities sell 10,000 deposits was quickly scaled back) and lingering stadium questions (the hope is to have special soccer stadiums with a capacity of 20,000–30,000 in place by the end of the century, though none currently exist; other issues involve artificial turf and concession leases) left MLS officials with no choice but to announce only seven markets. Two franchises were awarded to the New York area – including Giants Stadium. MLS plans to close off the upper deck, halving its capacity to 34,235 – a far cry from the 77,000 who crammed its three tiers during the Cosmos' glory days of Pele and Beckenbauer.

YOUNG GUNS *Heroic defeat for the U.S. in this 1992 Olympic game vs. Italy*

But those are not the only stumbling blocks. Criticism has been leveled not only at MLS' leaders: Many soccer people feel it was an inherent conflict of interest for U.S. Soccer Federation president – and World Cup USA 1994 chairman and chief executive officer – Alan Rothenberg to simultaneously head up the professional organization.

Another problem concerns the league's structure. The plan is for MLS to own all 12 franchises, a unique situation. Such central management, marketing and control may lead, many feel, to a sterility that is antithetical to a viable sports league. Too, the MLS business plan calls for a minimum of $50 million in initial capital, yet no information on the league's investors was forthcoming during the World Cup summer – nor was it in the weeks immediately afterward.

Furthermore, the MLS faces competition from a competing league, announced by Chicago entrepreneur Jim Paglia. Little news has been heard about that effort, but Paglia has promised to fight MLS for players and television contracts.

There are also several lesser known leagues – some regional, others nationwide (the biggest is the 71-team United States Interregional Soccer League) – that have scraped hard for several years to survive. They are unlikely to cede their turf, athletes and fan base to the upstart MLS.

WORLD CHAMPIONS *The women's national team brought America its first-ever world soccer championship*

In fact, it is the players themselves who could sabotage the MLS. Most of the top American names are already committed to European teams; others are under contract to U.S. sides, or are still in college (and thus ineligible to sign professional contracts). Where the MLS can find enough quality players – players with the name recognition to draw fans, the talent to keep them coming back and whose transfer fees are not prohibitively expensive – is an as-yet-unanswered question.

A Bright Future

Yet despite those formidable obstacles, the future of soccer in America appears bright. The game is not limited simply to the few dozen elite athletes who play in professional leagues. U.S. youth teams have performed exceptionally well in the world arena of late; for example, the Under-23 side won the gold medal at the Pan-American Games in Cuba and advanced to the 1992 Barcelona Summer Olympics; the Under-20 team finished eighth at the 1993 World Youth Championship in Australia (including a 6–0 demolition of Turkey, Europe's top seed), and the Under-17s made it to the quarterfinals of FIFA's 1991 and 1993 World Championships. In fact, the U.S. and Italy are the only countries in the world to have qualified for every FIFA championship from 1990–94.

Among those events is the Women's World Championship – and the American women are the reigning champs. They captured the crown in China in 1991, the first and so far only time an American team has won a world title. Women represent an important constituency in U.S. soccer, as players, coaches and spectators. Their numbers continue to grow rapidly.

MAN WITH A MISSION *Alan Rothenberg, U.S. Soccer president*

But for the brightest take on soccer's future in the United States, one simply needs to see numbers. According to the Soccer Industry Council of America, nearly 16 million Americans play soccer annually. Nearly three million of them play at least 52 days a year, about the same number as claim soccer is their favorite sport. Among participants under the age of 12, soccer trails only basketball as the most popular sport; it is third (behind basketball and volleyball) among boys and girls under 18. Soccer is the fifth most popular high school sport (after basketball, American football, outdoor track and baseball), and it is played in over 1,000 colleges and universities (far more than play gridiron football).

Adults show a 34 percent increase in soccer participation since 1987, helping make it the fastest-growing team sport in the United States. Today the nation boasts more than 50,000 state-level coaches and 9,000 national-level coaches; the number of certified referees is nearing 60,000 (one of the largest among the 178 nations belonging to FIFA).

Soccer still has a ways to go become a major American sport. The number of spectators lags well behind the number of participants. But the World Cup clearly spurred interest. Virtually every World Cup attendance record was shattered (save for the unreachable single-game mark, set in 1950 in Brazil's vast Maracana stadium); high television ratings, far above competing baseball, golf and Wimbledon tennis, stunned nearly everyone

Most importantly, youngsters growing up today understand that soccer is every bit as "American" a sport as the traditional Big Three: gridiron football, basketball and baseball. They play it, they understand it, they appreciate it and they love it. All that remains now is for them to win at it.

U.S. NATIONAL TEAM ALL-TIME RESULTS

FULL INTERNATIONAL MATCHES

Date	Opponent	Result	Site
1916			
Aug. 20	Sweden	3–2	Stockholm, Sweden
Sept. 3	Norway	1–1	Oslo, Norway
1924			
May 25	Estonia (OGF)	1–0	Paris, France
May 29	Uruguay (OGF)	0–3	Paris, France
June 10	Poland	3–2	Warsaw, Poland
June 16	Ireland	1–3	Dublin, Ireland
1925			
June 27	Canada	1–0	Montreal, Canada
Nov. 8	Canada	6–1	Brooklyn, U.S.
1926			
Nov. 6	Canada	6–1	Brooklyn, U.S.
1928			
May 30	Argentina (OGF)	2–11	Amsterdam, Holland
June 10	Poland	3–3	Warsaw, Poland
1930			
July 13	Belgium (WCF)	3–0	Montevideo, Uruguay
July 17	Paraguay (WCF)	3–0	Montevideo, Uruguay
July 26	Argentina (WCF)	1–6	Montevideo, Uruguay
Aug. 17	Brazil	3–4	Rio de Janeiro, Brazil
1934			
May 24	Mexico (WCQ)	4–2	Rome, Italy
May 27	Italy (WCF)	1–7	Rome, Italy
1936			
Aug. 3	Italy (OGF)	0–1	Berlin, Germany
1937			
Sept. 12	Mexico	2–7	Mexico City, Mexico
Sept. 19	Mexico	3–7	Mexico City, Mexico
Sept. 26	Mexico	1–5	Mexico City, Mexico
1947			
July 13	Mexico	0–5	Havana, Cuba
July 20	Cuba	2–5	Havana, Cuba
1948			
Aug. 2	Italy (OGF)	0–9	London, England
Aug. 6	Norway	0–11	Oslo, Norway
Aug. 11	Northern Ireland	0–5	Belfast, Northern Ireland
1949			
June 19	Scotland	0–4	New York, U.S.
Sept. 4	Mexico (WCQ)	0–6	Mexico City, Mexico
Sept. 14	Cuba (WCQ)	1–1	Mexico City, Mexico
Sept. 18	Mexico (WCQ)	2–6	Mexico City, Mexico
Sept. 21	Cuba (WCQ)	5–2	Mexico City, Mexico
1950			
June 25	Spain (WCF)	1–3	Curtiba, Brazil
June 29	England (WCF)	1–0	Belo Horizonte, Brazil
July 2	Chile (WCF)	2–5	Recife, Brazil
1952			
April 30	Scotland	0–6	Glasgow, Scotland
July 16	Italy (OGF)	0–8	Tampere, Finland
1953			
June 8	England	3–6	New York, U.S.
1954			
Jan. 10	Mexico (WCQ)	0–4	Mexico City, Mexico
Jan. 14	Mexico (WCQ)	1–3	Mexico City, Mexico
April 3	Haiti (WCQ)	3–2	Port-au-Prince, Haiti
April 4	Haiti (WCQ)	3–0	Port-au-Prince, Haiti
1955			
Aug. 25	Iceland	2–3	Reykjavik, Iceland
1956			
Nov. 28	Yugoslavia (OGF)	1–9	Melbourne, Australia
1957			
April 7	Mexico (WCQ)	0–6	Mexico City, Mexico
April 28	Mexico (WCQ)	2–7	Long Beach, U.S.
June 22	Canada (WCQ)	1–5	Toronto, Canada
July 6	Canada (WCQ)	2–3	St. Louis, U.S.
1959			
May 28	England	1–8	Los Angeles, U.S.
Oct. 8	Mexico (OGQ)	0–2	Mexico City, Mexico
Nov. 22	Mexico (OGQ)	1–1	Los Angeles, U.S.
1960			
Nov. 6	Mexico (WCQ)	3–3	Los Angeles, U.S.
Nov. 13	Mexico (WCQ)	0–3	Mexico City, Mexico
1961			
Feb. 5	Colombia	0–2	Bogota, Colombia
1963			
April 20	Chile (WCQ)	2–10	Sao Paulo, Brazil
April 22	Argentina (WCQ)	1–8	Sao Paulo, Brazil
April 28	Brazil (WCQ)	0–10	Sao Paulo, Brazil
May 2	Uruguay (WCQ)	0–2	Sao Paulo, Brazil
1964			
March 16	Surinam (OGQ)	0–1	Mexico City, Mexico
March 18	Panama (OGQ)	4–2	Mexico City, Mexico
March 20	Mexico (OGQ)	1–2	Mexico City, Mexico
May 27	England	0–10	New York, U.S.
1965			
March 7	Mexico (WCQ)	2–2	Los Angeles, U.S.
March 12	Mexico (WCQ)	0–2	Mexico City, Mexico
March 17	Honduras (WCQ)	1–0	San Pedro Sula, Honduras
March 21	Honduras (WCQ)	1–1	Tegucigalpa, Hon.
1967			
May 21	Bermuda (OGQ)	1–1	Hamilton, Bermuda
May 27	Bermuda (OGQ)	0–1	Chicago, U.S.
1968			
Sept. 15	Israel	3–3	New York, U.S.
Sept. 25	Israel	0–4	Philadelphia, U.S.
Oct. 17	Canada (WCQ)	2–4	Toronto, U.S.
Oct. 20	Haiti	6–3	Port-au-Prince, Haiti
Oct. 21	Haiti	2–5	Port-au-Prince, Haiti
Oct. 23	Haiti	0–1	Port-au-Prince, Haiti
Oct. 27	Canada (WCQ)	1–0	Atlanta, U.S.
Nov. 2	Bermuda (WCQ)	6–2	Kansas City, U.S.
Nov. 10	Bermuda (WCQ)	2–0	Hamilton, Bermuda
1969			
April 20	Haiti (WCQ)	0–2	Port-au-Prince, Haiti
May 11	Haiti (WCQ)	0–1	San Diego, U.S.
1971			
July 18	El Salvador (OGQ)	1–1	Miami, U.S.

July 25	Barbados (OGQ)	3–0	Miami, U.S.
Aug. 15	El Salvador (OGQ)	1–1	San Salvador, El Sal.
Aug. 22	Barbados (OGQ)	3–1	Bridgetown, Barbados
Sept. 18	El Salvador (OGQ)	1–0	Kingston, Jamaica

1972

Jan. 16	Jamaica (OGQ)	1–1	Kingston, Jamaica
Jan. 23	Mexico (OGQ)	1–1	Guadalajara, Mexico
April 16	Guatemala (OGQ)	2–3	Guatemala City, Guatemala
April 25	Guatemala (OGQ)	2–1	Miami, U.S.
May 10	Mexico (OGQ)	2–2	San Francisco, U.S.
May 14	Jamaica (OGQ)	2–1	St. Louis, U.S.
Aug. 20	Canada (WCQ)	2–3	St. John's , Canada
Aug. 27	Morocco (OGF)	0–0	Augsburg, W.Germany
Aug. 29	Malaysia (OGF)	0–2	Ingolstadt, W.Germany
Aug. 29	Canada (WCQ)	2–2	Baltimore, U.S.
Aug. 31	W.Germany (OGF)	0–7	Munich, W. Germany
Sept. 3	Mexico (WCQ)	1–3	Mexico City, Mexico
Sept. 10	Mexico (WCQ)	1–2	Los Angeles, U.S.

1973

March 17	Bermuda	0–4	Hamilton, Bermuda
March 20	Poland	0–4	Lodz, Poland
Aug. 3	Poland	0–1	Chicago, U.S.
Aug. 5	Canada	2–0	Windsor, Canada
Aug. 10	Poland	0–4	San Francisco, U.S.
Aug. 12	Poland	1–0	New Britain, U.S.
Sept. 9	Bermuda	1–0	Hartford, U.S.
Oct. 16	Mexico	0–2	Puebla, Mexico
Nov. 3	Haiti	0–1	Port–au–Prince, Haiti
Nov. 5	Haiti	0–1	Port–au–Prince, Haiti
Nov. 13	Israel	1–3	Tel Aviv, Israel
Nov. 15	Israel	0–2	Beersheba, Israel

1974

Sept. 5	Mexico	1–3	Monterrey, Mexico
Sept. 8	Mexico	0–1	Dallas, U.S.

1975

March 26	Poland	0–7	Poznan, Poland
April 4	Italy	0–10	Rome, Italy
April 20	Bermuda (OGQ)	2–3	Hamilton, Bermuda
April 27	Bermuda (OGQ)	2–0	San Francisco, U.S.
June 24	Poland	0–4	Seattle, U.S.
Aug. 19	Costa Rica	1–3	Mexico City, Mexico
Aug. 21	Argentina	0–6	Mexico City, Mexico
Aug. 25	Mexico (OGQ)	0–8	Toluca, Mexico
Aug. 25	Mexico	0–2	Mexico City, Mexico
Aug. 28	Mexico (OGQ)	2–4	Wilmington, Mexico

1976

Sept. 24	Canada (WCQ)	1–1	Vancouver, Canada
Oct. 3	Mexico (WCQ)	0–0	Los Angeles, U.S.
Oct. 15	Mexico (WCQ)	0–3	Puebla, Mexico
Oct. 20	Canada (WCQ)	2–0	Seattle, U.S.
Nov. 10	Haiti	0–0	Port–au–Prince, Haiti
Nov. 12	Haiti	0–0	Port–au–Prince, Haiti
Nov. 14	Haiti	0–0	Port–au–Prince, Haiti
Dec. 22	Canada (WCQ)	0–3	Port–au–Prince, Haiti

1977

Sept. 15	El Salvador	2–1	San Salvador, El Salvador
Sept. 18	Guatemala	1–3	Guatemala City, Guatemala
Sept. 25	Guatemala	0–2	Guatemala City, Guatemala
Sept. 27	Mexico	0–3	Monterrey, Mexico
Sept. 30	El Salvador	0–0	Los Angeles, U.S.
Oct. 6	China	1–1	Washington, U.S.
Oct. 10	China	1–0	Atlanta, U.S.
Oct. 16	China	2–1	San Francisco, U.S.

1978

Sept. 3	Iceland	0–0	Reykjavik, Iceland
Sept. 6	Switzerland	0–2	Lucerne, Switzerland
Sept. 20	Portugal	0–1	Benfica, Portugal

1979

Feb. 3	Soviet Union	1–3	Seattle, U.S.
Feb. 11	Soviet Union	1–4	San Francisco, U.S.
May 2	France	0–6	East Rutherford, U.S.
May 23	Mexico (OGQ) *	2–0	Leon, Mexico
June 3	Mexico (OGQ) *	2–0	New York, U.S.
Oct. 7	Bermuda	3–1	Hamilton, Bermuda
Oct. 10	France	0–3	Paris, France
Oct. 26	Hungary	2–0	Budapest, Hungary
Oct. 29	Ireland	2–3	Dublin, Ireland
Dec. 2	Bermuda (OGQ)	3–0	Hamilton, Bermuda
Dec. 12	Bermuda (OGQ)	5–0	Ft. Lauderdale, U.S.

1980

March 16	Surinam (OGQ)	2–1	Orlando, U.S.
March 20	Costa Rica (OGQ)	1–0	San Jose, Costa Rica
March 25	Costa Rica (OGQ)	1–1	Edwardsville, Costa Rica
April 2	Surinam (OGQ)	4–4	Paramaribo, Surinam
Oct. 5	Luxembourg	2–0	Dudelange, Luxembourg
Oct. 7	Portugal	1–1	Lisbon, Portugal
Oct. 25	Canada (WCQ)	0–0	Ft. Lauderdale, U.S.
Nov. 1	Canada (WCQ)	1–2	Vancouver, Canada
Nov. 9	Mexico (WCQ)	1–5	Mexico City, Mexico
Nov. 23	Mexico (WCQ)	2–1	Ft. Lauderdale, U.S.

1982

March 21	Trin. & Tob.	2–1	Port of Spain, Trinidad

1983

April 8	Haiti	2–0	Port–au–Prince, Haiti

1984

May 30	Italy	0–0	East Rutherford, U.S.
July 29	Costa Rica (OGF)	3–0	Palo Alto, U.S.
July 31	Italy (OGF)	0–1	Pasadena, U.S.
Aug. 2	Egypt (OGF)	1–1	Palo Alto, U.S.
Sept. 29	Neth.Antilles (WCQ)	0–0	Curaçao, Neth. Antilles
Oct. 6	Neth.Antilles (WCQ)	4–0	St. Louis, U.S.
Oct. 9	El Salvador	3–1	Los Angeles, U.S.
Oct. 11	Colombia	1–0	Los Angeles, U.S.
Oct. 14	Guatemala	0–4	Guatemala City, Guatemala
Oct. 17	Mexico	1–2	Mexico City, Mexico
Nov. 30	Ecuador	0–0	Long Island, U.S.
Dec. 2	Ecuador	2–2	Miami, U.S.

1985

Feb. 8	Switzerland	1–1	Tampa, U.S.
April 2	Canada	0–2	Vancouver, Canada
April 4	Canada	1–1	Portland, U.S.
May 15	Trin. & Tob. (WCQ)	2–1	St. Louis, U.S.
May 19	Trin. & Tob. (WCQ)	1–0	Torrance, U.S.
May 26	Costa Rica (WCQ)	1–1	Alajuela, Costa Rica
May 31	Costa Rica (WCQ)	0–1	Hawthorne, U.S.
June 16	England	0–5	Los Angeles, U.S.

1986

Feb. 5	Canada	0–0	Miami, U.S.
Feb. 7	Uruguay	1–1	Miami, U.S.

1987

May 23	Canada (OGQ)	0–2	St. John's, Canada
May 30	Canada (OGQ)	3–0	St. Louis, U.S.
June 8	Egypt	1–3	Seoul, South Korea
June 12	South Korea	0–1	Pusan, South Korea
June 16	Thailand	1–0	Chongju, South Korea
Sept. 5	Trin. & Tob. (OGQ)	4–1	St. Louis, U.S.
Sept. 20	Trin. & Tob. (OGQ)	1–0	Port of Spain, Trinidad
Oct. 18	El Salvador (OGQ)	4–2	San Salvador, El Salvador

1988

Jan. 10	Guatemala	0–1	Guatemala City, Guatemala
Jan. 13	Guatemala	1–0	Guatemala City, Guatemala
May 14	Colombia	0–2	Miami, U.S.
May 25	El Salvador (OGQ)	4–1	Indianapolis, U.S.
June 1	Chile	1–1	Stockton, U.S.
June 3	Chile	1–3	San Diego, U.S.
June 5	Chile	0–3	Fresno, U.S.
June 7	Ecuador	0–1	Albuquerque, U.S.
June 10	Ecuador	0–2	Houston, U.S.
June 12	Ecuador	0–0	Ft. Worth, U.S.
June 14	Costa Rica	1–0	San Antonio, U.S.
June 16	Soviet Union	0–1	Seoul, South Korea
June 19	Nigeria	2–3	Kwangju, South Korea
July 13	Poland	0–2	New Britain, U.S.
July 24	Jamaica (WCQ)	0–0	Kingston, Jamaica
Aug. 13	Jamaica (WCQ)	5–1	St. Louis, U.S.
Sept. 18	Argentina (OGF)	1–1	Taegu, South Korea
Sept. 20	South Korea (OGF)	0–0	Pusan, South Korea
Sept. 22	Soviet Union (OGF)	2–4	Taegu, South Korea

1989

April 16	Costa Rica (WCQ)	0–1	San Jose, Costa Rica
April 30	Costa Rica (WCQ)	1–0	St. Louis, U.S.
May 13	Trin. & Tob. (WCQ)	1–1	Torrance, U.S.
June 4	Peru	3–0	East Rutherford, U.S.

June 17	Guatemala (WCQ)	2–1	New Britain, U.S.
June 24	Colombia	0–1	Miami, U.S.
Aug. 13	South Korea	1–2	Los Angeles, U.S.
Sept. 17	El Salvador (WCQ)	1–0	Tegucigalpa, Honduras
Oct. 8	Guatemala (WCQ)	0–0	Guatemala City, Guatemala
Nov. 5	El Salvador (WCQ)	0–0	St. Louis, U.S.
Nov. 14	Bermuda	2–1	Cocoa Beach, U.S.
Nov. 19	Trin. & Tob. (WCQ)	1–0	Port of Spain, Trinidad

1990

Feb. 2	Costa Rica	0–2	Miami, U.S.
Feb. 4	Colombia	1–2	Miami, U.S.
Feb. 13	Bermuda	1–0	Hamilton, Bermuda
Feb. 24	Soviet Union	1–3	Palo Alto, U.S.
March 10	Finland	2–1	Tampa, U.S.
March 20	Hungary	2–0	Budapest, Hungary
March 28	East Germany	2–3	Berlin, East Germany
April 8	Iceland	4–1	St. Louis, U.S.
April 22	Colombia	0–1	Miami, U.S.
May 5	Malta	1–0	Rutgers, U.S.
May 6	Canada	0–1	Burnaby, Canada
May 9	Poland	3–1	Hershey, U.S.
May 10	Mexico	0–1	Burnaby, Canada
May 30	Liechtenstein	4–1	Sport Eschen-Mauren, Liechtenstein
June 2	Switzerland	1–2	St. Gallen, Switzerland
June 10	Czech. (WCF)	1–5	Florence, Italy
June 14	Italy (WCF)	0–1	Rome, Italy
June 19	Austria (WCF)	1–2	Florence, Italy
July 28	East Germany	1–2	Milwaukee, U.S.
Sept. 15	Trin. & Tob.	3–0	High Point, U.S.
Oct. 10	Poland	3–2	Warsaw, Poland
Nov. 18	Trin. & Tob.	0–0	Port of Spain, Trinidad
Nov. 21	Soviet Union	0–0	Port of Spain, Trinidad
Dec. 19	Portugal	0–1	Porto, Portugal

1991

Feb. 1	Switzerland	0–1	Miami, U.S.
Feb. 21	Bermuda	0–1	Hamilton, Bermuda
March 12	Mexico	2–2	Los Angeles, U.S.
March 16	Canada	2–0	Los Angeles, U.S.
April 7	South Korea	0–2	Pohang, South Korea
May 5	Uruguay	1–0	Denver, U.S.
May 19	Argentina	0–1	Palo Alto, U.S.
June 1	Rep. of Ireland	1–1	Foxboro, U.S.
June 29	Trin. & Tob.	2–1	Pasadena, U.S.
July 1	Guatemala	3–0	Pasadena, U.S.
July 3	Costa Rica	3–2	Los Angeles, U.S.
July 5	Mexico	2–0	Los Angeles, U.S.
July 7	Honduras	0–0	Los Angeles, U.S.
Aug. 28	Romania	2–0	Brasov, Romania
Sept. 4	Turkey	1–1	Istanbul, Turkey
Sept. 14	Jamaica	1–0	High Point, U.S.
Oct. 19	North Korea	1–2	Washington, U.S.
Nov. 24	Costa Rica	1–1	Dallas, U.S.
Jan. 25	C.I.S.	0–1	Miami, U.S.

1992

Feb. 2	C.I.S.	2–1	Detroit, U.S.
Feb. 12	Costa Rica	0–0	San Jose, Costa Rica
Feb. 18	El Salvador	0–2	San Salvador, El Salvador
Feb. 26	Brazil	0–3	Fortaleza, Brazil
March 11	Morocco	1–3	Casablanca, Morocco
April 4	China	5–0	Palo Alto, U.S.
April 29	Rep. of Ireland	1–4	Dublin, Ireland
May 17	Scotland	0–1	Denver, U.S.
May 30	Rep. of Ireland	3–1	Washington, U.S.
June 3	Portugal	1–0	Chicago, U.S.
June 6	Italy	1–1	Chicago, U.S.
June 13	Australia	0–1	Orlando, U.S.
June 27	Ukraine	0–0	Piscataway, U.S.
July 31	Colombia	0–1	Los Angeles, U.S.
Aug. 2	Brazil	0–1	Los Angeles, U.S.
Sept. 3	Canada	2–0	St. John's , Canada
Oct. 9	Canada	0–0	Greensboro, U.S.
Oct. 15	Saudi Arabia	0–3	Riyadh, Saudi Arabia
Oct. 19	Ivory Coast	5–2	Riyadh, Saudi Arabia

1993

Jan. 30	Denmark	2–2	Tempe, U.S.
Feb. 6	Romania	1–1	Santa Barbara, U.S.
Feb. 13	Russia	0–1	Orlando, U.S.
Feb. 21	Russia	0–0	Palo Alto, U.S.
March 3	Canada	2–2	Costa Mesa, U.S.
March 10	Hungary	0–0	Nagoya, Japan
March 14	Japan	1–3	Tokyo, Japan
March 23	El Salvador	2–2	San Salvador, El Salvador
March 25	Honduras	1–4	Tegucigalpa, Honduras
April 9	Saudi Arabia	2–0	Riyadh, Saudi Arabia
April 17	Iceland	1–1	Costa Mesa, U.S.
May 8	Colombia	1–2	Miami, U.S.
May 23	Bolivia	0–0	Fullerton, U.S.
May 26	Peru	0–0	Mission Viejo, U.S.
June 6	Brazil	0–2	New Haven, U.S.
June 9	England	2–0	Foxboro, U.S.
June 13	Germany	3–4	Chicago, U.S.
June 16	Uruguay	0–1	Ambato, Ecuador
June 19	Ecuador	0–2	Quito, Ecuador
June 22	Venezuela	3–3	Quito, Ecuador
July 10	Jamaica	1–0	Dallas, U.S.
July 14	Panama	2–1	Dallas, U.S.
July 17	Honduras	1–0	Dallas, U.S.
July 21	Costa Rica	1–0	Dallas, U.S.
July 25	Mexico	0–4	Mexico City, Mexico
Aug. 31	Iceland	1–0	Reykjavik, Iceland
Sept. 8	Norway	0–1	Oslo, Norway
Oct. 13	Mexico	1–1	Washington, U.S.
Oct. 16	Ukraine	1–2	High Point, U.S.
Oct. 23	Ukraine	0–1	Bethlehem, U.S.
Nov. 7	Jamaica	1–0	Fullerton, U.S.
Nov. 14	Cayman Islands	8–1	Mission Viejo, U.S.
Dec. 5	El Salvador	7–0	Los Angeles, U.S.
Dec. 18	Germany	0–3	Palo Alto, U.S.

1994

Jan. 15	Norway	2–1	Phoenix, U.S.
Jan. 22	Switzerland	1–1	Fullerton, U.S.
Jan. 29	Russia	1–1	Seattle, U.S.
Feb. 10	Denmark	0–0	Hong Kong
Feb. 13	Romania	1–2	Hong Kong
Feb. 18	Bolivia	1–1	Miami, U.S.
Feb. 20	Sweden	1–3	Miami, U.S.
March 12	South Korea	1–1	Fullerton, U.S.
March 26	Bolivia	2–2	Dallas, U.S.
April 16	Moldova	1–1	Jacksonville, U.S.
April 20	Moldova	3–0	Davidson, U.S.
April 24	Iceland	1–2	San Diego, U.S.
April 30	Chile	0–2	Albuquerque, U.S.
May 7	Estonia	4–0	Fullerton, U.S.
May 15	Armenia	1–0	Fullerton, U.S.
May 25	Saudi Arabia	0–0	Piscataway, U.S.
May 28	Greece	1–1	New Haven, U.S.
June 4	Mexico	1–0	Pasadena, U.S.
June 18	Switzerland (WCF)	1–1	Detroit, U.S.
June 22	Colombia (WCF)	2–1	Pasadena, U.S.
June 26	Romania (WCF)	0–1	Pasadena, U.S.
July 4	Brazil (WCF)	0–1	Palo Alto, U.S.

All-Time Record: 100 wins, 164 losses, 78 ties
World Cup Record: 4 wins, 9 losses, 1 tie
World Cup Qualifying Record: 19 wins, 24 losses, 13 ties
Olympic Record: 2 wins, 10 losses, 4 ties
Olympic Qualifying Record: 18 wins, 9 losses, 9 ties

KEY

WCF – World Cup finals
WCQ – World Cup qualifier
OGF – Olympic Games finals
OGQ – Olympic Games qualifier
PAG – Pan-American Games
NAC – North America Championship

Note: * In 1979 the U.S. was awarded its final two qualification matches against Mexico by forfeit because Mexico illegally used professional players. The U.S. lost the actual matches 0–4 and 0–2.

NORTH AMERICAN SOCCER LEAGUE CHAMPIONS

Year	*Team*	*Year*	*Team*
1968	Atlanta Chiefs	1969	Kansas City Spurs
1970	Rochester Lancers	1971	Dallas Tornado
1972	New York Cosmos	1973	Philadelphia Atoms
1974	Los Angeles Aztecs	1975	Tampa Bay Rowdies
1976	Toronto Metros	1977	New York Cosmos
1978	New York Cosmos	1979	Vancouver Whitecaps
1980	New York Cosmos	1981	Chicago Sting
1982	New York Cosmos	1983	Tulsa Roughnecks
1984	Chicago Sting		

SOCCER CHRONOLOGY

1848: First code of rules compiled at Cambridge University, England
1855: Sheffield FC, world's oldest club, formed (England)
1862: Notts County, world's oldest league club, formed (England)
1863: English FA formed, Oct 26
1871: English FA Cup inaugurated
1872: Size of ball fixed
1872: Scotland ties 0–0 with England in first official international at West of Scotland cricket ground
1873: Scottish FA and Cup launched
1874: Shin guards introduced by Sam Weller Widdowson of Nottingham Forest and England
1875: Crossbar replaces tape
1876: FA of Wales formed
1878: Referee's whistle used for first time at Nottingham Forest's stadium
1878: Almost 20,000 people watch first floodlit match, between two Sheffield teams, with lighting provided by four lamps on 30 ft wooden towers
1883: Two-handed throw-in introduced
1885: Professionalism legalized in England
1888: English League, brainchild of Aston Villa director, William McGregor, founded, and first matches played on Sept 8
1888: Scottish Cup winners Renton beats English FA Cup winners West Bromwich for the "Championship of the World"
1889: Unbeaten Preston, "The Invincibles," becomes first club to win English League and FA Cup double
1890: Scottish and Irish Leagues formed
1891: Goal nets and penalties introduced
1891: Referees and linesman replace umpires and referees
1892: English League Second Division formed
1893: Genoa, oldest Italian League club, formed
1895: FA Cup, held by Aston Villa, stolen from Birmingham shop window and never seen again
1897: Players' Union formed (England)
1897: Juventus formed
1898: Promotion and relegation introduced in English League
1899: Barcelona formed
1901: Southern League Tottenham Hotspur becomes first professional club to take FA Cup to London
1901: First 100,000 attendance (110,802) at FA Cup final, venue Crystal Palace
1901: Argentina beats Uruguay 3–2 in first international between South American countries
1902: Ibrox Park disaster: 25 killed when part of new wooden stand collapses at Scotland vs. England match
1902: Real Madrid formed
1902: Austria beats Hungary 5–0 in Vienna, the first international between teams outside Britain and Ireland
1904: FIFA formed with seven members
1905: England joins FIFA
1905: Goalkeepers ordered to stay on goal line at penalties
1905: First $1,500 transfer: Alf Common, from Sunderland to Middlesbrough
1908: U.K. beats Denmark to win first Olympic title at Shepherds Bush, London, England
1908: England travels to Vienna to beat Austria 6–1 in their first international on outside the U.K.
1910: Argentina wins the first South American Championship
1919: English League extended to 44 clubs
1920: Third Division South formed (England)
1921: Third Division North formed (England)
1923: First Wembley FA Cup final: Bolton 2, West Ham 0
1924: First Wembley international: England 1, Scotland 1
1924: Goal can be scored direct from corner kick
1925: Offside rule change: a player needs two, not three, players between him and goal to stay onside
1926: Huddersfield complete first hat trick of championships

GOAL GLUT

Arbroath beat Bon-Accord 36–0 on September 5, 1885 in the first round of the Scottish FA Cup, which is still a record score for a British first-class match. But it was little wonder the visitors went down by a cricket score, for the Aberdonians from 30 miles up the coast were actually cricketers, playing in their working clothes and not possessing a pair of soccer shoes between them. Their goalkeeper, who had never played soccer before, was injured and replaced at half time by a half-back. The Arbroath goalkeeper was not called upon to touch the ball, and winger John Petrie scored 13 goals — a record for an individual. It was not a good day for Aberdeen: Dundee Harp beat Aberdeen Rovers 35–0.

1927: Hughie Ferguson's goal against Arsenal makes Cardiff first club to take FA Cup out of England
1928: The four U.K. countries withdraw from FIFA
1928: Bill "Dixie" Dean scores 60 English First Division goals, still a record
1929: Goalkeepers ordered to stay on goal line until penalty is kicked
1930: Uruguay wins first World Cup
1933: Numbered shirts worn in the FA Cup final for first time, winners Everton wearing 1–11, Manchester City 12–22
1934: Sudden death of Arsenal manager Herbert Chapman on Jan 6
1936: Joe Payne's 10-goal record (Luton Town 12, Bristol Rovers 0)
1938: First live television transmission of FA Cup final (Preston 1, Huddersfield 0)
1939: Compulsory numbering of players in English League
1946: British Associations rejoin FIFA
1946: 33 killed and 500 injured as wall and crowd barriers collapse at Bolton vs. Stoke FA Cup match
1947: First $30,000 transfer: Tommy Lawton, from Chelsea to Notts County
1949: England's first home defeat by a non-U.K. nation (0–2 vs. Republic of Ireland at Goodison Park, Liverpool)
1949: Entire Torino team wiped out when airplane taking them home from Lisbon crashes near Turin
1950: English League extended from 88 to 92 clubs

1950: U.S. humbles England 1–0 in World Cup group match, and world record crowd (203,500) sees Uruguay beat Brazil 2–1 in the final in Rio de Janeiro

1950: Scotland first beaten at home by non-U.K. team (Austria, 1–0)

1951: White ball comes into use

1951: First official match under floodlights played at Highbury: between Arsenal and Hapoel Tel Aviv

1952: Newcastle becomes first to win successive FA Cup finals at Wembley

1953: Hungary beats England 6–3 at Wembley

1954: Hungary beats England 7–1 in Budapest

1955: First floodlit FA Cup match (replay): Kidderminster vs. Brierley Hill Alliance

1956: First floodlit English League match: Portsmouth vs. Newcastle

1956: Real Madrid, from an entry of 16 teams, wins first European Cup

1956: South Korea defeats Israel to win first Asian Cup

1957: First African Nations Cup final: Egypt 4, Ethiopia 1

1958: Electrified field used by Everton to beat frost

1958: Munich air disaster kills 19, including eight Manchester United players

1958: English League restructured into four divisions

1958: Barcelona beats a London Select team 8–2 over two games to win first Inter City Fairs Cup

1959: Billy Wright of Wolves, first man to reach 100 caps for England, retires on 105

1960: English League Cup introduced

1960: European champions Real Madrid wins first World Club Championship, beating South American champions Penarol over two legs

1960: Soviet Union wins the first European Championship

1960: Penarol of Uruguay wins first Copa Libertadores

1961 Tottenham completes first English League and FA Cup double this century

1961: First British $150-a-week wage paid to Johnny Haynes by Fulham

1961: Spurs pays $150,000 for striker Jimmy Greaves from Torino

1961: First $150,000 British transfer: Denis Law, from Manchester City to Torino

1961: Fiorentina beat Rangers 4–2 over two games to win first European Cup-winners' Cup

1961: Hapoel Tel Aviv defeats Selangor of Malaysia 2–1 to win first Asian Champions Cup

1962: Manchester United pays record $157,000 to bring Denis Law back from Italy

1963: Tottenham beats Atletico Madrid 5–1 in Cup-winners' Cup final to become first British club to win European trophy

1963 English FA centenary

1964: First televised "Match of the Day" on BBC television (Liverpool 3, Arsenal 2, August 22)

1964: 318 die and 500 injured in crowd riot over disallowed goal during Peru vs. Argentina Olympic match in Lima

1964: Oryx Douala of Cameroon defeats Stade Malien of Mali 2–1 to win first African Champions Club Cup

1965: Ten English League players jailed and banned for life for match-fixing

1965: Stanley Matthews knighted

1965: Substitutes allowed for injured players in English League matches

1966: England wins World Cup, beating West Germany 4–2 after extra time at Wembley

1967: Alf Ramsey, England manager, knighted

1967: Celtic beats Internazionale 2–1 to become first British winner of European Cup and complete unprecedented grand slam: European Cup, Scottish League, League Cup, Scottish Cup and Glasgow Cup

1967: First substitutes in FA Cup final (Chelsea vs. Tottenham), but neither is used

1968: 74 die at Nunez, Buenos Aires, when panic breaks out during River Plate vs. Boca Juniors match

1968: Alan Mullery becomes first England player sent off, vs. Yugoslavia in European Championship

1968: Manchester United becomes first English winner of European Cup beating Benfica 4–1 after extra time

1970: Brazil beats Italy 4–1 to capture World Cup for third time and win Jules Rimet trophy outright

1971: 66 fans trampled to death and 100 injured in second Ibrox disaster, as they tumbled down stairway just before end of Rangers vs. Celtic New Year's Day game

1972: Fairs Cup becomes UEFA Cup and is won by Tottenham, which beat Wolves 3–2 over two games

1974: English League football played on Sunday for first time

1974: Last FA Amateur Cup final

1974: Joao Havelange succeeds Sir Stanley Rous as FIFA president

1977: Liverpool wins League Championship and European Cup

1978: Freedom of contract accepted for English League players

1978: Liverpool first English club to win successive European Cups

1978: Ban on foreign players in English football lifted

1979: First all-British $750,000 transfer: David Mills, from Middlesbrough to West Bromwich Albion

1979: First $1.5 British transfer: Trevor Francis, from Birmingham City to Nottingham Forest

1981: Tottenham wins centenary FA Cup final

1981: Liverpool wins European Cup, becoming first British side to hold it three times

1981: Three points for a win introduced in English League

1981: Record British transfer: Bryan Robson, from WBA to Manchester United for $1.75 m

1981: QPR installs first artificial field in English football

1981: Death of Bill Shankly, legendary Liverpool manager

1982: 340 fans crushed to death during Spartak Moscow vs. Haarlem UEFA Cup match at Lenin Stadium

1982: Aston Villa becomes sixth consecutive English winners of European Cup

1982: Tottenham retains FA Cup, first time since it also did so in 1961–62

1982: Italy defeats West Germany 3–1 in Madrid to complete third World Cup triumph

1983: English League sponsored by Canon for three years

1984: Aberdeen takes Scottish Cup for third successive season and wins championship

1984: Tottenham beats Anderlecht in penalty shootout to win UEFA Cup

1984: Liverpool wins European Cup in penalty shootout and completes unique treble for an English club, with Milk Cup and League title

1984: Northern Ireland wins last British Home Championship

1984: France wins their first honor — the European Championship

1984: Britain's biggest score this century: Stirling Albion beats Selkirk 20–0 in Scottish Cup

1985: Bradford City fire disaster kills 56

1985: Kevin Moran (Manchester United) becomes first player sent off in FA Cup final

1985: Heysel disaster: 39 die as a result of rioting at Liverpool vs. Juventus European Cup final in Brussels. UEFA bans English clubs indefinitely from European competition

1986: Sir Stanley Rous dies, aged 91

1986: Wales FA moves HQ from Wrexham to Cardiff after 110 years

1986: Luton bans all visiting supporters as a measure against hooliganism

1986: Two substitutes allowed in FA and League Cups

1987: The 18-strong squad plus youth players and officials of Alianza Lima die in airplane crash

1989: Hillsborough disaster: 95 crushed to death at Liverpool vs. Nottingham Forest FA Cup semifinal

1989: Goalkeeper Peter Shilton creates England caps record of 109

1990: International Board amends offside law (player level no longer offside); FIFA makes professional foul a sending-off offense

1990: English clubs (Manchester United and Aston Villa) restored to European competition

1990 Guiseppe Lorenzo of Bologna creates world record by being sent off after 10 seconds for striking Parma opponent

1991: End of artificial fields in English Division One (Oldham and Luton)

1992: Premier League of 22 clubs launched; English League reduced to 71 clubs in three divisions

1992: 15 killed and 1,300 injured when temporary stand collapses at Bastia, Corsica, during Bastia vs. Marseille in French Cup semifinal

1993: Marseille are the first French team to win European Cup, but cannot defend their trophy following bribery scandal

1993: Manchester United wins inaugural Premier League championship

1994: Manchester United wins "double" of English League and FA Cup

1994: Brazil wins World Cup for record fourth time, beating Italy in a penalty shootout at the Rose Bowl, Pasadena, Calif.

MAJOR SOCCER AWARDS

FOOTBALLER OF THE YEAR

FIFA WORLD FOOTBALLER OF THE YEAR

1991 Lothar Matthäus (Germany)
1992 Marco Van Basten (Holland)
1993 Roberto Baggio (Italy)

WORLD FOOTBALLER OF THE YEAR (WORLD SOCCER MAGAZINE)

1982 Paolo Rossi (Juventus & Italy)
1983 Zico (Udinese & Brazil)
1984 Michel Platini (Juventus & France)
1985 Michel Platini (Juventus & France)
1986 Diego Maradona (Napoli & Argentina)
1987 Ruud Gullit (Milan & Holland)
1988 Marco Van Basten (Milan & Holland)
1989 Ruud Gullit (Milan & Holland)
1990 Lothar Matthäus (Internazionale & West Germany)
1991 Jean-Pierre Papin (Marseille & France)
1992 Marco Van Basten (Milan & Holland)
1993 Roberto Baggio (Juventus & Italy)

EUROPEAN FOOTBALLER OF THE YEAR (FRANCE FOOTBALL MAGAZINE)

1956 Stanley Matthews (Blackpool)
1957 Alfredo Di Stefano (Real Madrid)
1958 Raymond Kopa (Real Madrid)
1959 Alfredo Di Stefano (Real Madrid)
1960 Luis Suarez (Barcelona)
1961 Omar Sivori (Juventus)
1962 Josef Masopust (Dukla Prague)
1963 Lev Yashin (Moscow Dynamo)
1964 Denis Law (Manchester Utd)
1965 Eusebio (Benfica)
1966 Bobby Charlton (Manchester United)
1967 Florian Albert (Ferencvaros)
1968 George Best (Manchester United)
1969 Gianni Rivera (Milan)
1970 Gerd Müller (Bayern Munich)
1971 Johan Cruyff (Ajax)
1972 Franz Beckenbauer (Bayern Munich)
1973 Johan Cruyff (Barcelona)
1974 Johan Cruyff (Barcelona)
1975 Oleg Blokhin (Dynamo Kiev)
1976 Franz Beckenbauer (Bayern Munich)
1977 Allan Simonsen (Borussia MG)
1978 Kevin Keegan (Hamburg)
1979 Kevin Keegan (Hamburg)
1980 Karl-Heinz Rumenigge (Bayern Munich)
1981 Karl-Heinz Rumenigge (Bayern Munich)
1982 Paolo Rossi (Juventus)
1983 Michel Platini (Juventus)
1984 Michel Platini (Juventus)
1985 Michel Platini (Juventus)
1986 Igor Belanov (Dynamo Kiev)
1987 Ruud Gullit (Milan)
1988 Marco Van Basten (Milan)
1989 Marco Van Basten (Milan)
1990 Lothar Matthäus (Inter)
1991 Jean-Pierre Papin (Marseilles)
1992 Marco Van Basten (Milan)
1993 Roberto Baggio (Juventus)

SOUTH AMERICAN FOOTBALLER OF THE YEAR (EL MUNDO NEWSPAPER, CARACAS)

1971 Tostao (Brazil)
1972 Teofilio Cubillas (Peru)
1973 Pele (Brazil)
1974 Elias Figueroa (Chile)
1975 Elias Figueroa (Chile)
1976 Elias Figueroa (Chile)
1977 Zico (Brazil)
1978 Mario Kempes (Argentina)
1979 Diego Maradona (Argentina)
1980 Diego Maradona (Argentina)
1981 Zico (Brazil)
1982 Zico (Brazil)

1983 Socrates (Brazil)
1984 Enzo Francescoli (Uruguay)
1985 Romero (Brazil)
1986 Alzamendi (Uruguay)
1987 Carlos Valderrama (Colombia)
1988 Ruben Paz (Uruguay)
1989 Bebeto (Brazil)
1990 Raul Amarilla (Paraguay)
1991 Oscar Ruggeri (Argentina)
1992 Rai (Brazil)
1993 Carlos Valderrama (Colombia)

AFRICAN FOOTBALLER OF THE YEAR (FRANCE FOOTBALL MAGAZINE)

1970 Salif Keita (Mali)
1971 Ibrahim Sunday (Ghana)
1972 Cherif Souleymane (Guinea)
1973 Tshimen Bwanga (Zaïre)
1974 Paul Moukila (Congo)
1975 Ahmed Faras (Morocco)
1976 Roger Milla (Cameroon)
1977 Tarak Dhiab (Tunisia)
1978 Karim Abdoul Razak (Ghana)
1979 Thomas N'Kono (Cameroon)
1980 Manga Onguene (Cameroon)
1981 Lakhdar Belloumi (Algeria)
1982 Thomas N'Kono (Cameroon)
1983 Mahmoud Al Khatib (Egypt)
1984 Theophile Abega (Cameroon)
1985 Mohamed Timoumi (Morocco)
1986 Badou Zaki (Morocco)
1987 Rabah Madjer (Algeria)
1988 Kalusha Bwalya (Zambia)
1989 George Weah (Liberia)
1990 Roger Milla (Cameroon)
1991 Abedi Pele (Ghana)
1992 Abedi Pele (Ghana)
1993 Abedi Pele (Ghana)

The inaugural African Confederation player of the year award in 1993 went to Rashidi Yekini of Nigeria.

ASIAN FOOTBALLER OF THE YEAR

1990 Kim Joo-sung (South Korea)
1991 Kim Joo-sung (South Korea)
1992 *no award*
1993 Kaziu Miura (Japan)

OCEANIA FOOTBALLER OF THE YEAR

1990 Robby Slater (Australia)
1991 Wynton Rufer (New Zealand)
1992 Wynton Rufer (New Zealand)
1993 Robby Slater (Australia)

ENGLISH FOOTBALLER OF THE YEAR (FOOTBALL WRITERS' ASSOCIATION)

1948 Stanley Matthews (Blackpool)
1949 Johnny Carey (Manchester United)
1950 Joe Mercer (Arsenal)
1951 Harry Johnston (Blackpool)
1952 Billy Wright (Wolves)
1953 Nat Lofthouse (Bolton Wanderers)
1954 Tom Finney (Preston North End)
1955 Don Revie (Manchester City)
1956 Bert Trautmann (Manchester City)
1957 Tom Finney (Preston North End)
1958 Danny Blanchflower (Tottenham Hotspur)
1959 Syd Owen (Luton Town)
1960 Bill Slater (Wolves)
1961 Danny Blanchflower (Tottenham Hotspur)
1962 Jimmy Adamson (Burnley)
1963 Stanley Matthews (Stoke City)
1964 Bobby Moore (West Ham United)
1965 Bobby Collins (Leeds United)
1966 Bobby Charlton (Manchester United)
1967 Jackie Charlton (Leeds United)
1968 George Best (Manchester United)
1969 Dave Mackay (Derby Co) *and* Tony Book (Manchester City)
1970 Billy Bremner (Leeds United)
1971 Frank McLintock (Arsenal)
1972 Gordon Banks (Stoke City)
1973 Pat Jennings (Tottenham Hotspur)
1974 Ian Callaghan (Liverpool)
1975 Alan Mullery (Fulham)
1976 Kevin Keegan (Liverpool)
1977 Emlyn Hughes (Liverpool)
1978 Kenny Burns (Nottm Forest)
1979 Kenny Dalglish (Liverpool)
1980 Terry McDermott (Liverpool)
1981 Frans Thijssen (Ipswich Town)
1982 Steve Perryman (Tottenham Hotspur)
1983 Kenny Dalglish (Liverpool)
1984 Ian Rush (Liverpool)
1985 Neville Southall (Everton)
1986 Gary Lineker (Everton)
1987 Clive Allen (Tottenham Hotspur)
1988 John Barnes (Liverpool)
1989 Steve Nicol (Liverpool)
1990 John Barnes (Liverpool)
1991 Gordon Strachan (Leeds United)
1992 Gary Lineker (Tottenham Hotspur)
1993 Chris Waddle (Sheffield Wed)
1994 Eric Cantona (Manchester United)

SCOTTISH FOOTBALLER OF THE YEAR

1965 Billy McNeill (Celtic)
1966 John Greig (Rangers)
1967 Ronnie Simpson (Celtic)
1968 Gordon Wallace (Raith Rovers)
1969 Bobby Murdoch (Celtic)
1970 Pat Stanton (Hibernian)
1971 Martin Buchan (Aberdeen)
1972 Dave Smith (Rangers)
1973 George Connelly (Celtic)
1974 Scotland World Cup squad
1975 Sandy Jardine (Rangers)
1976 John Greig (Rangers)
1977 Danny McGrain (Celtic)
1978 Derek Johnstone (Rangers)
1979 Andy Ritchie (Morton)
1980 Gordon Strachan (Aberdeen)
1981 Alan Rough (Partick Thistle)
1982 Paul Sturrock (Dundee United)
1983 Charlie Nicholas (Celtic)
1984 Willie Miller (Aberdeen)
1985 Hamish McAlpine (Dundee United)
1986 Sandy Jardine (Hearts)
1987 Brian McClair (Celtic)
1988 Paul McStay (Celtic)
1989 Richard Gough (Rangers)
1990 Alex McLeish (Aberdeen)
1991 Maurice Malpas (Dundee United)
1992 Ally McCoist (Rangers)
1993 Andy Goram (Rangers)
1994 Mark Hateley (Rangers)

U.S. SOCCER FEDERATION

U.S. MALE AND FEMALE ATHLETES OF THE YEAR

U.S. Male and Female Athletes of the Year are selected by the U.S. Soccer Federation on the basis of "competing and excelling at the highest level of soccer offered by U.S. Soccer for the calendar year, exhibiting decorum on and off the field which reflects well on U.S. Soccer, and contributing toward the popularization, acceptance and credibility of soccer in the United States." The male award began in 1984; the women's in 1985.

Men		Women
1984	Rick Davis	*not awarded*
1985	Perry Van der Beck	Sharon Rerner
1986	Paul Caligiuri	April Heinrichs
1987	Brent Goulet	Carin Jennings
1988	Peter Vermes	Joy Bielfeld
1989	Mike Windischmann	April Heinrichs
1990	Tab Ramos	Michelle Akers-Stahl
1991	Hugo Perez	Michelle Akers-Stahl
1992	Marcelo Balboa	Carin (Jennings) Gabarra
1993	Thomas Dooley	Kristine Lilly

INDEX & ACKNOWLEDGEMENTS

Numbers in italics refer to captions

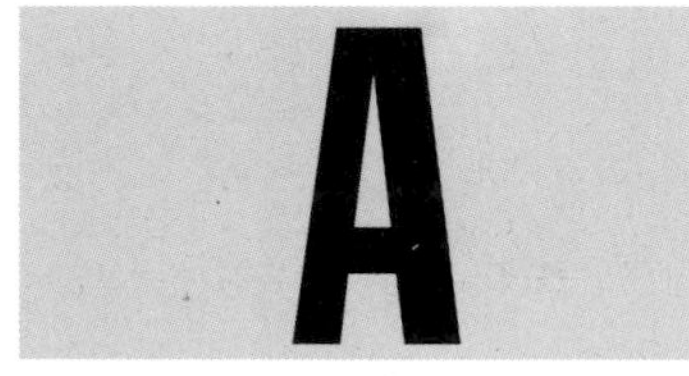

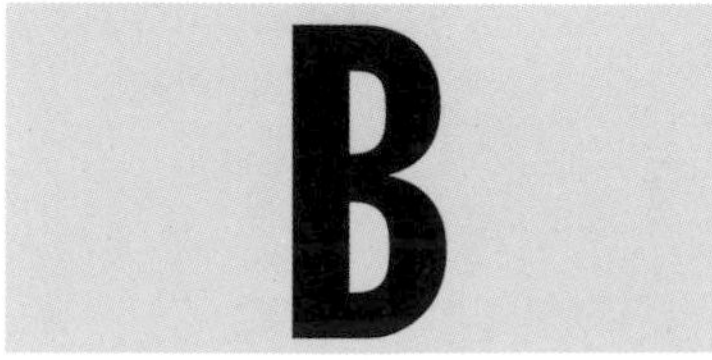

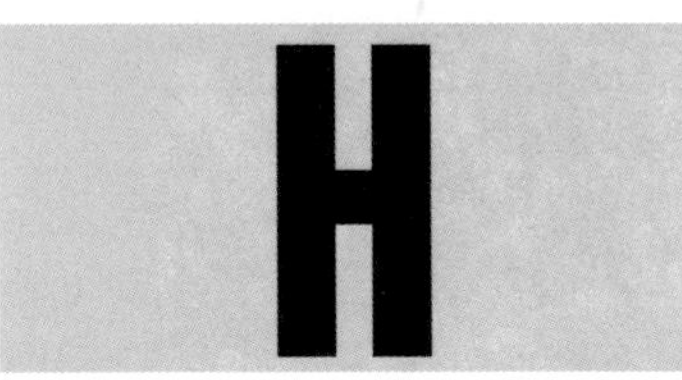

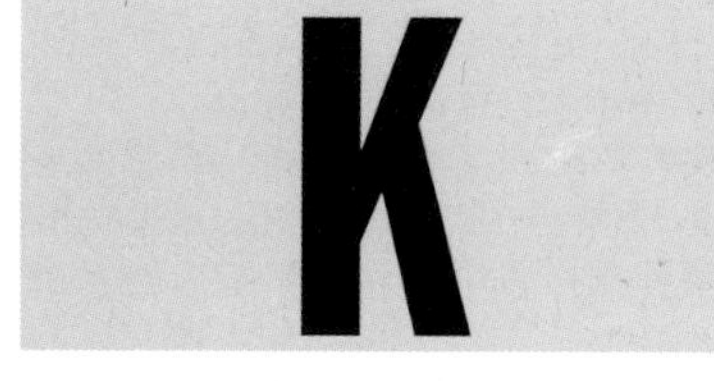

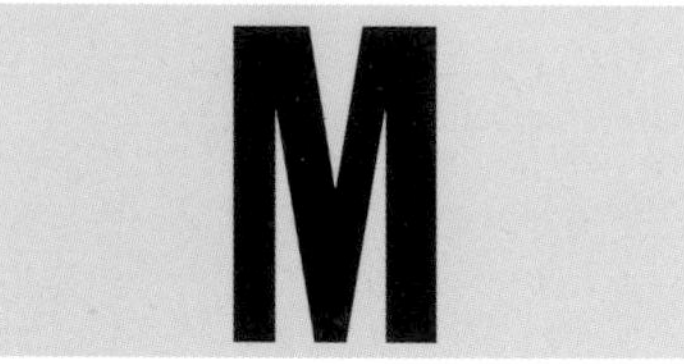

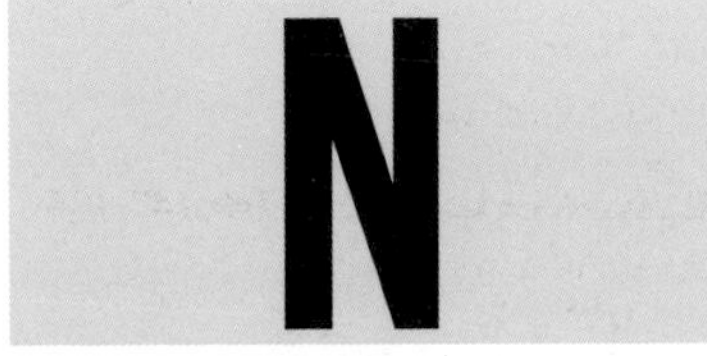

P

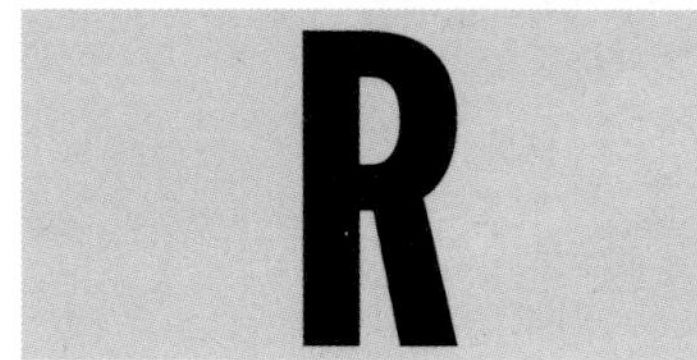

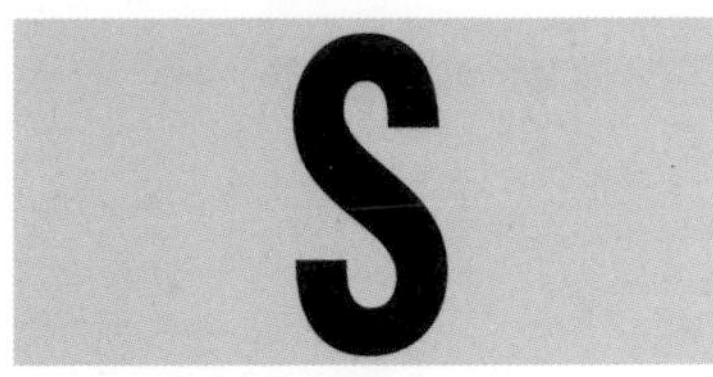

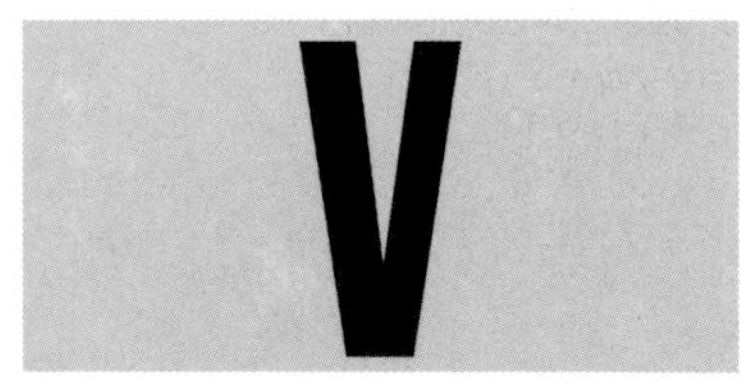

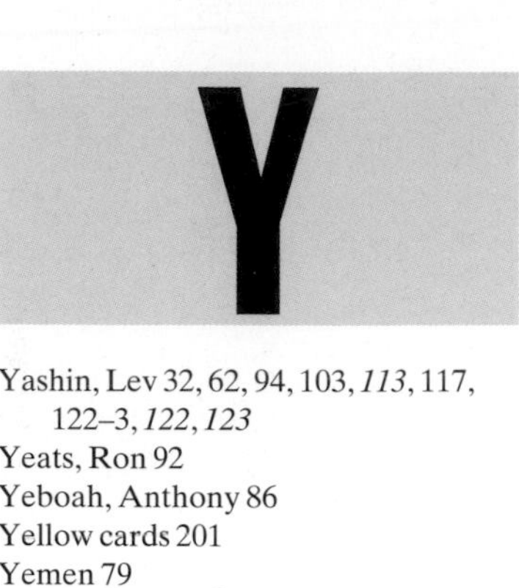

PHOTO CREDITS

The Publishers would like to thank the following sources for their kind permission to reproduce the pictures used in this publication:

Allsport/Shaun Botterill, Simon Bruty, Chris Cole, Mike Hewitt, Gray Mortimore, Ben Radford; **NS Barrett**; **Colorsport**/Gadoffre, Rick Rickman, Norbert Rzepka, SIPA, Varley, Zabci; **Mary Evans Picture Library**; **Hulton Deutsch Collection**; **Illustrated London News**; **Mirror Syndication International**; **Popperfoto**; **Bob Thomas**/Shaun Botterill, Clive Brunskill, Tony Feeder, Stuart Forster, Gamma-Barrault, David Joyner, Dave Rogers, Tempsport, Mark Thompson.

Thanks are also due to Matthew Impey at Colorsport and Andrew Wrighting at Bob Thomas.

In addition a number of individuals very kindly loaned their memorabilia from their collections for special photography:

p.207 tl P. Stacey – 1909 FA Cup Final shirt
p.207 cl Charlie Mitten – 1948 FA Cup Final shirt
p.207 bl Frank Stapleton – Brazil shirt
p.207 tr Mrs I. Beevers – 1911 England Trials shirt
p.207 cr Harry Gregg – 1960 Real Madrid goalkeeper's shirt
p.208 t Mrs I. Beevers – boots
p.208 cl Alf Kirchen – 1936 socks
p.209 tr Alf Kirchen – 1936 shin pads
p.211 bl Mrs M. Whittaker – ball, 1958 FA Cup game
p.211 tr Dennis Viollet – 1961 England cap
p.211 cr George Wall – 1910 England cap
p.211 br Tony Hurley – 1930 FA Cup-winner's medal